NEW CHALLENGES TO THE EUROPEAN UNION: POLICIES AND POLICY-MAKING

New Challenges to the European Union: Policies and Policy-Making

Edited by

STELIOS STAVRIDIS
The University of Reading

ELIAS MOSSIALOS
London School of Economics and Political Science

ROGER MORGAN
European University Institute, Florence

HOWARD MACHIN
London School of Economics and Political Science

Dartmouth

Aldershot • Brookfield USA • Singapore • Sydney

Published by
Dartmouth Publishing Company Limited
Gower House
Croft Road
Aldershot
Hants GU11 3HR
England

Dartmouth Publishing Company
Old Post Road
Brookfield
Vermont 05036
USA

British Library Cataloguing in Publication Data
New challenges to the European Union : policies and
    policy-making.
    1.European Union 2.Europe - Economic policy 3.Europe -
    Social policy
    I.Stavridis, Stelios
    341.2'422

Library of Congress Cataloging-in-Publication Data
Library of Congress Catalog Card No: 96-84762

ISBN 1 85521 455 5 (Hbk)
ISBN 1 85521 955 7 (Pbk)

Printed and bound in Great Britain by
Biddles Limited, Guildford and King's Lynn

Contents

Contributors

Professor Brian Abel-Smith (1926-1996) was appointed Professor of Social Administration at the London School of Economics in 1965. He served as a member of the regional and local hospital boards of the British National Health Service. Between 1968 and 1970, and again between 1974 and 1978, he was a Senior Adviser to the British Secretary of State responsible for the National Health Service. From 1982 he was chairman of the Advisory Committee on 'Health for All' the European Region of the World Health Organisation. Between 1978 and 1985, he was a Senior Adviser on the economic strategy for 'Health for All' to the Director General of the World Health Organisation. He was the author or joint author of 35 books and over 130 articles.

Dr Richard Collins is a Lecturer in Media and Communications in the Department of Social Psychology at the LSE. His publications include *Broadcasting and Audio-Visual Policy in the European Single Market* (John Libbey, 1994).

Dimitris N. Chryssochoou is a Lecturer in European Studies in the School of Social and Historical Studies at the University of Portsmouth. He has published a number of articles on democratic theory and European integration in leading academic journals (*West European Politics, Journal of European Integration, Current Politics and Economics of Europe*), and is the co-author (with Michael Tsiniszelis) of *Democracy in the European Union* [in Greek] (Sideris, Athens, 1995).

Nilesh Dattani is Joint Lecturer in International Relations in the Department of International Relations and the Interdisciplinary Institute of Management, both at the LSE.

Dr Walter Deffaa is Head of the Unit on 'Budget Procedure and Financial Programming' of the European Commission in Brussels where he has worked since 1983 on different assignments.

Dr Alain Guyomarch is Lecturer in European Politics in the Department of Government, and Deputy Director of the European Institute, at the LSE.

Debra Johnson is Senior Lecturer in Economics and European Studies at the University of Humberside. Prior to her employment at the University, she worked for twelve years as a professional economist, advising governments and business about the impact of the European Union on their activities, especially in relation to energy, chemicals and transport. She is currently working (with Colin Turner) on *Trans-European Networks; the Political Economy of Integrating Europe's Infrastructure* (Macmillan, forthcoming 1996) and on an FT Management Report on trans-European energy networks.

Panos Kanavos is Lecturer in Health Policy in the Department of Social Policy and Administration at the London School of Economics. He specialises in Health Economics & Policy, Industrial Economics of High Technology Industries, in particular pharmaceuticals and biotechnology and aspects of Macroeconomic Policy, including taxation. He has advised the European Parliament and is currently adviser to the Organisation for Economic Co-operation and Development (OECD) - Biotechnology Unit. His publications include: with B. Abel-Smith and E. Mossialos *American and Japanese pharmaceutical investment in Europe* - 1995, European Parliament; *Determinants of market structure in the International Biopharmaceutical Industry*, OECD, 1996.

Dr Matthias Kipping is Lecturer in European Economics and Comparative International Management in the Department of Economics at The University of Reading. In the past he worked for an international management consultancy. He holds a PhD from the University of Munich and his thesis has been published by Duncker & Humblot in Berlin. He has published on the origins of European integration, business government relations, and the role of management consultants in English, French and German academic journals and edited volumes.

Professor John Loughlin, who recently returned from Erasmus University of Rotterdam where he was Associate Professor of Public Administration, currently holds the Chair in European Politics at the School of European

Studies, University of Wales College of Cardiff. He is the co-editor of *Regional and Federal Studies: an International Journal* (Frank Cass, London), and one of the convenors of the ECPR Standing Group on Regionalism. His most recent book (co-edited with Sonia Mazey) is *The End of the French Unitary State: Ten Years of Regionalisation in France 1982-1992* (Frank Cass, London, 1995).

Dr Howard Machin is Director of the European Institute at the LSE, he has lectured on French and European Community policy-making since 1977 at the School, except for short periods as Visiting Professor at Cornell, New York, Paris 1, Paris 3, Bordeaux and Rennes Universities. His publications include: (with Peter A. Hall and Jack Hayward) *Developments in French Politics*, London, Macmillan, 1990; (with V. Wright) *Economic policy and policy-making under the Mitterand Presidency*, 1981-4., London, Pinter 1985; *The Prefect in French Public Administration*, London, Croom Helm, 1977. In 1989 the French Government honoured him with the distinction of *Officier des Palmes Académiques*, for services to French culture.

Dr Steen Mangen is Lecturer in European Social Policy in the Department of Social Policy and Administration at the LSE. Since 1985 he has been joint editor of *Cross-National Research Papers*. His recent publications include 'The Impact of Unification' in J. Clasen and R. Freeman (eds.): *Social Policy in Germany* (Harvester Wheatsheaf, 1994), 'Beveridge et le Plein Emploi' in *Les Politiques Sociales* (vol III 1994), pp. 102-109, and 'Urban Polarisation in European Contexts and Concepts' in *Cross-National Research Papers in the Social Sciences* (Pinter, London, 1996). He is also the author of *Spain After Franco: Regime Transition and the Welfare State* (Macmillan, 1996).

Dr Moshe Maor is a Research Officer in the European Institute at the LSE. His publications include: *The Institutional Determinant of Coalition Bargaining: Intraparty Conflicts and Coalition Bargaining in Western Europe* (Routledge, London, 1996) and *Political Parties and Party Systems: Comparative Approaches and the British Experience* (Routledge, London, forthcoming). He is also co-author of *Barriers to Entry into Political Systems* (Papirus, Tel-Aviv, 1988), and has published a number of articles in various journals and edited volumes. His field of specialisation is comparative political parties and comparative administrative systems. He is currently conducting research on 'The Convergence of West European Party Systems', as well as an ESRC-funded project on 'Converging Administrative Systems: Training, Recruitment and Role Perceptions'.

Alan Marin is Lecturer in Economics in the Department of Economics at the LSE. He has published articles in various journals, and has recently co-edited *Essential Readings in Economics* (Macmillan, 1995).

Professor John Marsh is Professor of Agricultural Economics in the Department of Agricultural Economics and Management, and Director of the Centre for Agricultural Strategy at The University of Reading. Since 1991, he has also been the Chairman of the Agricultural Wages Board for England and Wales. In June 1993 he was awarded the CBE.

Professor Roger Morgan is Professor of Political Science at the European University Institute, Florence. He previously held teaching and research appointments at a number of British and American institutions, including the Royal Institute of International Affairs. His most recent publications (as co-editor and contributor) include: *New Diplomacy in the Post-Cold War World* (Macmillan, 1993), *The Third Pillar of the European Union* (Brussels, European Interuniversity Press, 1994), and *Parliaments and Parties: the European Parliament in the Political Life of Europe* (Macmillan, 1995).

Dr Elias Mossialos is Director of LSE Health, and Senior Research Fellow in the Department of Social Policy and Administration at the LSE. In the past, he has worked for the European Commission and the European Parliament as Visiting Fellow to the EP's Scientific and Technological Options Assessment Programme. He was also an adviser to the WHO Regional Office for Europe. His recent publications include: (with B. Abel-Smith et al.) *Choices in Health Policy: An Agenda for the European Union* (Dartmouth, Aldershot and the Office for Official Publications of the European Communities, 1995).

Dr Helene Sjursen is a Lecturer in Politics and International Relations at the University of Glasgow. She was previously Assistant Lecturer in Politics at University College Dublin. Her recent publications include, [in Norwegian]

'Gamle problemer i ny klesdrakt? EFs utvidelsesprobleme i 1990-arene' (Old Problems in a new disguise? The EC's enlargement policy in the 1990s), *IFS-Info*, no. 3, 1993.

Dr Stelios Stavridis holds the Jean Monnet Chair in European Political Studies in the Department of Politics, and is the Director of the Centre for Euro-Mediterranean Studies in the Graduate School of European and International Studies, both at The University of Reading. His publications include 'The 'second' democratic deficit in the European Community: the process of European Political Co-operation' in F. Pfetsch (ed.): *International Relations and Pan Europe,* (Lit Verlag, Munster, 1993), and *Looking Back to See Forward: Assessing the CFSP in the light of EPC* (LSE European Institute Paper, London, April 1994). He has also co-edited with Chrisopher Hill, and contributed to, *Domestic Sources of Foreign Policy: West European Reactions to the Falklands Conflict* (BERG, Oxford 1996).

Dr Paul Taylor is Professor in International Relations in the Department of International Relations at the LSE. He is also editor of the *Review of International Studies*. His most recent publications include: *International Organisation in the Modern World* (Pinter, London 1993): *UN and the Gulf War* with A. J. R. Groom (Royal Institute of International Affairs 1992).

Dr Mark Thatcher is a Lecturer in Public Administration and Public Policy in the Department of Government at the LSE. His publications include the conclusion of 'Policy Networks: Bilan d'un Sceptique' in Le Galès, P. and Thatcher M. (eds.), *Policy Networks et Communities: débat sur leur apport aux politiques publiques* (l'Harmattan, Paris, 1995); 'Regulatory reform and internationalisation in telecommunications', in J. E. S. Hayward (ed.), *Industrial Enterprise and European Integration. From National to Internationalised Champions: Firms and Governments in the West European Economy* (OUP, Oxford, 1995).

Christopher Thomas is a Barrister in an independent practice at Skadden, Arps, Slate, Meagher & Floh in Brussels. Educated at Queen's College, Cambridge and the College of Europe, Bruges, he is a former stagiaire of the Legal Service of the European Commission and the Court of Justice of the

European Communities. He currently advises clients in Europe and the United States on various aspects of European Community law, in particular antitrust, state aids and procurement.

Colin Turner is Lecturer in Economics and European Studies at the University of Humberside. Prior to taking a position at the University, he was a merchant banker and researcher into EC competition policy at the Research Unit for Economic Liberalisation at the University of Exeter. His publications in the area of EU policy relate to EMU, policy towards utilities, especially telecommunications, and trans-European networks. He is currently working (with Debra Johnson) on *Trans-European Networks: the Political Economy of Integrating Europe's Infrastructure* (Macmillan, forthcoming).

Professor Thomas Weyman-Jones is Professor of Industrial Economics at Loughborough University. He has published books on British and European energy policy and on electricity privatisation.

Stephen Woolcock is Senior Research Fellow at the European Institute at the LSE. He was previously Senior Research Fellow in the European Programme at the Royal Institute of International Affairs (Chatham House). This chapter draws on research work carried out while the author was at the RIIA, which formed part of the Economic and Social Research Council's Single European Market Initiative co-ordinated by Professor David Mayes. The results of this research were summarised in the publication *Regulation in the Single European Market: centralisation or competition among national policies*, RIIA, 1994, and 'Competition in the European Union' in David Mayes (ed.) *The Evolution of Rules in the Single European Market*, (forthcoming).

Series Preface
European Political Economy

The first concern of the editors in establishing this series, is to encourage the study of issues of fundamental importance to the development, strength and prosperity of Europe, both East and West. Hence, we are using the term "European Political Economy" in the broadest sense, and inviting contributions from experts in many social sciences and from all European States.

With encouragement from the European Commission, many researchers are working together in interdisciplinary and international teams or networks to produce policy-relevant research of the highest academic standards. This second volume of the series is the product of such a team.

We are also concerned that these research findings should be available to the entire research community which uses English as an international language. Our aim is to produce texts which are easily comprehensible to readers of English who do not have the current cultural points of reference, or contemporary jargon of the USA, UK or any other English-speaking country.

The series editors are based in the European Institute of the London School of Economics and Political Science.

May 1996

Howard Machin
Chairman of the Editorial Board

Introduction

ROGER MORGAN

The great American statesman Dean Acheson once compared the federal government in Washington to a dinosaur, adding: 'the answer you get about what its policies are depends on which part of the brute you tap'. The European Union (EU)[1] often gives outside observers the same impression: in Puchala's celebrated image, descriptions of it are like descriptions given by blind men of an elephant.[2] The objectives of the Commission's Directorate-General for Competition Policy are sometimes in conflict with the aims of the DG for Industrial Policy; the Commission, the Council and the Parliament often speak with different voices; and the Union's member-states occupy a wide and contrasting range of positions on many of the major issues which the Union tries to handle.

Beyond the question 'What are the EU's policies?', there are deeper ones. If we ask 'What *is* the EU?', the answer is likely to be given in institutional terms, describing the function of the EU's various organs and how they are supposed to interact. If we ask 'What does the EU *do*?', the answer will be in terms of its various policies - economic, social, or international. Again, if the question is 'What is the EU *for*?', the answers will be very diverse indeed: optimistic and pessimistic, maximalist and minimalist, enthusiastic, sceptical, and hostile.

All of these different questions, and others, have a tendency to come up at the EC's or EU's periodic inter-governmental conferences. The next of these major review exercises,[3] when the governments and institutions of the EU take stock of where they are and try to decide where they should be going, will take place in 1996-97. It will thus be held at a time when the violent controversies stirred up by the EU's last inter-governmental production, the Maastricht Treaty of 1991, are still raging, and when the European policies of some if not all of the major member-states are very hard to predict. Despite these uncertainties, the IGC of 1996-97 will try to determine the EU's future course on a number of critical, indeed fundamental, issues. Do the institutional reforms agreed at

1

Maastricht now need further amendment, or is a period of quiet consolidation required? Should the Commission's powers be further restrained, in the name of 'subsidiarity', or does Europe expect it to give more forceful leadership? What can the EU do to protect the employment prospects of Europeans against rising global competition? Should the role of the Western European Union as the EU's military agency be upgraded, or not? What should the strategy and the tactics of the EU be for bringing the countries of Central and Eastern Europe nearer to, and eventually into, the Union? And finally, following from the last question, what is the role and purpose of the EU itself in a Europe where many long-standing problems and challenges now co-exist with a host of new ones?

The aim of this book, planned in the aftermath of Maastricht and completed as Europe awaits the Inter-governmental Conference of 1996-97, is to reflect on these and related questions, and to shed light on the nature of Europe's future policy options by placing them in the context of the present and the recent past. As will be seen, the questions of 'What *is* the EU?', 'What does the EU *do*?', and 'What is the EU *for*?', are all inter-connected; to give sensible answers to them, we must also give some attention to the question 'Where did the EU come from, and how has it developed into what it is now?'

One of the bitterest controversies hanging over the negotiation and ratification of the Maastricht Treaty concerned the question of how extensive the powers of the European Commission, and indeed the collective powers of the Union as a whole, should in fact be. As Paul Taylor shows in his contribution to this book, the apparently arcane question of the meaning and implications of the concept of 'subsidiarity' was one which reflected very deep rifts. These rifts became apparent at different levels and between many actors: between the Commission and some member-states; between some member-states and others; and even within individual member-states, where certain social or political forces supported a more interventionist role for the EU (in social policy or defence policy, for instance), and others resisted it.

Conflicts of this kind will certainly pose a challenge to the IGC of 1996-97, as they did in that of 1990-91, and they will not be easy to resolve. One reason for this is that, underlying the already complex controversy about whether or how far the EU should intervene in this or that policy area, there is the much deeper and wider-reaching conflict of opinion over how far governmental or quasi-governmental authorities should intervene in economic or social affairs at all. The profound gap between economic and social *dirigistes* and 'liberals' is one which is all too familiar in the public life of all modern industrial (or 'post-industrial') societies. Indeed, those who are optimistic about the development of the EU might argue that the fact that this issue now appears also at the European level confirms that the EC/EU is developing into a mature and serious polity (whereas pessimists might be inclined to stress only the negative fact of evident dispute and conflict as such).

The existence of deep differences of opinion on such fundamental issues of public policy is indeed not surprising when we recall how the EC/EU, throughout its history, has been open to 'inputs' from both the right and the left (from both extreme free-traders and trade unions concerned about their members), as well as from a wide variety of national traditions and attitudes. This last point might be illustrated by recalling that the early years of the European Community were marked by an endemic tension between a basically 'French' vision of indicative economic planning at the European level (Monnet himself, after all, came directly from the French Planning Commission to inspiring and implementing the Schuman Plan) and, on the other hand, a fundamentally 'German' commitment to free market forces, represented by Ludwig Erhard's Ministry of Economics. This dichotomy between two opposing national economic philosophies (presented here much too crudely) goes far to explain the EC/EU's central conflicts on economic policy, from the early debates over industrial policy and competition to the later controversies between French 'monetarists' and German 'economists' over Economic and Monetary Union (EMU).

The central issue of whether economic and social policies should be market-led or subject to governmental planning, as indicated above, runs through many of the areas of European policy analyzed in this book. As the relevant chapters show, the element of *dirigisme* tends to be particularly marked in the policy areas in which the Community was involved in its early years. European policies for such sectors as agriculture, regional development and energy first took shape in a period of European history - roughly the quarter-century after 1945 - when there was a widespread belief in the efficacy and even the necessity of political intervention to counterbalance market forces. It is therefore not surprising that elements of *dirigisme* still characterize the EU's policies in some of these areas, even though the more market-oriented philosophy of the 1980s and 1990s has (again not surprisingly) made its mark. As Matthias Kipping points out, the current approach to industrial policy, laid down in the Maastricht Treaty, expressly forbids any policy actions whose effect would be to distort competition, and also - most significantly - requires that decisions in this area should be taken unanimously.

There are several reasons why the EC/EU, since the early 1980s, should have reduced its earlier emphasis on spending programmes - whether in agriculture, regional or industrial policies, or in research and development - and given a higher priority to policies of a regulatory kind. One reason is that regulatory policies carry much lower budgetary costs than redistributive ones, and that taxpayers' resistance to high public spending has increased in recent years. Another reason has a deeper philosophical basis: it is that the belief in interventionist policies has been challenged by the view that economic goods (and even social ones) are best developed and distributed by 'the market', leaving only a regulatory role to the public authorities, whether national or European. The effects of this approach, which was explicitly emphasised by some of the EMU convergence criteria enshrined in the Maastricht Treaty, are to be seen in current EU policies in areas as diverse as the free movement of goods and services, or policies on public procurement, broadcasting and information technology (particularly telecommunications). As the relevant chapters in this book show, policy-making in many of these areas is marked by a continuing interplay between interventionist and market-oriented approaches, but the emphasis in recent years has been firmly on the latter.[4]

Another fundamental problem which dominated the Maastricht process has been variously described by such concepts as the EU's 'democratic deficit', the failure to create a 'citizens' Europe' and a communications gap between governments and the people. This problem arose in an especially acute form after the Maastricht Treaty had been signed and the process of parliamentary ratification had begun. Two of the governments which put the question to a referendum - France and Denmark - experienced disagreeable surprises;[5] the German government was allowed to ratify the Treaty after the Federal Constitutional Court had attached significant strings to it; and in Britain the ratification process dragged on in a bitter controversy which revealed deep political divisions and forced the Prime Minister John Major and his colleagues to make substantial commitments against further integration in the future.[6]

These events of the years 1991-93 led many commentators to conclude that something had gone fundamentally wrong with the project of integration as it had been preached and practised by Europe's leaders from Monnet to Delors. The lesson of Maastricht appeared to be that even when the negotiating governments took great care to carry their domestic critics along with them (Chancellor Kohl including the German Land governments in the Brussels process, President Mitterrand showing great caution on political union, and Prime Minister Major appeasing the 'sceptics' by 'opt-outs' on social policy and the single currency), they might still be faced with a backlash of opposition from those who felt they were going too far. The problem, as always, took different forms in different countries: whereas Kohl could legitimately be surprised at the reluctance of many Germans to follow his resolute lead along the Euro-federalist path, it could be argued that Major and his colleagues were themselves partly to blame for stirring up 'Euro-scepticism' by their assiduous continuation of the anti-European rhetoric of Mrs Thatcher. In any case, for whatever mixture of reasons, many European citizens showed considerable hesitation about supporting the projects their leaders had agreed to in Maastricht.

Some of the questions and polemics which followed from this were historical ones: it began to be widely argued that 'the construction of Europe' had been essentially a conspiratorial affair of élite-run deals concluded by the brokers of power (no doubt in the proverbial smoke-filled rooms), and that the only reason these élites had got away with so much was that they had successfully hidden their machinations from the public. Now that the peoples of Europe were at last getting a chance to express their justified resentment at the whole reckless project, it was argued, it would speedily be brought to a halt.

The extent to which European integration was a cabalistic undertaking promoted by Europe's leaders behind the backs of their citizens has been seriously exaggerated. Over the decades the pros and cons of 'Europe' have been debated in parliaments, in countless conferences of political parties and trade unions, in the media, and through innumerable channels representing interest groups, professional associations and local authorities. Anyone who wanted to learn about the subject had ample opportunities of doing so.[7] Monnet himself, as the recent biography by François Duchêne makes clear, by no means limited himself to trying to influence top-level leaders, but did his best to ensure that representatives of trade unions and political parties were associated with his efforts, as well as ministers, industrialists, and officials.[8]

However, the fact remains that the citizens of Europe in the 1990s have been, and still are, confused and perplexed about the issues of European integration - partly because many of their leaders are confused and perplexed themselves. It is true, as several contributors to this volume point out, that the EC/EU is responsible for policies which have directly benefited Europe's citizens - though essentially, perhaps, in their capacities as consumers or employees. As consumers, they have gained from European measures of consumer protection (for instance in relation to pharmaceutical products, as Elias Mossialos shows); and as employees, they benefit from the legislation associated with the Maastricht Treaty's Social Chapter, as well as earlier provisions concerning the labour market and industrial relations in general.

It has to be said, however, that the achievements of the EC/EU in the field of social policy (including social security, as Steen Mangen's contribution shows) have been very limited, for a number of reasons, and this has prevented Europeans from developing the kind of positive feelings about the EU which many of them feel for the 'welfare state' at the national level.

As Moshe Maor's chapter reminds us, the EU contains fifteen 'separate blocs', each representing a distinct national identity reflected in, and shaped by 'its own beliefs, schools, newspapers, political parties, trade union organizations, and voluntary associations'. However strong the forces of transnational interdependence - economic, social and political - which are breaking down the separateness of these national identities, they are constantly renewed, and the 'construction of Europe', if it is to proceed, has to find a way of balancing the European reality and the national ones.

Moshe Maor's contribution examines the implications of two alternative strategies for the development of European political union, and Dimitris Chryssochoou, starting from an analysis of the fundamental significance of democracy, discusses the problems of establishing a 'European *demos*, a 'nascent *Gemeinschaft*', developing from the 'managed *Gesellschaft*' which the member-states have maintained (more or less) so far.

A further factor dominating Western Europe's situation at the time of the Maastricht debates, and still doing so today, is the radically-changing international context. Essentially, the sudden replacement of the Cold War world - a world of relative certainties - by the confused pattern of the 1990s, has disoriented not only the purposes of Europe's leaders but also the understanding of their citizens. The Maastricht Treaty's bold affirmation that 'a common foreign and security policy is hereby established' sounds very impressive, and so does the commitment by the EU's leaders to move towards a common defence policy (after years in which the system of 'Political Cooperation' between the EC's foreign ministries was strictly limited to the political and economic aspects of security policy, excluding the military ones). However, as the chapter by Stelios Stavridis shows, the member-states still have clear divisions of interests, and the Maastricht Treaty's actual provisions governing the new Common Foreign and Security Policy are extremely restrictive, requiring unanimity before action can be taken. If we add to this assertion of member-states' rights the fact that the CFSP appears to be dominated by bureaucratic confusion and cross-purposes, both within the Commission and between the Commission and other institutions, its prospects do not look promising.

We must however stress that a fundamental reason for the failure of the member-states to put together a strong collective position on any major foreign policy issue is that they are faced with an unrecognisably different world from that of the recent past. Decades of talk about Europe 'speaking with a single voice in the world', or about the urgent need to 'create a European pillar of NATO', took place against a relatively unchanging background: that of an East-West confrontation in which the Soviet Union acted as a menacing 'external federator' for Western Europe, and the United States as a military protector which encouraged at least some aspects of Europe's unification. This context made it logical and desirable for Western Europe to develop at least the general ambition to have a specific foreign policy of its own. There were also, of course, ex-colonial and other areas of importance to Europe - the Middle East and North Africa, for instance - where a common policy for Europe seemed possible and desirable, and the slow progress of European Political Cooperation in the 1970s and 1980s appeared to bring such a policy within sight.

However, the end of the East-West confrontation and its replacement by new challenges, such as those represented by Iraq's invasion of Kuwait, or the disintegration of Yugoslavia, appear to be too much for Europe's divided leaders, subject to conflicting pressures from their domestic publics, so that the rhetoric of Maastricht on the 'CFSP' sounds distressingly hollow. It remains to be seen whether the forthcoming IGC can bring any improvement in this respect; but one has the uneasy feeling at present that the disappearance of the familiar Cold War landmarks has disorientated Europe's leaders in their attempt to define the EU's external interests, just as the changes of the 1990s apparently have on other issues too. It might have been expected, for instance, that the economic challenge to Europe from Japan, and from other centres of competitive industrial power, would galvanize Europe into a collective reaction of self-protection. In fact, however, Europe's reactions to these new economic challenges have been as diverse as they have to the more 'classic foreign policy' issues posed by the Gulf War and the end of Yugoslavia. The prospects for an influential EU presence on the world scene, in either economic or political terms, do not look good.

Uncertainty also hangs over an even more pressing dimension of the EU's relationship with its outside environment, that of its possible enlargement to take in Central and Eastern Europe. It is easy to see why Europe's leaders would like, in principle, to respond to the unsettled region to the East by welcoming the ex-Communist states into the benefits of the relative stability and prosperity offered by EU membership, which now extends virtually throughout Europe's Western part. It is even easier to see why the leaders and the peoples of the states in question, from the Baltic to the Balkans, are keen to join the Union. However, as the analysis by Helene Sjursen confirms, the conflicting economic, political and other pressures involved are very substantial, so that the EU's progress in bringing in these new partners (all of them very different from the recent intake of 'Eftans') will be extremely difficult and laborious. It is however a task which the Union must undertake if it is to have any hope of giving Eastern Europe the benefits now enjoyed in the West, and of making Europe as a whole more stable and secure.

The enlargement of the EU is linked, in turn, with the broader and deeper question of what exactly the EU *is*, and, as we indicated at the outset, the related questions of where it came from, where it is going, and what we judge its purpose to be. As Paul Taylor's chapter underlines, the many-sided debate surrounding Maastricht provided the first occasion in the Community's history when a substantial body of opinion argued that the process of integration was approaching its natural end, or that it *should* do so, or even that it should be reversed. This introduced a new note into a debate which for decades had assumed that the process of integration was unilinear and irreversible. Behind the arguments about 'subsidiarity', as we have seen, lie much deeper issues of what it is that the Europeans have created the EU to do for them, and what they expect of it in the future.

This book, by surveying the current state and future prospects of the EU's institutional structure, its policy performance and its place in Europe and in the world, aims to help readers to understand what the Inter-governmental Conference of 1996-97 will be about, and perhaps to decide what they think it *ought* to be about.

Notes

1   The term EU refers to the European Union which was set up by the Maastricht Treaty of 1992 and came into being on 1 November 1993. The term EC refers to the European Communities (formerly the European Economic Community, the ECSC and Euratom) before November 1993 and to the European Community (the first 'pillar' in the Maastricht architecture) after that date.

2   D. Puchala: 'Of Blind Men, Elephants and International Integration', in *Journal of Common Market Studies* (vol.IX, 1972), pp. 267-284.

3   These conferences are needed as Maastricht did not solve all the problems that European integration is facing, and also because integration is a dynamic process.

4   One should note here the paradox that the anti-Maastricht sympathisers find themselves in a situation where they call for nothing more that a common market (free trade) at a time when economic cooperation in Western Europe has reached the point where political cooperation is required.

5   The third country to hold a referendum was Ireland, where 69% voted 'yes' on 18 June 1992. Denmark needed a second referendum in May 1993 to overturn the negative result of June 1992, and the September 1992 referendum in France produced a very close result in favour of Maastricht (51.04%).

6   It is worth noting that this division was so deep that it forced the Prime Minister to make it a question of confidence within his party when he forced a leadership contest in the Commons in the early part of the summer of 1995.

7   The latter phenomenon is further reinforced by new technological developments which can link the citizen to the decision maker more directly than ever before (cf. Information Society Conference in Brussels in February 1995). Of course, it is assumed that the use of these technological developments will have mainly positive effects.

8   François Duchêne, *Jean Monnet, Statesman of Interdependence*, London, Norton, 1994, esp. pp. 284-8, 330-1.

SECTION A: NEW DIMENSIONS FOR THE EUROPEAN UNION:
Political and Institutional Developments

1   Prospects for the European Union

PAUL TAYLOR

One of the consequences of the long a often acrimonious debate that accompanied the ratification of the Maastricht Treaty was the identification, for the first time in the history of European integration, of an end to the process. Hitherto the idea that this was a matter of establishing an 'ever-closer union' of the peoples of Europe appeared to be just that, both to supporters and opponents of union: it was difficult to see any end, or how far it would get towards a tight federal union. But what seemed evident was that it could move in that direction. Some thought this had to be stopped: others welcomed it.

In the debate about the Single European Act there had been a similar problem, but those in favour of continuing with the *journey to an unknown destination* won the argument.[1] There were in the Act several indications of that outcome: there were to be economic and monetary Union, economic and social cohesion, a union of peoples, and further steps towards a common foreign policy. More important in some ways, however, was the absence of any explicit challenge to the traditional view of the process. Despite Mrs. Thatcher's efforts, the subtext of the Act, revealed in the style of its language and expressions, was that of the Euro-enthusiasts. In the Maastricht Treaty this was still the case, as was to be expected from the kinds of proposals which were considered in the diplomacy leading up to the decisive meeting of the European Council in December 1991.

But in the Maastricht Treaty a different tune was also to be heard. There was the statement of subsidiarity. And there was also the successful opposition of the British, and other countries, like Denmark, to the inclusion of the Federalist ambition in the Treaty. It might be argued that it is hard to see much practical difference between that and the idea of a European Union, as it was accepted, but the differences were real. The latter implied an association of sovereign states; the former suggested a move to European sovereignty.

The fierce determination to resist the former, in so many member states as ratification proceeded, was such that the President of the Commission, Jacques Delors, played down for a while the goal of a Federal Europe. The problems of giving the doctrine of subsidiarity any clear legal content were overwhelming, but that was not the point. Subsidiarity was always more important politically than legally. The Germans liked the idea, but it was also a concession to Britain; it allowed John Major a stronger hand in persuading the doubters in the House of Commons to go along with the Treaty. But it was essentially an injunction on behaviour, an assertion that some doctrine other than unification would now prevail, rather than a hard rule.

It was helpful in the more cautious states to let it be supposed that it also meant a repatriating of some functions of the Community, but that was never a practical possibility. In effect - though this was not the intention of the Eurosceptics in Britain - it stripped the integration process of ideological content, and replaced it with a utilitarian concept: that things should only be done at the European level if they were better done there.   Anything which was the exclusive competence of the Community would stay with the Community, and if strict legal criteria were applied it was hard to see how this could justify repatriating anything. But it implied a way of working for the future in the Commission and in the Council: that nothing would be transferred to the Community on the basis of the doctrine that doing things at that level was of necessity a good thing.

Subsidiarity

In 1992 and 1993 an extended discussion of three related concepts concerning subsidiarity took place in the European Community. These were the central principle of subsidiarity, and the related notions of proportionality and transparency. These could be translated into three kinds of concern, which were, respectively, with the level at which decisions about particular policies were to be made, the powers which were to be assumed by the agency entrusted with carrying out the policy, and the degree to which the policy-making process was to be open to the inspection of the public.

A series of declarations concerning these issues were produced by the Community's leaders in 1992, at meetings of the European Council in Lisbon in June 1992, at a special meeting in Birmingham in mid October, and at the meeting in Edinburgh in December 1992. In addition there were a number of pronouncements by other authorities, such as Jacques Delors, President of the Commission, as, for instance, in a speech to the European Parliament in June 1992. The Commission also produced two major texts on the subject to which reference will be made later.

The level of the discussion was sharply differentiated between a set of rather theoretical arguments, which did, however, help to clarify the constitutional character of the system and its direction of evolution, a set of claims and counter-claims by politicians and journalists, intended primarily to boost their preferred cause in the domestic electoral context, and a set of heated ideologically based arguments from lobbies about the nation, the state and Europe.

Typical of the latter was the fierce campaign mounted by the sentimental nationalists of the Bruges group - the Eurosceptics - in Britain, the campaign of the right wing opponents of the ratification of the Maastricht Treaty in France, exemplified in a number of articles in *Le Figaro* before the referendum in France in September 1992, and the corresponding anti-European groups in Denmark. The arguments of the politicians obviously had to take these views into account, as well as those of the authorities. The views of the politicians and journalists were obviously bound up with the perceptions of the wider electorates, and these may be encapsulated in what might be called the mood of the times. This seemed to be ebbing with regard to integration in the mid-1990s, and more will be said of this later. But discussion of subsidiarity was the most obvious symptom of this development, and this is discussed in more detail first.

Concern with subsidiarity was not new: it was discussed earlier in the Draft Treaty on European Union which had been approved in the European Parliament in February 1984.[2] But it moved up the agenda in the period before the agreement of the Maastricht Treaty in December 1991 primarily because of the concerns of the British government about what it saw as an excessive transfer of powers to the Brussels institutions, especially the Commission. The idea also became of importance in Germany; it arose out of the concern of the Laender (the main sub-units of the German federal system) for their powers, which they argued were being lost to the Federal Government in response to membership of the European Community, in breach of the division of powers stated in the German constitution. The British policy reflected an intensifying antipathy especially on the right, towards what seemed to be an increasing trend towards federalism, a position which for a while was reflected in some of the proposals of Jacques Delors. There were reports of Commission moves to significantly extend its own powers as a way of managing the Community if its membership was greatly increased. Delors did, however, quickly realize the unpopularity of such a strategy, and moved strongly to support the idea of subsidiarity.

In narrower political terms it was very important to John Major, the then recently appointed British Prime Minister, in his first intergovernmental conference in the Community, that he should be seen to have obtained significant political concessions from his partners. He had to achieve tokens of success at Maastricht, regardless of their merits, in order to outflank the Thatcherites in his party, and subsidiarity was one of them. He could claim, as did his Foreign Secretary, Douglas Hurd, that the inclusion of the concept in the treaty, was a triumph for the British, for a moderate intergovernmentalism in Europe, and a defeat for the Federalists. The others were happy to give him these concessions: it was congenial not to have to deal any longer with Mrs Thatcher, and there seemed to be a general recognition that the time had come to rein in the head-long move to further integration implied by the '1992 process'. For instance on 11 June 1992 M. Delors was reported as having supported a 'steady state Community' in a speech to the European Parliament, and, in contrast to his claims four years earlier, set out a 'vision of a decentralized union'.[3]

Accordingly the concept of subsidiarity was formally enshrined in December 1991 in the Maastricht Treaty which legally constituted an amendment of the Treaty of Rome. That was not ratified until the October of 1993, but a number of declarations and Summit communiques in effect introduced the doctrine. There was constant allusion to the relevant parts of the Treaty, the preamble and Article 3b, and it is instructive to examine the text directly in detail.

From the Preamble

> Article b. The objectives of the Union shall be achieved as provided in this Treaty and in accordance with the condition and the timetable set out therein while respecting the principle of subsidiarity as defined in Article 3b of the Treaty establishing the European Community.
> The Union shall be served by a single institutional framework which shall ensure the consistency and the continuity of the activities carried out in order to attain its objectives while respecting and building upon the 'acquis communautaire'.

From Article 3b

> The Community shall act within the limit of the powers conferred upon it by this Treaty and of the objectives assigned to it therein. In areas which do not fall within its exclusive competence, the Community shall take action, in accordance with the principle of subsidiarity, only if, and in so far as, the objectives of the proposed action cannot be sufficiently achieved by the Member States and can, therefore, by reason of the scale or effects of the proposed action, be better achieved by the Community. Any action by the Community shall not go beyond what is necessary to achieve the objectives of this Treaty.

A preliminary comment might be made at this stage about the form of words used in this text. It contained reference to both a new principle - only transferring to the Community what could be better done at that level - but also an assertion of the continuity and coherent quality of Community mechanisms and commitments in the form of the reference to the *acquis communautaire*. This was the first time that the latter had been mentioned in a Community text, though it had been in common usage by diplomats and specialists.

This was another example of the duality of Community arrangements which is discussed in more detail below. Assertions of Community, and acceptance of schemes for further integration, had often accompanied assertions of national identity and simultaneously agreeing procedures which protected the separate governments. Now the act was repeated but the lines were in reverse order: an explicit reference to the protection of the separateness of states had been accompanied by a *sotto voce* assertion of the continuity of the integration process and the inviolability of what had been achieved. Revealingly all the existing member states insisted that any new members must accept the *acquis communautaire* in full: even the British and the Danes did this, despite their various opt-outs in Maastricht and at the Edinburgh European Council meetings.

The principle of subsidiarity was enunciated in the two sentences in paragraph one of Article 3b, and that of proportionality was enshrined in the separate, single sentence, paragraph. These were the key references and were the subject of considerable discussion by lawyers and political scientists after the conclusion of the treaty about what they meant and how they were to be applied. Perhaps the most authoritative text written in interpretation of the principles was that prepared by the Commission of the European Community for the Edinburgh Summit in December 1992, and the following discussion relies heavily upon this.[4]

The meaning of the principles

First the meaning of the concepts is discussed. With regard to subsidiarity a key question was that of what was to be regarded as falling within the exclusive jurisdiction of the Community. The point should be stressed that it is impossible to allocate responsibility to the Community or the states on the basis of this principle: such an allocation is determined by the Treaty itself. A distinction had to be made between the formal allocation of powers and the manner in which they were to be exercised. With regard to the *exercise* of competencies:

> the Community should do only what is best done at that level, and the burden of proof should be on the Community institutions to show that there is a need to legislate and take action at the Community level at the intensity proposed.

The introduction to the above mentioned Report puts the main points succinctly:

> The first sentence [of Article 3b] underlines that the competencies are given by the Treaty and the limits of these competencies must be respected. Within these limits the Community has an obligation to

achieve the necessary results: to attain the objectives which the Treaty assigns to it.

The second sentence concerns the areas where the Community has not an exclusive competence and deals with the question whether the Community should act in a specific case. This article requires that the Community should only intervene if and so far as the objectives of the proposed actions cannot be realized sufficiently by the member states. This implies that we have to examine if there are other methods available for member states, for example legislation, administrative instructions or codes of conduct, in order to achieve the objectives in a sufficient manner. This is the test of comparative efficiency between Community action and that of member states.

The factors which could be examined in such cases are the effect of the scale of the operation (transfrontier problems, critical mass, etc.), the cost of inaction, the necessity to maintain a reasonable coherence, the possible limits on action at national level (including cases of potential distortion where some member states were able to act and others were not able to so) and the necessity to ensure that competition is not distorted within the common market.

If it were concluded that a proposal passes the test of comparative efficiency, it would still be necessary to respond to the question 'what should be the intensity and the nature of the Community's action?'. This recalls the principle of proportionality which is already an element of the case law of the Community. It is necessary to examine carefully if an intervention by legislative means is necessary or if other means which are sufficiently effective can be used. If it is necessary to legislate the Commission will as far as possible favour framework legislation, minimum norms and mutual recognition and more generally avoid a too detailed legislative prescription.

The third sentence of Article 3b applies not only to the area of shared competencies but also to the area of exclusive competence. It reaffirms that the principle of proportionality, for which certain criteria are set out above, should apply, but does not alter the attribution of competence.

There are large areas, primarily, but not exclusively, related to the four fundamental freedoms - the free movement of goods, persons, services and capital - where the Community had come to have exclusive competence. In addition the common commercial policy, the rules of competition, the common organization of agricultural markets, the conservation of fisheries resources, and the essential elements of transport policy, had over time been placed on this list.

But later in the Report the possible variations in such intensity, where powers are shared between the states and the Community, were spelled out. There were *legislative measures*, which were necessary to smooth the operation of the internal market and the common policies, where the Community's powers were very strong; there were *joint measures*, where they were also very strong, which were necessary to achieve economic and social cohesion, and in the future, common foreign and security policy; *supportive measures*, as regards certain social and environmental measures, where the Community's powers might be weaker, and *complementary measures*, where there was only modest political resolve to grant powers to the Community on the part of the states.

The Report also outlined ways in which the separate states might be brought into the process of monitoring the process of applying Community rules within their frontiers. More could be done through annual reports on compliance prepared by the states, or through the work of an ombudsman, which was proposed in the Maastricht Treaty, Article 107d, to check that states and individuals were doing what they said they were doing. Where firms or individuals had not complied with the rules regarding transparency in submitting tenders for contracts, governments should have the power to suspend the process. But, to help with transparency, the Report stated that Community legislation should be more accessible, both in terms of intelligibility and in terms of physical availability. It should not need to be reinterpreted.

The application of the principles

Writing a few years after Maastricht, it is difficult to avoid the conclusion that the discussion of these principles had clarified a number of issues but that it had not led to much alteration in the practice of the Community. But it had served to remind those who were involved in the process of making the rules that they needed to bear in mind the new directions. Douglas Hurd stated in February 1992 to the Foreign Affairs Select Committee that the Commission had in practice been sensitized to the need to act on the basis of subsidiarity, though specific rules and injunctions to this effect were hard to detect, either in the work of the Commission or of the Council of Ministers.[5] But what was important was that the discussion about subsidiarity had focused attention upon the need to find instruments among those available to the Community to distribute competencies in a more sensitive way than hitherto between the states and the Community wherever possible, and certainly not to pursue a crude strategy, which sentimental nationalists had found in the integration process hitherto, of transferring powers to the centre whenever possible, and seeing that as a good in itself.

The discussion had indeed contributed to a broad alteration in the course of the development of the Community away from centralist Federalism. (The implications of position statements from late 1994 are discussed below.) In the course of the discussion in 1992 the Community did acknowledge the primacy of the states in the Community, although paradoxically the federalists did find some comfort in the prospect it allowed of stronger links between the Community and the regions within the state: if things were to be done at the lowest possible level, even state governments might need to hand powers downwards, and this in turn would facilitate closer relations between the Commission and the regions within states. The British government failed to acknowledge the irony that, although they had prompted the idea of subsidiarity, they had also become in the 1980s one of the most highly centralized states in the Community, and one of the most resistant to the transfer of powers back to local authorities, least of all to regions. Subsidiarity could lead back to London but not to the counties or the boroughs.

But that the powers of the state had primacy was now explicitly asserted, one of the very few occasions in the history of the Community when this had appeared in a Community text. At the Birmingham summit, it was stated that the subsidiarity principle concerned purely the exercise and not the conferment of powers, which 'is reserved for the authors of the Treaty, namely the national governments'.[6] In the Report mentioned above, however, the authors stated that the 'conferment of powers is a matter for the writers of our constitution, that is to say of the treaty. *A consequence of this is that the powers conferred on the Community, in contrast to those reserved to the members, cannot be assumed...national powers are the rule and the Community's the exception'. [my italics]* This seemed to be a considerable alteration in the Commission's public stance compared with a few years earlier, and the lack of any rebuttal of the report by any of the member states in the European Council suggested that it represented the general view. It recognized that the powers of the states were superior, that they were the conferring agency, and that they could de-confer: in other words it asserted the continuing sovereignty of the states.

Indeed the general tone of the Edinburgh report implied a recognition of injunctions on behaviour of a relatively non-specific kind, or it made explicit that this was already the way of working of the Community. The lawyers had agreed that it could not be otherwise, as the principles were hard to translate into formal rules. Subsidiarity was a political not a legal concept. In a number of countries, however, the primary objective was for the anti-Europeans to be satisfied that something had been done and to stop the trend to Federalism: presentation was the important thing.

This was the spirit of the conclusions at the end of three summit meetings in 1992. The June meeting in Lisbon did little more than acknowledge the issue and to agree that something concrete should be done before the next meeting. This turned out to be the special meeting at Birmingham on 15 -16 October 1992, which on these issues produced a text of unexceptional blandness. It was affirmed that decisions must be taken as closely as possible to the citizen, and that making this principle work should be a priority for all the Community institutions without affecting the balance between them. The leaders also agreed at Birmingham that the foreign ministers should look at ways of making the work of the institutions of the Community more transparent. A report on these issues, the Sullivan Report, had been prepared, but attracted little attention. In this the Maastricht treaty had already made a start, as, for instance, when it required that the Commission should inform national parliaments of proposals for legislation on the assumption that they would express an opinion.

According to the *Financial Times*[7] just before the Edinburgh summit a European Commission official had said he expected the EC 'would be able to agree a text sufficiently meaningless to satisfy everyone on subsidiarity,' so as to cut through the artificially pumped up debate on how to divide power between the Community and the member states. The conclusions were that there would be no fundamental changes in the Community's method of working, though members of the Community's institutions would have to demonstrate that action at the EC level was in response to real needs in the member states.

This was in accordance with the main thrust of the debate from the start. The general interpretation among the Eurosceptics had been that Art. 3B meant a return of powers to the national level, and indeed the politicians in Britain had rather encouraged this view; that it would allow a clawing back of powers. But at Edinburgh there was no 'bonfire of the 71 items of EC law' which it had been reported would be struck down on the grounds of the subsidiarity principle. Only 20 planned measures from the Commission were modestly affected and there was no deletion of any significant legislation on these grounds. One cynical interpretation was that as the French referendum was now over and as John Major had achieved a majority in the House of Commons in favour of the principle of ratifying Maastricht, there was now no need to push too hard on subsidiarity, but merely to do enough so as not to seem to have been duplicitous.

The point should be stressed that the precise wording of Article 3b did not categorically lay down a requirement for preserving the powers of the states, and therefore for protecting their sovereignty, which was what the Eurosceptics had wanted. It could indeed imply precisely the opposite: a transfer of more powers to the Community level for reasons of scale or effect. The Eurosceptics view implied sacrificing efficiency in order to preserve national competence, whereas the Article actually implied the sacrifice of sovereignty in order to achieve greater efficiency.

Yet there were concessions to the Eurosceptics, though little evidence to suggest that they were acknowledged or even understood. In addition to those already mentioned there was also to be an inter-institutional accord to confirm that all power was vested in the states except where otherwise specified. As the question of the specification of these powers was a matter for the states anyway, and this fact had been stressed in Community documents, the net effect was again a reassertion of the underlying principle that the Community rested upon the separate constitutional orders of the sovereign member states.

The same general conclusions applied to transparency; the appearance of concessions without much achievement. There were minimal changes in the general practice. It was agreed that some Council debates would be televised for journalists, and that votes in the Council of Ministers would be made public (they had in fact been known since 1987). But this could be seen as simply providing further encouragement for the existing habit of making deals in the Council to allow agreement on the basis of consensus, even in areas where majority voting was formally allowed. The standard working practice of the Community of making deals in smoke-filled rooms was not affected. There were no proposals to strengthen the role of the European Parliament beyond those agreed in the Maastricht Treaty itself.

The habit of secret diplomacy was confirmed in April 1994 when *The Guardian* sought to persuade the Foreign Ministers in the General Council to accept the release of Council documents concerning the governments' positions on proposals for rules governing the employment of children. Despite the initial release of the documents to the newspaper the Council insisted that this had been an error, and that in future no papers about the positions adopted by governments regarding issues before the Council could be released.[8] The furthest move towards a more open approach by the Council was the acceptance that it would be routine to make public a record of the voting of governments.

In the event the debate on subsidiarity also had little to do with the concessions made by the Community to Denmark to allow that country to resubmit the Maastricht Treaty for the approval of the Danish people through a referendum. The Danes did have major concessions, which certainly affected other areas of the Community's business, such as enlargement. Denmark was permitted to opt out of the Maastricht provisions on a future common defence policy, common citizenship and a future European Monetary Union, but the subsidiarity text had no specific reference for Denmark, although obviously the Danish 'no' in the earlier referendum had encouraged those who wished to set in place a more specific application of subsidiarity.

Nature of the Reaction against Integration

The debate on the related concepts of subsidiarity, proportionality and transparency helped clarify aspects of the Community's general direction of movement, and the role of the various levels of decision-making, and probably helped to head off, for the time being, any further trend to a more centralized form of federalism. The range of specific adjustments in procedures, and the amount of legislation that was modified or abandoned was extremely limited. But it marked the reaching of another plateau in the Community's evolution in the first years of the 1990s. Such a cycle of development, a new phase of integration followed by a period of consolidation, had occurred on at least two earlier occasions, and indeed can be said to be a feature of the historical process of regional international integration: a period of *lourdeur* followed the crisis in 1965, and also marked the late 1970s, on both occasions, as in the 1990s, following after a period of enthusiasm. There is in this an historical dialectic, as well as a structural one, which is discussed below.

What explains the appearance of the hesitations which led to subsidiarity? The Maastricht Treaty was an illustration, not so much of spillover, but of overspill from the period of integrative momentum which culminated in the Single European Act and led on to the completion of the 1992 single market process. But well before this had happened a range of doubts and difficulties had appeared. These took a different form and mix in the different member states of the Community, and it is obviously impossible to discuss each case in detail here.

But they were generally coloured by a certain *ennui*, not to mention disillusion, with the political process in member countries, especially in Britain, France, Germany, and, as always, Italy. There was an impatience with national governments which was easily diverted,   sometimes deliberately by national authorities, to a European level. This background contributed to the success of the anti-Europeans in stirring up popular interest, which was readily focussed on the evidence of inefficiency and waste at the European level. This may be linked with a realization that things had indeed got to the point at which bonds could be forged between the member states which would be hard to break. In Britain, for instance, Maastricht was the occasion of the realization, for the first time, that the choice of Europe was not just a tactical move, a living in sin, which could be revoked at will, but more of a marriage in which, regardless of legal or constitutional realities, the national will itself could be subverted.

The Maastricht Treaty appeared to pose stark alternatives: whether it did in fact was beside the point. The Community never prospered when it seemed to be involved in a zero sum game with the nation state, if governments had to choose one or the other. Progress was always more likely when it appeared possible, even by resort to some subterfuge, to link the strengthening of the Community with the well-being of the separate states: to pose integration in terms of a structural dialectic. But at a time of recession in the 1990s the alternative routes to recovery - common action through the Community, or competitive unilateralism in individual states - did indeed pose a stark and destiny laden choice. Clearly neither public nor elite attitudes could sustain the former without hesitation; there was therefore a hankering after the latter, as a convincing dialectic form of the relationship between state and Community could not be presented .

But this was not anything unusual: the same thing had happened in the mid 1970s, when Europe could have solved the problems resulting from the weakness of the dollar by moving quickly to a joint response in the form of monetary union. The governments simply did not have the mutual confidence to make that jump. Nor did they in the mid 1990s when it came to dealing with recession: measures for joint recovery could have been planned at the level of the Community, and the rational technical option would have been to work together at that level. But governments were happy to use the context of the recession to reassert national identity: this would strengthen their power base among their electorates at home, though it was an uncertain route to economic recovery. The historical dialectic took precedence over the structural one.

Occasionally there were complaints from national governments about the difficulty of doing something in the face of Brussels opposition. Frequently in Britain this was linked with the demonizing and externalising of the Community institutions. There were Brussels Directives which did not suit our interests - or the interests of some group or other - now defined as sacred to our culture![9] Such judgements were made without regard to the fact that the national authorities had necessarily been involved in making the Directives in the first place. Feelings of subjugation by external forces which were beyond their control chimed well with the anger of those who were the victims of the recession: unemployment was running at record levels, and even the principle of public welfare itself was under attack. And governments liked the implication, as they pulled the strings, that they were also merely puppets.

There was also the reappearance of what Stanley Hoffmann had called the *logic of diversity*.[10] The ending of the Cold War sharpened a general awareness of a shadow of the past, in which states had different relationships with the outside world. For a number of states new possibilities for choosing between European and other roles emerged. Germany appeared in an older suit of clothes as a middle European power, and the Kohl government was having to deal with those who preferred a more active Ostpolitik to a continuing active Westpolitik. At a time of difficult relationships between Prime Minister Major and President Clinton, some anti-Europeans in Britain argued that the 'special relationship' with the USA was preferable to involvement in a European foreign policy arrangement that had failed over ex-Yugoslavia. Greece was clearly following its own line in the Balkans, and Italy under the new Prime Minister Berlusconi was also less positive about Europe than it had been, but nevertheless very sensitive to being sidelined in the EU.

It was not just that the logic of diversity was visible, but a perverse feeling that perhaps it might pay to develop that diversity further. For the Eurosceptics, as the 'special relationship' weakened, it seemed more important to cultivate it as an alternative to European Union. In April 1994 the US Ambassador to the UK, about to retire from London, pointed out that ' if Britain's voice is less influential in Paris or Bonn, it is likely to be less influential in Washington'.[11] As President Kennedy had told Harold Macmillan a third of a century earlier so Ray Seitz said to John Major in 1994: the 'special relationship' with the US and full participation in the European Union should not be seen as alternatives. The special relationship had a future if Britain was an active partner in Europe. Several other governments had to deal with comparable dilemmas.

For all the states, in this time of recession, there was also a hesitation about exactly how valuable the European markets were, and notes of discord in demanding separate national efforts with regard to commercial opportunities in the Far East and elsewhere. Just as the resurgence of integration in the early 1980s had been in large part a response to the challenge from the Far East in high-technology products, so ten years later, the limits of that collective response were visible. The markets which had developed in the Far East alongside the increasing productive capacity in high-tech products were now the target of intra - European competition about market shares. Economic take-off in the Far East was taking place precisely when recession in Europe seemed to be deepening, and doubts about the role of the European Community increasing. Thus development at the opposite end of the continent of Eurasia reinforced the logic of diversity in the European Union. The concern with subsidiarity, and the increased visibility of the limits of integration, were a product of these underlying developments.

The Measures of Integration

The European Union in the 1990s should not, however, be understood as being merely an intergovernmental arrangement, which continuously recreated the ancient and unchanging differences between the member states. As always the task facing the student of integration in Europe was to identify the balance between the states and the Community, rather than a straightforward rescue of the nation state. In the preceding discussion a backward thrust in the integration process was described, but this in the mid 1990s had to be seen in the context of the balance of the times. That was very much more in favour of integration than it had been in, say, 1957, or even 1974, and it is very important to form some measure of this achievement.

What are the measures of the achievement of integration? It is possible to propose some specific measures, in the light of which Europe can be said to have moved towards more integration. These concern, first, popular attitudes. Second they are to do with the way of working of the institutions of the Union. Third to do with the way in which the interests of governments and parties have moved; fourth to do with developments in the ways in which the civil servants of the member states engage with each other and with officials in the Brussels institutions; fifth to do with the emergence of an increasing range of common principles, norms and rules in the economic and social arrangements of the member states i.e. we have witnessed the emergence of a Community regime; and sixth there has been an increase in the level of economic interconnectedness and interdependence, not least, of course, in trade.

Changes in attitudes were fundamental to the development of an integrated economic zone. They were relevant to the mobility of labour, to the preparedness of those in work to move around the Community to protect their employment. They were also crucial in the development of a habit of not balancing the books of one participating state or territory with others: short term outflows from one to the other were not significant when attitudes moved towards the pattern found in a socio-psychological community. It was clear that this was not yet the case in the European Union in the mid 1990s, but that there had been some movement in that direction. Without that there could be no redistribution, and continuing complaints by those in areas showing a net outflow of resources.

But there was indeed evidence that public attitudes supported the transferring of competence to perform significant tasks, including the conduct of foreign policy, to the Union. Even in the more cautious states like Britain there was evidence of support for the extension of further competences to the Union, including support for creating a European Central Bank, a common defence, and a common foreign policy. The claim by the Eurosceptics that public opinion in Britain had become fiercely nationalist was simply not true.[12] And there was also evidence of the appearance of what Karl Deutch had called a 'security community' among the older core states. In other words citizens of one country were more discriminating in their judgements of the sub-groups forming the population of another; and they were more likely to reject military force as a way of settling differences with them. The Franco-German frontier was not now fortified. Neither were the frontiers between the other member states.

The institutional arrangements of the European Union in the 1990s represented a considerable achievement for those who had worked for their adaptation and development. It was unlikely that the Community could have survived had the Treaty of Rome been a clearly federalist document. States would quickly have realized that such a prospect was more than they could accept, and its reality more than could be obtained. Over the years the Treaty proved capable of being adapted to the purposes of both federalists and intergovernmentalists. By the mid 1980s, however, a crucial change in perceptions of the potential of the Community had taken place: that both purposes could be pursued at the same time and held in a dynamic positive relationship with each other. The sovereignty of states and the development of their sense of distinctive identity, the consolidation of national autonomy, were paradoxically capable of reconciliation with the strengthening of the Community.

In the early 1990s, this duality in the Community was evident in a number of the central institutions. The doctrine was that the Commission defined the interest of the Community and stood above the interests of states. Yet it also unofficially embodied a principle of representation. States were concerned to get their quota of officials, and they insisted on having 'their' Commissioners, who frequently embodied a kind of quasi-representativeness in that they came from a particular tendency within states: for instance, in Britain, one was from the left and the other from the right of the political spectrum. It was common knowledge that coalitions of officials of particular nationalities in the Commission tended to work particularly closely with governments and other organizations of the same nationality with regard to issues which concerned them. This could not be too obvious and discriminatory, but it happened. Hence the Commission was itself an embodiment of a symbiotic relationship between state and community.

Conversely the Presidency was superficially an embodiment of the principle of intergovernmentalism: each member, as a separate state, was placed in charge of the affairs of the Community for six months, i.e. once every six years in a Community of 12. Yet states which had the Presidency generally recognized that they could not simply use this opportunity to pursue national interests: they also needed to push for the interest of the collectivity. They became defenders of the Community and upholders of the interests of their own state, a duality of purpose which was partly the result of socialization - the consolidation of the regime's injunctions on behaviour - and partly the result of the rational calculation that to pursue national interests too blatantly would be counter productive.

Such a duality was, however, a valuable, and indeed, essential aspect of the working of the Community's institutions in the 1990s. It represented a stable relationship between two necessary imperatives which served the member states well. There has been at one and the same time both integration and state building, which is particularly evident in the new democracies of southern Europe, but which is in fact the case for all member states. This is a great achievement for the Community's institutions, and one which could be too easily thrown away with over rapid expansion from the existing core.

With regard to the external interests of states the Community members passed through a long period of adjustment and convergence. They had slowly evolved a philosophical basis of Community foreign policy, the result of a refocussing of expectations and loyalties upon the Community, going beyond the habit of consultation in matters of foreign policy to the appearance of a preparedness to put partnership ahead of interest on occasion in order to protect the regime. This was evident in the wording of Title 3 of the Single European Act called *Provisions on European Cooperation in the Sphere of Foreign Policy*. In Article 30, 2(c), the governments agreed to 'ensure that common principles and objectives are gradually developed and defined'; and that they would 'endeavour to avoid any action or position which impairs their effectiveness as a cohesive force in international relations or within international organizations'.[13]

Even the more cautious states had moved closer to Europe. In Britain Eurosceptics were afraid that in the elections to the European Parliament in June 1994 a massive swing against the Conservatives would be seen as a vote for Europe. Britain had focused increasingly upon Europe and away from the Commonwealth. Similarly the Danes had gone through a period of adjustment of their policy of semi-attachment. The French also became less involved with the zone of *'francophonie'*, and more with Europe, especially under President Mitterrand. This gradual consolidation of the underlying philosophy of collective action of the Community had taken a long time and had involved a progressive adjustment of views about the world and related interests.

It was impossible in the early 1990s that the newly independent states of Eastern Europe could fully understand this adjustment: as yet they did not share a similar view of the world, because they had not been in a context in which it had to be learned. The injunctions on behaviour which formed regimes could not be learned overnight. But the philosophy underpinning collective action among the member states was not all-encompassing: it was, as with attitudes, a matter of an increasing unity in diversity. But in the mid 1990s the logic of diversity had to be balanced against a logic of convergence.

The growth of converging economic interests coincided with changes in the working arrangements of national civil servants and in their attitudes towards transgovernmental cooperation. The evidence was overwhelmingly that civil servants even in countries such as Britain had got used to working in the numerous joint working committees with their counterparts in Brussels and other national administrations. There had indeed been a socialization of the bureaucrats, though arguably this had been at the expense of democracy. That a serious democratic deficit had appeared in Europe was hard to refute, though a crucial qualification of this was that such a deficit was a feature of modernized democracies in general - despite the delusions of potency among some elected representatives. As economic arrangements had become more technical, and more susceptible to international influences, so they had become more detached from the scrutiny of generalist members of elected assemblies.

But there had certainly been an increasing economic interconnectedness between the member states, shown in such developments as the increasing value of mutual trade, and the increasing value of Community, compared with national, budgetary flows. Inevitably, and despite the efforts of the more cautious states, this was matched by a greater weight of regulation at the Community level, and an increasing interpenetration of bureaucracies. The changes in the attitudes and behaviour of bureaucrats and politicians alike, and the increasing level of economic connections and transactions, justified the conclusion that in terms of formal rules and in terms of informal conventions of behaviour there had emerged by the mid 1990s a Community-wide system of governance. There was a Community regime.

Theories and Images of Europe in the mid-1990s

In the theoretical terms of the 1990s the likeliest end-situation in the Community - now called, after Maastricht, the European Union - was a modified form of intergovernmentalism. This remained the case as events began to move towards the next Intergovernmental Conference in 1996. As indicated above, for the first time in the Community's history there was a sense that the form of the end-situation was visible. Previously that had not been the case, and whatever stage was reached it had always seemed, to enthusiasts and antagonists alike, that progress towards closer union could continue indefinitely. Indeed the onus usually seemed to be on the latter to oppose rather than on the former to promote.

There were theories and images of Europe. A spectrum of outcomes in theoretical terms was conceivable. These ranged from traditional intergovernmentalism - the view that the Union was like traditional international society, dominated by separate and antagonistic sovereign states - to, at the other end of the spectrum, the federal outcome, still desired by some Euro-enthusiasts, but increasingly seeming to be unrealistic. The key difference in structural terms between these two end-situations was that federalism involved a transfer of sovereignty to the centre, whereas intergovernmentalism kept it at the state level.

In between, but on the federalist side, was neo-federalism, being the development of decision-making procedures with regard to specific task areas, within which it looked as if authority had in practice been transferred to a new centre - there had been partial authority - legitimacy transfer, and a partial relocation of sovereignty.[14] This approach assumed that the location of ultimate authority varied with the particular issue: that it could ebb and flow according to the emerging conventions of the Union.

On the intergovernmental side of the spectrum, between neo-federalism and intergovernmentalism, was a view of the end-situation which has been called consociationalism.[15] Consociationalism has been described by Lijphart as having four features, each of which, it is argued here, was reflected in the European Union of the 1990s.[16] First there must be a number of groups which are in some sense insulated from each other, in that their interests and associations are more inwardly directed than overlapping with those of members of other groups in the same state: there are relatively few cross-cutting cleavages, and authority within that state is segmented in relation to such groups. (In the European Union the distinctive polities of the separate states).

Secondly the state is dominated by what Dahrendorf called a *cartel of elites*:[17] the political elites of the various segments are each involved in some way on a continuous basis in the process of decision making and decisions are the product of agreements and coalitions among the members of that cartel. None is placed into the ranks of the opposition in decision-making, as, for instance, in the event of defeat in an election, which would be the case with a majority system. (In the European Union, the need to maintain a legitimizing consensus among leaders remained fundamental in the mid-1990s, despite the introduction of majority voting on some issues in the Council of Ministers by the Single European Act and the Maastricht Treaty). The third feature is a logical extension of the cartel principle: it is that all the political elites must have the right of veto over decisions of which they disapproved. (In the European Union, no state could be *compelled*).

In other words the majoritarian principle in the system as a whole, which is characteristic of other forms of democracy, is suspended in favour of the requirement of consensus, though it may be found within the segments, or, on some issues which are contentious, among the members of the cartel. (In the European Union the crucial point was that the formal agreement of majority voting was always conditional, and this must be so as the actors were states; it was accepted on the basis of a political consensus, and not by constitutional or legal fiat. A state might always withdraw from that consensus unilaterally, as with the French insistence on a right to veto the GATT agreement in late 1993 in defiance of the rule agreed earlier that it could be approved by qualified majority vote.)[18]

Finally there must be a law of proportionality, which means that the various segments of the population must have proportionate representation among the major institutions, the bureaucracy, legal systems, and so on, of the state. These features then ensure that the rights and interests of the subordinate sections of society, as interpreted by or filtered through the members of the cartel of elites, are safeguarded. Indeed political arrangements are so contrived that each minority is protected from the dictatorship of the whole. Each of these features was observable in some form in the institutions and procedures of the European Union. As argued in the previous section, even the Commission involved a compromise with the doctrine that it it was supranational; states insisted upon their quotas of staff, and Commissioners were from various tendencies in their home states.

This was the vision of the European Union in the mid 1990s which seemed to the present writer to be closest to the realities of the situation. But this was an academic vision, informed by the theories of the student of politics. What were the images of the practitioners? How far did they conform with the academic insight?

By the beginning of December 1994 papers outlining attitudes to the European Union, with implications for the next intergovernmental conference in 1996, had appeared in Germany, in a policy paper published by the CDU,[19] in France, in a *Manifesto for Europe* issued by Prime Minister Balladur,[20] and in Britain, in a number of statements by Ministers, but especially in Prime Minister John Major's speech in Leiden on 7 September 1994, and in the positions prepared by the Conservatives for the elections to the European Parliament earlier that year. There were clearly differences in stress among the three statements of position, but account should be taken of the domestic political context in which each was made, and of the different linguistic and rhetorical usage in each country. When these factors were allowed for, what emerged was a set of positions that had a surprising amount in common. The main points in the positions of the three may be summarized as follows:-

i. Balladur, Major and Kohl, all wanted the state to survive, and to maintain position in the Council. All three stressed the idea of the 'basic equality of the member states' (CDU paper), though the German view was explicit about wanting more votes in the Council for more people. That is it argued for stronger representation for itself as a state.

ii. All three saw the Council as maintaining a key role in the legislative process, and acknowleged that there was an irreducible core of intergovernmental interests (*intergovernmental field* in the German version).

iii. All three admitted the prospect of 'deeper monetary, commercial, cultural and defence coooperation'(Balladur paper) as part of an open list of options. But it was 'open' to Major in the sense that he carefully declined to rule anything out: he avoided positive support, which was the best he could do in the internal political context in the UK in the mid 1990s. He was particularly determined in not ruling out monetary union, the *most* 'federalist' goal, despite constant pressure from the Eurosceptics.

iv. Kohl and Balladur were clear about wanting the positions of national parliaments in the EC system to be reinforced. (Balladur: 'national parliaments must have more voice'. CDU: 'this [strengthening institutions] should be accompanied - not preceded - by efforts to engage participation by national Parliaments in the EU decision-making process.') The UK position was distinctive in that there was little call for Parliament's role in the EU system to be strengthened; the UK seemed to want the EU system to be a system for governments, which minimized any direct connections between the Parliament and Community institutions. There was also evidence from elsewhere that leading British parliamentarians were hostile to the new assembly of parliaments proposed in the Maastricht Treaty, as something which would dilute parliament's role.[21] There was hostility to strengthening the role of Parliament in the EU system.

v.   All three stressed the importance of subsidiarity: Germany most of all, despite the German useage of the word Federalism, which was much more extensive than in the other documents. The UK had the most restricted view of subsidiarity, as it excluded extensions of powers to regions and other areas within the state.

vi.   The CDU paper was the most explicit about the need for a core of states to go ahead, and not be restricted by the slowest in the convoy. There was strong support for a two or three tier Europe, and vigorous rejection of the British proposal of a 'Europe à la Carte'. Balladur, in the context of jockeying for position in the lead up to the French Presidential election - seeking to attract the Gaullist vote - said there should be a 'Europe of flexible circles inside the Union': there would be various circles of members which wanted closer union in certain areas. But what areas? It was quite likely that the upper tier would emerge clearly from this - at least in Balladur's text this was not excluded. (Since Chirac won the Presidential election in France, eliminating Balladur, the latter's attempted fudge on the EU was clearly in vain. It remains to be seen what Chirac's actual policy will be in the longer future).

Without the domestic constraints the chances were that Major would have said the same: the statements by Hurd and Major at the Party Conference in November, echoing the Leiden speech, were transparently for home consumption. It was an attempt to assuage the Eurosceptics - a necessary move in view of the government's narrow majority - without explicitly excluding policies which could have been preferred but which might later have to be accepted. They recognized that they would struggle to avoid being marginalized from a core if that emerged, and avoided - naturally - any indication that they would accept marginalization.

If the three positions are compared, and allowances made for context and usage, the sub-text, the differences between them begin to shrink. All three insisted upon the survival of the nation state, all three saw the prospect of more integration. All three supported the principle of subsidiarity. Indeed the German position, which used the word Federal most frequently, was adamant about this. The Germans were, however, committed to a constitution for Europe, which by implication would include some kind of final settlement of powers and competences: but they were also explicit about the need for more powers for national parliaments in this constitutional order. The Germans were also explicit in demanding appropriate controls, including democratic controls, for those competences that went to the centre. The French did not exclude further moves towards more integration, but were not specific about the nature of the final order: they wanted to reserve their position about its principles. The British were not averse to more competences going to the centre, but most insistent upon limiting institutional development there. They could not exclude the core idea, but were not prepared to face its institutional implications. It was also arguable that in resisting the core idea, the British strategy was counter-productive: it invited the Germans to positively reject the alternative which they proposed, and to firm up their preference for a core. There was little to suggest that the French, even under Mr. Balladur, were against this.

The image that appeared from the three positions was, therefore, that the superstate idea had been headed off by the mid-1990s. When examined closely proposals for federation, as in the CDU paper, began to look more like proposals, not for federalism, in the sense of a highly centralized superstate, dominated by a supremely powerful Commission - the anathema of the Eurosceptics - but more like a rather carefully decentralized association of states, which was a federation only in the sense that there would be some settlement of the powers of the collectivity and the constituents. The various statements by the Commission, and others, in the course of the negotiations about subsidiarity (mentioned above), were confirmed by these images. The point should be stressed: the German image was a federation only in the sense that it involved a formal settlement, embodied in an agreement between states, about what should be done where. It said nothing about ultimate responsibility or the location of sovereignty, though more than was liked by the British about what might be necessary to achieve proper governance, like public accountability. Indeed such an arrangement even in its most ambitious current versions, though not a form of traditional international society, looked more like a confederation, or consociation.

The major differences between the three concerned the degree of explicitness about the end situation. Indeed in resisting the German arguments as a start for negotiations leading up to the 1996 Intergovernmental Conference, the British strategy (yet again!) was counter-productive: it meant losing an opportunity to set in place the kind of Europe they preferred, for instance in terms of the location of sovereignty or the ways of managing the system. As it was, their opposition to any discussion of a constitutional settlement on terms such as those in the CDU paper meant that the Europe of which they disapproved remained on the agenda. The state was safe in Europe, but the British were helping to keep the threats to it alive.

Conclusions

Modified intergovernmentalism seemed to the present writer to be the most widely held image in the mid-1990s of the probable shape of the European Union of the future: it was a tightly managed community of states, among which the conventional conditions of sovereignty had been altered. The most significant element of the alteration was the acceptance of the possibility of separating the performance of functions from the condition of national autonomy. National autonomy became a means of participating in the common decision-making process, and much less an expression of separateness in the performance of specific tasks. But this end-situation also involved a paradox: that the Community did not challenge the identity of the member states, but rather enhanced that identity. The states became stronger through strengthening the collectivity. This perception was inherent in the idea of the European Union by the mid-1990s, and was one of its strengths.

It was indeed remarkable that in Western Europe in the mid-1990s some of the oldest fundamental conditions of sovereignty had been weakened without this being seen as challenging sovereignty. Complete independence in the conduct of foreign policy and defence had in earlier centuries been regarded as fundamental to the idea of sovereignty. There was now an *obligation* to attempt to coordinate foreign policies at the Community level, and the first steps towards a common defence structure and policy had also been taken. But these changes had taken place precisely at the point in the emergence of the European Community when the member states' leaders and publics had been brought to place more explicit limits upon integration.

The obvious conclusion was that the latter was a consequence of having gone too far with the former. More likely, reflecting the themes of this chapter, was that the Maastricht crisis was yet another example of the dialectic of the integration process: that there was a symbiotic relationship between the growth of the Community and the nation state. Any assertion of the former was likely, in the pattern of the historical evolution of the latter, to be accompanied by its countervailing development. Thus was the symbiotic relationship between the collectivity and the member states.

Notes

1   Taken from the Reith Lectures, delivered by Andrew Shonfield in 1971, published as *Europe: Journey to an Unknown Destination*, Harmondsworth, Penguin Books, 1972.

2   Marc Wilke and Helen Wallace, *Subsidiarity: Approaches to Power-sharing in the European Community*, RIIA Discussion Paper, Number 27, Royal Institute of International Affairs, Chatham House, 1990.

3   *The Guardian*, 11 June 1992.

4   Commission of the European Communities, *The Principle of Subsidiarity*, SECK(92) 1990, Final, Brussels, 27 October, 1992.

5   See Douglas Hurd's comments in *Evidence* on the implications of the Maastricht Treaty, given to the House of Commons Foreign Affairs Select Committee, February 1992, published March 1992 by House of Commons as HC (1991 - 92 223 - (ii).

6   *Financial Times*, 13 October 1992.

7   *Financial Times*, 16 December 1992.

8   *The Guardian*, Monday 18 April 1994.

9   See Melanie Philipps in *The Observer*, 14 March 1994 and Bernard Levin in *The Times*, 4 March 1994.

10   Stanley Hoffmann, 'Obstinate or obsolete: the fate of the nation state and the case of Western Europe', *Daedalus*, Vol.95, 1966, pp. 862 - 915.

11   *The Times*, 20 April 1994.

12   Commission of the European Union, *Eurobarometre*, July 1994, P.A13, Table 3.

13   Commission of the European Communities, *Bulletin of the European Communities*, Supplement 2/86, Single European Act, Brussels, 1986, p.18.

14   See A. Sbragia (Editor), *Euro -Politics:Institutions and Policy-making in the New European Community*, The Brookings Institution, 1993.

15   The following four paragraphs are modified extracts from the author's, *International Organization in the Modern World*, Pinter 1993, pp. 81 - 82.

16   Arend Lijphart, 'Consociation and Federation: Conceptual and Empirical Links', *Canadian Journal of Political Science*, Vol. XXII, No. 3, 1979, pp. 499- 515.

17   R. Dahrendorf, *Society and Democracy in Germany*, Garden City, 1967, p.276.

[18] For a fuller argument on this question see Paul Taylor, *International Organization in the Modern World*, Pinter, 1993, Chapter 4. For an opposing view see Anthony L. Teasdale, 'The life and death of the Luxembourg Compromise', *Journal of Common Market Studies*, Vol. 31, No. 4. December 1993, pp 567-579.

[19] See *The Guardian*, 7 September 1994.

[20] See *The Times*, 30 November 1994.

[21] See Select Committee evidence cited in note 5 above.

2 Towards Political Union: Assessing Two Strategies of EPU

MOSHE MAOR

Introduction

With the decisions taken at Maastricht, the Community has advanced in three respects; it completed the internal market, established the contractual grounds for EMU, and set the constitutional stage for EPU. The debate over the political link between these aspects which has followed the signing and the ratification of the Treaty has so far focused primarily on the appropriate balance of power between the institutions of the Community and those of the member states, that is, the extent to which the Community is, or ought to be, a federal institution.[1] The main tensions have been twofold; between those advocating increased powers for the supranational elements of the policy process and those wishing to strengthen its intergovernmental characteristics, as well as between those advocating 'deepening' the Community and those favouring 'widening' it.[2]

Whatever judgement one makes of the Treaty on European Union, everything depends on how it will be implemented. Thus, understanding the political link between the internal market, EMU and the constitutional stage for EPU requires also a consideration of the interaction between EPU and elite-mass relationships.[3] 'Elite' refers to national political leadership (i.e. party leaders), and elite-mass relationships refer to the process and the mechanisms by which the preferences of the citizens are taken into account by the national leadership. Elite-mass relationships, in our view, constitute an important dimension of EU politics, and are a key factor in promoting or inhibiting EPU. The questions which arise, and to which this chapter will pay attention, include: what characteristics of EU politics are important for understanding integration processes more generally?; what impact different

43

EPU strategies have on elite-mass relationships; and how these changed relationships, in their turn, affect EPU?

What do we mean by 'EU politics' and 'EPU'? *EU politics* refers to the politics of inter-bloc (i.e. inter-state) compromise.[4] It implies that elites of national identity-based blocs are willing and able to compromise over divisive issues with the result of promoting inter-bloc integration. *EPU* refers to an evolutionary process through which inter-governmental and/or supranational bodies are allocated governmental power directly affecting the citizens. This implies, on the one hand, the need to create a 'space without internal frontiers'. In other words, the removal of border controls over persons to enable EU citizens to exercise their right to move and reside freely in the Union, as well as the introduction of a fresh set of citizenship and political rights attached to the distinct supranational citizenship status (for instance, the right to vote in national elections for citizens who are long-term residents in a Member State). On the other hand, EPU also implies the need to move towards EMU and to strengthen the supranational elements in CFSP (for instance, enlarging the scope of the Commission's right of initiative). In terms of the differences between Member States, the first EPU strategy is to move forward by *moderating inter-bloc differences* since the free movement of people encourages the development of inter-bloc social and cultural links, alongside the economic ones. By contrast, the second EPU strategy is to advance by *maintaining inter-bloc differences*. What comes first is a matter of strategic choice.

The distinction between the two EPU strategies may, or may not, correspond to the intergovernmental/supranational dichotomy. Both moderating and maintaining inter-bloc differences could be implemented, for example, by introducing supranational dimensions (e.g. a supranational citizenship status, and supranational elements of CFSP, respectively). Thus, my analysis shifts the focus of interest away from the way decision-making processes are structured by looking at the *content* of EPU strategies and the effects they may have on elite-society relationships.

The central issue to which we now turn is the consequences the implementation of each strategy may have on elite-mass relationship. The argument advanced is that each of the above strategies may lead to a particular outcome which reflects the interests of the actor dominating the process of EPU. The first strategy - the creation of a 'space without internal frontiers' and the establishment of citizens' rights at the supranational level - would enlarge the scope and scale of transnational interest groups as well as those of European institutions, thereby undermining the control of the national political leaders over the political agenda. By contrast, we shall argue that the second strategy - the completion of EMU and the strengthening of the supranational elements in CFSP - would maintain inter-bloc differences, thereby sustaining the predominance of national political leaders. In the light of policies pursued so far by recent British governments (except the SEA) and the vitality of the Franco-German axis, the paper argues that a two-speed EMU as well as a two-speed free-movement-of-people area seems imminent, with the result of increasing significance of interest groups in shaping European policy in each of the countries in the 'fast lane'. Our first business is the nature of EU politics from the perspective of elite-mass relationships.

What is EU Politics?

The European Union represents the most significant example of economic and political integration which is developing under conditions of extreme pluralism of national identities. The fragmentation of the Community along territorial lines produces fifteen separate blocs, each a sharply bounded national identity with its own beliefs, newspapers, schools, political parties, trade union organisations and voluntary associations. How can we account for the development of economic and political integration in the Community despite these differences in national identities?

The explanation lies in the nature of EU politics as the politics of inter-bloc compromise. This is the secret of its success so far. This view commits us to all these ideas:

(i)   divisive issues are settled or postponed in the EU.
(ii)   the settlements are between blocs which are geographically
       defined.
(iii) political competition within blocs is 'self-contained'.
(iv)   these blocs have leaders, who are responsible for negotiating
       settlements or postponing divisive issues.
(v)   the bloc leaders must be convinced of the need for settlements.

(vi)   there is a causal connection between the fact that political competition is 'self-contained' and the fact that the process is dominated by party political elites.

Whereas the first, fourth and fifth ideas are derived from Lijphart's model of 'consociational democracy'[5] and remain unaltered, the second and third elements have been modified to take account of our view of the nature of EU politics. The sixth idea is not made explicit in Lijphart's studies.

What we mean by this formulation is that political leaders of national identity-based blocs are willing and able to compromise over divisive issues. At the EU level, this process is sustained by facilitating practices in the form of 'consociational' arrangements for conflict resolution by which all important political decisions require agreement among the leaders of the Member States.[6] Lijphart has identified four mechanisms of conflict resolution. Although taking different forms in different countries, 'the first and most important element is government by a grand coalition of the political leaders of all significant elements of the plural society'.[7] A classic example of the application of this mechanism at the European level is the voting by Qualified Majority in the Council of Ministers, as well as the introduction of the Cooperation Procedure in the European Parliament. The second mechanism is the mutual veto: decisions affecting the vital interests of a Member State are not taken without the agreement of its leaders. In this way, unanimity in the Council of Ministers, as well as the possibility of invoking the Luxembourg Accord of 1966, constitutes a minority veto as well as a rejection of majority rule. Lijphart's third mechanism, proportionality, is variously satisfied at the European level: the Member States are represented in decision-making bodies roughly in proportion to their population size and this proportionality may also extend to civil service appointments. Member State representation in the European Parliament, the European Commission and its top bureaucracy is proportionate to the population size of Member States. Fourth, each Member State enjoys a high degree of autonomy in dealing with matters that are its exclusive concern. This principle 'is the logical corollary to the grand coalition principle. On all matters of common interest, decisions should be made by all of the segments with roughly proportional degrees of influence. On all other matters, however, the decisions and their execution can be left to the separate segments'.[8] At the European level, the principle of segregated autonomy is most evident, for example, in the controversial concept of 'Subsidiarity' - rooted in the Maastricht Treaty - which is supposed to provide a guide for the distribution of responsibility between the Community level and Member States.

The EU bears testimony to the success of these mechanisms in reducing inter-bloc competition, upgrading common interests, promoting cooperation, and thereby minimizing the potentially destabilizing effects of national identity-based conflicts. As European political elites came to believe that such arrangements were highly desirable and feasible, they have gradually developed the skills and incentives to make them work. This was helped, among other factors, by the existence of overarching recognitions during the 1980s concerning the need for economic integration in light of the globalization of world trade. A commitment to democratic institutions resulting from the region's experience of destructive conflicts during the first half of the twentieth century further contributed to the development of conciliation practices. Traditions within the political elites favouring conciliation, mutual accommodation and compromise have also developed as the relative strength of the different elites became balanced, or not so widely out of balance that one could nurture realistic hopes of governing without the cooperation of one or more of the others .[9] In the EU, when negotiations take place among Member States, each Member can be represented by political leaders who reflect the orientations of that State, who therefore seem trustworthy and whose agreements are likely to be acceptable to the mass followings. If the national leadership is also centralized, political leaders are likely to possess the authority to enter readily into binding agreements and to isolate their negotiations from public discussion and participation. As a result, agreements may be reached, and later accepted by the public, that could not have been reached in public or through the direct participation of the public during the stages of the negotiation.

Not surprisingly, the institutional development of the EU so far has been dominated by the national leadership in each of the Member States. It has been mainly what Nordlinger[10] calls 'structured elite predominance', and conversely, a passive and deferential role of all non-elite groups, which determined the direction and the pace of integration. Specifically, when an issue on the agenda of the Council of Ministers and the European Council is highly divisive, national leaders will be faced with conflicting pressures from different class and sectoral forces as they are required to act at the European level. The short-run costs and benefits associated with the implementation of social policies, for instance, would be immediately apparent to workers, firm owners, or both. Domestic interest associations representing workers and firms are likely therefore to perceive potential costs or benefits derived from policy implementation and seek to promote their constituents' interests in the appropriate political arena. National leaders will have to choose between which domestic interests to accommodate and which to resist.

This decision could be taken without destabilizing effects only if political competition is *'self-contained'*, that is, when political actors and issue-dimensions during party competition are domestically-based. One important reason for this lies in the enhanced ability of the elites, in such a 'self-contained' condition, to balance electoral self-interest, especially regarding economic performance, with loyalty to traditional core constituencies and with the power of more ideological party activists.[11] Obviously, the balance struck can be expected to vary considerably across Member States and the parties within them. What seems certain is that a balance could be struck with minimum destabilizing pressures from alienated groups. In such a context, parties of left and right can fit the complex configuration of national interests - as transmitted by domestic interest groups - into the framework of their policy stances. Once the leaders of these parties have disciplined their supporters into following them by striking such a balance, they can use the free hand this gives them to settle similar issues at the European level.

Good evidence from all EU countries combined with common observation strongly supports the judgement that consociational arrangements for overcoming deep conflicts during the process of economic and political integration have invariably been directly created and managed by leaders, not by the general public, among whom passionate conflicting beliefs may remain strong even as their leaders pursue pragmatic and accommodating tactics. When such passionate conflicting beliefs have arisen on the public agenda, the main parties have been quick to subsume the issues within the dominant dimension of party competition, namely, the left-right divide, or to divert public attention to other issues.[12] In addition, major parties have consistently avoided competing over the issue of European integration throughout the national electoral campaigns of the

1980s and early 1990s.[13] Instead they have tended to compete over resource-related aspects (i.e. matters of allocation, distribution and redistribution) of the topic (the Social Chapter, for instance), which can easily be accommodated by the left-right dimension. Only when intra-party conflicts emerged over the issue of European integration, as in the French case, did the battle transfer to the public domain, in the form of a referendum rather than an electoral competition. Furthermore, in the case of Denmark, after an initial referendum which yielded a 'No' vote, a second referendum was initiated by the political elite. Overall, by avoiding *electoral* competition over the issue of European integration, the major parties have largely neutralized the potentially destabilizing effects of voter preferences in this area on their own electoral strength.[14] According to Taylor,[15] consociational mechanisms create 'special opportunities for elites to resist the development of cross-cutting cleavages'. Such mechanisms contribute to the consolidation of their power base, enhance their capacity to reward key domestic interest groups and amplify their capacity to influence the definition of such interests. Development of cross-cutting cleavages may encourage inter-bloc social and cultural links as well as cross-border collaboration. In turn this may undermine the homogeneity of the bloc, and thereby the ability of national leaders to shape voter preferences. We may reasonably conclude, then, that as long as inter-bloc differences are maintained - with the result of reducing inter-bloc competition - the process of economic and political integration will be dominated by national leaders. This conclusion is consistent with actual experience in different Member States, where political elites have adopted a variety of different strategies and practices which block the development of European cross-cutting cleavages.

The Dynamics of Political Integration

The analysis so far has been based on an implicit assumption that the institutional development of the European Union results from purely internal factors. However, as experience shows, countries are not static and external as well as internal conditions may change, with implications for the process of European integration. External conditions that initially favour political integration may alter and thereby cause a blockage of the process, as with France's veto of British entry which was related to the question of US influence in Western Europe. Conversely, external conditions may consolidate and thus enhance the stability of the integration process. A classic example is that global monetary uncertainty has created problems for European states who then have accepted the need for German leadership in the field - as evidenced in the construction of the EMS.[16] It represented the Member States' willingness to be pegged to the Deutschmark and to accept German priorities - anti-inflation - as their own for the sake of the system from which they also benefit. The result of such events is a consolidated basis for consensus upon which further demands for European integration can rest. This basis is strengthened, as Hoffman notes,[17] by the perceived failure among national elites of the nation-states to solve single-handedly the problems arising from economic and financial crises.

Increasingly favourable conditions may widen the scope of integration, extending it to countries with little or no prior exposure to it. The collapse of the communist regimes in Central and Eastern Europe, for instance, created the prospect of a new, much enlarged Union which could include the Central and East European states and also possibly Slovenia, and the Baltic Republics which have close historical ties with Scandinavia. In addition, the concept of political union, present but ill-defined, was brought into sharper focus by the disarray among Member States during the Gulf War, in the lead-up to Maastricht and by the civil war in Yugoslavia.

No satisfactory explanation of why the integration process varies between countries can ignore the pivotal role of principal leaders. Early in 1990 Jacques Delors expressed some ideas on constitutional reform in which he maintained that the subject justified its own IGC. This won the support of both the French President and the German Chancellor. In April 1990 the two issued a joint appeal for European Union. They also called for a second IGC 'to strengthen the democratic legitimacy of the Union, render its institutions more efficient, ensure unity and the Union's economic, monetary and political action and to define and implement a common foreign and security policy'. This appeal led to the IGC on EMU and European Union which was duly convened in December 1990 in Rome, and the continued negotiations in Luxembourg (June 1991) which led to a definite conclusion at the meeting in Maastricht in December 1991.[18] On the other hand, a negative view on the process was expressed by Prime

Minister Margaret Thatcher who, in her Bruges speech in 1988, declared that her first guiding principle was that 'willing and active cooperation between independent sovereign states' was the best way to build a European Community. While federalism was not mentioned in her critique of Europe's future, she made her feeling plain when she expressed her opposition to the suppression of nationhood and to the fitting of British customs and traditions into an 'identikit European personality'.

To adapt to the changing internal and external conditions, Member States have tended to delay committing themselves on specific issues. European integration has therefore proceeded with a certain amount of ambiguity in the Treaties. One or two illustrations suffice. The inclusion of the old term *'acquis communautaire'* in the Maastricht Treaty, for instance, is neither translated, nor has it been defined. It has generally been used in relation to enlargement, i.e. that an applicant State not only has to accept the rules of Community Law, but also its traditions and policies. Another example is the principle of 'subsidiarity', namely, the Community shall take action 'only if and insofar as the objectives of the proposed action cannot be sufficiently achieved by the Member States and can therefore, by reason of the scale or effects of proposed action, be better achieved by the Community'.[19] In the Treaty as a whole, the principle of subsidiarity has not been reflected in any particular curtailing or prescription in advance of the form or scope of Community actions. It remains therefore a general political concept, both very difficult to apply in practice and to use to mount any effective legal challenge for non-application.[20]

The conclusion we draw from the discussion so far is that conditions favouring and inhibiting European integration would tend to both co-exist and alternate. Short of a major catastrophe such as a deep and prolonged economic collapse, integration will continue in the large core countries where pro-European orientations have existed for a generation or more. If this argument is valid, one ought to recognize that whatever judgement one makes of the Treaty on European Union everything depends on how it will be implemented. The following section explores two alternatives: the first views the creation of a 'space without internal frontiers' and the establishment of citizens' rights at the supra-national level as the keystones of EPU, the second sees the completion of EMU and the strengthening of the supra-national element of CFSP as the cornerstones of EPU. Thus, the analysis shifts the focus of interest away from the way decision-making processes are structured by looking at the *content* of EPU strategies and the effects they may have on elite-society relationships.

Strategies of EPU

Creating a 'space without internal frontiers'

A convenient starting point is the introduction of 'citizenship' in the Maastricht Treaty (Article 8) which seemed to be one of the most radical, for until the signing of the Treaty this was an idea which only had substance in the context of the nation state. The Treaty concept of citizenship is based on the existing principle, as interpreted by the European Court of Justice, that nationals of member states have certain rights in some circumstances to move freely across national borders in the common market. Various rights - such as an autonomous right of circulation and establishment, free movement and establishment, voting and standing in municipal and European elections in whichever member state a citizen resides, the right to diplomatic protection in a third country where the citizen's nation is not represented, and the right directly to address grievances to the European Parliament and the Ombudsman - were also introduced. According to Close,[21] the right to move and reside freely can be counted as a 'citizenship right' on the grounds that it has been universally awarded to all adults, so it is possessed equally by all member states citizens.

However, the Treaty's provisions regarding this right are an uneasy compromise between the need to cooperate and a reluctance to give up controls. The compromise is reflected in the preamble to the Treaty, in which the signatories reaffirm 'their objective to facilitate the freedom of movement of persons while ensuring the safety and security of their people'. It is therefore hardly surprising that there was no trace in the Treaty of the commitment at Rome to fight against racism, as well as of the commitment to the Union adhering to the Council of Europe Convention for the Protection of Human Rights. These two commitments, amongst others, are essential in facilitating free movement of people within the European Union. Perhaps the main obstacle for free movement is the fact that it was an intergovernmental approach which was retained when it came to the attempt at Maastricht to incorporate into the EC Treaties comprehensive provisions on all matters related to the abolition of internal border control. The existing conventions were retained and together with all other related issues (except visa policy) they were now to be governed by procedures and institutions laid down in the Provisions on Cooperation on Justice and Home Affairs. According to Anderson, den Boer and Miller :[22]

> This part of the Treaty will profoundly affect the way in which the citizenship provisions operate. Citizenship 'proper' comprised amendments to the EEC Treaty and thus falls under the normal Treaty structures and procedures, which means, most importantly, that the rights comprising citizenship will be enforceable by citizens before the courts. But the key condition for the exercise of these rights will be the ability to cross borders between member states unhindered: this is what formally triggered the operation of European citizenship and provides for its trouble-free operation.

At the time of writing, this condition is far from being fulfilled, with controls in place at many internal borders. Efforts to eliminate controls on travellers at the EU's internal borders have run up against a categorical rejection from the UK, and also from Ireland and Denmark, albeit to a lesser extent. A policy of systematic checks is still in effect in the EU's ports and airports, even in those not offering connections to destinations outside the Union. The work by intergovernmental bodies to prepare free movement measures applicable to people (rather than their luggage) were marked by delays. Three measures have still not taken effect: (i) The Dublin Convention on the right of Asylum has so far not been ratified by all Member States; (ii) The EU's draft External Border Convention has not yet been signed due to the continuing conflict between the UK and Spain over Gibraltar;[23] and (iii) The Convention on the European Information System is still being drawn up. A notable exception is the group of Member States - namely the Benelux states, Germany and France - which have decided under the Schengen Agreement of 1985 to go ahead alone to try to formulate their own rules with regard to border controls. Italy became a signatory to this agreement in 1990, followed by Spain and Portugal in 1991, and Greece in 1992.[24] This basic agreement was complemented by the Schengen Convention of 1990 on the gradual suppression of internal border controls, which laid down the necessary measures for the application of the original accord. This is accompanied by increased cooperation in matters related to justice and home affairs and a tightening of external border controls.

The question which arises is the impact a 'space without internal frontiers' has on elite-mass relations? Free movement of people would encourage the development of inter-bloc social and cultural links, alongside the economic ones. This, in turn, may significantly enlarge the scope and scale of interest group activity. European interest groups will be formed across national borders as federated organizations on the markets where their interests are at stake. The web of domestic, specialized trade associations, trade unions and farmers' organizations would extend in a horizontal direction, managing the flow of influence between national governments and the Community institutions. In the past the dividing line between parties and interest groups was often drawn by pointing to a difference in functions. Groups were expected to convey to the party elites the total claim of a supposedly homogeneous membership, while parties were to select, aggregate, and thereby transform the raw demands of an electorate.[25] With the moderation of inter-bloc differences, transnational interest groups, and especially the elaborate structure which many of them form for effective action, may become so complex that they would be able - as parties do - to sift claims and establish preferences.

Moderating inter-bloc differences - enlarging the scope and scale of transnational interest groups - may undermine the control of the party elites over the political agenda. Policy positions of interest groups might not just be adopted to present a support-maximizing case to their members, but also as weapons to blunt the preference-shaping strategies of national political leaders. By vigorously contesting party leaders' positions through all stages of EPU, a viable interest group may significantly change how EPU is perceived by citizens and voters. In a broader way, transnational interest groups may influence the distribution of voter preference by building up voter expectation about what is feasible and/or desirable. In the nexus between economic, social and political integration, interest groups may translate their economic power into social power, and share with the party leaders the function of transforming social power into political decisions. As an outlet of anti-EPU energies by members, interest groups could become agents of innovation, by mobilizing such attitudes into political decisions. This may occur against a *status quo* which is achieved by agenda-setting carried out by party elites. Interest groups could therefore destroy a 'set' consensus over EPU as well as prepare for a new one.

As the legitimization of interest group activity depends on groups establishing preferences in line with their clientele, and since they are not responsible for the direct management of government, they may be willing to develop a partisan wing, or, more probably, to strengthen their links with European party federations. In their formative stage, such parties would have to rely on the support of interest groups in order to make their appeal to the electorate effective, indeed to ensure survival and growth. Once such parties are established in the political process at the European level, the relations would probably become more interdependent; interlocking leadership and membership, a common policy orientation etc.

Needless to say, such developments may significantly undermine the ability of political elites to segregate major areas of decision-making in order to minimize the aggravation of intra-bloc dissatisfaction. As their ability to reverse the centrifugal forces within the bloc declines, political elites may find themselves forced to adapt to, rather than shape, inter-elite and inter-bloc networks of relationships and transactions. Consequently, EU politics may be moving towards a system of shifting alliances. The idea - already enshrined in the Maastricht Treaty in the British and Danish opt-outs - would work in a 'bottom-up' way, through coalitions of consenting European interest groups (or their partisan wings) which will opt in to a particular area of joint decision-making (over EP powers, for instance) and initiate democratic reforms.

To sum up, the moderation of inter-bloc differences would increase the scope and scale of transnational interest groups. This, in turn, may undermine the control of national political leaders over the political agenda. Such control has so far enabled the party elites to operate in an electoral context of an agenda which fails to address voters' concerns over European integration and the constitutional conceptions of Europe. Thus, a viable interest group may significantly change how EPU is perceived by citizens and voters in these countries by introducing the dimension of European integration into the electoral agenda. Such interest groups are likely to play a significant role in shaping European policy.

Advancing towards EMU and the introduction of a supra-national element in CFSP

A convenient starting point is the likely future direction of CFSP and EMU. There is little doubt that at the heart of CFSP and EMU there is a readiness and indeed eagerness to develop a single foreign policy, a coordinated fiscal policy and a single monetary policy. The CFSP, however, is counter-balanced by an equally fierce desire on the part of Member States not to be caught up in the full Euro-machine of the European Commission, Parliament and Court of Justice. The compromise is to put joint policy on an intergovernmental footing rather than a supra-national one. Regarding EMU, the solution is a centralization of monetary policy through the European Central Bank, leaving fiscal policy in the hands of national governments working together through Ecofin. National fiscal policies, while differing both in detail and size and sign of change, will be largely determined by the requirement of a policy mix in which the monetary component is already given.

The relevant question in the context of this chapter is what impact the implementation of these reforms has on inter-bloc differences, and thereby, on elite-mass relationships. The answer is that the implementation of the above-mentioned reforms are unlikely to affect elite-mass relationships. A substantial reason for this is that the provisions of the Treaty regarding EMU - and to a lesser extent CFSP - put in place or strengthen federal elements. This, in turn, facilitates inter-elite links, thereby reinforcing segmental autonomy and hindering the development of cooperation amongst interest groups across Member States.

Specifically, EMU provides for a rigorous scheme for a federal currency system, with an independent central bank to manage the single currency, the ECU, and rules to ensure the sound management of the Member States' economies. Similarly, the Community's external economic policy, with substantial achievements to its credit, is also an important federal element. In this light, the CFSP can also be seen as a starting point with potential for federal steps in security and defence.[26] The introduction of federal mechanisms in these areas strengthens consociational practices at the level of the political elite, and fosters inter-elite links, cooperation and coordination. These effects, in turn, produce pressures which tend to reinforce segmental autonomy since they tend to sustain the predominance of national political leadership over the policy areas in question.

Sustaining inter-bloc differences - minimizing the scope and scale of transnational interest groups - is likely to maintain the control of the party elites over the political agenda. As no interest groups would be able to contest vigorously party leaders' positions through all stages of EPU, national political leaders would be able to determine how EPU is perceived by citizens and voters. In a broader way, political leaders may influence the distribution of voter preference by bidding up voter expectation about what is feasible and/or desirable. This would sustain a *status quo* which is achieved by agenda-setting carried out by party elites.[27]

It is helpful at this point to state the terms of the argument advanced here. Essentially it is that the premise underlying the completion of EMU and CFSP before creating a 'space without internal frontiers' is the need to maintain, rather than moderate, inter-bloc differences. As long as the distinction between the blocs remains a considerable barrier for the development of European interest groups, there is still enough leverage for national political leaders to reform the structure of EU institutions, accept new members, and determine the EU agenda for the next millennium. If this is the case, perhaps the most crucial step in the political development of the EU would be predominated by national political leaders, with a minor role for interest groups.

The discussion so far has focused on the impact the implementation of each EPU strategy has on elite-mass relationships, and its consequences for the future development of EPU. The questions to which we now turn are what may be the likely scenario, and in what ways could the two EPU strategies be accommodated?

The Growing Likelihood of a Two-Speed Europe

The gradual erosion of national autonomy provides a convenient starting point for the analysis of the likely EPU scenario. According to Skolnikoff,[28] the increase of economic interdependence, the rise of multinational corporations, the growing role of international institutions, the intensified worldwide communications and the threat of nuclear attack or proliferation - all of which are stimulated or made possible by technological change - are the primary causes of the erosion of national sovereignty. The emergence of these phenomena on the world scene results in growing limitations and constraints on the authority and autonomy of national governments:

> There is no doubt of the reality of this conclusion; there is today a large and expanding sector of national and international activities not under the direct control of governments, nor accountable to them, that impinge on the authority of governments and constrain to varying degrees their freedom of action or ability to order events. This is arguably the most significant aspect of the evolution in international affairs that has accompanied technological change.[29]

The derived conclusion is that Member States will find it difficult, if not impossible, to act autonomously, in disregard of the actions of external forces over which they have little or no control. Mature nations will continue to experience increasing constraints on their autonomy and authority as advances in the integration process encourage the growth of non-state organizations and activities.

As experience shows, the implication of increasing constraints on Member States with roughly similar economic and political conditions is a growing willingness to sacrifice major elements of their autonomy when the benefits are seen as substantial and the alternatives sufficiently undesirable. Security, for instance, was the prime motive for the first step: the integration of heavy industries under the ECSC umbrella in order to ensure that France, Germany and their neighbours would never go to war with each other again. Economic prosperity was the more prominent among the motives for the second great step: the foundation of the EEC which created the SEA. Enhancing both security and economic prosperity seem to be the prime motives for the third step; the Maastricht Treaty may be seen to confirm the Community as a valid framework for dealing with the growing interdependence among Member States. 'The weight of the evidence', Pinder (1994: 270)[30] argues, 'is that the Treaty will help significantly to deal with the problems of interdependence; and a failure to deal with these problems would be disastrous for the people of our countries, because the forces underlying the growth of interdependence are among the most important that determine the quality of their life'.

The negotiations leading to the fourth step (i.e. during the 1996 IGC) and the underlying motivations are more complicated. Member States face a number of issues that were only partly addressed during the

Maastricht debate. These revolve around the following fundamental questions: (1) the basic direction of the EU: will it become a complete pan-European institution or will it maintain its original Western European characteristics?; (2) the institutional character of the EU and the balance between European institutions; (3) the composition and the role of European-level institutions; (4) the constitutionalization of the treaties: will the ECJ begin more formally to assume the role of a supreme court? and (5) the autonomy of subnational representative and governmental entities.[31] These questions are clearly too divisive to be resolved at a single IGC. It is therefore very likely that the aim of the IGC will be modified in a way which will introduce the need - given the circumstances at that time - to make the Maastricht Treaty work as well as possible. This implies that the IGC would improve the working of the Union in the light of experience, ensure the enlargement to Central and Eastern Europe, and prepare EU institutions so that they are sturdy enough to accommodate the new members.

The likely attempt by the British government to impede some of the principal reforms proposed will make the IGC less effective, more complicated and less capable of dealing with problems such as the third stage of EMU and the anchoring of Central and East European states within the Union. This raises the prospects for a two-speed EMU, as well as a two-speed free-movement-of-people area. For the former, the Maastricht Treaty already differentiates between two groups of countries - those that will and will not participate in Stage III. Although the Treaty allows all Member States to become involved in decision-making, a core group of countries, probably the original six Member States minus Italy, could form a currency union and coordinate their economic policies closely, without regard for their partners in the slow lane. Regarding the 'space without internal frontiers', the removal of border checks within the Schengen zone implies a two-speed free-movement area. Interestingly enough, some countries which have already implemented the Schengen agreement (e.g. France, Germany and the Benelux countries), and possibly Denmark, Austria and Sweden are likely to enter into the fast lane of EMU.[32] The reason for this is that interdependence is intense among the Member States which do over half of their trade with each other. The grain of this interdependence has at its root the need for a wide market to tap the potential of specialization and skills, which require free movement of people and establishment of citizen's rights at the supranational level.

The implications for the Member States who are located in the fast lane (i.e. applying both EPU strategies simultaneously) are the strengthening of inter-elite links and the moderation of social and cultural differences amongst these countries. Based on our previous analysis, the moderation of differences would enlarge the scope and scale of transnational interest groups. This, in turn, may undermine the control of the party elites in these countries over the political agenda. Such control has so far enabled the party elites to operate in an electoral context of an agenda which fails to address voters' concerns over European integration and the constitutional conceptions of Europe. Thus, a viable interest group may significantly change how EPU is perceived by citizens and voters in these countries by introducing the dimension of European integration into the electoral agenda. Such interest groups are likely to play a significant role in shaping European policy in each of these countries.

Member States which are located in the slow lane of both EMU and the free-movement-of-people area are likely to maintain their traditional elite-mass relationship. This implies that interest groups in these countries are likely to play a much less significant role in shaping the European policies (i.e. in these countries) compared to the role played by interest groups which operate in the countries located in the fast lane. In sum, the role of interest groups in shaping European policy of the Member States within which they operate is likely to be increased as the members move into the fast lane of European integration.

Another implication for Member States which are in the fast lane in creating 'a space without internal frontiers' is likely to be related to citizen rights. Steps would probably be taken to define and strengthen the fundamental rights of nationals of Member States, especially if they are resident in another Community country. It would be reasonable to expect the establishment of legislation cum judicial review in the core countries (i.e. fast lane), under a written constitution that specifies certain fundamental rights.[33] Beyond political rights strictly linked to choice, a number of other provisions would probably be introduced: the right to cultural expression and the obligation to respect that of others; the right 'to enjoy a healthy environment and the obligation to contribute to protecting it'; a guarantee of every citizen's right to equal treatment and equal opportunities, the enjoyment of social rights and an obligation to display solidarity with all citizens of the core countries, respect for the dignity of others and the rejection of any form of social marginalization.[34]

Conclusion

The purpose of the Maastricht summit was to draw up the Treaty on European Union. It remains vital to ask, every now and again, how we should proceed in constructing the Union. An attempt to explore different alternatives has been the goal of this discussion. The upshot of our exploration of EPU strategy, then, is this: the quest for EPU may roughly proceed along two different strategies, each leading to a particular outcome which reflects the wishes of the actor dominating the process. The first sees the completion of EMU and the strengthening of the supranational element of CFSP as the cornerstones of EPU, whereas the second approach views the establishment of a 'space without internal frontiers' and the establishment of citizens' rights at the supra-national level as the keystones of the process. The latter may enlarge the scope and scale of transnational interest groups, thereby undermining the control of the party elites over the political agenda, whereas the former strategy would maintain inter-bloc differences, thereby sustaining the dominant position of national political leaders in their relationship with the demos.

The likely scenario - a two-speed EMU and a 'space without internal frontiers' - derives from the driving forces of integration, namely, interdependence. National political leaders however often make it harder for the societies they influence to come to terms with the realities with which people have to live. This has too frequently been the case with respect to British governments and their resistance to the implications of interdependence as reflected in the development of the Union. This analysis suggests that the increasing worldwide interdependence encourages Member States to defend their interests through close cooperation and coordination of policies. The political motives for the implementation of EMU are underpinned by economic forces favouring integration. At the same time, the economic motives for the implementation of EMU are underpinned by political forces favouring the creation of 'space without internal frontiers', as well as the establishment of citizens' rights at the supranational level. In light of policies pursued so far by recent British governments (except the SEA), a two-speed EMU as well as a two-speed free-movement-of-people area seems imminent, with the result of increasing significance of interest groups in shaping European policy in each of the countries in the 'fast lane'.

Notes

This paper was presented at the International Political Science Association, Berlin 1994. The author wishes to thank Albert Weale, Sidonie Beresford-Browne, and Rebecca Stokes for their comments.

1   Barratt Brown, M. (1991), *European Union: Fortress or Democracy?*, Nottingham: Spokesman; Bogdanor, V. (1990), *Democratising the Community*, London: Federal Trust.; Gillespie, P. and Rice, R. (1991), *Political Union*, Dublin: Institute of European Affairs; Haas, E.B. (1958) *The Uniting of Europe: Political, Social and Economic Forces. 1950-57*, London: Stevens & Sons; Haas, E.B. (1961), 'International Integration: The European and the Universal Process', *International Organization*, vol. 15, no. 3. Haas, E.B. (1964), *Beyond the Nation State: Functionalism and International Organisation*, Stanford, Ca: Stanford University Press; Hass, E.B. (1970), 'The Study of Regional Integration: Reflections on the Joy and Anguish of Pretheorising', in: Lindberg, L.N. and S.A. Scheingold (eds.) Regional Integration: Theory and Research, *International Organization*, vol.24, no. 4; Hass, E.B. (1976), *The Obsolescence of Regional Integration Theory*, Berkeley, Ca: Institute of International Studies; Harrison, R.J. (1974), *Europe in Question: Theories of Regional International Integration*, London: Allen and Urwin.; Hoffman, S. (1966), 'Obstinate or Obsolete? The Fate of the Nation-State and the case of Western Europe', *Deadalus*, vol. 95, no. 3. Keating, P. (1991), *Political Union*, Dublin: Institute of European Affairs; Keohane, R.O. and Hoffmann, S. (1990), 'Conclusions: Community Policies and Institutional Change', in: W. Wallace (ed.) *The Dynamics of European Integration*, London: Pinter; Keohane, R.O. and Hoffmann, S. (1991), 'Institutional Change in Europe in the 1980s', in: Keohane R.O. and Hoffmann, S. (eds.), *The New European Community: Decision-Making and Institutional Change*, Boulder, Co.: Westview Press. Lindberg, L.N. (1963), *The Political Dynamics of European Economic Integration*, London: Oxford University Press; Lindberg, L.N. (1970), *Europe's Would-Be Polity*, Englewood Cliffs, N.J.: Prentice Hall; Lodge, J. (1989), *The European Community and the Challenge of the Future*, London:Pinter; Rummel, R. (1992), *Toward Political Union: Planning a Common Foreign and Security Policy in the European Community*, Boulder: Westview Press; Pinder, J. (1986), 'European Community and Nation-State: A Case for Neo-Federalism?', *International Affairs*, vol. 62, no. 1; Wistrich, E.

(1990), *Steps Towards European Political Union*, London: European House Publishers.

2   For an interesting analysis of European scenarios, see Jacquamin, A. and Wright D. (eds.) (1993), *The European Challenges Post-1992*, Aldershot: Edward Elgar.

3   For recent analyses of these relationships Andeweg, R. B. (1993), 'Elite-Mass Linkages in Europe: Legitimacy Crisis or Party Crisis', Paper delivered at the European Conference, The Institute of European Studies, University of Oxford. Bogdanor, V. (1993), 'The European Community, The Political Class and the People', Paper delivered at the European Conference, The Institute of European Studies, University of Oxford. Hine, D. (1993), 'Political Parties and the Public Accountability of Leaders', Paper delivered at the European Conference, The Institute of European Studies, University of Oxford. Pasquino, G. (1993), 'A Most Difficult Task: Mediating Between The Powerless and the Powerful', Paper delivered at the European Conference, The Institute of European Studies, University of Oxford.

4   Throughout the text, 'bloc' means member states.

5   Lijphart, A. (1977), *Democracy in Plural Societies*, New Haven: Yale University Press; Lijphart, A. (1968), *The Politics of Accommodation: Pluralism and Democracy in the Netherlands*, Berkeley.

6   Taylor, P. (1991), 'The European Community and the State: Assumptions, Theories and Propositions', *Review of International Studies*, 17, pp. 109-125. Taylor, P. (1993) *International Organization in the Modern World*, London: Pinter Publishers.

7   Lijphart, A. (1977: 26), *op. cit.*

8   Lijphart, A. (1977: 41), *op.cit.*

9   Wallace, H. (1983), 'Negotiation, Conflict and Compromise: The Elusive Pursuit of Common Policies', in: Wallace, H. Wallace, W. and C. Webb (eds) *Policy-Making in the European Community*, 2nd ed., Chichester: John Wiley, pp.43-80.

10   Nordlinger, E.A. (1972), *Conflict Resolution in Divided Societies*, Cambridge, Mass: Center for International Affairs, Harvard University.

11   Lange, P. (1992), 'The Politics of the Social Dimension', in: Sbragia, A.M. (ed.) *Euro-Politics: Institutions and Policymaking in the 'New' European Community*, Washington, D.C.: The Brookings Institute, pp. 225-57. Maor, M. (1995a) 'Intra-Party Determinants of Coalition Bargaining', *Journal of Theoretical Politics*, 7:1 pp. 65-92. Maor, M. (Forthcoming) *Political Parties and Party Systems: Comparative Approaches and the British Experience*, London: Routledge.

12   Maor, M. and Smith, G. (1993a), *Government-Opposition Relationships as a Systemic Property: A Theoretical Framework*, Paper delivered at the ECPR Joint Sessions of Workshops, Leiden, April; Maor, M. and Smith, G. (1993b), 'On the Structuring of Party Competition: The Impact of Maverick Issues' in: Bryder, T. (ed.) *Party Systems, Party Behaviour and Democracy*, Copenhagen: Copenhagen Political Studies Press, pp. 40-50.

13   Note that the 1992 elections in Norway are the exception.

14   For preference-shaping strategy see: Dunleavy P. (1991), *Democracy, Bureaucracy and Public Choice: Economic Explanations in Political Science*, Hemel Hempstead: Harvester Wheatsheaf.

15   Taylor, P. (1991: 115), *op.cit.*

16   Wallace, W. (1990), *The Transformation of Western Europe*, London: Pinter.

17   Hoffmann, S. (1989), 'The European Community and 1992', *Foreign Affairs*, Fall, p. 30.

18   Laursen, F. and Vanhoonacker, S. (1992) *Intergovernmental Conference on Political Union*, Dordrecht: M. Nijhoff.

19   Article 3b of the EC Treaty, as inserted by the Maastrict Treaty, Article G(5).

20   Venables, T. and Martin, D. (1992), *The Amendment of the Treaties*, London: Butterworths, p. 24.

21   Close, P. (1995) *Citizenship, Europe and Change*, Houndmills: Macmillan.

22   Anderson, M. den Boer, M. and Miller, G. (1994: 105) 'European Citizenship and Co-operation in Justice and Home Affairs', in: Duff, A. Pinder, J. and Pryce, R. (eds.) *Maastricht and Beyond: Building the European Union*, London; Routledge, pp. 104-122.

23   Spain does not want the British colony to be considered an external border of the EU and proposes that Spain and the UK share customs and policy duties in Gibraltar.

24   When enlargement negotiations began in February 1993 with Austria, Finland and Sweden, these countries were invited to adhere to the Schengen Agreement and its Implementing Convention, *Agence Press Europe,* 5 February.

25   Anderson, M. den Boer, M. and Miller, G. (1994) 'European Citizenship and Co-operation in Justice and Home Affairs', in: Duff, A. Pinder, J. and Pryce, R. (eds.) *Maastricht and Beyond: Building the European Union*, London; Routledge, pp. 104-122.

26   Pinder, J. (1993) 'The New European Federalism: The Idea and the Achievements', in: Burgess, M. and Gagnon, A-G. (eds.) *Comparative*

Federalism and Federation, Hemel Hempstead: Harvester Wheatsheaf, pp. 45-66.

27   Maor, M. (1995 b) 'Party Competition in Interlinked Political Markets: The European Union and its Member States', in: Dowding, K. and King, D. (eds.) *Preferences, Institutions and Rational Choice*, Oxford: Clarendon Press, pp. 114-33.

28   Skolnikoff, E. B. (1993), *The Elusive Transformation: Science, Technology, and the Evolution of International Politics*, Princeton, N.J.: Princeton University Press p. 224.

29   Skolnikoff, E.B. (1993: pp. 224-5), *op.cit.*

30   Pinder, J. (1994) 'Building the Union: Policy, Reform, Constitution', in: Duff, A. Pinder, J. and Pryce, R. (eds.) *Maastricht and Beyond: Building the European Union*, London; Routledge, pp. 269-85.

31   Leonardi, B. (1995) *Convergence, Cohesion and Integration in the European Union*, Houndmills: Macmillan. pp. 262-3.

32   Note that Spain and Portugal have implemented the Schengen agreement but at this stage they are unlikely candidates for EMU.

33   Among the rights that might justify the autonomy of supranational institutions on certain matters, four are particularly relevant: (i) some political rights are necessary to the democratic process, in the sense that infringing these rights would constitute an impairment of the democratic process itself; (ii) the right of citizens with common problems to manage and make decisions that essentially affect only themselves; (iii) a freedom of choice (on matters such as abortion etc.); and (iv) the right to own property, and thus, to use one's property as one chooses.

34   Initial contributions by the Commission to the Intergovernmental Conference on political union, composite working paper. (SEC(91)500) of 15 May 1991.

3 Rethinking Democracy in the European Union: The Case for a 'Transnational Demos'

DIMITRIS N. CHRYSSOCHOOU

Preliminary Remarks on an Emerging Debate

This essay aims to assess the relationship between democracy and integration in the European Union (EU). It suggests that the coming into force of the Treaty on European Union (TEU) has embodied a new 'democracy dynamic' in the various attempts to further the range and depth of European integration in the 1990s. Whatever the legal maze surrounding its 'constitutionality', the new Treaty generates crucial questions for the democratic viability of the Union as a unique experiment in multinational shared rule, especially now that a new challenge seems to be confronting leaders and leads in the process of 'rethinking Maastricht': that of developing *democracy* among *democracies*, by inserting a stronger dose of decisional openness, policy responsiveness and popular control to the mechanisms responsible for the political management of EU affairs.[1]

Prospectively, the package agreed at Maastricht provides some of the necessary political infrastructure upon which the development of a *transnational demos* can be realized: a self-conscious and politically aware body of citizens capable of directing its democratic claims to, and via, the central institutions. This unique process of democratic self-transformation from an amorphous aggregate of the 'component' national *demoi* to an 'inclusive' European *demos* aims at the creation of a new civic 'we-ness' among the member publics, based on the formation of collective political identities, cross-national allegiances and multiple group affiliations.

Welcome as these might be for those subscribing to the dictum 'Power to the People' - itself a refined version of older democratic claims like 'No Taxation Without Representation' or 'Let the People Govern Themselves' - a Realist's reading of the TEU is likely to be somewhat different. In particular, s/he could argue that the constituent populations, and now citizens of the Union, still remain a largely fragmented and 'semisovereign' collection of individuals who lack either the means to set the integrative political agenda or influence in any substantive terms the making and taking of 'joint decisions' which nevertheless bear a direct impact on their lives.

This last observation brings us to the central question posed in this essay: which interpretation better fits the present-day EU? To provide an answer, and given Cohen's remark that 'Rational discourse about any particular democracy presupposes some understanding of the community in which that democracy is (or could be) realised',[2] it is essential to explore the basic properties of the new European 'body politic'.

Defining the Union: the Concept of Confederal Consociation

It seems fair to suggest that the search for political unity through the provisions of the TEU was an uneasy compromise between federal principles, confederal structures and consociational processes. A series of mutual concessions were taken by the states to meet the challenges of joint decision-making without losing sight of the growing quest for autonomous action within their own substructures. This point sharpens our viewing of the EU as a *Confederal Consociation*: a compound polity whose distinct culturally defined and politically organized units are bound together in a consensually pre-arranged form of 'Union' for specific purposes, without either losing their national identity or resigning their individual sovereignty to a higher central authority.[3]

Mainly due to its unique blend of consensual mechanisms for accommodating varying degrees of cultural distinctiveness and territorial autonomy within a nascent, but still highly fragile, framework of *mutual governance*, the Maastricht process has furthered the joining together of diverse entities in a 'single institutional system' that nevertheless preserves their respective integrities. Indeed, the peculiar nature of the political edifice created by the TEU challenges the organic view of the polity without relying entirely on the properties of 'segmented differentiation'. Hence, its greatest merit is that it does not question the separate constitutional order of the states, whilst allowing for a less rigid understanding of statehood so that the states can enjoy the fruits of the common management of merged sovereignties in a consociational manner, that is, through a coalescent-style of leadership in a 'cartel of elites'.[4]

This is made possible by applying a mixed system of consensus and majority government so designed as to bridge the tensions arising among the sub-units from a classical interpretation of the principles of self-determination and state sovereignty. In fact, the TEU offers an advanced conception of the practice of *co-determination* in a system of democracies that aims to reconcile the challenges of 'constitutional' change with the need for systemic stability - the latter term referring to the ability of the segment elites to accommodate a number of divergent expectations in joint decisions. As little doubt exists among its students that the EU remains largely unclassified as a political system, Confederal Consociation emanates as a promising analogy in filling the existing gap between state-centric and federalist-inspired approaches to EU integration, suggesting that the constituent governments have discovered new ways for strengthening their position both regionally and internationally. Indeed, the 'temple-model' created by the TEU helps to maximize the states' influence in the taking of decisions on matters of common concern, whilst allowing them to enjoy what Lijphart has earlier defined as 'a high degree of secure autonomy in organizing their own affairs'.[5]

Segmental autonomy, therefore, supported by an accommodative mutual veto, a proportional representation of all states to the central institutions, and an increased propensity of national leaders to rely on what Taylor calls 'government by alliance'[6] through *reversible dissensus* practices in joint decision-making, highlights the determination of the 'relevant elites' to exercise *managerial control* over integration even if this actually implies the striking of less ambitious settlements amongst them. Comparatively speaking, Confederal Consociation has an interesting analogue with a system of *horizontal* 'Cooperating States' in that the collective power of constituent governments is well preserved by making progress towards further formal integration dependent upon the convergence of national preferences - i.e., in the European Council as the Union's 'grand coalition' forum for striking interstate compromises.

This polycentric and multilogic pattern of federalism co-exists with a more favourable version of intergovernmentalism as a method of promoting unification, and is based on the premise that the defence of each separate interest coincides with the need to strike a deal in the context of an intersegmental positive-sum game. It may be best defined as a case of *inverse federalism*: a situation in which political authority tends to be decentralized as much as possible to the component units and away from the collectivity.[7] This mode of political interaction should be recognized as a discernible overall integrative stage in which the dynamics of *elite governance* shape the forms transnational federalism is allowed to take. In brief, territorial politics in the EU is becoming stronger as the scope of joint decisions is being extended, thus bringing its point of decision closer to the domain of state agents.

The last property of Confederal Consociation, that of *controlled pluralism*, highlights the elite-dominated character of the Union in that the members of the *elite cartel* are induced to adopting the working principles of 'joint consensual rule'. This cooperative dynamic conflicts with the 'winner-takes-all' ethos which subsists in the majoritarian Westminster model, whilst deviating from normative democratic theory and its insistence on 'rule by the many'. However, it accords with the development of consensus-building practices at the leadership level, supported by the emergence over time of a transnational political culture among the national governing elites.

In overall terms, by dismissing an 'either/or' conception of regional politics, Confederal Consociation sharpens the point that the extension of the Union's jurisdictional competences is compatible not only with the very idea of statehood itself, but also with further national state-building processes, subnational community-strengthening and multiple identity-holding. Further, it contains a suggestion both of the non-conflictual character of power-sharing and of the means through which the separateness of the segments is compatible with processes of 'institutionalized compromise'. Hence, the preservation of 'pluralism-within-unity' is conditioned by an overarching concern at the elite level for meeting the conditions of *stable governance*.

Finally, by emphasizing elite-driven, as opposed to *demos*-led integration, the model suggests that the dialectical co-existence of a plurality of forces pressing simultaneously for a more centralized or decentralized, loose or coherent, technocratic or democratic EU, passes through the ability of states to retain ultimate control over the process of building the new constitutional structure in a common framework of power. This system of *consensus elite government* in which high levels of interconnectedness co-exist with territorial segmental autonomy, approximates to the type of 'community' detected by Taylor as 'managed *Gesellschaft*'.[8] What is striking in this unique interplay between coordinated interdependencies and diffused political authority, is that the interests of the 'territorial state' co-exist with those of the central institutions insofar as they are products of consensually-predetermined inter-elite negotiations.

However, being a transitional arrangement, Confederal Consociation may give way, in time, to a politically organized community at the popular level which might be termed *nascent Gemeinschaft*. This could be achieved through the application of the TEU (possibly as amended by the 1996 IGC), not least due to the democratic aspirations embedded in the common citizenship provisions.[9] Before passing on to the implications that the new Treaty entails for the quality of democracy in the EU, it is important to throw some light on democracy's transnational dimension.

On Transnational Democracy: Setting a Framework

The evident need to respect the tradition of representative and responsible government at the Union level requires the incorporation of the fundamental principle of public accountability or *indirect demos control* in the arrangements that are to shape the relationships between the collectivity and its component states/citizens parts. This, however, requires the Union to affirm the role of its citizen-voters as the decisive subject in determining EU politics. This currently missing property from its political structures we term *transnational civic competence*.

From this view, democracy in the European Union refers to the gradual but stable building of a multilevel and polycentric system of mutual governance based on the power of commonly shared democratic arrangements among the member publics. This conception of democracy, however, implies that if a more civil, participatory and well-considered process of integration is ever to materialize, it must link different domains of political authority in such an elaborate way so as to accommodate the quests for democratic diversity of the parts and 'ever closer union' of the whole. Thus, the term 'transnational democracy' should be used as an analogy to illuminate the main features of a primarily organizing method, through which *the demos of the 'inclusive' polity can exercise control over all decisions that directly concern the lives of its members*.[10]

This definition is fully in line with the view that a common property of all forms of democracy is that sovereignty should rest with the *demos* itself and nowhere else. It also suggests that an optimal model for EU-level democracy would have to satisfy the following two criteria: the achievement of prior agreement by the larger, composite *demos* on 'the democratic rules of the game'; and the existence of mutually reinforcing legitimation structures to compensate for any loss of *national democratic autonomy* that further integration might entail. The latter term is defined as the ability of the constituent *demoi* to control EU activities through their national parliaments.

Thus sketched, far from being equated with a static system of axiomatic principles, norms and values, transnational democracy is more closely related to a set of procedural arrangements through which citizens share in the governing function of the larger entity. To that end, the establishment of the necessary machinery - including institutional and informational avenues - for effectively and continuously supervising the making of common policies and taking of joint decisions becomes an essential precondition for keeping them in close contact with public preferences.

To summarize, the more open the process of arriving at EU 'outcomes', and the more these are subject to the control of its *demos*, the more operationally meaningful transnational democracy is. For the incorporation of the accountability principle in the workings of transnational institutions becomes all the more relevant in the case of the EU since the latter represents a constellation of *democracies* embarked on a difficult journey of 'power-sharing' based on the collective management of 'pooled' competences. This said, we wish to turn our attention to a closer consideration of the problems that European governance generates for transnational democracy or, alternatively, to the question of a 'democratic deficit' in the EU system.

Reflections on 'The Other' Democratic Deficit 'Within'

A major but frequently concealed effect of West European integration is that it has often functioned as a contemporary *deus ex machina* for member governments to establish themselves as the principal actors of the national governing process. Indeed, a significant *recentralisation* of national political power has gradually taken place in favour of executive-centred elites and at the expense of traditional representative institutions which, at least so far, have failed to establish effective methods of controlling their executives in their conduct of relations with European institutions.

Hence, a deep-seated concern for a 'democratic deficit' has emanated in EU structures, pointing to the *growing dissonance between the essential requirements of democracy and the conditions upon which the governance of the Union actually rests*. Interestingly, one may trace in the relevant literature more than a dozen definitions of such a 'deficit', all converging on the same basic assumption: that the transfer of decision-making power from national to EU institutions was not matched by a corresponding degree of popular control over the new centres of authority either by national or transnational parliamentary structures. This, combined with the fact that publicly binding decisions are reached *in camera* in the Council of Ministers, and that it is only the member governments that are empowered to revise the context of the central arrangements and extend the scope of their collective action, make for a 'democratic deficit' in EU political structures.

But this is not all there is to the democratic 'pathology' of the European regional system. For the preceding description confines such a 'deficit' almost exclusively to the inadequacy of present central arrangements to bestow the Union a parliamentary capacity patterned on the familiar governing processes of its subsystems. From this 'orthodox' view, the deficit in question constitutes a structural/institutional deficit; its equally crucial socio-psychological component being ignored. That is, the absence of a civic-minded and politically active citizenry whose individual members have become conscious of their collective existence as one *demos*, whilst characterized by a lively sense and deep-rooted feelings of belonging together in a purposive whole.

But why should one be concerned with this aspect of the democratic deficit? A first answer is that the analytical foci of the *acquis academique* have failed so far to link any identity-related issues with the conditions of furthering transnational democracy. A second might be that unless questions relating to the political identity of EU citizens are immediately addressed, the next review conference due to start in 1996 will fail to make any impact on the democratization of the polity. These critical assertions serve as a reminder of the greatest challenge to democratic theory: that of focusing on new patterns of democratic reasoning so as to provide the missing link of the Union's qualitative transformation from *democracies* to *democracy*.

Little doubt exists that, for some, to speak of the end objective of European integration in the form of a transnational *demos* might be a somewhat presumptuous line of argument, and even a contradiction in terms, since it could presuppose the emergence of a new European 'political nation' as a prelude for the development of new forms of (supra)nationalism. Others might perceive the idea as detrimental to the preservation of segmental civic autonomy in a *par excellence* 'union of diversities' such as the EU. The response of this essay to these concerns is that if there is indeed a 'democratic deficit' in the EU, it is as much a *structural deficit*, reflecting the current asymmetry in the allocation of power between the core central institutions, as it is a *socio-psychological* one, reflecting the apparent lack of a 'sense of community' among the European peoples.

Moreover, if the Union is ever to evolve into a political system which deserves the term 'democracy', this is not to be achieved soleley by elevating the status of the European Parliament (EP) from a 'junior partner' to a full co-legislator with the Council or, in general, by any further constitutional amendments to the original treaties concerning the polity's institutional re-orientation. However essential, these steps will fall short of bearing the expected fruits if they are not accompanied by substantive changes in popular political sentiments and attitudes in relation to the recognition of democracy as a prerequisite for furthering the range and depth of European integration. Rather, the making of a truly democratic Union passes through the capacity of its citizenry to be transformed into a civic-minded 'all-body' in the form of a fully-fledged *demos*.

Such a determination, however, should first and foremost be shown by the anonymous member publics rather than by any documents signed by the states, confirming yet again their commitment to the democratic cause. Thus, the coming of democracy in the EU will result from the spread of new ideas and ways of relating the citizens to integration processes. For according to a revealing observation made by Schattschneider: '*democracy is first a state of mind*'.[11] In short, the envisaged order of events for realising EU-level democracy is for EU citizens to develop an active public awareness and formulate transnational democratic aspirations, whist directing their common democratic claims to, and via, the central institutions. This, together with the necessary institutional reforms, summarizes the road to greater and better democracy in the EU. Put bluntly, the democratic awakening of its member *demoi* will provide the popular base upon which a certain philosophy of democratic governance be reflected in its political processes: that of *transnational democracy*.

The point being made here is that the scholar ought to shift the emphasis from an elitist conception of EU politics to grass-root developments as a guide to revealing the widening chasm between democratic theory and practice in the integrative system. This relates to the question of what should the role of EU citizens be in a system of governance which can be classified best as an *unfulfilled democracy*, possessing some of the qualities found in the consolidated democracies of the sub-units.[12] Yet, one that should open up its political processes to a citizenry which still lacks the vantage point from which to see the larger edifice as a coherent political whole and cultivate its civic consciousness by transcending pre-established national ideologies and frontiers.

It is thus our contention that the struggle for transnational democracy will be won in the EU when the present collection of apathetic voters develops a common political personality of its own and sees a clear purpose of its activities in the larger configuration. For as long as it acts as a passive receiver and not as an active transmitter of ideas about the way in which EU affairs should be handled, the distinctive pattern of *executive elite dominance* currently evident in its structures will remain unchallenged to steer the Union, control the fate of its citizens and command the hierarchies of power by enforcing a more sophisticated version of Michels' 'iron law of oligarchy'.[13] This time, however, not in the form of dominant party structures, but of a 'regional regime' led by a management coalition of *co-operative elites*.[14]

The preceding diagnoses are not to suggest that one should turn to radical democratic prescriptions to revive the organic conception of political organisation. Rather, the aim is to find appropriate ways to stop the Union from falling short of accountability and responsiveness by means of involving more closely its incipient *demos* to the integration process. The object is to stress the potentialities of conscious community-strengthening by encouraging EU citizens to develop a sense of civic 'we-ness'. The importance of doing so is that formal constitutional engineering, far from being an end-in-itself, presupposes a self-conscious unit within which institutional reform can take place. And since no single democratic blueprint can claim to have the final word on how democracy can be made operative in the EU, it might be better to focus directly on popular political sentiments, beliefs and aspirations. To borrow again from Schattschneider:

> 'Unless we know, why it is supremely important that people participate in their own government, the great effort required to make democratic government work will not seem worth the pains'.[15]

In this way, at least, one should be hardly disappointed in discovering how much EU reality deviates from elaborate academic definitions of this unique object of study called 'democracy'.

Before moving on to examine some of the 'prerequisites' of democracy in the EU, let us stress that although the latter provides a kaleidoscope of multiple overlapping authority structures whose dynamic interaction springs from different constitutional traditions, diverse historical experiences, unlike political identities and distinct cultural affinities, the possibilities of enhancing its democratic properties by means of transcending popular political fragmentation are indeed limitless.

The '*Gemeinschaft* factor' and the Making of a Transnational *Demos*

Where does the preceding analysis deviate from existing academic approaches to the *problematique* at hand? To give a preliminary answer, it is possible to argue that without the existence of a 'political community', no democracy, whether taken as a theoretical or as a workable system, can be said to exist.[16] A second fundamental premise is that the underlying structure of relations which develop within a political community should be closer to a *Gemeinschaft* than to a *Gesellschaft*, in Tönnies' sense of the terms.[17] One reason for this is that the members of the former have developed to a sufficient degree a 'community spirit' strong enough to overcome most of democracy's potentially disturbing effects such as unequivocal compliance to the rule of majority. Equally, where such feelings are less profound, democracy is less secure in that the members of a political community lack the necessary bonds of unity in and through which all types of societal conflict might be amicably resolved.

To give a relevant example: the application of majority rule in a democratic system presupposes the existence of certain levels of social unity among its members. In Cohen's words: 'There can be no larger part unless the larger part and the smaller part are indeed parts of one whole'.[18] For acceptance of majority rule implies an *a priori* recognition that the 'opponents' who constitute 'the many' are also an integral part of the same community. Indeed, the concepts of democracy and *Gemeinschaft* refer to the same 'desirable' state of affairs in that they are ultimately expressions of an overarching relation which takes place between the members of the political community and between them and their governors. In particular, whereas democracy is an expression of these relations as viewed 'from within', *Gemeinschaft* becomes an expression of them as seen 'from outside'. Yet, what they both share in common is that they have to be formed 'from below' instead of being imposed 'from above'.

Moreover, in both cases authority is not viewed as a coercive centre which produces binding decisions on a given population without its prior consent, but rather as a form of structuring civic relations within a defined territory. Thus, authority in a *Gemeinschaft* becomes a by-product of a *dialectical public process of interaction* between 'decision-makers' and 'decision-receivers'. More importantly, *Gemeinschaft* rests on the concept of 'one people', and in political terms of one *demos*, pointing to the joining together of separate wills - with the collectivity not being considered as the sum-total of its parts but rather as an 'all-body' made up of smaller collectivities.

Moving the debate on to the Union level, a strong link exists between the '*Gemeinschaft* factor' and the democratic dimension of European integration. For the more positive the feelings of citizens, the greater the propensity of the Union to overcome any divisive issues which may arise as integration proceeds. From this view, the relationship between EU-level democracy and *Gemeinschaft* can be classified as a *symbiotic* one, suggesting that the more the viability of the Union relies on the *quality* of democracy exhibited by the central institutions, the more it remains dependent upon the extent to which elements of *Gemeinschaft* have been developed within the overall framework of shared rule. Accordingly, the formation of citizens' identities patterned on a core-set of democratic values is imperative for preserving the collectivity from the perils of popular fragmentation, whilst providing the frame within which citizens perceive themselves as part of a self-conscious political unit.

Applied to the EU, this process of *transnational demos-formation*, far from suggesting a legally-based merger of previously independent people into a new formally amalgamated entity, let alone to a centrally-planned strategy towards the construction of a *homo Europeaus* through assimilationist practices of 'consciousness-raising', points at a self-instituting process of political identity-building forged out of compatible democratic 'belief-systems'. This dynamic in the relationship between the member publics as individual units and as a composite but yet identifiable *demos* overrides any 'territorial' conception of EU politics, whilst being directed by the assertion of its collective existence as the only source of sovereign power: a 'body politic' which does not only share in civic entitlements, but is also capable of taking a prominent position in, and exercising control over, the transnational political process.

This observation is crucial for it suggests that a fully-blown EU *demos* has the political awareness of the individuals forming it, and not the will of a common central authority, to thank for its existence. Indeed, a transnational *demos* exists only if a community of politically organized people composed of different nationalities consider themselves as such. Put simply, *demos-*

formation should not be seen as part of a melting process where distinct collectivities are forced to undergo a process of 'national deculturation' and confirm their allegiance to a larger 'us' of an incipient nation. Should that be the case, it would be as if we were to accept that the emerging transnational political culture which sustains EU integration, for all its boundary-transcending implications, is a culture detached from the separate national and subnational cultures and identities of the 'uniting' parts.

In conclusion, the process of transnational *demos*-formation in the EU reflects the transformation of *a plurality of demoi to a pluralistic demos*, whose component parts actively share in a commitment to influence those relationships which, directly or indirectly, contribute to their daily lives. Therefore, it refers both to a process of *self-transformation*, insofar as the pursuit of democratic aspirations entails adherence to novel conceptions of citizen participation, and one of *self-transcendence*, insofar as pre-existing national traditions get in the way for achieving better conditions for large-scale democratic rule. Without this basis, there can be neither meaningful contacts between governors and governed *in* and *between* countries, nor solid institutional grounds for allowing citizens to identify with EU decisional 'outcomes'.

From a democratic theory viewpoint, *demos*-formation addresses the question not only of 'Who Governs?' and 'How?', but also of 'Who is to be Governed?', suggesting that no democracy has ever existed, exists or can exist without a *demos*. As Sartori put it: '*demos* precedes *cracy*'.[19] Tautological as it may sound, we find this argument sufficient to support the case for a transnational *demos* as a *praesumptio juris et de jure*. From this, after all, stems our contribution to the current debate: that the current democratic 'pathology' of the EU can only be remedied by paying attention simultaneously to the implications of, on the one hand, the process of transnational *demos*-formation, as the socio-psychological component of the democratic deficit, and, on the other, to those resulting from European constitutional reform, concerning itself with the structural facets of such a deficit.

Transnational Citizenship and Europe's would-be-*Demos*

The central question posed here asks whether Maastricht represents a breakthrough in the process of democratizing the EU by means of addressing both dimensions of the democratic deficit as identified previously. In general terms, the 'conventional' aspects of such a deficit were meant to be tackled through the introduction of a new legislative procedure, granting the EP the right to an 'unconditional' veto in certain policy areas. As for its socio-psychological part, the establishment of a common European citizenship was meant to provide a solution. In fact, it was believed that the combined impact of these measures would act as a prelude for further democratic reforms through the operations of the 1996 IGC. Hence, partisan polemics against the whole project aside, this set of democratic innovations represents a welcome, albeit moderate, development in transnational democracy-building. Since, however, the institutional remedies of the TEU have been extensively discussed elsewhere,[20] we should limit our analytical insight to their socio-psychological counterparts.

Citizenship, a legal prerequisite of democratic participation, is no longer the prerogative of nation-states. Having symbolized for some centuries now an 'internally-oriented relationship' which people as individuals have with national political institutions,[21] it has finally acquired in the context of the EU a multinational dimension. Whether a direct challenge to the very idea of statehood, the granting of member states' nationals of the right to be involved in European and local elections of other member states - especially those with a federal structure where subnational elections are taken as serious business - does signify that the era of the national state as the only legitimate actor for determining the conditions of citizenship is long gone.

Compared with the other provisions of the TEU for addressing the polity's legitimacy problems, and for all their legal shortcomings and limited sphere of application, Articles 8-8e EC carry an undisputed political weight, perhaps with the most far-reaching implications for the embodiment of a stronger *Gemeinschaft* element in integration processes. For one thing, they set in train the conditions for the development not only of what Groom calls 'psycho-political community',[22] but also the means for the nurturing of a European civic 'we-ness' as an essential requirement for the configuration of a shared democratic identity among the constituent publics. The civic element underpinning these assertions is that citizenship designates one of the most celebrated properties of democracy: the definition of the political rights and duties of the *demos* in the governmental process. In practice, this is achieved by a set of procedural arrangements that aim to fulfil the participative potential of the *demos* in the exercise of political power via the electoral process. Thus, citizenship entails a feature central to the democratic process: access to the realm of political influence.

Our viewing of EU citizenship as an element *par excellence* of nascent *Gemeinschaft* springs from a two-fold assumption: first, the setting up of a system of political rights at the Union level can further induce integrative sentiments at the grass-roots, thus offering the long-needed motive for greater public engagement in EU processes; and second, it reinforces the bonds of belonging into a purposive unit, whilst facilitating the process of EU awareness-formation on the part of its fledging *demos*. Symbolic as these may sound today, the 'democracy dynamic' embedded in the citizenship provisions should not be underestimated, all the more so in view of Article 8e EC which entitles the Council 'to adopt provisions to strengthen or to add to' the existing citizenship rights. This reference to possible future improvements does render the process of transnational *demos-formation* an open-ended one.

As with the rest of the TEU, however, so here, much will depend on the *quality* of proposals to be tabled down at the next 'deepening' round. Of such measures to build on the occurrence of a common political personality, the following can be mentioned: the introduction of a 'political citizenship' at the Union level in the sense that EU citizenship should not be conditional on the 'nationality requirement' but on new and independent civic properties of public participation in EU processes; the institutionalization of citizens' right to information on all EU issues that directly affect them; the drafting of a 'European social public order' based on the principle of solidarity to impose obligations on institutions and corporations;[23] the creation of protective legal mechanisms against any infringement of explicitly stated fundamental rights including all forms of discrimination; the enrichment of the citizens' social and economic rights, especially those relating to free movement, social welfare and working conditions; the establishment of a 'co-operative business system' for citizens to be involved in management-participation schemes; and the recognition of electoral rights to third country nationals residing legally in a member state of the Union.

This array of proposed entitlements as complementary to the new European *status civitatis* aims at the creation of a 'new political body' summed up in the notion of one *demos*. Perhaps, the political dynamics of the present citizenship arrangements will prove strong enough to foster *horizontal* ties among the constituent *demoi*, whilst signalling the birth of a more direct relationship between the Union and its publics. As O'Keefe put it: 'The importance of the TEU citizenship provisions lies not in their content but rather in the promise they hold out for the future'.[24] In short, if we define democracy as *the highest form of civic association for embracing the participation of the demos in the shaping of its political environment*, then, the implications that transnational citizenship generate for Europe's would-be-*demos* assume particular importance, whilst pointing to the assumption that the relationship between them is a *synergetic* one in that it involves the building of higher levels of political congruence among the European peoples and of citizen identification with the central institutions.

By way of conclusion, the triptych *symbiosis - synergy - osmosis*, as elements directly relating, respectively, to the basic properties of 'managed *Gesellschaft*', nascent *Gemeinschaft* and, ultimately, complete *Gemeinschaft*, can be also seen as the three stages in the making of a transnational *demos*: the first, describing the current nature of integration in terms of the relationship between the Union and the states (mutual dependence); the second, pointing to the concurrent development of horizontal links among the European peoples (compact structure) as well as a strengthening of existing ones among the dominant political elites (co-determination); and the third, representing a culmination of the previous two, and hence of earlier phases, in a genuinely representative and responsible 'Union of Peoples' (transnational democracy). From this perspective, transnational citizenship is a point of departure for the development of a new European 'public sphere' through which democratic considerations become firmly established in the 'civic culture' of its members. This, however, presupposes that a more 'communitarian' approach to EU politics prevails over any consociationalist-inspired tendencies to sustain consensus elite government.

The following diagram aims to capture the range of possibilities open to the interested parties in the context of the next round of multilateral negotiations in 1996 for furthering transnational democracy in the EU:

Democracy and the Politics of European 'Constitutional' Change

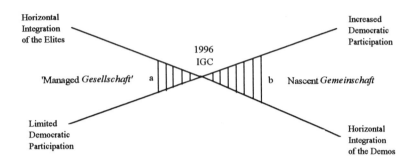

Note: a=democracy in input and b=democracy in output.

As the above diagram illustrates, the move from the upper left to the lower right side of the diagram points to the strengthening of horizontal links among EU citizens, whilst the second process stresses the quality of democratic participation in European integration processes. Taken both together, these tendencies can be seen as forming part of the wider qualitative leap of the Union - structural and socio-psychological - from 'managed *Gesellschaft*' to nascent *Gemeinschaft*.

Towards a Conclusion

A final point on the dialectics of democracy in the EU is in order: against the background of a mounting *crise de confiance* at the grass-roots, the EU finds itself, once more in its journey to political union, in front of an essentially political dilemma: that of consolidating the *acquis communautaire* so as to contemplate any possible anxiety of the states to preserve the integrity of their polities, or striking a radical break with existing practices by consciously and actively investing in the development of a transnational *demos ab intra*.

From our part, we claim that if the process of democratizing the collectivity is to be properly linked with the requirements of a nascent *Gemeinschaft*, it need not be a reflection of yet another compromised settlement by the governing elites between the advantages of collective action and the costs of autonomous decision-making. Rather, there is now a strong case for reversing the roles between those who have traditionally determined the direction of the European polity and those who have passively accepted the political and 'constitutional' choices of the former. All this amounts to the making of a new 'civic contract', flexible enough to accommodate high levels of democratic diversity within the substructures, but yet solid enough to stand firm against the politics of ministocracy, comitology and technocratic elitism.[25]

The timing for the Union to redress its acute democratic deficiencies, could not have been better, now that it is a handful of years away from the new millennium. This can only be achieved by redefining and rebalancing the democratic potential of its currently fragmented citizenry as one European *demos* conscious of its political identity. This way forward will guarantee the democratic physiognomy of the parts and realise, in the process of managing the common affairs, the most renowned aspiration of the democratic idea, recently epitomised by Dahl thus: 'Whatever form it takes, the democracy of our successors will not and cannot be the democracy of our predecessors'.[26] It is up to the shapers of the new European Union to provide some of the ends and means for making this wish come true, as it is for future generations to enjoy the fruits of its fulfilment.

Notes

1   Chryssochoou, D. N. (1994): 'La Democrazia Transnazionale nella Teoria e nella Pratica: Il Caso dell'Unione Europea', *Pace, Diritti Dell'Uomo, Diritti Dei Popoli*, Anno VI, No. 3, pp. 99-110.

2   Cohen, C (1971): *Democracy*, The Georgia University Press, p. 41.

3   For further details see Chryssochoou, D. N (October 1994): 'Democracy and Symbiosis in the European Union: Towards a Confederal Consociation?', *West European Politics*, pp. 1-14.

4   On this term see Dahrendorf, R. (1967): *Society and Democracy in Germany*, Weidenfeld, p. 269.

5   Lijphart, A. (September 1979): 'Consociation and Federation: Conceptual and Empirical Links', *Canadian Journal of Political Science*, p. 506.

6   Taylor, P. (April 1975): 'The Politics of the European Communities: The Confederal Phase', *World Politics*, p. 346.

7   This has been described elsewhere as an 'inverse pyramid'. For further details see Tsinisizelis, M. J. and Chryssochoou, D. N. (May 1995): *Reflections on the State of Democracy in the EU: The Concept of Confederal Consociation*, University of Leicester Discussion Papers in Federal Studies, FS95/3, p. 10.

8   Taylor, P. (April 1975), *op. cit.*, p. 336.

9   Chryssochoou D. N. (Winter/Spring 1995): 'European Union and the Dynamics of Confederal Consociation: Problems and Prospects for a Democratic Future', *Journal of European Integration*, pp. 279-305.

10   Chryssochoou, D. N. (December 1995): *The Theory and Practice of Democracy in the European Union*, Reading Papers in Politics, Occasional Paper No. 15, The University of Reading, pp. 12-13.

11   Schattschneider, E. E. (1969): *Two Hundred Million Americans in Search of a Government*, Holt, Rinehart and Winston, p. 42.

12   Chryssochoou, D. N. (July 1994): *The Consociational Dimension of European Integration: Limits and Possibilities of Transnational Democracy*, Occasional Research Paper No. 6, Institute for International Relations, Panteion University, p. 27.

13   On this term see Michels, R. (1915): *Political Parties*, Free Press.

14   There is of course a general problem of public apathy in democratic systems but its effects are particularly actute in reference to EU. For an account of the term 'regional regime' see Taylor, P. (1993) *International Organization in the Modern World: The Regional and the Global Process*, Pinter, pp. 2-3.

15   Schattschneider (1969), *op. cit.*, p. 43.
16   On this point see Cohen (1971), *op. cit.*, p. 41. Of course, one has to keep in mind that the inherently 'contested' nature of democracy eliminates any 'absolute truths'.
17   Tönnies, F. (1887) (1974): *Community and Association*, Routledge and Kegan Paul.
18   Cohen (1971), *op. cit.*, p. 46.
19   Sartori, G. (1987): *The Theory of Democracy Revisited*, Chatham House Publishers, p. 34.
20   Tsinisizelis M. J. and Chryssochoou, D. N. (Spring 1995), 'From 'Gesellschaft' to 'Gemeinschaft'? Confederal Consociation and Democracy in the European Union', *Current Politics and Economics of Europe*, pp. 1-33.
21   Close, P. (1995): *Citizenship, Europe and Change*, Macmillan, p. 2.
22   Groom, A. J. R. (1993): 'The European Community: Building up, building down and building across', in *People's Rights and European Structures*, Centre Unesco de Catalunya, p. 47.
23   European Parliament, 'Report on the functioning of the Treaty on European Union with a view to the 1996 Intergovernmental Conference', Doc EN/RR/273/273375, p. 68.
24   O'Keefe, D. (1994): 'Union Citizenship', in O'Keefe, D. and Twomey, P. M. (eds): *Legal Issues of the Maastricht Treaty*, Wiley Chancery p. 106.
25   Ministocracy refers to dominance of cabinet politics; comitology refers to the process of delegating legislative powers to specialized committees; and technocratic elitism refers to government by experts.
26   Dahl, R. A. (1989): *Democracy and its Critics*, Yale University Press, p. 340.

4   The Common Foreign and Security Policy of the European Union: Why Institutional Arrangements Are Not Enough

STELIOS STAVRIDIS

Introduction

The European Union (EU) is the largest, and one of the richer trading blocs in the world, and, together with the USA, the largest international humanitarian aid donor. Hence, the question of whether or not it has a 'single voice' in the world is important not only for itself and its member states, but also for the world as a whole. The international role of the EU is all the more vital now that the 'heavy lead weight' which the Cold War was imposing on most national and international conflicts has been lifted; further the 'glue' that kept the Western Alliance together has gone, and there is only one super-power left.

The question of a common European foreign policy has always been a factor in the construction of a more integrated Europe, even though it has not always been its dominant theme. Since 1945, foreign and security policy issues have regularly dominated the political agenda in Western Europe (e.g. NATO's successive 'crises' since the late 1940s; the European Defence Community in the early to mid-1950s; the Fouchet Plans in the early 1960s; the development of European Political Cooperation between 1970 and 1993; and the Western European Union, especially since the early 1980s). As a result, these events have affected the development of the European Communities - now European Union - and the pace of integration both directly and indirectly. It is therefore fair to say not only that decisions on a common foreign policy often act as 'a catalyst' for the constitutional arrangements of Europe,[1] but that for many years the actual discussions on Political Union really amounted to no more than discussions on foreign policy.[2]

The relevance of the Common Foreign and Security Policy (CFSP) mechanism for the future of integration in Europe is all the more important now that the 1996 Inter-Governmental Conference (IGC) is approaching fast, and that public support for, and interest in, the overall process of integration is rather problematic. This is evident by the controversial nature of the ratification processes of the Maastricht Treaty in Denmark, France, Germany and Britain, by the poor turn-outs at the latest Euro-elections in June 1994, by the emergence of 'anti-Maastricht' groupings inside and outside the European Parliament, and by the negative vote on EU membership in Norway in late 1994. All these questions will be further compounded by the need to enlarge the Union in the fairly near future (see following chapter on Enlargement). Any such development will inevitably bring a whole new set of issues onto the CFSP agenda.

Last, but by no means least, the EU's repeated failure to intervene effectively in the conflict in ex-Yugoslavia means that, in the late 1990s, together with the debates over a single currency and democracy, the CFSP has become one of the most dominant issues in Europe.

This chapter begins with a critical analysis of the Maastricht Treaty provisions for a CFSP and then reviews its record since it came into being following the implementation of that Treaty on 1 November 1993. It then considers the reasons for the rather limited impact of the new arrangements on the emergence of a European voice in world affairs, and, finally, assesses a number of recent proposals for improving that situation.

The double aim of this chapter is to show the limitations of the current arrangements but also, perhaps more importantly, to emphasize the fact that any approach that puts too much emphasis on the institutional arrangements of the CFSP, and ignores the politics (and the national interests behind them), runs the risk of presenting a false diagnosis and therefore of proposing the wrong solutions for change. This chapter takes the alternative view that the real problem is the non-convergence of national foreign policy interests *despite* nearly a quarter of a century of institutionalized efforts in that direction. To a certain extent this is due to the fact that diverging national interests have to be considered not as an impediment for the emergence of a common European international stance, but instead as the starting point from which such a development might occur. To try to impose a European 'strait-jacket' in foreign and security issues can only lead to a 're-nationalisation' of European foreign policy. Any over-harmonization which might result from qualified majority voting or from the 'imposition' of a foreign policy line favoured by the European Commission will unavoidably have a negative effect on all those years of foreign policy cooperation among member states. Any changes to the existing CFSP arrangements in the forthcoming IGC must take these factors into consideration. Any attempt to ignore them would perhaps promote a more reassuring line, which fits well with the traditional 'package deals' that have undoubtedly promoted European integration in the economic field, but which will at the same time antagonize far too many member states and their respective publics for the continuing well-being of European integration as a process which encompasses both economic and political matters, including foreign policy and security issues.

Assessing the Common Foreign and Security Policy

Assessing the CFSP provisions of the Maastricht Treaty

The first caveat that one must make at this stage is the obvious, though important - point that the period being assessed only covers about two years, i.e. 22 months (the period covers 1 November 1993 to 1 July 1995). Such a limitation means that this can only be an interim assessment. Having said that, it is a necessary exercise as the 1996 IGC will try to amend the CFSP provisions of the Treaty in the light of the experience accumulated until then. In other words, this is not only an 'academic' effort in the best sense of the word, but a contribution to the more general debate that is taking place in Europe prior to the IGC next year. The huge number of documents being presented recently by governments, political parties, European institutions and academics reflects the importance of this exercise. This is partly linked to the fact that the consensus now appears to be that the 'Monnet' method of integration has been replaced by the need for a more open, democratic approach which requires a longer, more complex, and less secretive debate on Europe.[3] The CFSP's future is equally affected by that new dimension.

The objectives of the CFSP provisions

In their most ambitious interpretation, the CFSP arrangements had three main objectives in mind. The arrangements in the Treaty represent a compromise between these ideals and various government views:

- firstly, to facilitate the emergence of common EU actions in the field of foreign and security policy by limiting the use of the rule of unanimity and the use of the national veto in the decision-making process;
- secondly, to 'integrate' the various external policies of the European Union by weakening considerably, if not totally eliminating, the previously existing legal and *de facto* dichotomy[4] between EC affairs (trade and aid policies) and EPC affairs (European Political Cooperation, i.e. foreign policy);
- thirdly, to move towards overcoming at long last the distinction between, on the one hand, the economic and political aspects of European security, and on the other, its military component (i.e. defence).

The Maastricht Treaty deals with the first problem by creating a distinction between principles and joint actions (Article J.3). In the former case, decisions will still be taken under the rule of unanimity but, once unanimous decisions have been arrived at, how they would be implemented would, if all states agree, come under majority voting decisions. With regard to the dichotomy between the then EC and EPC affairs, some progress has also been made by the incorporation for the first time of a right of co-initiative granted to the Commission, but the formal dichotomy is maintained, albeit under different names and acronyms (respectively European Union for EC, and CFSP for EPC). As for the military question, Maastricht faces up to this fact by adding a security-defence dimension to the European Union by allowing military issues to be discussed for the first time within the EU albeit within its second 'Pillar' and under the EU's newly declared 'defence arm', namely the WEU (Western European Union).[5]

In terms of new procedural arrangements, the Maastricht Treaty has created a number of new devices for the CFSP. Old EPC declarations and communiqués are replaced by CFSP Statements. Article J.2 institutes 'Common Positions' and Article J.3 creates 'Joint Actions'. This division is important for at least two reasons:

- the former also requires that 'Member States shall ensure that their national policies conform on the common positions';
- the latter provides for the possibility of 'decisions [...] taken by a qualified majority'.

The CFSP produced 15 Statements between 1 November 1993 and 31 December 1993, and 110 in 1994. This is consistent with the past record of EPC declarations and communiqués, although their final number is obviously affected by international events. Since November 1993, 11 Common Positions have been agreed, dealing with Former Yugoslavia (four to date), Ukraine, Haiti (two), Rwanda, Sudan, Libya, and Burundi. With the exception of those concerning the Ukraine and Burundi, the common positions dealt mainly with economic sanctions and other political use of trade.[6]

In addition, 15 Joint Actions have been adopted in the same period: 8 dealing with the Former Yugoslavia, 2 for the Stability Pact (the so-called 'Balladur Plan'), and one each on South Africa, the Middle East Peace Process, Non-Proliferation, the Russian Parliamentary Elections of 1993, and the control of exports for dual-use goods. The Joint Actions on Yugoslavia dealt with humanitarian aid and the administration of Mostar. As for South Africa and Russia, the Joint Actions really amounted to the sending of observers for the elections held in those countries in December 1993 and in April 1994 respectively.[7]

The limitations of the new arrangements

There are obvious inherent problems with these developments: the most important problem is of course the artificiality of the distinction between objectives and actions. This will not be easy to maintain in the real international world. As Christopher Hill has noted, it is extremely difficult to:

'sustain the distinction between policy (to be decided by unanimity) and implementation (to be subject to majority voting). A position which states set out as a policy goal in itself has the habit of soon becoming a step towards something else, in an unending chain of indistinguishable ends and means'.[8]

Similarly, it has been argued that

'different issues overlap. What would have been the position over the 1989 Tiananmen Square massacre in Peking, if human rights were under common action but relations with China were not?'.[9]

A further complication, which confirms the unsatisfactory nature of the CSFP arrangements, is the existence of an 'opt-out' clause which will simply make any agreement over a common stance extremely weak and impair the emergence of a common European policy. Thus, Article J.3 Paragraph 2 reads: 'The Council shall, when adopting the joint action *and at any stage during its development*, define those matters on which decisions are to be taken by a qualified majority' (emphasis added). Moreover, Paragraph 6 of the same article says that if a state is not conforming to the agreed position, it should simply inform the Council and, in case it decides to take urgent unilateral measures, these should simply have 'regard to the general objectives of the joint action'. The phrasing is far weaker than the one included in the second Dutch draft of November 1991 which had called for these actions to be 'in accordance with' the objectives of the joint action, and which was abandoned after the furore it created.

In other words, the Treaty has enough in-built ambiguity to avoid watertight definitions of what can - and what should - be done in foreign policy. This dimension continues to a certain extent the flexibility of the EPC arrangements; but one may wonder whether what in the past was a virtue has not been turned into a vice. It may be the case that the future use of majority voting will, as the EC's past experience has shown in other areas, facilitate the emergence of compromises and therefore of agreements, but it seems foolish to expect that a mechanism will create consensus, especially in such a sensitive field of national sovereignty. In that respect, the CFSP provisions have put the cart before the horse. Furthermore, the belief that a mixture of unanimous decisions and majority decisions will create a common stance betrays wishful thinking and a fundamentally mistaken interpretation of the past record of EPC, which, unquestionably, has not been particularly successful in defining clear foreign policy principles over the years (see below).

In terms of procedural arrangements, the confusion remains about the means available under the CFSP provisions, as there seems to be no logical division of labour between common positions and joint actions. All of them are now published in the *Official Journal of the European Union* (under series L - for Legislation), but the European Court of Justice is explicitly excluded from Pillar Two,[10] and the roles of the European Commission and of the European Parliament are limited. Furthermore, a recent Council report has complained about the unsuitability of the existing arrangements for 'the preparation and adoption of legal texts by COREU [which] causes difficulties' as their main purpose is communication and not to produce legal texts.[11]

Moreover, as a recent Commission report points out,

'Les 'positions' peuvent couvrir à la fois des orientations fondamentales et des actions concrètes tandis que les 'actions' peuvent se limiter à des mesures diplomatiques ou administratives ad hoc'.

Practice seems to have confirmed the most pessimitic predictions made in the past. The report also complains about the fact that a number of devices that are available have not been used in practice. Thus, an indirect form of majority voting was only used once (over the joint action on anti-personnel mines).[12]

Decision-making frameworks and procedures

With regard to the removal of the distinction between the decision-making frameworks and procedures for the external economic relations of the Union and those for its political affairs, although some limited progress has indeed been made, a number of important problems remain.

The absence of a clear definition of what each institution is supposed to be doing under the new arrangements is further complicated by Article A which states that 'The Union and its member states shall define and implement a CFSP'. This is quite different from the abortive and controversial Dutch plan of 24 September 1991 already mentioned above, which would have fully extended the Commission's traditional EC exclusive right of initiative to the CFSP. The Council and the Union are given the pre-eminent role, and the Commission shall act in full association with the work carried out in CFSP. The wording here is important as it implies that the Commission should not be seen as the key actor in the CFSP, even if Maastricht gives it for the first time the right of co-initiative in foreign and security issues. Only practice will show how the Commission will be allowed to use its new formal powers. So far, there seems to be little evidence that the Commission itself is willing to use them.

The problem was further complicated by the fact that it took the European Community/Union some time to reorganize its institutional arrangements with regard to the CFSP back-up infrastructure. The Political Secretariat, which took so long to materialize in the first place,[13] has now been 'merged' with the Council Secretariat in Brussels, although the distinction between CFSP and external economic affairs remains.[14] The number of officials has expanded from 5 in 1987 to nearly 30 in 1995, half of them being seconded from national foreign ministries and the remainder being full-time officials of the Secretariat General of the Council of the European Union which has now moved to its new (and massive) headquarters on the other side of Rue de la Loi. Similarly, it is not clear, at this stage, what will be the long-term implications of having given COREPER the final say over the preparation of Council meetings on all issues (including CFSP matters), while the Political Committee remains in charge of planning and formulating the EU's foreign policy. Especially when one bears in mind that the Foreign Ministers Report of 29 October 1993 has 'invented' a way to re-establish the primacy of the Political Committee over COREPER in CFSP matters: the former can issue an 'avis' (opinion) which cannot be altered by the latter.[15]

This situation is further complicated by the establishment in November 1993 of a second Directorate-General, alongside DGI, within the European Commission dealing with foreign affairs at the political level (DGIA). In addition to the nightmarish implications for internal Commission reorganization, such a development has created new antagonism in the midst of the Commission bureaucracy. In the last months of the Delors Presidency, the latter was also fuelled by the somewhat contrasting views and personalities of the Commissioners who were dealing directly with international affairs (Holland's Hans Van der Brock, Britain's

Sir Leon Brittan, and Spain's Manuel Marin).[16] Under the new Presidency of Jacques Santer (which began in January 1995), the same three Commissioners (but with slightly different portfolios), plus another two of their colleagues (Portugal's Joâo de Peus Pinheiro and Italy's Emma Bonino) all cover various aspects of international affairs. At the request of the European Parliament, following the first vetting of the new Commission in early January 1995 under the new Maastricht Treaty arrangements, the new Commission President, Jacques Santer, was also given a formal role in the CFSP .

The Commission has also just finished the second reorganization of its DGI and DGIA structure this time according to geographical lines, albeit some functional differentiation will remain. Thus, DGI, which used to cover all economic aspects of external relations with both sectoral and geographical units, now includes all aspects of relations (both political and economic) with North America (USA, Canada, but also NAFTA), Australia and New Zealand, and the Far East (Japan, China, Taiwan, Korea, Hong Kong, and Macao). DGI also deals with sectoral and thematic issues such as anti-dumping, and with relations with other international economic organizations such as the OECD or the World Trade Organization (ex-GATT). The non-European Mediterranean countries, Latin America, and all the other Asian states come under the brand new DGIB. As for relations with the countries in Europe which are not part of the EU, they now belong to DGIA, which covers both economic and political issues with them (Central and Eastern Europe, Russia, ex-Yugoslavia, the Mediterranean applicants, and what is left of EFTA after the 1995 EU enlargement). DGIA also covers the CFSP as a whole, relations with the UN, NATO, the Council of Europe and other international organizations, and also deals with questions of planning, COREU, and, finally, relations with the many Commisson offices around the world (delegations).[17]

Directorate General VIII (Development) remains in charge of the Commission's overall development and aid policy, and also covers relations with the ACP (Lomé Convention) countries; but if some aspects of these relations are dealt under the CFSP, then they come under DGIA. There is also a specially created office within the Commission dealing with humanitarian aid (ECHO: European Community Humanitarian Office) which began its operations in early 1993. All this adds some more confusion in the overall picture of what European foreign policy is and who decides it.

Another important implication of the creation of the CFSP, which has yet to be fully clarified and implemented, is the question of who finances CFSP operations? This is of particular importance as budgetary considerations have often dictated the final source of power in any organization not simply because of the fact of the 'who pays the piper ...' principle, but also because any financial contribution to the CFSP from the EC budget brings in, or reinforces the role of, the Community institutions, mainly the Commission and the European Parliament. This leads to the introduction into the debate over the future of the CFSP of the political power game that has characterized the process of European integration over the last forty years. This is not to say that other issues such as the question of the democratic control of European foreign policy are not important,[18] but it implies that the daily bargaining and power politics that takes place between the various EU institutions will impinge upon the future working arrangements of the CFSP in a manner that is not *necessarily* the most effective for the formulation, adoption, and implementation of a European common foreign and security policy.

The situation, for the time being, is that administrative expenditure incurred by the EU institutions under the CFSP arrangements will be financed through the EC budget. Operational expenses will come from either the national budgets or the EC budget.[19] In practice, the question of the financing of the CFSP - and of the way the current debate will evolve over the next few months - represents another problem that the 1996 IGC will have to take into consideration.

Even if in the past the artificiality of the distinction between the economic and political aspects of security, and its defence dimension, had been blurred *de facto*, as a number of incidents reveal,[20] the Maastricht Treaty has included the military aspects of security on the EU's agenda for the first time since the abortive attempt at creating a supranational defence community in the early 1950s (EDC).

More importantly possibly than the question of the non-coincidence of membership between the EU and the WEU (see below) or the fact that the taboo over defence issues has been lifted, is that Maastricht has failed to address the full implications for NATO of bringing the WEU into the EU. Although it is always difficult to define precisely which countries agree with which particular point, it is possible to argue a broad dividing line grouped on the one hand the UK, the Netherlands, Portugal, and Denmark, and, on the other, France, Germany, Italy, Spain, Greece, and Belgium on the question of the 'WEU vs NATO'. [21] The recent addition of three 'neutral' states has further complicated the debate but has not diminished its intensity significantly.

The Maastricht Treaty also lacks clarity over the nature of the future defence arrangements. Such vagueness is accompanied by some contradictions which mean trouble for future cooperation in that field. The open-ended nature of the commitment to achieve eventually the 'framing of a common defence policy, which might in time lead to a common defence' (Article J.4.1) only adds to the uncertainty. Even if the current phrasing is less demanding than the 'ought to lead' of the previous draft, the text of the Treaty also includes an inherent paradox. On the one hand, the WEU becomes 'an integral part' of the Union and is given the task of elaborating and implementing decisions and actions of the Union which have defence implications (Article J.4, paragraph 2). On the other, Paragraph 4 of the same Article states that the CFSP shall

> 'not prejudice the specific character of the security and defence policy of certain Member States and shall respect the obligations of certain Member States under the North Atlantic Treaty and be compatible with the common security and defence policy established within that framework'.

However, the wording of paragraph 2 is much stronger than in the previous Dutch draft of November 1991 which used the far less committing words of 'may be *wholly or partly* implemented in the framework of the Western European Union, *in so far as they also fall* within the organization's sphere of competence' (emphasis added). This seems to be a clear departure from the NATO communiqué of 8 November 1991 (Rome) where British officials were reported to have said that Mitterrand's scheme for the WEU had been through 'two uncomfortable days' when the primacy of NATO in European defence matters had been reiterated.[22] In addition, the CFSP provisions do not duplicate the WEU's activities as no defence council or CFSP troops are set up, and there is clear reference to the WEU treaty in the revision clauses.

The forthcoming IGC in 1996 has 'upped the stakes', as the WEU Treaty comes to the end of its initial 50 years of existence which gives the right to all its members to reassess their membership. In addition, the WEU has expanded, following the Petersberg Declaration of June 1992, which responded positively to the request made by the European Council in Maastricht in December 1991 to try and bring the respective EU and WEU memberships closer together. As a result, yet another EU member has become a WEU member state (Greece since 7 March 1995; whilst Spain and Portugal had joined the WEU in March 1990 only four years after joining the then EC), and other EU members have opted for the less controversial status of observers (Ireland and Denmark), whereas non-EU members of NATO have obtained an associated status (Turkey, Iceland and Norway). Undoubtedly this renders the whole debate about the related question of enlargement (see below) all the more complicated, especially if one adds the further question of NATO enlargement and its current arrangements with associate partners through the NACC (North Atlantic Cooperation Council) and PFP (Partnership For Peace). How all these points relate to the future enlargement of the EU and of WEU reinforces further the existing confusion.[23]

Assessing the CFSP'S Record

The CFSP, the conflict in ex-Yugoslavia, and the Macedonian question

It has been argued elsewhere that '[t]he cumulative impact of the Gulf and Yugoslavia does give pause for thought about the future [of the then EPC]'.[24] The former falls under the EPC era and will not be assessed at this stage, but the latter, though it began under EPC, falls squarely into the CFSP's existence. As for the Macedonian issue, it has been particularly prominent in the last two years, and is given special attention in this section because it represents an excellent test case for the CFSP. Our selection of the following case-studies is meant to illustrate the basic problems that the CFSP has faced, is facing, and will face in the future.

As far as the on-going conflict in ex-Yugoslavia is concerned, it is possible to argue that the sending of EC peace monitors was the first real common action of the then Community. The EC/EU has also sponsored a peace conference under the chairmanship of Lord Carrington, a series of unsuccessful ceasefires, and a constant mediation by Lord Carrington, then Lord Owen, and now Carl Bildt. To a certain extent, it was probably wrong to *expect* the EC/EU to play a role in peace-keeping operations when the United Nations's long standing experience could have been put to better use. Similarly, it was perhaps a mistake for the EC/EU itself to try to do peace-keeping operations in that region in the first place.[25] Moreover, once the real issue became one of peace-making also involving peace keeping by military means, organizations such as the WEU or NATO would have been better suited for such an action if and when it was willed.[26]

Where EPC *did fail* dramatically is in relation to the question of the recognition of new states. From the beginning of the Yugoslav crisis, the EC failed to recognize that the old Yugoslavia was doomed to disappear. In fact, it has been argued, rightly or wrongly, that the initial declarations made by the European foreign ministers on this question were interpreted by the Serbs and the Yugoslav Federal Army as a *carte blanche* for keeping the country united, by force if necessary. The American position being similar at that time meant that there was no apparent risk for those who believed that a military solution could work. Once the Germans pushed (especially after September 1991) for the recognition of Slovenia and Croatia, EPC cohesion ended. Only two days after the Treaty on European Union with its ambitious provisions for a common foreign and security policy had been agreed, the decision taken in Maastricht to promise recognition if certain criteria had been met on 15 January 1992 did not last for long. The Germans announced that they would recognize the two breakaway states irrespective of whether they passed the test set by the Badinter Committee. EPC's success at keeping the Twelve together for so long turned into a farce, even if Germany has been at pains by trying to argue that it had not 'single-handedly' forced recognition.[27]

The claim that keeping the Twelve together can be considered to be a success is unconvincing.[28] Surely after so many years of trying to get a common position, and, having provided *their own new criteria* thanks to the Badinter Report, EPC's failure to present a common front should be regarded as a major setback. The other countries, especially Britain and France showed their disappointment vis-à-vis the German independent line by not opening official diplomatic links with Slovenia and Croatia on the day they recognized them. This was not something that worried the German government too much, at least in the short run. Furthermore, Croatia was recognized even though it did not meet the criteria established by Badinter. President Tudjman's written assurances were deemed sufficient, and this recognition further damaged the credibility of Europe. Finally, the former Yugoslav Republic of Macedonia was not recognized although it did meet the criteria (see below).[29] Of course, all this could be dismissed as evidence of the respective power of the member states, but again, Germany's activism was difficult to understand for the other countries only a few months after Germany's failure to contribute militarily to the liberation of Kuwait, and because of the so-called constitutional restraints which the Germans continually referred to while calling for more action. The resurgence of nationally-driven foreign policies within the framework of the CFSP cannot be easily ignored. More and more governments are ready to promote their national foreign policy interests than was the case in the past. Big states obviously dominate this new trend. The Germans have been identified by many as the main 'villains'[30] but this criticism is by no means limited to them.[31]

What has been described above equally applies to small(er) states when they perceive, rightly or wrongly, that their vital national interests are at stake. The unilateral and unexpected imposition of an embargo on 'Macedonia' by the Greek Prime Minister on 16 February 1994 and the subsequent reactions within the EU deserve some attention as they summarize well the lack of commonality of views *despite* nearly a quarter of a century of dogged efforts at achieving precisely that. The fact that this most important conflict did not get onto the CFSP agenda, and the fact that it was not even considered (at the Greek government's behest), further highlight the difficulties that the new foreign and security policies arrangements within the EU are facing.

What actually happened on 16 February 1994 was the culmination of a long saga over the recognition and the name of the republic which came out of the collapse of the old Yugoslavia and which used to be called the Yugoslav Republic of Macedonia.[32] As the new state entered the United Nations, the name agreed in April 1993 was that of the Former Yugoslav Republic of Macedonia (or FYROM for short). This was the first time that a new UN member had joined the organization with a temporary name, but, at that time, this was seen as the only solution considering Greece's opposition to the use of the historic name of Macedonia. There was also provision for continued negotiations to try and find a diplomatic solution to that specific problem. As a result, all the EU members continued to abide by the decision taken in Lisbon in June 1992 not to recognize FYROM formally, although relations were *de facto* entered into once FYROM joined the UN.

On 15 October 1993, the new Greek government of Andreas Papandreou (PASOK had won the early elections of 10 October 1993) decided to withdraw from the UN-brokered negotiations with FYROM over the republic's future name. The Greek government claimed at the time that no progress was being made and, therefore, that there was no point in continuing the discussions.

This unilateral withdrawal was seen by some third states as breaking off the promise to try and settle the dispute diplomatically and, subsequently, as bringing the decision taken in Lisbon in 1992 to an end. Thus, Belgium, which was holding the Presidency of the Council at the time, announced on 21 October that it recognized FYROM. This opened the way to a number of other EU states to follow suit (Denmark, France, Germany, Italy, the Netherlands and the UK in December 1993).[33] The Greek government saw this as a renunciation of the agreed policy adopted in Lisbon and was furious about it.

The fact that Belgium was holding the Presidency just before Greece was seen by Athens as a clear rebuff to the incoming administration which had just been elected. The additional fact that the other EU states followed the Belgian lead just before the beginning of the Greek Presidency was seen by some as further evidence of an anti-Greek 'plot'. Before the recognitions, Mr Pangalos had warned against such a development which would be regarded in his view as 'highly regrettable [and as] a hostile act towards Greece, [which] will create problems in the area'.[34] After the recognitions, a Greek government spokesman, Mr Evangelos Venizelos, had described the December 1993 recognitions as 'a blow to European solidarity'. Mr Papandreou had also suggested that Greece might impose an embargo against FYROM as a result of diplomatic recognition by friendly countries.[35]

There were many reactions to the Greek decision to impose the embargo in February 1994[36] which included a number of critical voices, both in most EU capitals and in the European Commission in Brussels. Some commentators also presented the embargo as further 'confirmation' of the fact that Greece was not a 'European' country. The often-related argument that it should not be a member of the EU either, was mentioned at that time. The fact that there is no clear logical or institutional link between how a state behaves in its foreign policy and whether it should be a member of the EU was conveniently overlooked.[37] If such a link were to be made, it would create an impossible situation for the CFSP as the countries that, more often than not, tend to prevent a common European voice in international affairs, are usually the big ones, and Britain and France in particular.

The comments made by Mr Pangalos on 29 November 1993 about Germany's role ('Germany [...] is like Pantagruel, a giant with bestial force and a child's brain') were quickly repeated in the media as further evidence of Greece's lack of Europeanness. Mr Pangalos had also said that the hasty German recognition of Slovenia and Croatia had eventually precipitated the bloodshed in Bosnia.[38] It has become clearer now that many EU member states' diplomats tended to agree with this view but were not ready to say so publicly then, and even now these comments are mainly 'off the record'.

The European Commission's reaction to the Greek embargo of February 1994 was even more important. Following a failed attempt to find a compromise solution by the then Commissioner for External Political Affairs, Mr Hans van den Broek, the Commission took the decision to bring the Greek government before the European Court of Justice in early April 1994 under the Common Commercial Policy (CCP) rules. This decision also stemmed from the fact that the Dutch Commissioner blamed equally Athens and Skopje for the lack of success of his 'shuttle' diplomacy. Mr van den Broek did not endear himself to the Greeks at the end of his failed diplomatic effort by declaring that 'Greece must lift the embargo [...this is] not negotiable'.[39]

This is not the place to assess the legal issue at stake.[40] Suffice it to say, that to bring the country holding the Presidency to Court over a foreign policy issue can only be seen as a political decision which, to be carried out, must have secured the tacit support of major EU states. This was perceived in Athens, rightly or wrongly, as an unacceptable act of interference in its internal affairs and an attack on its sovereignty. The additional fact that the Commissioner dealing with the embargo decision at the EU level was a former Dutch foreign minister was not lost in Greece where, perhaps not surprisingly, it was linked to the fact that, at that time, the Dutch Parliament had not ratified Greece's accession to the WEU Treaty.[41]

The debate that took place in the European Parliament illustrates the limitations of the CFSP arrangements well. Mr Pangalos, who had the unpleasant role of trying to defend the Greek position on 23 February 1994 during a heated debate in Brussels, insisted that there was no Presidency view because there was no agreement in the Council. Pangalos himself admitted that 'most members of the Council - but not all of them - levelled criticism at the Greek government for its decision'. Some MEPs mainly from the ARC group (e.g. the Belgian Vandemeulebroucke) but also senior MEPs such as the veteran Leo Tindemans, a former Belgian prime minister, emphasized the Presidency's failure to come up with a statement on the situation. All the hullabaloo hid the more important fact that, on such an important issue for one of its member states, the EU could not produce a common view because there was no solidarity with, or from Greece.

To sum up, this section has shown that national perspectives continue to dominate the formulation of a European foreign policy. The procedural arrangements cannot *by themselves* produce a common position for the European Union. The examples of the conflict in Bosnia and the question of Macedonia were used here to illustrate this point. The main conclusion however extends to other areas of international relations. These two cases remain of primary importance for the EU in the 1990s. But the previous record of EPC also shows a similar picture. In other words, these two recent examples fit well into a pattern that can be discerned in European foreign policy cooperation: that is that there has been very little progress towards a common European stance in world affairs, despite nearly 25 years of efforts in that direction. The key question is that not enough attention has been paid to the really important issues of divergent national perspectives.

Explaining the Reasons for the Lack of Progress

European Political Cooperation (EPC)'s past record

As was mentioned above, there is a clear lack of evidence of any real progress in terms of substance of European foreign policy since the CFSP provisions were implemented. The best example is Yugoslavia, both at the level of the paralysis experienced by the EU in its efforts to find a peaceful solution to the conflict, and more importantly, with regard to the problem of the recognition of new states.

The following section examines briefly the lack of a single voice in the past in an attempt to explain why it has been so difficult to achieve that objective, and also in order to show that the real problem does not lie with the institutional arrangements of the CFSP now and of EPC in the past, but rather with the fact that member states have different views and priorities in the world. The non-coincidence of views cannot easily be dismissed, and it is even possible to argue that, in the last few months, this view has begun to have some influence with a number of European Commission officials: institutions are not enough.

If one examines carefully whether EPC successfully promoted a cohesive foreign policy stance for the European Community in the past, a balanced assessment shows some real progress but equally some important limitations.[42]

On the 'plus' side

On the one hand, it can be argued that, in procedural matters, EPC did create a foreign policy cooperation machinery. This in turn helped the emergence of a European coordination reflex between the various foreign ministries of the member states, which, in turn, has led to a degree of Europeanization of national foreign policies.[43] The existing literature also identifies 'quelques resultats'[44] on several important international issues, such as East-West relations (especially at the height of the 'second' Cold War during the Reagan years[45]), the Middle East, the Conference on Security and Cooperation in Europe (CSCE),[46] or Central America in the 1980s.[47]

In all those cases, the Europeans presented a unified front (often in opposition to a more hawkish American line, and of course, opposed to the Communist views as expressed primarily by the Soviets at the time). Thus, in the Middle East, as early as October 1973, EPC had called for a cease-fire with a reference to the legitimate rights of the Palestinians. This relatively pro-Palestine line culminated in the June 1980 Venice Declaration which confirmed the PLO's right to self-determination and participation in negotiations. All this was of course strongly criticized by the USA.[48] In Central America, the EC, initially through its EPC machinery (and despite the reservations of some of its members), supported the 1979 Sandinista revolution because it saw it as a removal of a dictatorship, thus opposing the US view that it was only a Communist takeover. Then, EPC gave its full support to the Contadora peace process, this effort culminating in the institutionalization of EC-Central American relations (the so-called San José process) with full economic and political links in 1984.

Even during the Gulf war of 1991, the Europeans were able to coordinate their policies rather well. In early August 1990, the Twelve imposed sanctions against Iraq, froze its (and Kuwaiti) assets, and stopped arms deliveries before the UN decision to do so. As for the contributions to the war effort in the liberation of Kuwait, even the attempt by Trevor Salmon to show the discrepancies in the responses of EC states in fact confirms that all states did at least something.[49] Furthermore, it is a bit misleading to expect EPC solidarity which did not deal with the military aspects of security to produce results in the military field.

And, as noted above, the EC/EU stance on Yugoslavia has had some positive features, as, for the first time, EC monitors were sent there to monitor the peace, and a European envoy tried, and is trying to find a solution to the problem.

Similarly, cooperation at embassy level or at the level of international organizations such as the United Nations has also increased.[50] It has however fallen short of Bonn's call in 1992 for joint EC embassies in the 11 Republics in the new Commonwealth of Independent States.[51] Such an idea is not really new and was first mooted in the 1970s. It would in fact be an extension of the existing practice whereby an EU state that does not have an embassy in a third country is represented by another EU member state (usually bigger).[52]

The limitations

All the events that have just been described represent rather limited progress in European foreign policy cooperation all the same, as there has been a high number of instances where no European voice has actually materialized. As important is the fact that the past record of EPC has not produced any clear goals or objectives for European foreign policy in the future as consistency in EPC reactions has not been the name of the game.

Even with the areas where some progress was made, there are powerful counter-arguments: the French recanting on the Venice Declaration on the Middle East only months after it had been adopted, persistent divisions on South Africa,[53] and, the German position on the recognition of some of the Republics of ex-Yugoslavia (see above). Moreover, the success story of the CSCE might have simply been due to a unique combination of helpful factors such as the fact that its preparatory work coincided with the early phases of EPC when enthusiasm for cooperation was easy to find or that the CSCE fits best what EPC actually was, namely, declaratory diplomacy.[54]

In addition, more often than not, EPC's rhetoric was not matched by the reality. In other words, whenever an EPC declaration condemned an event in the world, the necessary action was not always taken as a result. To some extent this was due to the fact that the means available to EPC were rather restricted, as most traditional foreign policy tools remained within the national prerogative, or fell under the competence of the Commission and the European Community. But this should not hide the fact that in many cases all that EPC did was to produce a series of communiqués and demarches on human rights abuses without any meat attached to them. Thus it is possible to argue that EPC often provided a useful means for claiming that something was being done when in fact all that was done was to issue declarations and communiqués. In the reality of EPC, words seemed to speak louder than action!

Even at the procedural level, the fact that more COREU messages are sent across Europe does not necessarily mean that there is more agreement between the EU states. Sometimes disagreements lead to an increased number of communications with no guarantee of success. The same point applies to the increased number of meetings between European diplomats. A meeting of minds may be the result of such efforts, but, similarly, the traditional clichés and stereotypes can also be reinforced by such meetings.

As for the Gulf war, *real* criticism of the EC response can be directed at *two* important incidents: the first was the lack of a common European position on the 'hostages' despite the fact that there was a common EC rhetorical condemnation of any attempt to negotiate separately decided at the Rome European Council Declaration in October 1990. Many states managed to get their own citizens (or some of them) freed directly or indirectly, clearly in contravention to that particular decision.[55] Secondly, the French, who had taken all along a more conciliatory line with Baghdad, totally broke solidarity with the Alliance - and with the Europeans - on the eve of the military hostilities in a last-ditch and failed attempt at finding a political solution to the conflict. What really matters here is the fact that a European decision to stick to the official UN position was bypassed, and occurred on a day when a foreign ministers meeting had taking place, and Prime Minister Major had 'had lunch with Mitterrand but again was told nothing'.[56] These two instances seem to be of far greater significance for any assessment of EPC than any complaints about the Spaniards withdrawing their ships at the time of the hostilities, the Belgians refusing to sell ammunition to the British, or the French sending 'slow' planes and aircraft-carriers with helicopters on them.[57] Europe's original coherence was painstakingly achieved, but did not last long, even *before* the hostilities had begun.

There has also been a plethora of cases where no common EPC reaction emerged because of the profound differences that existed between the various governments. Thus, the shooting down of KALOO7 in September 1983 did not lead to any EPC condemnation because of Greek reservations. Similarly, the 1986 US bombing of Libya in retaliation of the La Belle discotheque bombing in Berlin came only hours after a European call for no military action. Moreover, although the US action had received full UK support, it has been said that the then British Foreign Secretary Sir Geoffrey Howe had, wittingly or unwittingly, misled his partners at a foreign ministers' meeting only hours before the action. Most significantly, no EPC communiqué came afterwards, once again because of Greek reservations, but this time well founded as Libyan involvement has since been dismissed in favour of Syria's.

In 1987, following the Hindawi affair, when the UK broke off relations with Syria over alleged Syrian involvement in an attempt to blow up an El Al jumbo jet leaving from Heathrow, no common stance materialized. In fact, Britain 'humiliatingly failed' to get the EC's full support for diplomatic and economic sanctions against Syria.

> 'All that Sir Geoffrey Howe succeeded in getting from his colleagues was a collective expression of concern and an agreement not to receive

the Syrian diplomats expelled from London. Greece would not even assent to this'.[58]

Even in the Falklands episode of 1982 where 'rarely had the Community moved with such a speed'[59] in its imposition of sanctions against Argentina, EC solidarity with Britain lost some of its coherence as soon as the fighting began in the South Atlantic.[60]

One important set of cases where it is extremely difficult to identify a common EC/EPC reaction despite the rhetorical commitment to a clearly defined principle has been the EC reactions to military intervention. EPC's claim that 'there are no 'justified' interventions or 'good' occupations, regardless of the validity of the motives invoked'[61] is not confirmed by its verbal reaction to most cases of military interventions. This was particularly damaging for EPC as it basically amounted to an exercise in declaratory diplomacy. In particular, *not* to issue common declarations on major international issues definitely was a setback for EPC. Examples abound and augur badly for the CFSP where principles are supposed to play such an important role. The following list sums up the most important cases where there was no common European reaction to a military intervention:[62]

- the French interventions in Chad in 1978 and in 1983;
- the US intervention in Grenada in October of the latter year;
- the US invasion of Panama in December 1989.

A final important factor is the lack of any real progress at the United Nations, where, after nearly a quarter of a century of political cooperation, the number of common positions at the General Assembly remains rather limited, and cannot qualify yet as a common European position. Thus, it is possible to dismiss the claim often made by the Presidency that the (then) Twelve had achieved a common position over 75 per cent of the time in 1988,[63] as it is rather unrealistic to use overall figures which include resolutions passed without vote, i.e. resolutions which attract agreement among 150 to 160 countries. It is evident that, in those cases, consensus among the EU states cannot possibly be regarded as an achievement if, say, Chile, Chad, China and Czechoslovakia are also in agreement.

More significantly, if one not only ignores the less controversial issues such as the Year of the Disabled or the United Nations University, but focuses instead on resolutions dealing with more sensitive issues such as decolonization, the right to self-determination, or disarmament, preliminary research findings show that the figures of EC consensus are both lower and more erratic: The most important result that can be drawn from this research is that over the last 22 years, there have been only 5 sessions of the General Assembly where there were 50 per cent or more resolutions where the EC achieved consensus on important issues. Other lessons show that the percentage in the early 1990s does not differ much from the percentage in the early 1970s although one must admit that the number of member states concerned has grown from five in 1970 (West Germany joined the UN in September 1973) to twelve by 1986. Even so, only 40 per cent of all the resolutions included here (1,103 of them) have produced consensus:[64] This is not the same result as those claimed by the Presidency above: 60 per cent of the time there was *no* EC consensus.

To sum up, it might be true to say that although EPC did

'not [...] constitute the foreign policy *of* the Community and its member states [but] at least it represent[ed] a foreign policy *for* Western Europe'.[65]

To be really accurate one should add 'from time to time' or 'occasionally'. The key point here is that no clearly identifiable and consistent principles have emerged so far. This is a critical point as it implies that irrespective of whatever institutional reforms come out of the forthcoming IGC, the absence of a common European view on international affairs remains the real issue and the real obstacle to the emergence of a European foreign policy.

Proposals for Reform

A critical assessment of some of the current proposals for change

Be it proposals for change emanating from the European Commission, or the European Parliament, or other influential institutions such as research centres, the most favoured reform is an end to the use of the national veto,[66] and the introduction of majority voting on most foreign policy issues (though not defence yet).[67] The additional argument used in that approach is the fact that the TEU has already provided for the possibility of having majority voting in the CFSP, and, therefore, all that is required is an extension of existing arrangements.

The most important criticism that can be levelled at these proposals is that all of them ignore reality. The mere fact that the existing provisions for majority voting have *not* been used shows that there is a much more fundamental problem that prevents the emergence of a common European foreign policy: namely, the divergent views among member states on a vast number of international issues. The most obvious and dramatic example is the current disaster in Yugoslavia where the absence of a clear European view of what needs to be done has indirectly contributed to the bloodshed. Of course, the main reason for it has to do with the various ethnic groups on the ground. The cacophony that has come out of Brussels has further reinforced the paralysis of Western policy towards the region. A weak US President and a rampant Republican Party still basking in their mid-term election glory have added to the problem more recently.

All current proposals point to the same conclusion: once more procedural alterations are being proposed with the hope that the end product of a common European foreign policy will materialise *despite* the past record of EPC and the CFSP's record to date. The fact that there is no clear view nor agreement between the fifteen is only presented as an obvious reason for more integration. Once again, as with Maastricht, the procedural and institutional 'obsession' that has dogged most of European integration in the last few decades is coming to the fore. Not surprisingly, the results of changes on these lines would be more of the same. Mechanisms seem to be more important than substance. This is in our view a mistake. In other words, they still miss the point. The machinery should be a means and not an end in itself. To quote from the Draft Council Report of early April this year: 'the provisions of the Treaty cannot alone provide ready-made solutions to problems, but only the means to tackle them'.[68]

Other suggestions

It is often argued that an effort should be made to produce a common European assessment of international events with a view to producing a common approach. This is usually done by the planning staff in foreign ministries whose role it is to produce a number of possible solutions to any given problem. The final decision is then taken by the government of the day after having taken into consideration the various views of other actors, although this varies according to how open the foreign policy system is.[69] In addition, closer collaboration among national foreign ministries and CFSP officials on issues that are of vital importance to one of the member states should be carried out. There is no point in trying to put all 15 EU views together if, say on a matter of vital importance to one of the member states, that member state is in a minority of one.

There are now five people dealing with planning in DGIA, one in the Council Secretariat, plus a number of other planners such as the Forward Studies Unit which is directly attached to the Commission President, several foreign policy advisers to other Commissioners, and an important number of national foreign ministries officials who are seconded to the Commission or to the Council. To a certain extent, this is inevitable as there is no obvious alternative pool of diplomats to bring to Brussels. Their role is obviously so limited in the current input on European foreign policy-making that it is not very significant.[70]

The way the whole system works is far more influential than any procedural arrangement that calls for, or prevents, majority voting. The bottom line remains that national foreign policy, and in particular that of the big(ger) EU member states - dominates the formulation of European foreign policy. Good evidence of that can be found in the recent decision[71] to rearrange the order in which the member states hold the Presidency in such a way that it favours bigger states. Whereas the arrangements for the Presidency rotation before they were changed in late December 1993 would have allowed a big state to hold it in 1996.1 (Italy), 2000.1 (UK), 2002.1 (Germany) and 2002.2 (France), 2003 (Spain), i.e. a gap of 4 years between the Italian and British Presidencies and then a concentration of big states in 2002 and 2003; the new arrangements have ensured that a big state holds the Presidency every one to two years (Italy 1996, UK 1998,

Germany 1999, France 2000, Spain 2002) even though Germany, France and Spain have held Presidencies in 1994 and 1995.

Simon Nuttall has argued recently that EPC has not been based upon the lowest common denominator but has produced rather a 'median' position between the two most extremist positions among the Twelve.[72] As a result, Nuttall argues that it is also more difficult then to reverse a decision adopted by the Twelve because it represents not only the interests of one state, but of most if not all states that are affected. There might be some truth in that statement. One can immediately think of exceptions (see above), but the real issue at stake here is whether such an approach does not promote the emergence of a common position for the sake of it which, more importantly, generates the marginalization of one member state on an issue of vital importance for that state. A more worrying development is that, if ignored, this situation will create a 'dictatorship of the majority' grouping most EU states with the largest populations. Democracy is not only about the rule of the majority. Minority views have to be protected otherwise diversity disappears.

In the longer run, as the number of international issues coming to the attention of the CFSP inevitably expands,[73] the ensuing creation of a constant but changing 'minority of one' cannot possibly lead to a common (i.e. accepted by all members) foreign policy. What it does produce is a view that is challenging the position adopted by one member state and, if more powerful, would overrule it. The future prospects for smaller states are to say the least going to be problematic. It seems ironic that the Commissioner who seems to have publicly complained about the imposition of the views of the bigger states on those of the smaller members[74] is the person who made all the running to prevent, unsuccessfully to date, the Greek decision to embargo FYROM from standing.

The main point here is that there is no European voice because there is no European 'demos' (see chapter on Democracy), and, therefore, the views of lobbies and public opinion can only be expressed through national structures. The national governments are the best representatives of the various national public opinions, not only because they have to win elections to stay in power (accountability in an indirect democratic system which is the norm in Western Europe at the end of the 20th century), but also because they put their own national viewpoint first. Whether this is correct or not does not alter the fact that there is no European demos, no

European voice, and, far more importantly, that neither the Commission nor the European Parliament can claim that they represent exclusively Europe's voice. In fact, the inter-institutional debate which is still raging after all those years is the best guarantee that no common European voice is expressed jointly by the European Commission and the European Parliament. This is one of the main points of this chapter, namely, that the attempt made by a number of people to present the lack of input by the Commission and the Parliament[75] into the CFSP as a question of 'democratic deficit' has been counteracted in recent years by the resurgence of the nation-state and of intergovernmental cooperation as a more acceptable means of integration.

Conclusions

This chapter has argued that the CFSP arrangements have failed to produce a common European foreign policy not only because of their complexity and unsatisfactory nature, but more importantly because the different national interests of the EU member states cannot be reconciled by procedural means alone. The past record of EPC also shows that perhaps the TEU was a Treaty too soon (as opposed to a Treaty too far), because it wrongly assumes the pre-existence of a number of factors that simply were not there: member states have different interests in the world. Moreover, despite many positive elements in both of them, neither the European Commission nor the European Parliament can claim that they represent a European voice in the world. As a result of their legitimate input into the formulation of European foreign policy, all they do in fact is add more voices - often not very coherent and rather confused - to the existing fifteen ones.

This chapter has not really dealt with the related question of European defence policy. This is not only due to the lack of space, but also because, in our view, such a policy will follow the eventual emergence of a European foreign policy, and will not precede it, unless, as a Dutch diplomat ironically put it recently:

> 'Perhaps we could start with a common European military force in order to compel the Member States to come up with a common foreign policy'.[76]

The process of integration in Europe seems to have reached that stage where uniformity and harmonization are no longer desirable and no longer feasible. It may, at long last, be the time to look for an alternative path that may result from a more open, democratic, and pluralist approach. As a result, all those interested in foreign policy should be given the opportunity to have more say in the way European foreign policy will be shaped in the future. Let us only express our hope here that the IGC of 1996 - which will be dominated by the EMU (Economic and Monetary Union) and the CFSP - does not gives us more of the old approach.

Notes

1   C. Hill: 'The European Community: towards a common foreign and security policy?', in *The World Today* (vol.47, no.11, November 1991), p.193.

2   See S. Nuttall: *European Political Cooperation* (Clarendon Press, Oxford, 1992).

3   See C. Tugendhat: 'Second thoughts on Europe', in *The World Today* vol.51, nos 8-9, August-September 1995, p.159. This is not necessarily the view shared by others, see François Duchêne: *Jean Monnet - The First Statesman of Interdependence* (WW Norton, New York, 1994), pp. 354-60.

4   The Paris and Rome Treaties (ECSC, EEC, EURATOM) and the Single European Act covered the external economic relations (trade and development policies) whereas EPC was based on a series of Reports and on Title III of the SEA. The decision-making machinery was also kept separate. See Nuttall, *op. cit.*, pp. 51-259.

5   The Maastricht Treaty has created a 3-pillar structure with EC affairs (mainly economic and financial) in the first pillar, the CFSP in the second pillar, and cooperation in Justice and Home Affairs in the third pillar. The main differences between the three pillars reflect the diverging views over the type of integration that was wanted for these three areas with, if one oversimplifies here, a more supranational and federalist slant in Pillar One, a more intergovernmentalist slant in Pillars Two and Three. For more details, see J. Monar, W. Ungerer, W. Wessels: *The Maastricht Treaty on European Union - Legal Complexity and Political Dynamic* (European Interuniversity Press, Brussels, 1993), esp. pp. 37-65.

6   *Draft Report of the Council on the Functioning of the Treaty on European Union* (Brussels, 5 April 1995).

7   *Ibid.*

8   Hill, *op.cit.*, p.191.

9   D. Usborne: 'Near hysteria at Castle de Haar', in *The Independent* (11 October 1991).

10 See note no.5 above.

11 *Draft Report*, *op. cit.*, p.27.

12 In some instances, it is possible to 'lift' the rule of unanimity if there is a qualified majority of member states in favour of a certain decision. The state(s) which is in a minority accepts then not to prevent the adoption of a joint action. *Rapport sur le fonctionnement du Traité sur*

l'Union Européenne (Commission Européenne, Brussels, 10 May 1995), p.66.

13   For more on that particular 'saga' in the history of European integration, see *inter alia* P. Sanchez da Costa Pereira: 'The Use of a Secretariat', in A. Pijpers et al. (eds): *European Political Cooperation in the 1980s*, pp. 85-103.

14   Within the Council Secretariat, the new CFSP Unit comes under DG E (External Relations) as does the Unit for External Economic Relations. The CFSP Unit is then divided into three sub-units (Directorates), one dealing with General Affairs and Planning, another one being divided on geographical terms (Europe, Africa, Asia, Latin America, and Middle East respectively), and a third covering multilateral issues such as security, human rights, the CSCE, the UN etc. The EC and EPC working groups have been, on the whole, totally merged into one working group according to functional or geographical criteria.

15   Interviews.

16   Interviews.

17   Interviews. The Commission Report of 10 May 1995 cited above describes it well: 'La mise en route de la politique étrangère et de sécurité commune a été *laborieuse*' (p.65, emphasis added).

18   See S. Stavridis: 'The 'Second' Democratic Deficit in the EC: The Process of European Political Cooperation', in F. Pfetsch: *International Relations and Pan Europe* (Lit Verlag, Münster, 1993), pp. 173-94.

19   *Bulletin of the European Union* (no.6-1994), pp. 83-6.

20   For instance, 'in October 1983, the foreign ministers in EPC discussed the Intermediate Nuclear Force (INF) talks in Geneva and the NATO policy of stationing Pershing and Cruise missiles in certain countries', in E. Kirchner: 'Has the Single European Act opened the door for a European Security Policy', in *Journal of European Integration* (Fall 1989), note 7, p.3. Similarly, at the United Nations, over the period 1987-88, the Twelve's adoption of common positions on disarmament was 'impressive: common positions were presented on conventional disarmament, on the necessity of objective information on military matters, on the relationship between disarmament and development, on the reduction of military budgets, in the general debate on disarmament, at the session of the United Nations Disarmament Commission and at the special session of the UNGA [United Nations General Assembly] on disarmament', in R. Dehousse: 'European Political Cooperation 1 July 1987 - 31 December 1988', in *European Journal of International Law* (1990), p. 390 (notes omitted).

21 P. Tsakaloyannis: "The Acceleration of History' and the Reopening of the Political Debate in the European Community', in *Journal of European Integration* (1991), pp. 100-101. The traditional division refers to an Atlanticist, versus a more Europeanist, European defence. The former implies an on-going US commitment to the defence of Western Europe. The latter's assumption is that Europeans should and could defend themselves without the Americans.

22 *The Times* (9 November 1991).

23 To confuse matters further, the WEU has also created the status of 'Associate Partner' to link itself to several Central and East European countries. This category should not be mistaken with that of an Associate Member.

24 T. Salmon: 'Testing times for European political cooperation: the Gulf and Yugoslavia, 1990-92', in *International Affairs* (vol.68, no.2, April 1992), p.253. See also M. Brenner: 'The alliance: a Gulf post-mortem', in *International Affairs* (vol.67, no.4, October 1991), pp. 665-78.

25 It should be noted that the fact that the European Community/Union needed to have the UN involved at the same time as its own efforts were being carried out (Vance and Stoltenberg) further reinforces the point that the EU lacks the means for qualifying as a full international actor.

26 As a female Slovenian official put it in October 1991 in more graphic terms: 'The EC are like the eunuchs who used to look after Turkish women (...) they know what to do and where to do it, but they can't', in *The Independent*, 11 October 1991.

27 H-H. Wrede: "Friendly Concern' - Europe's Decision-making on the Recognition of Croatia and Slovenia', in *The Oxford International Review* (vol.IV, no.2, Spring 1993), p.30. The European decision to recognize followed a letter (on 11 December 1991) by the UN Secretary-General to the Dutch Presidency saying that a recognition could only worsen things.

28 Salmon, *op. cit.*, p.253.

29 This paper does not discuss the merits of the case. See J. Pettifer: 'The new Macedonian question', in *International Affairs* (vol.68, no.3, July 1992), pp. 474-85; S. Economides: 'Riding the Tiger of Nationalism: the question of Macedonia', in *The Oxford International Review* (vol.IV, no.2, Spring 1993), pp. 27-29. Suffice it to say that the Badinter Report states that: 'Given that the republic has denied territorial ambitions and is committed not to engage in hostile acts with other states, the name 'Macedonia' is in itself no evidence of territorial

ambition`. Reproducing the latter statement should in no way be seen as agreeing with it. See Pettifer, *op.cit*, pp. 481-82.

30 W. Horsley: 'United Germany's Seven Cardinal Sins: A Critique of German Foreign Policy', in *Millennium* (Vol.21, no.2, Summer 1992), pp. 225-41; M. Thumann: 'Between Ambition and Paralysis: Germany's Balkan Policy 1991-94', in *Eurobalkans* (No.16, Autumn 1994), pp. 36-43; C. Bluth: 'Germany: defining the German interest', in *The World Today* (vol.51, no.3, March 1995), pp. 51-5. For a more sympathetic view, see W. Wallace: 'Germany as Europe's leading power', in *The World Today* (vol.51, nos 8-9, August-September 1995), p.164 where he argues that 'Germany may be Europe's central power, but it is also its reluctant leader (...). Anti-Americanism was an integral element within the Western Alliance; anti-Germanism was already visible before the end of the Cold War within the European Community (...). All this the new leader of Europe must learn to live with. It is tough at the top, but it is tougher for all if the central power is unwilling to accept the burdens of its leading position'.

31 Hence, the new international activism expressed by France following the election of Jacques Chirac to the French Presidency in May 1995. The announcement of the resumption of nuclear testing in Mururoa or the more active involvement in Bosnia are but two recent examples. See also M. Sutton: 'Chirac's foreign policy: continuity - with adjustment', in *The World Today* (vol.51, no.7, July 1995), pp. 135-38.

32 For a good account of recent Greek foreign policy, including on the Balkans and 'Macedonia', see Y. Valinakis: 'La Grèce dans la nouvelle Europe', in *Politique Etrangère* (no.1/94, Spring 1994), pp. 223-32. For a different view on the Macedonian question, see D. Perry: 'Une crise en gestation? La Macédoine et ses voisins', in *Ibid.*, pp. 179-207.

33 Although the Belgian recognition did not concern itself with the question of the name of the country it had just formally recognized.

34 *The Independent* (3 December 1993).

35 For more details, see Greek press at the time.

36 The full text is available in *Statement by the Prime Minister to the [Greek] Ministerial Council on the Issue of Skopje* (Secretariat General for Press and Information, Foreign Services Department, Athens, 16 February 1994). 'Skopje - the FYROM capital city - is the name used in Greece for FYROM. The embargo included the closing down of the Greek Consulate General in Skopje and the 'interruption' of trade to and from FYROM through the port of Salonica. The sanctions did not include humanitarian supplies.

37 Even if one ignores the fact that there is no expulsion mechanism in the Treaties.

38 The original text by T. Pangalos is in N. Frangakis et al. (eds): *The Third Greek Presidency of the Council of the European Union* [in Greek] (Estias, Athens, 1994), pp. 23-34; the quotation is on p.29 (the translation comes from *The Independent* of 3 December 1993).

39 *Agence Europe* no.6205, 7 April 1994.

40 E.g. the use of Article 224 or Article 225 of the Rome Treaty, the 30 June 1994 preliminary ruling by the European Court, or the Advocate-General Jacobs' opinion of 6 April 1995, which can be interpreted as harbingers of a judgement in favour of the Greek government.

41 The Greeks, rightly or wrongly, suspect an 'anti-Greek' campaign in the EU. The whole issue came to a head at the Cannes European Council meeting in late June 1995 when Papandreou expressed his outrage at the new French policy towards Serbia following Jacques Chirac's election to the French Presidency. See *The Independent* (30 June 1995).

42 For full details and references, see S. Stavridis: *Looking back to see forward: assessing the CFSP in the light of EPC* (LSE European Institute Paper, London, April 1994), pp. 3-14.

43 See F. de la Serre: 'The scope of national adaptation to EPC' in A. Pijpers et al (eds): *European Political Cooperation in the 1980s - A Common Foreign Policy for Western Europe?* (Martinus Nijhoff, Dordrecht, 1988), pp. 194-210. For an earlier account, see C. Hill (ed.): *National Foreign Policies and European Political Cooperation* (George Allen & Unwin, London, 1983).

44 P. de Schoutheete: *La Coopération politique européenne* (Labor, Brussels, 2nd ed., 1986), p.67.

45 For details, see D. Allen, M. Smith: 'West Europe in Reagan's World: Responding to a New American Challenge', in R. Rummel (ed.), *'The Evolution of an International Actor-Western Europe's New Assertiveness'*, Westview, Boulder Colorado, 1990, pp. 201-40.

46 De Schoutheete, *op. cit.*

47 W. Grabendorff: 'Relations with Central and Southern America: a question of over-reach?', in G. Edwards, E. Regelsberger (eds): *Europe's Global Links* (Pinter, London, 1990), pp. 84-96.

48 De Schoutheete, *op. cit.*; P. Ifestos: *European Political Cooperation* (Gower, Aldershot, 1987).

49 Salmon, *op. cit.*, p.243.

50 There also are regular working groups and parties of experts which deal with sectoral matters like the CSCE, the Mediterranean, the Middle

East, the United Nations, or Asia: over one hundred such meetings take place every month, in R. Ginsberg: *Foreign Policy Actions of the European Community - The Politics of Scale* (Reinner, Boulder, 1989), p.51.

[51] Genscher in an interview in the German press; He also argued that if not all EC states were ready for that, it would be possible to start with only a few of them, reported in *The Independent* (4 January 1992).

[52] Such an arrangement is particularly useful for a country with limited international resources at the time when it holds the Presidency of the Council.

[53] See M. Holland: *The European Community and South Africa: European Political Cooperation under Strain* (Pinter, London, 1988), and his 'European Political Co-operation and Member State Diplomatic Missions in Third Countries - Findings from a Case-Study of South Africa', in *Diplomacy and Statecraft* (vol.2, no.2, July 1991), pp. 236-53.

[54] Other useful factors were the fact that the three Baskets allowed for a clear cut separation of tasks with the Commission leading in Basket II, NATO in Basket I, and EPC in Basket III; blocs were the means *par excellence* in the overall process and therefore bloc cooperation was at a premium; Europe's lead was facilitated by the lack of enthusiasm of the USA.

[55] For details, see Salmon, *op. cit.*, p.247.

[56] *Ibid.*, p.240; Brenner, *op. cit.*, pp. 673-74. For more details on the Mitterrand position, see J. Howorth: 'The President's special role in foreign and defence policy', in J. Hayward (ed.): *De Gaulle to Mitterrand - Presidential Power in France* (Hurst & Co, London, 1993), pp. 184-188.

[57] Indeed, such a view mistakingly pretends that the EC was a world power like the USA.

[58] C. Hill: 'European Preoccupations with Terrorism', in A. Pijpers et al, (eds), *op. cit.*, p.178.

[59] G. Edwards: 'Europe and the Falkland Islands Crisis 1982', in *Journal of Common Market Studies* (Vol.XXII, No.4, June 1984), p.295.

[60] *Ibid.* For a detailed account, see S. Stavridis, C. Hill (eds): *Domestic Sources of Foreign Policy: West European Reactions to the Falklands Conflict* (BERG, Oxford, 1996).

[61] Statement by the Presidency on behalf of the Ten on Cambodia at the 36th session of the UN General Assembly, New York, 19 October 1981, *EPC* (FRG Government, Bonn, 1982), p.286.

62 See Stavridis (1994), *op. cit.*, pp. 9-13 for further details and full references.

63 Report on European Union (EPC aspects), 6 December 1988, in *European Political Cooperation Bulletin* (Vol.4, no.2, 1988), p.335.

64 *European Political Cooperation at the UN: A critical assessment 1970-1992*, Reading Papers in Politics no. 20, Department of Politics, The University of Reading, June 1996. See also Nuttall, op. cit., esp. pp. 138-9. Of course, such an exercise comprises a number of limitations related to the special nature of UN politics; see Stavridis. Pruett, op. cit., and B. Tonra: *Ireland, Denmark and the Netherlands in European Political Cooperation* (Paper presented to the ECPR Madrid Joint Sessions, 17-22 April 1994), pp. 13-16.

65 R. Rummel: 'Speaking with one voice - and beyond', in A. Pijpers et al. *op. cit.*, p.129.

66 For instance:
- Commission Report of 10 May 1995, p.66;
- Matutes Report, Committee on Foreign Affairs, Security and Defence Policy, European Parliament, 24 April 1995, p.6;
- Bertelsmann Foundation Interim Report of a Working Group on *CFSP and the Future of the European Union* (July 1995), p.2.

67 For more on that question, see *European security policy towards 2000: ways and means to establish genuine credibility* (High-level group of experts on the CFSP, First Report, Brussels, 19 December 1994), p.19.

68 *Draft Report of the Council, op. cit.*, p.25.

69 For a review of the existing literature, see S. Stavridis: *Foreign Policy and Democratic Principles: The Case of European Political Cooperation* (unpublished PhD thesis, LSE, London, 1991), pp. 97-133.

70 A proposal that is being discussed nowadays is that of a joint Commission (DGIA)-Council Secretariat planning cell. (interviews).

71 1 means first half of the year and 2 means second half of the year. The initial decision was taken at the December 1993 European Council meeting in Brussels.

72 Nuttall, *op. cit.*, p.314.

73 The subject-area is not limited any more. Art J.1.1 reads that the CFSP is 'covering all areas of foreign and security policy'.

74 Mr Van den Broek complained that although 'we have a foreign policy [...] my main problem is becoming more and more whether we have a *common* foreign policy . Who is taking the decisions? a new *troika*'

[France, UK, Germany]' in *Financial Times* (19 April 1995, emphasis added).

75 Most of the recent EP reports and resolutions on that subject make that point quite explicitly.

76 Mr Willem Andrae, Minister Plenipotentiary at the Dutch Embassy in Paris, during a Conference on 'Beyond Maastricht' organised by the Philip Morris Institute for Public Policy Research in Paris in January 1995; the quote is from the Conference Proceedings, p.15. For a different view on whether European defence should precede the emergence of a European foreign policy, see L. Martin, J. Roper (eds): *Towards a Common Defence Policy* (European Strategy Group and The Institute for Security Studies, WEU, Paris, 1995).

5 Cooperation in the Fields of Policing and Judicial Affairs

ALAIN GUYOMARCH

The inclusion of the first formal Treaty provisions for common policy-making between all twelve member-states of the European Union (EU) in the area of law and order - by Title VI (article K) of the Treaty on European Union (TEU) - provokes three questions. The first is that of analyzing exactly what the Treaty does. The second is the explanation of how the Treaty provisions were made: for what reasons did the member-state governments which had hitherto minimized linkages between economic integration and cooperation in such a sensitive area of state sovereignty as the maintenance of law and order decide formally to recognize a law and order dimension of Community membership? The third question concerns the restricted scope and almost obsessive intergovernmentalism of article K: why was common policy-making made so limited in scope and so difficult to accomplish, especially in relation to joint implementation procedures?

These three questions are addressed across the four sections of this chapter. The first section analyzes the provisions of the TEU in detail, considering the nature and extent of the changes it enacted. The second section places the changes of the TEU in the context of previous attempts by European governments to organize cooperation in judicial and internal matters before 1991. The experience of those attempts - the Pompidou, Trevi and Schengen groups - was that agreement between governments of European states on limited common objectives concerning law and order, was far easier to achieve than consensus on any practical common policy at the European Union level.

The third section considers the factors which influenced the member-state governments in 1991 to include judicial and internal affairs as a policy-area of common concern in the TEU. The estimations of the impact of four changes on both crime and population migrations - the implementation of freedom of movement of persons and capital within the Single Market, major technological developments, the recession and the end of the East-West divide - are identified as key explanatory variables.

In the final section, the problem of finding common ground between the very varied institutional approaches to imposing law and order in the different member-states is explored. The limited nature of the TEU provisions, however, is shown not only as a consequence of this practical difficulty, but also as a reflection of very different political approaches to the problem and the desire of at least some member-state governments to relinquish as little as possible of their sovereign power in justice and policing.

The conclusion returns to the implications of the decision by the writers of the TEU not to use the institutional framework of the Community for decision-making in judicial and internal affairs, despite their acknowledgement of the existence of a common European interest in that area. By creating the distinct structures of the 'Third Pillar', they continued the loose, intergovernmental approach of earlier frameworks of collaboration and ensured that actually deciding and implementing any common policy will be a slow and difficult process.

The Maastricht Treaty Provisions

In creating a 'citizenship of the Union' and constructing a new framework for cooperation in the domain of justice and internal affairs - the 'Third Pillar' of the institutional architecture of the Union - the TEU went far beyond all earlier Treaties, in that it formally recognizes the 'European' nature of at least some aspects of law and order problems and policies. At the same time, however, the Treaty also reaffirmed the sovereign responsibility of the member-state governments for maintaining law and order and laid down a strictly intergovernmental framework for most aspects of joint policy-making with a very limited - or sometimes nonexistent - role for the supranational institutions, the Commission, Court and Parliament. Hence, whilst 'judicial and home affairs' are now in the Treaty, they are treated in an almost schizophrenic way.

A first innovation of the TEU was article 8 which gives the formal citizenship of the new Union to all those holding the nationality of the member-states, and thereby extends voting rights, in any one member state, to resident nationals of other member states for municipal and European elections. Furthermore, that provision is complemented by a measure designed to create a common policy on the entry and exit of nationals of third countries; article 100c allocates responsibility for determining policy on visas to the Community framework, with qualified majority voting in the Council after 1995.

Of equal importance is Article K (Title VI) of the Treaty, which establishes the complex framework for cooperation in judicial and internal affairs as an integral part, a 'Third Pillar', of the Union. The Treaty lists nine law and order policy domains which are explicitly recognized as being of common interest and subjects for policy-coordination by the Council of Ministers, with a view to making common policies. However, whilst creating machinery for making common policies, the Treaty does not lay down any aims or objectives for those policies. The policy areas listed in the TEU are: asylum policy, rules concerning the crossing of external borders of member states, immigration policy and policy relating to nationals of third states, action against drug abuse, action against international fraud, judicial cooperation in civil matters, judicial cooperation in criminal matters, customs cooperation, and police cooperation. That last item is the most specific, in that the TEU not only provides for common action for the prevention and repression of terrorism, drug trafficking and other forms of international crimes, but also for the establishment of an 'information exchange system within a European Police Office, or Europol'. In practise, the TEU means that some features of earlier informal arrangements (the Trevi Group) are retained and given formal existence.

The distinction between the Third Pillar decision-making process and that of the Community is marked in two ways. The first is that article K4 establishes a 'Coordinating Committee' of senior officials to prepare the work of the Council (instead of COREPER); bizarrely, this Coordination Committee must work with COREPER in preparing visa policy decisions under Article 100c. The second is that the Council may draw up conventions for joint policies which do not provide for the resolution of disputes by the European Court of Justice.

As a whole, the Third Pillar provisions remain deliberately ambivalent. Whilst they allow for the possibility of joint policy-making in judicial and internal affairs, such policies are dependent upon unanimous decisions in the Council of Ministers. Furthermore, article K1 sub-divides judicial and domestic policy-areas into different categories which are dealt with in slightly different ways. Only six of the nine policy-areas listed as subjects for common action are deemed to fall within the policy competence of the European Commission; the others remain in the sphere of sovereignty of the member-state governments. For the first six policy-areas, the Treaty stipulates involvement of the Commission in the decision-making process and gives it joint responsibility with the Presidency of the Council of Ministers for informing the European Parliament about decisions taken. In contrast, initiatives for joint policies in matters of criminal justice, customs cooperation and police cooperation can only be made by the governments of the member states, and the Parliament may - or may not - be informed by the Council. There is, however, a further complication, since article K9 allows for the possibility of an eventual shift (by a unanimous decision in the Council) of responsibility for policy-making in the first six policy-areas to the Community framework (article 100c); in contrast, only by the signing of a new Treaty can criminal justice, customs and police cooperation be shifted from the Third to the First Pillar.

Another area of ambivalence is that of Europol, the common police information system. On the one hand, the Treaty does not integrate Europol and the Schengen Information System (SIS); indeed, article K7 allows for the continued operation of the SIS distinct from but in parallel with Europol. On the other hand, the Treaty does not stipulate how the activities of Europol will be organized and financed. Since the ratification of the TEU, this latter question has proved particularly difficult. In late 1994, despite the determined efforts of the German Presidency of the EU, the essential convention on the scope, organization and financing of Europol was still hotly contested. Unresolved issues included the rights of access to information and the role of common EU institutions (the Court of Justice, the Court of Audit and the Parliament) in supervising Europol's operations. The joint efforts of the French and British governments to restrict the role of Europol and to minimize the influence of supranational Community institutions[1] have blocked the agreement which must be unanimous on these questions. At the Cannes Summit of June 1995, British objections to the supervision of Europol by the Court again blocked any agreement. Although in practise there has been growing cooperation between police forces in the 15 member states in allowing mutual access to their computer data bases, especially since April 1995, proposals for closer cooperation have met renewed opposition from the British and French governments. A Dutch proposal for a European Law Enforcement Network met a stormy reaction from the French and the British.

In May 1995, the Commission, in its report on the implementation of the TEU, indicated that the lack of cooperation and transparency in the 'Third Pillar' raised serious questions about the practicality of further enlargements. Clearly, the unanimity requirement and the institutional disagreement between governments of member-states were preventing any real progress in making policies in the domain of justice and internal affairs. The same month complaints were voiced in the European Parliament that it was not receiving information about the planned Europol Convention. Furthermore, the Council was criticized for attempting to create a police structure without first defining its rules and powers. MEPs even argued that the normal protection of individual rights was at risk in the Europol discussions.

Hence, if the Maastricht Treaty marks an important step in a long slow process of evolution in that all twelve member-states have recognized the need for some common policies in justice and policing, it is a very hesitant step. The Treaty only provides for one specific common policy, that of granting visas to citizens of third countries, and even here it delays the use of qualified majority voting in the Council until 31 December 1995. This curious institutional architecture not only separates asylum policy, immigration policy and the rules concerning crossing external frontiers of the Community (under Article K1), from visa policy (under Article 100c), but even prevents the customs union from allowing its executive agency, the Commission, to suggest policy changes relating to cooperation between customs services. Thus, the creation of a formal structure within the EU institutions for making common judicial and domestic policies is a complex, cautious and limited change. If the Governments of Britain and France remain committed to making intergovernmentalism work, the experience of both the Community and the Schengen Group suggests that in 1996, reaching unanimity amongst the fifteen will not be easy.

The Limited Structures for Cooperation on Law and Order before 1992

The early attempts in post-war Europe to organize cooperation in policing and justice usually took a functionalist approach. Hence, international agencies were set up with strictly limited responsibilities for common services in specific policy-areas where common objectives could be defined. The delimitation of membership was determined by shared policy aims, which ranged from those of controlling a common border (the object of many bilateral pacts) to those of sharing useful information on particular types of activity. When information-pooling was the goal, the scope of the agencies created could be global (Interpol) or regional (the Pompidou Group of the Council of Europe).

With the establishment and development of the European Community, the process of setting up common policies and executive bodies took on a more neo-functional character as cooperation to police the free movement of persons was treated as an essential complement to economic integration, the Single Market programme and the free movement of goods, services and capital. The creation of the Trevi Group reflected the recognition by all member-state governments of a need for some forms of cooperation in policing. The Schengen Group was set up by an inner core of member-state governments which hoped to abolish all controls at internal borders.

Early developments of limited international police cooperation resulted from clearly delimited functional goals. Before 1945, most joint international actions between European states to deal with law and order problems concerned either cross-border controls or mutual extradition treaties. Most governments felt they had no interest in facilitating criminal behaviour by harbouring criminals from neighbouring states. In the late nineteenth century, there were also a number of attempts to institutionalize police cooperation to deal with terrorism, reflecting the common concern of governments with socialist or nationalist revolutionary movements and anarchism.[2] The first major international meeting between police leaders took place in 1898[3]. Only in 1923, however, was the first permanent international agency created - the International Criminal Police Commission (ICPC), based in Vienna. With thirty-four member-countries (mostly European) the ICPC provided a joint information service for ten years, until the Nazi occupation of Austria effectively ended its activities[4].

In 1946, a new international body was established by nineteen of the former ICPC states. The new body, with headquarters in Paris (as Austria was partly under Soviet occupation) soon became known by its telegraphic address, 'Interpol'. During the post-war period Interpol grew from a small, largely West European body into a global organization. After the 'Fall of the Wall' most East European states were admitted as members. By September 1990, membership totalled 150 countries. The growth in size, however did not change the functional nature of the body. The agreed functions are two-fold. The first is to promote mutual information and assistance between criminal police authorities. The second is to develop common services for the prevention and suppression of crimes.

Interpol can only assist national police forces in cases which clearly fall within the criminal codes of laws of the member countries and are in the spirit of the Universal Declaration of Human Rights; any assistance with cases of a political, military, religious or racial character is prohibited. The organization is primarily a data coordination centre for the police forces of the member countries. Its officials, though seconded officers from national police services, do not carry out any normal police operations and have no powers of arrest. In each member-state there is one 'central bureau', which provides the sole communication link between national police forces and Interpol. If the limited functions of Interpol have made it an attractive body to join, they have also made the organization unsuitable for adaptation for other purposes. Hence, there have been many critics of the inadequacies of Interpol[5], but in particular, European police leaders and criminologists have noted the difficulty of creating a 'European Regional Group' within Interpol for other joint activities and tighter coordination.

Three other institutions - the United Nations, the Council of Europe and the European Community - all created in the post-war decade had the potential of developing as frameworks for international cooperation in criminal justice policy. The United Nations was soon too bitterly divided on international questions to attempt any development in this area. During its early years, the Council of Europe was concerned with the definition and defence of human rights. In that context, some comparative crime studies were undertaken. However, the Council's responsibilities for coordinating judicial and police cooperation in Europe did not develop during the 1950s and 1960s, largely as a result of the numerous internal divisions between its members which, given the inter-governmental nature of its decision-making, blocked any institutional growth.

The third international body, the European Community, had a smaller and more homogenous membership than either of the other organizations, and its institutional framework provided mechanisms for enacting common laws and ensuring their respect by the European Court of Justice. The Treaty of Rome also included a general enabling clause, article 235, but its use depended on unanimity in the Council of Ministers and as de Gaulle, President of France from 1959 to 1969, was opposed to any measure which might undermine national sovereignty, the evolution of the Community as a framework for cooperation in such sensitive policy-areas as policing and criminal justice was blocked.

De Gaulle's successor at the Elysée Palace, Pompidou, recognized that a European police coordination agency could be useful, but, sensitive to the anti-EC sentiments of many of his supporters, promoted a Group to Combat Drug Abuse and Illicit Traffic in Drugs within the inter-governmental Council of Europe. His idea met a warm response from the other governments and the new body, a consultative study group of ministers and senior civil servants from all nineteen member countries became known as the Pompidou Group. Reports were prepared on the control of drug trafficking, on the role of criminal justice systems in responding to the problems of drugs abuse and on methods to combat traffickers by dealing with money laundering. Studies were carried out on collecting and evaluating data for common policy formulation and on educational initiatives against drug abuse. There was, however, no strong demand for the Pompidou Group to perform any other activity than the study and coordination of policies on drug-related crime.[6]

Within a few years, proposals for cooperation in other law and order policies were being made, but in a different institutional framework, that of the European Community. In 1974, Pompidou's early death and the election of a non-Gaullist, Giscard d'Estaing, to the French Presidency, meant that the growth of joint policy-making in this domain within the EC framework was no longer blocked. Furthermore, the first enlargement of the Community was accomplished in 1973, thereby providing a wider base for joint policy-making. At the Council of Ministers of the Interior meeting in Rome in 1975, there was unanimous agreement to create a permanent group for cooperation in policing and criminal justice.

At the first meeting of this intergovernmental group of ministers and officials, held in Luxembourg in 1976, the new body became known as the Trevi Group. The main aim in the 1970s was cooperation between police forces of the member-states of the EC to fight terrorism. However, from the start, when issues considered in the Trevi Group concerned non-EC countries, representatives of the governments or police forces of those states have been invited to participate.

The Trevi Group operated at three different levels: ministerial, senior officials and working groups. At ministerial meetings, held once every six months, each member state of the EC was represented by its minister responsible for police and security matters (usually the Justice or Interior Minister). At the next level, a committee of senior officials, plus a small number of chief police officers, met more frequently to prepare policy advice for the ministers and to coordinate the work of the working groups. These working groups, composed of specialists, officials and detectives or examining magistrates, met regularly to prepare reports for the ministerial meetings, and their meetings often took the form of conferences or seminars.

The first working group, set up in May 1977, was responsible for centralizing information about, and coordinating the fight against, terrorism. Regular meetings were organized to analyze terrorist groups, their structures, strategies and tactics, and to discuss procedures for improving communications networks. Subsequently other working groups have been established to deal with police equipment and aspects of public order, serious and international crime and drug trafficking, and the crime and policing implications of the Single European Market. In the Trevi II working group, police forces exchanged information on a wide range of topics, including training, equipment, public order problems, and after the 1985 Heysel Stadium tragedy, football hooliganism. The Trevi III working group, on serious crimes, developed a loose network for cooperation between the Drug Liaison Officers of all member states, for the pooling of appropriate information and for mutual assistance when necessary. A National Drugs Intelligence Unit was set up in each member-state, with a European Drugs Intelligence Unit as coordinating body. This working-group also discussed the improvement of cooperation to combat other serious international crimes, notably bank fraud and the theft of vehicles. Between 1988 and 1992, a fourth working group was established to consider the policing implications of the reduction of border controls in the Single Market programme.

As an informal intergovernmental body, Trevi had no permanent administrative staff, headquarters or budget. The operations of the Trevi groups, at all levels, were directed in the same way as those of the Council of Ministers of the European Community. The organization of business was the responsibility of the member state holding the Presidency for the current six-month period. At the ministerial level, the minister responsible for police or justice of the state which held the Presidency of the Council of Ministers set the agenda and took the chair. At lower levels, officials from that same member state led all activities and chaired all meetings. To ensure continuity between presidencies a 'Troika' - a committee composed of the past, present and future presidents of the Council of Ministers of the Interior and Justice - acted as an executive agency. In Rhodes in December 1988, the European Council stressed the importance of the Trevi group activities in the official Declaration, which noted that the achievement of Community goals was dependent on cooperation between judicial and police authorities to combat terrorism, international crime, narcotics and illegal trafficking. In Madrid, in May 1989, the Trevi ministers decided to improve their organization by sharing the continuity and administrative support functions more widely; they instituted a 'Piatnika' of five member-states, those holding the current presidency, the two previous presidencies and the two next presidencies of the EC to replace the 'Troika'.

The 'Paris Declaration' of the European Council in December 1989 also underlined the importance of freedom of movement as a core feature of the European Community. Once again, the Trevi ministers noted that freedom of movement for persons and capital increased the risk of a development of crime across frontiers and increased the possibility for professional criminals to exploit the gaps in cooperation between the agencies of the member states. The Trevi ministers outlined plans for improving the communication of information, assigning liaison officers, exchanging police intelligence and examining the viability of a common information system. The Dublin 'Programme of Action' by the Trevi ministers, in June 1990, re-affirmed these plans: exchanges of personnel were increased, regular meetings between the agencies involved in the policing of frontier posts were organized, both to pool information and to discuss options for allowing 'hot pursuit' across frontiers and studies for creating a joint information system were launched[7]. Despite these ambitious goals, a constant problem of the Trevi Group was the absence of a secretariat, a central organization with an 'institutional memory', or even a common information point. The effectiveness of the organization was impaired and coordination was difficult in the implementation, monitoring, evaluation and amendment of decisions.

Trevi was a forum in which representatives of the member-states exchanged information and benefited from each other's experience of dealing with problems. It also had a role in identifying European 'best practises' and improving the effectiveness and efficiency of police work. Furthermore, Trevi was highly regarded by police leaders as it provided a useful framework on which to build close multilateral police cooperation. Although the membership was restricted to the countries of the European Community, Trevi was also successful in establishing links with neighbouring countries, notably Switzerland, Austria and Sweden. As an inter-governmental organization, parallel to, but not part of, the EC institutional framework, Trevi was not subject to the control of the Court or accountable to Parliament. A formal linking of policing and criminal justice policy-making arrangements to Community institutions had to await the Maastricht Treaty, and even then these questions of control and accountability were not clearly addressed.

The Trevi Group, however, was not the only predecessor of the Third Pillar of the TEU. Since 1985, another structure, the Schengen Group, had been negotiating for close cooperation in criminal justice and policing to deal with the complete abolition of internal border controls. This Group eventually included the majority, but not all, member states of the EC. The governments of the Benelux states were the first to abolish internal border controls, as early as 1958. In 1984, after massive trans-European traffic jams provoked by lorry-drivers' protests at the slow and bureaucratic border controls still in operation 27 years after the signing of the Treaty of Rome, the French and German governments signed the Saarbrucken Agreement, providing for the abolition of border controls between the two countries[8]. One year later, in June 1985, the Schengen Treaty was signed by representatives of the governments of the Netherlands, Belgium, West Germany, France and Luxembourg, with the explicit goal of abolishing all border controls between those states. At that first meeting, in Schengen (Luxembourg), the ministers agreed that a second agreement would be necessary to define the precise changes needed to policing organizations to deal with freedom of movement across internal borders and to immigration arrangements at the single external border. Thus, the 1985 Agreement provided for a second Agreement, to be signed in or before 1989.

In practise, however, reaching unanimity between the governments of the Schengen states on these crucial practical questions proved much more difficult than envisaged. Negotiations were complicated by the reunification of East and West Germany, and the changing relations between the EC and Eastern Europe. The second Agreement was finally signed in June 1990, but its implementation was postponed until certain conditions were fulfilled and at the earliest in 1993. That 'Complementary Agreement' also provided that other member states of the EC could join the Schengen Group - on the condition that their governments accept the total 'package' without any modification. In November 1990, Italy was admitted to the Schengen Group and the governments of Spain, Greece and Portugal also applied to join.[9] In April 1995, the Austrian Government signed to become the tenth member country.

In March 1993, however, the French Government announced that, as the conditions for the complementary Schengen Agreement to be implemented had still not been achieved, a further unspecified delay was needed. In January 1994, the governments of the nine Schengen states agreed to suspend - 'sine die' - the implementation agreement. In November 1994, the governments were at last discussing the possibility of a 'trial period' of operations, and on 22 December 1994, the nine member-governments meeting in Bonn agreed to implement the Schengen agreement on 26 March 1995 for a three month trial period between seven of the nine members: France, Germany, Netherlands, Belgium, Luxembourg, Spain and Portugal.[10] The contrast between the rapid signature of the first

Schengen Agreement and the slow process of negotiating an implementation agreement reflects the difference in the contents of those two deals. The 1985 Agreement laid down the goals of gradually eliminating all controls at mutual borders and making the necessary legal changes - which each national parliament would need to ratify - for applying common policies at external borders and joint policing arrangements. In contrast, the June 1990 Agreement concerned concrete measures, rather than idealized goals. Agreeing precise rules for the reinforcement of external border controls, for close and effective cooperation between judicial systems, police forces and administrative services of the members and for common policies on visas, immigration and the right of asylum was a far more difficult and politically sensitive challenge, which involved almost all the governments concerned in changing established policies.

The problems encountered in two areas of the implementation arrangements exemplify the complexity of the negotiations. One element in the 1985 Agreement was the establishment of a common, central, computerized information system, the Schengen Information System (SIS). The studies and negotiations for creating SIS commenced in 1988. A first problem was to define what the contents of the database should be. After long discussions the accepted delimitation of the database contents were: aliens classed as undesirable in any one of the Schengen states, asylum applications and refused applications, wanted criminals, persons under surveillance and details of firearm and vehicle ownership. A second problem was that of differing data protection restrictions between the Schengen states which required for a common system of protecting individual rights to be negotiated. Very practical details of financing, and choices of hardware, software, the main-frame location and the number of access terminals had also to be agreed. The final choice for the location of the central SIS computer was Strasbourg.

A second problem area was that of 'hot pursuits', since, when border controls no longer exist, police officers chasing fleeing criminals must either be able to continue their pursuit across any border they cross or have such excellent communications with the police forces in neighbouring states that their officers can immediately take over the pursuit. In theory it may be logical for the officers of the police in the first

Schengen state to continue their pursuit onto the territory of the second state until the police of that state take over the chase. In practise two difficult questions arise: how far can a foreign police officer conduct a pursuit into another country? and which national law should the pursuing police officer apply in this 'pursuit zone'? The 1990 Complementary Agreement finally included a 'hot pursuit' clause which provides the right for the police officers of one country to pursue suspects into the territory of another country, but they do not have the power to carry out an arrest on foreign soil.

The negotiations in the Schengen Group have been carried out at two levels; at the higher level there have been biannual meetings of ministers, whilst, at the lower tier, working-groups of civil servants and police officers of the member countries have done most of the long and detailed work of negotiating the policies and institutional agreements. Once negotiated the Schengen agreements required ratification in all member countries. Hence it was not until 1992 that the 1990 Schengen Agreement was finally ratified by the parliaments of all member countries, after long delays and several challenges to its constitutionality.

In April 1995 two incidents took place, one on the Belgian border, the other on the German frontier, which illustrated the legal complexities created by the Schengen Agreement. In both cases, 'hot pursuits' onto French territory were not authorized and the government in Paris admitted that the further legislation necessary to allow such 'hot pursuits' would take several months to prepare and to pass. In late June 1995, however, when the agreement was finally due to come into full force, the new government of President Chirac decided to opt out for a further six month 'trial period', and to retain the option of reintroducing full border-checks if crime problems were seen to increase.

Ironically, at the same time that French Governments were hesitating about the basic principles of the Schengen Agreement, the five Nordic countries expressed serious interest in joining the project. One complicating element, however, was the pre-existing cooperation convention between these five countries and the fact that only three of them are members of the EU. Only these three could be given 'observer status', whereas a lower level, 'Associate membership' is possible for the others.

The non-integration of EU and Schengen institutional arrangements has created further problems in relation to East European states. Although some countries, like Bulgaria, have association agreements with EU, the control of their citizens crossing Schengen external borders have been reinforced. This has given rise to the criticism that the raising of the 'iron curtain' on the Eastern side of these frontiers after 1989 has been replaced by the lowering of a 'feather curtain' (of visa requirements and strict border checks) on the Western side.

In short, the negotiations of the TEU provisions on judicial and domestic affairs, which took place whilst the Schengen Complementary Agreement was still in the process of ratification, reflected some of the goals of that agreement, but in only one policy-area, that of visas, was there any move away from pure intergovernmental decision making. The evidence of the Pompidou, Trevi and Schengen groups was all too clear: it was easy to agree on common objectives, but far more difficult, if not impossible, to agree on common policies and institutions to achieve those goals, at least as long as unanimity between the governments of all the member countries was required to take any decision.

The Case for Common Policies on Law and Order

The factors which influenced the member-state governments to include judicial and domestic affairs as a policy-area of common concern and for joint policy-making were essentially the shared estimations of four changes - the freeing of movement of persons and capital within the Single Market, major technological developments, the recession and the end of the East-West divide - and their impact on both crime and population migrations. Hence, governments which had hitherto denied any obvious logical linkages between economic integration and cooperation in the maintenance of law and order decided at Maastricht formally to recognize, albeit in a limited way, a judicial and domestic policy dimension of the European Union. Nonetheless, the EU borders were of only small relevance in dealing with many of these major problems.

Since its foundation, the EU has not only become the world's largest trading block, but movements of persons and goods between member states have multiplied rapidly, and those movements are becoming even more frequent with the reduction - and eventual abolition - of internal border controls. At the same time, the growth of crimes of many kinds has been massive and mass immigration, both legal and illegal, has taken place in most member states[11]. Members of national criminal communities are all too willing to learn 'best practises' from each other by comparison, but also to internationalize their own activities, or at least to practise European cooperation of a kind never envisaged by Jean Monnet. The removal of internal border controls on persons and goods and the ending of national controls on capital movements has provoked anxiety in many EU governments about the likely ineffectiveness of purely national approaches to maintaining law and order.

There is clear evidence that some of the most 'newsworthy' crimes - including drug trafficking, electronic-financial fraud, thefts of works of art, and terrorism - have increased in number in Europe during the 1980s, and all these types of crime often have transnational characteristics. It is in no way surprising that one major challenge to law and order - that of international drug trafficking - was the first reason for European cooperation and has remained an essential element in the debate on common European policies on law and order. The drugs trade has developed with the general growth of international travel and trade, and the freeing or abolition of border controls between EU member states facilitated that evolution. In Western Europe, growing prosperity and the movements of immigrant workers have also contributed to that development. Drug networks are often complex organizations of producers, processors, carriers, dealers and money-launderers, of various nationalities and operating in many different countries. The Medellin Latin American cartel, the Chinese 'triads', and the Sicilian-USA mafia (Cosa Nostra) and its Italian sister networks (Ndrangheta and Camorra), are merely the most famous of the multi-national drug syndicates. With the abolition of internal border controls, the member-states of the EU are facing this problem more acutely than many other parts of the world.[12]

The major technological development with an impact on the growth of internal law and order problems has been the development of international computerized financial transactions. The computerization of many banking and other financial operations has allowed the growth of criminal activities which have international characteristics and hence are very difficult to police within any national structures. Frauds involving credit cards, and bank computers as well as tax evasion and insider-trading are typical examples of the recent cross-border crimes. The Single Market, by allowing free movements of persons, capital and services, has made it easier for the criminal community to exploit the new technologies.

During the 1980s, large-scale legal and illegal immigration into Europe has been increasingly viewed by many member-state governments as a major problem requiring common European solutions. Ironically, three decades earlier it had been labour shortages in booming liberal economies in Western Europe which led many governments to encourage immigration from former colonies, usually in the third world. Similarly in the 1950s, many West European governments condemned the leaders of the Soviet Bloc states for imprisoning their peoples; indeed, free international movement was hailed as a basic human right. The governments of Germany and France proclaimed their countries to be 'terres d'asile', and promised political asylum to all dissidents willing to respect their national laws. The West German government even offered its citizenship to anyone of German descent, from East Germany or anywhere else in the Soviet Bloc. However, if in theory free entry into many West European states was possible in the 1950s and 1960s, in practise political repression meant that few who wished to move could actually do so.

Political and economic changes of the 1970s and 1980s in particular, changed both the nature of migration and the perception of the problem by West European governments. The post oil-crisis recessions and the technological restructuring of industry brought mass unemployment to Western Europe. Even brief periods of recovery did not significantly reduce the levels of the unemployed. Not only were new immigrants unwelcome, but in some countries government policies attempted to persuade established immigrants to return to their countries of origin. Such policies produced few results, except stirring up resentment amongst second generation immigrants, and established migration circuits from North Africa and the Indian subcontinent could only be broken with considerable difficulty and cost. The 'Fall of the Wall' in 1989, however, exacerbated the problem as the threat of a massive migration of populations from the former Eastern Bloc countries to West European states seemed imminent. Whenever the process of establishing market economies or democratic governments in post-communist states appeared to be unsuccessful, there were widespread Western fears of mass emigration[13]. Indeed, in June 1995, a number of Bulgarian businessmen protested that the Schengen Group's attempts to toughen restrictions on illegal immigrants were disrupting their normal business travel arrangements.[14] In contrast, the exclusion of Italy from the operational 'trial period' of the Schengen Agreement was motivated by the ineffectiveness of Italian border policing to stop the entry of illegal immigrants. To attempt to check the unofficial night ferries arriving on the extensive Adriatic frontier, Italian authorities have deployed the army to reinforce the coast-guard and border police.[15]

In 1991 at Maastricht, many EU political leaders recognized the existence of serious 'European' law and order problems for which 'European' solutions seemed more effective and efficient than 'national' solutions. Nonetheless, robust data about the exact extent of the problems was in short supply. Assessing the extent of the practical problems for which common European policies were appropriate is fraught with difficulties. Although the rates of recorded crimes have risen in all EU member-states since 1958, there have been similar, or in some cases greater, increases in non-EU states. In some member states, notably France, Germany, Britain and the Netherlands, the incidence of certain types of crime stabilized or declined in the late 1980s - the period of increased freedom of movement by the Single Market programme. Furthermore, when increases in crime rates have occurred, they have generally concerned crimes which are not directly related to the Single European Market, namely burglary, car theft, robbery with violence and sexual offences.

There is still little evidence of a massive rise in trans-frontier criminal behaviour, and the spectre of cross-border commuting muggers and burglars may sell Europhobic newspapers, but, in 1995, remains largely a myth. Even the international nature of the narcotics syndicates may be exaggerated. Certainly, the success of the Mafia and other drug networks has often depended on exploiting cultural features of particular national diaspora groups, so that whilst the suppression of European border controls may facilitate their expansion, they still face a problem of adapting to different national cultures.[16] Nor is the problem of immigration essentially a common 'European' challenge. The 'frontline' state, Germany, has faced a massive demand from asylum seekers: over 250,000 in 1991 and over 400,000 in 1992, and immigrants of German descent totalled another 400,000 in 1992. In contrast, the French and British authorities both faced fewer than 60,000 demands for asylum in 1991.[17]

Although the available data about crime rates and population migrations does not clearly indicate that the EU is the most relevant framework for joint action in judicial and domestic affairs, the government of almost every EU member state has become increasingly afraid of its inability, acting alone, to deal with the effects of the removal of internal border controls on persons and goods and the ending of national controls on capital movements. The decision, in the TEU, formally to give the EU a role in judicial and domestic policy-making, albeit a limited one, was not taken easily, given its implications for national sovereignty. However, the institutional framework for cooperation, as set down in article K, demanded unanimity to adopt common policies. This was inevitably difficult to achieve since amongst the member-states there existed a great variety of institutional arrangements and approaches to policing and justice -common policies implied changing some or many of those arrangements.

The Different National Approaches to Law and Order

The limited nature of the TEU provisions in part reflects the desire of member-state governments to relinquish as little as possible of their sovereign power in justice and policing. Equally important, however, was the real difficulty of finding common ground between the very varied approaches to imposing law and order in the different member states. Police and judicial systems have been increasingly under pressure to respond to their 'market', to work together and to adopt each others' technological and methodological advances. Given that all member states share both the economic legislation of the EU and the civil liberties principles of the European Convention on Human Rights the importance of this problem may appear surprising. Nonetheless, the practical problems which impede formulating and implementing common policies at the European level are considerable, and are matched by the political obstacles to joint policy-making in these domains.

These practical and political obstacles to joining European policy-making are exemplified in the experience of the Benelux partners. The governments of Belgium, the Netherlands and Luxembourg made the agreement, in the Benelux Treaty, to abolish all internal border controls between their countries after 1960. Each state, however, retained its own immigration laws and its own methods of enforcing those laws. One clause of the Treaty provided for 'hot pursuits' by police officers of fleeing criminals to be continued across borders. Debates on the precise rules for implementing this provision showed the extreme sensitivity of allowing the police of one country to operate on the territory of its neighbour, and only in 1976 was the clause finally implemented, and then its application was limited to two border provinces and a one-kilometre penetration zone. Mutual suspicions about the zeal and competence of different national agencies were also revealed. In 1976, the Dutch immigration authorities convinced their government that Belgian immigration officials were not effectively controlling the Franco-Belgian border; in response the Dutch government posted officers of the Royal Marechaussée just inside the Dutch-Belgian frontier to carry out non-border checks. Since then some cross-border police cooperation in exchanging information, joint border checks, access to communications networks and contingency plans has developed. Nonetheless, there has been very little harmonization of police methods or of the criminal law codes. In short, after thirty years of promises to work together, joint policy-making in judicial and domestic affairs has been very limited.

Differing laws and rules of criminal procedure are a major source of practical difficulties for attempts at making common policies by governments of member states. Although there is widespread agreement on the need for joint policies to deal with international drugs cartels, the making of actual policies is hampered by very different rules concerning both the ownership and trading of narcotics and the treatment of addicts. In the Netherlands, for example, the possession of 'soft drugs' is not a criminal offence, whereas in Britain, France and Germany it is. Equally, the acknowledged need for common action to deal with the rise of violent crimes and terrorism faces the reality that different member states have very different rules about the sale and ownership of guns.

The considerable diversity of rules of evidence and the codes of conduct for police officers and investigating magistrates also poses many problems. Clearly 'hot pursuit' across a non-controlled border becomes very problematic if the code of conduct for police officers changes markedly at that border. Although extradition treaties have existed for many years, different standards of admissibility of evidence continue to cause problems.

Differences over immigration policies and problems are also important and reflect very different national histories and definitions of nationality and citizenship. Most immigrants to Britain came from the Commonwealth countries, mainly India and the West Indies; in most cases they either acquired voting rights with permanent resident status or simply took British nationality. French immigrants mostly originated in former North African colonies or in Algeria when it formed an integral part of France. In contrast Germany at first recruited cheap labour for its economic miracle from Turkey, but the acquisition of nationality was rare and difficult. Since the late 1980s, however, the source of the vast immigrant population in Germany is the former Communist block, and many of the newcomers have automatic access to German nationality on the basis of their German descent.

Differences of police and judicial structures merely compound the problems arising from differences of legislation. In all countries the police forces and the courts are involved in three types of functions. The first is that of administrative policing - crime prevention, traffic flow, petty offences and emergencies. The second is that of criminal justice, dealing with the investigation, trial and punishment of serious crimes. The third is that of national security, which includes everything from border controls to defending politicians and protecting military secrets. In all three types of function, professional police and judicial services interact with elected officers of government, both local and national, with professional bureaucrats and with specialized emergency services including the military. The diversity of arrangements is enormous, making all forms of joint action and policy-making between member-states of the European Union complex and difficult.

When police officers or examining magistrates in one member state seek the collaboration of their functional equivalents in another state, they frequently find that functional responsibilities are distributed very differently across the border. An Anglo-Italian comparison is illustrative of the extent of this problem: a detective from the Criminal Investigation Department of a unitary geographical police force in Britain might - according to the circumstances - require the collaboration of an examining magistrate, or an officer of the Vigile Municipale, the Polizia Nazionale, the Carabinieri or even of the Guardia di Finanze. In general, magistrates and police officers have little knowledge or understanding of the law and order structures outside their national boundaries. Furthermore, acquiring such a knowledge is not easy, given the numerous traditional conflicts of competence between the various police and judicial authorities in many of the member states. In France, for example, the rivalry between the Gendarmerie, the National Police and the municipal police officers is matched only by the traditional demarcation dispute between examining magistrates and police detectives in general.

Anxiety over the suppression of border controls is not the same in Britain as in most continental European states. In Britain (and Ireland) the myth of the 'island fortress' leads to a widespread belief in the real capacity of customs officers and immigration officials to keep drugs, guns, rabies and illegal immigrants out of the country. In contrast, most continental ministers acknowledge that only border controls on the scale of the former East Germany can impose effective supervision of who or what enters their countries.

Overcoming differences of national traditions to make joint European policies on law and order depend on political choices taken by the governments of the fifteen member states. Decisions to make such joint policies depend in part on elite beliefs and attitudes about European integration. Governments formed by parties with strong nationalist beliefs and suspicions of common European policies - the British Conservatives and the French Gaullists are good examples - seek to minimize European solutions or initiatives. In general Dutch and German leaders are much more willing to increase the scope of collective European decision-making than Danish politicians. Justice and policing are particularly sensitive issues as they are traditional 'regalian' functions of the State, and highly symbolic in debates over sovereignty.

If the variety of pro- or anti-integrationist ideologies amongst the ruling parties is one source of division in the Council of Ministers and the European Council, so too is the diversity of views about the desirable nature of joint policies and policy instruments. Some see the major challenge for the EU to be that of providing effective means for investigation and repression of crimes and criminals. For others, however, the priority is crime prevention and civil rights. Such differences of approach are most visible when asylum and immigration policies are under discussion. Those taking the repressive approach urge an increase in discretionary powers for police and immigration authorities to prevent the entry of illegal immigrants and to deport all those who managed to get in without a proper permit. Liberals, in contrast, stress that would-be immigrants and asylum seekers should have full access to 'due legal process' to defend their case for entry. In general, Centre-Right French governments have been repressive, whilst German governments, whether led by the CDU or the SPD, have been liberal.

Conclusions

The TEU provided the first formal institutional arrangements for common policy-making in justice and domestic affairs and authorized the creation of an institution whose very title, Europol, suggests a federal European police organization or an integrated policy on policing. However, although the Treaty legitimized the establishment of common policies in 'judicial and internal affairs', it did not use the institutional framework of the Community for decision-making, but created the distinct structures of the 'Third Pillar'. In short, in the TEU, the member-state governments retained the intergovernmental approach which had characterized all earlier common policy-making in these policy areas. That approach was also taken in the Schengen Group since its creation in 1985 with the aim of dismantling internal border controls.

Six main conclusions can be drawn from this analysis of the changes, their context and their prospects. One is the absence of any provision relating to justice or domestic affairs in the Treaties of Paris and of Rome. There was indeed almost no Treaty base for any policy initiatives by the two supranational Community institutions, the Commission and the Court of Justice. In the absence of any drive for common policies from the Commission, cooperation depended on initiatives from national government. Even the TEU, whilst allowing the Commission a right of initiative in areas covered by article K1 (1) to K1(6), excluded it in the other crucial policy domains (articles K1(7) to K1(9)). In short, leadership in policy-making has to be very largely the task of member-state governments.

A second conclusion is that the growing awareness of some common and shared policy challenges in criminality and immigration by governments of the member states has not weakened the 'national' perceptions of crime problems and solutions by most politicians and professionals. Only in Germany - with its federal structure and tradition, open frontiers for political refugees and German descendants, and strategic location at the border with the former Eastern Bloc - have numerous politicians and professionals argued the case for common European policies. Not surprisingly, German governments have often taken the lead in proposing common solutions to shared problems in law and order or border controls and have shown greater willingness than several of their partners to create common services (notably the French and British Governments).

A third conclusion is that the diversity of organizations which deal with problems of law and order in the various member states is a major obstacle to even simple cooperation between services. Inevitably common policies are difficult to construct when institutional approaches are based on very different premises.

In contrast, a fourth conclusion is that the effectiveness of the limited types of cooperation and joint policy-making which have been undertaken has been widely recognized. The gradual growth of common activities - in all cases adopted by unanimous decisions of the member-state governments - reflects the shared perception by many policy-makers (of different nationalities and political parties) that existing joint policies have brought benefits. If some national and nationalist politicians have been reluctant publicly to admit that joint policies actually produce positive benefits for citizens, they have nonetheless drawn the practical implications of that conclusion.

A fifth conclusion is that the TEU, far from reducing institutional incoherence in the EU, has actually reinforced it. The distinction between the Community process and the parallel intergovernmentalism of Trevi and European Political Cooperation have been formally maintained. In places, however, (notably articles 100(c) and K9) the borderline has been blurred. A new intergovernmental body, Europol, has been created but previously existing organizations, have been neither integrated nor formally linked with it. The possibility of developing a Europol information system in parallel to that of Schengen, clearly has no policy rational - although it may have a political logic. The existence of parallel or overlapping policy frameworks and agencies is inevitably both costly and inefficient. Ironically, the same politicians who demand greater transparency - 'to make European institutions more easily comprehensible to ordinary citizens' - are often the ones who insist on the maintenance of this Byzantine architecture.

The final conclusion is that the symbolic importance, in debates on sovereignty, of law, order and justice as a 'regalian' function of the state, has not declined, but probably increased. The TEU, by merely providing a framework for making common policies in these very sensitive policy areas has called into question an element of the logic and legitimacy of the nation-state. Hence, the institutionalization of policing and justice cooperation by the Maastricht Treaty, however limited its immediate policy results, has inevitably provoked the wrath of those opposed to any further Europeanization of public policy-making. It is ironical that in most member states, those on the right of politics who are most obsessed with 'law and order issues' and effective police action are frequently the same politicians who most actively oppose the adoption of joint policies which might improve policing and justice in all parts of the EU.[18]

Notes

1   German Hopes for Europol Dashed, *Financial Times*, 1st December 1994. *Newsbytes New Network*, 20 April 1995.
2   Fijnaut, C. (1991), in Heidensohn, F. and Farrell, M. (eds), *Crime in Europe* London, Routledge.
3   *Ibid em.*, p.104.
4   Fijnaut, C. (1987), 'The Internationalisation of Criminal Investigation in Western Europe', in Fijnaut, C. & Hermans, R. (eds), *Police Cooperation in Europe*, Lochem: van den Brink J.B.
5   Huins, J.M.M. (1980) 'The Need for Effective International Police Cooperation in the fight against Increasing International Crime: an examination of the Effectiveness of Interpol in Fulfilling the Needs of the United Kingdom at the approach of the 1980s', unpublished manuscript, Bramshill: Police Staff College.
6   Bigot, D. (ed), (1992) *L'Europe des Polices et de la Sécurité Intérieure*,
    Espace International, Paris:Edition Complexe, p.48.
7   'Programme of Action Relating to the Reinforcement of Police Cooperation and of the Endeavours to Combat Terrorism or Other Forms of Organized Crime,' issued by the Trevi Group of Ministers, Dublin: June 1990.
8   Hreblay, V. (1994), *La libre Circulation des Personnes, les Accords de Schengen*, Paris: Press Universitaires de France, p.1.
9   Blanc, H. (1991), Schengen: Le Chemin de la Libre Circulation en Europe, *Revue du Marché Commun*, pp. 722-26.
10 *Libération*, 23 December 1994.
11 Clutterbuck, R. (1990), *Terrorism, Drugs and Crime in Europe after 1992*, London: Routledge, pp.108-118.
12 Jamieson, A. (April 1992), 'Drug Trafficking after 1992', *Conflict Studies*, Special Report. Lacoste, P. (1992), *Les Mafias contre la Démocratie*, Paris: J.C. Lattès.
13 Quick no. 19 - 92, 29 April 1992.
14 Reuters, Sofia, 2 June 1995.
15 *The Independent*, 20 May 1995.
16 Falcone, G. (1992), 'Qu'est ce que la Mafia?, *Esprit*, 10, 111-118; Lacoste, *op. cit.*
17 Stewart, A. (June 1992), 'Migrants, Minorities and Security in Europe', *Conflict Studies*, 252.

18   For further references: Anderson, M. (1989) Policing the World: Interpol Politics of International Police Cooperation. Oxford: Clarendon Press; Anderson, M. and Den Boer, M., eds (1994) Policing Across National Boundaries London: Pinter; Den Boer, M. and Walker, N. (1993) European Policing after 1992. *Journal of Common Market studies,* 31/ 1; Latter, R. (1991) Crime and the European Community after 1992. London: HMSO (Wilton Park Papers, 31); Lindberg, L. (1963) The Political Dynamics of European Economic Integration. Stanford: Stanford University Press; Monar, J. and Morgan, R. (eds), (1994), *The Third Pillar of the European Union,* Brussels, European University Press; Van Reenen, P. (1989) Policing Europe after 1992: Cooperation and Competition, *European Affairs,* 2.

6 Enlarging the Union

HELENE SJURSEN[1]

Introduction

The European Union (EU)[2] is living through a period of radical change. At the centre of changes is the issue of enlargement. The prospect of a vast increase in the number of member states in the EU raises important, and also difficult, questions of a political, economic and institutional character. It highlights the need for internal reform of the EU's institutions and policies and raises the question of whether, or to what extent, the Community of Six, established in 1958, can provide a satisfactory basis for a Union of twenty states or more at the turn of the Century. At the same time, the issue of enlargement cannot be kept separate from the wider debate on the reorganization of Europe after the end of the Cold War. Since 1989, the European Union has become one of the few devices for peace, stability and prosperity in Europe. The way in which the EU responds to demands for enlargement will greatly affect the continent as a whole.

The chapter starts with a brief overview of previous enlargements. It then turns to look at the problem of enlargement in the context of the end of the Cold War. Finally, the last section assesses the EU's approach to enlargement half way through the 1990s. It is suggested that although the prospect of enlargement in the 1990s presents the EU with a more complex set of issues than previous enlargements, the European Union's policy does not differ radically from the period prior to 1989. This policy does not consist in a deliberate choice between widening and deepening. Rather, it is in the context of a wider compromise including the interests and perspectives of the actors inside the EU and the overall debate on the future direction of European integration that the EU's enlargement policy has to be understood.

Enlargement and European Integration: a Brief Review

Enlargement is a declared objective of the Treaty of Rome. The Preamble of the Treaty asserts that the member states are 'Determined to lay the foundations of an ever closer union among the peoples of Europe'. Furthermore, according to article 237, 'any European State may apply to become a member of the Community'. However, increasing the number of member states has rarely been a priority for the European Union. Rather, enlargement has been considered as contradictory to the process of integration. As pure logic would indicate, increased membership leads to a more heterogenous and less cohesive community and reduces the probability of achieving agreement. Consequently, membership applications to the EU have usually been discussed with reference to the threat that enlargement or 'widening' might represent for further integration or 'deepening' inside the EU. This image created through the notions of widening and deepening is important because it highlights the inherent characteristics of enlargement. However, it does not fully explain the EU's enlargement policy, neither does it give a clear idea of the impact of enlargement on the process of integration.

The EU's policy on enlargement has rarely been the result of a clear-cut choice or balancing act between widening and deepening. In effect, the process of enlargement involves and affects actors at three separate but interconnected levels within the EU: firstly, at the level of specific sectorial interests (the interest of various industries may be jeopardized by the arrival of new and possibly more competitive products from the new member states); secondly, at the level of the 'national interest' (enlargement affects the position of the member states and their ability to influence Community decisions); and finally, at the level of the Community system itself (especially on its institutional structure, its component elements and its decision-making process). A brief look at previous enlargements will indicate that decisions on enlargement have usually been the result of a complex interaction between actors at these three levels and the political debate inside the European Union at the time.[3]

Enlargement to the North

The first applications for membership to the European Community came already in 1961, only four years after the signing of the Treaty of Rome. It was nevertheless to take eleven years and a lot of institutional and political wrangling before Great Britain, Denmark and Ireland actually became part of the Community.[4]

The main reason why these countries had to wait so long to join the Community was the French President de Gaulle's reluctant attitude to British membership. There has been some debate about the reasons for his strong opposition to the British application. Most authors agree that although economic issues had some influence on de Gaulle's position, his main motive was political, and specifically related to his policy of 'independence' from the United States. British membership was seen as tantamount to allowing the USA to enter the Community through the back door.[5] Also important in understanding the French position, as well as that of the other actors inside the EC, is the situation inside the Community in the early 1960s. The French refusal of British membership can be seen as part of a more general struggle over the future direction of European integration. After his accession to power in France in 1958 de Gaulle was determined to shape the Community according to his own vision. Two of the constituent elements of de Gaulle's Community were respect for the sovereignty of the member states and independence from American influence. British membership was, in the eyes of de Gaulle, an obstacle to this vision of Europe. From the perspective of the Commission and the other member states, who did not altogether share de Gaulle's view of the future of Europe, British membership was seen as an effective counterpole to French dominance. In other words, the attitude of the member states to enlargement was influenced by the ongoing struggle about the future orientation of the Community. It was seen as a factor that might strengthen or weaken the position of the different actors and, together with it, their vision of the Community, rather than as an issue examined exclusively on its own merits.

In the long run France could not prevent enlargement. At the summit in the Hague in 1969 the new French President Georges Pompidou agreed to the reopening of membership negotiations with Great Britain, Denmark, Ireland and Norway. France's change of policy should not however be seen solely as a result of de Gaulle's resignation in April 1969. The decision to enlarge was in effect part of a 'package deal' aiming at satisfying the interest of all Community members. Hence France agreed to enlargement as a trade-off against the other Community members' commitment to the completion of the Common Agricultural Policy.[6]

Enlargement to the South

If the political desirability of British membership was disputed, those of Greece, Spain and Portugal were, from a political/strategic viewpoint generally considered both positive and necessary.[7] The fact that with three new member states the Common market would include 314 million consumers and open for closer links with former colonies must also be mentioned in order to appreciate the Community's positive attitude.

The enlargements to the Mediterranean states have often been seen as a means to support the transition to democracy and also to ensure stability in Western Europe.[8] However, there was at the same time concern about the economic and institutional consequences of the Mediterranean enlargement. The level of economic development in these countries was lower than the Community average. Concern was also expressed about the risk of a dilution of the efficiency of Community institutions and its decision-making process with increased membership. But most importantly, the Mediterranean enlargement was affected by the internal difficulties of the Community in the early 1980s. The conflict inside the Community was centred around the question of the British contribution to the Community budget. However, this dispute was at the same time a symptom of a more general conflict over the future direction of European integration.[9] The continuing disagreements inside the Community delayed negotiations on enlargement, and the Community repeatedly failed to set a specific date for the accession of Spain and Portugal.[10] It was only when the internal dispute was resolved, at the Fontainebleau summit in 1984, and the future course of integration in the form of the Single Market was agreed upon, that a final date (1 January 1986) was set for enlargement. In this context some have argued that '... the Single European Act can [even] be seen as partly a way of completing arrangements for the enlargement of the Community to twelve members.'[11]

It may be suggested then, that although concern about the effects on the cohesion of the Community system was present both during enlargement to the North and to the South, enlargement has in practice not prevented further integration. Rather, the prospect of enlargement has provoked the EU into putting its own house in order. And, most importantly, decisions to enlarge have been made against the backdrop of a wider compromise between competing interests and views inside the Community, rather than as a direct response to the risks that widening might entail for the prospects of further deepening.

At the beginning of the 1990s the Community was at the brink of not one, but several, waves of enlargement. The great number of new membership applications presented the Community with considerable opportunities. For the first time in its history it could envisage the possibility of encompassing the whole of the European continent. Nevertheless, difficulties were also abundant.

The general gist of these problems, such as the question of the resilience of the Community system, the concern about increased economic competition from new member states or the impact of enlargement on the role and influence of particular member states, were similar to previous enlargements. However, the issue of enlargement at the beginning of the 1990s was qualitatively different from previous enlargements, partly because of the high number of applicants and partly because of the changes in the external environment in which enlargement would take place.

Setting the Scene for Enlargement in the 'New Europe'

The Community was at the beginning of the 1990s the central focus of attention for a collection of national objectives and interests that diverged to a much larger extent than under previous enlargements. Geographically the prospective member states spread from the Arctic Circle to the Mediterranean. In size they varied from the micro-states of Cyprus and Malta to the giants Turkey and Poland. The needs of these countries are as different as their size and geographical location. Their economic, political and social structure is diverse, and so were the challenges they presented to the Community framework. Consequently, cohesion would be more difficult to achieve both at a political and an economic level. It would demand an even larger expression of solidarity inside the Community than what already existed. The new international context in which enlargement would take place further raised the stakes in the Community's policy choices in the early 1990s. With the end of the Cold War and the end of the political division of Europe, the EU became a dominant actor on the European continent and one of the few devices for maintaining peace, prosperity and security in Europe.

The next section first looks in turn at each group of applicants and the questions that their application raised for the European Community. Subsequently, it outlines the conditions set out by the European Union for enlargement in the 1990s.[12]

A diverse group of applicants

EFTA

Relations between EFTA and the European Union had, since 1972, been governed by bilateral free trade agreements. These agreements were replaced by the European Economic Area (EEA) agreement in January 1994. Before the EEA-agreement came into force, however, the five main EFTA-states had applied for full membership in the European Community.

The existence of the EEA agreement meant that, in economic terms, the EFTA-applicants were better prepared for membership than many of their predecessors. Much of the Community acquis was already accepted and implemented by the EFTA states through this agreement.[13] What is more, despite high budget and trade deficits, in particular in Sweden and Finland, the EFTA-states were on the whole all rich enough to be net contributors to the EC budget.[14] Finally, EFTA was the Community's most important trading partner and, conversely, the EC was also EFTA's most important market.[15]

It was chiefly in political terms that the EFTA-states were seen to have the potential to create problems for the European Community. Although their motivation for joining the Community was not exclusively economic (the collapse of the Soviet Union and the end of the Cold War were also important in placing membership in the EC on the political agenda), neither governments nor public opinion at large in the EFTA states could be accused of overwhelming enthusiasm for the concept of a federal Europe. The EFTA countries have a pragmatic and utilitarian approach to European integration. Indeed, the Swiss rejection of the EEA agreement and the Norwegian rejection of membership seemed in retrospect to confirm the image of Northern and Alpine scepticism to European integration.[16] It might well be, then, that, in the long run, enlargement to the EFTA Countries would hinder efforts toward further integration. Finally, the possibility that Finland's, Sweden's and Austria's status as neutrals might prevent the strengthening of cooperation in the area of security and defence was also a cause for concern.

There is little reason however to assume that these states would automatically take a negative stand on further integration. Firstly, membership was easily approved in Austria, Finland and Sweden.[17] Secondly, the candidate states pronounced a strong interest in the issues of transparency, accountability, social policy and environmental policy. A commitment to these questions might in reality lead the new member states to advocate a strengthening of EU policies, rather than a loosening of integration. Thirdly, the meaning and importance of neutrality has much changed as a result of the end of the Cold War. Indeed, the neutrality of both Austria and Finland were a result of the Cold War itself. As for the 'active neutrality' of Sweden, there is little indication that it would prevent the country from participating fully in the Common Foreign and Security Policy (CFSP).

On the other hand, the orientation and general outlook of EU foreign and external relations is likely to be influenced by Nordic and Alpine enlargement. Ironically, where this will probably be felt most strongly is in relation to the question of future enlargement, not only to Central and East Europe, but also to the Baltic states. The EFTA-states, geographically closer to these regions, are all sensitive to their economic and security concerns.[18]

Table 1. Enlargement in the 1990s

	status with EU	application	negotiations open	accession
EFTA				
Austria	EEA (1994)	1989 (July)	1993 (Feb)	1995 (Jan)
Sweden	EEA (1994)	1991 (June)	1993 (Feb)	1995 (Jan)
Finland	EEA (1994)	1992 (May)	1993 (Feb)	1995 (Jan)
Switzerland	[a]	1992 (May)	[b]	
Norway	EEA (1994)	1992 (Nov)	1993 (Apr)	[c]
Mediterranean				
Turkey	assoc.	1987(Apr)	[d]	
Malta	assoc. 1971	1990 (Jul)	after IGC	?
Cyprus	assoc. 1973	1990 (Jul)	after IGC	?
Visegrad				
Hungary	EA	1994 (Apr)	2000?	?
Poland	EA	1994 (Apr)	2000?	?
Czech Republic	EA	1996 (Jan)	2000?	?
Slovakia	EA	1995 (June)	2000?	?

[a]   Rejected the EEA agreement in a referendum on 7 December 1994.

[b]   Against the backdrop of the negative vote on the EEA, negotiations were not opened.

[c]   Rejected membership in a referendum on 28 November 1994, by 52.2% of the votes.

[d]   Enlargement negotiations have been postponed, agreement to establish a customs union has been achieved.

Central and Eastern Europe

Poland, Hungary, Rumania, Slovakia, the Czech Republic, Bulgarian, Estonia, Lithuania and Latvia have officially applied for membership to the European Union. Slovenia is likely to do so in the near future.

Relations between the European Union and the Central and East European countries (CEEC) are regulated by association agreements (the Europe Agreements), and by the so-called 'structured relationship' between the associated states and the institutions of the Union.[19] The Europe Agreements are 'second generation' agreements, building on the trade and cooperation agreements signed in the immediate aftermath of the fall of the communist regimes in 1989.[20] They are framework agreements within which cooperation may be gradually intensified and expanded. Indeed, since their signature, they have already been improved in significant ways, chiefly in response to criticism that, focusing too much on the protection of the Community, they did not address the real needs of the associated states.[21] The central concern of the Europe Agreements is the establishment of a wider European market, encompassing all the associated states. The onus is on the associated states to adopt the internal market rules, to restructure their economies and perform the necessary macro-economic adjustments. Financial support is provided through the Phare programme, as well as the European Investment Bank and the European Bank for Reconstruction and Development. A minimum budgetary figure of 1.1 bn ECU per year for the Phare programme, was set for the first time for 1995.[22]

The 'structured partnerships' aim at establishing a dialogue between the EU and associated states in areas which are considered to have a 'trans-European dimension'. The EU emphasizes in particular the need for a dialogue in the areas of energy, environment, transport, science and technology, as well as in home and judicial affairs and foreign and security policy. Annual meetings have been scheduled for the Heads of State and Government and semi-annual meetings for the Foreign Minsters and Justice and Home Affairs-ministers.[23]

For the Central and East European states membership in the EU offers a framework of support for the process of transition to a market oriented economy and liberal democracy. The prospect of being part of a wider Western security community is also important.[24] But although the practical gain expected from membership is vital, its symbolic value must equally be underlined. Membership in the EU would symbolize the definite end to the division of Europe and the final re-inclusion of the East European states into the European 'family'. Hence, the issues raised by the prospect of an eastern enlargement are different from those raised as a result of a Nordic and Alpine enlargement.

The first issue is related to the 'cost' of such an enlargement. One unofficial Commission's estimate of the cost to the EU budget of enlarging to the four Visegrad states (Poland, Hungary, the Czech Republic and Slovakia) is of 80 bn ECU. By way of comparison, the existing EU budget amounts to 70 bn ECU. As one may see from table 2, the largest difference between the CEEC economies and the EU is in the national income. Inflation is also high, although it is declining in all four states. The economic situation is perhaps not, however, as bleak as one might expect. In terms of budget deficit, which is also one of the indicators for participation in the Monetary Union, the situation in the CEEC compares well with the EU average.

Table 2. Central and Eastern Europe: Key Indicators

	population (m)*[e]	GDP/ capita $[f]	real GDP ann. % change[g]	inflation*	external debt % of GDP**[h]	public deficit % of GDP**
	38.5	4880	4.5	32.2	54.5	2.8
Hungary	10.26	5740	1.0	18.8	67.3	6
Czech Republic	10.3	7160	1.5	7.0	27.5	+0.1
Slovakia	5.3	5620	-4.1	13.5	27.4	6.8
EU average		17000	2.1	3.7[i]	5.8[j]	6.6[k]

[e]*   1994, Preliminary EUI estimate.

[f]   1992, The Economist, 5 November 1994.

[g]   1994, IMF staff estimates (1993 for Slovakia). IMF World Economic Outlook, October 1994.

[h]**   1993 year-end figure. All remaining figures from 'Is the West doing enough for Eastern Europe?' Philip Morris Insitute, November 1994, p.41.

[i]   May 1994.

[j]   1992.

[k]   May 1994.

In order to catch up with the economies of the European Union, it is necessary for these states' economies to grow faster than the EU average. Central to the growth of their economies are exports as well as foreign investment. Hence the importance of the Europe Agreements. Yet there are clear restrictions in these agreements to the opening of trade: farm products, for example, which represent a large proportion of the CEEC's exports, do not have free entry into the Union. Sensitive sectors such as textiles, iron, steel and coal are also affected by restrictive measures.

The reluctance of the EU to speed up trade liberalization confirms that enlargement to Central and Eastern Europe does not depend only on the level of economic development in these states. There is also concern inside the EU about increased competition from Central and East Europe in certain economic sectors. What is more, the prospect of an Eastern enlargement reinforces the need for a restructuring of some of the existing policies of the EU, such as agricultural and regional policies.[25] Membership applications from the CEEC also raise the question of how to define Europe. In principle, the EU is open to all European states.[26]

However, as William Wallace has pointed out, there are no clear criteria for defining what a European state is, or where Europe stops.[27] The signing of the Europe Agreements might indicate that rather than a criteria of European identity, the borders of the European Union will be determined by a combination of strategic, economic and political considerations. Hence, the Baltic states have signed Association agreements and are thus, according to the Copenhagen summit declaration, potential members in the Union, whereas Ukraine, too large, too poor and too close to Russia, has not been offered such an agreement.[28] There is also the question of timing. When should enlargement start and which states should be integrated first? In turn, this highlights the question of security: does membership in the EU automatically open for membership in the West European Union (WEU)? If this is so, what might the consequences of enlargement be for those states which do not enter the EU and, perhaps most importantly, what would be the effect of such an enlargement on Western relations with Russia? A final issue raised as a result of the prospect of enlargement to Central and Eastern Europe is the risk that this might lead the Union to neglect the Mediterranean region. There is concern amongst the Mediterranean states that such a reorientation is already taking place. It is no doubt essential that this does not occur.[29]

The South

Malta, Cyprus and Turkey constitute the third group of applicants. However, if their geographic proximity link these three countries together, they do not raise the same type of problems with regard to EU membership. In terms of its population, Turkey, with its 57.7 million inhabitants would be the second largest European Union member.[30] Malta and Cyprus on the other hand are micro-states with respectively 360,000 and 700,000 inhabitants.[31] Thus, whereas Turkey might threaten to become too dominating by its size, the two other Mediterranean applicants represent all the problems related to a micro-state member of the Union.

In addition to, and more importantly, than the question of population size, is that of the level of economic development. Figures have raised doubts as to whether or not Turkey would be able to take on the obligations that result from the Union's economic and social policies. The Union is also concerned about the burden that Turkish membership would impose on its own resources.[32] With regard to the political issues, although positive developments have taken place in terms of constitutional reforms and improvements of the situation of human rights, there are still doubts as to whether the situation in Turkey has reached the EU's requirements.[33] Finally, the political divergency between Greece and Turkey, and in particular the dispute about Cyprus, is in itself a hindrance to membership negotiations with Turkey.[34]

Cyprus' and Malta's applications do not imply the same economic problems as their Turkish counterpart. Adoption of the 'acquis communautaire' would not pose insurmountable problems for these states. The main issue in their case is that of their size and how their roles in the institutional framework should be defined. The European Commission has questioned the ability of these states to take on the responsibilities of the Presidency. One might also raise the question of whether or not Malta's constitutional status as a neutral and non-aligned country would be compatible with the Common Foreign and Security Policy (CFSP). The Malta Labour Party (in opposition) opposes Maltese membership and is still strongly attached to the status of neutrality.[35]

Procedures and conditions for membership

Political control with the process of enlargement lies with the member states, represented by the General Affairs Council. Applications for membership are addressed to the Council which decides unanimously, on the basis of a Commission opinion, whether or not to open negotiations.[36] The Council is also responsible for negotiating the accession agreement with applicant states.[37] It does so in close cooperation with the Commission, which produces much of the preparatory work. Significantly in this respect, during the enlargement negotiations with the EFTA states, the Commission set up a task force for enlargement. The European Parliament has the power to reject enlargement by an absolute majority.

Building on the provisions of the Treaties, the European Council in Lisbon (June 1992), set out the criteria according to which future enlargement should take place. In order to qualify for membership in the Union, applicant states must satisfy a series of strict economic and political conditions. Firstly, they must fulfil the conditions of European identity, democratic status and respect for human rights. Secondly, the applicant states must accept the Community system and have the capacity to implement it. This requires the applicant to have 'a competitive market economy, and an adequate legal and administrative framework in the public and private sector'. Thirdly, applicants must accept and have the ability to implement the Common Foreign and Security Policy 'as it evolves over the coming years'.[38]

These conditions are not entirely clear cut and are open to different interpretations. They constitute an effort to impose logic and rationality on a process which sometimes lacks both. For example, the definition of what constitutes 'Europe' is, as we have already pointed out, open ended. The economic criteria appear more easily applicable. Essentially, bearing in mind the implementation of the Single Market and the commitment in the Treaty of Maastricht to Economic Monetary Union, the economic obligations for membership are more difficult to fulfil than under previous enlargements. Based on our overview of the applicant states, it would appear that the Central and East European states are not yet economically ready for membership. Poland has however argued that one should most of all take into consideration the health of the economy of applicant states, rather than its overall wealth, thus indicating room for manouvering also in this area.[39] Most importantly, the EU underlines that enlargement will depend on 'the Union's capacity to absorb new members, while maintaining the momentum of European integration'. This establishes a close link between the internal developments of the EU and the prospect for enlargement. Turning now to assess the Union's approach to enlargement in the 1990s, we shall suggest that rather than a particular state's ability to conform with specific economic and political criteria, enlargement depends on processes internal to the European Union, and most of all on the ability of the Union to put its own house in order. In this respect, the European Union's response to demands for enlargement does not differ radically from the period prior to 1989, despite the qualitative differences to this issue in the 1990s.

Enlargement in the 1990s: an Interim Assessment

In anticipation of a rush of membership applications in 1989, Helen Wallace outlined three different scenarios for future EC enlargements. The scenarios were the following: (i) consolidation of the existing Community and close partnerships with the rest of Europe; (ii) completion of the internal market and widening with no further deepening; (iii) extensive enlargement and building a new European structure.[40] These scenarios are useful yardsticks against which one can now, halfway through the 1990s and in anticipation of the 1996 Intergovernmental Conference (IGC) assess the response of the European Union to the problem of enlargement.

The first scenario would mean the creation of new forms of close partnerships between the EC and the rest of Europe, including both economic and political elements, and a continuation of the process of integration in the Community proper. It might also indicate that completion should be conducted with the aim of contributing to the refashioning of Europe. It would not rule out enlargement in the long term. The second scenario would mean abandoning the emphasis on further integration, and enlarging in the short term to EFTA and in the medium term to Central and Eastern Europe. A return to integration might be envisaged in the long term, but would not be given priority. The third scenario would mean the end of West European integration and the creation of a looser pan-European structure including all European states, with intergovernmental institutions and coordination rather than common policies.

As Helen Wallace points out, the real choice of the then European Community was between the first and the second scenario. Evidence leads us to suggest that the European Community's initial approach came closest to the first scenario of consolidation and close, open-ended association. The European Union has since 1989 established a network of institutional links with potential member states. The most important institutional frameworks are the already mentioned Europe Agreements, the EEA agreement and the association agreements with the Mediterranean states. But there are also, in the area of security and defence, the Stability Pact and the associate memberships in the WEU, and in the economic sphere, Eureka, Esprit and, most recently, the prospect of extending the trans-European networks to Central and Eastern Europe.[41]

Questions have arisen quickly, however, as to how useful these networks are, and as to whether or not they can be considered to be anything more than transitory for a majority of the European states.[42] The experience of both the European Economic Area Agreement and the Europe Agreements indicate that to most states these agreements are not, in the long term, a satisfactory alternative to membership. As we have seen, Sweden, Finland and Austria turned their back on the EEA and acceded to the EU on 1 January 1995. Membership negotiations with Malta and Cyprus are expected to open after the Intergovernmental Conference in 1996.[43] With regard to the Central and East European states, the Union has proposed 'pre-accession strategies' within the framework of the Europe Agreements.[44] These do not substantially change the existing framework of relations between the EU and the associated states. The importance lies in the acceptance, in principle, of future enlargement and in the fact that further developments of the Europe Agreements will be designed with the explicit purpose of assisting the CEEC in preparing for membership. It is only Turkish membership which has been postponed and where, as an alternative to membership, the Association agreement, signed in 1963, has been reactivated. It thus looks likely that association has generally become a transitional measure, and that, as a permanent solution, it is relevant only to a few European states. Indeed, even from the perspective of the European Union itself, these agreements may chiefly have been instruments aimed at delaying enlargement for as long as possible, rather than substitutes for it.

One of the principal reasons for the associated states' disenchantment with their status is their exclusion from participation in EU policy-making. In fact, despite the establishment of close cooperation, the European Union has maintained a clear distinction between membership, which provides participation in policy-making, and association, providing access to the single market, as well as the possibility of aligning policies in other areas with those of the Union, but no influence on policy making. The decision of the EFTA states to seek full membership was to a large extent provoked by disappointment with this aspect of the EEA-agreement.[45] The importance of participation at the level of policy-making was also clearly felt by Norway once the results of the referendum in November 1994 were made official. Norway was overnight cut off from the EU's political networks and working groups, leading a well informed observer to comment that Norway 'is politically more isolated than at any time since 1905'.[46] Udgaard's point is that despite participation in a wide network of European agreements, Norway's political influence is dramatically reduced as a result of its decision to turn its membership back.

The first scenario, initially favoured by the EU, has been overtaken, or redefined, by events. This does not mean that the second scenario, of widening, but no further deepening, ignored in 1989, is now the closest to reality. The European Union's conditions for enlargement indicate that there is a wish for the process of integration to continue. The EU stresses that enlargement will depend on the Union's capacity to absorb new members while maintaining the momentum of integration. Also, the pre-accession strategies for the CEEC put economic cohesion between the EU and the applicant states at centre stage, and the onus for change is on the applicants themselves. In fact, the logic of events has led the EU to undertake a more complicated bargain in which both the process of enlargement and the process of further integration will have to be accommodated.

In this context, the concept of differentiation, as a means to manage a Union of twenty states or more, has received increased attention. This concept is not new. Throughout the history of the EU there has been a multitude of proposals centred around this theme.[47] Looking at the European Union post-Maastricht, it is arguable that differentiation, despite the fact that it is not recognized as an organizing principle or applied in a systematic way, is already the de facto reality of the Union. The Economic and Monetary Union, to which all member states have subscribed, introduces a differentiation in time, and accepts that some member states might reach the ultimate destination before others. In social policy, for which Britain has not signed, there is a differentiation in space. Previous to the Treaty of Maastricht, the Schengen agreement and the European Monetary System were already based on the principle of differentiation. With regard to enlargement the concept is significant because it indicates that flexiblibility is possible in dealing with new and potential member states.[48] It is also significant in that it highlights the fact that deepening, or integration, is not a one way street toward a predetermined goal.

Yet, it is unlikely that the EU will make a deliberate choice to adopt a specific strategy of differentiation. In this sense, it is the existence of such a large number of proposals related to the management of widening and deepening which is significant. One of the first German proposals, albeit not from the government, but from the CDU/CSU faction in the Bundestag, was of the creation of a 'hard core'.[49] The French appeared for some time to favour 'concentric circles'. Indeed, this is at the heart of the whole problem of enlargement. It is not only a matter of the ability of the system as such to cope with a higher number of members, or of the ability of the applicant states to fulfil certain political and economic criteria. The difficulty lies in the European Union's own aptitude in dealing with its internal disagreements, in the existing members' aptitude in agreeing amongst themselves on the choices to be made, both with regard to the future direction of European integration and with regard to the balance to be established between demands for enlargement and concerns about protecting their own interests and perspectives. And most importantly, the difficulty lies in the absence of a consensus on the purpose and future shape of the Union.

The perspective of member states on enlargement is influenced by their own economic and political constraints, by how they perceive enlargement to affect their position and interests within the EU, as well as by their views on the future direction of European integration. Hence, Germany puts a successful eastern enlargement of the EU high on the agenda. It sees enlargement as a major instrument in the effort to stabilize democracy in its neighbouring states.[50] France, on the other hand, is concerned that enlargement might reduce its influence in the EU, by tipping the balance in the Franco-German partnership further in Germany's favour. It also underlines that the Mediterranean region, closer to its own concerns, should not be ignored as a result of a discussion on an eastern enlargement.[51] Britain is pleased with the notion of enlargement in general, but mostly, it would seem, because it is considered as a way of reducing the chances of further integration.[52] Finally, the beneficiaries of the regional funds are concerned about possible revisions in these policies in the case of enlargement.[53]

The main question is how enlargement can be accommodated into these priorities. And as during previous enlargements, it is against the backdrop of a compromise between the interests and priorities of the EU actors, their view of the future of European integration and the pressure for enlargement, that the EU's enlargement policy in the 1990s is emerging.

Conclusion

view of Integration and enlargement Relations.

The prospect of enlargement is usually discussed with reference to the consequences that it might have for future integration. It is difficult to escape this logic of an inherent contradiction between widening and deepening when examining the question of enlargement, yet, the relationship has usually been more complex. Firstly, widening does not have to lead to a dilution of the EU, and has not always done so: widening and deepening have often gone hand in hand, with the prospect of widening forcing the EU to take steps toward further deepening. What is more, new states, through a commitment to specific policies, might contribute to strengthening integration, rather than weakening that same process. Secondly, the widening-deepening dichotomy gives the impression that deepening is a 'one way street' moving in a clearly specified direction. One should not ignore that there are different roads to deepening, and that in reality it has been difficult for the EU to refuse widening even when it was seen to threaten deepening. Thirdly, and most importantly for our argument, the EU's policy toward enlargement in the 1990s, as well as in previous years, is not only the result of an assessment by the EU of the risks that widening might entail for deepening, but also, and predominantly, a function of the internal policy-making processes of the European Union.

Notes

1   The author is grateful to Christopher Hill for comments on an earlier draft of this chapter.

2   The term European Union (EU) will be used for the period after the ratification of the Treaty of Maastricht. For the period prior to this, the term European Community (EC) will be employed.

3   For a detailed account of all the enlargements of the Community, see F. Nicholson and R. East, *From the Six to the Twelve: the enlargement of the European Communities*, Keesings International Studies, Harlow, Longman, 1987.

4   Norway also applied in 1962 but eventually rejected membership in a national referendum in 1972.

5   See for example P. Gerbet *La Construction de l'Europe*, Paris, Imprimerie Nationale, 1983, pp.291-315.

6   C. Franck 'New Ambitions: From the Hague to Paris summits (1969-72)' in Roy Pryce (ed.) *The Dynamics of European Union*, London and New York, Routledge, 1987, p. 132.

7   Greece presented its application in 1975, and Spain and Portugal in 1976.

8   L. Tsoukalis, *The European Community and its Mediterranean Enlargement*, London, Pinter, 1981, p. 255.

9   P.Taylor, *The limits of European integration*, London, Croom Helm, 1983.

10   Greece, as the only Mediterranean state, entered the EC in 1981, apparently as a result of the intervention of French President Valery Giscard d'Estaing.

11   R. Keohane and S. Hoffmann 'Institutional Change in Europe in the 1980s' in Keohane and Hoffmann, *The New European Community*, Boulder, Westview Press, p.21.

12   For a chronology of enlargement in the 1990s, please refer to table 1.

13   The 'four freedoms' as well as the areas of transport, competition, consumer protection, research and development, education and company law were, with minor exceptions, fully covered. Social policy, environmental policy, energy, agriculture and fisheries were partly covered. The Customs Union, external relations, development policy, taxation, industrial policy, regional policy, institutional and budgetary provisions, as well as the new policies of the Maastricht Treaty (CFSP, JHA and EMU), remained to be dealt with. See F. Granell, 'The European Union's Enlargement Negotiations with Austria, Finland, Norway and Sweden', *Journal of Common Market Studies*, vol 33, no 1, March 1995, pp. 117-141.

14   Sweden's budget deficit in 1993 was 12.9% of its GDP, in Finland it was 7.9% of GDP. *The Economist*, November 5, 1994, 'The Nordic countries'.

15 For a detailed overview of the EFTA states and their relations with the EC, see Helen Wallace (ed), *The Wider Western Europe*, London, Pinter, 1991.

16 Membership was rejected in a referendum in Norway on 28 November 1994 by 52.2% of the votes. Switzerland rejected the EEA agreement in a referendum on 7 December 1992. For a discussion on Norway's rejection of membership, see I. Sogner and C. Archer, 'Norway and Europe: 1972 and now', *Journal of Common Market Studies*, vol 33, no. 3, September 1995, pp.389-410.

17 Membership was approved in Austria by 67%, in Finland by 57 %, in Sweden by 52.5%. Also, the French referendum on the ratification of the Maastricht Treaty has shown that scepticism in public opinion with regard to European integration is not necessarily the 'prerogative' of the more recent member states.

18 Yet, at the Madrid summit, it was the Danish delegation which pressed the case of the Baltic states, not the Swedish and the Finnish ones, and which successfully achieved acceptance for the principle that the Baltic states' applications will be treated in the same way as those from the Central and East European states. See *Jyllandsposten*, 15 December 1995.

19 This notion was introduced at the Copenhagen summit in June 1993.

20 So far, association agreements have been signed with Poland, Hungary, the Czech Republic, Slovakia, Bulgaria, Rumania and the Baltic states. A similar agreement is being negotiated also with Slovenia.

21 For this view see for example H. Kramer 'The EC and the Stabilisation of Eastern Europe', *Aussenpolitik*, Volume 43, 1/92 and H. Kramer, 'The European Communities response to the New Europe', *Journal of Common Market Studies*, vol 31, no.2, June 1993.

22 *Agence Europe Bulletin*, 10 December, 1994, p. 6.

23 European Council in Copenhagen, 21-22 June 1993, Conclusions of the Presidency; *Europe Document*, 21 July 1994, 'Strategy Aimed at preparing the CEEC for accession to the EU'; *Europe Document*, 14 September 1994, 'European Commission suggestions on the strategy to prepare the CCEE for accession to the EU'.

24 Hanna Suchocka, 'L'Europe centrale et la Communauté européenne', *Le Monde*, 11 June 1993. Hanna Suchocka was Polish Prime Minister at the time the article was published.

25 Early reports on content of the Commission's studies on the effect of enlargement on agricultural and structural policies confirm this. See for example L. Barber, 'Brussels keeps the gates to the east shut', *Financial Times*, 16 November 1996. Also, *Financial Times*, 4 March 1995.

26   Article 'O' in the Treaty of Maastricht.

27   W. Wallace, 'From twelve to twenty four? The challenges to the European Community posed by the revolution in Eastern Europe', pp. 34-51 in C. Crouch and D. Marquand, *Toward Greater Europe*, Oxford, Blackwell, 1992.

28   The role of Ukraine is raised in Zbigniew Bzrezinksi, 'A plan for Europe', *Foreign Affairs*, vol. 74, no 1, Jan/Feb 1995, pp. 26-42.

29   D. Moisi and M. Mertes, 'Europe's map, Compass and Horizon', *Foreign Affairs*, vol 1, no 1, Jan/Feb 1995, pp.122-34. Also, E. Mortimer, 'Pulled in all directions', *Financial Times*, 26 January 1995.

30   For an overview of EU relations with Turkey, see W. Hale, 'Turkey: A Crucial but Problematic Applicant', in J. Redmond (ed), *Prospective Europeans*, London, Harvester Wheatsheaf, 1994, pp.113-32.

31   The EU's response to Malta's and Cyprus' applications is dealt with in J. Redmond, 'Cyprus and Malta: Still the Mediterranean Orphans?', in Redmond, *op. cit.*, pp. 133-147.

32   *European Parliament Session Documents*, March 1991, Report of the Political Affairs Committee on the Community Enlargement.

33   'Declaration of the EU Presidency on customs union with Turkey', *Europe Documents*, 28 February, 1995.

34   The fact that a compromise has been found on this issue with regard to the customs union between the European Union and Turkey does not necessarily guarantee that the question will not be reopened in the case of membership negotiations.

35   Commission Opinion on Malta's application for membership, Com (93) 312 final, Brussels, 30 June 1993; Commission opinion on the application by the Republic of Cyprus for membership, Com (93) 313 final, Brussels, 30 June 1993.

36   In the case of Greece's application, the Commission's opinion was 'overruled' by the Council of Ministers.

37   Under previous enlargements, individual technical Councils were involved, thus enhancing the likelihood that special interests would inhibit the process of negotiation.

38   *Bulletin of the EC*, Supplement 3/92, Commission of the European Communities, 'Europe and the Challenge of Enlargement' and European Council Lisbon, 26-27 June 1992, 'Conclusions of the Presidency'. Conditions for enlargement were further developed in the Copenhagen summit, after the enlargement to CEEC was accepted in principle. See Conclusions of Presidency, *op. cit.*

39   See table 2.
40   H. Wallace, *Widening and Deepening: the European Community and the New European Agenda*, RIIA Discussion Papers, no 23, London, 1989.
41   *Europe Document*, Atlantic Document no 96, March, 1995, 'Final Document on Stability Pact in Europe'; *Europe Document*, 14 December 1994.
42   *The Independent*, 20 March 1995.
43   European Council in Corfu, 24-25 June 1994, Conclusions of the Presidency.
44   *Europe Document*, 14 December 1994, 'Strategy for preparing the CEEC for accession, defined by the General Affairs Council and adopted by the Essen summit'; *Agence Europe*, 11 December 1994, 'Essen summit special edition' (9-10 December 1994).
45   A. Michalski and H. Wallace, *The European Community: the challenge of enlargement*, European Programme Special Paper, RIIA, London, 1992, p.57.
46   N. Morten Udgaard, 'En politisk kastrert stat i Europa' ('A politically castrated state in Europe'), *Aftenposten*, 28 March 1995.
47   H. Wallace, *Europe: the Challenge of Diversity*, London, Routledge, 1985.
48   Indeed, Ludlow and Ersbøll point out that the notion of derogation has been a central feature of every enlargement. P. Ludlow and N. Ersbøll, 'Towards 1996: The agenda of the Intergovernmental Conference', CEPS Paper, Brussels, 10 November 1994, p. 10.
49   CDU/CSU-Fraktion des Deutschen Bundestages, Bonn, 1 Sept. 1994, 'Reflections on European Policy'. One might add that, according to recent press reports, the CDU/CSU paper has now been 'watered down'.
50   Mertes and Moisi, *op. cit.*, p.130.
51   *Financial Times*, 20 February 1995.
52   Its position during the EFTA enlargement on the issue of deciding the size of the blocking minority in the Council of Ministers is indicative of this. Likewise, Spain held up negotiations with EFTA out of fear that with three or four wealthy northern European states in the EU, its own chances of qualifying for the EMU would be reduced.
53   *Irish Times*, 30 January 1995.

7 The EC Budget

WALTER DEFFAA

The Community Budget from its Beginning: Basic Figures and Concepts

Since its foundation, the European Community's budget expenditure has been in steady increase, but has, at the same time, remained relatively modest compared to the total of public expenditure in its Member States and the Community's overall economic output, measured for instance by its gross domestic product. (graph 1 and 2). The historical evolution of public expenditure at Community level up to 1994 reflects both the development of Community policies and the successive enlargements increasing the number of its members from the original six to twelve since 1986.

In 1960 Community expenditure (including the European Coal and Steel Community (ECSC) and the European Development Fund (EDF), which continue to have autonomous budgets separated from the 'General Budget of the European Communities') amounted to ECU 59 million and represented 0.03 per cent of Community GDP or 2.5 ECU (in 1994 prices) per capita of the EC population. In the meantime total expenditure has been rising to ECU 720,377 million in 1994, but representing some relatively modest 1.28 per cent of GDP or 207 ECU per capita and 2.5 per cent compared to public expenditure in the Member States.

During this period important policies have been developed which also have had a major impact on Community expenditure, such as:

- the creation of the European Agricultural Guidance and Guarantee Fund in 1962 establishing the Common Agricultural Policy
- the research policy, initially based on the Euratom Treaty, but since then extended to many other fields on the basis of the EEC Treaty
- the reform of the European Social Fund in 1971
- the establishment of the European Regional Development Fund in 1975
- the development of the Common Transport Policy
- the reform of the Structural Funds in 1988

- the establishment of the Cohesion Fund in 1993
- in budgetary terms, agricultural expenditure has been remaining redominant, but loosing importance in recent years and thus creating space for increasing appropriations in particular for the structural funds, but also for research, external policies etc.

On the revenue side (graph 3), the Community's General Budget[1] was financed until 1970 by a system of Member States' contributions under Article 200 of the EEC Treaty. From 1971 a system of own resources applied for the General Budget which comprises:

- customs duties
- agricultural levies
- VAT revenue, initially limited to 1 per cent of a commonly defined VAT base and raised to 1.4 per cent in 1985.

In 1988 a so-called fourth resource was introduced, which was determined as a percentage of the total Community GNP.

Whereas the traditional own resources (customs duties and agricultural levies) played an important role in the early days and accounted for some 50 per cent of the budget revenue by the end of the 1970s, this role diminished afterwards following the steady increase in self-sufficiency for agricultural produce and reductions in customs tariffs in the context of the successive GATT negotiations. The third resource, VAT, became more and more important and still accounts for more than 50 per cent of total revenue in 1994 despite the introduction of the fourth GDP-resource in 1988 destined mainly to alleviate the regressive impact of the VAT resource discriminating the poorer Member States.

The figures presented so far hide a very complex decision process which governs the budget procedure at Community level. The role of the Commission of the European Communities is formally limited to its making budgetary proposals ('preliminary draft budget' - PDB) to launch the budget procedure in which the Budget Authority (Council and Parliament) decide - both arms of the budget authority after two interconnected readings - on the final appropriations

Graph 1: Community expenditure as a percentage of Member States' budgets and of Community GDP.

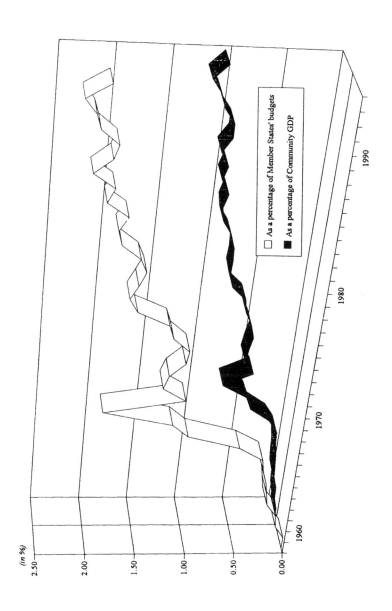

Graph 2: Community expenditure from 1958 to 1994 at current prices and 1994 prices.

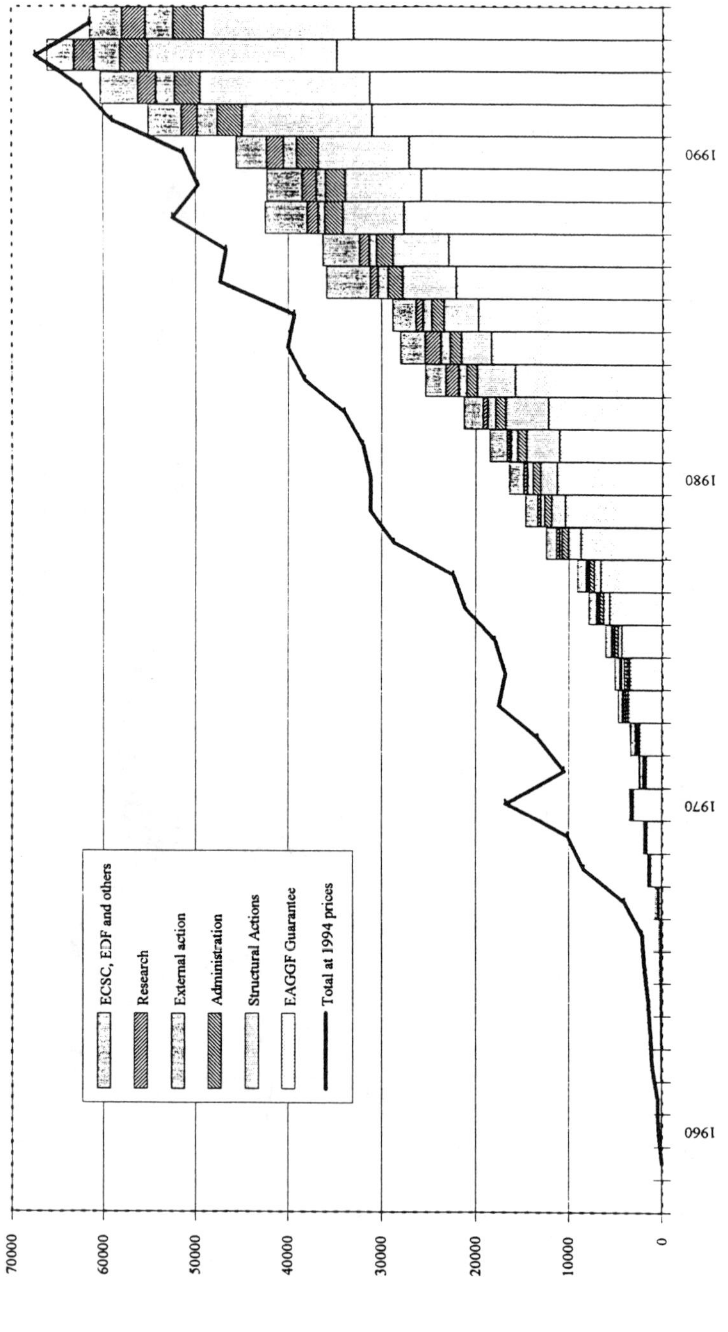
ECSC, EDF and others
Research
External action
Administration
Structural Actions
EAGGF Guarantee
Total at 1994 prices
70000
60000
50000
40000
30000
20000
10000
0
1960
1970
1980
1990

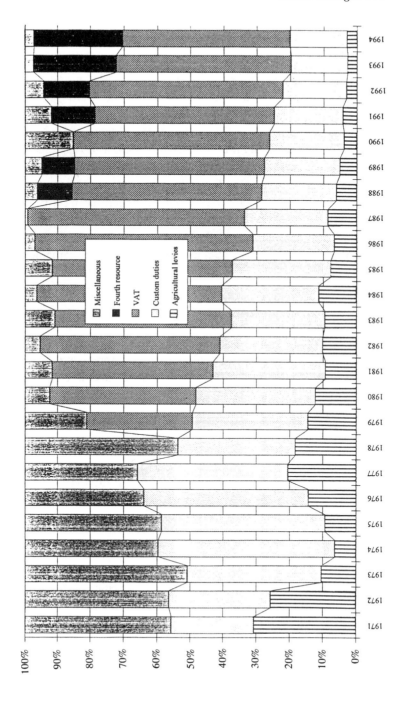

Graph 3: Community revenue from 1971 to 1994.

to be entered into the budget which will consequently be implemented by the Commission.

As indicated, the budget authority is split between Parliament and the Council of Ministers. The latter is deciding definitively on so-called compulsory expenditure $(CE)^2$, whereas Parliament has the 'last word' on non-compulsory expenditure (NCE), but the appropriations voted can only exceed compared to the preceding financial year the maximum rate of increase for NCE^3, if Council agrees. Parliament's margin of manoeuvre (without the agreement of Council) is, however, guaranteed to a certain extent in the sense that it can increase the NCE proposed by Council in the draft budget (Council's first reading) by up to half a maximum rate - in the limit of an overall increase of NCE of 150 per cent of the maximum rate. [4] To sum up, it can be argued, that power is not evenly balanced between Council and Parliament in the budget procedure, since Council can decide on more than half of the budget and Parliament's say as far as NCE are concerned is limited by the provisions of the maximum rate of increase. Parliament has, however, the right to reject the draft budget as a whole, if there are important reasons for doing so. Parliament's budgetary decisions are furthermore constrained; on the one hand, by the fact that Council has the final legislative authority and that Community expenditure has, in principle, to be based on a specific legal base authorizing the expenditure in question; and on the other hand, since it has no specific competence (nor is it accountable for decisions) on the revenue side, but can only exercise its powers in accordance with the ceiling for own resources fixed by the Member States and ratified by all national parliaments.

The separation of legislative power (eventually belonging to Council) and budgetary powers, being split between Council and Parliament, was one reason for the dispute between Community institutions which marked the permanent budget crisis since the late 1970s which became worse and worse by the mid-1980s. Eroding own resources and failing attempts to contain agricultural spending added to the problems.

The Community budget is implemented by the Commission. Its financial management is subject to internal control under the authority of a financial controller. The Commission has also set up a specific unit for combating fraud. The Commission's financial management is furthermore subject to external supervision of the Court of Auditors and to a discharge procedure conducted by Parliament on the recommendation from the Council.

The Single European Act and the Delors-I-Package [5]

A wide ranging financial reform was essential in order to deal with the crisis which seemed increasingly to threaten the very foundations of the Community. The main aims of the reforms, known as the Delors-I-package were as follows:

-    to provide the Community with stable and sufficient resources to achieve the objectives set out in the Single European Act (i.e. completion of the internal market, economic and social cohesion, development of Community research with the research framework programmes)
-    to ensure, as a kind of quid pro quo, that stricter budgetary discipline was applied and to limit the growth in expenditure, particularly on agriculture
-    to ensure compliance with the procedure for adopting the budget, given that none of the budgets since 1985 had been adopted on time before the beginning of the financial year.

The reforms, geared towards achieving these objectives, were set out, both in Community legislation[6] and in an Inter-institutional Agreement between Council, Parliament and Commission[7] which defines commonly agreed rules of conduct in the budget procedure. The financial perspective forms an integral part of the Interinstitutional Agreement and sets compulsory ceilings, given in ECUs at constant 1988 prices, for six categories of expenditure (headings) for each financial year of the period 1988-92. The ceilings for the individual headings are expressed in terms of commitment appropriations[8], while there are ceilings for both commitment appropriations and payment appropriations[9] for the overall totals (table 1). Both arms of the Budget Authority committed themselves to accept the rate of increase of NCE resulting from applying the ceilings for the financial years 1988-92. Thereby they avoided, by advanced agreement, the yearly dispute over exceeding the maximum rate of increase which had for so long undermined the efficiency of the budgetary procedure. Equally the distinction between compulsory and non-compulsory expenditure lost most of its importance.

Provision was initially made for a 3.9 per cent average annual increase in commitment appropriations rising from ECU 45,303 million in 1988 to ECU 52,800 million (at 1988 prices)[10] in 1992, and a 3.4 per cent average annual increase in payment appropriations from ECU 43,779 million to ECU 50,100 million (assuming that the ceilings were reached for each individual heading).

Table 1. Inititial Financial Perspective 1988-92

		1988	1989	1990	1991	1992
						(in million d'écus)
Appropriations for commitments						
1. EAGGF Guarantee		27,500	27,700	28,400	29,000	29,600
2. Structural operations		7,790	9,200	10,600	12,100	13,450
3. Policies with multiannual allocations		1,210	1,650	1,900	2,150	2,400
4. Other policies		2,103	2,385	2,500	2,700	2,800
of which: non-compulsory expenditure		1646	1,801	1,860	1,910	1,970
5. Repayments and administration		5,700	4,950	4, 500	4,000	3,550
of which: stock disposal		1240	1,400	1,400	1,400	1,400
6. Monetary reserve		1,000	1,000	1,000	1,000	1,000
	Total	**45,303**	**46,885**	**48,900**	**50,950**	**52,800**
of which:						
- compulsory expenditure		33,698	32,607	32,810	32,980	33,400
- non-compulsory expenditure		11,605	14,278	16,090	17,970	19,400
Appropriations for payments						
Appropriations or payments required		**43,779**	**45,300**	**46,900**	**48,600**	**50,100**
of which:						
- compulsory expenditure		33,640	32,604	32,740	32,910	33,110
- non-compulsory expenditure		10,139	12,696	14,160	15,690	16,990
Appropriations or payments required		1.12	1.14	1.15	1.16	1.17
as % of GNP						
Own resources ceiling as % of GNP		1.15	1.17	1.18	1.19	1.20

Source: M.Nucci 'XIX/277/91' 13 December 1991

Since these increases exceeded anticipated GNP growth, provision had to be made for an increase in the own resources ceiling from 1.15 per cent of GNP in 1988 to 1.20 per cent in 1992. Agricultural expenditure in heading 1 is restricted not only by the ceiling in the financial perspective but also by the agricultural guideline, under which agricultural spending may not increase by more than 74 per cent of the GNP growth rate. The purpose of the guideline is to contain the increase in agricultural expenditure. The impact of sharp fluctuations of the ECU-dollar exchange rate on agricultural spending is to be covered by the monetary reserve (heading 6).

The increases for heading 2 and 3 were far higher than the average. The 17.6 per cent annual growth rate in heading 2 (structural operations) is the result of the European Council Decision in 1987 to double the size of the Structural Funds by 1993. These extra resources were intended to strengthen economic and social cohesion in the Community and to promote economic development in its poorer regions. Provision was also made for significant increases in resources allocated to research, a major category under heading 3.

The financial perspective 1988-92 reflected the political compromise behind the decisions taken at the Brussels European Council in 1988. The completion of the internal market was to be accompanied by a substantial transfer of resources - in the form of programme-based Structural Funds - and other Community flanking policies, such as enhanced research. The increase in expenditure in the Community budget was to be kept within certain limits by containing agricultural spending, with total expenditure not exceeding the relatively modest level of 1.20 per cent of GNP.

The Interinstitutional Agreement did provide for changes to be made to the financial perspective. There were six revisions in total, primarily in order to take into account the impact of German unification in 1990 on the Community budget, in order to finance new tasks arising from changes on the international scene (e.g. aid for the new democracies in Central and Eastern Europe - PHARE programme - and technical assistance to the republics of the former Soviet Union - TACIS programme) and to enable the Community to respond appropriately to international crises (e.g. assistance during the Gulf crises, special food aid for Africa)[11]. The revised financial perspective applicable in the financial years 1988-92 are presented in table 2, which shows that all the revisions referred to could be financed within the given own resources ceiling which was never reached.

On the revenue side, the 1988 reform made some important steps towards a system of own resources that is less regressive than the existing one which was mainly based on VAT-contributions. The rate for the VAT-resources was, however, maintained at 1.4 per cent, but the VAT base was capped at 55 per cent of GNP. Thereby the discrepancies in the VAT base/GNP ratios of Member States were neutralized to a certain extent, and hence the distortions in their contributions to the Community budget. A fourth resource fully based on GNP was introduced in order to provide the revenue required to cover expenditure in excess of the yields of the two traditional own resources and the third VAT resource. Since the overall economic performance was more abundant than initially expected, the fourth resource could not have the full expected impact in making the system of own resources more linked to Member States' ability to pay.

The overall experience with the Interinstitutional Agreement was largely positive, even so one has to admit that the overall economic environment and in particular the evolution of agricultural markets played a rather favourable role.[12]

Every budget since 1988 has been adopted on time, before the start of the financial year. 'Budgetary peace' has been restored between the institutions. Budgetary discipline has worked and succeeded in containing the increase of agricultural spending.

It was possible to finance, under the fixed own resources ceiling, not only the ambitious objectives of social and economic cohesion as well as the flanking policies of the internal market programme, but also to absorb the financial impact of German unification and to finance new assistance programmes for third countries in particular in Central and Eastern Europe.

The Maastricht Treaty and the Delors-II-Package [13]

The new reality of the budget procedure, governed by the Interinstitutional Agreement 1988-92, which resulted in a de facto suspension of the annual application of key provisions of the Treaty, could have led to an indepth reshaping of the Treaty provisions concerning the Community Budget in the new Treaty on European Union. In fact the Maastricht treaty has amended the Treaty only marginally in this respect. It is, however, true that the application of the subsidiarity principle which figures so prominently in the Maastricht treaty will also have an impact on budgetary management and the evolution of public expenditure at Community level.

Even if the Maastricht treaty does not fundamentally change the budgetary provisions laid down in the Treaty, it nevertheless has - through its policy orientations - some impact on the Community budget. These priority tasks comprise:

-        economic and social cohesion - by reinforcing the structural funds and setting up a cohesion fund

Table 2. Final Financial Perspective 1988-92

(ECU million; current prices)

	1988	1989	1990	1991	1992	Annual Real Increase
Appropriations for commitments						
1. EAGGF Guarantee	27,500	28,613	30,700	33,000	35,039	1.15%
2. Structural operations	7,790	9,522	11,555	14,804	18,109	17.56%
3. Policies with multiannual allocations	1,210	1,708	2,071	2,466	2,905	18.51%
4. Other policies	2,103	2,468	3,229	5,648	5,936	23.41%
of which: non-compulsory expenditure	1,646	1,864	2,523	4,738	5,029	25.88%
5. Repayments and administration	5,700	5,153	4,930	4,559	3,893	-13.45%
of which: stock disposal	1,240	1,449	1,523	1,375	810	-14.41%
6. Monetary reserve	1,000	1,000	1,000	1,000	1,000	- 4.79%
Total	**45,303**	**48,464**	**53,485**	**61,477**	**66,882**	**4.95%**
of which:						
- compulsory expenditure	33,698	33,764	35,454	37,199	38,503	-1.56%
- non-compulsory expenditure	11,605	14,700	18,031	24,278	28,379	19.06%
Appropriations for payments						
Appropriations or payments required	**43,779**	**46,885**	**51,291**	**58,458**	**64,081**	**4.72%**
of which:						
- compulsory expenditure	33,640	33,745	35,372	37,195	38,435	-1.57%
- non-compulsory expenditure	10,139	13,140	15,919	21,263	25,646	20.07%
Appropriations or payments required as % of GNP	1.08	1.06	1.08	1.13	1.19	
Own resources ceiling as % of GNP	1.15	1.17	1.18	1.19	1.20	

Source: M.Nucci XIX/277/91   REV.8 24.2.1992

- creation of a favourable environment for competitiveness - by developing research and technological development programmes as well as transeuropean networks in transport, telecommunications and energy
- external actions - by responding to the increased responsibilities of the Community for keeping peace, promoting democracy and providing humanitarian aid.

These enlarged tasks had to be taken into account in the Commission's proposal for the Delors-II-package destined to succeed the Delors-I-package from 1993 - the first Interinstitutional agreement and the financial perspective expiring by the end of 1992. The Commission tabled its proposals in February 1992 under the leitmotiv, 'From the Single Act to Maastricht and beyond: The means to match our ambitions'. The subsequent difficult process of negotiations among Member States culminated in the conclusions of the European Council in Edinburgh, 11-12 December, 1992.[14] It took, however, until October 1993 to conclude a new Interinstitutional Agreement in which not only Council and Commission but also the European Parliament accepted the ceilings of the Financial Perspective agreed in Edinburgh and committed itself to respect them when exercising its powers.

The new financial perspective covers the seven year period of 1993 to 1999. It has been largely built upon the rationale and the structure of the financial perspective 1988-92 of the Delors-I-Package (table 3).

Overall Community expenditure could rise from ECU 69.2 bn in 1993 to ECU 84.1 bn in 1999 by 3.3 per cent p.a. in commitments, and from ECU 65.9 bn to ECU 80.1 bn, i.e. by 3.3 per cent p.a. in payments - the annual increase being 0.6 per cent points and 1.6 per cent points respectively lower than in the initial and final financial perspective for 1988-92.

The own resources ceiling will only moderately rise from 1.21 per cent in 1995 to 1.27 per cent of GDP in 1999, leaving a small margin of 0.01 per cent for unforeseen expenditure in 1994 and in subsequent years. The Commission had initially proposed 1.37 per cent for 1997 and then modified its proposals later to 1.32 per cent in 1999 assuming a margin of 0.03 per cent for unforeseen expenditure. Therefore the Edinburgh compromise is very close to the Commission's revised proposals.

Furthermore the Commission's proposals have been largely accepted as far as the structure of the new Financial Perspective is concerned. Expenditure is broken down, as in the Delors-I-Package, by six main headings, but which are slightly reorganized in order to ensure greater budgetary and political transparency.

Heading 1 still refers to the European Agricultural Guidance and Guarantee Fund, Guarantee Section, but has been reshaped by including, in addition to all expenditure under the reformed common agricultural policy, expenditure under the European Fisheries Guarantee Fund (heading 4 in 1988-92) and expenditure on income aid (heading 2 in 1988-92). The total of heading

1 continues to be covered by the agricultural guideline of which neither the growth rate nor the base level have been changed. Heading 1 expenditure is complemented by the monetary reserve, which remains in heading 6; both headings account for some 52 per cent of the total in 1993 which will go down to 46 per cent in 1999 following the trend of containing agricultural expenditure noted already under the former Financial Perspective 1988-92. The monetary reserve will undergo modifications both in its amount and its destination. Since exchange rate fluctuations will have a more limited impact on agricultural spending under the reformed Common Agricultural Policy which relies less on price support, the amount has been reduced to ECU 500 million from 1995, with a reduction of the franchise from ECU 400 million to ECU 200 million.

The monetary reserve will in the future not only cover the impact of exchange rate movement between the ECU and the US-dollar, but also the impact of exchange rate movement among EC currencies. If agricultural expenditure exceeds the agricultural guideline and the coverage provided by the monetary reserve, due to the consequences of internal monetary realignments and the application of the 'switch-over' mechanism, 'appropriate steps to fund the EAGGF Guarantee will be taken by Council'.

Heading 2, Structural Operations, comprises all expenditure for strengthening of the economic and social cohesion of the Community and is devoted exclusively to the financing of the Structural Funds and the newly established Cohesion Fund. Appropriations for this heading will increase by nearly 6 per cent per year (in constant prices), thereby increasing their share in the total budget from 31 per cent to 36 per cent from 1993 to 1999.

Appropriations for objective 1[15] regions will increase by 75 per cent from ECU 12,328 million in 1993 to ECU 19,280 million in 1999; the new German Länder and Est-Berlin will be included in the list of objective 1 regions.

The newly established Cohesion fund will assist the four countries (Greece, Ireland, Portugal and Spain) with a GNP per capita below 90 per cent of the Community average provided they have a programme leading to the fulfilment of the economic convergence conditions set out in the Maastricht treaty. The fund will provide support for environmental projects and transport infrastructure project at a Community co-financing rate of between 80 and 85 per cent. The appropriations earmarked for the Cohesion fund will increase from ECU 1,500 million in 1993 to ECU 2,600 million in 1999. For the four Cohesion Fund countries the funding from the Structural Funds and the Cohesion Fund will permit a doubling of commitments under Objective 1 and the Cohesion Fund between 1992 and 1999.

Table 3. Financial Perspective 1993-1999 (EUR 12)

(ECU million - 1992 prices)

	1993	1994	1995	1996	1997	1998	1999	Annual Increase 1999/93
Appropriations for commitments								
1. Common agricultural policy	35,230	35,095	35,722	36,364	37,023	37,697	38,389	1.5%
2. Structural operations	21,277	21,885	23,480	24,990	26,526	28,240	30,000	6.8%
2.1. Structural Funds	19,777	20,135	21,480	22,740	24,026	25,690	27,400	6.4%
2.2. Cohesion Fund	1,500	1,750	2,000	2,250	2,500	2,550	2,600	12.2%
3. Internal policies	3,940	4,084	4,323	4,520	4,710	4,910	5,100	4.9%
4. External action	3,950	4,000	4,280	4,560	4,830	5,180	5,600	7.0%
5. Administrative expenditure	3,280	3,380	3,580	3,690	3,800	3,850	3,900	3.2%
6. Reserves	1,500	1,500	1,100	1,100	1,100	1,100	1,100	-4.4%
Monetary reserve	1,000	1,000	500	500	500	500	500	-8.3%
Loan guarantees	300	300	300	300	300	300	300	0.0%
Emergency aid	200	200	300	300	300	300	300	8.3%
Commitment appropriations - Total	**69,177**	**69,944**	**72,485**	**75,224**	**77,989**	**80,977**	**84,089**	**3.6%**
Payment appropriations - Total	**65,908**	**67,036**	**69,150**	**71,290**	**74,491**	**77,249**	**80,114**	**3.6%**
Total payment appropriations (% GNP)	1.20	1.19	1.20	1.21	1.23	1.25	1.26	
Margin (% GNP)	0.00	0.01	0.01	0.01	0.01	0.01	0.01	
Own resources ceiling (% GNP)	1.20	1.20	1.21	1.22	1.24	1.26	1.27	

Source: M.Nucci XIX/277/91 13 December 1991

Heading 3 comprises all internal policies other than the Common Agricultural Policy and structural actions strengthening the cohesion in the Community. Many of them are considered essential in promoting the competitiveness of the European economies, such as research and technological development programmes and the development of trans-European networks. According to the Edinburgh conclusions the proportion of appropriations for research and technological development must remain between one half and two thirds of the overall appropriations for this heading. A specific priority has been given to trans-European networks by the Treaty on European Union. Appropriations reflecting this priority would fund the development of networks in the following areas: transport, energy and telecommunications and promote access to, and interconnection between, national networks and pay attention to the need to link peripheral regions with the centre. Even if appropriations will increase considerably (1994: ECU 290 million), the Community contributions can only have a knock-on effect by financing feasibility studies and interest subsidies, given the sheer size of this kind of investment absolutely essential for the efficient functioning of the internal market.

The other policies under this heading account for not even 2 per cent of the entire budget, i.e. ECU 1.4 billion in 1994, and comprise for instance education, training and youth policy, social policy actions, energy and environment policy, consumer protection and the internal market. Community action in these fields has to respect fully the subsidiarity principle and is thus mostly limited to demonstration projects or pilot programmes with knock on effects to be taken up later at lower levels as well as cross-border projects and programmes where important externalities impede efficient implementation at a national level.

Community expenditure for external action has quadrupled between 1988 and 1994, corresponding to the new role of the Community on a rapidly changing international scene. These increasing efforts will continue in the future and the priority for external actions set out in the Maastricht treaty is fully reflected in the high increase in heading 4 of the Financial Perspective which also includes the external aspects of the common fisheries policy, i.e. the international fisheries agreements, and of environment policy and operational expenditure to be entered in the budget in respect of the Common Foreign and Security Policy, but excludes the European Development Fund which itself provides aid of some ECU 2 bn per year to developing countries in the Third World.

The Community has been stepping up aid to the countries of central and eastern Europe and the independent States of the former Soviet Union and it will in parallel strengthen its Mediterranean policy. The Community will also continue to help its partners in Africa, Latin America and Asia. Finally the Community will continue to provide help in cases of emergency and distress occurring anywhere in the world as a result of war, natural disasters or epidemics. For the latter actions, a reserve for emergency aid has been established in heading 6 of the Financial Perspective. In total, external expenditure will rise from ECU 4.5 bn in 1993 to 6.2 bn in 1999.

Administrative expenditure of all Community institutions is the only component of heading 5 in the new Financial Perspective, whereas it shared the old heading 5 together with repayments and reimbursements to Member States. The evolution of the ceiling is broadly in line with the overall totals allowing to finance not only supplementary administrative resources necessary to manage increasing Community activity, but also retirement pensions the cost of which is rapidly increasing due to the demographic structure of the Community officials.

Finally, heading 6 (reserves) now contains three reserves, for which resources will be called only if the need arises during the financial year. The first two have already been mentioned: the monetary reserve for the EAGGF-Guarantee and the emergency aid reserve. A third reserve provided for financing a loan guarantee fund in order to cover the increasing risks related to the Community's borrowing and lending activities in favour of third countries.

On the revenue side, the Edinburgh conclusions continue to follow the orientations of the Delors-I-package, but do not basically reorganize the existing system of own resources.[16] The rate for the VAT-resource will be reduced from 1.4 per cent to 1 per cent while at the same time VAT bases will be capped at 50 per cent of Member States' GNP, compared to 55 per cent at present. Both provisions will be introduced gradually from 1995 and will both bring VAT contributions more in line with the contributive capacity of individual Member States and increase the overall weight of the fourth GNP-resource, which furthermore automatically increases with rising expenditure, thereby rendering the system of own resources less regressive.

The system for the correction of the UK's budget imbalances, introduced in 1984, was entirely confirmed. Thereby the UK is, basically, reimbursed two thirds of the difference of its share in Community expenditure and its share in VAT- and GND-contributions to the Community budget.

Budgetary Impact of the Adhesion of Austria, Finland and Sweden to the European Union

On the revenue side the maximum financial capacity of the Community will grow through enlargement in the same proportions as the GDP of the Union, ie some 7 per cent or some ECU 5 bn in 1995 increasing to nearly ECU 6 bn by the end of the century.

On the expenditure side there are of course new requirements resulting from enlargement that have to be covered by the Community budget. For an important part of the supplementary expenses the amounts have been laid down in the Act of Accession. For the rest, requirements had to be evaluated. On the basis of a Commission proposal the Financial Perspective was adjusted in December 1994 in accordance with Article 24 of the Interinstitutional Agreement (table 4). The main adjustments are the following: as far as category 1 of the Financial Perspective is concerned, the agricultural guideline has been raised by 74 per cent of the increase in Community GNP resulting from enlargement, ie by 5.2 per cent. In other words, enlargement is treated in the same way as an annual adjustment of the guideline.

The increases of the ceilings for category 2 correspond to the amounts laid down in the Act of Accesion plus ECU 200 million for the financing of a new initiative for the peace process in Northern Ireland. The annual increases amount to some ECU 1 bn and cover the interventions of the structural funds in the new member states for both existing objectives 1 to 5b and the new objective 6, which is specifically intended for regions with a very low population density (eight persons per square km or less). Under this heading the Community will also take over the commitments entered into by the acceding countries under the EEA financial mechanism.

The ceilings for internal policies increase by some 7 per cent and those for external policies by 6.3 per cent - these increases correspond to the GDP and respectively population share of the new member states. In the light of important additional needs in terms of linguistic services (the number of official languages increasing from 9 to 11 and the number of language combinations going up from 72 to 110) the increase for administrative expenditure is relatively small and represents only 4.33 per cent.

A new category 7 has been set up comprising the temporary and gradually delcining budgetary compensations for the new member states that are provided for in the Act of Accession and should help the new member states to take internal measures cushioning the implementation of the common agricultural policy in their countries.

Globally speaking, total expenditure will rise by 5.2 per cent over the period 1995 - 1999 as a result from the recent enlargement. As the own resources ceiling increases by 7 per cent, the difference presents a valuable and very welcome safety margin which will allow the very tightly calculated margin for unforeseen expenditure contained in the initial financial perspective adopted in Edinburgh, to be restored and even substantially increased by the end of the period. The enlarged Community will thus be better equipped to face any unexpected macroeconomic evolutions and to cope with unforeseen events in the future.

Table 5 presents the 1995 budget voted in December 1994 in detail and according to the structure of the new Financial Perspective.

Outlook

Since 1988 the Community budget has been consolidated both in terms of a smoother decision process and in terms of improved overall efficiency and equity. The Community budget reflects largely its policy priorities, while at the same time respecting budgetary discipline and offering increasingly better value-for-money. The financing of the budget takes more account of the ability to pay of individual Member States. But major challenges remain to be met.

The revenue system has not undergone fundamental changes in the Delors-II-Package, while already the own resources decision of 1988 contained an allusion to the possibility of obtaining a new type of own resource and while Parliament has constantly been pressing for a real Community tax. Even if the existence of own resources is one of the main legal characteristics of the present system, in economic terms the VAT- and the GNP-resource very much resemble national contributions to the Community budget, which are constantly criticized in some Member States in the national budgetary debate. Therefore the reform of the present system of own resources will be on the political agenda of the years to come. Complex financial and institutional issues are at stake.

Today major changes in the conduct of the budgetary procedure have been introduced by interinstitutional agreements, which are in conformity with the Treaty but not explicitly reflected in it, e.g. multi-annual ceilings for certain categories of expenditure of binding nature for both arms of the budget authority. Important improvements have been achieved, but further reform could streamline the budget procedure and make it more efficient; for instance the first reading in Council has a very limited impact on the non-compulsory expenditure eventually entered into the budget. In order to reduce the often quoted democratic deficit in the Community, the role of Parliament could be strengthened by giving it more competence for the budget as a whole and at the same time responsibility and accountability (e.g. for the revenue side). The Interinstitutional Conference in 1996 could be an occasion to develop further the budgetary provisions of the Treaty in order to reflect better today's budgetary reality and to take into account the future role of the different Community institutions.

Table 4. Financial Perspective for the enlarged Union 1995-1999

(ECU million - 1992 prices)

	1995	1996	1997	1998	1999
Appropriations for commitments					
1. Common agricultural policy	35,354	37,245	37,922	38,616	39,327
2. Structural operations	24,477	26,026	27,588	29,268	30,945
Structural Funds	22,369	23,668	24,980	26,610	28,345
Cohesion Fund	2,000	2,250	2,500	2,550	2,600
Financial Mechanism EFTA	108	108	108	108	0
3. Internal policies	4,702	4,914	5,117	5,331	5,534
4. External action	4,549	4,847	5,134	5,507	5,953
5. Administrative expenditure	3,738	3,859	3,974	4,033	4,093
6. Reserves	1,100	1,100	1,100	1,100	1,100
Monetary reserve	500	500	500	500	500
Loan guarantees	300	300	300	300	300
Emergency aid	300	300	300	300	300
7. Compensations	1,547	701	212	99	0
Commitment appropriations	**75,467**	**78,692**	**81,047**	**83,954**	**86,952**
- Total					
Payment appropriations - Total	**72,020**	**74,605**	**77,372**	**80,037**	**82,778**
Total payment appropriations	1.21	1.21	1.22	1.22	1.24
(% GNP)					
Margin (% GNP)	0.00	0.01	0.02	0.03	0.03
Own resources ceiling (% GNP)	1.21	1.22	1.24	1.26	1.27

Source:M.Nucci XIX/277/91 13 December 1991

Table 5. Budget 1995 (Commitment Appropriations)

Item FP 95	Heading	Budget 94 (1)	FP 95 (2)	Budget 95 (3)	Var. % (3)/(1) (4)	Var. (3)-(1) (5)
1	Common Agricultural Policy					
	Market Expenses (B1-1 To B1-3)	34. 520.000.000		35.559.000.000	3.01%	1.039.000.000
	Accompanying Measures (B1-4 and B1-5)	267.000,000		1.416.500,000	430.52%	1.149.500.000
	Reserve Enlargement (B1-7)			950.000,000	9.02%	950.000.000
	Total Heading 1	34.787.000,000	37.944	37.925.500,000		3.138.500.000
	Margin			18.500,000		
2	Structural Operations					
	EAGGF-Guidance (B2-10)	3.343.000,000		3.316.000,000	-0.81%	-27.000,000
	Financial Instrument Fisheries (B2-11)	419.000,000		439.000,000	4.77%	20.000,000
	ERDF (B2-12)	9.030.000,000		10.593.000,000	17.31%	1.563.000,000
	ESF (B2-13)	6.457.000,000		6.444.000,000	-0,20%	-13.000,000
	Community Initiative Programmes (B2-14)	1.706.000,000		2.144.000,000	25.67%	483.000,000
	Transitional Measures and Innovation Schemes (B2-18)	368.000,000		242.000,000	-34,24%	-126.000,000
	Other Structural Operations (B2-2)					
	Cohesion Fund (B2-3)	1.853.000,000		2.152.000,000	16.14%	299.000,000
	EEA Financial Mechanism (B2-401)			108.000,000		108.000,000
	Reserve Enlargement (B2-400)			891.000,000		891.000,000
	Sub-Total Structural Funds	21.323.000,000	24.069	24.069.000,000	12.88%	2.746.000,000
	Sub-Total Cohesion Fund	1.853.000,000		2.152.000,000	16.14%	299.000,000
	Subtotal EEA Financial Mechanism		108	108.000,000		108.000,000
	Total Heading 2	23.176.000,000	26.329	26.329.000,000	13,60%	3.153.000,000
	Margin			0,000		
3	Internal Policies					
	Research (B6)	2.472.423,000		3.118.696,000	26.14%	646.273,000
	Other Agricultural Operations (B2-5)	205.825,000		207.700,000	0.91%	1.875,000
	Other Regional Policy Operations (B2-6)	31.000,000		51.300,000	65,48%	20.300,000
	Transport (B2-7)	16.000,000		24.000,000	50,00%	8.000,000
	Common Policy on Fisheries and Sea (B2-9)	25.640,000		26.100,000	1,79%	460,000
	Education, Vocational Training and Youth Policy (B3-1)	287.500,000		361.450,000	25,72%	73.950,000
	Audio-Visual Section and Culture (B3-2)	151.900,000		137.700,000	-9,35%	-14.200,000
	Information and Communication (B3-3)	47.500,000		57.000,000	20,00%	9.500,000

Table 5. continued

	Heading	Budget 94 (1)	FP 95 (2)	Budget 95 (3)	Var. (3)/1 4	Var. (3)-(1) (5)
	Other Social Operations (B3-4)	156.630,000		174.645,000	11,50%	18.015,000
	Energy (B4-1)	83.000,000		62.000,000	-25,30%	-21.000,000
	Euratom Nuclear Safeguards (B4-2)	19.480,000		18.800,000	-3.49%	-680,000
	Environment (B4-3)	133.450,000		137.000,000	-9.35%	-14.200,000
	Consumer Protection (B5-1)	16.000,000		20.750,000	26.69%	4.750,000
	Aid for Reconstruction (B5-2)	9.250,000		6.300,000	-31.89%	-2.950,000
	Internal Market (B5-3)	173.800,000		152.530,000	-12.24%	-21.270,000
	Industry (B5-4)	40.450,000		117.700,000	190.98%	77.250,000
	Information Market (B5-5)	12.000,000		13.000,000	8.33%	1.000,000
	Statistical Information (B5-6)	30.000,000		33.000,000	10.00%	3.000,000
	Trans-European Networks (B5-7)	259.800,000		411.000,000	58..20%	151.200,000
	Cooperation in Justice (B5-8)	2.000,000		5.000,000	!50.00%	3.000,000
	Steel Research (B5-9)					
	Reserve Enlargement Research	150.000,000		-150.000,000	-200.00%	-300.000,000
	Reserve Enlargement Networks	30.000,000		-30.000,000	-200.00%	-60.000,000
	Reserve Enlargement Internal Policies			100.000,000		100.000,000
	Sub-Total Research	2.622.423,000		2.986.698,000	13.20%	346.273,000
	Sub-Total Trans-European Networks	289.800,000		381.000,000	31.47%	91.200,000
	Sub-Total Others	1.441.425,000		1.705.975,000	18.35%	264.550,000
	Total Heading 3	4.353.648,000	5.060	5.055.671,000	16.12%	702.023,000
	Margin			4.329,000		
4	External Action					
	EDF(B7-1)	-		-		
	Food and Humanitarian Aid (B7-2)	855.100,000		847.900,000	-0.84%	-7.200,000
	Cooperation with ALA Countries (B7-3)	648.700,000		670.500,000	3.36%	21.800,000
	Cooperation with Mediterranean Countries (B7-4)	399.850,000		487.400,000	21.90%	87.550,000
	Other Cooperation Measures (B7-50)	587.000,000		646.783,000	10.18%	59.783,000
	Cooperation with CEEC and CIS States B7-6	1.463.000,000		1.582.600,000	8.17%	119.600,000
	Cooperation with Other Third Countries B7-7	50.000,000		52.000,000	4.00%	2.000,000
	External Part of Some Community Policies (B7-8)	284.190,000		294.200,000	3.52%	10.010,000
	C.S.F.P (B8-1)	20.000,000		110.000,000	450.000%	90.000,000
	Reserve Enlargement External Policies B7-95)			190.000,000		190.000,000
	Total Heading 4	4.307.840,000	4.895	4.881.383,000	13.31%	573.543,000
	Margin			13.617,000		

Table 5. continued

	Heading	Budget 94 (1)	FP 95 (2)	Budget 95 (3)	Var. (3)/1 4	Var. (3)-(1) (5)
5	Administrative Expenditure Institutions					
	Commission (Part A without Pensions)	2.093.962.000		2.153.175, 356	2.83%	59.213,356
	Pensions	334.761,000		351.147,000	4.89%	16.386,000
	Reserve Enlargement (A0-X5)			87.000.000		87.000.000
	Total Other Institutions	1.205.877.000		1.416.999,817	17,51%	211.122,817
	Total Heading 5	3.634.600.000	4.022	4.008.322,173	10,28%	373.722,173
	Margin			13.677,827		
6	Reserves					
	Monetary Reserve (B1-6)	1.000.000.000		500.000.000	-50.00%	-500.000.000
	Guarantee (B0-23)	318.000.000		323.000.000	1.57%	5.000,000
	Emergency Aid (B7-91)	212.000.000		323.000.000	52.36%	111.000.000
	Total Heading 6	1.530.000.000	1.146	1.146.000.000	-25.10%	-384.000.000
	Margin			0,000		
7	Compensations					
	Compensations (B1-7)			1.547.000.000		1.547.000.000
	Total Heading 7		1.547	1.547.000.000		1.547.000.000
	Margin			0,000		
	Commitment Appropriations Grand Total CE	37.222.094.000		41.420.470.000	11.28%	4.198.376.000
	NCE	34.566.994.000		39.472.406,173	14.19%	4.905.412,173
	Total Appropriations for Commitments	71.789.088.000	80.943	80.892.876,173	12.68%	9.103.788,173
	Margin			50.123,827		
	Payment Appropriations Grand Total CE	37.203.484.567		41.402.270.000	11.29%	4.198.785,433
	NCE	31.151.116,876		35.124.810,173	12.76%	3.973.693,297
	Total Appropriations for Payments	68.354.601,443	77.229	76.527.080,173	11.96%	8.172.478,730
	Margin			701.919,827		

Notes

[1]   The following text refers to the General Budget of the European Communities only and does not take account of the ECSC budget and the EDF.

[2]   Defined in Article 203 of the EEC Treaty as 'expenditure necessarily resulting from this Treaty or from acts adopted in accordance herewith'. At present compulsory expenditure covers more than half of the budget, mainly the EAGGF Guarantee Section, expenditure for the Mediterreanean Protocoles and international fisheries agreements' pensions.

[3]   The maximum rate of increase is calculated as a simple arithmetic average between the nominal GNP growth in the Community and the average variation in Member States' budgets for the year (t-2).

[4]   In principle the overall limit of 150 per cent of the maximum rate has never been practically applied in this context, since Council has set as its rule of conduct to limit the increase of NCE in its draft budget to 50 per cent of the maximum rate.

[5]   See P. Zangl: The Interinstitutional Agreement on Budgetary Discipline and Improvement of the Budgetary Procedure, in: Common Market Law Review, Vol. 26, 1989, pp. 675-678; E. Flores, P. Zangl: La structure financière de la Communauté face aux défis présents et futurs, in EUI Working Papers, EPU No. 9, European University Institute, Florence, 1991, pp. 9-26.

[6]   Council Decision of 24 June 1988 on the system of the Community's own resources (88/376/EEC, EURATOM); Council Decision of 24 June 1988 concerning budgetary discipline (88/377/EEC).

[7]   Interinstitutional Agreement of 29 June 1988 on Budgetary Discipline and Improvement of the Budgetary Procedure.

[8]   Commitment appropriations cover the total cost in the financial year of the legal obligations entered into in respect of operations to be carried out over a period of more than one financial year.

[9]   Payment appropriations cover cash expenditure resulting from the commitments entered into during the financial year and/or previous financial year.

[10]   The expenditure ceilings are converted into current prices by means of a technical adjustment which the Commission makes before the budget procedure begins.

[11]   cf. W. Deffaa, The 1992 Community Budget - a Sound Basis for Community Finances? INTERECONOMICS, March/April 1992.

[12] For a rather critical assessment, see H.-J. Timmann: Haushaltsdisziplin und politische Entscheidungsmechanismen, in: Europarecht, Vol. 2, 1991, pp. 133-9.

[13] Cf. Ph. Jouret, Les Conclusions d'Edimbourg sur le Paquet 'Delors', Revue du Marché Commun et de l'Union Européenne, n° 368, May 1993 and P. Zangl, The Financing of the Community after the Edinburgh European Council, INTERECONOMICS, May/June 1993.

[14] The 1993 budget was voted in December 1992 in conformity with the Edinburgh conclusions, but Parliament did not accept at that stage the table of the financial perspective for the financial years 1994 - 99.

[15] Objective No. 1: promoting the development and structural adjustment of the regions whose development is lagging behind, i.e. GDP per capita below 75 per cent of the Community average.

[16] The Commission was invited, at the request of some Member States, to carry out a study on a new 'fifth resource'.

SECTION B: TOWARD ECONOMIC AND MONETARY UNION:
From the Single Market to a Single Currency?

8 Economic and Monetary Union

NILESH DATTANI

In the immediate aftermath of the Maastricht Summit in December 1991 and the signing of the Treaty on European Union on 7 February 1992 it seemed that the European Community (now to be renamed the European Union) was set to embark on a conveyor belt which would lead to Economic and Monetary Union (EMU) by 1 January 1999 at the very latest. The treaty was expected to be ratified by all twelve member states without a hitch during the course of 1992 in order to bring it into force on 1 January 1993. This was not to be so, and subsequent events proved that the initial euphoria about the desirability as well as the feasibility of EMU as charted in the Maastricht Treaty seemed to be somewhat naive.

The outcome of the Danish referendum on 2 June 1992 which was a narrow majority against the Maastricht Treaty derailed the ratification process. The narrowness of the positive vote in the subsequent French referendum and the events leading up to the ejection of the pound sterling and the Italian lira from the Exchange Rate Mechanism (ERM) of the European Monetary System (EMS) during September 1992 raised doubts about the feasibility of the Maastricht Treaty timetable. Confidence was further impaired by the growing severity of the economic recession which was enveloping almost the entire membership of the European Community and, the crisis of credibility in the foreign exchange markets from early spring 1993 onwards which culminated in the widening of the fluctuation margins to 15 per cent for all ERM currencies.[1]

Eventually the Treaty came into force on 1 November 1993 but it is no exaggeration to say that for a time it was difficult to decide whether the Maastricht plan for EMU was an economic dream that had become a political nightmare or whether it was a political dream that had become an economic nightmare.

This chapter seeks neither to provide a chronological account of the evolution of European monetary integration to date [2] nor to assess the workings and achievements of the European Monetary System (EMS).[3] Instead it aims to provide a background to and the logic for the advocacy of plans for creating EMU; it then comments upon the costs and benefits of a single European currency and examines the Maastricht Treaty programme for EMU; finally it concentrates on analyzing the implications of implementing the Maastricht plan for EMU and concludes by identifying a number of broader economic, financial and political issues that are of relevance to this particular issue area. The underlying thesis of this chapter is that analyses of the topic of EMU which rely (almost) exclusively either on economic and financial logic however sophisticated,[4] or on the political dynamics of the process of European integration[5] fail to capture the essential realities of this topic. The economic, financial and political rationale and ramifications of EMU are impossible to disentangle and only a multi-faceted approach provides real understanding of the issues and enables a proper appraisal of the way ahead. [6]

The Background

The priority of the Treaty of Rome in 1957 was the creation of a common market and monetary integration was only a marginal concern with emphasis placed on macro economic policy cooperation especially with regard to balance of payments and exchange rate policy.

The Bretton Woods international monetary system and limited capital mobility between states gave national governments pre-eminence in the realm of monetary policy and the US dollar was the undisputed international key currency. The notion of a regional European currency and an economic and monetary union in the EC were not mentioned in any major discussion in the first decade of the Community's existence.

The Werner Report of October 1970, and the EC exchange rate arrangement known as the 'snake' which was initiated in March 1972 in the dying months of the Bretton Woods international monetary order, marked a watershed in the EC's orientation towards EMU. Whereas the former charted the route to achievement of EMU in stages by the end of a decade, i.e. 1980, the latter was an attempt by certain West European countries to create a regional zone of exchange rate stability in a new era of initially wider permissible exchange rate fluctuations under the Smithsonian Agreement of December 1971 and then floating exchange rates globally after March 1973.

The Werner plan rapidly became irrelevant as it fell victim to the economic and financial turbulence of the 1970s and the 'snake' had a very chequered history both in terms of the participation of currencies in the mechanism as well as its ability to deliver economic convergence across a range of West European countries.[7] However a major achievement of both these episodes was that they helped set the scene for the creation of the European Monetary System in March 1979 which had the objective of creating 'a zone of exchange rate stability' in the EC with the dual aim of safeguarding and enhancing intra - community trade and, insulating Western Europe from the adverse effects of dollar volatility and the general United States policy of 'unbenign neglect' in the international monetary and financial system. The EMS also had the goal of achieving policy convergence in the economies of member countries and this would be ensured by the imperative for economic and financial discipline in order to uphold the exchange rate commitments in the Exchange Rate Mechanism of the EMS.

The Logic

The relative success of the EMS and the inauguration of the Single European Market programme led to an intensification of the debate about EMU from the mid - 1980s onwards. For many EMU was a necessary adjunct to the '1992' programme of free movement of goods, services, people and capital in the European Community. Only a single currency could guarantee the creation of a genuine single market in goods, services and factors of production within the Community, according to these proponents. The analogy most frequently made is with the US economy with its large 'continental' market, immense mobility of goods, services and factors of production, all crucially facilitated by the existence of a single currency. However it is important to note that economic theory does not support this assertion: a genuine common market can exist without a single currency.[8] Hence this rationale for EMU is based on little more than gut feeling or instinct.

A more convincing case for a single currency for some people rests on the fact that by the early 1990s nearly 60 per cent of the *total* EC members' external trade was with other members and that over 25 per cent of EC members' GDP on *average* was accounted for by intra-EC trade.[9] Since a single European currency would help save on transaction costs, it is quite desirable.

Moreover the completion of the internal market will increase trade and capital mobility and this enhanced economic interdependence reduces the effectiveness of the exchange rate as an instrument for balance of payments correction.

A very logical underpinning for EMU was provided by the Italian economist cum bureaucrat Tommaso Padoa-Schioppa who identified what he called the 'inconsistent quartet' of economic objectives. A group of countries cannot simultaneously achieve free trade, free capital mobility, stable exchange rates and monetary antonomy - something in this quartet has to be sacrificed.[10] For example, in an economy experiencing high unemployment, the government might decide to cut interest rates to boost the level of economic activity and thereby alleviate the problem of unemployment. But with free trade, this might lead to an increase in imports and a decrease in exports, and free capital mobility will lead to an increase in the outflow of capital and a reduction in the inflow of capital. Thus a deterioration in the trade and capital accounts will jeopardize exchange rate stability. Padoa-Schioppa argues that since the internal market, the decision to liberalize capital movements, and the EMS are already in place, monetary autonomy would have to give way and EMU makes this possible. Furthermore it is argued that in an era of liberalized and vast capital movements monetary autonomy for states has been eroded considerably and thus this sacrifice is more of form rather than substance.

The Benefits and Costs of a Single Currency

Since an economic and monetary union eventually results in a single currency for the participating countries it is necessary to examine the major costs and benefits of such an edifice. The European Commission published a major study of this topic in October 1990 with the title, *'One Market, One Money'*.[11] Many people make an analogy between this report and the 1988 Cecchini Report which tried to advance the case for the Single Market Programme by quantifying its potential benefits. The *'One Market, One Money'* report has been criticized on methodological and empirical grounds but it is useful in identifying the pros and cons of EMU.[12]

Three major benefits are highlighted by this report. Firstly, a single currency would eliminate foreign exchange transaction costs within the Union and it is estimated that the EC as a whole could save at least 0.5 per cent of its GDP a year (worth between ECU 13 bn and ECU 19 bn) from this gain. Secondly, lower inflation rates and reductions in interest rates coupled with fewer risks for investment could boost the EC's real output by some 5 per cent of GDP.[13]   Thirdly, the external role of a single European currency could produce some seigniorage gains and reduce the EC's need to hold foreign currency reserves by some ECU 160 bn because intra-community trade and financial flows would all be in ECUs. Such a large windfall could be used imaginatively by the EU to regenerate its industrial base or to enhance its participation in global multilateral institutions. [14]

The benefits of a single market are coupled with those of a single currency and the report emphasizes that though the direct static or once-and-for-all gains might be relatively small, the longer term dynamic gains could be considerable though unquantifiable. Such gains could be in terms of having price stability, a higher sustainable rate of economic growth, or superior capacity to adjust to economic shocks. Other benefits such as enhanced financial integration in the EC and the improved prospects for global economic co-ordination in a tripolar world (the EU, the USA, and Japan) are also stressed.

Against this range of benefits are two main costs: firstly, the loss of the exchange rate as an instrument of policy and the sacrifice of independent monetary policy; secondly, the loss of monetary financing of budget deficits and of seigniorage (which is the revenue generated by the issuance of money). A single currency would circumscribe the ability of national governments to deal with certain economic problems and force societies to undergo painful economic measures to achieve adjustment to economic shocks.[15] However, the report argues with reference to recent economic theory (such as rational expectations and time-consistency) and current economic realities (such as financial liberalization and capital mobility) that these policy options which are now to be sacrificed have a diminished scope in today's world and therefore the value of these costs is far less than that of the potential benefits of a single currency.

Leaving aside the question of whether or to what extent the EU constitutes an optimum currency area,[16] it has to be acknowledged that there is considerable disagreement among economists about issues such as the effectiveness of exchange rates, the extent of national monetary policy autonomy, the efficiency of markets in general and financial ones in particular, the perception of inflation as a credibility problem, the susceptibility of EU economies to similar shocks, etc. Therefore any assessment of the economic costs and benefits of EMU is likely to be both speculative and controversial.

The discussion hitherto has focused exclusively on the economic dimension of the costs and benefits of a single currency. Important as this is it misses a vital aspect of the debate about the desirability of EMU. As one author has put it,

> '.....Not a single monetary union in the past came about because of a recognition of economic benefits of the union. In all cases the integration was driven by political objectives.' [17]

For many, a single currency is desirable irrespective of its economic merits, because it signifies not just an integrated European economy but a common European identity and perhaps a single European polity. This strand of thought has always been present ever since the 1950s and its effect on the course of events hitherto and in the future can only be omitted at the risk of being politically naive.[18] For others EMU is a road to EPU (European Political Union) because the dynamics and imperatives of the former will automatically lead to the latter.[19] In this context it is instructive to note that a prominent economist [20] concluded a study of EMU with the following words:

> '.....neither the costs nor the benefits of monetary union are in principle as great as critics and advocates respectively have made out. In fact, from a purely economic perspective, it seems to me something of a storm in a teacup. Why then has so much fuss been made over it? I think the answer is primarily political ...... A separate currency is an important symbol of nationhood, while a common currency is an equally potent symbol of a shared political destiny. This is why anti-federalists such as Margaret Thatcher chose to make their stand here rather than on issues of greater economic significance.'

Two further points need to be mentioned briefly with regard to placing the costs and benefits of a single currency in their proper perspective. Firstly, there is little doubt that for individual countries in the EU, political considerations are at least as significant as economic logic in determining their attitude to EMU.[21] For Germany the Maastricht Treaty had the dual merit of making German unification more palatable to her West European partners and of making further European political integration more likely. For France the Maastricht plan for EMU gave some possibility of regaining monetary influence by participating in the decision-making in the European Central Bank and ECOFIN (the Council of Ministers of Economics and Finance). For the Benelux countries, EMU reinforces West European political integration whereas for the four southern Mediterranean countries (including Portugal) and Ireland EMU provides an external macro-economic discipline, the prospect of larger regional, structural and cohesion funds and a tangible sign of the modernization of their countries. The United Kingdom and Denmark are in a unique position because of their 'opt-out' clauses but for them too the political advantages of agreeing to the Maastricht Treaty were important.

Secondly, even if the overall economic benefits of a single European currency are plausible and non-trivial, for some individual regions and countries, certain costs would exceed some benefits and therefore there is a distributional issue involved here. Trade-offs and compensations will therefore have to be made and a failure to recognize the inherently political nature of the issue here will ensure that the practical realities of EMU are likely to diverge substantially from the theoretical blueprints for achieving EMU.

The Plan

The Maastricht Treaty envisages a three-stage approach to EMU with irrevocably fixed exchange rates and a single monetary policy, leading eventually to the adoption of a single European currency.

During the *first stage*, which began on 1 July 1990, all remaining restrictions on capital flows were to be abolished and all EC currencies were to participate in the ERM. Direct central bank lending to the public sector was to be terminated. Member states were to endeavour to achieve convergence of economic performance and seek to achieve improved policy coordination. In essence, the first stage consolidated the status quo and involved no institutional changes.

The *second stage*, which is a transitional stage, started on 1 January 1994. It involved the setting up of a new institution, the European Monetary Institute (EMI), located in Frankfurt, which will prepare the way for the future European Central Bank (ECB). The EMI will strengthen coordination of member states' monetary policies though the ultimate responsibility for monetary policy will remain with national authorities. Member states can entrust their foreign exchange reserves to the EMI which will not intervene in foreign exchange markets nor oblige members to hold reserves with it. In order to prepare the ground for the ECB, the EMI will conduct preparatory work in a number of areas of central bank activity such as the conduct of monetary and foreign exchange policies, the collection of financial statistics, the setting up of payments systems across the EU and the issuance of currency notes. The EMI is led by an independent full-time president and its top decision-making body is the EMI Council which is composed of the President of the EMI and the Governors of the central banks of the EU member states. [22]

Stage two entails two other things. At its start the currency composition of the ECU basket was frozen.[23] During this stage national central banks will be made independent of their governments if they are not already so.[24]

The *third and final stage* of EMU is planned to begin either on 1 January 1997 or, at the latest, 1 January 1999. For the first date to be achieved, a majority of the EU states must qualify by fulfilling the necessary conditions for stage three; [25] otherwise this stage will begin on the latter date irrespective of how many countries qualify.

At the start of stage three, exchange rates between participating currencies will be fixed irrevocably and a single monetary policy will be implemented by the European System of Central Banks (ESCB) which will consist of a European Central Bank (ECB) and national central banks all of whom will be independent of national governments. The ECB would be responsible for managing a single currency which would eventually replace national currencies.

The primary objective of both the ESCB and the ECB will be the achievement of *price stability*[26] and both these institutions will be free of interference from EU institutions or member governments.

The most crucial aspect of the Maastricht programme for EMU is the *convergence criteria* which set out the conditions for admission to the final stage. These five criteria are quite explicit and they concentrate exclusively on monetary variables. They are:

- *Price stability*. To qualify for EMU a country's inflation rate should be no more than 1.5 per cent above the average of the three best performing EU countries in terms of inflation;

- *Interest rates*. The interest rates on long-term government securities should not exceed by more than 2.0 per cent the average of interest rates on similar securities in the three EU countries with the lowest inflation rates;[27]

-   *Deficits*. National budget deficits must be less than 3 per cent of GDP;
-   *Debts*. The public debt should not exceed 60 per cent of GDP;
-   *Currency stability*. A country's currency must have maintained its membership in the normal band of the ERM for two years without having initiated a devaluation of its currency.

Although these criteria seem to be laid down unambiguously and a strict enforcement is possible, this is highly unlikely. Firstly the relevant articles of the Maastricht Treaty are worded such that there is an element of discretion in their interpretation.[28] The phrasing of Article 104C allows budget deficits to exceed 3 per cent of GDP provided this is 'exceptional and temporary', and a country can be deemed to have met the convergence criteria even when its public debt exceeds 60 per cent of GDP provided this higher ratio has 'declined substantially and continuously' and 'at a satisfactory pace'. Secondly it is highly likely that political considerations will influence judgements about whether a particular country has met the convergence criteria or not - for example few can conceive of an EMU without German or Dutch participation. Thirdly it is obvious that trade-offs will have to be made between the different criteria e.g. if Belgium or the Netherlands fulfils all the convergence criteria except the one regarding outstanding public debt then surely they will be deemed to qualify for entry to stage three. Fourthly, given the severity of the recent recession in the EC and the existence of 18 million people unemployed, an increasing number of commentators are asking for a distinction to be made between structural and cyclical deficits, primary and overall deficits and capital and current expenditures in national budgets. Fifthly, assessment of the currency stability criterion is bound to be a judgemental exercise because of the proviso regarding membership in the normal band of the ERM without having initiated a devaluation of a country's own currency.

Recently there has been some debate about whether the 'nominal' convergence criteria of the Maastricht Treaty need to be supplemented by some 'real' convergence criteria.[29] The Maastricht paradigm is very much a creature of its time. It assumes that output, employment and growth cannot, at least in the long run, be influenced by monetary policy; what determines these outcomes are structural factors in an economy. The only thing that monetary policy can fundamentally influence is the rate of inflation. Thus the only macro-economic objective that a government can and should aim to deliver is low inflation. This would then provide a stable environment for the market economy to operate efficiently. Leaving aside the criticisms of this albeit, simple exposition of 'the Maastricht paradigm', we can now understand why governments are willing to surrender their control of monetary policy to a ECB. As one author has put it:

> 'First, because countries cannot permanently solve an unemployment problem by adopting an expansionary monetary policy, they are not abandoning anything important by ceding monetary policy to a supra-national entity. Second, because monetary policy affects inflation and nothing else in the long run, countries might as well cede control of that policy to an entity that would pursue a low inflation objective with maximum credibility...Third, there need be no convergence in unemployment rates between countries, since either inside or outside a monetary union, differences in unemployment would be determined entirely by structural factors in the labour market...Fourth, ...countries cannot make permanent gains by devaluing their currencies since a decline in the exchange rate will be quite rapidly washed away by a rise in domestic prices, leaving the real exchange rate unaltered.' [30]

Thus the Maastricht convergence criteria are based on these beliefs. The criteria require a convergence of inflation rates among the participating countries and this would be sustained over time by imposing constraints on governments' ability to endanger monetary stability especially in terms of running excessive fiscal deficits. Such a framework would enhance the private sector's belief in the permanance of low inflation over time and provide the right conditions for generating economic growth and employment in the economy. Hence the Maastricht Treaty does not require that unemployment rates, or growth rates, be convergent across the Union before the single currency can be introduced.

Proponents of 'real' convergence argue that it is possible to have a convergence of nominal variables such as inflation rates, or interest rates, or debt ratios, etc., with divergences in real variables such as unemployment rates, output and growth, competitiveness, and current account balances. This would, it is argued, throw up immense strains for certains regions in an EMU and in the absence of political integration and fiscal federalism lead to general instability. Sooner or later the monetary union would disintegrate in the face of such regional problems. Thus a realistic approach to achieving EMU needs to incorporate additional criteria. The article by the author quoted above suggests the following supplementary 'real' convergence criteria to the Maastricht criteria:[31]

	Real GDP[1] 1994	Unemployment rate[1] 1994	Current A/C as per cent of GDP[1] 1994	Index of competitiveness vs Germany (Feb 87=100) end 1994
'Real' Convergence Criteria				
Suggested criteria	Within 1.5 per cent of trend growth [2]	12.9 [3]	No less than -2.0 [4]	90-110 [5]
Germany	2.3	7.3	-1.8	-
France	2.4	11.3	0.8	108.3
Italy	2.4	11.8	1.5	123.9
UK	3.9	9.4	-0.4	93.9
Spain	1.8	22.4	-1.0	109.5
Netherlands	2.4	10.0	1.8	108.3
Belgium	2.3	10.0	4.8	103.9
Denmark	4.6	10.2	2.8	103.1
Portugal	1.0	6.1	-1.6	-
Greece	1.0	10.2	-0.8	97.7
Ireland	5.0	17.7	7.9	106.3
Luxembourg	2.6	3.3	28.6	110.9
Finland	3.5	18.7	2.4	112.1
Sweden	2.0	7.7	0.4	113.9
Austria	2.8	6.0	-1.1	105.5

[1] Goldman Sachs estimates, OECD Dec 1994, European Commission Dec 1994.
[2] Trend growth taken to be average of 1984 - 1994.
[3] Unemployment rate no more than 2 percentage points above EU average.
[4] Any current account deficit no more than 2 per cent of GDP.
[5] Competitiveness against Germany within 10 per cent of the level in February 1987 (when the ERM was last 'voluntarily' realigned). Higher numbers indicate greater competitiveness against Germany.

Source: Goldman Sachs

In this connection it is pertinent to note that Article 109J (1) of the Maastricht Treaty enjoins the EC Commission and the EMI to take into account not just the five 'nominal' convergence criteria but also "the development of the ECU, the results of the integration of markets, the situation and development of the balances of payments on current account and an examination of the development of unit labour costs and other price indices" in preparing their respective regular reports for monitoring progress towards convergence by EU member countries for consideration by the ECOFIN Council. It remains to be seen how these additional criteria will be interpreted and what they will be worth.

Mention must also be made of a long standing debate between the so-called 'monetarist' and 'economist' schools of thought in this context.[32] The debate is to do with whether economic convergence is a consequence or a pre-requisite of monetary union. The latter view, represented by countries like Germany and the Netherlands, argues that you need an appreciable degree of co-ordination of economic policy and convergence of economic performance in order to have a stable basis for inaugurating a monetary union with a subsequent transfer of political and fiscal powers to a federal centre. Thus EMU is the culmination of the process of economic convergence. The former view, argued by countries such as France, Italy and Belgium, believes that the inception of EMU would hasten economic convergence because of its dynamics and momentum. Hence in this preception EMU delivers economic convergence (through the imposition of economic and financial discipline on the governments of the participants) and not vice versa. It can be said that the story of European monetary integration from the Werner Report to the Maastricht Treaty is one which has only superficially reconciled the two sides in this debate. In the negotiations leading up to the Maastricht Treaty, the power and influence of Germany and in particular the Bundesbank ensured that the 'economist' school of thought which believes that economic convergence is a prerequisite for EMU coloured the Maastricht edifice.

With respect to the current position of EU member countries in relation to the Maastricht convergence criteria it is clear that the situation for some countries in relation to particular criteria is not promising as the table below illustrates.

What the table indicates is that at present Germany and Luxembourg fulfil all five convergence criteria,[33] while France comes very near to it. Austria, Denmark, Finland and the Netherlands should have little difficulty in achieving fulfilment of all the criteria. The UK is in a unique position because although she can conceivably fulfil all the criteria, there is the 'opt-out' clause, the Bank of England is not independent of the government and there would be the political hurdle of having to re-join the ERM. Countries such as Belgium,

Ireland and Sweden have a difficult though not an impossible task ahead of them.

Economic Indicators and the Maastricht Treaty Convergence Criteria

Data refers to calender year 1994

Criterion → Denomination →	Inflation	Long-Term Interest Rate	General Government Budget Position	General Government Gross Debt	Member-ship of ERM
	per cent P.A	per cent P.A	per cent of GDP	per cent of GDP	Exchange Rate
Austria	3.0 ✓	7.0 ✓	-4.4	65.0	Yes ✓
Belgium	2.4 ✓	7.7 ✓	-5.5	140.1	Yes ✓
Denmark	2.0 ✓	7.8 ✓	-4.3	78.0	Yes ✓
Germany	3.0 ✓	7.0 ✓	-2.9 ✓	51.0 ✓	Yes ✓
Greece	10.8	20.8	-14.1	121.3	No
Finland	1.1 ✓	9.1 ✓	-4.7	70.0	No
France	1.6 ✓	7.2 ✓	-5.6	50.4 ✓	Yes ✓
Ireland	2.4 ✓	7.9 ✓	-2.4 ✓	89.0	Yes ✓
Italy	3.9	10.6	-9.6	123.7	No
Luxembourg	2.1 ✓	6.4 ✓	1.3 ✓	9.2 ✓	Yes ✓
Netherlands	2.7 ✓	6.9 ✓	-3.8	78.8	Yes ✓
Portugal	5.2	10.4	-6.2	70.4	Yes ✓
Spain	4.7	10.0 ✓	-7.0	63.5	Yes ✓
Sweden	2.4 ✓	9.5 ✓	-11.7	81.0	No
United Kingdom	2.4 ✓	8.1 ✓	-6.3	50.4 ✓	No

Source: European Monetary Institute (April 1995), Annual Report 1994 p.40 and p.49

✓: Criterion satisfied (author's assessment)

Note: The reference values for Inflation and Long-Term Interest Rates are 3.16 per cent and 10.03 per cent (this is calculated by averaging the rates for the three best performing countries in terms of price stability, viz., Finland, France and Denmark, and adding the permissable margins of 1.5 per cent and 2.0 per cent respectively).

Greece, Italy, Portugal and Spain are going to find it very difficult to meet the necessary criteria. What it all sums up to is three things: there is little chance of EMU commencing on 1 January 1997 because a majority of EU countries are unlikely to qualify for stage 3; the main problem is the worrisome state of most EU countries' fiscal positions;[34] and, when EMU starts on 1 January 1999 a not insignificant number of EU countries are likely to qualify for membership.[35] It might be ironic to note that should the EU enlarge its membership to incorporate certain formerly planned economies of central and eastern Europe then countries such as the Czech Republic, Poland, Hungary and Slovenia are likely to have little difficulty in fulfilling the Maastricht convergence criteria.

The Implications

There is little doubt that, contrary to what the EU leaders had been saying during the ratification process of the Maastricht Treaty, EMU is inevitably going to lead to a multi-speed Europe at least in two senses. Firstly, not all EU countries are going to qualify for EMU on current criteria and hence we will either have a distinction between those who form an inner core EMU and those who are in the outer ring of EMU, or we will have a distinction between those who join EMU and those who cannot or will not join in.

Secondly we will see a divergence within the European economic and monetary union between the prospering regions and the regions that lag behind. A single European currency will enhance the competitiveness of the former by attracting investment and activity while the latter will have few means at their disposal to improve their condition.[36]

A common currency and a single central bank does imply a sacrifice of monetary sovereignty for participating countries. As one author[37] has put it,

> 'European integration has already extended beyond trade; and the 1992 process represents both a quantitative and qualitative shift towards the creation of a regional economic system. Yet EMU is something very different. In terms of national sovereignty, the stakes are infinitely higher... the plans for the creation of EMU could not be camouflaged as a technical matter with limited political consequences. *"Money is, after all, at the heart of national sovereignty."'* (Emphasis added).

However it can be argued that for EMU this is a difference of degree rather than kind since for EU countries, the openness of their interdependent economies coupled with capital mobility, has already appreciably circumscribed national monetary sovereignty.

A monetary union implies that a country which is a part of it cannot now resort to using the exchange rate instrument to solve its macro-economic problems. It now needs to rely on other mechanisms and theoretically they are: wage-price flexibility, labour mobility, built-in stabilisers to cushion regional shocks, and intra-regional transfers of funds. Given the social and institutional realities of Western Europe, wage-price flexibility exists only to a moderate extent and depressed regions are unlikely to create demand and jobs via this mechanism. As for labour mobility in the European Union, this is pretty low because of distinct national cultures, history and languages as well as risk aversion and ignorance of job opportunities on the part of the unemployed. It is estimated that in 1992, less than 5 per cent of the total resident population in EU member countries was foreign, and only one third of them originated from other EU countries. [38] Monetary union in the United States, for example, relies on much greater labour mobility than what the EU has. One empirical study of how the US states adjust to regional shocks came to the following conclusion:

> 'Of the 100 workers who lose their job, 30 stay unemployed, 5 drop out of the labour force and 65 leave the state...It is out-migration of unemployed workers, rather than in-migration of companies attracted by low wages, that explains how US states adjust to regional shocks'. [39]

An alternative mechanism for alleviating regional shocks is built-in stabilisers. These are automatic tendencies which come into play to diminish the intensity of booms and slumps through the operation of the tax and welfare systems. A frequently quoted, though challenged study,[40] of how regional shocks are cushioned in the US argues that a fall of one dollar in average state income per head results in an actual fall of 60 cents in per capital disposable income because federal tax payments would decrease by 34 cents and federal welfare transfers would rise by 6 cents as a consequence of the initial one dollar decline in state income. Even if these American figures are an exaggeration, the absence of an EU wide tax and welfare regime suggests that European regions have few built-in stabilisers to ameliorate the effects of regional shocks.

The final mechanism in terms of intra-regional transfers to compensate regions which suffer from high unemployment and low growth has limited potential since the size of the EU budget currently amounts to less than 1.25 per cent of EU GDP (compare this with the fact that national government spending in EU countries accounts for, on average, about half of GDP). In the aftermath of German Economic and Monetary Union in 1990, fiscal transfers from the western to the eastern part of Germany have amounted to 4 per cent of all German GDP.[41]

Thus the extent to which these alternative mechanisms to exchange rate instrument for regional economic adjustment obtain in the EU is limited and therefore regions which experience high unemployment and low growth are going to find life very difficult. Moreover if the monetary policy and exchange rate instruments are non-existent for individual countries in EMU then a greater burden falls on fiscal policy. Yet the convergence criteria regarding public debt and budget deficit levels, the constraints on deficit financing and the implications of the Single Market for tax harmonization and budgetary discrepancies all diminish the scope for using fiscal policy instruments.

Turning briefly to the external dimension of EMU, two issues stand out. The EU's foreign exchange reserves would be held by the ESCB but it would not decide on the external exchange rate policy - that would be the preserve of ECOFIN. This could lead to problems as it is highly unlikely that all participating countries in EMU will have a uniform view about the single European currency's exchange rate against non-EU currencies. Moreover ECOFIN decisions on the external exchange rate policy are bound to have an impact on internal monetary conditions and its not clear how this will fit in with the ECB's mandated objective of maintaining price stability.[42]

Finally EMU is likely to have important consequences for the international monetary system. A single European currency could challenge the dollar's global dominance and lead to a multi-currency standard in the global financial system. It could also enhance international co-operation and economic policy coordination though this assumes that the EU will speak with one voice. As Peter Kenen[43] has asked, who will represent the EU in the G7 when national finance ministers retain primary responsibility for fiscal policies, ECOFIN decides exchange rate policy, and the ECB has the responsibility for monetary policy and for intervening on foreign exchange markets? Moreover, as the same author has commented, if the United States frequently is not particularly interested in policy coordination because its economy is large and relatively closed, what guarantee is there that the EU will behave differently when it becomes a single economy, not much different in size and openness from the US.

Conclusion

A distinguished American economist [44] who is a critic of EMU has argued that the proper question that needs answering in the debate about the desirability of a single European currency is not,

> 'Are the economic benefits great enough to outweigh the political disadvantages of the federal structure for Europe that would follow the adoption of a single currency?',

but rather,

> 'Would the political advantages of adopting a single currency outweigh the economic disadvantages?'

While this might be an unfair dichotomy it highlights the thesis of this chapter which is that EMU is as much a political issue as it is an economic and financial one. [45] Rather than summarizing the contents of the preceding sections of this chapter, this conclusion identifies a number of broader economic, financial and political concerns that will emerge if EMU is realized. In an EU in which some member states are members of an EMU and others not, there is a danger of EMU fracturing the Single Market because there could be conflict between the hard currency countries (i.e. those that are part of a single currency group and thus cannot unilaterally depreciate their currency) and the soft currency countries (who can engage in competitive devaluations). Already the strains are beginning to show; if press accounts are to be believed, at the Cannes European Summit in June 1995, President Chirac complained to the Italian and Spanish Prime Ministers of the unfair advantage their tomato and strawberry farmers were gaining in the French market due to the depreciation of the lira and the peseta in the last couple of years. The Belgian Finance Minister is on record as saying that

> 'participants in a single currency zone would not sit idly by if certain other members wanted to enjoy all the advantages of a Single Market without the disciplines of a single currency'. [46]

Such feelings, if widespread, could lead to trade sanctions being imposed by the participating on the non-participating states. It will be essential to design a system of rules and obligations to enable the core EMU countries to live with the non-members, otherwise the achievement of a Single Market will be in jeopardy.

If EMU is created without any alteration in the political institutions of the EU and if the basis of its composition continues to be nation-states with claims to political sovereignty then questions of democratic accountability and credibility are bound to rise over time. What faith will citizens retain in national electoral processes if the government they have chosen lacks the capacity in certain fundamental respects to deliver on its manifesto promises? If EMU of the Maastricht Treaty variety is realized then important policy instruments of governments such as monetary, fiscal and exchange rate instruments will be eliminated or severly curbed, and the only policy instruments left to national governments will be microeconomic ones such as, for example, structural changes to labour markets. Such policies at best show results only in the longer term. Unless the citizens settle for minimal expectations of their governments they are bound to be disillusioned. Moreover a question mark hangs over the future of a pluralistic multi-party national polity since how will political parties differ in terms of their fundamental ideology if their country is part of EMU?

Once EMU is created how sustainable will it be? Little thought has been given to this because the prime focus of attention hitherto has been on how EMU will be created. Yet the question of EMU's sustainability is a profound one because history shows that monetary unions once created are not guaranteed continual survival. In an instructive article Benjamin Cohen [47] undertakes a comparative analysis of six currency unions during the nineteenth and twentieth centuries to determine what essential factors are required for their sustainability. His conclusion is that while economic and organizational factors are relatively unimportant, the political factors are crucial for the longevity of currency unions. By political factors he means the presence of a dominant state - a regional hegemony - which is able and willing to use its influence to keep a currency union functioning effectively; it also means the presence of sufficient ties and a community of interests which make the participants willing to accept the loss of monetary autonomy. He states,

> 'Judging from my six cases, it seems clear that one or the other of these two factors is necessary for the sustainability of currency integration among sovereign states. Where both are present, they constitute a sufficient condition for success. Where neither is present, currency unions tend to fail' [48]

He goes on further to state:

> '...studies of currency integration that principally emphasize either economic variables or organizational characteristics miss the main point. The issue is only secondarily whether the members of a monetary union meet the traditional criteria identified in the theory of optimum currency areas or whether monetary management and the issuing of currency happen to be centralized or decentralized. The primary question is whether there is likely to be either a local hegemon or a fabric of related ties with sufficient influence to neutralize the risk of time-inconsistency. Sovereign governments require incentives to stick to bargains that turn out to be inconvenient. The evidence from my historical sample suggests that these incentives may derive either from side - payments or sanctions supplied by a single powerful state or from the constraints and opportunities posed by a broad network of institutional linkages. One or the other of these political factors must be present to serve as an effective compliance mechanism.'[49]

What such an analysis implies is that for EMU to be sustainable over time either hegemony needs to be exerted by some actors, or the interests of sovereign states need to coincide for a long time, or there needs to be fundamental institutional developments.

Finally, it is pertinent to note that the European Union has embarked on a journey that has few historical parallels. Monetary unions have usually followed the political unification of societies (sometimes as states otherwise as regionally integrated units) not preceded it. Furthermore no major money has ever existed without a state behind it. A single European currency as envisaged now will be the first example of a major currency coming into existence without the prior existence of an issuing state.

Notes

1 Germany and the Netherlands however agreed bilaterally to keep their currencies within the narrow margin of fluctuation of +/- 2.25 per cent.

2 For a detailed account up to 1992 see Gros, D. and Thygesen, N. (1992), *European Monetary Integration*, London: Longman.

3 For concise accounts see Tsoukalis, L. (1993), *The New European Monetary Integration*. London: Longman, and also Artis, M. J. and Lee, N. (1994), *The Economics of the European Union*, Oxford: Oxford University Press.

4 See, for example, De Grauwe, P. (1994), *The Economics of Monetary Integration*, (2nd. Re. Ed.). Oxford: Oxford University Press.

5 See Dyson, K. (1994). *Elusive Union*, London: Longman. For an older account see Guerrieri, Paolo and Pier Carlo Padoan (1989). *The Political Economy of European Integration*, Hemel Hempstead: Harvester Wheatsheaf.

6 As Pauly, L. W. (Winter 1991-2) has concluded 'The Politics of European Monetary Union: national strategies, international implications'. *International Journal* Vol. XLVII No. 1: pp. 93-111): '... European monetary union should finally be seen as effectively merging arcane matters of internal economic management with the deepest concerns of statecraft in a unique political environment. Behind it lies not an automatic economic or bureaucratic logic but an intricate and historically rooted political process...'.

7 See Gros and Thygesen (1992) *op.cit.*

8 See Feldstein, M. (1992) 'Europe's Monetary Union: The Case against EMU' *The Economist*, 13 June, pp. 23-6.

9 See Tsoukalis (1993) *op.cit.*

10 See Padoa - Schioppa, T. 'The European Monetary System: A Long-term View' in Giavazzi, Francesco, Stefano Micossi and Marcus Miller (eds.) (1988). *The European Monetary System*. Cambridge: Cambridge University Press. See also Padoa - Schioppa, (1987). *Efficiency, Stability, and Equity*. Oxford : Oxford University Press.

11 European Commission. (October 1990), 'One Market, One Money: An Evaluation of the Potential Benefits and Costs of Forming an Economic and Monetary Union', *European Economy* No. 44.

12 The report is extremely detailed but relies almost exclusively on economic logic and empirical evidence, some of which is extrapolated. For a theoretical assessment of the costs and benefits of a single currency see De Grauwe (1994) *op.cit.*; for a simpler treatment see Emerson, M. and Huhne, C. (1991), *The ECU Report*, London: Pan Books. A good political economy

approach to the topic is contained in Crawford, M (1993), *One Money for Europe? - The Economics and Politics of Maastricht*, Basingstoke: Macmillan. For a sceptical assessment of the report see Bean, C. (1992), *Economic and Monetary Union in Europe*, London: LSE Centre for Economic Performance Discussion Paper No. 86.

13   Note that unlike the first benefit which would be an ongoing gain, the 5 per cent increase in GDP would be a once-for-all gain achieved by moving to a new environment of price stability and less uncertainty.

14   See Pauly (Winter 1991-2), *op.cit.* p. 108.

15   See a latter section of this chapter on The Implications of EMU.

16   Since the early 1960s this has been the traditional theoretical apparatus used by economists to assess the merits of a single currency. The theory has undergone considerable refinements and there is a lot of debate about the importance of various factors (such as wage/price flexibility, resource mobility, sectoral and geographic trade patterns, the openness of economies and the nature and source of potential balance of payments disturbances) which should govern the choice of currency regime by political authorities. The *One Market, One Money* report *op.cit.* argues that the theory of optimum currency areas is not very useful for analyzing the costs and benefits of EMU. *op.cit.*

17   De Grauwe, P. (November 1993), 'The Political Economy of Monetary Union in Europe' *The World Economy* vol. 16. No. 6: pp. 653-62, here p. 656.

18   For examples of this view see some of the contributors in Steinherr, A. (ed.) (1994), *Thirty Years of European Monetary Integration*, London: Longman.

19   The two views are not mutually exclusive.

20   Bean (1992) *op.cit.*

21   See Sandholtz , W. (Winter 1993), 'Choosing union: monetary politics and Maastricht,' *International Organisation,* for a detailed account. De Grauwe, P. (November 1993) *op.cit.* and Tsoukalis (1993) *op.cit.* provide a brief account.

22   The President of the Council of the EU and a member of the European Commission may participate in the EMI Council meetings but have no right to vote.

23   The European Currency Unit is a centre piece of the EMS and is a composite currency that contains specific amounts of the currencies of the twelve members of what was the European Community. The logic behind the decision to freeze the currency composition of the ECU was to enhance

the ECU's stability and increase its usage in the run up to the introduction of a single European currency.

24   With the notable exception of the Bank of England, every EU central bank is already or is about to be independent. See European Monetary Institute (April 1995) Annual Report 1994, Frankfurt.

25   Unless the UK and Denmark revoke their 'opt-out' from stage 3 of the Maastricht Plan for EMU they will not be included in the majority calculation. Hence a 1997 start to stage 3 may require a majority of 7 out of 13 countries and not 8 out of 15 countries. See Gros and Thygesen (1992) *op.cit.*

26   It is noticeable that the Maastricht Treaty does not define this term precisely. Does it, for example, mean zero inflation, low inflation or steady inflation?

27   There is a slight ambiguity about the wording of the Treaty in this respect because it is unclear whether the reference value for the price stability and interest rate convergence criteria is the average of the best three performers or the rate achieved by the third country in the ranking. See Gros and Thygesen (1992) *op.cit.* and EMI Annual Report 1994. *op.cit.*

28   The European council will decide on whether the convergence criteria have been achieved or not. This will be on the basis of regular reports from the ECOFIN Council where the assessment for each country's performance will be done by a qualified majority vote. ECOFIN's assessment in turn will be based on regular reports to it from the EC Commission and the EMI on progress towards convergence.

29   See Bank of England Quarterly Bulletin (May 1995) 'The economics of EMU', Vol. 35 No. 2: pp. 192-6. and also Davis, G (1995) 'Time to review Maastricht blueprint on covergence', *The Independent,* Monday 27 February, p. 25.

30   Davis, G. (1995) *op.cit..* See also Charles A.E. Goodhart, 'The Political Economy of Monetary Union' in Kenen, Peter (ed.) (1995), *Understanding Interdependence: The Macroeconomics of the Open Economy.* Princeton: Princeton University Press.

31   Davis, G. (1995) *op.cit.*

32   See Tsoukalis (1993) *op.cit.* and Gros and Thygesen (1992) *op.cit.*

33   And could theoretically initiate stage 3 of the Maastricht Plan on their own on 1 January 1999.

34   See *EMI Annual Report* 1994. *op.cit.*

35   For optimistic scenarios see *Financial Times* Monday 1 August 1994 p. 15 and *Guardian* Tuesday 8 August 1995 p. 14.

36 See Masera, R. S. (May 1994) 'Single Market, Exchanges Rates and Monetary Unification.' *The World Economy*, Vol. 17 No. 3. pp. 263 - 74.

37 Tsoukalis (1993) p. 176, *op.cit.*

38 Bank of England Quarterly Bulletin (May 1995) p. 196, *op.cit.*

39 See *Financial Times* Monday 18 May 1992, Canzoneri, Matthew B., Vittorio Grilli and Paul R. Masson (eds.) (1992), *Establishing a central bank: issues in Europe and lessons from the US.* Cambridge: Cambridge University Press.

40 See Xavier Sala-i-Martin and Jeffrey Sachs, 'Fiscal federalism and optimum currency areas: evidence for Europe from the United States' in Canzoneri, Mathew B., Vittorio Grilli and Paul R. Masson (eds.) (1992), *Establishing a central bank: issues in Europe and lessons from the US*, Cambridge: Cambridge University Press. See also De Cecco, Marcello and Alberto Giovannini (eds.) (1989), *A European Central Bank?* Cambridge : Cambridge University Press.

41 Bank of England Quarterly Bulletin (May 1995) p. 196. *op.cit.*

42 See Goodhart, C.A.E. (1992), *EMU and ESCB after Maastricht* London: LSE Financial Markets Group.

43 Kenen, P. (ed). (1992). *EMU after Maastricht.* Washington: Group of Thirty.

44 Feldstein (1992), p. 23, *op.cit.*.

45 See, for example, Gros and Thygesen (1992) pp. 460 - 7 *op.cit* for an argument as to why EMU does not need political union.

46 Quoted in Tugendhat (August - September 1995), 'Second thoughts on Europe' in *The World Today* Vol. 51 Nos. 8-9: pp. 159-61.

47 See Benjamin J. Cohen, 'Beyond EMU: The Problem of Sustainability' in Eichengreen, Barry and Jeffrey Frieden (1994), *The Political Economy of European Monetary Unification.* Boulder : Westview Press.

48 Cohen (1994) *Ibid.*, p. 159.

49 See Panic, M. (1992), *European Monetary Union - Lessons from the Classical Gold Standard.* New York: St. Martin's Press, for an interesting argument regarding the viability of EMU over time which contrasts it with the workings of the pre-1914 international gold standard.

9 Is a Single European Market Still Credible?

STEPHEN WOOLCOCK[1]

Introduction

The initial credibility of the single European market (SEM) initiative of the European Community resulted from a combination of market and policy-led factors, which gave it the momentum needed to overcome the inertia of national policies and preferences. After 1990 the European Union (EU) lost both political and economic momentum. This paper first considers whether a single European market is still credible given this loss of momentum. Sustaining the credibility of the SEM also requires effective implementation of the legislative measures in national legislation and their enforcement. The second half of the paper therefore considers the crucial question of implementation and enforcement. Having analyzed these two factors in the credibility of the SEM, the chapter concludes that the SEM has broadly withstood the loss of momentum during the period 1991-94. On the question of implementation and enforcement however, a continued and consistent commitment from national governments, regulatory authorities and European institutions will be required if the objective of creating a genuine internal market is to be achieved.

The internal market programme was launched at a time when the political and economic climates were favourable for European integration. Since 1990 political support for integration has weakened. There is now a broadly held view that the more technocratic or functionalist approach to integration which predominated up to the end of the 1980s is no longer sufficient. The heightened awareness of the issues in European integration in the general public now requires a different, more political approach. The economic environment also changed from one of steady or even vigorous growth during the second half of the 1980s to one of economic slow down and recession in the first half of the 1990s.

The internal market is important for European integration as a whole and it was no accident that the SEM initiative achieved prominence. The SEM covered an area of policy in which there was a broad consensus on the need for common action among governments and economic actors. Although trades unions were critical of the absence of a social dimension to the SEM proposals. The internal market is also at the core of the EC in the sense that it builds on the common market. In the past it was possible to proceed with market integration even when more ambitious political projects failed. Thus agreement could be reached on the establishment of the four freedoms in the Treaty of Rome, in the aftermath of the failure of the European Defence Community.

At the peak of the euphoria over 'Europe 1992', it was a widely held view among public and private sector commentators, that the internal market process was 'irreversible'. Indeed, for a time it appeared that much of what the functionalist theory suggested about the spill-over effects of integration would in fact come about. Decisions in one area did lead to pressure for the creation of a single market in related areas in order to create the 'level playing field'. For example, the adoption of EC Directives creating a single passport for banking, created pressure for similar legislation for investment and other financial services. Rather than play safe through resisting change, the safe option became one of pressing ahead. National governments holding the Presidency of the EC competed to pass the most pieces of legislations during their terms.

By mid 1992 things had changed. Indeed with hindsight it is possible to identify a change, at least during 1991 as the economy in a number of EC member states began to slow. By 1992 it was the neo-realist school of thought which appeared to be in the ascendence. As the responses to the political and economic shocks which hit Europe during the period 1989 - 1992 showed, the nation state was still alive and well. The stalling of economic and monetary union (EMU), second thoughts over the Maastricht Treaty on European Union (TEU), not to mention the absence of an effective EU response to the crisis in the former Yugoslavia, all showed that integration was not inevitable. In the wake of Maastricht, there has been much discussion of the prospects for monetary or political union, but relatively little attention has been focused on the internal market. This chapter seeks to redress this imbalance, by considering whether the internal market is still credible.

Before discussing the details of the internal market programme, it is first necessary to look at some of the main developments which have resulted in the loss of momentum in the EU. These include economic recession and the associated problems of the European Exchange Rate Mechanism (ERM), the difficulties ratifying the Maastricht treaty on European Union, recent and future enlargement and thus possible dilution of the EU, and difficulties defining a coherent external trade policy for the EU. The paper then briefly summarizes the position with regard to the legislative programme for the internal market and explains the reasons why there has been no agreement on the few outstanding issues such as company law. It then turns to what is now the more important question of implementation and enforcement.

External Shocks and the Credibility of the Market

The impact of the recession

Past experience with European integration has shown that developments are sensitive to the general state of the economy. The EC's internal market initiative was timely in the sense that it corresponded with a period of strong economic growth during the second half of the 1980s. The 1980s had begun with recession and slow growth. By the time the policy initiatives of the Cockfield White Paper (1985) on 'Completing the Internal Market and the Single European Act' (1987) were taken, however, the economy had picked up. Average growth in GDP for the EC as a whole was 2-2.5 per cent between 1984 and 1987. In the period 1988-89 economic growth in the EC exceeded 3 per cent peaking at 4 per cent in 1988. This had a twofold effect. First, market liberalization was easier under conditions of economic growth, because those representing industrial and sectoral interests were more interested in getting access to new growing markets than defending stagnant or declining existing markets. Second, increased investment went hand-in-hand with economic growth and there was, especially during the period 1987-89, a rapid rise in cross border investment both within and beyond the European Community. This growth in cross-border investment meant that structures were being created which no longer corresponded to the pattern of national industries. The combination of policy initiatives and market-led developments in 1987-88 gave the SEM credibility which in turn led policy-makers and investors to base decisions on the assumption that the SEM would be created. This in turn created a momentum for integration.

GDP growth in the EC declined to 1 per cent in 1990. In 1990, and to some extent in 1991, the locomotive effect of massive transfers from west to eastern Germany sustained the EC economy, but this was only a temporary benefit. In 1992/3 the German economy slid into a recession and the general EC economic recovery was delayed. Cross border mergers and acquisitions came to a grinding halt as companies consolidated or struggled with the deteriorating economic climate. Despite the recession the legislative programme for the establishment of an internal market continued. There was a slowing in the pace of adoption of directives, but this was to be expected as many of the more difficult decisions had been put off and had to be tackled towards the end of the programme. As will be showed below the legislative programme was, more or less, completed on schedule.

In terms of the programme therefore the impact of recession does not seem to have been that great. The real test will be whether the legislative programme will be implemented and enforced. The pressure of the recession was felt in more indirect ways than in the adoption of EC Directives. For example, state subsidy programmes, which had been generally on the decline during the 1980s, were reactivated in efforts to help major firms in difficulties. But even here the overall level of subsidy did not rise significantly.

Problems with the EMS

The Delors Committee on EMU was established at the Hanover European Council meeting in 1988, a time when the economic growth cycle was approaching a peak. From the outset there were two clear schools of thought on EMU. One argued that a single currency could only follow real economic convergence, the other that a treaty commitment to create EMU was needed to help provide the discipline needed to bring about economic convergence. The real economic convergence school of thought was supported by most economists. The views of central bankers, business and politicians varied more between countries. An important leading proponent of the economic convergence school was the German Bundesbank. It was supported in this by most of German industry. The institutional approach incorporating commitments to a timetable for a single currency was supported by politicians committed to European Union. The German Chancellor, Helmut Kohl, was a leading proponent of this view and he was supported by President Francois Mitterrand of France. There was also a more general French interest in gaining control over European monetary policy, which meant, in practice, integrating the Bundesbank into a European Central Bank. The opening of the Berlin Wall, followed by German unification, served to strengthen the German desire to accelerate European integration in order to ensure that German unification took place within the context of deeper European integration. This strengthened the Franco-German interest in a deal which involved France accepting elements of political union, such as a Common Foreign and Security Policy (CFSP) and more power for the European Parliament (EP), in return for German support for monetary union. In other words during 1990 the political support for an acceleration of efforts to create EMU overcame the long established opposition from economists and the Bundesbank.

The credibility of the institutional approach to EMU soon suffered a series of major setbacks. First, the economic slow down resulted in economic divergence which put the convergence criteria included in the Maastricht Treaty (at the insistence of the central bankers), out of reach, at least for much of the 1990s. The recession resulted in increased budget deficits as tax revenue fell and unemployment benefit payments increased. Further public spending cuts to meet the convergence criteria became politically untenable in the face of high and rising unemployment. Second, there was German unification. The rapid collapse of the east German economy following its immediate opening to competitive markets in the West, required massive fiscal transfers from the German Federal Government. In the absence of equivalent cuts in expenditure in the western German states, there was a major fiscal expansion in Germany. As noted above this stimulated growth in Europe during 1991, but when the Bundesbank moved to control the resultant inflationary pressures by increasing interest rates, the deflationary effect was felt throughout Europe, where economic growth was in any case already in decline or stalling.

The third shock came in the shape of the rejection of the Maastricht Treaty by Denmark in June 1992. This precipitated a fierce debate on the treaty, which questioned the credibility of achieving EMU and a single currency via institutional or treaty means. Once the credibility of the EMU timetable was questioned, market speculation intensified. The commitment to support the narrow exchange fluctuation band of the European Exchange Rate Mechanism (ERM) then provided speculators with a one way bet in which they could buy currencies on forward spot markets prices and sell to the central banks in the fairly safe expectation that certain currencies would be forced to devalue. Once the credibility of the deadlines had been undermined such speculative pressure grew.

A fourth external factor which did not figure highly in the commentaries of the time, was the external pressure on the EMS as a result of record low US interest rates. Divergence between US and European (or rather

German) interest rates has always created pressures within the EMS. These pressures became intense during the course of 1992 as the US Federal Reserve reduced interest rates to a 20 year low (3.5 per cent discount rate) in an effort to stimulate the, still sluggish, US economy. This coincided with a rise in German interest rates as the Bundesbank was forced to act to control inflation. The result was a divergence between German and US interest rates and a resultant inflow of funds from Dollars into Deutsche Marks in spring and summer of 1992. This weakened the other European currencies and added to the pressure to maintain high interest rates in other European countries in order to retain currencies such as Sterling or the French Franc in the ERM bands. The inability to reduce interest rates meant that economies like the British and French slid into recession while retaining high interest rates. The intense pressure on the weaker currencies resulted in 'Black Wednesday' in September 1992, when Sterling and the Lira were forced out of the ERM and the Peseta and Irish Punt were realigned. For another year the French government maintained its support for the policy of the *Franc fort*, but in August 1993 it too was forced to accept that something had to give. As a result the ERM currency fluctuation band was increased from a maximum of 2.5 per cent to 15 per cent for most of the countries remaining in the ERM.

Therefore in the face of these external pressures the EC experienced divergence rather than convergence. National interests shaped policy, whether in the form of maintaining tight monetary policy or devaluation. The recession pushed all but Luxembourg beyond the 3 per cent of GDP maximum budget deficit permitted under the convergence criteria for EMU (Italy 12 per cent and Britain 10 per cent). In 1993 inflation also exceeded the convergence criteria for EMU in half the member states. Stage three of EMU (a single currency) which also requires participant countries to have been operating within the narrow (2.5 per cent) band of the ERM for two years, seemed at best a distant prospect.

Despite these external shocks most of the member states maintained policies which kept the Maastricht convergence criteria within sight. In practice exchange rates did not fluctuate by the 15 per cent allowed by the new band. Indeed, France and Germany decided, in the summer of 1993, to work towards a closer cooperation of economic policies in order to promote economic convergence. Even in Britain, where many saw the EMU as a dead-letter, the economic policies pursued ensured that interest and exchange rates did not diverge too much from the rest of the EC. By the end of 1994 the economic prospects for the European Union had improved, with 2 per cent growth in the year and projected growth higher in 1995 and 1996. This offered the prospect of reduced public deficits. Inflationary pressure was also contained in most countries during the period, thus enabling more optimism about the ability of a critical number of member states meeting the convergence criteria for EMU by the late 1990s. Thus although the events of 1992/93 have profoundly shaken the credibility of the EMU and confirmed the 'real economic convergence school' as predominant, they have not resulted in the massive exchange rate fluctuations and economic divergence, which would have made a nonsense of the single market. While the EMU crisis had a profound impact on the EU, the impact on the SEM was muted.

The wider European market

Another exogenous development to be considered was the enlargement of the EC. The conclusion of the European Economic Area (EEA) agreement between the EC and the EFTA countries in May 1992 in Oporto, effectively extended the single market to include all the EFTA countries, except Switzerland, whose electorate voted against it in a referendum in late 1992. With the exception of agriculture and fishery policy the EEA extended the existing *acquis communautaire* as of August 1991 - (that is the sum of EC Directives, Regulations and case law) - to cover the whole of western Europe. The EEA was followed by the accession of Austria, Sweden and Finland to the European Union in January 1995.

Although the enlargement of the European Union may have weakened the momentum for political and monetary integration within the EU, it has had little impact on the internal market. There was already significant market integration between the EFTA countries even before enlargement. The major EFTA-based companies, such as ASEA, Volvo, or Hoffmann La Roche, have long had a presence across the European market and have, if anything, been more active in extending this to meet the 'challenge' of the internal European market than many companies based in the existing members of the EU.

Future enlargement to include central and east European countries raises more questions, especially from an institutional point of view, but, as the 1995 White Paper on eastern enlargement made clear, compatibility with the European Union's *acquis* and thus SEM will be a condition for the membership of these countries. In other words enlargement may potentially weaken the EU by dilution, but insofar as it consolidates the existing European approach to market integration, and subject to effective implementation and enforcement, it consolidates the SEM.

One final potential source of tension within the EC was external commercial policy. This was particularly marked during the closing stages of the Uruguay round of GATT negotiations in 1993 when differences among the 12 threatened the credibility of the EU and elements of the internal market. In general a common commercial policy in areas covered by the SEM is required, if the SEM is not to be eroded by individual member states 'competing' to conclude trade agreements with third parties. On most SEM issues the European Commission was firmly in control of the negotiations in the GATT even when competence for some issues, such as trade in services, was shared between the European Community and the national governments. The conclusion of the Uruguay Round in December 1993 and its signing in April 1994 removed most of the immediate tensions between the member states over commercial policy and thus any potential threat to the SEM. The November 1994 ruling by the European Court of Justice clarified the competence issue in the areas of services and intellectual property, but did not remove all the potential for clashes over competence between the Commission and Member States. For example, the insistence by some national governments on their right to conclude agreements with third countries in civil aviation could undermine the efforts to complete the SEM in that sector.

The Completion of the Single Market

By the middle of 1995 all but a few of the legislative provisions required for the internal market had been adopted by the Council of Ministers. But little progress was made in getting member state agreement on the remaining measures. In 1994 only two measures were adopted, leaving fourteen of the original 282 provisions in the Cockfield White paper outstanding. The main areas in which agreement was still to be reached in mid 1995 were:

border controls on individuals: This is of symbolic and political importance, but has less effect on the internal market. Agreement has been blocked by Britain, Denmark and Ireland, which are determined to retain controls on individuals indefinitely for reasons of public policy (immigration and asylum policy). The European Commission has argued that Article 8a of the Single European Act (SEA) requires member states to remove all border controls both on commerce - which were removed on 31 December 1992 - and people. The remaining member states of the EC signed the Schengen agreement with the aim of removing border controls. Even here there were, however, delays in the removal of barriers. Originally controls of individuals were to be removed by the end of 1993 but problems concerning the coordination of internal security measures in the signatory countries meant a delay into 1995 and even then France could still not comply fully for 'technical' reasons. Border controls will still remain between the Schengen countries and the three non-participating countries, but the impact on the internal market is limited. Commercial vehicles already cross borders without controls and stopping to show a passport has little impact on commerce.

Company law: Three Directives, the 2nd, 5th and 13th company law directives (CLDs) as well as the European Company Statute (ECS) are still to be agreed. The main problem has been over provision for employee representation in 2nd and 5th CLDs and the ECS. Germany insists there must be provision to ensure its national laws requiring co-determination are not undermined. Germany's concern is that EC legislation will provide German firms with an opportunity of avoiding co-determination requirements. On the other hand, Britain is equally insistent there should be no co-determination introduced in Britain via European law.

Agreement on the company law directives has also been held up because of differences between the continental and British structures of company law. Britain remains committed to a system based on unitary boards, whereas the predominant continental model is a two tier board structure. Compromises concerning requirements for non-executive directors, which would enable the representation of different stakeholders in a company, have failed to make progress, again largely because of British suspicion.

The 13th Company Law Directive was intended to provide a common rule for takeovers in the SEM. Here progress was blocked by the antipathy of many member states to a system based on the British City Take-Over-Panel, and paradoxically the determination of the same Panel to resist any EC legislation for fear of statutory EC provisions in place of self regulation. Thus even though the Commission's proposed 13th Company Law Directive is essentially based on the British model, the City of London and the British government opposed its adoption. In 1995 the German regulators announced that they would also move to adopt the British model. This may precipitate other member states to follow suit.

Lack of agreement on these company law directives will mean that the structure of company law and corporate control will continue to differ within the EU. The absence of common company laws should not be overplayed. Indeed, even if company law were to be established at a European level, national practices and structures would, in all probability, continue. Some change may come about as a result of market factors. Indeed, the situation that exists currently is that different companies using different forms of company law and corporate control are competing with one another within a single market for goods and services. This competition may produce some convergence, but in the meantime takeovers and acquisitions may be harder in some countries, such as Germany, Italy or France, than others. This may result in competitive distortions.

Company taxation: Two important Directives are still to be adopted in the field of company taxation. One would enable the losses incurred in a subsidiary in another member state to be off-set against profits in the home state. The other covered double taxation of royalties, but was withdrawn by the European Commission in November 1994, because of opposition from member states. These are important Directives which will remove some of the remaining bias against cross-border investment which currently exists and was identified in the 1992 Ruding Committee report on company taxation.

Apart from these measures the initial Cockfield White Paper provisions have been more-or-less completed. Until the end of 1993 there was a delay over the adoption of measures concerning trade marks and intellectual property, which was due to a political deadlock over the location of the European trade mark office, which was in turn linked to the decisions on the location of a range of other EC offices, such as the European Pharmaceutical Agency (EPA) (registration of new pharmaceutical products), the European Environmental Agency (EEA) (monitoring of the environment) and last but not least, the European Monetary Institute (EMI) (preparation for stage three of the EMU). The latter was, of course, particularly difficult because the city which succeeded in getting the EMI would be well placed to get the European Central Bank wherever it is established. A 'package deal' covering these agencies was finally reached in late 1993 with the Trade Mark Office going to Spain, the

EEA to Denmark (Copenhagen), the EPA to Britain and the EMI to Germany (Frankfurt).

Implementation and Enforcement

Although it is important to complete the legislative programme, the key to the credibility of the SEM is the effective implementation and enforcement of the legislation that has been adopted. The majority of SEM legislative measures take the form of Council Directives. These must be implemented in national legislation after they have been adopted by the Council of Ministers. The obligation is to satisfy the objectives set out in the Directive, not to reproduce the Council Directive word for word in national legislation. Article 189 (EEC) specifies that 'a Directive shall be binding, as to the result to be achieved, upon each Member State to which it is addressed, but shall leave to the national authorities the choice of form and methods.'

Implementation therefore means the passage of legislation in each member state. The flexibility provided by the use of Directives, as opposed to Regulations in which common provisions apply directly in all member states, is intended to provide scope for different national traditions and laws. This flexibility has never been more important than today because of the concern about undue centralization in Brussels. This has led national governments as well as the European Commission to seek ways of reassuring public opinion that centralization will be limited. On the other hand, there is a strong desire, especially on the part of the European Commission but also business, to ensure that the SEM provisions are implemented properly in each member state. National diversity raises doubts about the even implementation and enforcement of EC law, unless there is an effective means of ensuring that the directives meet the objectives of legislation.

The task of ensuring effective implementation is complicated by the fact that the implementing measures are a succession of texts of different legal hierarchy (i.e. some statute, some government regulations). These implementing measures are issued by different authorities (sometimes national government, sometimes regional or state government and sometimes by regulatory agencies) in different legal systems. As a result it is difficult to compare the effects of the some 2000 pieces of implementing legislation in the nine official languages of the EC.

By the end of 1994 implementation was in the order of 90 per cent. In other words 90 per cent of the total transposition measures required in national legislation had been carried out. Implementation is poor in some areas because national governments have not adopted implementing legislation or passed national legislation incompatible with the objectives set out in Directives. This is the case in such areas as public procurement, insurance, intellectual property and pharmaceuticals. Some of the 282 measures in the Cockfield Paper do not require transposition in national legislation. Implementation rates between member states vary, but in general terms the degree of variation has declined since the early 1990s. The national implementation rates vary between 96 per cent in Denmark, to 80 per cent in Greece and 85 per cent in Germany.[2]

National legislation implementing the Directive must still be enforced. Therefore differences in the rigour of enforcement could undermine the credibility of the SEM as easily as the non-implementation of Directives. For example, if one country fails to ensure that its industries comply with costly minimum standards, it would provide a competitive advantage for the national industry. Furthermore, the concept of mutual recognition would be undermined, since there would be no confidence that products originating in the country concerned met the minimum requirements. In such circumstances, it is likely that national tests would be reintroduced, which would result in a move backwards towards national barriers to trade.

There is diversity in national approaches to enforcement. In some cases the bodies responsible for enforcement are at the national level and in others at the regional level. For example, in metrology (the measurement and calibration of measuring equipment) the responsibility is shared between central and regional bodies in France, Italy and Spain, between central and local government in Britain and Ireland (which have no effective regional government) and in The Netherlands and Denmark testing is carried out by the private sector. There is also a diversity between member states with regards to the resources available for enforcement. To take the metrology case again, Germany has 20 scientists and 100 engineers working on type approval at the federal level as well as strong state level resources. France has 30 engineers, Britain 20 and Spain 20 for type approval and generally weaker engineering and technical backup than Germany. Ireland has only 1 type approval engineer. Similar diversity exists in most areas.

The Sutherland Report

The need to ensure effective implementation and enforcement was recognized at the beginning of 1992. Indeed, the focus of work on the internal market shifted to implementation and enforcement. In March 1992 the European Commission established an independent review committee under the chairmanship of Peter Sutherland, ex Vice President of the EC Commission, to consider what changes should be made to ensure the full implementation and enforcement of the internal market. The Sutherland Report was published in October 1992.

During the period the Sutherland committee was deliberating, the EC was in the midst of the debate on the ratification of the Maastricht Treaty on European Union. This debate highlighted the gap between decision-making in the EC and concerns among the general public about the lack of transparency and accountability of decision-making on the EC level. A number of ideas were put forward to fill this gap. One concerned a greater openness in EC decision-making, the other was the concept of *subsidiarity* i.e. the effort to determine the most effective and efficient level (EC, national or sub-national) at which to regulate and legislate.

When the Sutherland report was published in October 1992 it picked up on this debate. The main recommendations of the Sutherland report were as follows:

- *improved information of the internal market:* This reflected concern about the gap between decision-making in the EC Council of Ministers and those affected by the decisions. Sutherland argued that the legislation had to be accessible to those potentially affected by it if the SEM was to find the broad support and legitimacy it needed to be credible.

- *impact assessment of EC provisions:* This second general recommendation called for better assessments of the impact of EC measures and more use of scientific advice to ensure that Directives, such as those on animal health or the environment, are based as much as possible on objective criteria and not merely the result of political compromise among the 12 member states.

- *a codification of rules:* The Sutherland report recommended that in order to make EC law more accessible for economic actors and legal practitioners alike, there should be a codification of existing EC provisions and the associated rulings of the European Court of Justice. At the time there was only limited consolidation of EC law with the result that it was not easily accessible for non-specialists.

- *greater transparency:* The complexity of the different enforcement bodies meant that it is often difficult to know which agency was responsible for the enforcement of any given directive. This was clearly important for any aggrieved party, especially as many cases of non-application or enforcement of Directives resulted from a lack of knowledge of the provisions rather than a wilful desire not to enforce EC legislation. If it was possible to identify the responsible agency quickly, direct representations may be made and thus time saved.

- *cooperation between national enforcement agencies:* One of the most important recommendations of the report was for closer cooperation between national enforcement agencies. Effective communication between national enforcement agencies was seen as a means of strengthening the weaker agencies, by providing them with access to expertise in the stronger, better resourced agencies. Such communication would also enable the development of best practices in monitoring and enforcement measures. It would also help ensure that diversity of administrative structures did not result in diversity in enforcement. Greater cooperation between the national agencies would also strengthen mutual confidence, a vital commodity if mutual recognition was to work effectively. The report also called for greater cooperation between the EC institutions, primarily the Commission and the national governments.

- *better access to remedies:* With thousands of pieces of EC legislation central monitoring of compliance and enforcement was not feasible. The Sutherland report recommended that the European Commission should ensure that the access to remedies or redress were equivalent in each member state. But the Report also argued that in a decentralized EC system, the national agencies and individuals must also share responsibility for ensuring enforcement. The Sutherland report therefore recommended a number of ways in which this could be done, including: (i) encouraging the use of national courts to seek redress, (ii) ensuring practising lawyers are aware of the possibilities under EC law, and (iii) providing informal advice on options for redress under EC law. At present only a limited number of EC provisions, mostly Regulations as opposed to Directives have *direct effect, i.e.* grant rights to individuals or companies. Such rights can, for example, be used to challenge decisions of the national or EC authorities. National governments are reluctant to see an extension of such rights, because they fear they will be forced into court by disgruntled citizens. In this sense the European countries are not as litigious as, for example, the United States. In some countries it is a novelty for a citizen to take the state to court. In one of its more radical suggestions the Sutherland report suggested that such rights should be extended and more Directives (which normally do not have *direct effect)* should become directly applicable.

By pressing for more extensive use of remedies the Sutherland report was going with the grain of European Court of Justice (ECJ) decisions. In one notable case, *Francovich v Italian Government,* the ECJ suggested that individuals may, in certain circumstances, be able to claim damages from a national government if the latter fails to implement properly an EC Directive. The ECJ laid down three conditions for claiming such damages:

i.   the *result* prescribed by the directive should confer rights to private individuals;

ii.   the nature of those rights should be ascertainable from the provisions of the directive; and

iii.   there should be a causal link between the failure of the State to fulfil its obligation and the damage sustained by the persons adversely affected.

This discussion of compliance and enforcement has illustrated some of the central issues in compliance and enforcement. These are:

-    how can the desire to contain the growth of centralized power that is associated with the concept of 'subsidiarity' be reconciled with the vital need to ensure that EC directives are enforced in an equivalent fashion in each region and member state of the EC?

-    does an effective system of enforcement and compliance require more extensive rights of access to remedies under EC law for individuals and companies, and if so how can this be reconciled with the desire of national governments not accustomed to being taken to court by their citizenry to limit direct effect?

The Sutherland report stressed that the desire to protect diversity must not result in different rules for different member states which would undermine the credibility of the internal market. On the second issue the Sutherland report appears to come down in favour of the EC evolving in such a fashion as to grant more rights for individuals and companies.

The Council and Commission responses

In response to these issues the national governments adopted a Council Resolution on 10 November 1992. This called for greater transparency in drafting new EC proposals and thus effectively endorsed the first of the Sutherland proposals. In order to help ensure effective implementation it called for the Commission to produce an annual report on the SEM and to come forward with more detailed recommendations on strengthening cooperation between national authorities. The Council also called for a general assessment of the effectiveness of the SEM by 1996.[3] On balance this represents an endorsement of more effective enforcement, but with a bias towards 'top-down' action by the national authorities.

At the same time efforts were under way on the subsidiarity issue. At the Edinburgh European Council meeting in December 1992 the Council of Ministers produced broad guidelines on subsidiarity and asked the Commission to prepare a comprehensive paper on the issue for the December 1993 European Council in Belgium. Each national government subsequently provided lists of amendments to existing EC legislation which the Commission considered in its document. The concern of the national governments was to satisfy local discontent about the intrusiveness of EC regulation by showing that the trend towards more and more EC level action was not irreversible. On the other hand, there is a concern among companies that decentralization should not result in divergent implementation and enforcement. The outcome is unlikely to reverse any important legislation or to undermine the ability of the Commission to fulfil its duty of acting as guardian of the treaties. The focus will be on politically sensitive issues and technical reviews of existing provisions, such as basing bathing water quality standards on more scientific criteria than the more politically determined criteria in the current directive. The national governments have shown no taste for enhancing access for individuals by extending direct effect to more directives.

The European Commission has also responded to the proposals.[4] In December 1992 it established an Advisory Committee for Coordination in Internal Market Field consisting of the member states and drawing on experts when required, to oversee the management of the SEM. This is intended to provide a forum for coordinating the efforts of the Commission and the Member States. The Advisory Committee is also intended to provide the means of promoting collaboration between the national enforcement agencies.

The Commission also produced ideas for a strategic programme on the internal market aimed at reinforcing its effectiveness and imparting it with renewed momentum.[5] The working paper, produced by the Commission for consultation with national governments and other interest groups, was part of a wider effort to revitalise the process of European integration after the trials of the Maastricht ratification process[6] The Commission accepted that it should monitor the implementing legislation in the member states, and proposed that this be done by first enhancing transparency through the publication of the texts of all implementing legislation. Because of the multiplicity of texts the Commission suggested that 'when the work of harmonization has been completed in a particular area and the situation regarding application by the Member States is convergent, directives could be consolidated in the form of a regulation.'[7] In other words the Commission assumes that the divergent national laws will ultimately converge at which point it would be possible to have one text. Consolidation would simplify matters because there would no longer be questions concerning whether national implementing measures satisfy the EC objectives. Although the Commission is not suggesting this should happen quickly, it would arguably mean a move towards a more centralized approach. The Commission document also stresses the role of the ECJ in ensuring implementation. After the ratification of the Maastricht Treaty the ECJ is able to fine Member States which do not comply with the judgements of the court on, for example, the implementation of an SEM directive. [8]

When it comes to enforcing the SEM provisions the Commission has limited powers. In certain areas concerning health, it has specific obligations to ensure public health provisions are met. The Commission also has a direct role in competition policy, subject to review by the ECJ, to enforce treaty provisions such as Articles 85 and 86 (EEC) (anti-cartel) and Arts 90-93 (EEC) (control of state subsidies). Outside these areas, it is the national administrations which usually carry out inspections and take action against infringements of Community law. In an effort to promote a common interpretation of the rules the Commission strategy paper suggested:

-    providing the national authorities with a common consolidated interpretation, (in line with the codification proposed by Sutherland). In December 1993 consolidated texts of the Directives on public procurement, medical diplomas and foodstuffs were agreed by the Council. Work is ongoing in a number of other areas;

-    organizing a network of information exchanges between national authorities along the lines of existing networks, such as those for customs and indirect taxation. Exchanges of national officials is taking place, but the take-up in terms of secondment to other national enforcement bodies is not as great as the Commission had expected, due to the reluctance of national governments to contribute their half of funding for EU schemes;

-    helping to identify the relevant national control authorities. The June 1994 Internal Market Council adopted a resolution on administrative cooperation and agreed on points of contact for public purchasing, telecommunications, taxation and transport. Further progress was made during 1995 with work in other sectors, but gaps still remain;

-    establishing audits of national control systems to provide a better evaluation of the problems and identify ways in which approximation of the different national control systems can be brought about.

With regard to access to remedies the Commission picked up the Sutherland Report's recommendation of improving knowledge of possible remedies available under EC law among national lawyers. The European Commission has subsequently made studies of the difficulties and was set to make proposals by the end of 1995, including recommendations that all practising lawyers have some training in EC law. It also agreed with Sutherland on the case for following up on the ECJ's decision in the Francovich case. In November 1993 the Commission produced a consultative Green Paper on access to remedies for consumers, which was discussed at a public hearing in December 1994.[9] This may help maintain the momentum behind the debate on wider remedies but national governments are likely to continue to resist any extension of direct effect.

In the short to medium term the measures needed to ensure effective implementation and enforcement as well as promote confidence in the functioning of the principle of mutual recognition are mostly procedural. As such they have not provoked much opposition from the national governments and have provoked less public debate than the adoption of the internal market Directives or other matters concerning Europe, such as the 1996 intergovernmental conference. But for the effectiveness of the SEM a sustained commitment to the kind of nitty-gritty issues of enforcement and administrative cooperation is essential. As the Sutherland report stressed, the active engagement of those affected by SEM provisions, namely the companies and customers, is a further condition for success. If there is slippage in implementation in some countries or some sectors, it will undermine the credibility of the SEM and thus the concept of mutual recognition. As the June 1994 resolution suggests, the Council has, to date, indicated that it is serious about carrying out the follow through measures required to make the SEM effective. But it is still too early to say whether the sustained effort needed will be forthcoming.

Preventing new obstacles

The Commission is proposing a wider application of Directive 83/198/EEC to cover all trade in goods and services. This, so-called information directive requires national authorities to inform the European Commission and thus the other member states, of any new regulation or national law. The directive was initially used in the field of national technical regulations. Since 1983 it has operated by requiring national authorities to notify the European Commission of any plans to introduce new technical regulations. The Commission informs the other member states, which then have time to consider whether there is a case for new EC regulation to cover the area. During this standstill period no national measures may be adopted. This has effectively established a filter for national technical regulations which might undermine future EC technical provisions.

In an adaptation of this idea, the Commission is suggesting that national authorities should notify the EC whenever they refuse to recognize the rules of other member states. As mutual recognition is central to the SEM, this would provide a means of identifying all instances when mutual recognition does not work and provide an opportunity for action to be taken. National governments opposed this during 1994, arguing that it was tantamount to asking transgressors to confess in public, but the Commission continued to press national governments to include mutual recognition clauses in draft legislation notified under 83/189/EEC and thus identify when they do not offer mutual recognition. In March 1994 the Council adopted a Directive (94/10/EC) strengthening 83/189/EEC by, for example, extending the definition of a technical regulation to include tax incentives and to extend the standstill period to 18 months.

Outlook for the Internal Market

The completion of 95 per cent of the legislation in the SEM programme within the deadline is a significant achievement for the EC, but it does not mean that a genuine single market has been established. For some years to come there will continue to be important local market characteristics. This will mean that effective market access to national or sub-national markets, could still require investment in a local presence. This is especially the case in the services sectors and other industries, such as those affected by public procurement, which formed the focus of the EU's SEM programme.

The momentum behind integration in the EU was arrested by the economic recession, the instability in the EMS and the troubled process of ratifying the Maastricht Treaty on European Union. But now that the treaty is ratified and following the Belgian Presidency's attempt to relaunch common efforts, some of the political dynamism has returned. This combined with the economic recovery towards the end of 1993 and during 1994 and 1995 has given the EU some forward momentum, which helps the SEM. But the credibility of the SEM will ultimately depend on the work behind the scenes on the implementation and enforcement of the legislation in each member state. This will take time and commitment from governments, regulatory agencies and economic operators. Work has begun on strengthening cooperation and enforcement mechanisms, but there is still a danger that backsliding by some member states could damage the credibility of mutual recognition and thus the SEM as a whole. There is also still a delicate balance to be achieved between maintaining the diversity sought by politicians and public opinion frightened by the ambition of the Maastricht agreement, and the need for effective EU level enforcement. On balance, the internal market seems likely to retain its credibility despite the difficulties of the last three years.

Notes

1   Stephen Woolcock is a Research Fellow at the London School of Economic's Centre for Research on the United States. This article is based on work he carried out while with the European Programme of the Royal Institute of International Affairs, which was funded by the Economic and Social Research Council under its Single European Market Initiative.

2   See Commission of the European Communities *The Single European Market in 1994* Report from the Commission to the Council and European Parliament, COM (95) 238 Final 15 June 1995.

3   Sectoral studies are now being carried out and findings will begin to emerge in early 1996.

4   For the initial response see European Commission Communication from the Commission to the Council and European Parliament on *The operation of the Community's Internal Market After 1992 Follow-up to the Sutherland Report* SEC(92) 2277 final 2 December 1992.

5   Commission of the European Communities *Reinforcing the effectiveness of the internal market* a working document of the Commission on a strategic programme on the internal market. COM (93) 256 final, 2 June 1993.

6   See European Commission *Making the most of the internal market* 22 December 1993. COM(93)632 final.

7   Commission of the European Community *Making the most of the internal market op.cit.*

8   In an associated move the European Commission has proposed that future SEM Directives will include a clause providing for financial penalties for non-implementation.

9   Commission of the European Communities *Green Paper on Access to Justice for Consumers* COM(93)576 16 November 1993.

10 The Free Movement of Goods and Services

CHRISTOPHER THOMAS

Introduction

The Treaty of Rome as concluded in 1957 contained a number of specific provisions designed to facilitate the free movement of goods and services between the Member States. But only in the Spaak Report[1] are the implications of those provisions made absolutely clear. Spaak called for 'la fusion des marchés.' The Community was not intended to secure free trade between national markets, but the merger of those markets into a single, common, market.

The thinking behind the common market was dominated by concern for the free movement of goods. This was to be secured by a variety of means, combining the dismantlement of the existing protection of the national economies of the Community with the legislative elimination of those barriers to trade which resulted merely from differences between the laws and practices of the Member States. But neither the Spaak Report nor the Treaty of Rome paid particular attention to the free movement of services. This was associated with the free movement of workers, and the freedom of the self-employed and corporations to establish themselves in other Member States. Rather than viewing the matter as the corollary of the free movement of goods, with its many intricate treaty provisions, services were dealt with in a separate and far less detailed way.

In due course, the Single European Act introduced the now famous declaration of intent contained in Article 7a of the EC Treaty, which calls for the establishment of an internal market which shall comprise an area without internal frontiers in which the free movement of goods, persons, services and capital is ensured in accordance with the provisions of this Treaty.

The Establishment of the Common Market in Goods

The first task of the Rome Treaty was to establish a timetable for the elimination of customs duties and all charges having equivalent effect between the original six Member States of the Community. This was done in Articles 12 to 17 of the Treaty, which also prohibited the introduction of new duties or equivalent charges - and increasing existing ones - during the period of reduction.

In accordance with the Spaak Report's rejection of the free trade area model, Article 9 provided that the rules on customs duties (and quantitative restrictions) were not limited to goods produced within the Community. Those from outside the common market were to be treated in exactly the same way, once they had been released from customs after payment of any duties owing under the Common Customs Tariff.

With respect to customs duties as such, all went according to plan. Export duties were removed by 1 January 1962, and duties on imports were eliminated ahead of the twelve year target, on 1 July 1968. The Court of Justice made a critical contribution to the process in 1963 with its *Van Gend en Loos* judgement in which it was held not only that the prohibition of increases in duties applied to the reclassification of a product so that it fell into a category attracting a higher duty, but also that individual importers might rely on the Treaty in their own national courts.[2] This latter development, the doctrine of direct effect, is nowhere mentioned in the text of the Treaty and is an early example of the Court's commitment to the practical realization of the free movement ambitions of the Community.

The pattern followed that the successive enlargements of the Community, were more or less the same, though the periods for adjustment were shorter. In the most recent enlargement, in 1995, there were no transitional periods for the elimination of customs duties.

In order to avoid evasion of the rules on customs duties the Rome Treaty provided for the elimination of 'charges having an equivalent effect to customs duties' in accordance with the same timetable as for customs duties proper. This expression was progressively defined in two judgements of the Court of Justice. In the *Gingerbread* case it established the essential principle that the purpose of the charge is irrelevant to its classification.[3] In that case the protective effect of the charge was clear, and strongly emphasized by the Court. But a protective effect is only possible if there is a domestic industry to be protected. In the subsequent *Diamantarbeiders* case, therefore, Belgium argued that since it had no domestic diamond extraction industry, a charge imposed on imported unworked diamonds to support a fund providing social benefits for workers in the domestic diamond finishing industry could not be a charge having equivalent effect. Indeed the domestic industry could only be disadvantaged by such a charge.[4]

In these circumstances the Court was led to declare that the purpose of the customs duties provisions of the Rome Treaty was not merely to remove the protective effect of import duties, but to secure the free movement of goods across frontiers. It set out a revised definition of a charge having equivalent effect:

> 'any pecuniary charge, however small and what-ever its designation and mode of application, which is imposed unilaterally on domestic or foreign goods by reason of the fact that they cross a frontier, and which is not a customs duty in the strict sense ... even if it is not imposed for the benefit of the State, is not discriminatory or protective in effect or if the product on which the charge is imposed is not in competition with any domestic product.'

Although most charges will in fact be imposed for protectionist reasons, the *Diamantarbeiders* case is important in that it established the distinction between the free movement of goods and the elimination of protectionism.

The formula adopted by the Court does not prevent fees being demanded for services rendered. This permits the provision of, for example, warehousing facilities, in return for payment. But it does not allow charges to be imposed for measures of public benefit, such as health inspections.

The second principal task to be carried out was the progressive elimination of quantitative restrictions on imports and exports (quotas). The Treaty established a timetable very similar to that for customs duties. The original Six agreed to a standstill on existing quotas and phased dismantling of import quotas (to be completed by 1 January 1970) and of export quotas (by 1 January 1962). All this was accomplished without substantial difficulty. The more general process of quota elimination in Europe enabled their immediate prohibition on the accession of new Member States, and now the absolute prohibition contained in Article 30 applies throughout the Community.

The third, and perhaps most difficult, task undertaken by the Rome Treaty concerned market regulation. The access of goods to a market depends not only on the ability of those goods to cross any international frontiers surrounding the market without restriction or taxation, but on the rules and regulations set down by the local public authorities to regulate that market. Every modern state intervenes in the market to protect its citizens from dangerous products or from morally outrageous activities, or to defend the cultural integrity of its society, or for a host of other reasons. Such intervention can also be used to exclude imported goods. Whether or not this is the intention, it is often the effect.

To deal with this problem, and the related one of regulations which restrict the export of goods so as to retain essential raw materials for domestic downstream industry, the Rome Treaty provided for both judicial and legislative action. Article 30 reads as follows:

> 'Quantitative restrictions on imports and all measures having equivalent effect shall, without prejudice to the following provisions, be prohibited between Member States.'

Article 34(1) provides:

> 'Quantitative restrictions on exports, and all measures having equivalent effect shall be prohibited between Member States.'

These prohibitions entered into force in relation to imports and exports between the original six on 1 January 1970 and 1 January 1962 respectively. A shorter transitional period was set for the first enlargement of the Community, and in the later enlargements there were no transitional periods at all.

In *Ianelli* and *Pigs Marketing* the Court held Articles 30 and 34 to have direct effect.[5] Measures caught by these prohibitions will prima facie, therefore, be struck down by national courts. But in order to protect legitimate state intervention a derogation is provided by Article 36:

> 'The provisions of Articles 30 to 34 shall not preclude prohibitions or restrictions on imports, exports or goods in transit justified on grounds of public morality, public policy or public security; the protection of health and life of humans, animals or plants; the protection of national treasures possessing artistic, historic or archaeological value; or the protection of

industrial or commercial property. Such prohibitions or restrictions shall not, however, constitute a means of arbitrary discrimination or a disguised restriction on trade between Member States.'

Article 36 does not exclude the matters referred to from the scope of the Rome Treaty, as for example Article XX of the GATT excludes a similar list of measures from that treaty. It merely provides temporary legitimation of measures otherwise unlawful under Article 30 or 34. The Rome Treaty intended that obstacles to free movement resulting from measures falling within Article 36 would be removed by harmonizing legislation under Article 100:

'The Council shall, acting unanimously on a proposal from the Commission, issue directives for the approximation of such provisions laid down by law regulation or administrative action in Member States as directly affect the establishment or functioning of the common market.'

The adoption of harmonizing legislation under Article 100 (or 100a) will normally 'pre-empt' Member State competence in the field governed by the Community legislation. As explained by the Court in its *Ratti* judgement, if a Member State then acts in such a way as to be caught by Article 30 or 34, then it cannot rely on Article 36 at all and is in violation of Community law.[6] The sole exception is where the Community legislation makes clear that it does not seek to establish an exhaustive set of rules in the area, as is the case, for example, with 'minimum standards' directives.

As will have been observed, the Treaty does no more than establish the principles: the details of which measures of market regulation will have to be removed, so as to ensure free movement, are not specified. Under Article 33(7) the Commission was granted a power to issue directives concerning the procedure and timetable for the abolition of measures of equivalent effect during the transitional period. It used this power, and continues to use its role in bringing infringement actions against Member States, to direct the debate as to what exactly constitutes a measure of equivalent effect. A few days before the end of the transitional period, the Commission issued Directive 70/50,[7] setting out a list of measures to be abolished. The Commission's analysis in that Directive has been confirmed by the Court of Justice in a number of aspects.

As the Commission claimed, not only are the laws of a Member State covered by Article 30, but also its administrative practices and any incitations to private individuals to act in a particular way. The Court has also made clear that the measures of all state authorities are included, be they national, regional or local. Article 30 even extends to certain professional bodies with statutory powers and private corporations financed by the state and run by the appointees of the state.

Measures which discriminate overtly against imports are prohibited, as well as more subtle forms of protectionism. For example, the UK was held to have breached Article 30 by requiring that all goods sold at retail level must bear an indication of their origin, thus enabling consumers to distinguish between goods on the basis of national origin alone.

But the Court has also departed from the original views of the Commission. The preamble to Directive 70/50 states that:

> 'the formalities to which imports are subject do not as a general rule have an effect equivalent to that of quantitative restrictions.'

This has not been accepted by the Court. In *Donckerwolcke* it held to be unlawful the establishment of a system by which France monitored imports of third country origin by requiring all goods crossing French frontiers to be accompanied with a request for an import licence (stating the origin of the goods), even though the licence was automatically granted.[8]

This ruling was the natural result of the Court's judgement in *Procureur du Roi v. Dassonville*.[9] This case concerned a prosecution for the irregular sale in Belgium of Scotch whisky imported from France. The Belgian law relating to designations of origin required that goods sold under recognized designations, such as 'Scotch Whisky,' had to be accompanied by a declaration from the customs authorities of the alleged country of origin that the product did indeed originate there. The UK authorities were quite prepared to make such a declaration, but unfortunately the cooperation of the UK producer or the French importer was required to identify the goods sold in Belgium as the ones exported from the UK. Since the producer had awarded an exclusive distribution contract to an undertaking in Belgium, and could exert pressure on its distributor in France, there was no realistic prospect of such cooperation being forthcoming.

The Belgian law did not clearly discriminate in favour of national production, nor did it in itself prevent the import of goods. But the clear result was that the Scotch whisky of this producer would not be imported from other EC countries into Belgium, thereby isolating the Belgian market from intra-brand competition. The Court responded with a very broad statement of principle:

> 'All trading rules enacted by Member States which are capable of hindering, directly or indirectly, actually or potentially, intra-Community trade are to be considered as measures having an effect equivalent to quantitative restrictions.'

In the present case, trade was restricted only indirectly - the measure created a situation in which a private undertaking was able to prevent importation into Belgium. But this was enough: the Belgian law was found to be contrary to Article 30.

The real importance of the decision is that the Court went beyond the specific case-by-case approach adopted (of necessity) by the Commission in Directive 70/50. From 1974 Community law had a comprehensive test to determine whether measures were caught by Article 30. The free movement of goods could now realistically be advanced by private litigation in national courts.

It will be recalled that 'measures of equivalent effect' to export quotas were also prohibited by the Rome Treaty. States usually wish to encourage exports rather than restrict them. For this reason, the prohibition of measures of equivalent effect to export quotas has always been fairly uncontroversial. In the *Groenveld* case the Court held that the prohibition concerned:

> 'national measures which have as their specific object or effect the restriction of patterns of exports and thereby the establishment of a difference in treatment between the domestic trade of a Member State and its export trade in such a way as to provide a particular advantage for national production or for the domestic market of the State in question at the expense of the production or the trade of other Member States.'[10]

This definition, which expressly requires discrimination against exports to be shown, is radically different from that relating to imports given in the *Dassonville* case, an indication perhaps that the Court shares the general lack of concern over export restrictions.

As mentioned above, the Treaty contains a temporary derogation from Articles 30 and 34. Article 36 can be invoked by a Member State to save measures of equivalent effect to import or export quotas, even if they treat imports or exports differently from domestic trade. But the Member States are not given carte blanche to restrict trade in the areas specified in Article 36. The national measure must be 'justified' by the grounds relied upon.

The measure must serve to achieve some particular objective falling within one of the grounds exhaustively listed in Article 36. Member States will normally have no difficulty in 'justifying' their measures in this sense: only if they are clearly unrelated to any of the grounds specified will problems arise. The measure must also be proportionate, in two ways. It must not be more restrictive than is required to achieve its objective (put another way, the objective must not be realizable by less restrictive means). Furthermore, the restriction on trade caused must not be out of all proportion to the objective pursued.

The measure must not constitute a 'means of arbitrary discrimination'. Mere differential treatment is not a disqualifying factor. Instead, the phrase is meant to indicate that a Member State may not invoke the grounds of Article 36 in relation to imports or exports if it does not apply the same reasoning to its domestic products or trade. It is arbitrary discrimination to ban a dangerous import for safety reasons, while allowing similar domestic products to be sold. Likewise, a Member State cannot restrict imports from another Member State if it does not treat similar imports from all Member States in the same way. Of course, the goods permitted to be sold may be different from the restricted goods. In this case differential treatment is justified and does not amount to arbitrary discrimination.

The measure must also not constitute a 'disguised restriction on trade between Member States.' This is intended to prevent Member States from invoking Article 36 when their actual intention is to restrict imports.

Article 36 was intended to provide only temporary respite: the Treaty assumed that legislation at Community level would gradually eliminate recourse to Article 36. But the Community's early attempts at harmonization were limited. Article 100 restricted the legislative effort to directives, which meant that the common market was dependent on the differential rates of adoption of national implementing measures. The direct effect of some directives is of course useful to those individuals prepared to go to court, but in practice the need for certainty tends to mean that national administrations and private businesses will rely on the national law as it stands.

The directives themselves could only be adopted by unanimity. Given the Commission's policy of taking particular sectors and trying to establish detailed and exhaustive rules, the unanimity requirement meant that progress was slow. Proposals could gather dust for decades.

The fourth major objective of the Rome Treaty was to eliminate discriminatory taxation of goods. A simple way to increase the price of imported products is to tax them more heavily than domestic ones. To prevent this, Article 95 of the Treaty of Rome provided that:

> 'No Member State shall impose, directly or indirectly, on the products of other Member States any internal taxation of any kind in excess of that imposed directly or indirectly on similar domestic products.'

> 'Furthermore, no Member State shall impose on the products of other Member States any internal taxation of such a nature as to afford indirect protection to other products.'

Article 95 is not a well drafted provision. It does not deal expressly either with discrimination against products manufactured outside the Community but in free circulation within it, nor with discrimination against products intended for export. In order to secure the general objectives of the Treaty, the Court of Justice therefore intervened with its *Co-Frutta* and *Statens Kontrol* judgements to extend the protection of Article 95 to such products.[11]

It will be noted that the prohibition relates only to discrimination. But obstacles to the free movement of goods are also caused by non-discriminatory measures. Such obstacles were intended to be removed by Article 99, which provides for harmonization of internal taxation, on the basis of unanimity. Unanimity on a subject as close to the heart of state power as taxation has proved very difficult to achieve, and the Court has reacted.

Without rejecting as such the test of discrimination, the Court has interpreted it in very novel ways. Article 95 was to a large extent based on the text of Article III of the GATT, but the rules now applied within the Community would be unthinkable in the context of ordinary international trade.

The Court has not limited Article 95 to overtly discriminatory taxation laws, or even to those which discriminate in fact if not in appearance. Under the Court's *Schul I and II*[12] jurisprudence, it is 'discriminatory' to impose VAT without subtracting VAT paid in the exporting country from both the assessment base (the price of the good) and the final amount calculated to be due. Double taxation, at least in relation to VAT, is therefore illegal.

The fifth task of the Treaty regarding the free movement of goods concerned 'commercial monopolies.' States may wish to create monopolies in the import or distribution of certain goods for a number of reasons. Putting such activities under the control of a single entity can enable better control of public health measures, or prevent tax evasion. It can also be used as a device to favour national production. Particularly where an exclusive right to import is granted to the national manufacturer, such monopolies can operate as a very effective form of protection indeed. For this reason, Article 37(1) of the Rome Treaty provided:

> 'Member States shall progressively adjust any state monopolies of a commercial character so as to ensure that when the transitional period has ended no discrimination regarding the conditions under which goods are procured and marketed exists between nationals of Member States.'

> 'The provisions of this Article shall apply to any body through which a Member State, in law or in fact, either directly or indirectly supervises, determines or appreciably influences imports or exports between Member States. These provisions shall apply likewise to monopolies delegated by the State to others.'

The extent of the obligation to adjust commercial monopolies is not immediately clear from the text. The Court of Justice has therefore acted to clarify matters. According to the Court, Article 37 compels Member States to abolish exclusive rights to import and to market imported goods. But they may maintain monopolies of production and of the marketing of domestic goods.

The Establishment of the Common Market in Services

The free movement of services was intended to be achieved by Article 59 of the Treaty of Rome:

> 'Within the framework of the provisions set out below, restrictions on freedom to provide services within the Community shall be progressively abolished during the transitional period in respect of nationals of Member States who are established in a State of the Community other than that of the person for whom the services are intended.'

'The Council may, acting by a qualified majority on a proposal from the Commission, extend the provisions of the Chapter to nationals of a third country who provide services and who are established within the Community.'

Although the benefits of this provision were limited to nationals of the Member States (subject to the intervention of the Council), those from outside could also benefit by creating a company under the laws of one of the Member States and providing services through that vehicle. Services themselves were defined by Article 60:

'Services shall be considered to be 'services' within the meaning of this Treaty where they are normally provided for remuneration, in so far as they are not governed by the provisions relating to freedom of movement for goods, capital and persons.

'Services' shall in particular include:

(a) activities of an industrial character;
(b) activities of a commercial character;
(c) activities of craftsmen;
(d) activities of the professions.

Without prejudice to the provisions of the Chapter relating to the right of establishment, the person providing a service may, in order to do so, temporarily pursue his activity in the State where the service is provided, under the same conditions as are imposed by that State on its own nationals.'

Inspired by the last paragraph of Article 60 the Council adopted Directive 73/148[13] guaranteeing individual citizens of the Member States the right to enter and stay in other Member States in order both to provide and to receive services. This right is subject to considerations of public policy, public security and public health, as set out in Directive 64/221.[14]

The Court of Justice approved the granting of rights to beneficiaries of services as well as to service providers in its *Cowan* judgement.[15] It also held that other transfrontier situations are included, such as that in which both the provider and the recipient remain in their own countries and the service in some way flows between the two. This was decided in the *Bond van Adverteerders* case, concerning the transmission of commercial television signals.[16]

In *Van Binsbergen* the Court held Article 59 to have direct effect.[17] This meant that even in the absence of much further legislation by the Council, the process of establishing the common market in services could go ahead by judicial action. Measures which discriminated in form or in effect against the providers or recipients of services protected by Article 59 would now be challenged in court. But national courts would also hear arguments that the measures were justified under Article 56 by reasons of public policy, public security or public health.

The Single Market Agenda

The common market programme as set out above was very ambitious and, in relation to other exercises in economic integration, very successful. But by the critical standard of the fusion of national markets into one, it was a failure. Even the considerable intervention of the Court of Justice could not make up for the inactivity of the Council. Without an intensification of legislative activity by the Community it was clear that the common market would not become a reality. That legislation was unlikely to be forthcoming, for two reasons. Firstly, the veto power reserved for each Member State in Article 100 meant that compromises between the national governments were very difficult to accomplish. Secondly, the detail in which the Commission sought to regulate economic life was resisted as such, particularly given the fact that the Community legislative process had no significant democratic element.

Fundamental dissatisfaction with the existing arrangements for the creation of the common market was first shown by the Court of Justice. In February 1979 it gave judgement under Article 30 in the *Cassis de Dijon* case. This concerned a German spirits importer, Rewe-Zentral AG, which wanted to sell in Germany Cassis de Dijon imported from France.[18] The Cassis contained 15 to 20 per cent alcohol, but the German Branntweinmonopolgesetz provided for a minimum alcohol content of 25 per cent. The Commission had submitted a proposal for harmonizing legislation in 1976, but nothing had so far come of it. In the meanwhile, the difference between the applicable French and German legislation meant that spirits lawfully produced and marketed in France could not be sold in Germany. It was the classic case of the failure of the Community legislative process holding up the establishment of the common market.

Instead of merely regretting the lethargy of the Community legislature the Court itself made an essentially legislative choice. It held first that:

> 'Obstacles to movement within the Community resulting from disparities between national laws relating to the marketing of the products concerned must be accepted in so far as those provisions may be recognized as being necessary in order to satisfy mandatory requirements relating in particular to the effectiveness of fiscal supervision, the protection of public health, the fairness of commercial transactions and the defence of the consumer.'

The Court then rejected the German argument that its law prevented consumers from being misled as to alcohol content, on the basis that this objective could be achieved by the simple fixing of an information label on the bottle. It concluded that:

> 'There is therefore no valid reason why, provided that they have been lawfully produced and marketed in one of the Member States, alcoholic beverages should not be introduced into any other Member State; the sale of such products may not be subject to a legal prohibition on the marketing of beverages with an alcohol content lower than the limit set by the national rules.'

The key point is that the Court rejected the test of discrimination. Now all national measures in some way restricting the sale of goods would have to satisfy a test of proportionality. Inherent in that test was the presumption that the rules applied by one Member State should be accepted by the others as equivalent to their own.

The significance of the judgement can be seen if the alternative legislative solution is considered. The Council would have had to have decided on the level of alcohol content at which spirits could be sold. This might have been higher or lower than the French level. But by establishing the principle of mutual recognition, the Court decided that at least in relation to French Cassis, the minimum level in the Community would not be higher than 15 per cent. This was of course subject to any particular public interest arguments that other Member States might make, but the fact remained that any higher limits were prima facie unlawful. No further Community legislation was required to establish the common market in Cassis.

After the Court, the next institution to react was the Commission. In June 1985 it presented a White Paper, 'Completing the Internal Market,' to the European Council.[19] In this it proposed a wide-ranging programme of legislation designed to make up for the inactivity of the past. But unlike its previous view, according to which the ultimate goal of legislation was harmonization, the Commission was much more selective.

The Commission proposed leaving some matters to be determined entirely by the mutual recognition doctrine of the Court. National courts would be expected to use Article 30 in order to establish free movement throughout the Community. Other matters would have to be harmonized, but this would be kept to a minimum: Community legislation would do no more than lay down essential health and safety requirements. Apart from this, the Community would delegate the fixing of standards to private organizations such as CEN, CENELEC and ETSI.[20]

This 'new approach' would have two advantages. It would enable the non-political aspects of the creation of common rules to by-pass the cumbersome legislative process of the Community, and it would reduce the intrusiveness of Community legislation. It was therefore a considerable advance in both practical and presentational terms.

The Member States made possible the legislative programme of the Commission by adopting in 1986 the Single European Act amending the Rome Treaty. A new Article 100a was introduced into the Treaty. As amended by the Treaty on European Union, paragraphs 1 and 2 of that article provide that:

1. By way of derogation from Article 100 and save where otherwise provided in this Treaty, the following provisions shall apply for the achievement of the objectives set out in Article 7a. The Council shall, acting in accordance with procedure referred to in Article 189b and after consulting the Economic and the Social Committee, adopt the measures for the approximation of the provisions laid down by law, regulation or administrative action in Member States which have as their object the establishment and functioning of the internal market.

2. Paragraph 1 shall not apply to fiscal provisions, to those relating to the free movement of persons nor to those relating to the rights and interests of employed persons.

The critical change made was, of course, the introduction of qualified majority voting (now in the form of the co-decision procedure, set out at Article

189b). Legislation facilitating the free movement of goods could now only be blocked by a group of at least three Member States. The negotiations in the Council became more fluid and less likely to reach stalemate. In addition, the Council could now issue regulations as well as merely directives. But tax harmonization was excluded from these provisions and continued to be governed by the unanimity rules of Article 99.

The Achievement of the Single Market

Given the nature of the Single Market as the realization of the original concept of the common market, it is not surprising that a significant element in its achievement was simply the continued application of the existing case law of the Court of Justice. The *Cassis de Dijon* jurisprudence was developed as the Court recognized other 'mandatory requirements' beyond those referred to in the original judgement. Significantly, the Court added such matters as social protection and the environment. The jurisprudence was also extended to services. In *Säger* the Court made clear that a restriction of the free movement of services, even if the result of an indistinctly applicable measure, is caught by the prohibition of Article 59 unless justified by a mandatory requirement.[21] It ruled in *Commission v. Germany* that when granting authority to provide a regulated service a Member State may not require satisfaction of conditions already met in the State in which the undertaking is established and must take account of supervision and verifications carried out in that State.[22]

In 1983 the Council had adopted a Directive setting up a procedure for the exchange of information between Member States on proposed national technical regulations and standards. The Directive was extended and refined twice, in 1988 and 1994.[23] It now applies to all industrially manufactured and agricultural products and requires Member States to notify new national norms to the others and to the Commission, and on request to delay application for six months (or twelve if Community legislation is proposed). This enables consultation to take place in order to eliminate any obstacles to free movement before they arise.

The procedure has proved very successful. It is premised on the fact that many technical barriers are not actually intended to restrict trade: this is merely a by-product of their being adopted in ignorance of the practice or plans of other states.

In May 1985 the Council adopted a Resolution on future practice in relation to technical standards.[24] It mirrored the Commission's proposals in the White Paper. The 'new approach' is the basis of the Community's '1992' legislative programme and has been successfully applied in numerous cases.

A recent example is the Council's Directive intended to facilitate the free movement of satellite earth station equipment. Directive 93/97[25] recites that the Council has decided only to legislate in relation to the essential requirements concerning satellite earth station equipment: the rest can be left to the application of Article 30 of the EC Treaty. The Directive sets out a number of requirements which must be met by such equipment, including for example the avoidance of harmful interference between space-based and terrestrial communications systems and other technical systems. It compels Member States to permit the marketing of equipment satisfying these requirements. CEN, CENELEC and ETSI are expected to draw up voluntary European standards implementing the requirements imposed by the Directive, and national standards organizations (such as the BSI in the UK or ELOT in Greece) to draw up national standards implementing the European ones. Member States must presume equipment manufactured in accordance with such national standards to be compatible with the requirements of the Directive.

The application of the Directive is assisted by procedures for the fixing of a 'CE' mark to the equipment. The mark indicates that the equipment has been approved by a national control authority as conforming to the national standard. Finally, should specific regulation be required, the Commission is delegated authority to adopt such measures under the regulatory committee procedure.

The Community is therefore now applying a very subtle blend of harmonization and mutual recognition in legislation and Article 30 in the courts.

In accordance with Article 7a of the EC Treaty the Council has acted to establish an 'area without internal frontiers.' Perhaps the most significant aspect of this is the abolition of fiscal controls on the frontiers between Member States. The Member States used to impose VAT and excise duties on all imports as they crossed the frontier and to repay it on exports as they left. This required the goods involved to be accompanied by a host of customs documents, which would be checked at the frontier where the taxes would be imposed or reimbursed.

In 1977 a regime of 'internal transit' had been introduced to enable goods to be exempted from taxation in all but the Member State of destination.

In 1988 all the various national customs documents were replaced by a Single Administrative Document. But as of 1 January 1993 both these measures were abolished (subject to transitional arrangements for Spain and Portugal), leaving goods free to cross internal borders without customs documents or the imposition of taxation. Instead Directive 91/680[26] creates a transitional arrangement according to which the exporter and importer declare the sale to their respective Member State authorities and the Member State of destination levies the VAT. The Directive records the intention to introduce a definitive system of taxation in the Member State of origin, but this is a very ambitious project. The definitive system can be accomplished only under Article 99, which requires unanimity among the Member States. On such a delicate issue, progress is likely to be slow.

In contrast, major progress has been made in the elimination of veterinary and plant health controls. The general rule is now that the control is made in the Member State of origin, with the State of destination being restricted to taking samples. The latter can oblige the former to follow its own standards if there are no harmonized Community rules.

Action has also been taken to remove or diminish other internal controls, such as those on vehicles and baggage. The Council is moving towards a common list of goods capable of both civilian and military use, so as to be able to eliminate internal controls on dual-use goods.

Differences in the various intellectual property laws of the Member States have long been recognized as an obstacle to free movement of goods. To a limited extent this can be dealt with by judicial action. A copyright law which reserves protection to nationals is unlawful as a discrimination against other Community citizens. Under Article 30, a patent cannot be used to prevent the resale in one Member State of goods sold by the patent holder in another.

But where one law provides for a different duration of protection, or protects rights not recognized at all in another Member State, problems arise which are difficult to solve in this way. The choice of what to protect and for how long is an essentially legislative choice. The Council has increasingly been making that choice. It has provided for the creation of numerous new intellectual property rights, for example for computer programmes (Directive 91/250[27]) and for the rental of video cassettes even after they have been sold (Directive 92/100[28]). It has also acted to harmonize for example the duration of copyright protection at 70 years (Directive 93/98[29]).

The Single Market programme also includes a variety of measures dealt with elsewhere in this book. The opening-up of public procurement and the liberalization of inland, maritime and air transport are of considerable importance. So too is fiscal harmonization, though here the successes of the Community are not numerous. Much progress has however been made in the field of financial services. The entry of the Community into the realm of environmental and social protection has reduced the motivation for protectionism by Member States.

Prospects for the Future

Two themes run throughout this study of the free movement of goods and services. The first is the debate over whether only discriminatory measures should be prohibited, or whether non-discriminatory restrictions should be included as well. The second concerns the changing perception of the relative roles of the national and Community judiciary and of the Community legislature. The two are inextricably linked.

It is clear that the signatories of the Treaty of Rome anticipated that the Council would have primary responsibility for the establishment of the common market. But the Council proved inadequate as a legislature, and the role of national courts, in conjunction with the Court of Justice, has expanded dramatically. This latter development results from the assumption by the Court of Justice of the role of a constitutional court in order to interpret the EC Treaty in such a way as to achieve its objectives. The means employed has been to shift areas which otherwise would have had to be left for legislation into the domain of the courts. Every judgement in which the Court of Justice extended the judicially enforceable prohibitions of the Treaty to non-discriminatory measures should be seen as a sign of its diminishing confidence in the Council.

It is against this background that the latest case law of the Court should be assessed. In its 1993 *Keck* judgement the Court held that 'certain selling arrangements', such as a general prohibition on resale at a loss, do not breach Article 30 if in law and in fact they affect domestic and imported goods in the same manner.[30] A distinction was made from those measures relating to requirements to be met by the goods themselves, such as packaging or labelling requirements, to which the old *Cassis de Dijon* judgement continued to apply. No reasoning was given. But it can perhaps be inferred that the Court is now confident in the Council and its 'new approach' to legislation relating to such non-discriminatory measures. The *Keck* judgement should not be seen as a step away from economic integration but rather as one towards integration more by legislation than by judicial action. In time it may have its equivalent in the services field, as the Court withdraws the judiciary from further areas of integration activity in order to make room for the legislative process.

In this respect, the Maastricht Treaty may be expected to play a substantial, although indirect role. The Treaty on European Union did not affect the substantive EC Treaty rules on the free movement of goods and services. However, by introducing the co-decision procedure for, inter alia, Article 100a, the Maastricht Treaty gave the European Parliament a decisive role in Single Market legislation. Now that the Community legislature contains a forceful democratic element, the Court may take the view that not only is Community legislation likely to be more acceptable to the population, but that the Parliament's elected politicians may actively resist limitation of their freedom to legislate by Court decisions 'interpreting' the Treaty.

There are, however, other indications of a genuine trend away from ever-continuing integration. The effect of the common market has always been undermined to some extent by state aids granted by the Member States. But through the structural funds and the new Cohesion Fund, the Community itself is now diverting resources away from the regions in which they would be employed if the (common) market was left to allocate resources itself. In the interests of environmental protection, even the Court of Justice has departed from the absolute nature of the Single Market principle. In the *Belgian Waste* case it declared that a regional law prohibiting the entry of non-toxic waste from outside the region was non-discriminatory because waste produced inside the region should be considered to be different from identical waste produced outside.[31] This distinction was made on the basis of the principle laid down by Article 130r(2) of the EC Treaty that environmental damage should as a priority be rectified at source. As a non-discriminatory measure, the law could then be justified on environmental grounds in accordance with the *Cassis de Dijon* jurisprudence.

These developments do not indicate a decline in enthusiasm for economic integration as such. But they do show that the Single Market has advanced to such an extent that, in the same way as such decisions have traditionally been taken in national economies, the Community is having to weigh the concerns of the market against other factors relevant to modern democracies.

Notes

1.   The Spaak Report was the result of the intergovernmental committee set up by the Conference of Messina in 1955 to examine the possibilities for a broader economic treaty between the Member States of the European Coal and Steel Community. It was the inspiration for the Treaty of Rome. Comité intergouvernmentale créé par la Conférence de Messine (1956), *Rapport des Chefs de Délégation aux Ministres des Affaires Etrangers* (the *'Spaak Report'*), Bruxelles.

2.   Case 26/62 *Van Gend en Loos* [1963] ECR 1.

3.   Joined Cases 2 & 3/62 *Commission v. Luxembourg and Belgium* ,(the *'Gingerbread'* case) [1962] ECR 425.

4.   Joined Cases 2 & 3/69 *Sociaal Fonds voor de Diamantarbeiders* [1969] ECR 211.

5.   Case 74/76 *Ianelli* [1977] ECR 557. Case 83/78 *Pigs Marketing* [1978] ECR 2347.

6.   Case 148/78 *Ratti* [1979] ECR 1629.

7.   *Commission Directive 70/50* based on the provisions of Article 33(7), on the abolition of measures which have an effect equivalent to quantitative restrictions on imports and are not covered by other provisions adopted in pursuance of the EEC Treaty, JO 1970 L 13/29.

8.   Case 41/76 *Donckerwolcke v. Procureur de la République* [1976] ECR 1921.

9.   Case 8/74 *Procureur du Roi v. Dassonville* [1974] ECR 837.

10.   Case 15/79 *Groenveld* [1979] ECR 3409.

11.   Case 193/85 *Cooperation Co-Frutta* [1987] ECR 2085; Case 142/77 *Statens Kontrol* [1978] ECR 1543.

12.   Case 15/81 *Schul I* [1982] ECR 140; Case 47/84 *Schul II* [1985] ECR 1491.

13.   *Council Directive 74/148* on the abolition of restrictions on movement and residence within the Community for nationals of Member States with regard to establishment and the provision of services, OJ 1973 L 172/14.

14.   *Council Directive 64/221* on the coordination of special measures concerning the movement and residence of foreign nationals which are justified on grounds of public policy, public security or public health, JO 1964, p. 850/64.

15.   Case 186/87 *Cowan* [1989] ECR 195.

16.   Case 352/85 *Bond van Adverteerders* [1988] ECR 2085.

17   Case 33/74 *Van Binsbergen* [1974] ECR 1299.

18   Case 120/78 *Rewe-Zentral AG v. Bundesmonopolverwaltung für Branntwein* (the '*Cassis de Dijon*' case) [1979] ECR 649.

19   Commission of the European Communities (1985), *Completing the Internal Market,* Luxembourg, OOPEC.

20   The Comité Européen de normalisation, the Comité Européen de normalisation électrotechnique and the European Telecommunications Standards Institute.

21   Case C-76/90 *Säger* [1991] ECR I-4221. In this case, a U.K. specialist in patent renewal services successfully challenged the reservation of such activities in Germany to persons holding a special professional qualification.

22   Case 205/84 *Commission v. Germany* [1986] ECR 3755.

23   *Council Directive 83/189* laying down a procedure for the provision of information in the field of technical standards and regulations, OJ 1983 L 109/8 (as amended by Council Directive 88/182, OJ 1988 L 81/75, and by European Parliament and Council Directive 94/10, OJ 1994 L 100/30).

24   Council of the European Communities (1985), *Council Resolution on a new approach to technical harmonization and standards,* OJ 1985 C 136/1.

25   *Council Directive 93/97* supplementing Directive 91/263/EEC in respect of satellite earth station equipment, OJ 1993 L 290/1.

26   *Council Directive 91/680* supplementing the common system of value added tax and amending Directive 77/388/EEC with a view to the abolition of fiscal frontiers, OJ 1991 L 376/1.

27   *Council Directive 91/250* on the legal protection of computer programs, OJ 1991 L 122/42.

28   *Council Directive 92/100* on rental right and lending right and on certain rights related to copyright in the field of intellectual property, OJ 1992 L 346/61.

29   *Council Directive 93/98* harmonizing the term of protection of copyright and certain related rights, OJ 1993 L 290/9.

30   Joined Cases C-267 & C-268/91 *Keck and Mithouard* [1993] ECR I-6097.

31   Case C-2/90 *Commission v. Belgium* (the 'Belgian Waste' case) [1992] ECR I-4431.

11 Tax Harmonization: The Single Market Challenge

PANOS KANAVOS[1]

Introduction

As the Member States of the European Union (EU) enter a debate phase on the future of Economic and Monetary Union, important tax policy issues, associated with further economic integration, will have to be encountered. These relate to the efficient allocation of resources, particularly in the light of the free movement of factors - mostly capital - and their sensitivity to tax differences among Member States. They also relate to the strictly national orientation of fiscal policy, which may at times result in Member States competing and setting aggressive tax rules in order to attract foreign investment. These issues also relate with the Member States' recognized autonomy and sovereignty over fiscal policy in the pursuit of national economic and social policy objectives.

Apart from the requirements of a common market which necessitate the free and unimpeded flow of goods, services and factors of production, the purpose of tax harmonization (or approximation) touches upon issues of fiscal policy and its redistributive effects. The continuing debate on tax harmonization therefore relates to whether or not the debate on Economic and Monetary Union will lead to any tangible results in the near future. This latter effect could not have been foreseen in the Treaty of Rome. Article 99 specifically mentions that approximation of tax structures is certainly an objective, but has left it to be tackled at later stages in the process of integration (Articles 100-102). In the same spirit, the Treaty on European Union agreed at Maastricht has not departed from the principle that the right to levy taxes is the exclusive preserve of the Member States.

This chapter attempts to capture this debate and, at the same time, provide a critical overview of the issues involved in the approximation of the tax structures of the 15 Member States of the Union. Reference will be made to policy issues relating to both indirect as well as direct taxation.

Necessity for Tax Harmonization

The necessity for tax harmonization[2] dates from the foundation of the European Community. The tax systems of the Member States of the EC were initially heterogeneous to a large extent[3], reflecting important differences in their economic and social structures and economic policy objectives. However, the free movement of goods, services, as well as factors of production, made compelling the abolition of all sorts of barriers put forward by the tax systems of Member States. In view of this conviction, the Treaty of Rome (article 95) clearly states that taxes on imported goods should not exceed the tax imposed on their domestically produced equivalent and authorizes (article 99) the European Commission to submit proposals for the harmonization of indirect taxes, so that differences between Member States be eliminated. However, there is vagueness regarding the meaning of the term 'harmonization', since, according to article 105, harmonization should not be more than an 'approximation of the laws in the Member States'.

Despite its importance, direct taxation[4] is not explicitly considered in the Treaty of Rome. Article 220 requires Member States to endeavour to eliminate double taxation by agreement between them. Direct tax measures involving corporations, therefore, are only possible under the provisions of article 100 of the Treaty, which permits the harmonization of laws generally to create a single European market and any fiscal measure has to be approved unanimously. On the other hand, the Maastricht Treaty, through article 73D, authorizes Member States to distinguish between residents and non-residents for tax purposes.

From a policy perspective, differences in taxation levels affect the relative prices of goods and this has an impact on the terms of trade within an economy and between the economy in question and other countries, so that the pattern and the volume of trade may also be affected. Such changes imply redistribution of income between the citizens of the country, the country and its partners in the economic union and the economic union and the outside world. The effects are similar to those derived from changes in tariff structures.[5] In addition, taxes are used by governments as instruments of budgetary, social and economic policy. With changes in taxes and rates consequent upon tax harmonization there will be effects on both the instruments and the objectives of economic policies. Hence, tax harmonization would have effects on tax revenues, and this may imply the requirement for public expenditure harmonization. In general, tax harmonization is multidimensional, affecting all the functions of the tax system, such as allocation of resources, economic stabilization, economic growth, income distribution, balance of payments and tax revenue. Every government's policies relate to these functions, but different governments have different sets of objectives and therefore different priorities and rankings of these functions. Tax harmonization affects both the functions of the tax system and the order of their priority.

The absence of efforts to harmonize tax structures unavoidably creates an environment for tax competition and this yields a number of harmful consequences for the efficiency of an economic system such as the EU: *firstly*, if competition is left to follow its course, Member States will set tax rates at a lower level than they would if acting cooperatively and by lowering tax rates Member States are following a beggar-thy-neighbour policy, which may result in undertaxation.[6] *Secondly*, differences in tax rates may provoke locational distortions, particularly with respect to decisions on where in the Union to produce, invest or collect capital income that would not be made in the absence of taxes.[7] Such distortions cause resource misallocation thereby weakening the Union's economic efficiency. *Finally*, distribution problems may emerge among countries of the tax proceeds from firms or individuals operating in more than one Member State, through the absence of common rules.

From a practical perspective, assuming that the EU will eventually enter the final stage of monetary union, new tax initiatives in the pursuit of the economic union goal become necessary, and it would then be preferable for the EC to go beyond its current resources and have direct access to other tax bases. A situation where the budget is primarily funded by national contributions is politically unsatisfactory in the long term as it makes the Community's financial dependence on national governments very apparent.

Indirect Taxation

The Value Added Tax

The first step towards the direction of approximation of laws described in the Treaty of Rome, was the Neumark Report (1963), which stated that because the tax systems of the Member States were non-neutral to intra-community trade, thereby exerting distortionary pressures, neutrality would be restored in intra-community transactions through the adoption of the value added tax, which would replace a series of cumulative taxes, and the destination principle as a method of taxation. In accordance with the above propositions, the Council of Ministers, upon recommendation of the European Commission, proceeded with the adoption of the value added tax (VAT) in 1967, in part to prevent Member States from using indirect taxation to favour domestic producers over foreign producers through the manipulation of border tax adjustments, and ruled that all Member States should adopt it[8].

The VAT contributed 17.3 per cent to the total tax revenue in the EU in 1993, (table 1). It is generally acknowledged that VAT has a number of attributes compared with other sales taxes, such as broader revenue base, neutrality and efficiency,[9] that make its introduction desirable to tax authorities and, to a certain extent, outweigh disadvantages such as regressivity and potential inflationary effects that most indirect taxes have.[10]

Although in principle, VAT rate differentials do not distort production location decisions as long as the destination principle is maintained, it has nevertheless been argued that the elimination of border controls requires convergence of tax rates because of the difficulty in enforcing the destination principle without such controls.[11] In addition to the implications that tax harmonization imposes on economic policy, the introduction of the VAT as the common sales tax, posed three very distinctive problems common to all turnover taxes; the *first* relates to the point at which the tax should be imposed according to the *origin* or *destination* principles of taxation. This issue relates to whether the tax is imposed on the production or the consumption stage respectively and has clear implications for the accrual of revenue.[12] The *second* problem relates to the coverage of the tax and equal treatment requires that the tax base be the same in the Member States of the Union. The *third* problem relates to exemptions that may defeat the aim of a sales tax like the VAT being a tax on consumption.

Legislation adopted aimed at achieving conformity between the different practices of the Member States. In particular, the guidelines were set with respect to the following three issues: *firstly*, the inclusion of the retail stage in the coverage of the VAT; *secondly*, the use of VAT levies for the financing of the EC central budget, a decision taken by the Commission in 1969 which led to the necessity of further harmonization of the VAT base amongst Member States. *Thirdly*, the achievement of greater uniformity in VAT structure.

Having institutionalized the above framework, the EC has also acceded to the destination principle.

Table 1. Tax Revenue as % of GDP in the European Union, 1993

	Belgium	Denmark	Germany	Greece	Spain	France	Ireland	Italy	Luxembourg
1. Taxes on income of individuals	13.9	26.0	10.6	3.8	8.4	6.1	11.6	11.9	9.2
2. Corporate Income Tax	2.2	2.2	1.4	2.1	2.0	1.5	3.0	4.1	7.2
3. Taxes on property	1.2	2.1	1.1	1.5	1.7	2.3	1.5	2.4	3.5
Total 1 to 3	*17.3*	*30.3*	*13.1*	*7.4*	*12.1*	*9.9*	*16.1*	*18.4*	*19.9*
4. VAT	7.0	9.8	6.8	9.5	5.1	7.5	7.0	5.6	6.7
5. Excise taxes	4.0	5.2	3.6	7.7	3.5	3.8	6.2	4.5	5.2
Total 4 & 5	*11.0*	*15.0*	*10.4*	*17.2*	*8.6*	*11.3*	*13.2*	*10.1*	*11.9*
6. Other taxes	0.0	0.9	0.5	0.9	0.8	0.4	0.7	1.2	0.1
7. Total 1 to 6	*28.3*	*46.2*	*24.0*	*25.3*	*21.5*	*21.6*	*30.0*	*29.7*	*31.9*
8. Social Security contributions	16.3	1.6	15.1	13.9	13.4	19.6	5.6	17.7	12.7
9. Total tax receipts	*44.6*	*47.8*	*39.1*	*39.2*	*34.9*	*41.2*	*35.6*	*47.4*	*44.6*
Personal income tax as % of total tax receipts	30.4	52.1	27.1	9.3	24.0	13.9	32.0	24.9	20.5
Corporate income tax as % of total tax receipts	4.8	4.4	3.6	5.0	5.7	3.4	8.1	8.5	16.3
VAT as % of total tax receipts	15.3	19.7	17.5	23.2	14.6	17.1	19.3	11.7	14.9
Excises as % of total tax receipts	8.7	10.3	9.1	18.7	9.9	8.7	17.0	9.4	11.7

Table 1. Continued.

	Netherlands	Portugal	UK	EC-12	Sweden	Finland	Austria
1. Taxes on income of individuals	12.2	6.3	9.3	10.8	18.4	16.3	9.4
2. Corporate Income Tax	3.3	2.3	2.4	2.8	2.2	1.2	1.5
3. Taxes on property	1.8	0.8	3.6	1.9	1.6	1.3	1.1
Total 1 to 3	*17.3*	*9.4*	*15.3*	*15.5*	*22.2*	*18.8*	*12.0*
4. VAT	7.0	6.2	6.6	7.1	8.5	8.6	8.3
5. Excise taxes	3.9	7.0	4.8	4.9	4.7	5.9	3.8
Total 4 & 5	*10.9*	*13.2*	*11.4*	*12.0*	*13.2*	*14.5*	*12.2*
6. Other taxes	1.2	0.2	0.5	0.7	0.5	0.2	0.6
7. Total 1 to 6	*29.4*	*22.8*	*27.2*	*28.2*	*35.9*	*33.5*	*24.8*
8. Social Security contributions	18.3	8.4	6.0	12.4	13.8	12.1	14.8
9. Total tax receipts	*47.7*	*31.2*	*33.2*	*40.6*	*49.7*	*45.6*	*38.6*
Personal income tax as % of total tax receipts	25.4	19.9	27.8	25.6	36.8	35.7	21.6
Corporate income tax as % of total tax receipts	7.0	7.2	7.2	6.8	4.5	2.7	3.5
VAT as % of total tax receipts	14.5	19.7	19.5	17.3	17.0	18.8	19.1
Excises as % of total tax receipts	8.2	22.3	14.1	12.3	9.4	12.9	8.8

Source: Revenue Statistics, OECD, 1995.[13]

Notes: (*) For Italy, available rates were for 1978. NB Greece introduced the VAT on 1 January 1987; Spain & Portugal were not members of the EC in 1982; they introduced the VAT on 1 January 1986.

With the issue of the 6th Directive in 1977 (Official Journal, L145, 13/6/77), all Member States were obliged to harmonize their VAT systems so that deviations regarding the tax base would be minimized.

Taxable transactions, persons and amounts were defined. Special schemes for small businesses and farmers were put forward and a list of the activities that could be exempted was set up, including insurance, banking, and other financial transactions, as well as services in the public interest. Arrangements allowing countries to deviate from the common tax base in several areas were incorporated, with the understanding that these deviations should eventually be eliminated. After its implementation the only element of difference between the Member States was the tax rates, where considerable differences existed (see table 2). At the same time huge differences were also observed regarding the coverage of the various rates, since most Member States seem to have different kinds, different levels as well as different exemptions from the tax.[14] Thus, the same product that is taxed at the low rate in one Member State, may be exempt in another.

The determination of the Member States to continue with the process of integration and the creation of the Single European Market from 1993 onwards, was reflected upon the common efforts to intensify the process of indirect tax harmonization. In the Commission's White Paper (COM(85) 310 final) the necessity was recognized to adopt a common VAT base, to coordinate its structure and coverage so that similar goods and services would be taxed alike in the Member States, and proposed the adoption of target rates. If transactions crossing frontiers within the EC were to be treated in exactly the same manner as those within a Member State, the introduction of a system of tax collection by the country of origin would be essential. The principle of origin would then need to be supplemented with an EU clearing mechanism to ensure that revenues would continue to accrue to the Member State where consumption takes place. And, of course, the narrowing of the differentials in national VAT rates is imperative in order to lessen the risks of fraud, tax evasion and distortions in competition.

The Cockfield proposals submitted to the Council in 1987 reflected this spirit[15]. The debate focused on equal numbers of VAT rates - a low rate between 4 per cent and 9 per cent for a number of basic needs goods, and a normal one ranging between 16 per cent and 20 per cent[16] but also flexibility as to their level, combined with the principle of origin as a point of collection. These proposals were seen as a compromise between the objective of realizing the internal market without trade distortions on the one hand, and avoiding disruptive budgetary consequences for certain Member States on the other.

The opposition from several Member States was fierce, on the grounds that the proposals intervened in national fiscal policy objectives. Apart from the complexity, manifested in a plethora of rates in several Member States (see table 2), the proposed boundaries restricted the revenue raising potential of the tax, particularly as many Member States imposed increased VAT rates on a large number of goods considered to be luxuries (cars, electronics, etc). The debate continued with the Commission communication of May 1989,[17] whereby a series of alterations were adopted that would provide more flexibility than the Cockfield proposals. These alterations included a transition period up to thè end of 1992 which would serve as a convergence period, provided that all Member States would undertake the responsibility of harmonizing their legislation with the proposed system. The new elements included provisions for some Member States to keep their zero rate for a number of goods and the adoption of only the low boundary of 15 per cent for the normal rate. The Council of Ministers decided that it is the long-term objective of the Community to replace the principle of the country of destination, by that of the country of origin in intra-community trade. Over the short-term and up to the end of 1996, the principle of the country of destination would have to be kept.[18] This compromise reflects the objective difficulties encountered by several Member States in terms of revenue losses due to tax rate convergence and the adoption of the principle of origin.

The current rules in intra-Community trade are set out in Council Directive 91/680/EEC.[19] These are to be applied between 1 January 1993 and 1 January 1997, when a definitive regime is to be introduced.

Under the transitional regime cross-frontier sales will be taxed in the country of destination of the goods, whereas under the definitive regime such sales will be taxed in the country of origin. The abolition of frontier controls and the fact that the VAT was, up to the end of 1992, charged at importation of goods at the frontiers, calls for a different collection system. The new system is based on the idea that purchases of goods moving between Member States are taxed as acquisitions in the hands of the purchaser. In this system the intermediate export and import stage through customs is eliminated and the collection of the tax is integrated into the domestic VAT collection system.

The entry of the transitional arrangements into force, since January 1993,[20] is a significant achievement if one considers the sensitivity of all

Member States regarding their taxation systems and their sovereignty over fiscal policy.

Table 2. VAT Rates Applied in the Community Member States

Country Member	Year	1982(*)			1993		
		Reduced Rate	Normal Rate	Increased Rate	Reduced Rate	Normal Rate	Increased Rate
Germany	1968	6.5	13	-	7	15	-
Belgium	1971	6	17	25	1/6/12	19.5	-
Denmark	1967	-	22	-	-	25	-
Spain	1986	na	na	na	6	15	28
Greece	1987	na	na	na	4/8	18	36
France	1968	5.5/7	18.6	33.3	2.1/5.5	18.6	-
Ireland	·1972	0/18	30	-	2.3/10/12.5	16/21	-
Italy	1973	2.8	18	38	4/9/12	19	38
Luxembourg	1970	2/5	10	-	3/6	15	-
Netherlands	1969	4	18	-	6	18.5	-
Portugal	1986	na	na	na	5	16	30
United Kingdom	1973	0	15	-	-	17.5	-

Notes: (*) For Italy, available rates were for 1978.

na   Greece introduced VAT on 1 January 1987; Spain and Portugal were not members of the EEC in 1982; they introduced VAT on 1 January 1986.

In the Commission's own words, however, 'the difficulties encountered by business are a reminder that firms and consumers do not yet enjoy all the advantages expected from a single market'.[21] It is a fact that businesses still need to prove the intra-Community nature of their operations, bear the burden of the identification and declaration requirements and the deterrent effect of certain provisions. These differences are important in determining the level of business compliance costs, and, combined with the large number of rules, the wide variation of rates and differing administrative procedures,[22] translate into complex mechanisms for applying the common system of VAT, despite the alleged simplicity of its operating principles.

It is understood that some of the problems associated with the current VAT system are due to its transitional nature. The definitive system, however, is unlikely to take effect on 1 January 1997, as originally planned. The Commission in its report to the Council and the Parliament on 15 June 1995,[23] would not give a definite date as to when such proposals and guidelines would be submitted.[24] One of the problems of course relates to the ongoing debate about the eventual principle of taxation.

An origin-based VAT system is strongly opposed by many Member States, on three accounts. *Firstly*, it implies loss of revenue to a number of Member States due to their export capacity being smaller than their propensity to import. Therefore, tax revenue accruing from exports will fall short of tax revenue payable on imports. *Secondly*, the origin principle implies that the tax will be levied at the production stage and tax revenue will accrue to the country of production. Thus, exports from a low-tax to a high-tax country enjoy an artificial comparative advantage. *Thirdly*, this effort may be seen as interference with the sovereignty of fiscal policy and, if adopted, will be a serious drawback in many Member States' policy objectives to reduce budget deficits and overall debt levels, unless its implementation coincides with the introduction of an efficient monitoring mechanism that would guarantee the same level of tax revenue under the new system.

The Commission argues that such a system will reduce dramatically all administrative charges and will simplify procedures, on the understanding of closer cooperation between the national tax authorities. It is questionable whether, such levels of cooperation can be achieved in a short period of time, despite positive steps taken in this direction.[25]

Excise Duties

Excise duties are mainly revenue-raising, single-stage taxes levied on products characterized by high consumption levels and low price elasticities of demand. For certain products, the revenue-raising function is associated with policies to discourage consumption of harmful products such as tobacco or alcohol. Excise rates diverge widely among Member States because they are subject to priorities as well as changes in economic policy, but are also dependent on individual consumption patterns. This is why differences in the rates applied across the EU will always exist and why greater tax coordination can be better achieved through the introduction of minimum rates. This particular strategy summarizes policy debate in this field.

Harmonization of excises has proved to be a difficult and slow process. This can be explained in part by protectionist pressures, but also by differences in consumer tastes, cultural attitudes towards drinking and smoking, as well as divergent social policies - for instance, income distribution - and policies relating to the environment, energy conservation and health. The Commission[26] views increases in the rates and extension in the scope of excise duties as a means of funding reductions in statutory charges on labour (in addition to assisting in other policy areas).

Traditionally, excise duties are intended fundamentally for revenue-raising purposes. Therefore, the issues raised by their harmonization are specifically those relating to their revenue-raising function and to the equity implications of these methods. Targeted products for this purpose include tobacco and its products, alcoholic beverages and mineral oils. Despite their uniform consideration as revenue instruments, the modern theory of public finance has stressed their qualities in achieving certain allocative objectives.[27] For this purpose there is a clear-cut distinction between taxation of demerit goods (tobacco and alcohol) that pose health risks to the population, and energy conservation and environmental control, (which applies to hydrocarbon oils), the consumption of which leads to pollution, health hazards and climatic changes.

With reference to the taxation of demerit goods, minimum rates for alcohol and alcoholic beverages, cigarettes and tobacco were introduced in 1992,[28] with the additional condition that every two years the Council will examine the minimum rates and, in so doing, take account of the proper functioning of the internal market and the real value of those rates. The large variety of rates in the Union indicates the different attitudes among Member States as well as support of local industries, with regard to corresponding policy goals (see table 3). Although a minimum degree of harmonization of structures is also necessary - alongside the approximation of the rates in force in Member States - to ensure the dismantling of tax frontiers and considerable progress has taken place,[29] the differences in structures have a less pronounced impact than the considerable discrepancies in rates. For this purpose specific allowances (for alcohol and tobacco) have been authorized on a transitional basis for Denmark, Ireland, Germany and Spain.

Energy taxation is more complex. The Commission has stated that fuel excises and motor vehicle taxes should bear some relation to the construction and maintenance cost of motorways.[30] Fuel taxes are also used to conserve energy, protect the environment, and reduce imports. There are, furthermore, international competitiveness considerations, whereby countries tend to levy higher rates on fuel used by final consumers and lower rates on fuel used as input in industrial production. This latter effect dominates the debate regarding the imposition of an environmental tax for carbon dioxide emissions. The Commission's proposals have met strong opposition from affected industries - particularly chemicals, steel- and Member States, which view the imposition of such a tax reducing their international competitiveness. A large number of Member States, in particular, insist that the base principle should remain the voluntary feature for introduction of this tax, without commitment as to its future potential harmonization.

Direct Taxation

Direct taxes and social security contributions are the most important components of total tax revenue. In the European Union, revenue from these two categories was 27.9 per cent of total EU GDP, in 1993, whereas for the same year direct taxes and social security contributions yielded 67 per cent of total tax revenue. However, considerable differences exist between the various Member States (see table 1). Some Member States put emphasis on direct income taxation (Belgium, Denmark, Sweden, Finland, Ireland), more so than others (France, Greece, Portugal, Spain, Italy); other Member States prefer to have high social security contributions than income taxes (France, the Netherlands, Germany, Spain, Italy), whereas in others social security contributions yield less revenue, partly because income tax is high (Denmark, and less so in Sweden and Finland), or because the overall weight has been shifted towards indirect taxation (as is the case of Greece and Portugal and, less so, the UK). Overall, there is a clear-cut North-South division, in that the latter exploit indirect taxes more intensely. Very importantly, variations in corporate income tax are quite considerable among Member States, although this source does not yield more than 6.8 per cent of total EU tax revenue.

Direct tax harmonization is an ongoing process and has focused attention in the capital tax structures of Member States, leaving out personal income tax. There is a distinct division between personal income and capital income taxes, relating to the mobility of the relevant factors. Income from financial assets can be shifted rapidly from one jurisdiction to another, with virtually no transaction costs.

In contrast, the scope for large-scale cross-border shifts is minor in the case of taxes on labour income and social security contributions since international labour mobility is likely to remain limited.[31] Thus, it is expected that personal income tax will undoubtedly remain the cornerstone of national fiscal policies, despite the implications that taxation of personal incomes from capital raise.

Taxation of capital income

As a result of the current distinction in fiscal treatment between residents and non-residents, the ongoing competitive process threatens to degenerate into a situation where each country acts as a tax haven for financial asset holders residing in the 14 other Member States, given the free movement of capital within the EU. This may imply tax competition among Member States and all the relevant consequences deriving from that.[32] Economic theory and empirical evidence suggest that differences in taxation on income from capital across countries can be expected to induce an inefficient allocation of capital and distort locational decisions of direct investors. Obviously, differential rates of taxation are not the only determinant of foreign direct investment and other factors help explain locational decisions of firms,[33] but, with reference to the attitude of individuals gaining from differences in the rates of return (arbitrage), the argument of differential taxation rates holds.

This issue is particularly relevant for the EU, as the drive to complete the Single Market fully exposes investment decisions to differences in tax burdens across Member States. The distortionary effects of such taxation are twofold and can directly be related to the difference between the gross and the net rate of return on capital: firstly, its size affects the degree of capital accumulation and, secondly, differences across countries distort the international allocation of capital and savings, and the location of financial intermediation. It is expected that individual Member States, because of their high direct taxes and low indirect taxes, must expect a capital outflow and a relocation of their firms in other countries and a reorganization of production in a way detrimental to their investment goods industry. It appears, therefore, that competition on the basis of comparative tax advantages rather than comparative cost advantages, is detrimental and this is why only harmonization agreed on

Table 3. Excise Rates in the EU for Certain Classes of Products, 1 January 1995, in ECU

Country	Wine[1]	Beer[2]	Cigarettes[3] in ECU	%	Spirits[4]	Unleaded Petrol[5]	Leaded Petrol[5]	Diesel Oil Used as a Propellant[5]	Gas Oil for Heating Purposes[5]
Belgium	37.22	1.49	67.23	57.76%	1606.7	409.89	479.47	296.03	5.31
Denmark	86.95	3,32	121.40	63.07%	3698.5	381.80	467.29	299.49	299.49
Germany	0.0	0.80	74.79	58.68%	1326.6	509.85	561.88	322.56	41.62
Greece	0.0	0.82	47.09	57.50%	550.0	389.04	406.10	245.71	133.09
Spain	0.0	0.75	22.17	56.40%	551.6	361.60	393.68	262.24	76.72
France	3.35	0.76	73.84	58.70%	1381.5	544.70	584.77	326.0	73.80
Ireland	271.58	8.75	101.37	58.58%	2757.3	345.82	378.16	297.46	47.11
Italy	0.0	1.40	45.72	57.00%	593.3	471.43	527.32	349.82	349.82
Luxembourg	0.0	0.81	51.02	57.95%	1037.4	354.48	407.62	253.02	5.31
Netherlands	49.94	1.82	59.85	57.00%	1540.1	502.43	566.45	295.09	47.66
Austria	0.0	1.48	61.10	57.00%	739.1	333.40	406.59	243.22	48.05
Portugal	0.0	1.31	44.60	67.17%	715.2	442.88	478.64	315.18	0.0

Table 3. Continued.

Country	Wine[1]	Beer[2]	Cigarettes[3] in ECU	%	Spirits[4]	Unleaded Petrol[5]	Leaded Petrol[5]	Diesel Oil Used as a Propellant[5]	Gas Oil for Heating Purposes[5]
Finland	284.24	11.37	95.72	57.54%	5016.1	456.97	532.21	298.46	33.91
Sweden	284.30	10.09	81.20	49.18%[6]	5131.7	440.63	498.01	313.10	168.78
UK	179.58	5.53	108.23	62.70%	2634.1	400.48	462.11	400.48	27.37
EU-min	*0.0*	*0.75*		*57.00%*	*550.0*	*287.00*	*337.0*	*245.0*	*18.0*

1   per hectolitre of product.

2   per hectolitre/ degree plato

3   per 1,000 cigarettes of the most popular price category; combination of specific and ad valorem elements, the minimum incidence of which should not be less than 57 per cent of retail selling price.

4   per hectolitre of pure alcohol.

5   per 1,000 litres.

6   Sweden has a derogation and need not apply the ad valorem tax until 1996 and need not be above the 57 per cent level before 1999.

Source: European Commission, COM(95) 285 final, 13 September 1995.

collectively at the level of the EC can prevent the potential benefits of integration turning into actual losses. The decomposition of the overall tax wedge on investment income into a corporate and a personal component is analytically convenient in addressing allocative issues amongst economies when international capital movements take the form of portfolio flows; i.e., transactions in foreign financial assets normally not involving controlling ownership. At the personal level a tax on capital income reduces the rate of return on domestic financial assets and affects saving behaviour. Differences in personal tax burdens across countries thus induce an inefficient allocation of saving, and distort the pattern of capital ownership. At the corporate level a tax on capital income affects the level of the gross rate of return on domestic real assets necessary to cover the cost of borrowing (interest payments). The existence of differential taxation rates (as suggested by the rates in table 4) of capital income at the company level implies unequal marginal rates of return from capital. In such cases, because capital movements between countries are propelled by tax differences rather than by financial and investment considerations alone, its allocation is inefficient.

Despite several proposals of the Commission to harmonize direct taxes dating back as early as 1969 - and, for the corporation tax, 1975[34] - slow progress has been made recently regarding the fiscal treatment of companies operating in more than one Member State and proposals put forward have consistently failed to obtain the necessary unanimous approval. The proposed directive regarding corporate tax rate harmonization was never adopted because the European Parliament stressed the prior need to harmonize the rules of computation of the company tax base.

However, the Commission no longer seeks to harmonize completely at any price company tax systems and rates. Efforts in the late 1980s were geared to the adoption of measures that would lead to the completion of the internal market, particularly the removal of double taxation of crossborder income flows. This led, in July 1990, to the adoption of three proposals by the Council; the 'Parent-subsidiary' directive,[35] the 'Merger' directive[36] and the 'Arbitration' convention,[37] whilst two other proposals were also put forward during this time for debate; the 'Interest and Royalty' proposal[38] and the 'Imputation of foreign losses' proposal.[39]

As documented in the Ruding report, but also previously in OECD,[40] effective corporate tax rates vary significantly between Member States on account of differences in the definition of the tax base, statutory rates, the fiscal link between firm and shareholder (the so-called system of imputation) and the rules on double taxation relief regarding income from cross-border activities. Furthermore, corporate tax pressure on outward and inward investment is, on average, considerably higher than that associated with domestic investment, pointing to important internal market imperfections still existing in the corporate tax field. The results of the survey conducted by the Ruding Committee suggest that Multinational corporations' (MNCs) decisions on where to locate an investment and how to finance it are indeed influenced by corporate tax considerations, although taxation is not the only determinant. Relevant to investment decisions by MNCs is the problem of privileged tax regimes. It is a fact that some Member States had introduced special tax schemes and concessions in order to attract internationally mobile business, typically in the service sector. The concern is that generous tax incentives can be carefully targeted to pull in new business from other Member States.[41] Finally, as for the problem of transfer pricing disputes which were identified as another important issue, the solution would be to improve the exchanges of information amongst tax authorities in different Member States, as a cost-effective measure.[42]

Following the results and recommendations of the Ruding report, the Commission laid down a number of guidelines and priorities,[43] which make out five broad areas of policy, as outlined below.

Elimination of double taxation on cross-border income and gains

Within a fully completed internal market, financial flows and transactions between companies established in different Member States, should take place under the same conditions as those between companies operating within a single Member State. The withholding tax levied on interest and royalty payments are tax measures impeding transnational cooperation between companies from different Member States. Although there are bilateral agreements amongst Member States aiming at eliminating double taxation of such income, these do not constitute a satisfactory solution, due to administrative formalities and because double taxation may occur wherever it is not stipulated that withholding taxes are deductible from the taxable profits of the recipient company.

The gradual abolition of withholding taxes was put forward on a two-step basis. Firstly, only withholding taxes on royalty payments and interest made between companies belonging to the same group should be abolished.

Table 4. Corporate Income Tax Rates in the EU (1 January 1995)

Country	Top tax rate %	Comments
Austria	34	
Belgium	40.17	A lower rate applies to companies owned more than 50% by individuals. The tax rate incorporates a 'crisis' levy of 3% and applies as of the tax year 1994
Denmark	34	Corporations must either pay corporation tax on account during the income year or pay a surcharge. There are no local taxes on corporations
Finland	25	In 1993 municipal tax was abolished and national income tax set at 25%
France	33.33	Long-term capital gains are taxed only at 18%, provided that the balnce (82%) is retained in the company as a long-term reserve. There is a proposal to increase this to 19% (with effect from Jan. 1, 1994), but, to date this has not yet been adopted by the French Parliament
Germany	58.95/ 46.13	Of the two rates quoted, the first applies to retained profits and the second to distributed profits. Both rates include corporate tax at 45/30 tax, and trace tax (which can be between 12 and 18%). From January 1, 1995, the corporate tax rates for both retained and distributed profits are increased by a surcharge of 7.5% of the corporate tax.
Greece	40	The 40% rate applies to unlisted companies with bearer shares and to foreign branches. All other companies are subject to a rate of 35%. Discounts of 5% are allowed to companies which pay their corporate tax in a lump sum at the time of filling the tax return. A 3% surcharge applies to gross rental income
Ireland	40	Most manufacturing and many service companies are effectively taxed at 10%. Closely owned companies suffer a surcharge at an effective rate of 12% on undistributed investment and professional income
Italy	52.2	Corporate income tax rate at 36% plus local income tax at 16.2%

Table 4. Continued.

Luxembourg	40.29	Includes municipal tax at effective rate of 9.09% (rate varies). The surcharge has increased from 2.5% for the 1995 tax year
Netherlands	35	The first DFl 100,000 of taxable profits is taxed at 40%
Portugal	39.6	Includes municipal tax at 3.6%
Spain	35	
Sweden	28	
UK	33	There is a small companies rate of 25% applicable to companies with taxable profits below £300,000 and marginal relief on profits up to £1.5m

Source: Financial Times, February 1995.

Subsequently, it would be appropriate to introduce arrangements for the gradual abolition of withholding taxes on such payments between companies not belonging to the same group.

It was further suggested that there should be mutual assistance between the authorities of different Member States, concerning the exchange of information where there appears to be a transfer of profits.[44] Despite extensive discussion in the Council, the proposals were withdrawn on 30 November 1994 by the Commission, due to considerable objections from different Member States.[45] The fundamental reason for their rejection is directly related to their fiscal implications for individual Member States. A number of Member States are net importers of capital and technology for which withholding tax on such payments represents an appreciable source of tax revenue. Considerable concerns were also voiced about abuse.

Introduction of a more neutral system of taxation of savings

The issue results from the liberalization of capital movements as from 1 July 1990 and from the realization that all Member States effectively act as tax havens for residents of other Member States because they do not impose withholding tax on interest paid to non-residents in a wide range of circumstances. The Commission proposed two directives in 1989 but these have not yet been adopted despite repeated discussions in the Council. The revival of the proposal to introduce such a tax has been promoted by Germany, following tax changes that were responsible for capital flight to Luxembourg. On the other side, Luxembourg and the UK are concerned that the introduction of such a system would lead to capital flight to non-EU countries. Luxembourg, in particular, would not agree to such measures unless most OECD countries adopted a common approach.

In view of the structural importance of savings in promoting employment and growth, the Economic and Social Committee[46] called for the establishment of an EU savings policy, on the grounds that a common approach to savings would help achieve economic convergence and greater capital mobility within the Single Market. Approximation of the taxation of savings and, in particular, the establishment of a generally applicable system of withholding tax, would make it possible to remove double taxation. The introduction of such policy should promote the channelling of savings into long-term investment, whilst at the same time pursuing the goals of protecting small savers and bringing about neutral taxation which is vital if capital movements are to be stabilized. Nevertheless, the differences amongst Member States still exist.

Realization of a neutral system of insurance services

Taxation is particularly important in the case of financial services; the attractiveness of a life assurance product is in most Member States determined by the tax regime applicable to it, as the deductibility of premiums can be crucial. Such deductibility may, however, depend on the domicile of the insurance company and non-residents may be automatically placed at a disadvantage. Following the recommendations of the Ruding Committee, the Commission recognized the need for intervention in the financial services sector[47] and this was achieved through the life insurance directive,[48] thereby opening up the possibility for life insurance companies to sell their products cross-border without having to be established in the Member States where they trade. However, there are still distinctions between the tax treatment of policies sold by an established insurer and the treatment of policies with a non-resident insurer, involving the tax deductibility of premium payments made by the policy holder. These differences remain a barrier to the cross-border sale of policies and hinder the internal market for insurance.[49]

Taxation of individuals who are resident in one Member State but earn their living in another

Unequal tax treatment of individuals living in one Member State, who receive the vast majority of their income from another, is contrary to the basic freedom of movement for workers provided by article 48 of the EC Treaty. The Commission has therefore recommended[50] that in these circumstances individuals should not be subject to tax on this income which is heavier than if they and their families were resident in that Member State. The rule is required where at least 75 per cent of the individual's total taxable income is earned in that state during the year. This recommendation comes after the failure of the Council to adopt a directive to harmonize the taxation of cross-border workers and has received legal validation by the European Court, after it has been challenged.[51]

Improvement of the fiscal environment of SMEs, which face particular problems in developing their activities beyond national boundaries

Due to their importance in creating employment opportunities and contributing to growth, a number of initiatives have been put forward by the Commission: *firstly*, a Communication was adopted in 1994[52] addressing important issues such as fiscal parity between incorporated and unincorporated enterprises, the reduction of administrative burdens on Small & Medium Size Enterprises (SMEs) beginning to engage in cross-border activities, the abolition of tax obstacles to the use of venture capital and the taxation of the transmission of enterprises; *secondly*, a recommendation was issued[53] inviting the Member States to correct the deterrent effects of progressive rates of income tax payable by partnerships in respect of reinvested profits and to eliminate tax obstacles to changes in the legal form of enterprises; and finally, a Recommendation was issued[54] inviting the Member States to take action to improve the fiscal environment relating to the transfer of ownership of SMEs, with the objective of safeguarding the structure of such businesses and saving jobs. Despite the above initiatives, SMEs are as yet unable to take full advantage of the single market and encounter difficulties in the legal and fiscal environment in which they operate. They are often taxed more heavily, and have to bear proportionally higher costs when they operate across borders than in the case of a purely national activity.

Concluding remarks

The creation of the single market and the removal of all outstanding impediments to intra-EC trade has a number of implications for intra-EC trade, and for the taxable income of individuals and companies. The steps undertaken so far in terms of approximating rates and tax structures in the fields of indirect and direct taxation are expected to have positive allocative and distributional effects and medium - to long-term efficiency gains.[55] It is true that progress has been slow in certain areas, particularly with reference to direct taxation, due to opposition from individual Member States. Nevertheless, the current state of affairs is compatible with the experience of other entities built on tight or loose federal ties.[56]

It is clear that the right to levy taxes lies at the heart of national sovereignty and one has to recognize that centralization of tax revenue would be far from easy to achieve because of the loss for national tax revenue it would imply. It is not surprising, therefore, that tax developments in the European Union mirror the struggle between the advocates of national sovereignty for individual Member States and the advocates of collective European decision-making. National governments are therefore likely to continue using taxes as instruments for achieving national policy objectives, and resist further harmonization attempts.

Although the Maastricht convergence criteria set strict rules regarding the acceptable levels of debt and fiscal deficit prior to currencies' forming an economic union, little or nothing is said about the conduct of fiscal policy and the role of the budget at the European level. The issue of taxation lies at the heart of economic policy-making at the national level. The Member States must decide whether or not economic and monetary union will eventually proceed. If this is the case, then it raises budgetary issues, namely who is going to be responsible for fiscal policy in Europe. If it is the national governments, then harmonization can really proceed along the track it has already followed and improve upon the current state-of-the-art, particularly corporate taxation. In this way, one safeguards a minimum efficiency in the movement of capital between Member States without severe distortions. If, however, fiscal policy is to be run by a supranational government, having at its disposal a 'federal' budget and, therefore, increased distributional potential, then further changes need to be introduced which also render the harmonization of direct taxes more compelling. The only way that a supranational government can administer fiscal policy is to have a sizeable budget in its hands; this is the only way fiscal policy will achieve its redistributive role within the 'European' society, rather than staying within national limits. This is an issue that the forthcoming Inter Governmental Conference must seriously address rather than skillfully evade.

Harmonization of the EU tax systems was thought to be an issue beyond redemption once the principle of subsidiarity was introduced. However, if a single currency is eventually adopted, this is likely to increase enormously the momentum for a fully harmonized, or even single, tax system for those Member States using the same currency.

Notes

1   I am grateful to Dirk Schelpe, of the European Commission - DGXV and two anonymous referees for useful comments and suggestions. All remaining errors are mine.

2   Primarily all sales (or turnover) taxes and excise duties.

3   Heterogeneity in terms of rates, administrative procedures, compliance and enforcement. For a brief overview, see Hitiris T., *'European Community Economics'*, 1991.

4   Includes income taxation, corporate taxation, taxes on wealth and social security contributions.

5   Krugman P. Obstfeld M., *'International Economics: Theory and Policy'*, Harper Collins, 1991.

6   Giovannini A., 'National Tax Systems versus the European Capital Market', *Economic Policy*, No. 9, pp. 364-384, October 1989.

7   Devereux M. Pearson M., *Corporate Tax Harmonization and Economic Efficiency*, Institute of Fiscal Studies, report series No. 35, London, 1989.

8   See Second Council Directive of 11 April 1967, 67/228/EEC.

9   Tait A. (ed.), *'Value Added Tax: Administrative and Policy Issues'*, International
Monetary Fund, OP/88/91, Washington DC, October 1991.

10   Frenkel J., Razin A., Symansky S., *'International VAT Harmonization: Economic Effects'*, International Monetary Fund, Research Department, WP/91/22, Washington DC, February 1991.

11   See COM(87) 320 final. This argument is based on evidence that international tax rate differentials may distort trade through various channels, for instance the existence of tax-exempt entities, traders and public and private institutions, the phenomenon of cross-border shopping by individuals, and the fraud or tax evasion caused by the absence of border controls. Bovenberg L.A., Horne J.P., 'Taxes on Commodities: A Survey', in Kopits G. (ed.), *Tax Harmonization in the European Community: Policy Issues and Analysis*, International Monetary Fund, OP94, Washington, 1992.

12   Musgrave R.A., *'Fiscal Systems'*, New Haven, London, 1969.

13   OECD, *'Revenue Statistics of the OECD Member States'*, Paris, 1995.

14   A further problem regarding the taxation of antiques and second-hand goods was successfully resolved with the adoption of the 7th VAT Directive in the 1980s.

15   These proposals are contained in a number of official EEC documents; see Commission of the European Communities, COM(87) 320 final/2,

COM(87) 321 final/2, COM(87) 322 final/2, COM(87) 323 final/2, COM(87) 324 final/2, COM(87) 325 final/2, COM(87) 326 final/2, COM(87) 327 final/2 and COM(87) 328 final/2.

16 Zero rating was opposed on the grounds that it was a temporary measure to be eliminated upon the completion of the internal market.

17 See Commission of the European Communities, COM(89) 260, final.

18 The compromise was confirmed in June 1991; see EC, Council of Economic and Finance Ministers (ECOFIN), *'Abolition of Tax Frontiers'*, Results of Working Sessions, Brussels, 24 June 1991.

19 Official Journal, L376, 31/12/91.

20 Particularly with respect to compliance of Member States with the legislation put forward by the Commission and agreed upon by the Council.

21 See Commission of the European Communities, *'The Single Market in 1994'*, report from the Commission to the Council and the European Parliament, COM(95) 238 final, Brussels, 15 June 1995.

22 In countries where a new organization has been set up for VAT, firms are dealing with several offices for their tax affairs. Most countries require monthly returns and payment of the tax though Ireland requires its returns bi-monthly and the UK and Denmark quarterly. Farmers in Denmark are allowed to make returns every six months. In general, the UK provides the most favourable treatment from a cash benefit point of view, though it has a system of heavy penalties for late payment of the tax.

23 Commission of the European Communities, *The Single Market in 1994* report from the Commission to the Council and the European Parliament, COM (95) 238 final, Brussels, 15 June 1995.

24 As opposed to its commitment to bring such proposals forward before December 1994 as stated in its 1993 report on the internal market, COM(94) 55 final, of 14 March 1994.

25 Such as the VAT Information Exchange System (VIES), the Standing Committee on Administrative Cooperation, the Central Liaison Office and the Matthaeus - Tax programme to attain closer cooperation between national administrations.

26 See European Commission, White Paper on Growth, Competitiveness and Employment, Office for Official Publications, 1994.

27 Spahn P.B., 'Consequences of EMU for fiscal federal relations in the Community and the financing of the Community budget', in 'The

Economics of Community Public Finance', *European Economy*, reports and studies, No. 5, 1993.

28   Council Directives 92/79/EEC of 19 October 1992 in OJ L 316 (cigarettes), Council Directive 92/80/EEC of 19 October 1992 in OJ L 316 (tobacco other than cigarettes) and Council Directive 92/83/EEC of 19 October 1992 in OJ L 316 (on alcoholic beverages and alcohol contained in other products).

29   Measures have already been taken towards this direction since 1974. For tobacco, Council Directive 72/464/EEC of 25 June 1974, as it was amended by subsequent directives 74/318/EEC, 75/786/EEC, 76/911/EEC, 77/805/EEC, 80/369/EEC, 80/1275/EEC, 86/246/EEC and 92/78/EEC; for alcohol and alcoholic beverages Council Directive. 92/83/EEC of 19 October 1992; and for mineral oils Council Directives 92/81/EEC, of 19 October 1992, and 92/108/EEC of 14 December 1992.

30   Commission of the European Communities, *Elimination of Distortions of Competition of a Fiscal Nature in the Transport of Goods by Road: A Study of Vehicle Taxes, Fuel Taxes and Road Tolls*, COM(86) 750 final, Brussels, December 1986.

31   The only progress in the field is a proposed directive of 1979 dealing with the taxation of migrant workers, which was withdrawn in 1992 and replaced by the recommendation of 1993 (OJ L 39 of 21 December 1993).

32   Sinn H-W., *'Capital Income Taxation and Resource Allocation'*, Amsterdam, North Holland, 1987.

33   See among others, Dunning J., *'Globalisation of Business'*, New York, 1993.

34   Commission of the European Communities, COM(69) 6 final, COM(69) 5 final, COM(75) 392 final.

35   Directive 90/435/EC of 23 July 1990 in OJ L 225 of 20 August 1990.

36   Directive 90/434/EEC, in OJ L 225, 20 August 1990; this directive eliminates the tax disadvantages of international mergers by deferring the taxation of any capital gains relating to the assets of the contributing or acquired company until they are realized, as done for domestic mergers.

37   As it appeared in OJ L 225 of 20 August 1990. This convention is a procedural instrument establishing a process to eliminate double taxation (not just the risk) resulting from the correction of transfer prices.

38 Proposal for a Council Directive on a common system of taxation applicable to interest and royalty payments made between parent companies and subsidiaries in different Member States, COM(90) 571 final of 28 November 1990 (OJ C 53, 28/02/1991), as amended by COM(93) 196 final of 10 June 1993 (OJ C 178, 30 June 1993.

39 Proposal for a Council Directive concerning arrangements for the taking into account by enterprises of the losses of their permanent establishments and subsidiaries situated in other Member States, COM(90) 595 final of 24 January 1991.

40 Ruding O. et al., '*Report of the Committee of Independent Experts on Company Taxation*', Office of Official Publications of the European Communities, Luxembourg, 1992. OECD, 'Taxing Profits in a Global Economy: Domestic and International Issues', *DAFFE/CFA*, (91)12, Paris, 1991.

41 The Committee for this purpose recommended a minimum corporate tax rate of 30% and also recommended that incentives should be unrelated to the tax base and be transparent.

42 Thereby complementing the arbitration convention.

43 See SEC(92) 1118 final: Commission communication to the Council and Parliament subsequent to the conclusions of the Ruding Committee indicating guidelines on company taxation linked to the further development of the Internal Merket, 26 June 1992.

44 In accordance to the Council Directive on Direct Taxation of OJ L336, 27/12/1977. This suggestion was only to make use of the 1977 Directive to combat abuse.

45 See Schelpe D., 'Present Position and Future Plans for Taxation by the European Commission', Brussels, 12 April 1994, personal communication.

46 Own-initiative of the Economic and Social Committee on Savings; No. CES 1018/94, Bulletin of CES 7/94.

47 See, for instance, the Communication from the Commission to the Council, COM(93) 632 final of 22 December 1993, and COM(94) 55 final, of 14 March 1994.

48 (92/96/EEC), which entered into force on 1 July 1994.

49 Despite Commission initiatives, Member States have not yet been able to agree upon a common approach; see COM(95)238 final, of 15 June 1995.

50 Commission Recommendation, OJ L 39 of 21 December 1993.

51   Decision in case No. C-279/93 (Finanzamt Koeln-Altstadt vs. Schumacker), 14 Febuary 1995.

52   Commission Communication on the improvement of the fiscal environment of SMEs, OJ C 187 of 9 July 1994, pp. 5-11.

53   94/390/EC.

54   COM(94) 3312 final of 7 December 1994.

55   Kopits G. (ed.), '*Tax Harmonization in the European Community: Policy Issues and Analysis*', International Monetary Fund, OP94, Washington, 1992.

56   Daly M. Weiner M., 'Corporate Tax Harmonization and Competition in Federal Countries: Some Lessons for the European Community?', *National Tax Journal*, Vol. 46, No. 4, pp. 441-461, 1993.

12 The Development of European Regulatory Frameworks: The Expansion of European Community Policy-Making in Telecommunications

MARK THATCHER

European Community (EC)[1] decisions in telecommunications provide an excellent example for the study of the processes and nature of Community regulation and industrial policy. National states have traditionally played a central role in telecommunications, notably by establishing legal monopolies given to publicly-owned service operators. In the 1980s and 1990s, however, the EC developed a wide-ranging policy framework that differed considerably from the industrial policies pursued before the 1980s by member states. Moreover, EC telecommunications policy has seen the application of the core of EC powers, namely competition law, to a strategic industrial and economic sector, a process in which member states and the Council of Ministers, the Commission and the European Court of Justice have all been important actors.

Three major features of the growth in EC activity are highlighted in tracing the development of EC policy making in telecommunications over the 1980s and early 1990s. First, the form and pace of the expansion of EC policy-making: the EC's role grew through a series of steps, with each step representing a limited increase in EC competence and the development of an EC regulatory framework; the expansion of EC competence was accompanied by compromises and temporary exceptions for difficult issues or countries; at each step, considerable agreement on the growth of EC activity existed amongst member states, with disagreement generally being limited to specific points of implementation, and not the principle of an expansion in EC activity. However, the steps in EC policy making rapidly succeeded each other, so that over a ten-fifteen year period, the cumulative effect was a major expansion of EC activity and indeed the creation of a wide-ranging EC regulatory framework. Thus EC policy making in telecommunications possesses features similar to those set out in models of incrementalism.[2] Second, the major features of the EC's regulatory framework are explored in order to show how they appear to significantly limit the ability of member states to pursue traditional industrial policies at the national level; in particular, the methods whereby EC regulation prevents member states from using policy tools to fulfil certain traditional policy functions in the sector are examined. The third feature highlighted is how the EC 're-regulated' the sector: EC regulation replaced national regulation; but, the nature of EC regulation differed from national regulatory frameworks before the 1980s, being strongly based on 'fair competition'.

Traditional National Policies in Telecommunications

Until the 1980s, policy in telecommunications was almost exclusively determined at the national level: international bodies such as the ITU (International Telecommunications Union) and CEPT (the European Conference of Postal and Telecommunications Administrations) had few powers over their members, and in any case were concerned only with international communications. In most EC member states, a similar regulatory framework existed, determined at the national level: a PTO (public telecommunications operator), which was usually publicly-owned and in most cases joined the postal services within a government department and hence formed part of the central governmental civil service,[3] supplied telecommunications services and certain types of equipment to customers. The PTO was given a monopoly over the public telecommunications infrastructure, and all services on this network by law or through an exclusive licence. The position of the PTOs over the supply of CPE (customer premises equipment - user equipment attached to the network) varied somewhat, but generally they held *de facto* or legal monopoly rights, whilst permitting supply by private firms of more sophisticated forms of equipment to businesses; in such cases, the PTO also acted as the regulatory body, issuing the few private licences needed and laying down norms for the equipment to be supplied. Equipment, both for the network and CPE, was generally manufactured by privately-owned suppliers. Strong regulatory bodies independent of the PTO and government did not exist; almost no competition was permitted and regulation was mostly implicit, with few explicit rules governing the supply of services and equipment, or the rights of users.

The regulatory framework permitted national policy-makers to pursue a range of policy aims; whilst some differences in these objectives were seen between countries and between different periods, certain common elements existed over time and cross-nationally. PTO tariffs were set to fulfil several policy objectives. One was to produce sufficient revenue; this level varied according to the investment plans of the PTO, the extent of PTO borrowing permitted and sometimes the needs of the general government budget, to which the PTO's spending and profits might make a contribution. Another aim, implicit or explicit, was to cross-subsidize certain users and/or services: some services were priced below cost, notably charges for access to the telecommunications network (connection and rental charges) and local calls, whilst others were priced above costs, mostly international and national calls. As a result, some groups were cross-subsidized by others, and in particular, PTO profits from large business users were used to subsidize losses from residential customers. The process of setting tariffs was linked to a third function of PTOs: the use of telecommunications prices for wider policy objectives, such as controlling inflation or influencing demand for telecommunications.

In most European countries, policy in network equipment manufacturing involved supporting selected 'national champions'. One policy instrument was the granting of PTO orders: this was an intensely political matter and in general, the majority went to 'national champions' such as Siemens in West Germany, CGE/Alcatel in France and Plessey and GEC in Britain. Another policy instrument was the establishment of very close relationships over research and development: PTOs and their 'national champion' suppliers would often jointly develop equipment, and PTO orders would virtually be guaranteed, frequently through a cartel arrangement whereby suppliers shared patents and PTO orders were divided according to pre-determined shares between 'approved' suppliers.

Research and development support to these privileged 'national champions' would be given both through PTO research establishments and through national research and development ('R&D') programmes financed by governments seeking a strong domestic subsector, jobs and exports. National governments and PTOs periodically sought to restructure the equipment subsector by altering the division of orders or altering the participants in R&D programmes, and hence allowing new entrants and encouraging or forcing mergers between firms.

EC Policy Making before the 1980s

EC policy in telecommunications was extremely limited in the 1960s and 1970s. Regulatory frameworks were regarded as a national matter, as were the decisions made within them, even though this involved the closure of telecommunications markets to potential suppliers from other EC member states. During the 1970s, the Commission began to call for change, and sought to link industrial policy with regulation of telecommunications. But, in practice, almost no major EC role developed.[4] The Commission appeared to have neither the will to act, nor the belief that the Treaty of Rome gave it the instruments to do so, whilst national governments treated telecommunications as a *chasse gardée*, seeing no need for EC activity. This situation was to greatly alter during the 1980s and 1990s.

EC Organizations and Powers in Telecommunications

The 1980s saw the establishment of new EC bodies involved in telecommunications policy making. In 1979, an Information Technologies Task Force was set up to provide the Commission with information concerning long-term R&D. Then in 1986, it was merged with other Commission departments to become a separate Directorate General for Telecommunications, Information Industries and Innovation, DG XIII which led Commission work on telecommunications and information technology R&D. It was also involved in telecommunications regulation, but its role was often subordinate to that of the competition Directorate General, DGIV, as the latter enjoyed legal powers to deal with public monopolies and abuse of a dominant position by organizations (notably EC Treaty Articles 90 and 86).

The Commission established bodies to provide links with other actors in telecommunications. Representatives of member states sat on various committees: in 1984, the Senior Officials Group on Telecommunications was set up, followed by the Senior Officials Group on Information Technology Standards and the Senior Officials Advisory Group for the Information Market.[5] The establishment and running of R&D programmes saw the involvement of industrialists, notably in the Information Technology Task Force. The EC played a crucial role in the creation in 1988 of ETSI (the European Telecommunications Standards Institute): although legally a private body, composed of different types of members (PTOs, manufacturers, administration and users), the EC made it one of the main organizations responsible for defining EC-wide norms and standards.[6]

The legal framework concerning telecommunications, and the powers of EC bodies, in particular those of the Commission and the Council, arise from various Treaty Articles. Telecommunications are not mentioned specifically in the Treaty of Rome. However, several of the general Articles are especially relevant. Articles 30-37 provide for the free circulation of goods, notably Article 30 which prohibits quantitative restrictions or measures having equivalent effect (including non-tariff barriers), whilst Article 59 provides for the freedom to provide services throughout the EC and Article 7 prohibits discrimination on grounds of nationality within the EC. Article 85 outlaws measures and activities which are capable of affecting trade between member states and which are aimed at or have the effect of impairing competition within the EC, unless falling within exceptions covered by Article 85(2), whilst Article 86 bans 'abuse of a dominant position'. The Treaty contains provisions specifically pertaining to 'national enterprises' such as publicly-owned PTOs. Article 90 is the most important. Article 90(1) forbids member states from introducing or maintaining any measures contrary to the Treaty, and specifically those which conflict with Articles 7 and 85-94, with respect to 'public undertakings' and those enterprises to which member states grant 'special or exclusive rights' (such as monopolies or protection from competition by a licensing system); thus member states cannot not use PTOs to avoid the competition provisions of the Treaty. This is qualified by Article 90(2), which states that for :-

'undertakings entrusted with the operation of services of general economic interest, the rules of the Treaty, and notably those concerning competition, apply insofar as they do not obstruct the performance, in law or fact, of the particular tasks assigned to them' (i.e. the undertakings).

Enforcement of the Treaty is covered by Article 90(3), which gives the Commission the responsibility of ensuring the application of the Article and the power to issue Directives or Decisions to member states, these not requiring approval by the Council or the European Parliament.

More specific mention of R&D and telecommunications came in EC Treaties after 1958. Telecommunications were included in the Single Market programme (1992); under the new Article 100A, introduced under the 1986 Single European Act, decisions for the creation of the Single Market can be passed by a qualified majority of the Council of Ministers. Moreover, under the 1986 Single European Act, the EC was given powers to undertake R&D programmes, a function developed in the 1993 Maastricht Treaty: an overall 'framework programme' was to be proposed by the Commission, requiring unanimous approval by the Council of Ministers and also acceptance by the European Parliament. However, specific programmes within the framework programmes only needed a qualified majority within the Council of Ministers. The Maastricht Treaty also provided a legal basis for EC action to create 'trans-European networks', including specifically in telecommunications (section XII of the Treaty), as well as general provisions on creating the conditions for industrial competitiveness.

Preparing the Terrain: EC Plans for Telecommunications Policy

The EC has distinguished between different fields within the telecommunications sector, with policy varying between them, especially in terms of speed of change. In particular, three fields have seen much EC activity. The first is the 'infrastructure', the fixed-line public telecommunications system run by PTOs, which consists of means of transmission (mostly cables, but also radio-transmission and satellite equipment) and public exchanges or 'switches', which ensure that calls are routed to the person called. The second is the supply of services, ranging from voice telephony to advanced services combining telecommunications and computing, such as telematics (whereby computer data bases can be consulted by linking terminals to them using the telecommunications system) and data processing and transmission services; linked to services is a range of accompanying Customer Premises Equipment ('CPE'), from telephone sets and fax machines to high complex computers. And, finally, there is the manufacture of switches and transmission equipment for the infrastructure.

The EC Commission began to argue in the 1970s that an EC industrial policy for the information and telecommunications sectors was essential for Europe's economic future.[7] After a series of general pronouncements, but few concrete plans, during the 1970s, the 1980s saw a series of increasingly ambitious proposals from the Commission. In 1980, it submitted three proposals to the Council, calling for harmonization in telecommunications, a common market in CPE and more open public procurement.[8] Although these were accepted by the Council, this only took place in 1984 and they were only translated into Recommendations, which are not legally binding.

Further Commission activity took place in 1983-84. In 1983, the Commission proposed to the Council six 'lines of action' in telecommunications, covering similar ground to that of 1980, but also including R&D and using telecommunications technologies to assist under-developed areas of the EC; the Commission suggested that increasing the EC's role in telecommunications would not affect the duties of PTOs nor the use of PTO revenues by member states.[9] These 'lines of action' formed the basis for a telecommunications action programme, put forward in May 1984 by the Commission and approved by the Council of Ministers in December 1984.[10] Its scope appeared limited. The market for CPE would gradually be opened up through the creation of EC standards (themselves based on international standards), the progressive introduction of procedures for mutual recognition between national authorities of type approval of CPE and the opening of a proportion of public procurement contracts to other EC suppliers. Advanced telecommunications services and networks were to be promoted through a development programme for a long-term wide-band network (i.e. a network with very high transmission capacity, thereby able to transmit not only voice telephony, but also sophisticated data and visual services) and discussions on infrastructure projects of interest to all member states.

More substantial change was suggested by a Green Paper issued by the Commission in 1987.[11] A common market in CPE should be established. This would involve the ending of PTO monopolies over the supply of CPE, 'fair procedures' for the approval of CPE, including mutual recognition of licences granted in other member states, and the establishment of EC standards. Similarly, a common market in advanced telecommunications services should be created: monopoly supply by PTOs would be ended; 'fair competition' in supply would be achieved by the EC defining the conditions of access to the telecommunications infrastructure, including standards and interfaces for interconnection, ensuring that the tariffs charged by PTOs were based on costs and by scrutiny of cross-subsidization between monopoly services and those open to competition by PTOs. EC rules for 'fair' access to the network would be known as ONP (Open Network Provision). More generally, 'fair competition' required a separation of regulation and supply, so that PTOs were not both competitors and regulators of other suppliers. Furthermore, public procurement of telecommunications equipment, notably network equipment, should be opened to competition from suppliers other than the 'national champion' manufacturer in each country. The EC would ensure this by establishing rules concerning standards and tenders and by action against unlawful discrimination.

However, the Green Paper also balanced these suggested measures for greater competition with others more compatible with the traditional 'public service' roles of PTOs. No change in public ownership would be required by implementation of the Green Paper. Decisions over the exclusive PTO provision of the infrastructure would equally be left to member states. Nationally-determined PTO monopolies over non-advanced or 'reserved services' could continue; since these included voice telephony, accounting for 85 per cent of the telecommunications services market, the bulk of telecommunications revenue could remain within the public monopoly. The Green Paper recognized the public service tasks of PTOs, and in particular the function of ensuring universal service to cover basic needs; it accepted that this required the financial viability of PTOs, and hence the possibility of some cross-subsidization between services. Thus whilst tariffs should be 'oriented' towards costs, there should be a 'fair trade-off' between this and offering an universal service; measures could be taken to prevent 'cream-skimming', whereby competitors to PTOs would undercut PTO tariffs on profitable routes, whilst leaving the PTO to shoulder the burdens of universal services. Furthermore, although competition in the supply of CPE and non-reserved services would be permitted, safeguards to ensure network integrity and the protection of 'reserved services' were envisaged. Hence it appeared that means of influencing the scope and form of competition would be available to member states.

Two distinct rationales for the Green Paper's proposals were put forward. First, the legal provisions of the Treaty of Rome were argued to require greater competition, especially Articles 30, 85, 86 and 90. Second, the measures were in the interests of the EC. Telecommunications were becoming more and more economically important. New technological and economic conditions were altering the nature of the sector, and failure to adapt the regulatory framework to these would entail severe consequences. Competition in CPE and advanced services was claimed to arise from the increasing mixing of telecommunications and computing and to be essential for the growth of new telecommunications applications. A common European market in CPE, network equipment and services, through fair competition and common standards, would allow EC firms to enjoy a large market necessary for economies of scale; hence they would be capable of meeting global competition from American and Japanese firms. The Green Paper noted that its proposals were part of a world-wide trend, and indeed that competition in many non-voice services and in most CPE had already been introduced in several EC countries.

After publishing the Green Paper, the Commission launched a 'consultation process', lasting six months. The results, it claimed, indicated a broad consensus on most of the measures proposed, with disagreement being limited to the continuation of PTO monopolies over the infrastructure and over reserved services.[12] The Commission then set out a timetable for implementing the Green Paper. In June 1988, the Council of Ministers gave its support to the aims of the Green Paper, by passing a Council Resolution.[13] The period between 1988 and 1992 saw the use of the Green Paper as the base for a series of measures. Then after 1992, EC activity began to extend beyond the original measures envisaged in the Green Paper.

EC Policy for Customer Premises Equipment

EC policy for CPE has involved three related elements: competition in the supply of CPE, mutual recognition of CPE licences between member states and the establishment of EC norms and standards. All three were envisaged in the 1987 Green Paper.

In 1988, the Commission issued a Directive on CPE, which became known as the Terminals Directive.[14] The Directive insisted that member states allow competition in the supply of all types of CPE. Those member states that had granted 'special and exclusive rights' (such as a monopoly) were to ensure that these were withdrawn. Member states were to make the necessary provisions to permit suppliers to import, sell, attach, put into service and maintain CPE, and a timetable was laid down whereby competition in the supply of different types of CPE would be allowed by the end of 1990. Member states could only insist that CPE should meet 'essential requirements', specified by the EC namely that equipment ensured the safety of employees and operators of public networks, protected public networks against damage and allowed inter-operability with other equipment.

The main principles and objectives of the Directive were not opposed in the Council of Ministers.[15] However, the Commission, and specifically DGIV, issued the Directive under Article 90(3), arguing that it was necessary for the enforcement of Article 90(1) as the special and exclusive monopoly rights of PTOs were contrary to Treaty Articles concerning competition (especially Articles 30, 85 and 86). The use of Article 90(3) meant that the Directive did not need to be passed by the Council of Ministers nor be scrutinized by the European Parliament, as would have been the case if, for instance, Article 100A had been used; it was also significant for future attempts by DGIV to enforce its view of the requirements imposed by Article 90. The Commission's choice of Article 90 was challenged by various countries, resulting in the important case of *French Republic, supported by Italy, Belgium, Germany and Greece v Commission of the European Communities*.[16]

The judgement of the European Court of Justice centred on the right of the Commission to issue the Directive under Article 90(3), on which point it upheld the Commission. Nevertheless, it also examined the meaning of Article 90(1) and (2) with respect to the substantive content of the Directive. The Court held that Article 90 was designed to reconcile the use by member states of certain undertakings, notably those in the public sector, as instruments of economic or fiscal policy, with the respect of EEC competition rules and the unity of the common market. It stated that the legality of 'special and exclusive rights' granted by member states depended on their compatibility with the Treaty Articles referred to in Article 90. The Court held that all regulatory measures which could, directly or indirectly, harm trade between member states were illegal, being incompatible with Article 30. It therefore held that 'exclusive rights' over the supply, attachment, maintenance and putting into service of CPE were unlawful. But, the Court appeared to distinguish 'special rights', which might not damage intra-Community trade; indeed, it annulled the Directive's provisions outlawing special rights on the grounds that the exact types of rights and the ways in which they contravened the Treaty were not specified. Nevertheless, on balance, the outcome of the case was favourable both to the power of the Commission to use Article 90, and to its approach (and that of the 1987 Green Paper) of ending or severely limiting the 'special and exclusive' rights of PTOs.

The second strand of EC policy was mutual recognition of licences granted in other member states; this would facilitate competition in supply in national EC markets, especially by other EC firms. A first step was taken in 1986, when the Council of Ministers adopted a Directive[17] whereby member states were to recognize the results of tests carried out in other EC countries to establish that equipment conformed to norms and standards applying throughout the EC. However, in practice this meant that only equipment for which norms had been established by the CEPT [18] was covered, which was only a very limited proportion of CPE. The second stage was full mutual recognition, under a Directive adopted by the Council in 1991.[19] CPE meeting the EC's 'essential requirements', and tested and licensed in one member state, can be marketed and attached to telecommunications networks throughout the EC without further testing or licensing.

The principle of mutual recognition of licences issued in other member states, who can only insist that CPE meets EC-defined 'essential requirements', was widely accepted in the Council. Disagreement was confined to two issues. 'Liberal' countries, such as Britain, (West) Germany, the Netherlands and Denmark wished to minimize the applicability of EC 'essential requirements', fearing that they would limit competition in practice, whereas other countries, notably France, Belgium, Italy and Spain favoured coverage of most CPE, claiming that regulatory protection against 'uncontrolled' competition was needed. The outcome was a compromise, whereby the Directive applied to CPE attached to public networks and to mobile equipment, but not to terminals attached to private networks. The second question was an attempt by France to restrict mutual recognition of equipment manufactured in non-EC countries; this suggestion was rejected.

Harmonization through the establishment of norms and standards applying throughout the European Community constituted the third element of EC policy. Already in 1983, a Council Directive imposed a duty on member states to inform the Commission of regulatory plans involving technical standards and norms, and allowed the Commission to intervene if it considered that such plans could constitute a barrier to intra-community trade. Then a Council Directive in 1986 (86/361/EEC) laid down procedures for the CEPT to draw up technical specifications, in order to allow equipment to be marketed throughout the EC. However, standard-setting was very slow. Thus in 1988 ETSI took over much of the work of EC standard setting. Nevertheless, unlike other areas of technical standards,[20] CPE must meet mandatory norms to fulfil the 'essential requirements' specified in the 1988 Terminals Directive: this means ETSI norms or, if none are specified for a particular type of equipment, national norms. If CPE meets the standards and tests laid down by ETSI and accepted by the Commission, it can be licensed in any member state and then freely traded and attached to public networks throughout the EC without any further licensing restrictions.

Services other than 'Reserved Services'

The 1987 Green Paper envisaged that EC law would allow competition in the supply of all services, other than 'reserved services' and the infrastructure. Such an approach had already been foreshadowed by the European Court of Justice, in the case of *Italy v Commission*, known as 'the BT case'.[21] It ruled that regulations issued by BT, acting under British law, to restrict the use of BT's network to supply telex forwarding services were contrary to Article 86 of the Treaty of Rome. Although the case only concerned regulations issued by a PTO, and not by public bodies independent of PTOs, it was important in that many national restrictions on supply were imposed by PTOs, and in that the Court made clear its belief that national rules limiting competition were in general undesirable, so regulations not covered by the judgement but falling under Article 90, might also be ruled illegal.

In 1990, the Commission formally issued a Services Directive,[22] acting under Article 90(3). 'Special and exclusive rights' were to be abolished for a wide range of services. Competition in the supply of all VANS ('value-added network services' - specialized services, whereby 'value' is added to mere transmission by some operations being performed on the signals sent) was to be permitted from the end of 1990. Member states could insist that VANS be licensed, but this could only oblige suppliers to meet EC-defined 'essential requirements', namely safeguarding the integrity of the public network, the safety of its operation, and the operability and protection of data; moreover, any restrictions had to be 'proportional' to achieving their aims, non-discriminatory, public and notified to the Commission for scrutiny. Services which merely involved the transmission of data were to be liberalized at the end of 1992. Finally, the simple resale of leased line capacity, whereby transmission capacity could be rented from a PTO and then resold to third parties, was to be permitted from the end of 1992.[23] The Directive did not apply to mobile and satellite services, for which separate Directives would be issued.

The general principle of greater competition in the supply of non-reserved services was accepted within the Council of Ministers. Disagreement centred on three issues. First, the powers of the Commission: its use of Article 90(3) was challenged by several countries, led by France, before the European Court of Justice. But, the Court ruled in favour of the Commission,[24] closely following its decision in the Terminals Directive case. A second issue was the coverage of the Directive: a group of Mediterranean countries, notably France, Italy, Spain and Greece, wished to exclude data transmission services, whereas Britain, (West) Germany, Holland and Denmark favoured their inclusion. The result was a compromise: data transmission services were included, but member states could insist on additional licence conditions to ensure non-interruption and availability of supply, quality of service and, most important of all, the pursuit of 'tasks of general interest'; such conditions were to be 'objective', public and without discriminatory effects, these being monitored by DGIV. Moreover, countries with 'under-developed infrastructures' could ask for extensions of the transition period until 1996.

The third matter concerned conditions of supply and the norms and standards imposed by the EC, which, as with CPE, accompanied the abolition of national 'special and exclusive rights'. Concurrently with the Services Directive, the Council passed the ONP (Open Network Provision) Directive. This laid down the general principles governing access to telecommunications infrastructure for service providers. It formed part of the compromise whereby greater competition in the supply of services was accepted: the 'liberal' countries wished to restrict the application and specificity of the ONP Directive, being concerned that it would be too prescriptive and hence prevent real competition, whereas other member states, such as France, pressed for maximum coverage and also insistence on EC-determined norms and standards in the licensing of services.

Technical norms and standards were to be decided by ETSI. They were to be voluntary, in keeping with the EC's general 'new approach' to standards, and hence their non-adoption could not be used to refuse a licence to a supplier. However, service providers adopting them were certain of meeting EC 'essential requirements' and hence could offer their services throughout the EC. Moreover, mutual recognition of licences between member states is being introduced, so that service providers who meet EC 'essential requirements' and obtain a licence in one country will be able to operate throughout the EC.[25]

The ONP Directive aimed to meet three concerns: to ensure the inter-operability and compatibility of services, allowing trans-European services to be offered; to permit implementation of the Services Directive; to deal with problems concerning 'fair competition' between PTOs and other firms, especially concerning tariffs and access to the infrastructure, as PTOs might both retain monopolies over the provision of the infrastructure and also be competitors in the supply of non-reserved services tariff policies.[26] The ONP Directive was a framework Directive, being followed by a series of specific Directives and Recommendations dealing with individual services. Nevertheless, certain principles are common to legislation flowing from the ONP Directive. Service providers are given the right to connect their equipment to the infrastructure and to supply their services on it; norms and standards, especially interfaces (the point of connection between the infrastructure and the service provider's equipment) are specified, so that suppliers know the technical conditions for access to the network, and PTOs cannot use such conditions to restrict competition; principles for tariffs are laid down, and in particular in the principle that prices must be based on 'objective' criteria, notably costs; discrimination with respect to conditions of usage and tariffs is forbidden. Thus in practice, ONP Directives have been a means of both ensuring the respect of minimum standards and also facilitating 'fair' and effective competition.

For satellite communications, the Commission published a separate Green Paper in 1990.[27] It proposed that competition be allowed in equipment and services, the harmonization of standards in equipment, mutual recognition of licences, service suppliers being able to buy space 'segments' or capacity directly from satellite organizations, and similarly the latter being permitted to directly market capacity to service providers other than PTOs. Directives to implement these proposals have been proposed by the Commission and have been enacted or are in the process of being passed.[28]

EC action in mobile communications has focused on reserving common radio frequencies in all member states, and common equipment standards, so that mobile equipment can be used throughout the Community.[29] In June 1993, the Council asked the Commission to produce a Green Paper on mobile communications. The Green Paper, produced in April 1994, set out the objectives of establishing the conditions for the development of a European-wide market for mobile services and equipment, the identification of common principles for the supply of mobile networks, terminals and services and the promotion of a mass mobile market. It therefore proposed that 'special and exclusive rights' should be abolished, albeit subject to 'appropriate licensing conditions', restrictions on the development of mobile networks and services should be ended and that type approval and mutual recognition of equipment should be further developed. Hence it followed closely the approach of extending competition used for services and voice telephony. Measures to implement the Green Paper should follow after 1994.

Reserved Services and the Infrastructure

The 1987 Green Paper envisaged that certain member states could maintain, if they wished, 'special and exclusive' rights over the provision of the network infrastructure and also the supply of 'reserved' services, and in particular voice telephony. The rationale was that safeguarding public service goals, and in particular the provision of voice telephony as a 'universal service', might require cross-subsidization between different types of service. However, the Green Paper argued that any restrictions imposed by member states on competition should be narrowly construed.

The 1990 Services Directive and ONP Directive followed the Green Paper, and excluded the infrastructure and supply of voice telephony and telex services from the requirements of competition. However, this represented a compromise between those urging more competition, notably Britain and DGIV, and those seeking to protect PTO monopolies, particularly France. The issue was left open, in two respects: first, the Commission was empowered to re-examine 'special and exclusive rights' in 1992; second, the issue of whether special and exclusive rights were legally compatible with Article 90 was not clarified.

After the compromise of 1990, the Commission advanced on three fronts. First, it claimed that regardless of the legality under Article 90 of 'special and exclusive' rights granted to PTOs, the behaviour of PTOs was covered by competition law, and in particular Articles 85 and 86. Thus PTO decisions over the supply of 'reserved services' and the infrastructure could be scrutinized for contravening EC law on anti-competitive agreements or for abuse of a dominant position. In September 1991, the Commission issued guidelines for undertakings in telecommunications, including PTOs.[30] Illegal agreements included those to divide markets or to set prices; hence PTO tariff-setting might be covered. Furthermore, agreements made by PTOs as part of international accords adopted by organizations such as the CCITT (International Telegraph and Telephone Consultative Committee, an important body in determining international norms and the prices of international services) were covered. A 'dominant position' under Article 86 was argued to include 'special and exclusive rights', whilst abuse could arise from not only refusal to supply a product or service without a legitimate reason, but also practising abnormally low prices in order to drive out competition. Hence the supply of the telecommunications infrastructure and reserved services by PTOs was open to challenge under competition law. An early indication of the possible implications came in 1991, when DGIV announced a formal investigation into prices charged for international communications by PTOs in the EC, an issue involving not only the decisions of PTOs, but also international agreements on tariffs and payments between PTOs for international services.

The second part of the Commission's approach was to propose an ONP Directive on voice telephony in 1992.[31] It dealt with the terms under which voice telephony and related services were supplied. It called for service targets to be set, for users to have an enforceable contract and for certain advanced features (such as freephone and caller identification services) to be available. It also covered terms for access to the public switched network, a crucial point if competition was to be possible. Its requirements included the availability of access to the network at certain points, non-discrimination in the provision of access and the possibility of intervention by national regulatory authorities if reasonable requests for interconnection were not being met. However, the Directive recognized that national regulatory authorities, such as Oftel in Britain, would have primary responsibility for enforcing the Directive.

However, the ONP Voice Telephony Directive became linked to the third element of the Commission's approach: extending competition. From January 1992 a committee, headed by the then Commissioner responsible for DGIV, Sir Leon Brittan, reviewed progress in establishing the ONP framework and the appropriateness of member states being able to maintain the remaining 'special and exclusive rights' allowed under the 1990 Directives. In October 1992, it published its report. It suggested that a true internal market in telecommunications and progress in the international competitiveness of European firms were being held back by international communication tariffs being too high and the lack of international networks, notably those using high capacity lines. It argued that 'liberalization' of telecommunications was needed to assist the sector. It put forward several scenarios for the future, but favoured the rapid extension of competition. It suggested that competition in intra-EC communications should be permitted in 1996, and, although national 'special and exclusive rights' in national communications would be permitted, other measures would follow to permit greater competition.

The Commission's proposals were supported by 'liberal' states, led by Britain, but also including Denmark and the Netherlands. However, they were opposed by other member states on two main grounds: first, France and Germany were concerned that greater competition would threaten the financial viability of their PTOs, and in particular their fulfilment of tasks of general economic interest, such as the provision of universal service, as other operators 'cream-skimmed' profitable services; second, poorer and smaller states, such as Greece, Portugal, Spain, Ireland and Luxembourg, feared that their PTOs were too small and under-developed to withstand foreign competitors.

The Commission then launched a six month consultation, as it sought the views of interested parties. After consultations with national regulators, companies, PTOs, users groups and professional associations, the Commission made new proposals in April 1993. These offered several compromises and changes compared with its original suggestions and were largely accepted by the Council, in June 1993.[32] Voice telephony, both international and within member states, would be opened to competition from 1998. However, Spain, Ireland and Portugal were given up to a further five years, during which time they could prepare their PTOs for competition, whilst countries with very small networks (notably Luxembourg, and perhaps also Belgium) could request an extension of up to two years. Moreover, certain principles were set out, notably that greater competition should be accompanied by measures to ensure the availability of 'universal service' throughout the EC at a reasonable price for the consumer and subject to a reasonable time scale for delivery. 'Access charges' for use of PTO networks should be possible, to help pay for this aim; the extent to which cross-subsidization between services would be permitted was unclear. 'Special and exclusive rights' over the telecommunications infrastructure and cable television networks were to be examined by the Commission before the end of 1995; in the meantime, national monopolies over these could remain. Furthermore, the head of DG XIII, Michel Carpentier, indicated that given an environment of greater competition, the application of competition law would have to be altered, to allow cooperation agreements and even mergers between PTOs without these being prevented by Articles 85 and 86.[33] Finally, largely at the insistence of France, EC markets would only be opened to firms from non-

EC countries to the extent that these other countries allowed reciprocal access to their national markets.[34]

The agreement on competition in voice telephony was incorporated in a revised ONP Voice Telephony Directive. But, the measure became entangled with other issues unrelated to telecommunications, in this case, a dispute between the European Parliament and the Council on the failure of the latter to accept any of the European Parliament's proposed amendments to the draft Directive under the new 'co-decision' procedures of the Maastricht Treaty. This was the first conflict involving these procedures, and, concerned to establish its rights, the European Parliament rejected the Directive in July 1994, even though the content of the measure appeared to enjoy wide support among MEPs. The Council is expected to produce a new but very similar Directive in 1995.

The spread of competition continued apace in 1994: in October 1994 the Commission produced the first part of its Green Paper on the Liberalization of the Infrastructure and Cable Television. It proposed that competition in the infrastructure should be introduced in two stages. From the first of January 1995, services which had already been opened to competition (such as data transmission or advanced services) could be transmitted not only on the networks of PTOs, but also on 'alternative networks', such as cable television networks and the private networks owned by bodies such as railway and electricity companies. Full competition in the infrastructure (i.e. choice of infrastructure for other services, principally voice telephony) would be introduced in 1998. This two-stage approach was supported by Britain, France, Germany and the Netherlands, but was bitterly opposed by 'Mediterranean countries' and Belgium. The Commissioner for competition, Karl van Miert, threatened to use Article 90 to ensure that competition began before 1998. In response, the Council in November 1994, accepted the principle that competition in the infrastructure should be established under EC legislation, but set 1998 as the date for implementation, thus giving time for PTOs to prepare themselves. Moreover, an extension was given to countries that had enjoyed one, for the introduction of competition in the supply of voice telephony, whilst the principles of the maintenance of 'public service' and reciprocity with non-EC countries were to be included in the Directives to implement the agreement. Hence the details of the ensuing Directives will be important for licensing and the form of competition that will develop.

Nevertheless, the expansion of EC policy in 'reserved services' and the infrastructure appears remarkable compared to the position in 1990: then, it seemed that in these fields, which account for the bulk of telecommunications revenue (85-90 per cent), national monopolies might persist for a long period and the EC would play a small role. But, by the end of the 1990s, EC law will insist that member states permit competition in voice telephony and the infrastructure, whilst the Commission and its competition rules will influence the way in which competition is conducted to ensure its 'fairness'.

R&D Policy

Effective EC policy making in R&D began in the 1980s. The Commission, and notably Viscount Davignon, began consultations in the early 1980s with large European Information Technology ('IT') firms, known as the 'Round-table firms'. As a result, a pilot R&D programme in IT was begun in 1982, named ESPRIT (European Strategic Programme for Research and Development in Information Technologies), approved by the Council of Ministers. This was followed by a full programme, ESPRIT Phase 1, approved by the Council of Ministers in 1984 with a budget of 750 million ECUS and designed to last five years, and to be followed by another five year programme. At the same time, in 1983, the Council of Ministers had approved a pluri-annual Framework Programme for the years 1984-87 with a budget of 3,750 million ECUs, covering various fields of research, but with the improvement of energy resources as the main budgetary element of spending.[35]

Telecommunications were not directly covered by either ESPRIT or the First Framework Programme, although the former involved combinations of telecommunications and computing. However, in 1984 the Commission put forward a telecommunications action programme[36] named RACE (Research and Development in Advanced Communications Technologies for Europe), which included a development programme for the long-term implementation of future wide-band networks. These are telecommunications networks with a very high transmission capacity, able to transmit speech, data and images simultaneously, in order to provide new advanced services; they are sometimes known as ISDN (Integrated Services Digital Networks). The Council of Ministers approved a pilot programme for RACE after the Commission agreed that finance would come from existing Commission budgets, that no commitment to a later full phase would be made and that the CEPT would play a central role.[37] The pilot programme would define the main fields of RACE, notably the development of a model of the new broadband network (including norms and standards for the network, terminal equipment attached to it and services which would be offered on it) and the priorities for long-term R&D. As with ESPRIT, EC funds (20 million ECU) were matched by the same sum provided by participating countries, and a large number of industrial companies, universities and PTOs were involved.

The Commission then put forward in 1986 the main phase of RACE, covering the years 1987-91, with the objective of the introduction of an EC-wide integrated broadband network by 1995. RACE would cover both Europe-wide agreement on norms and standards and also the mobilization of European R&D resources. RACE now formed part of the Commission's wider EC R&D programme, the Second Framework Programme (covering the years 1987-91), which would include ESPRIT and IT, and also RACE; its budget was fixed at 5,396 million ECUs, for the years 1987-91. The Programme secured widespread acceptance but was only accepted by the Council of Ministers in 1987, after protracted negotiations involving other matters.[38] RACE enjoyed the third largest budget within the Second Framework programme with 550 million ECUs; moreover, this sum was to be matched by participating companies, so that the total volume of spending was to be 1,100 million ECUs. RACE's first phase involved three main elements: developing broadband systems; supporting broadband technologies; aiding the supply of advanced services on the network, providing access for users and allowing the attachment of user terminal equipment to the network.[39] RACE was then included within the Third Framework Programme (for the period 1990-94), when its budget was slightly reduced to 489 million ECUs. Its objectives for this second phase particularly concern the development of artificial intelligence in networks, communications with mobiles, transmission of images (including High Definition Television) and the use of optical fibre. In June 1993, a fourth Framework Programme (for the period 1994-98) was approved by the Council of Ministers, which included 3,900 million ECUs for information and communication technologies, out of the total of 13.1 billion ECUs. The RACE programme was succeeded by a programme for ACTS

(Advanced Communications Technology and Services), which enjoyed a budget of 630 million ECUs. It will continue the work of RACE, but greater emphasis is to be given to operational trials of advanced services and networks.

Despite the billions of ECUs being spent, EC R&D programmes represent only a tiny proportion of total European R&D.[40] However, arguments for their importance rest on their capacity to act as a catalyst in promoting R&D in Europe and cooperation between Europe firms.[41]

Public Procurement

Telecommunications were excluded from the 1977 Directive on the opening of public procurement supply contracts.[42] A Council Recommendation[43] was passed in 1984 whereby member states were to ensure that PTOs provide opportunities for firms from other member states to tender for at least 10 per cent of the value of annual orders for PTO switching and transmission equipment, but it was not legally binding. The 1987 Green Paper envisaged that this provision would be extended, and that national barriers would be weakened by common EC standards and type approval of equipment.

Finally, in 1990, a Council Directive[44] laid down rules for procedures for public procurement supply contracts. It covered public bodies enjoying 'special and exclusive rights' and activities relating to public telecommunications networks or the supply of 'public telecommunications services'.[45] Operators and service providers are obliged to ensure that sufficient information is given to potential suppliers, that selection procedures are clear and non-discriminatory, that technical specifications refer to and give priority to EC-wide norms, that if other specifications are used, that they are non-discriminatory in their effects, and that if quality criteria are used (as opposed to price criteria), that they be objective and available to all enterprises concerned. Moreover, a 'Remedies Directive'[46] was passed in 1992 to provide potentially aggrieved parties with methods of seeking redress, including damages.

Nevertheless, the scope of the public procurement Directive was limited in several respects. Although it was due to come into force on 1 January 1993, later dates apply to Spain (1996), Greece and Portugal (1998). It only covered contracts for works over five million ECUs and those for the supply of equipment over 600,000 ECUs. Moreover, whilst tender procedures had to be fair, purchasers could choose the method for allocation of contracts, including open tenders, tenders restricted to candidates already selected by some qualification or by negotiation with a supplier, with or without rival tenders.

National Institutional Arrangements for PTOs

The EC laid down a few stipulations for the institutional arrangements in member states for telecommunications and their operation. In particular, two important provisions are specified in several Directives, notably those on CPE supply and services supply. First, the functions of regulation and the supply of services and equipment must be separated. Thus regulatory decisions must be taken by bodies separate from PTOs. Second, decisions must be made according to public, non-discriminatory and 'objective' criteria. These requirements were upheld by the European Court in the Terminals Case.

EC requirements for national institutional frameworks were, however, notable by their absence. The EC did not attempt to specify the institutional framework for PTOs, nor under the Treaty of Rome can it decide whether PTOs should be publicly or privately owned. Most of the legislation was in the form of Directives, which required member states to transpose them into national legislation, but gave them freedom over the means of meeting EC requirements.

Telecommunications, Trans-European Networks and 'Electronic Highways'

EC policy in the 1990s has increasingly emphasized that telecommunications are a central element in the creation of trans-European 'information networks' or 'electronic highways'. Before the Maastricht Treaty, and following an initiative by the Commission, the European Council adopted a Resolution in 1990 calling for EC action in favour of trans-European networks. The Commission then pressed for an action programme, a position aided by the inclusion of trans-European networks within the Maastricht Treaty. Information networks were included within the programme for trans-European networks agreed at the Edinburgh and

Copenhagen summits, at which the principle of combining EC and private sector funds was agreed, together with sources of EC finance. The impetus for an extension of EC activity continued with Jacques Delors' *White Paper on Growth, Competitiveness and Employment* in December 1993, in which he argued that it was essential for European competitiveness to develop a 'common information area', notably through the establishment of trans-European 'electronic highways', which would provide wide and inexpensive access to large quantities of information for European users.

In order to provide greater precision concerning concepts such as European 'information infrastructures' and 'the information society', to examine the financial implications of programmes to implement the Delors Report's vision and to provide practical measures, a high-level group of European industrialists was established, known as the 'Bangemann Group', as it was chaired by the EC Commission Vice-President, Martin Bangemann. Its report, *Europe and the global information society,* of May 1994, made several recommendations. Some followed existing policies, such as continuing the extension of competition, notably to the provision of the telecommunications infrastructure. Others involved the application of policies in other fields, such as intellectual property and rules on media ownership, to telecommunications and the supply of information. Finally, measures to ensure the development of Europe-wide telecommunications networks, services and applications were proposed, including the continued use of Europe-wide standards and the creation of EC programmes for the application of telecommunications services on an EC-wide basis. The report was well-received at the Corfu summit of the European Council in June 1994.

Thus it appears that the expansion of EC policy in telecommunications is being increasingly linked to a broader approach concerning 'information', including infrastructure, networks, services and norms.

Conclusion

EC activity in telecommunications grew steadily in the 1980s and then rapidly in the early/mid 1990s. A pattern to its development can be discerned, which applied to almost all areas of telecommunications policy. Limited plans, which appeared to imply only minor changes in the supply arrangements of member states were announced, followed by correspondingly circumscribed legislation; examples include the supply of CPE, public procurement and R&D programmes. Considerably more ambitious plans were then put forward by the Commission, the most notable example being the 1987 Green Paper and the Second Framework Programme; these were then implemented by a series of Directives covering CPE, services, ONP and public procurement, and also the research and development programmes. Nevertheless, member states retained important powers over the bulk of the sector, and in particular voice telephony and the infrastructure. Finally, in the 1990s, the coverage of EC activity was widened, to cover voice telephony, the behaviour of PTOs and satellite services. Further EC measures in the remaining parts of the sector, particularly the infrastructure and mobile communications are being undertaken. R&D offers an exception, in that EC expenditure remains only a fraction of national spending.

Thus by a series of steps, the EC transformed its role in telecommunications. At the beginning of the 1980s, the EC played almost no part in regulating the sector. By the 1990s, EC legislation insisted on competition in the supply of all services and CPE, 'fair procedures' in norm setting and public procurement, independent and 'fair' regulation and respect of Articles 85 and 86; moreover, the EC was undertaking large-scale R&D programmes. The process of EC policy making bears many resemblances to that described in theories of 'incrementalism': the steady development of policy; the gradual accretion of powers by the EC; limited concessions being made to obtain maximum acceptance; the final sum of the series of steps being very great change over a relatively limited period of time.

The expansion of EC policy making was marked by a high level of agreement by member states and an evolution in their positions. The early steps in EC policy seemed limited. Greater conflict arose over the implementation of the more ambitious plans in the late 1980s, but these centred on the powers of the Commission, and particularly its use of Article 90, and some specific elements of the legislation. Nevertheless, there was broad agreement with respect to the general direction of change and the legitimacy of the EC extending its field of activity. During the 1990s, this consensus was accompanied by publicly stated views that national monopolies in voice telephony and the infrastructure, the heart of the telecommunications sector, would be allowed to remain. But, the position altered, so that by 1992, all member states were prepared to accept the end of 'special and exclusive rights' in voice telephony, and the reappraisal of national monopolies for the infrastructure in 1995, whilst by 1994, they agreed that EC legislation should enforce competition in the infrastructure by 1998.

Taken as a whole, the EC's policies have severely reduced, if not virtually ended, the regulatory scope for member states to pursue their traditional industrial policies in telecommunications under EC law. National monopolies have been progressively outlawed. Licences and norms cannot be used to favour certain suppliers. The freedom of PTOs to set their tariffs is limited by the pressure of actual or potential competition, by EC rules on cost-based pricing and by Commission surveillance using Articles 85 and 86. As a result, the ability of member states to use PTO tariffs to cross-subsidize certain services and groups of users or to produce a certain level of revenue for purposes such as raising revenue for the government, controlling inflation or raising sums for investment, has been reduced. Although the EC's R&D expenditure has only been a small proportion of that undertaken in the EC, it has offered an alternative method of undertaking R&D and of cooperation with other EC firms to that provided by national programmes. Furthermore, the traditional guarantees of PTO orders for certain suppliers are now confronted by EC rules on public procurement, whilst national governments wishing to restructure domestic equipment manufacturers by altering the distribution of PTO orders, face the obstacles of EC procurement rules and a more competitive environment for PTOs.

Assessing the extent to which EC activity has actually constrained member states or will constrain them, is difficult for two particular reasons. First, it requires an examination of whether and how effectively EC law is implemented. Second, and more importantly, it depends on the position of member states: EC legislation may already have been implemented at national level, or may have been desired by member states, or elements within the latter. Thus, far from an imposition, EC legislation may have been regarded as desirable by member states.[47] Nevertheless, it is clear that EC legislation greatly limits autonomous regulatory activity by member states.

EC policy has not merely involved the ending of national 'special and exclusive rights', but also the establishment of a framework for the supply of services and equipment. This framework has several key elements: EC law permits competition in the supply of services and equipment; only limited 'essential requirements' are imposed on suppliers; EC rules insist on mutual recognition of licences between countries; the EC defines the terms of use of the telecommunications infrastructure; the principle of cost-based pricing is enunciated; independent and 'fair' regulatory bodies and procedures must be established by member states Although this can be described as 're-regulation', it is important to note that its fundamental aim is 'fair competition', and legislative clauses dealing with the pursuit of general economic goals and 'public service' are vague. The 'logic' of the system is thus very different from that of traditional national regulatory frameworks and industrial policies in telecommunications.

Notes

1   Almost all decisions concerning telecommunications have been taken under the EC 'pillar' of the European Union.

2   For a discussion of incremental analysis, incremental change and 'partisan mutual adjustment', see Lindblom, C.E., 'The Science of 'Muddling Through' in *Public Administration Review*, vol.19 (1959), pp.79-88, Lindblom, C.E., 'Still Muddling, Not Yet Through' in *Public Administration Review*, vol.39, pp.517-26, Lindblom, C.E., *The Intelligence of Democracy* (New York: the Free Press, 1965), and Braybrooke, D. and Lindblom, C.E., *A Strategy of Decision* (New York: The Free Press, 1963).

3   The most notable exception was in Britain, where the Post Office was a public corporation from 1969.

4   See Schneider, V., and Werle, R., 'International regime or corporate actor?' The European Community in telecommunications policy' in Dyson, K. and Humphreys, P. (eds), *The Political Economy of Telecommunications* (London and New York: Routledge, 1990), and Sandholtz, W., *High-Tech Europe* (Berkeley, Los Angeles and Oxford: University of California Press, 1992, pp.92-9.

5   Ungerer, H. and Costello, P., *Telecommunications in Europe* (Brussels: Commission of the European Communities, 1988), p.130.

6   See Hawkins, R.W., 'Changing Expectations: Voluntary Standards and the Regulation of European Telecommunication', *Communications et Stratégies*, no.11, 3rd. Quarter 1993, pp.53-86.

7   For details of the various proposals made, see Schneider and Werle, *op. cit.*, pp.87-91.

8   COM(80)422 Final.

9   *Communication from the Commission to the Council on Telecommunications: Lines of Action*, COM (83), 573 final; see Schneider and Werle, and Sandholtz, *High-Tech Europe, op. cit.*

10   *Communication from the Commission to the Council on Telecommunications*, COM (84) 277.

11   *Towards a dynamic European economy - Green Paper on the development of the common market for telecommunications services and equipment*, (COM(87) 290, June 1987).

12   COM (88) 48.

13   *Council Resolution of 30 June 1988 on the development of the common market for telecommunications services and equipment up to 1992.*

14   Commission Directive 80/301/EEC.

15   *Financial Times* 28 April 1988 and *Le Monde* 30 April 1988.

16   Case C-202/88 [1990] ECR I-223; for a summary and discussion, see *Common Market Law Review* 28, Winter 1991, pp.964-88.

17   91/263/EEC.

18   European Conference of Postal and Telecommunications Administrations.

19   86/361/EEC.

20   For an explanation of the EC's changing general approach to standard setting, see Schreiber, K., 'The New Approach to Technical Harmonization and Standards' in Hurwitz, L. and Lequesne, C. (eds), *The State of the European Community* (Harlow: Longman, 1991); for telecommunications specifically, see Hawkins, *op. cit.*

21   Case 41/83 (1985), 2 CML Rep 368; for a discussion, see Schulte-Braucks, R, 'European telecommunications law in the light of the British Telecom judgement' in *Common Market Law Review* 23 (1986), pp.39-59.

22   Commission Directive on competition in the markets for telecommunications services 90/388/EEC.

23   This was important for 'cream-skimming' and indirect competition to PTO monopolies over voice telephony, as private suppliers could provide in effect an alternative supply to the PTO by re-selling capacity on certain routes; it was particularly important as PTOs often charge a fixed price for a leased line, irrespective of usage.

24   Joined cases C-271, C-281 and C289/90 *Spain, Belgium, Italy v Commission* [1992] ECR I-5883.

25   By 1994, the Council had adopted a Common Position on a draft Directive, which was before the European Parliament.

26   Delcourt, B. 'EC Decisions and Directives on information technology and telecommunications' in *Telecommunications Policy,* vol.15, no.1, February 1991, pp.15-21 and Madurand, F., 'ONP: its past, present and future' in *XIII Magazine,* no.11, September 1993, pp.11-13.

27   *Green Paper on a common approach in the field of satellite communications in the European Community* (COM(90)490 final).

28   The most important Directive, 94/46/EC, extended the provisions of the Services Directive, including competition in supply, to satellite services; for other measures, see Verhoef, P., 'Satellite Communications' in *XIII Magazine*, no.11, September 1993, pp.25-32.

29   See Maduraud, F. 'Mobile Communications', *XIII Magazine*, no.11, September 1993, pp.20-4.

30 *Guidelines on the application of EEC competition rules on the telecommunications sector* (91/C233/02).

31 *Proposal for a Council Directive on the Application of Open Network Provision (ONP) to voice telephony,* COM(92)247 final; for a discussion, see Higham, N., 'Open Network Provision in the EC', in *Telecommunications Policy,* May/June 1993, pp.242-9.

32 *Communication to the Council and the European Parliament on the consultation on the review of the situation in the telecommunications services sector* (Doc COM(93) 159) *and Council Resolution on the review of the situation in the telecommunications sector and the need for further development in that market* of 16 June 1993; see also *Messages* no.427, September-October 1993, pp.19-23, *AFP Communiqué* 17 June 1993 and *Libération* 18 June 1993.

33 *AFP Communiqué* 18 June 1993 and *La Tribune Desfossés* 21 June 1993.

34 *l'Agefi* 17 June 1993.

35 For analyses of ESPRIT and the various Framework programmes, see Peterson, J, 'Technology Policy in Europe: Explaining the Framework Programme and Eureka in Theory and Practice', *Journal of Common Market Studies,* vol. XXIX, no.3, March 1991, pp. 269-90, Sandholtz, W., ESPRIT and the Politics of International Collective Action, *Journal of Common Market Studies,* vol.XXX, no.1, March 1992, pp.1-21, and Cattelain, M., 'Les recherches initiées et financées par les communautés européennes: evolution et tendences', *Réseaux,* no. 58-60, 1990, pp.171-90.

36 *Communication from the Commission to the Council,* COM (84) 277).

37 Sandholtz, *High tech Europe* , *op. cit.,* pp.243-44.

38 *Ibid.*

39 For details, see Ungerer and Costello, *op. cit.,* pp.154-7.

40 One estimate was that the second Framework Programme accounted for just over 4 per cent of civil public sector R&D spending, whilst they represented less than 3 per cent of the EC's total budget - Gaster, R., 'Research and Technology Policy' in Hurwitz and Lequesne, *op. cit.*

41 See Sharp, M., 'The single market and European technology policies' in Freeman, C., Sharp, M. and Walker, W. (eds), *Technology and the Future of Europe* (London and New York: Pinter, 1991) and for ESPRIT, see Sandholtz, *High-Tech Europe, op. cit.,* pp.186-207.

42 Directive 77/62/EEC.

43 84/550/EEC.

[44]   *Council Directive of 17 December 1990, on the awarding of contracts in the water, transport and telecommunications sectors* 90/531/EEC, 'the utilities Directive'.

[45]   Ravaioli, P. and Zourabichvili, M., 'Telecommunications', *XIII Magazine,* no.10, May 1993, pp.7-9.

[46]   Directive 92/13/EEC.

[47]   The clearest example is provided by Britain, where competition in the supply of CPE, services and the infrastructure had already been introduced in the 1980s, and whose Government wished to 'export' Britain's regulatory framework at EC level; for an analysis of the interaction between national developments and policy making at EC level, see Thatcher, M., 'Regulatory reform, national enterprises and internationalisation in telecommunications: the interaction between the European Community and its member states' in Hayward, J.E.S. (ed), *From National to International Champions in the West European Economy* (Oxford: OUP, 1995).

13 Unity in Diversity? The European Single Market in Broadcasting and the Audio-Visual 1982-1994

RICHARD COLLINS

> The audio-visual sector is of great importance to the cultural identity of peoples, regions and nations. It is also a rapidly growing sector of the world economy, significant in its own right and with considerable multiplier effects on other sectors such as electronics, telecommunications, the space industry and publishing.[1]

Introduction

This paper examines the development of the European Community's[2] audio-visual[3] and broadcasting policy. This story is complicated and therefore difficult to tell. It involves shifts in the balance of power and level of activity between Community institutions (for the Community whilst grammatically singular is institutionally plural) and Community Member States; in the priority given to different sectors in the domain of broadcasting and audio-visual policy; changes in the Community's high policy goals (with consequential effects on audio-visual policy), between the instruments chosen for the realization of policy goals; and in the relations between the Community and other European agencies (notably the Council of Europe and the European Broadcasting Union).

Broadcasting and the audio-visual might be thought to be relatively unimportant to the Community's affairs. By some measures they are: the budget for the MEDIA programme, (Community's support for film and television production), amounted to 48,262,000 ECU in 1992.[4] Whereas expenditure on the Common Agricultural Policy was budgeted at 35.3 bn ECU in 1992 - about 53 per cent of the Community's budget. The Commissioners charged with responsibility for DG X, (the Directorate General for the Audio-visual,

Information, Communication and Culture), have come from small Community countries, reflecting the low prestige of DG X. By such measures broadcasting and the audio-visual are singularly unimportant. But other measures suggest a greater importance for the sector. The inability of the USA and the European Community to agree on the inclusion of the broadcasting and audio-visual sector in the GATT international trade regime threatened completion of the round; The Financial Times headlined its report - two days before the final Uruguay Round deadline - 'GATT deal hopes hinge on US audio-visual demands'.[5] A notable testimony from the European Parliament to the sector's importance heads this chapter and Jacques Delors, the President of the Commission of the European Communities, specifically acknowledged the importance of the audio-visual and broadcasting sectors in his first speech to the European Parliament when taking up office as President in 1985. Delors affirmed the importance of the cultural industries for both the culture and the economy of the Community.

> 'the culture industry will tomorrow be one of the biggest industries, a creator of wealth and jobs. Under the terms of the Treaty we do not have the resources to implement a cultural policy; but we are going to try to tackle it along economic lines. It is not simply a question of television programmes. We have to build a powerful European culture industry that will enable us to be in control of both the medium and its content, maintaining our standards of civilization, and encouraging the creative people amongst us.'[6]

Delors' emphasis on the economic reflected both the Commission's recognition that, as advanced countries increasingly shifted towards becoming 'information societies',[7] sectors such as film and television were increasingly important loci of wealth and job creation, and the necessity, prior to the Maastricht Treaty on European Union, for the Commission's actions in the cultural sphere to be presented as *economic* rather than cultural measures. Even Article 235,[8] the main provision in the Treaty of Rome to have enabled the Commission and Community to exercise powers outside the economic domain, (albeit only on the basis of unanimous consent by the Member States), specifies that such action is legitimate only 'in the course of the operation of the common market'. Delors' statement (and Community policy) should therefore not be understood as necessarily attributing *greater* importance to the economic than to the cultural. Indeed important Community initiatives in broadcasting and the audio-visual have been taken in order to realize essentially *cultural* goals. And the inclusion of Article 128, the 'Culture' article in the Maastricht Treaty extends the Commission's powers in the cultural domain.

The European Community's broadcasting and audio-visual policy effectively dates from 1982 when the first directly elected European Parliament passed the Hahn Resolution on Radio and Television Broadcasting in the European Community.[9] It has focused on three distinct, but interdependent sectors; on hardware, notably the setting of television transmission standards, and software, notably film (and to a lesser extent television programme) production, and on a mediating third sector, distribution (principally television broadcasting). Community policy has been a notable locus for conflicts between proponents of interventionist and market instruments for the achievement of goals; that is between 'dirigistes' and 'liberals'. And, in the decade between 1982, when the Hahn Resolution was adopted, and 1992, when the Single Market was implemented, policy priorities shifted significantly; between cultural and economic policy goals and between the use of film and television to foster unity and diversity in the Community.

The most important of the Community's policy initiatives, creation of a single Community television market - a 'Television without Frontiers', has run in parallel with initiatives (within both Community and national contexts) to redress the undesired effects of market integration.[10] The Community's broadcasting and audio-visual policy has thus both sought to promote market integration on the basis of 'supply specialisation' and to inhibit it.[11] And, because the EEC Treaty (Treaty of Rome) did not provide the Community with powers to pursue cultural objectives, (except on a basis of unanimous agreement), Member States have used 'European variable geometry'[12] to achieve outside the Community, goals that were impossible to secure within it.

Community broadcasting and audio-visual policy must be understood, not simply as the resultant of negotiation and compromise *within* the European Community and between its institutions, (the Commission, the Council and the Parliament in order of importance), but also as the product of shifting institutional alliances and initiatives which extend *outside* the bounds of the Community. If we are to understand European Community broadcasting and audio-visual policy we must recognize that it cannot be defined in a neat and tidy way and that we must consider the changing balance of political forces within the community.

Dirigism and Free Markets

There have been two principal, and rival, instruments adopted for the realization of Community policy goals in the audio-visual sector. Dirigism, or political intervention in markets to secure specific outcomes, and liberalism, the creation of conditions in which competitive markets function without overt political intervention. The conflict between these rival systems of resource allocation and their sponsors has been one of the 'grand narratives' of the European Community. As is well known these differences, (between Adam Smithian advocates of an economic Darwinism, where markets allocate resources on the basis of competition, and Colbertians who invest the state with the role of allocating resources) are loosely mapped onto the differences between the policies (and interests) of Community Member States and between Directorates within the Commission of the European Communities.

Some Members, and some Directorates, are customarily seen as dirigiste and some as liberal, or pejoratively as 'ultra liberal'. A Commission official (and a French national) stated that the UK and France are the 'ideal types' of liberal and dirigiste Member States.[13] The UK is at the liberal, and France at the dirigiste ends of the liberal/dirigiste spectrum.[14] This Commission official also stated that he believed 'the information industries are central to this policy debate' and that therefore the disputed issues in Community policy in the audio-visual sector were representative of more significant 'high policy' questions. The European Parliament has made similar judgements:

> 'European media policy...is a touchstone for judging whether the Member States...are prepared to take European unification seriously and adopt a common policy on the media'.[15]

A senior UK government official[16] lent support to the Commission official's judgement that the UK and France were usually at odds in their approaches to audio-visual and broadcasting policy. The UK official stated that the UK's first priority in respect of Community broadcasting and audio-visual policy was to secure a 'free market (qualified by the requirements of taste and decency)' and went on to say that the policy goal of the UK for the Commission's most important dirigiste initiative in respect of audio-visual software, (and one strongly supported by France), the MEDIA programme, was to 'close it down'.[17]

A free market policy is likely to serve the UK well. For the UK has long had a stronger audio-visual sector than have other Community states. Its audio-visual sector has a very much healthier international balance of trade than have those of other Community countries.[18] Its most notable strengths include a comparative advantage over other Community states (except Ireland) in speaking the world's most important language. And the UK has competitive advantages based on market size and wealth and the long standing presence in the UK of the factors required for audio-visual production. London is Europe's most important centre for the media industries and one of three (all anglophone) global centres for cultural production (and for audio-visual production in particular).

Community measures promulgated by dirigistes have principally been directed towards supporting the audio-visual sector in peripheral Community states, productions in minority languages and fostering co-productions involving several Community Member States. They have therefore been supported by those Member States which perceive their languages and cultures (and audio-visual industries) to be threatened by the global internationalization of audio-visual markets and the integration of Community markets. For the most part such policies have been supported by the Community's small countries and by France (which, in spite of being a large and powerful Community member, perceives its language, culture and audio-visual industry to be threatened by globalization and the integration of Community cultural markets. The recent promulgation of the Loi Toubon, requiring use of the French language, testifies eloquently to the power of these concerns). Whereas the UK has consistently opposed such initiatives and has thus been regarded as 'ultra liberal' by interventionists.

The Community's dirigiste measures, (some clearly aimed at augmenting diversity others at fostering unity) are centred in the MEDIA programme and are likely to be enhanced following the signing of the Maastricht Treaty which includes Article 128 which provides, inter alia, that 'The Community shall contribute to the flowering of the cultures of the Member States'. The UK opposed to Article 128 of the Treaty, (which extends Community competence into the cultural field), but although not successful in excluding the culture article from the Treaty did succeed in limiting its scope. Article 128 confines the Community's competence in the audio-visual to 'artistic and literary creation, including *in* (my emphasis) the audio-visual area' rather than opening the whole of the audio-visual sector to Community intervention.[19]

Community Policy

The practical implementation of the Community's broadcasting and audio-visual policy was described by a Commission official[20] as having three aspects; establishment of rules, (notably through the issue of Directives), promotion of programme production and circulation, and development of the technological competence and productive capacity of the Community. The policy landscape can be triangulated from three major landmarks. The Directives on satellite television transmission standards,[21] and on television broadcasting, that is the Television without Frontiers Directive,[22] and the establishment of the MEDIA programme of support for the European audio-visual sector.[23]

The goal of a Single European Market by 1993 was introduced by Jacques Delors during his first period of office as President of the Commission of the European Communities. This policy chimed with the pervasive UK assumptions of free trade and free markets and which were held particularly strongly by the UK governments of the 1980s. The Single Market is the single major Community initiative which has been wholeheartedly supported by the UK Government. A single audio-visual and broadcasting market appeared to offer Europe the key competitive advantage of market size on which it was believed the enduring success of the United States' audio-visual industry had been based.

The two chief Community initiatives to establish a Community wide television market were the Television without Frontiers Directive (which emanated from DG III the Directorate General for the Internal Market), and the satellite television transmission standards Directive (from DG XIII the Directorate General for Telecommunications, Information Technology and Innovation). Their integrative purpose (and to some extent effect) has called up a compensatory response (largely designed to compensate for the integrative effects, and the consequential decline in diversity, of a single market) the MEDIA Programme (located in DG X the Directorate General for the Audio-visual, Information, Communication and Culture).

Co-ordination of Community policy is effected at regular Commissioner meetings attended by the President of the Commission and the Vice-Presidents and Commissioners for DG I, III, IV, X, XIII and XIX.[24] The

Commissioner meetings are chaired by the Commissioner responsible for DG X which is responsible for preparation and documentation of Commissioner meetings.[25]

Television without Frontiers

Ivo Schwartz of DG III, the Commission official who took the leading role in progressing Television without Frontiers from Green Paper to Directive, stated that *Television Without Frontiers* was conceived to secure access for all Community Member States to broadcast signals emanating from any other Member State, and to harmonize Community broadcasting advertising standards. Achievement of these goals would assist the establishment of the single market in broadcasting services and would also serve the *cultural and political* goal defined in the EEC Treaty of promoting 'ever closer union among the peoples of Europe'.[26]

However cultural objections to the single market became more and more important. Schwartz attempted to rebut them by arguing that 'the EEC Treaty applies not only to economic activities but also to all social and cultural activities carried out for remuneration'.[27] Later, such liberal arguments provided a basis (before the Maastricht Treaty on Political Union) for dirigiste intervention in the broadcasting and audio-visual sector, notably through DG X's MEDIA programme.

One importance of *Television Without Frontiers* lay therefore in the Commission's acknowledgement that cultural matters were indeed part of its jurisdiction and that cultural concerns had a legitimate place in broadcasting policy. However a conflict grew between the cultural goals the Community defined (seeking unity in diversity) and the economic logic of a single broadcasting market in which an intensified division of labour and competition would tend to eliminate cultural production by less efficient producers - often those whose linguistically or geographically peripheral status made them vulnerable - led to a redefinition of Community cultural goals.

Unity before Diversity

A single broadcasting market was initially advocated for its integrative effects in the political, cultural and economic domains. The Television without Frontiers Green Paper stated 'Cross-frontier radio and television broadcasting would make a significant contribution to European integration'.[28] And cited the celebrated syllogism of the Hahn Resolution [29] to legitimize its advocacy of a single market

> 'European unification will only be achieved if Europeans want it. Europeans will only want it if there is such a thing as a European identity. A European identity will only develop if Europeans are adequately informed. At present, information via the mass media is controlled at national level'.[30]

During the early 1980s the themes of a single market and a unified European culture were dominant in European Community policy making. The goal of unity rather than diversity was uppermost. For the classic nationalist syllogism, that political institutions survive only when they are congruent with cultural communities, (states are robust and legitimate only insofar as they are isomorphic with nations, and nations are communities differentiated from other communities by cultural difference) was believed to be true.[31] If the Community was to survive it needed a common culture and a shared European identity.

But the most important effect of the Television without Frontiers initiative has not been that which was anticipated. Television without Frontiers was designed to establish a single Community television market. However Community television markets have remained largely separate (where integration has occurred it has been a relatively modest consolidation of adjacent markets of states using the same language) but the changed regulations which followed Television without Frontiers have permitted an increase in competition within national (or more precisely single language) television markets of Community Member States. The Television without Frontiers Directive has shown that the most important barriers separating Community television markets are not regulatory or technological but linguistic and cultural, and Community audio-visual markets remain separated on national and linguistic lines.

The Directive on Satellite Television Transmission Standards

In keeping with the goal of establishing a single market and supporting the Community's electronics industry the Commission also proposed a Directive on satellite television transmission standards (the Directive - Council of the European Communities 1986 - was promulgated in 1986). Here the

Commission's reasoning was two fold; that both European cultural integration and the Community's electronics industry had been disadvantaged by the existence of two incompatible transmission standards - PAL and SECAM - used for broadcasting terrestrial television, and that early establishment of a European standard would make possible an incremental approach to a Community standard for High Definition Television (HDTV). HDTV would in turn provide a defensive screen behind which the Community's electronics industries could shelter from Japanese (and United States) competition.

The Directive to establish MAC satellite transmission standards as a Community norm was promulgated; first,[32] to restructure what was perceived to be a failed satellite television market; second, to establish a viable market, based on a single technical standard for (some parts of) the European consumer electronics industry; and third, to facilitate the incremental development of HDTV in Europe. However the decision to prioritize the D2-MAC standard meant that transnational, Community wide television services reaching audiences of different language communities became more, rather than less, difficult than with a different standard.[33] Promotion of a single hardware market necessitated trading off creation of a single Community software market.

The MAC standard was opposed by many Community broadcasters, by sections of the electronics industry (Philips and Thomson were the leading lobbyists for MAC, opponents included those, such as Amstrad, with a base in PAL standard manufacturing and others that saw the MAC standard as inferior to emerging digital transmission standards) and by the few and rather weak consumer interest groups which commented on this seemingly recondite aspect of Community policy. The satellite transmission standard Directive[34] expired on 31 December 1991 without having achieved its goal of a large population of MAC standard satellite television receivers and MAC standard television services, (largely due to the pre-emptive effect of the successful early establishment of PAL standard services transmitted from the Astra Satellite). Political agreement on a new Directive was reached at the Council of Ministers meeting on 27 January 1992. The sponsoring Commissioner, Pandolfi, (then responsible for DG XIII), attempted to win support for a new Directive which would establish D2-MAC as a mandatory standard for television satellite transmissions in the Community.

On 26 June 1991 the Commission issued a draft directive which, as an interim measure, permitted 'grandfathering' of established PAL and SECAM channels. However new channels, from 1992, were to transmit in MAC. The effect of the proposals in the draft directive would be to advantage established channels (because they would be receivable by the established population of European satellite television viewers whereas new, MAC, channels would not be) and thus inhibit the development of a 'single market' for satellite television within the Community. The UK, Spain and Ireland opposed the draft directive (as did commercial television interests in Germany). Successive revisions of the draft Directive weakened the requirement to use MAC and eventually political agreement was reached in the Council of Ministers on a 'common position' to be enshrined in a new directive.

The 'common position' adopted by the Council, which formed the basis of a new Directive,[35] establishes a formal commitment to the MAC route to the establishment of a single Community HDTV standard, to single standards for satellite transmission and conditional access equipment and to the use of HD-MAC as a standard for non digital services. However the 'common position' opened the door, hitherto closed, to a non-MAC, digital, route to HDTV.[36] Moreover the Directive does not prohibit use of PAL (or SECAM) transmission standards but provides only that new services established after 1995 must use the MAC transmission standard (however new services are permitted to simulcast in PAL and/or SECAM). Effectively, therefore, the search for a common standard was abandoned.

The Council of Ministers agreed an action plan for development of HDTV, including incentives for programme production in MAC and 16:9 ratio, in June 1993. The plan, which earmarked subsidies of 228m ECU over four years, reflected a compromise devised to accommodate UK objections to an interventionist policy. Production subsidies will be limited to ECU 160m between 1993 and 1997 with a further 68m ECU earmarked for HDTV/16:9 production in small Member States. Producers must provide 50 per cent of the additional costs of HDTV/16:9 production from commercial sources, (although in the case of small countries this requirement is relaxed and only 20 per cent of additional production costs must be procured from commercial sources), the whole programme, including private and Community funds, is to amount to 405m ECU.[37]

The basis on which the Directive was promulgated, and production subsidies agreed pleased 'ultra liberal' interests. The UK official interviewed by the author on 10 February 1992 expressed satisfaction at the outcome of negotiations and commented 'the UK did very well' in the negotiations about the content of the new Directive by establishing a blocking minority with

Denmark, Spain and Ireland against the efforts of France, Germany and the Netherlands to re-establish a Community requirement for the mandatory use of MAC satellite television transmission standards. The UK was also perceived to have reneged on an agreement on Community subsidies for HDTV/16:9 production concluded at the Edinburgh summit during the UK's presidency of the Community in 1992. The final agreement reached in the Council of Ministers during the Danish Presidency in early 1993 was less generous to producers than proponents of subsidy had wished, (though more generous than the UK had hoped).

Thus, (although the Television without Frontiers Directive only came into effect in 1991), the two Directives[38] expressed the dominant assumptions in the Community of the early and mid 1980s; that a single broadcasting market would unify the Community culturally (and therefore politically) and would assist the development of the Community's audio-visual hardware and software industries. However neither Directive established the single market which they were conceived to implement. Cultural and linguistic barriers ensured that Community broadcasting and audio-visual markets remained separate. Although Television without Frontiers has assisted trans-border broadcasting which has led to some restratification of broadcasting markets on a linguistic basis and to an increase in competition within distinct markets.[39] But it has done little to assist the development of Community wide television services.

Divisions between different sectors of the electronics industry and between the broadcasting and electronics industries (and between the Member States which are their sponsors) have, thus far, frustrated the harmonization of transmission standards which was the goal of the satellite broadcasting directive. In spite of a new 'common position', on the basis of which a new directive on satellite transmission standards has been promulgated,[40] the goal of a single Community television transmission standard has remained elusive. The achievement of a single market in broadcasting has been frustrated by the determined defence of the different interests of different sections of the European electronics industry by their national governments.

Diversity over Unity

There were powerful forces opposed to both the satellite television transmission standards and the Television without Frontiers (single market) Directives. From the first publication of the Television without Frontiers Green Paper in 1984 countervailing, dirigiste, pressures were mobilized against the single market in broadcasting. Thus, alongside attempts to establish a well functioning integrated European broadcasting market (as yet no such initiatives have been launched for other audio-visual sectors such as film), policy initiatives have been launched to countervail the effects of the single market. To understand these initiatives we must examine their origins in the discussions in the European Parliament in the early 1980s.

The Hahn Report

The European Parliament's Hahn Report of 1982 has been described as the 'premiere pierre' of Community broadcasting policy.[41] Hahn argued that 'Information is a decisive, perhaps the most decisive factor in European integration' and judged that integration was unlikely to be achieved whilst 'the mass media is controlled at national level'. Hahn favoured the new technology of satellite television as a means to European integration and argued that 'television satellites will lead to a reorganization of the media in Europe; the new technical facilities will break down the boundaries of the national television networks and enforce the creation of wide-ranging transmission areas'.[42]

Those who sought an instrument for the making and dissemination of a unified European culture were quickly disabused of their faith in television. Attempts to establish transnational television services (whether commercial or public service) in the 1980s failed,[43] and the large scale nationalist conception of a unified European culture to complement and sustain a European polity became discredited as perceptions of a threat from television to indigenous national Community cultures grew. If we follow Kedourie's reasoning about the nature of the relationship posited by nationalism between language, culture and political identity we can see why the vision of a unified European culture took on the aspect of a nightmare. For Kedourie:-

> 'language is the means through which a man becomes conscious of his personality. Language is not only a vehicle for rational propositions, it is the outer expression of an inner experience, the outcome of a particular history, the legacy of a distinctive tradition'. [44]

Language is then co-extensive with culture and identity. If, as nationalists believe, political structures require to be congruent with cultural communities if they are to be stable and legitimate (the core of the argument

Hahn and others were advancing in the context of Community audio-visual policy during the early 1980s) then the European Community required not only a common culture but a common language if it was to survive and develop satisfactorily. There could be no question that were there to be a common language of the Community it would have to be English. There was, therefore, a retreat from the notion that a common Community culture (and thus language) was required; diversity rather than unity became the slogan under which cultural dirigistes fought thereafter.

However Hahn also explicitly warned against broadcasting becoming 'an article of merchandise in the framework of the Common Market'[45] and foresaw a possibility of satellite television *threatening* a broadcasting war in which European culture would be annihilated as well as *promising* a vehicle for European integration. And it is this perspective (with its consequential emphasis on regulation and political intervention in markets), rather than that advocating use of the media for European integration, to which those (such as Barzanti), who have argued for a Community policy now tend to have recourse. Hahn is now cited to legitimize calls for political intervention to ensure *diversity* rather than *unity* .

Mariano Maggiore, formerly the Deputy Head of DG X's Audio-visual Directorate, stated 'We have no interest in promoting a melting pot. We want to preserve European identities'.[46] The stress on diversity in contemporary Community policy reflects both the failure of transnational broadcasting by satellite in the 1980s, (and the consequential recognition that Europe was inescapably culturally and linguistically diverse) and the threat to national audio-visual and broadcasting markets, (and thus to national media industries) presented by a single market. These threats were perceived to come from anglophone services and productions. Maggiore also stated 'we don't want to leave the audio-visual to the English language media'.

The MEDIA Programme

In consequence of the perceived threat to cultural diversity within the Community (a threat that comes from the United States *outside* the Community and from the United Kingdom, thanks to the single market, *within* the Community) there has been a steady growth of intervention in the Community's audio-visual and broadcasting markets in order to redress the effects, perceived to be undesirable, of a single market. The MEDIA programme is the most important of such initiatives and eloquently exemplifies the predominant emphasis on diversity, rather than unity, which has latterly informed Community policy. However, as Maggiore recognized, the support the Community has offered under the MEDIA programme is unlikely to be sufficient to enable audio-visual industries to survive in small Community countries. Whilst selective aid to individual national initiatives, notably to the small countries, is unacceptable within a single market so too, Maggiore stated, is the use of the same criteria for allocating Community resources to small countries as are used with big countries. This, he said, 'ends up with ridiculous injustices'.

For the logic of the single market is that English language producers will prevail, endowed as they are with powerful advantages over producers in other languages. There will be limits to the success of anglophones for the 'cultural screens' which separate European audio-visual consumers are only partly permeable. However the limits will be set by consumers rather than by national rule making and the changed limits set by consumer preferences are likely to disadvantage non-anglophone producers. Hence the shift in emphasis in Community policy from unity to diversity, for more producers in more Community member states are likely to lose by unity in broadcasting and audio-visual markets than are likely to gain from it.

The MEDIA 92 programme was established in 1988 by the Commission of the European Communities using its own discretionary expenditure funds. MEDIA was established in two phases; a preparatory phase and a second, realization phase which required the approval of the Council of Ministers to be put into effect. The preparatory, or pilot, phase ended in 1990 and continuation of the MEDIA programme until 1995 was endorsed by the Council in December 1990 when MEDIA 92 was granted 200m ECU for a period of five years commencing 1 January 1991 (Council of the European Communities 1990).[47] Following the Council decision MEDIA 92 was renamed MEDIA 95.

The role of MEDIA is to promote 'the production and dissemination of audio-visual works throughout the Community'.[48] Its specific focus is 'training, preproduction, multilingualism of programmes, use of nex (sic) technologies, distribution and commercial promotion, the creation of a 'second market' and easier access to venture capital'.[49] During the pilot phase of MEDIA 92 eleven projects or programmes were launched. To them have been added a new set of priorities ('priority will be given to co-operation with professionals from Central and East European countries'), and new institutions.[50]

MEDIA is an excellent example of the Community's recent attention to a middle stage between hardware and software production, that is to distribution, which was formerly neglected. Extensive, if ungenerously funded, though MEDIA's initiatives are limited to funding pre-and post-production (and in particular to the promotion of improved distribution and circulation) of films and television programmes. MEDIA does not support production as such but has emphasized cultural pluralism within the Community by supporting the circulation of Community productions, particularly those made in minority languages.

Competition and the Single Market

The development and implementation of Community broadcasting and audio-visual policy cannot be fully understood from examination of regulations and policy documents. For important aspects of policy and practice have emanated from the case by case rulemaking of the Directorates of the Commission of the European Communities responsible for Competition (DG IV) and the Internal Market (DG III). DG III and DG IV broadly divide responsibilities so that DG III makes rules and DG IV enforces them. However these are not clear and categorical distinctions, there are areas where DG IV lacks jurisdictional standing (and where DG III has enforcement functions) and others where DG IV's enforcement of regulations has set standards and thus made rules.

For example DG IV, the Competition Directorate, has made important interventions in respect of broadcasters' acquisition of rights to sporting events and cinema films and thus has made, rather than enforced, rules. There have been two particularly important cases where DG IV has set the terms on which broadcasters have established rights to programmes. First, in overturning the principal German public service broadcaster's, the ARD's, deal with MGM/United Artists, and second, in the *Eurosport* case.[51] The UK company W H Smith Television (the principal investor in the satellite television channel Screensport) complained that Eurosport, (a satellite television channel established under an agreement between the Eurosport Consortium - a group of European Broadcasting Union (EBU) member broadcasters including the BBC - and Sky Television), infringed Community competition requirements and thereby disadvantaged Screensport. The nub of the dispute was whether

Screensport was improperly disadvantaged in the acquisition of rights to screen sports events by EBU member broadcasters with a stake in Eurosport, the Commission ruled in favour of Screensport.[52]

In 1991 DG III was involved in extensive discussions with the Government of France in order to reconcile French national television programme content quotas (which required 50 per cent French programme content) with those prescribed in the Council Directive on television broadcasting (the Television without Frontiers Directive) which requires 50 per cent of programming of Community origin.[53] However these discussions, and France's revision of its regulations to conform to the requirements of the Directive, took place before the Directive assumed the force of law. The case of national quotas is an example of enforcement responsibilities lying with DG III rather than DG IV. When the organization in question is an enterprise DG IV has jurisdiction, where a Member State then DG III is responsible. However a section of DG IV is responsible for scrutiny of state aid to enterprises (and ruled against the reservation of government subsidy to film makers in Greece to Greek nationals).[54]

Intergovernmental Initiatives

In contrast to the European Community's regulations (which are based on the jurisdiction of a supranational entity) the Council of Europe's co-production support scheme Eurimages and the Audio-visual Eureka (a 'marriage bureau' for European co-productions) have been established by intergovernmental agreement using 'European variable geometry'. The Audio-visual Eureka was established with direct participation by the Commission of the European Communities and Eurimages by member states of the European Community (notably France) in order to achieve through intergovernmental agreement outside the Community what they had been unable to achieve inside the Community.

France is not the only European Community state to have recourse to the Council of Europe's 'variable geometry'. The UK, for example, actively supported the development of the Council's Convention on Transfrontier Television because it preferred the wider reach and fewer compromises of sovereignty which a Convention (achieved by intergovernmental agreement in the Council of Europe) rather than a Community Directive offered.

The European Support Fund for the Co-production and distribution of Creative Cinematographic and Audio-visual works (Eurimages) was established (following an initiative of France) on 26 September 1988 in order to develop European cinematographic and audio-visual production. (Resolution (88) 15 modified by Resolution (89) 6 of the Committee of Ministers of the Council of Europe). Its purpose was described by the Council as the achievement:

> 'of a genuine and diversified European audio-visual production capable of meeting the needs of television viewers and of encouraging closer unity between peoples as well as the mutual enrichment of cultures...Without increased and competitive audio-visual production, there is a real risk that the new channels will be fed by re-broadcasts of existing programmes or extra-European programmes'.[55]

Ryclef Rienstra, when Executive Secretary of Eurimages, explained[56] that Eurimages was established as a consequence of the lack of success in establishing a co-production support scheme as part of the European Community's MEDIA programme. The Audio-visual Eureka was established in 1990 as a cultural parallel to the technological Eureka [57] (HDTV was a common focus of the technological and audio-visual Eurekas). Miyet described the Audio-visual Eureka as inspired by

> 'a realization of the existence of structural weaknesses in the production and circulation of European programmes: insufficient capacity, especially in drama, Europe's marginal position on world markets, imbalance in exchanges, political mobilization still confined to a few isolated concerted actions'.[58]

Thus far pro-active measures by the Community (notably the MEDIA programme) have been less important than those designed to establish a single television market. Both the Community Directives on Television without Frontiers and on satellite transmission standards were in keeping with the goal of a single market (though the latter can less readily be reconciled with the goal of fostering a competitive market). The dirigistes have been unable to command the political clout necessary to promulgate an interventionist Directive in respect of 'software' in the broadcasting and audio-visual sector. However significant alliances and institutions (notably Eurimages and the Audio-visual Eureka) have been established *outside* the European Community to secure these dirigiste goals.

Conclusion

Whilst the European Community has formally had an audio-visual and broadcasting policy for only a little more than five years (since the Council's Resolution in 1988) or, if one dates the inception of a policy to the Hahn Report and Resolution of 1982, for just over a decade it is clear that audio-visual and broadcasting policy has been of great importance within the Community. It has both had an enormous symbolic importance and it is anticipated that the audio-visual sector (including broadcasting) will play an increasingly important economic role within the Community. Moreover, because of widely held beliefs among Community members that cultural production and consumption are strongly linked to political identities, it is believed that the political integrity (and thus the economic health) of the Community depend on . audio-visual and broadcasting policy.

Yet we have seen that the interests (and beliefs) of Community Member States are profoundly different. From the point of view of the UK economic interest and political ideology suggest continuing support for the integration of markets and an absence of intervention. France, for reasons of economic interest and political ideology, has taken the opposite view. Some other Member States have consistently allied themselves with either liberal or dirigiste groupings. Belgium, for example, has consistently favoured intervention, subsidy and political control of markets. Denmark has consistently opposed Community actions in the cultural domain but, like other small member states in the Community, fears for the future of its own audio-visual sector in circumstances of competition and an intensified division of labour similar to that promoted by Television without Frontiers.

A retrospect on developments in the Community over the last decade shows that in both hardware and software dirigistes have lost relative to free marketeers. However, whilst in hardware dirigistes continue to espouse a single Community standard, a single Community electronics market and Community unity; in software the emphasis of dirigistes has changed. Whereas in the early 1980s intervention was directed towards the construction and dissemination of a single European culture and identity latterly it has been directed towards ensuring that the Community remains culturally diversified. Curiously both interventionists and free marketeers now emphasize 'diversity' whereas in the early 1980s both emphasized unity.

For economic, political and cultural reasons the audio-visual and broadcasting sectors are likely to remain an arena of conflict within the European Community. So too are they likely to continue to remain a site of conflict between the Community and the United States. Although negotiators surmounted the final hurdle of an audio-visual agreement and at last brought the GATT Uruguay Round to a successful conclusion in December 1993. It was conflicts between the European Community and the United States over the audio-visual trade regime that nearly caused the Round to fail. The Financial Times reported,[59] two days before the GATT deadline, that 'Successful completion of the Uruguay Round of trade talks appeared to hinge on proposals...detailing US demands on access to Europe's television and film markets.'

The GATT conflict between the Community and the USA over the audio-visual trade regime epitomized the conflict which took place within the Community between dirigistes and liberals and in the international, as in the intra-Community, conflict France was the leading opponent of free trade, (and was particularly strongly supported by Ireland and Spain).[60] Yet the exclusion of the audio-visual sector from the Uruguay Round, (thus permitting the continuance of Community subsidy and quota regimes), is unlikely to satisfy the USA. The cultural industries (including film and television) are second only to the aerospace industry in returning a positive balance on the USA's international trade, (which is in chronic deficit). And restrictions on the free flow of information are incompatible with cherished US values. The United States' chief GATT negotiator, Mickey Kantor, contended that European Community doctrines of 'cultural exception' enshrine 'the principle of limiting viewers' rights to see what they wish ... and recognized a system which denies artists and producers the right to funds legally earned through royalties.[61] 'Fortress Europe' is a major threat to United States' economic interests and doctrines of freedom of information.

Not only is the 'ever closer union' prescribed in the Treaty of Rome difficult to achieve in respect of broadcasting and the audio-visual *within* the context of the Community (because of the different interests of Community Member States) but the achievement of that closer union, (realized through European content quotas, subsidies for European production and the like), is likely to alienate one of the Community's most important trading partners.

Although the audio-visual and broadcasting sectors were excluded from the GATT Uruguay round they are likely to remain a bone of contention between the Community and the USA and a site of conflict between proponents of rival visions of the Community itself. For the lynch pin of the Community's broadcasting and audio-visual regime, the single television market - Television without Frontiers - is perceived by powerful forces within the Community to be a Trojan Horse for the destruction of the European Community's audio-visual economy and culture. As Jack Lang stated in the Community's semi-official publication 'European Affairs':

> 'The countries of Europe, encumbered as they are with all sorts of historic, linguistic and sociological barriers, were more or less impervious to each other, while the European market - unified - existed only for the Americans'[62]

Eloquent testimony to the continuing differences in values within the European Union is given by the contrast between two papers published in early 1994 by the European Union. These were the Bangemann report,[63] and the Audio-visual Green Paper, properly titled 'Strategy Options to Strengthen the European Programme Industry in the Context of the Audio-visual Policy of the European Union'.[64] In its first paragraph the Bangemann report unequivocally urged that 'the European Union... put its faith in market mechanisms' and explicitly rejected the use of 'public money, financial assistance, subsidies, dirigisme, or protectionism' as policy instruments.[65] Whereas the authors of the Green Paper emphasized the comprehensive failure of audio-visual markets and the consequential need for intervention to secure desired ends. The Green Paper's authors refer to the impact of film and television on 'national and regional cultures',[66] to the importance of 'cultural and linguistic diversity' in determining outcomes,[67] to the deficiencies of the European audio-visual sector and the threat posed by exogenous products notably from the USA,[68] and the problems posed by 'television production [which] has focused on satisfying national audiences with very little by way of programme circulation within the Community'.[69]

Clearly the divisions apparent in the European Community's broadcasting and audio-visual policies continue to characterize those of the European Union. Thus far liberals have enjoyed considerably more success in implementing their policies than have dirigistes; the establishment of a single television market, the determined assaults by DG IV on European public service broadcasters in the name of competition have done far more to reshape the European broadcasting and audio-visual sectors than have either the dirigistes' modest initiatives to support production (MEDIA 95, Eurimages and the Assises); or their Directives on satellite television transmission standards. However the successful campaign to keep the cultural industries, including broadcasting and the audio-visual, outside the GATT regime suggests that dirigistes may enjoy further policy successes. Not least because the European Union Treaty, the Maastricht Treaty, invests the Commission with cultural powers - modest though they are. But whether liberals or dirigistes are in the ascendent it is clear that broadcasting and audio-visual policy is likely therefore to remain a neuralgic point both in the European Community's external trade relations and between Community Member States. For the interests of the Community and its major trading partners are no easier to reconcile than are the interests of its Member States in respect of broadcasting and audio-visual.

Notes[70]

1   European Parliament (1989) Report on the European Community's film and television industry (*The de Vries Report*). PE 119.192/fin. 9 January 1989.

2   Now properly referred to as the European Union.

3   The term 'audio-visual' is an awkward one in English though familiar to speakers of other European languages. Strictly, and usefully, it signifies all the sound and imaging sectors - television, film, radio, recorded sound etc. But the term is customarily used to signify film, television and associated activities. However the usage 'audio-visual' in European Community parlance suggests that the user of the term may be a supporter of intervention in film and television markets. It connotes a 'dirigiste' approach to policy for the sector.

4   OJ L 26 p. 710 3 February 1992.

5   Financial Times 14 December 1993 p. 18.

6   Delors, J, (1985) Address to the opening of the European Parliament 12 March 1985. Commission programme for 1985 in Debates of the European Parliament. OJ No 2-324. p. 64.

7   Bell, D. (1976 [1973]) The Coming of Post-Industrial Society. Penguin. Harmondsworth.

8   Article 235 states, 'If action by the Community should prove necessary to attain, in the course of the operation of the common market, one of the objectives of the Community and this Treaty has not provided the necessary powers, the Council shall, acting unanimously on a proposal from the Commission and after consulting the Assembly, take the appropriate measures'.

9   European Parliament (1982) Report on Radio and Television Broadcasting in the European Community. (The Hahn Resolution). OJ 87/82, pp. 110-12.

10   Commission of the European Communities (1984) '*Television Without Frontiers*' Green Paper on the Establishment of the Common Market for Broadcasting especially by Satellite and Cable. COM (84) 300 final. Office for Offical Publications of the European Communities. Luxembourg; Council of the European Communities (1989) Directive on the coordination of certain provisions laid down by law, regulation or administrative action in Member States concerning the pursuit of television broadcasting activities. 89/552/EEC. OJ No L 298. 17 October 1989. pp. 23-30.

11   CEC (1984) *op.cit.* p. 38.

12   A term used to signify the use of fora other than the Community, (and notably the Council of Europe), to secure ends impossible to realize within the Community because of the requirement for unanimity imposed by Article 235 of the Treaty of Rome.

13   Interviewed by the author on 7 November 1991.

14   Maggiore (1990 p. 108) states that Denmark, Germany and the United Kingdom have been 'most pugnacious' in their opposition to interventionist initiatives in broadcasting and the audio-visual sector.

15   European Parliament (1985) p. 35.

16   Interviewed 10 February 1992.

17   In general the UK has traded off concurrence with pro-active Community financial support for the audio-visual sector against increased harmonization and integration of Community audio-visual markets. The UK's specific concern in relation to the MEDIA programme, that money should not be wasted, was shared by Germany (see the statement by the German Delegation to the Council of Ministers of 20 December 1990 Document 10927/90 ADD 1). But the UK/Germany alliance has not held good for all broadcasting and audio-visual issues. For commentary on French policy perspectives see Storey in Crouch, C. and Marquand, D. (1990) *The Politics of 1992. Beyond the Single European Market.* Basil Blackwell. Oxford.

18   The OECD placed the UK second only to the United States as an international trader in audio-visual works (OECD Observer (1986) No. 141 July pp. 23-25 Paris), the Bank of England stated that 'earnings from film and television amounted to 2.8 per cent of exports and 3.5 per cent of imports of financial and other services in 1984 and showed a surplus of £131m. Real growth in this sector has been strong but somewhat erratic, in recent years' Bank of England (1985) Quarterly Bulletin. N 100. September. London. p 413. Maggiore (1990 p. 45) estimates that the UK accounted for 68.5 per cent of total Community audio-visual exports in 1985. In 1990 the Central Statistical Office (CSO 1991) Overseas Transactions of the Film and TV Industry. (CSO. Newport) estimated that the UK had an overall surplus on its overseas trade in film and television programmes (television making a slight loss which was more than compensated for by a surplus on the film account). For discussion see Collins, R. Garnham, N. and Locksley, G. (1988) *The Economics of Television. The UK Case* pp. 50-78. Sage. London.

19   Article 128 extends Community jurisdiction, for the first time, to the cultural domain. Under the Rome Treaty Community dirigiste cultural initiatives (which as we shall see have been very important in the unfolding of

broadcasting and audio-visual policy) had to be legitimized under the vague and dubious rubric of the Treaty's provision for the promotion of 'ever closer union' among Community members. The provisional text of the treaty on political union provides new authority for cultural initiatives and specifies that: The Community shall contribute to the flowering of the cultures of the Member States, while respecting their national and regional diversity, and at the same time bringing the common cultural heritage to the fore. Action by the Community shall encourage cooperation between Member States and, if necessary, support and supplement their action in the following areas: i) improvement of the knowledge and dissemination of the culture and history of the European peoples: ii) - conservation and safeguarding of the cultural heritage of European significance; iii) non-commercial cultural exchanges; - artistic and literary creation, including in the audio-visual sector.

20   Interviewd by author 11 November 1991.

21   Council of the European Communities (1986) *Council Directive on the adoption of common technical specifications of the MAC-packet family of standards for direct satellite television broadcasting*: OJ L 311, 6 November 1986; Council of the European Communities (1992) *Directive on the adoption of standards for satellite broadcasting of television signals*. 92/38/EEC 11 May 1992. OJ L 137. 20 May 1992. pp. 17-20.

22   CEC (1989) *op.cit.*

23   Council of the European Communities (1990). Decision concerning the implementation of an action programme to promote the development of the European audio-visual industry (MEDIA) (1991-1995). OJ L 380. 31 December 1990. p. 37.

24   DG I is responsible for the External Affairs of the Community and DG XIX for its budget.

25   Sources: Interviews by the author November 1991, Burgleman, J.P. and Pauwels, C. (1991). La Convergence de L'Audiovisuel et des Telecommunications en Europe. La Politique des Communautes Europeennes. CSNMIT. Free University of Brussels. Mimeo.

26   Which the Commission claimed was a requirement of the Treaty of Rome - see, inter alia, Bruhann, U. (1985) Address to the IBA Television without Frontiers conference 30 April 1985. p.2. IBA mimeo. London; and Schwartz, I. (1985) The Policy of the Commission of the European Communities with respect to Broadcasting in European Broadcasting Union Review. Programmes Administration, Law. Vol. XXXVI No. 6. p. 26. November.

27   Schwartz (1985) *op.cit.* p. 26.

28   CEC 1984. *op.cit.* p. 28.

29   Wilhelm Hahn was a German Christian Democrat Member of the European Parliament whose resolution on radio and television broadcasting in the European Community is often seen as marking the beginning of a Community broadcasting policy. In September 1980 the European Parliament's Committee on Youth, Culture, Education, Information and Sport established a committee of enquiry (with Hahn as rapporteur) whose *report on Radio and Television Broadcasting in the European Community* (European Parliament 1982) was submitted to the Parliament on February 23rd 1982. The report contained two draft resolutions (one emanating from Hahn and one from a parallel initiative on broadcasting - the Schinzel initiative - of another parliamentarian) which were composited between the Parliament's receipt of the report and its promulgation of a Resolution (European Parliament (1982a) Report on Radio and Television Broadcasting in the European Community. OJ 87/82, p 110-12), now usually known as the Hahn Resolution.

30   Cited in CEC (1984) *op.cit.* p. 28.

31   See, inter alia, Gellner, E. (1983) *Nationals and Nationalism* Blackwell. Oxford.

32   Council of the European Communities, (1986) *op.cit.*

33   The Directive authorized use of three MAC standards, C-MAC, D-MAC and D2-MAC. But D2-MAC was the only standard approved for both cable and satellite use. D2-MAC was better fitted to use on many existing cable systems than were either C or D MAC standards, however D2-MAC has capacity for only two stereo (or four mono) sound channels. Multilingual services, aimed at audiences in more than two separate language communities, were thus rendered difficult to provide.

34   Council of the European Communities, (1986) *op.cit.*

35   Council of the European Communities, (1992) *op.cit.*

36   The Parliament, reflecting its customary dirigiste rather than liberal line on audio-visual policy matters, opposed this permissive policy and called for a common standard, rather than a common format, for HDTV (OJ C150 31 May 1993).

37   XIII Magazine News Review N 11 p. 3. Quarterly. Commission of the European Communities. Brussels.

38   Council of the European Communities (1986) and (1989), *op.cit.*

39   Moeglin, P. (1991) 'Television et Europe' in *Communication* Vol. 12 No. 2 pp. 13-51.

40   Council of the European Communities (1992), *op. cit.*

41   By the former Chairman of the European Parliament's Committee on Youth, Culture, Education, the Media and Sport [interview 7 November1991] Roberto Barzanti.

42   European Parliament (1982) p 8.

43   Collins, R. (1993) 'Public Services Broadcasting by Satellite in Europe: Eurikon and Europa' in *Screen* Vol. 34. No. 2, pp. 162-75.

44   Kedourie, E. (1966) *Nationalism.* Hutchinson. London. p. 62.

45   European Parliament (1982) *op.cit.* p. 23.

46   Interview with author 11 November 1991.

47   Council of the European Communities (1990) Decision concerning the implementation of an action programme to promote the development of the European audio-visual industry, MEDIA 1991-1995. OJ 380. 31 December 1990. p. 37.

48   OJ C 115 29 April 1991. p. 18.

49   Council of the European Communities 1990, p. 174.

50   See Commission of the European Communities (1991) *MEDIA Guide for the Audio-visual Industry.* Edition 6. Commission of the European Communities. Brussels. p. 3.

51   See Decision 15 September 1989 in OJ L 284 p. 36-44. 3 October 1989.

52   See Decision 19 February 1991 in OJ L 63 p. 32-44. 9 March 1991.

53   Article 4.1. OJ No L 298, 17 October 1989. p. 18.

54   See OJ L208/38 20 July 1989.

55   Council of Europe (1991) Council of Europe activities in the media field. p. 17. Council of Europe Directorate of Human Rights. Strasbourg.

56   Interviewed 17 December 1991.

57   The Technological Eureka was established as a Community initiative at the instigation of France in 1985 in order to foster collaboration between European (including non-members of the EC) electronics and high technology enterprises.

58   Miyet, B (1990) The European Audio-visual Conference. In *European Broadcasting Union Review.* Programmes Administration Law. V XLI N 1 January. p. 10.

59   *Financial Times* 14 December (1993) p. 18.

60   *Financial Times* 6/7 November (1993) p. 4.

61   *Financial Times* 15 December (1993) p. 6.

62   Lang, J. (1988) 'The Future of European Film and Television. In *European Affairs* V 2 No. 1 p. 18.

63 Bangemann, M., et ai, 1994 'Europe and the Global Information Society. Recommendations to the European Council' (Brussels).

64 Commission of the European Communities (1994) *Strategy Options to Strengthen the European Programme Industry in the Context of the Audio-visual Policy of the European Union.* (The Audio-visual Green Paper). Brussels.

65 Bangemann, M. [et al] (1994) *op.cit.* p. 3.

66 European Commission (1994) *op.cit.* p. 4.

67 European Commission (1994) *op.cit.* p. 5.

68 European Commission (1994) *op.cit.* p. 6.

69 European Commission (1994) *op.cit.* p. 7.

70 This bibliography contains works cited in the text above and other works relevant to this subject. Readers who are interested in the regulation, structure and performance of the European Community's audio-visual sector are referred to Assises europeennes de l'audiovisuel. Projet Eureka audiovisuel (1989). Ministere des affaires etrangeres, Republique Francaise and Commission of the European Communities. Paris; Lange, A and J-L Renaud (1989) The Future of the European Audio-visual Industry. European Institute for the Media. Manchester; Maggiore, M (1990) Audio-visual Production in the Single Market. Commission of the European Communities. Luxembourg; Shaughnessy, H. and C. Fuente Cobo (1990) The Cultural Obligations of Broadcasting, European Institute for the Media. Manchester; UNESCO (1989) World Communication Report. UNESCO. Paris; and to the author's 'Broadcasting and Audio-visual Policy in the European Single Market'. John Libbey. London. 1994.

The research on which this paper is based was supported by the Economic and Social Research Council under award R 00023 2159 and was undertaken when the author was a member of the Department of Media and Communications at Goldsmiths' College, University of London. The author is grateful to the Council for its support and to Goldsmiths' College for its hospitality.

14 The Regulation of the European Pharmaceutical Industry

ELIAS MOSSIALOS, BRIAN ABEL-SMITH[†]

The regulation of pharmaceuticals is the result of the interplay of decisions taken at the level of the Community and the decisions of each Member State. The relationship between them is subtle. Member States are primarily concerned to contain the cost of pharmaceutical consumption as part of publicly financed health care. To a varying extent, Member States are also concerned to encourage an industry which has been growing rapidly at the global level. The central aim of the Community is to remove obstacles to the free movement of goods, while at the same time encouraging research and development to promote exports. At the EC level, the pharmaceutical industry is viewed as one of Europe's best-performing high-technology sectors. Yet this potentially European-wide market remains considerably partitioned along national lines. In examining systems of regulation at European and national levels later in this chapter, it is important to analyze the characteristics and the size of the pharmaceutical market. We next examine the actions which have been taken at Community level and then turn to examine the policies of Member States. Then we discuss several pending issues related to pricing of pharmaceutical products. The final section draws the main conclusions and examines policy options for the future.

[†]   This chapter is attributed to Professor Abel-Smith who sadly died before this book was published.

The Peculiarities of the Pharmaceutical Market

The market for ethical pharmaceuticals is unlike ordinary markets where consumers can be left to buy from competing producers on the basis of quality and price.[1] This is partly because the consumer only pays part of the price and the agency which pays the major part (the government or insurer) does not determine what or how much is bought. Furthermore, the consumer's ability to transform information into knowledge is limited. Many types of treatment are not repeated and as health care is an inherently technical subject, there are very few consumers, who could 'prescribe' without themselves becoming doctors. In addition, new drugs are covered by patent protection for twenty years which can be extended. In the case of patented products, companies compete on the basis of product suitability and differentiation, but price competition could be important where there are several therapeutic alternatives. The nature of the majority of the industry's products is perceived to be a matter of 'life and death'. Medicines are seen as essential in ways that most goods are not. Some may fear that as a result of this, pharmaceutical firms can set whatever price they like. Delegating decision-making power to a public regulatory agent is driven by the notion that profit incentives and market competition are insufficient to generate a socially optimal level of information or to produce socially desirable decisions by the pharmaceutical companies. State intervention concerns the safety of products, profit or price controls, the regulation of marketing and advertising and the regulation of overall pharmaceutical consumption. Intervention is generally exercised by a variety of agencies and in pursuit of a multiplicity of aims. The objective of these regulations is to supplement the working of the market. However, these regulations are very much concerned with the means and not concerned with the evaluation of performance in relation to the ends.

As a result of this absence of the normal market forces of competition, many governments intervene to fix prices. A second reason why they do so is because drugs are in part paid for out of public expenditure.

The European Pharmaceutical Market

The pharmaceutical industry in the EU is not geographically clustered and one reason for this has been the historical record of barriers to completely free trade within the EC. It is expected that a relocation of the industry, if Europe becomes a truly single market, will be beneficial to the EU economy in aggregate and will allow firms to achieve efficiency gains. Even if this change is beneficial in aggregate, there will be winners and losers. In this process a number of employees will lose their jobs. But governments may be able to negotiate lower prices or keep prices at reasonable levels.

One of the most important features of the European pharmaceutical market is its dominance by a relatively small group of large multinational research oriented companies. With the notable exception of Germany, they account for over 50 per cent of sales in Member states and a large share of exports. Two-thirds of the world market in 1992 was supplied by only 30 companies of which only eight were of EU origin - four German, three British and one French. Fifteen of the companies were based in the United States and this country supplies about half the world market, though its share has fallen slightly over the last decade. The three leading EU countries (Germany, the United Kingdom and France), have suffered a fall in the share of the world market from 31 per cent in 1981 to 26 per cent in 1984, followed by a recovery to 28.8 per cent in 1991. Firms in the top 30 have remained relatively unchanged over the 1980s, but since the early 1990s there have been significant changes in the rank order as a result of an increasing number of merges and acquisitions.[2] On average, 21 per cent of the revenue of the top 30 companies came from the sales of a single product in 1992.[3] Over a third of their revenue came from only one therapeutic category of drugs and over 60 per cent from only two such categories. Only a handful of companies compete in the same therapeutic categories. Within the therapeutic categories there are sub-markets where there are only a few 'real' competitors.

There are also 2,500 smaller companies specializing in generic and Over the Counter (OTC) products or operating within local markets. The industry is highly concentrated in the therapeutic sub-markets with the large companies controlling over 85 per cent of the therapeutic sub-markets in most EU Member States. Productivity in the Union's firms, measured as sales per employee, was 50 per cent of that in the United States industry and 45 per cent of that of Japan in 1991. The majority of the firms are small or of medium size: only 17 per cent had over 500 employees in 1991. In all six Member States (Belgium, Germany, France, Italy, UK, Denmark) for which data is available from Eurostat, over 45 per cent of pharmaceutical companies employed between 20 and 99 employees, over the 1981-89 period. On average 37 per cent were of medium size employing between 100 and 499 employees.[4]

The European pharmaceutical industry is at serious risk of losing out in the market for ethical drugs, relative to its major global competitors. Over the past decade the proportion of new and innovative drugs developed in Europe has been falling.[5] European investment in research and development, taken as a proportion of the industry's sales, is considerably below that of the United States and much below that of Japan.[6] Insofar as the future of pharmaceutical research is believed to lie in the new field of bio-technology, developments in this field in Europe are very seriously behind those in the United States.[7]

Action at the Community Level

Community regulation of the pharmaceutical sector raises questions of potential conflict between industrial policy and health and social protection policy objectives.

The legal framework within which the European Union may take action in the field of health has evolved considerably since the founding of the Community. The 1957 Treaty of Rome did not mention health specifically, although Article 118 enabled the Commission to promote close cooperation in the social field and particularly in matters relating to social security, prevention of occupational accidents and diseases, and occupational hygiene. The Euratom and European Coal and Steel Treaties also contained provision for cooperation in the field of occupational health in respect of the industries concerned.

The 1986 Single European Act amended the earlier Treaties and, in Article 100A(3), required the Commission to take, as a base, a high level of protection in its proposals concerning health, safety and environment and consumer protection, as they relate to the working of the single European market. This Article was used by the Commission services to initiate legislation in the field of pharmaceuticals and since 1986 a significant number of directives and regulations have been produced.

The most significant provision in the fields of health and industry were introduced in the 1992 Treaty on European Union (TEU). The Treaty gives the Union a new competence in public health (Articles 3(o), 129, and 129a). The Treaty also introduced Article 130 on industry, charging the Community with ensuring that the conditions necessary for the competitiveness of the industry exist.

In essence, Article 129 enables the Community to take action to co-ordinate national policies on the prevention of major scourges, as well as health information and education and the incorporation of health protection requirements in the Community's other policies. But the Treaty did not alter the fact that the provision of health services would remain exclusively the responsibility of the Member States. Harmonization of the laws and regulations of the Member States are specifically excluded.

The Commission's DG on Industrial Policy - DGIII - is mainly responsible for the development of pharmaceutical industrial policy. But there are other Directorate Generals which have competence in several areas that relate less directly to pharmaceutical policies. These span a significant number of Directorate Generals. They include, amongst others, DGV (Employment, Industrial Relations and Social Affairs), DGXII (Science, Research and Development), DGXIII (Telecommunications, Information Market and Exploitation of Research), and DGXV (Internal Market and Financial Services).[8] It is worth noting that in 1994 the European Commission Communication on the outlines of an industrial policy for the pharmaceutical sector, was jointly signed by DGIII Commissioner Bangemann and DGV Commissioner Flynn.[9] But the Treaty also introduced the concept of subsidiarity that has important implications for many areas of national policy. Under the principle of subsidiarity, health services, including pricing and financing of medicines, are the responsibility of each Member State.

Consolidating the European internal Market

The European Commission has made significant efforts to push the Union towards a 'Single Market' in medicines. It has tried to create a multistate procedure for marketing approval for medicines. It has achieved agreement on directives on product's classification,[10] advertising and sales promotion,[11] good manufacturing practice[12] on provisions relating to labelling and package inserts[13] and on wholesale distribution.[14] But the implementation of these directives was left to the relevant authorities of Member States. Nevertheless, existing divergent national policies combined with the inherent peculiarities of the pharmaceutical market and the structure of the industry make the completion of a single European market a particularly difficult task. For a Single Market to become a reality it would be necessary to remove further barriers to trade by standardizing pack sizes, dosages and the names of products marketed under different names in different countries. This should reduce costs and allow a pan-European wholesaler to stock less products.

However, there would still remain opportunities for Member States to discriminate in favour of national companies by the provisions they make with regards to the systems of regulation of prices/profits, patient's co-payments and the number of products reimbursed by the Health Insurance of the National Health System.

Price harmonization within the Community will be affected by the degree to which pressure can be lifted off companies to expand local manufacturing facilities unnecessarily, thus providing an opportunity for companies to achieve more economies of scale. Public procurement policies in various Member States also systematically tend to favour domestic over foreign suppliers.

Standardizing systems of patient payment or drug lists would be seen by Member States as a precedent-setting invasion by the Commission into the province of health care organization, which Member States see as protected by the principle of 'subsidiarity' enshrined in the Treaty of the European Union [15] - that governmental functions should be undertaken at the lowest practicable level - which they keenly want to maintain.

If the aim were to introduce competition in final selling prices rather than just ex-factory prices, then it would be necessary:-

- to deregulate wholesale and retail margins,

- to remove the restrictions which prevent the development of cost-cutting chains of pharmacies under common ownership,

- to align the levels of VAT.

Attempts to coordinate the level of VAT have so far met with only limited success.[16] It has been a major effort to try and further standardize tax coverage. Standardizing pharmacists' retail margins would lead to the closure of a large number of pharmacies in some Member States which would be far from being politically popular.

If one wanted to reduce the risks facing a potential pan-European wholesaler, there would in addition need to be monetary integration, via a single currency, which cannot, now, be taken for granted. In addition, the

European Union proposes a structure which implies the assignment of the control of price inflation to a central monetary authority and the assignment of the control of budgetary balances to the Member States' fiscal authorities. Any strategy which would imply the conduct of monetary policy so as to control inflation without regard to its effect on the balance of payments, and of conducting fiscal policies so as to control budget balances without regard of their effect on price inflation, could turn out to be a recipe for economic and monetary instability.[17]

Moreover some other factors are also important concerning the free movement of medicines in the European Union in relation to price control and reimbursement systems:

First, the elasticity of demand for drugs of a given category varies extensively between countries due to different medical practices and prescribing habits, epidemiological patterns and consumption patterns.

Second, the number of products on the market in the twelve Member States differs significantly, and the same applies for the information contained in the leaflets. Significant problems still exist in the classification of medicines as Prescription only Medicines (POM) and Over the Counter (OTC) products, although in March 1992 the EC adopted a Council Directive Concerning the Classification for the Supply of Medicinal Products for Human Use.[18] Only seven common OTC products were found in the top fifty sales in four EC Member States in 1992 (Italy, France, Germany and the United Kingdom).[19]

Third, depending on country-specific medical practices, the rates of reimbursement and the price levels or price increases granted by insurance funds vary due to different value judgements made on the relative benefits of specific drugs. It is also worth noting that some countries have already started grouping medicines with similar or the same therapeutic outcomes (interchangeable medicines) or according to the pharmacological and therapeutic similarity of the ingredients of the active substance. But the criteria employed in the classification process differ extensively among Member States.

Fourth, even if a common price could be imposed on similar drugs the prices for the consumer would vary considerably due to the extensive divergences in patient contribution schemes.

New Developments towards a Single Market

Progress towards a Single Market has been given a new impetus with the adoption by the Council of two new Regulations establishing the European Medicines Evaluation Agency (EMEA) in London and the Supplementary Protection Certificate (SPC).

Market Authorization and the Development of The European Medicines Evaluation Agency (EMEA)

In 1975 the Commission established a Committee of representatives of national authorization authorities, the 'Committee for Proprietary Medicinal Products' (CPMP)[20] and set up a multistage 'CPMP procedure' for medicines approval.[21] The aim of the CPMP was to facilitate a company that had obtained a marketing authorization in one Member State to obtain marketing authorization in another Member State. A multiple authorization was established with the objective to avoid duplication of procedures and reduce delays in the authorization procedure. Applicants who had obtained authorization in one Member State could apply for an extension of the authorization to the authorities of five or more other Member States. In case of an objection from Member States the CPMP would have to make a non-binding recommendation.

The CPMP procedure was not used extensively by the pharmaceutical industry. During its existence from 1976 to 1985 only 41 applications were submitted. One reason may have been the fact that most of the rules governing pharmaceuticals in the EC have not been harmonized yet. The reaction of the Commission was to introduce amendments to the Directive 83/570/EEC and create the 'Multistate Procedure'. The minimum number of States that could be approached for an extension of the original approval was reduced from five to two. CPMP opinions remained non-binding but companies had access to CPMP hearings to present their application. The 'Multistate Procedure' was more successful than 'Mutual Recognition'[22] procedure but the progress had been slow, with different decisions depending on the Member State, even though it allowed the company the choice of the rapporteur.[23]

National medicines regulatory systems in the EU Member States have traditionally been developed as a means of protecting consumers. The proposals of the European Commission to establish a European Agency for the Evaluation of Medicinal Products were criticized because although some attention was paid to health and safety issues, the basic principles underlying the proposals are those of the free market. [24]

At the time of the inauguration of the Agency, the Commission emphasized that 'the creation of the Agency is firstly a benefit for the European patient'. It should be, however, noted that five years ago no one thought seriously of selling the idea of establishing an Agency as a patient benefit.[25]

The change in the Commission's statements reflected the pressure of different consumer associations which argued that the new system lacked transparency and that there was no consumer representation in the decision-making procedures.[26]

Three registration procedures for pharmaceuticals were established according to the Regulation establishing a European Agency for the Evaluation of Medical Products[27]:-

-   a centralized procedure, reserved for innovatory products and leading to a single Community wide authorization valid for all 15 Member States. The use of the centralized procedure will be compulsory for all medicinal products derived from biotechnology but available only at the request of companies for other innovatory products. Under this procedure applications will be processed by the Agency in London.

-   a decentralized procedure, which will apply to the substantial majority of products, based upon the principle of mutual recognition, and covering a variable number of Member States.

-   a national procedure, limited in principle to applications of local interest concerning a single Member State.

The national authorities have lost their regulatory powers in the case of biotechnology products. The Agency will also be dealing with the authorization of innovatory pharmaceutical products and it is expected that one of the issues that will be raised in the near future will be the definition of an innovative product. Policy implications related to this matter will be important in years to come.

Definition of Innovation

There are two different procedures where the definition of innovation is very important. The Centralized Procedure in the EMEA and the application for a Supplementary Protection Certificate. In the Centralized Procedure, the EMEA is going to decide if a product constitutes a significant innovation in order to be evaluated under the provisions stated in Part B of the Annex to the Regulation establishing the Agency. Criteria for the evaluation of the therapeutic value of medicines have already been developed in Germany, the Netherlands, the United States and Japan. Commissioner Bangemann defined as innovative products those which are new world-wide products resulting from a specific inventive activity. [28] But this constitutes a very broad definition and could actually cover the majority of the new chemical introductions on the market.

The Agency has not yet clarified if it plans to develop specific criteria for the assessment of new chemical entities. Professor G. Benzi, the European Parliament's representative on the EMEA's Management Board, submitted a paper to the Board in December 1995, suggesting a more formal recognition of innovation in the context of new medicines. A clear definition is expected to raise opposition from the pharmaceutical industry whose representatives usually argue that it will lead to an additional regulatory hurdle or have a rebound effect on reimbursement decisions. [29] But there are additional problems concerning the definition of what is an innovative product at European level and these reflect the multiplicity of the regulatory mechanisms in the Community. Countries which have established criteria for the evaluation of the therapeutic effectiveness and innovativeness of new products have a single regulatory organization and they do not currently use these criteria for pricing and reimbursement decisions. The problem with the centralized system is that it will not be able to deal with all the applications submitted. [30] It is not clear, however, how the officials will 'prioritize' their decision-making and how drugs not being processed through the centralized system should be assessed for marketing. There will be two different categories of products: those which are innovative but are not going to be authorized due to limited number of applications the centralized system will be processing and those not meeting the innovation criteria.

The new system is, therefore, inherently unstable and represents a halfway house between the establishment of a European Food and Drug Administration, with increased decision-making powers and what is currently possible, given the developments in the regulatory process at European level, which reflect the objective of several Member States to participate in and influence decision-making. This is inevitable, since market authorization of products is part of the Member States portfolio to sustain pharmaceutical manufacturing within their borders.

Intellectual Property

In 1992 the Council adopted Regulation 1786/92 concerning the creation of a Supplementary Protection Certificate (SPC) for medicinal products,[31] to allow a protection period of up to fifteen years from the date of the first market authorization in the Community. The original proposal of the Commission suggested a Supplementary Protection Certificate of up to ten years with an effective patent protection of up to sixteen years in the first Member State in which the product was launched. The UK suggested an SPC of five years with an effective protection of up to 14 years. The Council finally agreed a five year extension with a maximum of fifteen years effective patent protection.

The SPC extends the period of patent protection initially conferred by a patent to allow for the period of the patent term erosion due to the time taken to obtain market authorization.

The maximum duration of the SPC has been substantially reduced by the Council from ten years, which was the initial proposal of the Commission, to five years with the compromise proposal put forward by the Dutch Presidency, thus reflecting the concerns of generic product manufacturers. There was disagreement amongst the Member States concerning the transitional arrangements. Germany opposed the retrospective character of the SPC, but finally a compromise has been achieved. It was agreed that the 'start-up' date for the restored patent protection would differ amongst Member States.[32]

According to the explanatory memorandum of the Commission's original proposal,[33] only 'innovative products' were to be covered by the

SPC. Despite the above definition, however, the issue of what constitutes an innovative drug is still quite vague and remains to be appropriately defined. As regards the possibility of generic producers to carry out research with a view to submitting an application for authorization to place their products on the market, before the end of the period of the protection conferred by the SPC, the Regulation provides only that the SPC shall confer the same rights as conferred by the basic patent[34] without further specification.

According to the Commission the courts in several Member states have ruled that the use of the patented product for obtaining authorization to place a generic product on the market does not constitute straightforward experimental use (which third parties are allowed in derogation from the exclusive rights of the patentee) but an act with commercial purpose and thus liable to be prohibited by the holder of the patent.[35]

In the U.S. the Drug Price Competition Patent Term Restoration Act of 1984, known as the Waxman-Hatch Act, exempts from patent infringement statute the 'uses reasonably related to the development and submission of information under a federal law which regulates ... drugs'.[36] The generic producer is therefore allowed to take a number of steps before the patent expires and perform all necessary testing and other regulatory activities in order to obtain approval by the Food and Drug Administration while the U.S. patent is still effective.

In the European Union generic competition will not start immediately after the expiry of the SPC, but a considerable period afterwards, i.e. the time it takes the generic manufacturer to undertake all the necessary scientific and regulatory preparations. The consequences of the above for independent generic manufacturers in Europe are not encouraging for a number of reasons:-

-       first, patent holders can clearly use this additional protection period, after the expiry of the patent or the SPC, to outpace the traditional generic competitor, by introducing immediately after the SPC expiry, their own generic formulation;

-       second, US generic companies, which are entitled to prepare their marketing authorization file during the patent period, will be ready to launch their own generic versions immediately after the expiry of the marketing exclusivity period, placing them potentially in a position to outpace EU-based companies in specific sub-market categories.

The SPC also prohibits the foreign supplier from making the shipments to the U.S. According to Senator David Pryor, it is expected that the SPC will delay entry on to the U.S. market of a generic version of a product from 3 to 6 years since preparatory activities would have to take place after the patent expiration.[37] It is also expected that the economic impact on the US health care system will be significant since the normal 40 per cent to 70 per cent cost savings from generic drugs will be delayed for a significant period of time. This cost is estimated to range from $20 to $50 billion. Approximately 80 per cent of all bulk active drug ingredients utilized by U.S. generic drug manufacturers is imported from EC countries.[38]

It is also worth noting that the implementation of the SPC since January 1993 will affect decisions on which approval procedure for new pharmaceutical products to use since each SPC will apply to the first indication approved in the first Member State. Companies with a new product to file would prefer to apply to the new centralized procedure, as approval will be granted in all member States at the same time. Alternatively they will have to choose the fastest procedure in one of the Member States and this may affect their decision on where to locate production and other facilities.

Pricing and Reimbursement Policies

While in some areas the Commission has managed to make considerable progress towards a Single market, it has had to accept that Member States retain substantial autonomy in the crucial area of pricing, reimbursement and user charges.

In addition, pricing and financing systems in the Union are far from similar. The Commission has attempted several times to introduce harmonizing legislation in this field, but it has failed to convince Member States to accept binding measures. The principle of subsidiarity, introduced in the Treaty on the European Union has imposed further impediments to the creation of a Single Market in the pharmaceutical sector.

In December 1988 the Council adopted a Directive relating to the transparency of measures regulating the pricing of medicinal products for human use and their inclusion in the scope of national health insurance schemes (henceforth the 'Transparency Directive').[39] The Commission acknowledged that the Directive was an initial step towards harmonization and that further measures should take place progressively.

The Commission considered these measures as appropriate given the 'inadequacy or absence of competition in the medicinal products market'. The Commission's 'White Paper on Completing the Internal Market' published in 1985 has also recognized that the pharmaceutical market has certain peculiarities which distinguish it from other consumer markets including the fact that the final consumer does not select the product the doctor prescribes and government pays for it.

The Commission also emphasized that the requirements of the Directive do not affect the policies of the Member States which rely primarily upon free competition to determine the price of medicinal products. The wording of this Directive rather contradicts that of the White Paper which suggests that there is no real competition in the pharmaceutical market. Thus, the co-existence of two diametrically different positions in the same document may reflect the influence of certain interest groups in the formation of the Directive.

The Directive requires that the national authorities adopt transparent, objective and verifiable criteria when deciding on price or profits regulations or the setting up of limited and positive lists of drugs. It defines a time limit of 90 days on national authorities to agree or set a price on newly introduced products and requires that they state the reasons if they fix a different price to that sought by the company. In addition, the Directive delimits the timing on processing applications for price increases, defines the steps following the introduction of a 'price freeze', requires by national authorities a classification of products by therapeutic category and demands from Member States to set up criteria for judging the fairness of transfer prices.

Finally, the Directive provides for the establishment of a Committee on Pharmaceutical Pricing Transparency to oversee the operation of the Directive.

In March 1992 the Commission launched its proposals for the amendment of the Directive. In this document the Commission while again underlying that there is no competition in the pharmaceutical market, argues that direct price control systems impede the development of true price competition and worsen the convergence of pharmaceutical policies in Europe. However, there is no explanation on how price competition systems are compatible with imperfect and non competitive markets.

The Commission argues that direct or indirect controls on medicine prices, as well as restrictive measures concerning the share of medicine costs covered by the public insurance systems, are legitimate since they pursue an unquestionable objective from the point of view of the Community Law. However the Commission asserts that these measures distort the integration of the market although the European Court has never accepted this position.

In January 1991 the Commission circulated a discussion document and a questionnaire to all interested parties - governments, industry, professional associations, - aiming at elaborating their considerations on the probable amendments of the Directive as they have previously suggested in Article 9 of the Directive. This document raised a number of issues related to the pricing and financing of medicines and suggested further inquiry into the possibilities of amendments of Articles 2, 3 and 4. The document provided for two sets of alternative measures aiming at either the greater depth of the transparency of policies of the measures taken by Member States on the pricing and reimbursement decisions or the alignment of the divergent policies by harmonizing a number of the aspects that they present.

Only six Member States[40] replied to the questionnaire. All Member States opposed the idea of a more energetic role of the Commission in the pricing and financing procedures. Moreover, the United Kingdom and the Netherlands questioned the emphasis given by the Commission on the transparency procedures. They suggested that the Commission examine measures concerning the demand policies of the prescription market.

The general comments from all, as well as the European Federation of Pharmaceutical Industries Association (EFPIA), were generally opposed to any direct involvement of the Commission in the national pricing and financing procedures. The discussion document also asked the interested parties to examine whether the amended Directive should include a method for the measurement of profits and a standard profit rate. The probability of enacting a system of control of profits at European level as an alternative to price control was also to be discussed. Both the EFPIA and the Member States suggested that the Commission not take actions leading to a common methodology for profit control.

The Commission finally came up with a draft recommendation which included a number of guidelines on deregulation and the promotion of competition in the market place. The recommendations included proposals for freedom of pricing for non-reimbursed medicines, progressive deregulation of direct price controls and removal from reimbursement of the Over the Counter medicines. The Commission again argued that the market is characterized by a lack of price competition, and further harmonization is distorted by price controls. It was also emphasized that greater price competition would contribute both to progressive harmonization of this sector with the normal conditions of the internal market. The Commission, therefore, moved away from its previous argument that the market for pharmaceuticals is not a competitive market.[41] The Commission had also prepared a proposal for a Council Directive on modifications to the Transparency Directive, but finally decided to withdraw it.

The proposals of the recommendation were discussed in the Committee on Pharmaceutical Price Transparency, and several Member States expressed reservations about the proposals on market deregulation, whereas other Member States[42] agreed in principle but could not see the point to those recommendations.

Following several meetings and consultations Commissioner Bangemann,[43] responsible for the internal market policies, suggested that the experience gained since the entry into force of the 'Transparency' Directive was not yet sufficient to enable the Commission to submit to the Council any definitive proposals on fuller approximation of national measures regulating the pricing and reimbursement of medicines.

In a paper presented at an Institute of Economic Affairs conference on pharmaceutical policies in Europe in December 1992 Commissioner Brittan, Commission Vice-President responsible for competition, emphasized that where dealing with national price-control systems the Commission is at the very crossroads between the creation of a common market and national sovereignty. He stated that at present it is neither possible nor desirable to attempt widespread harmonization in this sector, though he encouraged an evolutionary process leading to a gradual convergence of the national systems insofar as necessary to create a single market.[44] The Commission finally decided to shelve the 'technical' amendments to the 'Transparency Directive' in December 1992. According to Commissioner Brittan the principle of subsidiarity influenced the Commission's decision.[45]

The response of Commissioner Bangemann was to initiate discussions with the industry on a wider package linked with the industrial policy for the pharmaceutical sector. The industrial policy discussion started in November 1992, when the Commissioner met with a group of industry leaders to discuss mutual concerns about the future of the pharmaceutical industry in Europe.

The result of that meeting was the establishment of a joint Commission-Industry Task Force (IPTF) which led to the March 1994 publication of the Communication to the Council and the European Parliament on the 'Outlines of an Industrial Policy for the Pharmaceutical Sector in the European Community.' [46]

The Industrial Policy Communication

At least ten different drafts of the Communication were prepared and its final text differs extensively from the initial drafts. The explanation is that Commissioner Flynn's cabinet in DG V (responsible for social policy) became involved or aware of the draft Communication at some stage and intensive discussions between DG III (Industrial Policy) and DG V started at the end of 1993. The title of the Communication may imply that the Commission might have abandoned its earlier ambitions to put forward policies on pricing and financing.[47] This, however, was probably not the initial plan since in the first drafts of the Communication there were significant policy recommendations regarding the pricing and financing systems. It would be impossible 'constitutionally' for DG III to bypass and ignore the 'Pharmaceutical Pricing Committee' which is responsible for discussing and evaluating the Commission's proposals relating to the Transparency Directive. A wider policy Communication, however, could be produced by another body in order to evade any policy impediments or the reluctance of the 'Pharmaceutical Pricing Committee' to re-examine the issue of harmonization in this field.

The Commission regards the Communication as a basis for discussion, rather than the expression of final policy. [48] The Commission stated that the European industry is facing stiffening worldwide competition. It was emphasized that the capacity of the EC firms to innovate appears to be declining, and that they are underrepresented in some new fields. It was also emphasized that for the first time in twenty years the total pharmaceutical employment in the pharmaceutical industry did not increase in 1993 and that within the next three years (1993-95), nearly 27,000 jobs could be lost in the European pharmaceutical industry. The Commission sent a warning message by underlying the fact that the industry will not be able to create 5,000 to 10,000 new jobs a year in the future, as in each of the last years.

Given the strong preoccupation of the Commission's officials and the increasing worries of the national governments with the increasing number of unemployed and the failure of successive policies to create further employment in the EU, the Commission's argument looked convincing. The Commission 'failed' to emphasize that further market harmonization would lead to the loss of a significant number of jobs given the low productivity and overemployment of the European companies.

The Commission also suggested that it planned to intensify its efforts to consolidate the internal market, establish better intellectual protection for genuine innovative therapies and create programmes better suited to pharmaceutical R&D. It underlined that its aims try to enhance competition in the pharmaceutical market, by rendering it more transparent and allowing generic medicines to stimulate competition on price.

But the final draft of the Communication did not include the proposals for drug price deregulation which were included in the initial drafts. According to an editorial published in the Wall Street Journal Europe[49] 'the purge was engineered by Social Affairs Commissioner P. Flynn, backed by President Delors and 'half the Commission'. The Communication is still under review in the European Parliament and it is not yet known if there will be a reaction from the Council. Once again the dilemmas the regulators are faced with - cost containment vs industrial development - left their imprints in the formation of policies and reflected the peculiarities of this market and the difficulties to harmonize it.

The Actions of Member States

The central concern of Member States has been to control pharmaceutical expenditure and a variety of measures have been adopted with this aim in view - operating on patients, doctors and the industry. Cost-sharing is intended to influence patients' behaviour, while attempts to influence doctors' behaviour include positive and negative lists, encouraging generics, monitoring doctors' prescribing and giving budgets to each doctor. Finally, operating on the industry are company budgets or agreed levels of total revenue for the industry and regulating or influencing prices. Information on the role of each of these is summarized below.

Cost-sharing

The role of cost-sharing in the fifteen Member States is shown in table 1. Italy and Spain are the countries which try to place the greatest weight on cost-sharing for drugs but in both cases there is considerable illegal evasion. The view taken by the Commission is that co-payment is an acceptable way for Member States to limit pharmaceutical consumption and that it is preferable to direct control over prices.

The Role of Positive and Negative Lists

A very limited positive list is in effect 100 per cent cost-sharing for those products excluded from it. Italy's decision, from 1994, to narrow this list from 4,545 to 771 has clearly this effect. Table 2 illustrates which countries have positive and negative lists. Some countries with positive lists may also have negative lists but a positive list is assumed here to also cover the negative one.

It is worth noting that in the judgement of the Duphar Case,[50] the Court of Justice decided that under a compulsory national health care scheme the Member States are entitled to exclude certain medicinal products from reimbursement or to allow reimbursement only for certain products on the condition that the choice of the excluded products (in the case of a negative list) or of the included products (in the case of a positive list) involves no discrimination regarding the origin of the products and is carried out on the basis of objective and verifiable criteria, and provided that it is possible to amend the lists whenever compliance with the specified criteria so requires.

Table 1. Cost-sharing in the Member States in 1995

Country	Percentage of Items Exempted	Charges
Belgium	None	flate rate plus 0/25/50/60/80/100% of price
Germany	NA	3, 5 or 7 marks depending on pack size based on days or treatment
Denmark	NA	0/25/50 per cent of price
Spain	62	0/10/40 per cent of price
Finland	None	FIM 25 or 45 and 0/25/50 per cent of price
France	9	0/35/65/100% or price
Greece	NA*	0/10/25% of price
Luxembourg	None	0/20% or price
Ireland	GMS-100**	none for GMS patients
Italy	32	flat rate of 3000 lire (£1.20) for first two items or 3000 lire for first two plus 50% of price
Netherlands	100	none
Austria	18	ATS 34 per time
Portugal	45	0/30/60 per cent of price (15 and 45 per cent for low income persons)
Sweden	Negligible	0/SEK 160 for the first item and SEK 60 for further items
United Kingdom	85	flat rate of £5.25

NA - not available
* - very low - just chronic sick
** - General Medical Service
Source: Authors' estimates

Table 2. Positive and Negative Lists

Positive	Negative
Austria	Germany
Belgium	Spain
Denmark	Ireland
Finland	Luxembourg
France	United Kingdom
Greece	
Italy	
Netherlands	
Sweden	
Portugal	

Source: Authors' estimates

Encouraging the Use of Generics

Generics were estimated in 1993 to be 12 per cent of sales in the United Kingdom, and about the same order of magnitude in the Netherlands and about 16 per cent in Germany. Only the Netherlands provides incentives for pharmacists to seek these lower prices, as a third of the savings can be retained.

In the United Kingdom, the government has been successfully promoting the use of generic drugs as one of the measures to keep the drug bill under control. It is not surprising that fundholding general practitioners prescribe generics more than non-fundholders. There is still room for a large growth in the generics market as there are wide variations in the extent to which doctors prescribe them.[51]

Much depends on the incentives facing the pharmacist. Clearly a pharmacist has no incentive to substitute them when he is paid on the basis of a percentage of the price even if this is regressive. This is one reason why generic penetration has been high in both the Netherlands and the United Kingdom where the pharmacist receives a fixed fee per drug item.

France, Spain, and Italy all have plans to develop the generic market. Italy is likely to change to a flat rate system of remunerating pharmacists to encourage their use.

Budgets for Doctors and the Industry

Despite their basic systems of influencing or controlling prices, such as price control, profit control or a reference price system, budget controls have been superimposed as shown in table 3. No less than five countries have budgets either agreed with the industry (and to be enforced by it) or with penalties for doctors or simply laid down by the government.

Table 3. The Role of Budgets in 1995

Country	Budget
Germany	Indicative budgets for each doctor and for each region (doctors at risk for DM 280 million).
Italy	Laid down by the government.
United Kingdom	Indicative for non-fundholding GPs but firm for fundholders.
France	Revenue maximum per company to achieve 3.2% growth in expenditure in 1994. From 1996, budgets for each doctor. If exceeded, the level of fees will be reduced. Medical references are to be extended to cover all doctors' activity.
Spain	7% growth of expenditure for three years to be enforced by the industry from 1995.

Source: Authors' estimates

Summary of the Methods of Regulating or Influencing Prices

The methods of regulating or influencing the prices of pharmaceuticals are summarized in table 4. The underlying mechanisms are shown in the left hand column, even though they have recently, as in France, been superseded by budgets. Presumably if the budget system does not work effectively or the industry is unwilling to continue it, France will revert to its old system.

Table 4. Main Means of Regulating or Influencing Medicine Consumption in 1995

Country	Underlying mechanism to regulate or influence prices	Price cut
Belgium	Prices based on improvement over existing therapy	--
Germany	Free pricing plus a reference price system excluding patented drugs	5% cut ended 1994
Denmark	Free pricing plus a reference price system	5 % ending April 1997
Spain	Prices based on 'cost'	3% cut ending 1997
Finland	Prices are regulated	
France	Prices fixed on medical effectiveness and negotiation with each company	--
Greece	Prices fixed based on cost, transfer price and 3 lowest in EU	--
Ireland	Average or prices in Denmark, France, Germany, the Netherlands and the UK	
Italy	Average prices of Germany, Spain, France and the UK	2.5% or 5% cut ended 1995
Luxembourg	Prices in Belgium, free pricing if no price in Belgium	
Netherlands	Prices are the average of those in Belgium, France, Germany and the United Kingdom. Reference price system including some patent drugs	5% cut ending June 1996
Austria	Price negotiation based on costs in a typical Austrian company of a comparable foreign product	
Portugal	Lowest price among Spain, France and Italy	In 1994, between 2.85 and 8 per cent. In 1995 an increase was granted of 1 per cent.
Sweden	Negotiated price and a reference price system excluding patented drugs	--
United Kingdom	Profit regulation	2.5% cut ending autumn 1996

Source: Authors' estimates

The Level of Prices

What is the apparent effect of these different systems of regulating prices/profits on the level of drug prices in the different countries? It is not possible to make accurate comparisons for a number of reasons. First, a high proportion of sales in one Member State may go on products not sold in other Member States. Secondly, products can be similar, or identical, but traded under different names in different countries. Thirdly, package sizes, strengths, dosages and presentations vary and there is the problem of combined ingredients. Fourthly, the importance of a product in the sales of one Member State may be very different from that in another Member State. Fifth, there are the variations in wholesale and retail margins and in the level of VAT. Finally, there is the difficulty of finding an exchange rate which fairly reflects purchasing power. Nevertheless, one attempt at comparison is shown in table 5.

Table 5. Index of Prices of Pharmaceuticals (EU=100)

Country	1988	1993
Germany	128.4	105.4
Italy	79.1	95.5
United Kingdom	115.9	122.7
France	71.5	63.4
Spain	71.6	93.5*
Netherlands	131.9	148.4*
Greece	73.8	84.7
Belgium	88.6	116.2
EU	100.0	100.0

* Provisional
Source: German Association of Pharmacists (ABDA, 1994)

This table, produced by the Association of German Pharmacists, is only based on 129 products chosen in 1988 and thus excludes many costly new products. The calculation has been criticized for this and other reasons. For example, it includes a number of 'over the counter' drugs which are not reimbursable and excludes generic drugs.[52] The results should be interpreted as only very broadly indicative for the above reasons.

The table does not reflect the major changes made in the systems of price control in France and Italy since 1991, nor the large price increases granted in Greece in recent years. But it indicates a very wide variation of prices with Greece and France well below the other countries. Germany comes out surprisingly low in view of its policy of free pricing, subject to the reference price system.

Parallel Imports

Price differences in the Member States have encouraged the growth of parallel imports. A parallel market has been developed by wholesalers who buy products in low-price countries such as Greece, Spain, Portugal and France and export them to high-price countries (Germany, U.K., The Netherlands and Denmark). Denmark and the Netherlands actively encourage parallel imports as a way of cutting down pharmaceutical expenditure but Germany has used measures to impede these imports.[53]

In the Netherlands savings which pharmacists make by buying parallel imports are passed on to the consumers but in the UK pharmacists cannot do the same because of the flat rate prescription fee although the Department of Health assumes a level of parallel import prescriptions when setting individual practice budgets.[54]

The Court of Justice has ruled in favour of parallel imports on several occasions, though only within the EU. In the 'De Peijper' case the Court of Justice, to which the matter was referred under Article 197 of the EEC Treaty, delivered a judgement on parallel imports of medicinal products. According to the Court's rule the authorities are not entitled to require from a parallel importer to provide them with documents which are only available to the manufacturer, especially when these documents were already given to the authorities by the manufacturer.[55] In addition the fact that the name of the product imported in parallel is not identical to that of the product already authorized does not allow the regulatory authorities to require a different new authorization procedure, since the imported product which was produced by a branch of the same company as the one already authorized in the country where it is imported, has the same therapeutic effectiveness. The German authorities are content in such cases to only verify that the products are identical concerning their therapeutic effectiveness.[56]

Following this judgement the Commission prepared and forwarded to the Council on 2 June 1980, a proposal for a Directive relating to parallel imports of proprietary medicinal products.[57] The aim of the proposal was to establish a system for the registration of parallel imports in order to prevent a manufacturer of a proprietary product or his duly appointed representatives from being allowed by regulation or practice to monopolize the importing and marketing of the product by simply refusing to produce the documents relating to the product in general or to a specific batch. The Economic and Social Committee raised several objections to the proposed Directive and the European Parliament voted against the proposal on 16 October 1981.[58] After these negative reactions the Commission decided to withdraw its proposal and issued a Communication on parallel imports of proprietary medicinal products for which marketing authorizations have already been granted.[59]

Companies have tried to reduce the impact of parallel imports by launching products into all European markets at a smaller time period than before and thus creating problems for governments in low price countries to use prices of other low price countries as benchmark prices. Thus, they achieved introducing products on many markets at roughly the same price. This policy was undermined by the devaluation of several currencies (i.e. the Italian lira was devalued in 1992 by 38 per cent) and extensive price cuts especially in Italy and Spain.

Pricing of Pharmaceuticals: Transparency Directive and Beyond

The 'Transparency Directive' was in reality a procedural directive setting out a framework of procedures for decision-making but it was not a harmonizing Directive. Several issues were raised before and after the introduction of the Directive which reflect the partial or incomplete harmonization in the pharmaceutical sector. These included, amongst others, the role of the level of prices as an impediment to free trade, price discrimination against imports, the use of average European prices and the definition of an excessive price.

Defining the Level of Prices

The level of pharmaceutical prices as an impediment to free trade was raised by the Commission in Case C-249/88 Commission v Belgium. The Commission[60] argued that the prices of pharmaceutical products in Belgium were lower than in other Member States as a supportive argument to its claim that the rules on the fixing of maximum prices for pharmaceutical products were incompatible with Community law. But later in a response to a written question by the Court, the Commission 'wished to state that it drew no inference in law from the data on the comparative level of prices of pharmaceutical products in the Member States and that the comparisons were merely intended to illustrate the economic consequences of the contested measures.'[61] The Court decided that this issue should be left out of account.

The proceedings also involved a system of maximum prices for pharmaceutical products fixed by the Belgian authorities. The Commission argued that the method of setting prices discriminated against imports, but the Court ruled that this allegation was unsubstantiated. The Commission also argued that the price was fixed at such a low level that imports were discouraged due to the low profit margins. The Court agreed that such a result would disclose a violation of Article 30 EEC, but found that the Commission had not proved its case.

The Court's long established view is that there is a form of discrimination to apply the same mandatory pricing regime to goods with different production costs. The Court has ruled that Article 30 is infringed when an import is denied the opportunity to undercut the domestic product (unlawful minimum price fixing)[62] or to trade at a reasonable profit (unlawful maximum price fixing).[63]

Price Discrimination against Imports

In the same Case the Court ruled that the Kingdom of Belgium failed to fulfil its obligations under the EEC Treaty by permitting price increases in return for undertakings on investment, research, employment and exports. The Belgian government introduced a system of programme contracts in 1983 and exempted pharmaceutical products covered by the programme from the rules barring pharmaceutical products from approval for reimbursement where their price exceeds that of similar products by a given per centage. These products may therefore have not been used as basis for comparisons for the purpose of approval of reimbursement of other products. This system was repealed in 1988 and only contracts which had not been expired were permitted to continue. The Court ruled that even though the default has been remedied after a period of time the Kingdom of Belgium failed to fulfil its obligations under the EEC Treaty.

By permitting prices to be granted in return for undertakings on investment, research, employment and exports pricing systems place imported products at a disadvantage and these measures are considered by the Court of Justice to have an effect equivalent to a quantitative restriction prohibited by Article 30 of the EEC Treaty.[64]

Article 30 of the Treaty precludes, inter alia, national price controls which fix price components differently for domestic products and for imported products, to the detriment of the latter, impede increases to the price of the imported product corresponding to the additional costs and charges of importation, or fix the prices of products solely on the basis of the cost price or the quality of domestic products at such level to create an impediment to importation.[65] According to the Court, such a hindrance occurs when imported products cannot be sold at a reasonable profit on the market of the State of importation.

The Use of Average Prices

Two Member States have introduced a system of average prices (Italy from 1994 and the Netherlands from 1996) and another three (Greece, Portugal and Ireland) 'look over their shoulders' at prices in other European countries.

In Italy, under the new system introduced in 1994, the prices are the average of those in Germany, Spain, France and the United Kingdom expressed in lire using the purchasing power parities for each country, which are considerably lower than the exchange rates. Companies complained that if they imported products, they would do so at a loss as they would have to pay at exchange rates and not purchasing power parities. The Commission sent a letter to the Italian government on 1 June 1995 pointing out that, under European Court case law, this could be interpreted as a quantitative restriction on imports. This allegation, however, is difficult to prove especially for big multinational companies, which have concentrated their production plants in a few countries and thus have achieved economies of scale in the production function.

At a later stage, the Commission stated that it has no objection in principle to the adaptation of Italian medicine prices to the average European price. The Commission suggested that it is for the Italian authorities to decide how they wish to calculate the average price of medicines, in compliance with the provisions of the 'Transparency Directive' and, as regards medicinal products imported from other Member States, Article 30 of the EC Treaty.

The Commission finally decided not to raise any concerns against the Italian system because it did not discriminate against particular products.[66] In addition, in a response to a parliamentary question on the impact of the average price system in the Netherlands on the long-term viability of the innovative pharmaceutical research in Europe, Commissioner Bangemann pointed out that the average price of medicinal products is much higher in the Netherlands than in the other Member States. He suggested that it is speculative to predict that changes in the prices charged in the Netherlands will inevitably lead to job losses and cuts in research and development. He therefore implied that prices in the Netherlands may be excessive. [67]

Excessive Prices

The issue of excessive prices in the pharmaceutical sector was raised by the Danish presidency of the European Council in 1993. The Danish government asked Health Ministers to examine ways of keeping down prices of new pharmaceutical products. The Danish government prepared a note warning[68] that the growth of pharmaceutical expenditure could threaten the development of health policy and the basic choices which all Member States have to make within the health sector. It also underlined that many Member States' expenditure on reimbursement for pharmaceuticals is continuing to rise far more than other health expenditure. Several effective products have been replaced by new products which do not provide major improvements but whose prices are higher than those of the old products. The Danish government also emphasized that many new innovative products are priced extremely highly and that the industry enjoys a quasi-monopoly situation reinforced by the Supplementary Protection Certificate which provides effective patent protection periods. The Danish government has called for discussions at Community level to ensure that Member States are not forced to accept unusually high prices for highly innovative products.

The response of the Commission was the establishment of a working party whose mandate was to clarify what is an excessive price. The working party failed to reach a definition but carried out a study which indicated that whatever system of control has been implemented at national level, the pharmaceutical product concerned has been placed on the market in the Member States at similar prices. The Commission pointed out that Member States introduced measures concerned with the level of reimbursement in order to contain expenditure, and that this action confirms the Commission's own conclusions that action on reimbursement is more effective and has less of a distorting effect on the market than action on prices. The Commission did not comment explicitly on the problem of excessive pricing and its study rather indicates that similar prices in the Member States may reflect the regulator's inability to intervene and set a fair price.[69]

Multinational companies that practice discriminatory pricing to different national markets are susceptible to the charge of excessive pricing. According to the Court of Justice overpricing is defined as 'charging a price which is excessive because it has no reasonable relation to the economic value of the product supplied'. The Court has also said that the onus of proof of overpricing rests with the Commission or other persons alleging it.

This requires a comparison of the price with the full production costs. However, it is not easy to determine production costs, in particular in multi-product companies such as pharmaceutical companies where fixed costs such as Research and Development, capital investment and administrative and promotion costs are allocated between several products. There are also additional problems concerning transfer prices from the mother and the subsidiary company. Since these data are difficult to obtain, evidence on excessive pricing may be produced by comparing ex-factory prices in different countries for the same products. However, this can only be done in countries where prices are not regulated.

But how is a fair price to be defined? What is an excessive price or profit? Article 86(a) of the EEC Treaty defines an abuse due to a dominant position in the market as 'directly or indirectly imposing unfair purchase or selling prices or other unfair trading conditions'. As far as unfairly high prices are concerned, the authority to support the position that excessive prices are prohibited under Article 86 is found in a number of judgements of the European Court of Justice and in particular in the United Brands ('Chiquita' Bananas) Case,[70] where the Court adopted a test of unfairness based on the relationship between the price and the economic value of the goods provided by the dominant firm. According to the Court, the economic value of goods concerned should be determined, inter alia, by taking into account the relevant costs actually incurred by the dominant firm and by examining comparable prices for comparable goods. The application of these criteria to the pharmaceutical market is problematic and raises specific issues related to the complexity of analyzing industrial research and development costs.

A company has to incur the sunk cost of a high initial investment in order to develop a new product. In other sectors, companies seek sufficient assurance that the risks undertaken are covered or that there are convincing expectations of this happening. Companies and regulators cannot accurately project the profits of a specific product since it is not easy to predict competition as new treatments may be introduced and there is uncertainty about future market conditions.

There are also limits to a direct comparison between products and prices and the problem is more difficult when comparing real innovative products. How can a threshold be determined beyond which the price of a product charged in one or more countries ceases to have a reasonable relation to the economic value of the product? When can the level of profit margin which the company achieves on a product legally be described as an abuse? These problems have defied resolution in the formation of an industrial policy at European and often at national level. It is also important to examine what is a fair price for a specific product by taking into account the impact on the total pharmaceutical budget. The establishment of guidelines for determining 'fair' prices for individual products is not a guarantee for the total fairness of the system. Regulators should take into account the available global budget and the 'objective' or 'real' value of each product in the decision-making process. However, this may be impossible to be done since regulators cannot always predict the potential market size of a new product, its impact on other sectors of the health system and the direct and indirect costs or benefits associated with its use.

Conclusions

The creation of a harmonized market for pharmaceuticals has been a long-standing Community objective, although it has received renewed impetus from 1985 onwards. A series of actions has been taken by the Commission to promote harmonization in the pharmaceuticals sector and a significant volume of legislation has been produced. But there are still considerable differences between Member States in the pricing and reimbursement of medicines, with multinationals being obliged to adapt to the specific requirements imposed by each national authority. In addition the incentives for efficiency in the pharmaceutical market tend to be perverse and induce both providers and consumers to act without due regard to costs. The peculiarities of this market 'obstruct' the function of a free market mechanism.

Pharmaceutical pricing is not just a matter of the health budget. It determines future jobs and exports in an area where Europe once held the leading position and has the potential to continue to do so in the future. The question of what is 'fair value' in terms of economic efficiency or 'a fair rate of return' is still controversial in other fields of the economy. It is more controversial in the pharmaceutical sector where little is still known about the cost-effectiveness and outcomes of different therapeutic alternatives or single therapies. The essential problem facing the European Union is how to reconcile conflicting policy objectives. On the one hand, the European Commission is concerned to secure the safety of products, to restrain over-consumption and keep health care costs under control. But on the other hand, incentives are needed for the industry to make useful innovations some of which may save long term health care costs, and generally increase exports and thus employment and income in the Member States. However, further harmonization may lead to a reduction of the workforce in exchange for efficiency gains.

Pharmaceutical companies fear that harmonization would force prices down to the lowest levels in any EU Member State, hitting profits in the world's largest but fragmented market. On the other hand, governments have been concerned that prices might be harmonized upwards, compressing already limited health care budgets.

The introduction of an EC supervisory authority, other than the Committee on Pharmaceutical Pricing Transparency, with responsibility in the pricing and financing of pharmaceuticals may help to ensure that rules apply in the same way in all Member States, but the creation of such a body would entail extensive amendment of the pharmaceutical legislation and would require consensus both from Member States and the pharmaceutical industry. Considering the debate within the Commission on the Industrial Policy Communication this seems unlikely in the near future. A policy option for the future in Europe, may be the introduction of a profit control system at the European level. However, there are several problems which may lead to ineffective regulation: the degree of the regulator's uncertainty about the cost structure of manufacturing and market conditions. The companies which are subjected to a return on capital, may choose overcapitalisation in building, equipment, research and development, whenever the allowed rate of return exceeds the company's true cost of capital. Excessive additional expenses are also a possibility if they are reckoned as a proportion of the cost function. It is unclear whether the regulator can have a precise knowledge of the cost structure and the production process. The expansion of the company may not always be profitable on the basis of welfare considerations since it may be more of a waste than a true investment on research and development and on new technology. It also does not provide an incentive for the company to minimize costs.

Another problem accruing from the implementation of a profit control system at European level is the location of pharmaceutical industries and especially that of production, research and development facilities. For the time being the pharmaceutical market is very partitioned due to the differences and divergences of national rules. Furthermore, in contrast to the situation in Federal countries, multinational companies' profits are allocated in the EU Member States, not on a basis of a formula, but following established international practices. Transfer prices, then, still remain a powerful tool for MNCs, through which they can achieve a wide range of corporate objectives. The determination of accurate taxable profits may be easier at the European level since separate accounting systems to determine them can give companies the opportunity to shift profits from high-to-low tax areas. However, it is very difficult to invent a formula to allocate corporate taxes between Member States.[71]

The implementation of a pharmaceutical pricing scheme at European level analogous to British Pharmaceutical Profit Regulation Scheme could lead to a concentration of pharmaceutical manufacturing industries in more strategic areas (e.g. in France and Germany) which could serve better for trade with other European countries, reduce wholesaling expenditures and save from economies of scale in all levels of the pharmaceutical production function. Although this is important from the point of welfare savings and gains at European level, it is highly improbable that it would be accepted both by the Member States and the majority of the pharmaceutical industries which prefer to enjoy good relations with each government and negotiate separately with each of them. In addition, if adopted, companies would then have to report their results to a Central Regulatory Authority, which would certainly encounter opposition from the Pharmaceutical Industry.

Thus, if a centralized profit control system is difficult to be implemented, is a central control on prices an alternative? But even if there was central control on prices on what criteria would prices be based? In addition, even if a Single Market were politically acceptable, how would it operate? On these important issues even the industry failed to find a consensus.

Many of the regulatory measures introduced by countries create opportunities to discriminate in favour of national firms or firms contributing to national investment or employment. Moreover some of these opportunities are exploited. And when a decision is taken on professional grounds by a professional committee, as may be the case with the last three of the above, it will be very difficult for the Commission to prove that discrimination has taken place.

Whether governments were willing to embark on new discussions to harmonize the pharmaceutical market is a political decision and will reflect their different priorities in industrial and health policy. It is expected, however, that in the near future most of the governments will revert to their short term policies of limiting pharmaceutical expenditure rather than consider the long term advantages of developing a coherent industrial policy. There are several Member States which are not interested in pursuing further their industrial policy in the field of pharmaceuticals, since they see no prospect of benefiting directly from such a development. Member States have different interests and priorities and there is no sign of these being likely to change. Such diverse attitudes are reflected in the reactions of Member States to the draft Industrial Policy Communication document. Moreover, with the political emphasis on subsidiarity, the Commission may not achieve consensus to harmonize price and reimbursement regulations throughout the Community.

Notes

1   For a discussion of the peculiarities of the pharmaceutical industry see, Mossialos E., Kanavos P., Abel-Smith B., *Policy Options for Pharmaceutical Research and Development in the European Community*, European Parliament, Brussels, 1993.

2   It is, however, worth noting that the role of the European Union owned companies in these merges and acquisitions is small except for the Glaxo-Wellcome merge in the UK and the Hoechst (Germany) and Marion Merrell Dow (USA) merge.

3   Mossialos E., Kanavos P., Abel-Smith B., The Pharmaceutical Sector in the European Union: An Overview, in Mossialos E., Ranos C., Abel-Smith B., *Cost Containment, Pricing and Financing of Pharmaceuticals in the European Community: The Policy-Makers' View*, LSE Health and Pharmetrica S.A., Athens, 1994, pp. 17-87.

4   Mossialos et al., 1994. *op cit.*

5   Over the past twenty years there has been a swing in the discovery of new chemical entities from Europe to Japan. The proportion originating in the United States has remained constant at around 22 per cent, while Japan's share has increased from 13 per cent between 1970 and 1974 to 26 per cent between 1988 and 1992.

6   Mossialos et al., *op. cit.*

7   Abel-Smith B., Mossialos E., *Regulation in Question: A Study of Regulating Expenditure on Medicines*, LSE Health, London 1996.

8   In addition DGVI (Agriculture) has responsibility for veterinary medicines while DGXI (Environment) deals with environmental protection issues, such as waste management and DG XXIV (Consumer Policy Service) with consumer protection. DGIV (Competition) has also a division dealing with competition issues related to pharmaceuticals, including policies related to merges and acquisitions, parallel imports and excessive prices.

9   Commission of the European Communities, 1994, 'Communication to the Council and the European Parliament on the Outlines of an Industrial Policy for the Pharmaceutical Sector in the European Community'. COM(93) 718, Brussels.

10   Directive 92/26, 1992, Official Journal of the European Communities, Vol. 113, 1992, p.5.

11   Directive 92/28, 1992, Official Journal of the European Communities, Vol. 113, 1992, p.13.

12   Directive 89/341 of May 1989, Official Journal of the European Communities, No. 142, p. 11.

13   Directive 92/27, 1992, Official Journal of the European Communities, Vol. 113, 1992, p. 8.

14   Directive 92/25, 1992, Official Journal of the European Communities, Vol. 113, 1992, p.1.

15   Article 3 (b).

16   VAT rates for pharmaceutical products differ extensively among Member States. There is no VAT rate in Sweden and the United Kingdom, whereas the rate is 20 per cent of the retail price in Denmark and 15 per cent in Finland.

17   Meade, J., The EMU and the Control of Inflation, *Oxford Review of Economic Papers*, Vol.6, No. 4, pp. 100-7, 1990.

18   Directive 92/26/EEC, Official Journal of the European Communities, Vol 113, p. 5.

19   Mossialos et al., *op. cit.*

20   Council Decision 75/320/EEC of 20 May 1975 setting up a Pharmaceutical Committee, Official Journal of the European Communities, Vol. 147, 9 June 1975.

21   Directive 75/319, 1975 Official Journal of the European Communities Vol. 147, p. 75.

22   Between January 1991 and December 1992, 119 applications were submitted to the CPMP corresponding to an equivalent of 752 national applications. It should also be noted that more than 90 per cent of the applications were submitted by companies manufacturing generic products. Generic manufacturers will not have the opportunity to use the EMEA system in the future, since only 'innovative' products will be processed through this procedure.

23   Commission of the European Communities, *Report on the Operation of the Committee for Proprietary Medicinal Products in 1991 and 1992*, Brussels, May 12, 1993.

24   Anonymous, (1991), 'European drug regulation - anti-protectionism or consumer protection?', *The Lancet*, Vol. 337, pp. 1571-72, June 29 1991.

25   See for a discussion of the changes of the Commission's approach: Albedo, (1995), Brussels - Still at the Centre?, *Pharmaceutical Technology Europe*, pp. 10-13, March 1995.

26   National Consumer Council, 1994, *Secrecy and Medicines in Europe*, National Consumer Council, London.

27   Regulation 2309/93, 1993, Official Journal of the European Communities, Vol. 214, p.1.

28   Joint answer to Written Questions No 2367/92, 2368/92, 2370/92 given by Mr Bangemann on behalf of the Commission, 26 November 1992.

29   See for a discussion of the industry's views: Anonymous, Call for EU definition of 'innovation', *SCRIP*, No 2106, p.4, 1996.

30   The Agency is expected to deal with up to 70 applications a year for market authorization in the first five years of its operation.

31   Regulation 1768/92, 1992, Official Journal of the European Communities, Vol. 182, p. 1.

32   For example, Italy, Belgium selected 1 January 1982 as the 'start-up' date from which products introduced on the market, whereas France, Ireland, Denmark, Luxembourg, The Netherlands and the United Kingdom selected 1 January 1985 and Denmark and Germany 1 January 1988.

33   Commission of the European Communities, Proposal for a Council Regulation (EEC) concerning the creation of a supplementary protection certficate for medicinal products, COM (90) 101 - final - SYN 255, Luxembourg, 1990.

34   See Article 5.

35   Joint answer to Written Questions No 2367/92, 2368/92, 2370/92 given by Commissioner Bangemann on behalf of the Commission, 26 November 1992.

36   See 35 U.S.C. § 271(e) (1).

37   David Pryor, Chairman, United States Senate, Special Committee on Ageing, Letter to Mickey Kantor, United States Trade Representative, March 9, 1993.

38   M. Matz, D. Weeda, Memorandum to Ira Shapiro, Esq., General Counsel, Office of the U.S. Trade Representative, on *European Community Supplementary Protection Certificate and the Resultant Delay on the Introduction of U.S. Generic Pharmaceuticals*, Olsson, Frank, and Weeda, P.C., Attorneys at law, Washington D.C., April 1 1994.

39   Directive 89/105, 1989, Official Journal of the European Communities, Vol.40, p. 8.

40   The United Kingdom, The Netherlands, Greece, France, Denmark and Spain.

41 Commission of the European Communities, *Recommendation of the Commission relating to the measures taken by Member States on the prices and the Reimbursement of medicinal products*, Brussels, December 1992.

42 The Netherlands, France, Germany and the United Kingdom.

43 See the Communication to the Commission from Mr Bangemann, Vice President of the Commission, on the Recommendation of the Commission relating to the measures taken by the Member States on the prices and the reimbursement of medicinal products, Brussels, December 1992.

44 Leon Brittan, *'Making a Reality of the Single market: Pharmaceutical Pricing and the EEC'*, Paper presented at an Institute of Economic Affairs Conference on Pharmaceutical Policies in Europe, December 1 1992, Brussels.

45 Abrahams P., Brussels shelves measures to harmonise drug prices, *Financial Times*, 2 December 1992, p.22.

46 Commission of the European Communities, 1994, op. cit.

47 Thompson R., 1994, *The Single Market for Pharmaceuticals*, Butterworths, London.

48 Deboyser, P., 'An Industrial Policy for the Pharmaceutical Industry in Europe: Current Issues', in Mattison N., Mossialos E., *Health Care Reforms and the Role of the Pharmaceutical Industry*, Pharmaceutical Partners for Better Healthcare, Basel, 1995.

49 Anonymous, Bad Medicine in Europe, *The Wall Street Journal Europe*, p. 8, 22 April 1994.

50 See judgement of 7 August 1984 in Case 238/82.

51 Audit Commission, *A Prescription for Improvement: Towards More Rational Prescribing in General Practice*, London, HMSO, 1994.

52 See *Scrip*, No. 1997, 7 February 1995.

53 In 1992 the estimated penetration of parallel imports as a percentage in values of total sales was 3 per cent in Denmark, 2 per cent in Germany, 12 per cent in the Netherlands and 9-10 per cent in the United Kingdom. see also for a discussion of impediments to parallel trade: Remit consultants, *Impediments to Parallel Trade in pharmaceuticals within the European Community: Final Report*, Office for Official Publications of the European Communities, Luxembourg, 1992.

54 Consumers in the European Community Group, 1993, *Pharmaceuticals in the Single Market*, CECG 93/5, London.

55 See Case 104/75 De Peijper [1976] ECR 613 and the Commission's interpretative Communication of 6 May 1982 on the parallel imports of proprietary medicinal products whose marketing has already been

authorized, Official Journal of the European Communities, Vol. 115, 6 May 1982.

56   See Commission of the European Communities, COM(94) 55 final, *The Community Internal Market: 1993 Report*, Brussels 14 March 1994.

57   See Proposal dated June 2 1980 for a Directive amending Directives 65/65/EEC and 75/319/EEC, Official Journal of the European Communities, Vol. 143, 12 June 1980.

58   The Parliament considered the Commission's proposal superfluous and not justified. The Parliament stated that the Court of Justice has clearly declared that laws and regulations standing in the way of parallel imports to be contrary to the EEC Treaty. The Parliament also stated that the general conditions governing the free circulation of medicines should be addressed, including the mutual recognition of marketing authorizations and the dismantling of economic barriers to trade. See for a discussion, Deleau M., *Report on the proposal from the Commission of the European Communities to the Council for a directive amending Directives 65/65EEC and 75/319/EEC on the approximation of provisions laid down by law, regulation or administrative action relating to proprietary medicinal products*, Doc. 1-303/81, European Parliament.

59   See Communication from the Commission to the Council, COM(81) 803 final on Parallel Imports of Proprietary Medicinal Products for which Marketing Authorizations have already been Granted, Brussels, 17th December 1981.

60   Case C-249/88 Commission v. Belgium, Judgement of March 19, 1991.

61   See Report for the Hearing in Case C-249/88, p. 24.

62   Case 82/77 Van Tiggele (1978), E.C.R. 25; (1978) 2 C.M.L.R. 528. and Case C-287/89 Commission v. Belgium, Judgement of May 1991.

63   Case 65/75 Tasca (1976), E.C.R. 291; (1977) 2 C.M.L.R. 183.

64   See judgement in Case 141/87 *Commission* v *Italy* [1989] ECR 943.

65   See Judgement in Case 56/87 *Commission* v *Italy* [1988] ECR 2919 and judgement in Case 181/82 *Roussel Laboratoria* v *Netherlands* [1983] ECR 38849, paragraph 17.

66   See the parliamentary answer given by Commissioner Bangemann, Official Journal of the European Communities, 349/23, 9 December 1994.

67   Written Question E-2292/95 by Karla Peijs (PPE) to the Commission (31 July 1995) on Pharmaceuticals: Netherlands Pricing Proposal Official Journal of the European Communities, 311/46-47, 22 November 1995.

68   See Council Document 6451/1/93.

69   See Commissioner Bangemann's response to a written question E-2093/95 by Mihail Papayannakis (GUE/NGL) to the Commission (18 July 1995) on Prices of New Pharmaceutical Products, Official Journal of the European Communities, Vol. 311/33-34, 22 November 95.

70   United Brands Case, ECR, February 14, 1978, 1978 ECR 207, p. 299-303.

71   For a discussion of the problems of allocating the corporate tax base between Member States, see, Daly, M., Weiner, J., (1993), Corporate Tax Harmonization and Competition in Federal Countries: Some Lessons for the European Community, *National Tax Journal*, Vol.46, No.4, pp. 441-61.

SECTION C: THE EUROPEAN ECONOMY AND EUROPEAN SOCIETY:
Challenges for existing and new policies

15 The Common Agricultural Policy

JOHN MARSH

Introduction

The European Community is based on the economic logic of a 'common market'. This allows for competition to operate within the Community by the removal of barriers to trade and for firms within the Community to enjoy a common level of protection in relation to the rest of the world. The net economic effect will depend upon whether the overall barriers to trade which remain are greater or less than those which existed before the common market was established. If the net effect is a reduction in the degree of protection the Community as a whole will be enriched.[1]

For agriculture the founders of the Community chose a different route. Instead of dismantling barriers between member states by abolishing internal protection they sought, by the use of agricultural policy instruments, to provide a common level of protection which would favour farmers within the EC. This system is authorized in the Rome Treaty, Articles 38 to 47, which make provision for a 'Common Agricultural Policy', (CAP). This chapter attempts to outline the main characteristics of the CAP and to consider its role within the Community of the 1990s. It falls into six parts:-

(i)   A background - why there is a CAP
(ii) The CAP system as initially conceived
(iii) The development and current shape of the CAP
(iv) The impact of the CAP on member states
(v)   The impact of the CAP on the rest of the world
(vi) Issues for the CAP in the 1990s.

The story which has to be told is one of continued, if often reluctant, adjustment as markets outflank the positions adopted by policy makers. That process of adjustment shows no signs of coming to an end.

The Background - Why there is a CAP

Every member of the Community had an agricultural policy before entry. It was judged that agriculture could not safely be left to the unfettered operation of market forces. The emphasis given to the various reasons for this judgement differed among member countries. Although there was no uniform degree or method of intervention there was a consensus that something more than the simple removal of barriers to trade in agricultural goods was needed. There were at least six reasons for this judgement:-

(i)   In the 1940s, as a result of the Second World War, many countries in Europe had experienced food shortages. Rationing systems had been applied and continued, at least in some countries, into the 1950s. A secure supply of food was recognized as a key responsibility of government and it was believed that this could best be ensured by a high level of domestic self-sufficiency. Thus agricultural policies offered higher inducements to farmers than markets alone would have provided. Sometimes this was in the form of higher prices. Sometimes it was provided by subsidies on products. In general governments sought to reduce the market risks facing producers and so encourage a higher level of investment in food production.

(ii)   Agricultural markets tend to be unstable. Demand changes relatively little from year to year but supply can alter significantly because of the effects of weather, pests and disease on production. In addition, there is generally a substantial lag between the decision to produce and the actual availability of a product. Once the production process is started the farmer faces a stark choice between abandoning the crop or the growing animal or continuing and selling the product for whatever price it will fetch. Thus, in the short run, despite low prices the quantity reaching the market may not change significantly. These characteristic 'price inelasticities of supply and demand' account for the fact that in an uncontrolled market prices may move violently up or down in a short period.[2] Such movements are damaging both to producers and consumers and they may also lead to an inappropriate level of investment and so reduce the real income of the economy as a whole. Actions to stabilize markets have thus been a common reason for agricultural policy.

(iii)   Agriculture as a long established industry offers a variety of opportunities for greater economic efficiency. Some of these arise because of technical advances which reduce costs - for example, methods which increase the yields of crops or animals. Some occur because, as economies grow, relative factor prices change. For example as real incomes rise economic efficiency may require the substitution of capital for labour. Governments have sought to exploit such opportunities. They have funded research, development and extension services. They have provided subsidies for the introduction of new methods and in some cases reduced the cost of capital to the sector. Special tax regimes, especially in relation to inheritance taxes, have been used to foster investment in farming and forestry.

(iv)   Trade in food has been an important objective for some governments. Those countries where more is produced than consumed have sought to expand exports as a means of generating foreign exchange. Net importers have looked to 'import substitution' as a device which improves their balance of payments position. Economic theory does not necessarily support such an approach.[3] It emphasizes rather the benefits to be derived from comparative advantage. However, this is a more difficult notion to grasp and politicians and many industry leaders continue to seek a larger share of agricultural and food markets as a means of improving their balance of payments[4].

(v)   Agriculture is a fragmented industry made up of small firms with virtually no ability to influence the terms on which they sell or buy. The firms who supply farm inputs and those who purchase farm outputs tend to be much larger. In recent years concentration in these sectors has greatly increased so that major retailers, processors and suppliers of farm inputs exercise considerable market power. The asymmetry of competitive strength has been seen as a reason for government intervention. Such concerns have justified support for co-operatives, for marketing boards and for state marketing agencies.[5]

(vi)   Agriculture world wide is the largest user of labour. Even within developed countries such as those of the Community it continues to be a significant employer. Its significance is greatest in rural areas where it is a primary source of employment, not only on the farm but also in agriculture's support industries. The share of agriculture in total employment has declined everywhere and in some EC countries is now relatively small but its political and cultural influence remains considerable.[6] As a result governments have sought to shield farmers from the sharp pressures of market forces. In the absence of such intervention it is likely that the numbers of people engaged in agriculture in the EC would have fallen very much more rapidly than has been the case.[7]

Despite agreement that some form of intervention in agriculture was needed, the policies of the member countries varied greatly as did the prices which prevailed within their markets. Simply opening up frontiers would have forced those governments which provided the greatest level of support to underwrite agriculture throughout the Community or to allow internal prices to fall to whatever level competition dictated. Such a prospect was not acceptable. Equally, however, it was unacceptable to leave agriculture outside the common market. It was too large a part of the EC economy. In 1956 it accounted for some 20 per cent of the workforce and some 10 per cent of gross domestic product. For member countries with low prices and the capacity to expand the inclusion of agriculture was an essential quid pro quo for opening their markets to imported industrial goods. The solution was to introduce a common policy.

The Initial Concept of the CAP System

The legal basis of the CAP is set out in Articles 38 to 47 of the Treaty of Rome. These include a statement of objectives for the CAP, Article 39.

The common agricultural policy shall have as its objectives:

(a)   to increase agricultural productivity by developing technical progress and by ensuring the rational development of agricultural production and the optimum utilization of the factors of production, particularly labour;

(b)   to ensure thereby a fair standard of living for the agricultural population, particularly by the increasing of the individual earnings of persons engaged in agriculture;

(c)   to stabilize markets,

(d)   to guarantee regular supplies; and

(e)   to ensure reasonable prices in supplies to consumers.

In working out the common agricultural policy and the special methods which it may involve, due account shall be taken of:

(a)   the particular character of agricultural activities, arising from the social structure of agriculture and from structural and natural disparities between the various agricultural regions;

(b)   the need to make the appropriate adjustments gradually; and

(c)   the fact that in Member States agriculture constitutes a sector which is closely linked with the economy as a whole.

Market management has dominated the debate about agricultural policy in the EC largely because it is by far the most expensive component of the policy. From the outset, however, the CAP system attempted to combine the manipulation of market prices with a number of structural objectives. Table 1 shows the distribution of budgetary expenditure between guarantee expenditure, in support of market prices, and guidance expenditure relating to structural change.

Table 1. EAGGF Guarantee and Guidance Expenditure (Mio ECU)

Year	EAGGF Guarantee Expenditure	EAGGF Guidance Expenditure	Total
1973 [EUR 10]	3,923.3	187.6	4,110.9
1981 [EUR 10]	11,141.2	725.4	11,866.6
1985 [EUR 10]	19,843.4	898.3	20,741.7
1986 [EUR 12]	22,137.4	971.7	23,109.1
1990 [EUR 12]	26,453.5	1,968.0	28,421.5
1994* [EUR 12]	36,465.0	2,864.0	39,329.0

*Preliminary draft budget
Source: The Agricultural Situation in the Community, 1986, 1991, 1993

Price support for farmers depended upon the limitation supplies of each major product, whether from domestic or foreign suppliers. For each major product, a separate regime was devised. The details of each product regime are of great importance to producers and traders and do vary, but the principles of the system are common.[8] Diagram 1 illustrates this approach, by restricting supplies reaching the market to q1 price is raised to p1.

Imports were controlled by a system of variable import levies. In simple terms the Council of Ministers set a level of price which they wished to see for internal markets. They then established a 'threshold price' which applied to goods entering the EC from outside. If the price in world markets was below the threshold price a levy which corresponded to the difference between the lowest world price offer and the threshold price was charged on all imports. In effect price competition by importers became impossible. For some products, in addition to the variable import levy there was also an import duty, expressing in Community jargon, the 'community preference' to be enjoyed by internal suppliers.

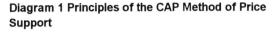

Diagram 1 Principles of the CAP Method of Price Support

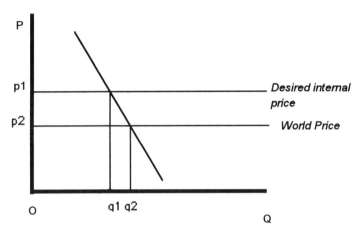

The collapse of market prices as a result of excessive domestic production was prevented by a system of withdrawing supplies from the market. For major products an 'intervention price' was set, somewhat below the 'target' or 'guide' price level the Council hoped would operate within the market. Farmers could offer goods, which met the appropriate standards, to official intervention agencies which were required to buy them at this floor price. Having acquired stock at intervention the agencies could sell them either within the EC, provided of course prices were not below the intervention level, or abroad. In that case exporters who could only secure the lower 'world' price for the goods they sold to other countries, were provided with subsidies in the form of 'export refunds' which enabled them to complete the deal. In addition to disposals abroad the Community could provide subsidies on sales of intervention stock to internal uses which did not compete with the commercial market within the EC. Thus wheat or milk powder might be used for animal feed, butter or meat provided on concessional terms to pensioners or used to feed school children, prisoners or the armed services.

Diagram 2 Some implications of CAP support systems

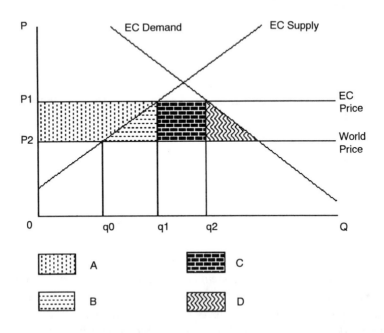

Diagram 2 sets out in a schematic form some of the consequences of applying the CAP support system in situations in which the EC remains a net importer of the product concerned. The shaded areas A and B represent additional revenue to the agricultural sector. However, the expansion of production from q0 to q1 requires additional resources. The shaded area B indicates the extent to which these resources are drawn from more productive uses elsewhere in the economy in order to allow expansion to take place. On the remaining imports, 0q2-0q1, revenue, represented by the shaded area C accrues to the government. So far as consumers are concerned, they lose, both because of higher prices and because of a reduction in consumption. The sum of the shaded areas A,B,C and D represent these losses in the Diagram. Of this, A is captured by farmers, C by the government and B and D, the so-called 'dead-weight losses', represent a reduction in national welfare.

Diagram 3 re-draws this diagram on the assumption, not unrealistic for the EC, that internal prices are fixed at levels which generate a higher level of production than can be absorbed within the EC itself.

Diagram 3 Some implications of CAP System with Net Exports

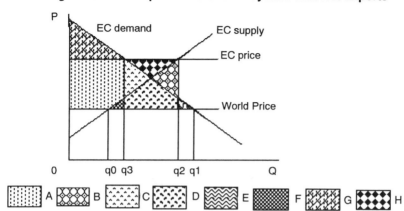

Again consumers face considerable losses, the shaded areas A,C,D,E,F and G all represent reductions in consumer welfare. Producer gains are considerable, A,B,C,D, F and H constitute additional revenue, of which F,D and B are consumed in additional costs. The most dramatic change, however, is in the position of the government, now the budget has to fund the difference between the amount paid to farmers and its value in other uses, at a minimum, the world price, on that quantity which is now produced within the EC but not consumed there. This includes the areas, B,C,D and H. From being a net contributor to the funds of the EC the product has become a net cost.

Diagram 4 provides an alternative visual illustration of the logic of the system. Given that the internal market is stabilized at a level higher than that of the prevailing prices in international markets, the effective instruments are the variable import levies and export refunds.

At the outset structural policy was limited to additional support for some national policies, in particular assistance relating to frontier areas. By the late 1960s a more positive approach to structural development emerged. Through a variety of schemes, stimulus was given to farm improvement, to the retraining of farm workers and to assist those who wished to retire. However, the development of structural policy owes much to the pressures which arose in relation to the CAP's market policies, and these are more conveniently described in the next section of this chapter.

Diagram 4 The Variable Levy System of the CAP

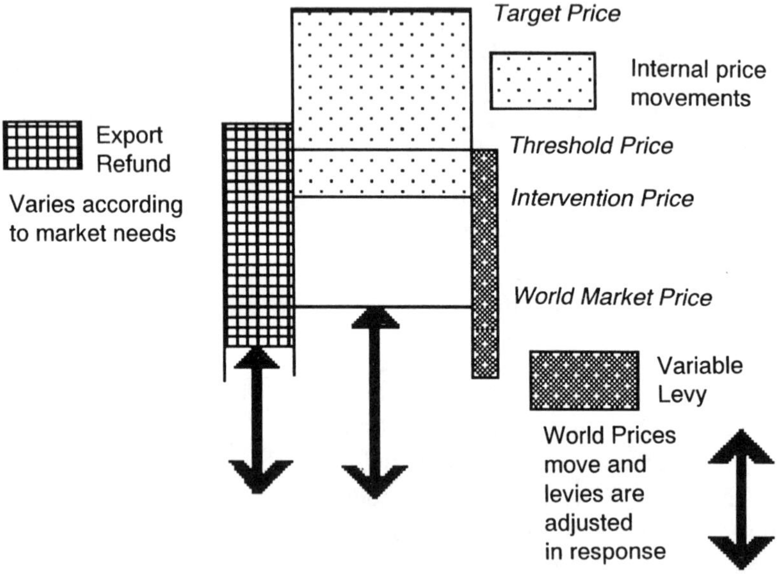

The Development of the CAP

The first product regimes were instituted in 1962 for Cereals and Milk. By 1968 it was already becoming clear that some fundamental revision of the policy was needed. The Commissioner for Agriculture set out radical proposals for a new structural policy which would encourage the development of modern, enlarged competitive businesses[9]. His proposals stemmed from a recognition of some basic flaws in the CAP as it then existed. These same problems have continued to trouble the Community.

First, the system of price support encourages increased production. Farmers only benefit if they have products to sell. New technology, since the 1960s, has permitted a great increase in productivity. Yields have risen, quality has improved and wastage, as a result of difficulties at harvest and in storage, has been reduced. As a result the EC has become increasingly self-sufficient. The consequence of this has been a persistent tendency for the budget cost to rise. Table 2 shows how this developed up to 1990 for major product sectors and in total. Price support has accounted for a very large share of total Community expenditure. Inevitably this has given rise to continuous criticism especially from consumers and from those countries which are net contributors to the EC budget.

Second, the system of price support does not meet the social needs of the EC. Higher prices benefit most those who have most to sell. The poorest farmers generally have very little to sell and so derive correspondingly small benefits. Indeed, because one of the means by which they might expand is to buy in feed to rear animals, the higher price of cereals may make it even more difficult for them to escape from poverty. Higher prices do not offer a long term solution to income problems even for larger farmers. They tend to be capitalized in the form of higher land prices. As a result new farmers, or existing farmers who wish to expand, face higher costs. Individual income is dependent upon how many people choose to remain in farming or to join the industry. Systems of support which are tied to continued agricultural production tend to retain people in the sector. As a result they have little success in their social objectives and may even be regarded as counter-productive.

Third, the system of price support requires payments to farmers in their own national currencies. Official EC prices are fixed in terms of the Community 'currency', originally a 'unit of account',(ua), but now the 'European Currency Unit', (ECU). This necessitates the use of exchange rates to determine the value of intervention and other official currencies in each of the national currencies involved. Problems arise when a national currency changes its value. If, as logic would suggest, official EC prices were adjusted accordingly at the same time, those countries which devalue their currencies, would have to put up prices to their farmers and consumers. Equally countries whose currency rose in value would need to reduce internal agricultural prices to their farmers and consumers. Neither adjustment was welcomed. Higher food prices were politically embarrassing and believed to add to inflationary pressures. Lower farm prices caused an outcry from agricultural lobby groups whilst receiving little support from consumers. However, if no price changes took place, trade between countries would be affected. Agricultural products produced in countries which reduced the value of their currency would seek markets, at intervention if necessary, in countries where the same nominal price in the local currency would now exchange for more units of the exporters currency. Countries where currency values appreciated would face the prospect of a deluge of imported agricultural products seeking intervention rather than be sold in markets closer to the point of production. Essentially such developments would force a single market price on the EC. However, given the political unacceptability of such an outcome, the Community invented a system of Monetary Compensatory Amounts, (MCAs). These placed a tax, broadly equivalent to the change in monetary values, on products moving from depreciating countries to the rest of the EC, and provided a corresponding subsidy on goods flowing in the reverse direction. In effect this cancelled out the effects of the changes in parities.

Table 2.   EC Budget Cost for Various Agricultural Products   (Mio ECU)

Product	1975	1980	1990
Cereals	620.8	1,669.0	3,856.0
Rice	4.2	58.7	94.2
Sugar	309.2	575.2	1,391.1
Oils & Fats (inc. olive oil)	231.4	687.3	4,646.6
Fruit & Vegetables	90.3	687.3	1,253.0
Wine	139.1	299.5	745.2
Tobacco	228.5	309.3	1,232.1
Milk Products	1,149.8	4,752.0	4,971.7
Beef & Veal	980.0	1,363.3	2,833.2
Sheepmeat & Goatmeat	-	53.5	1,452.3
Pigmeat	53.8	115.6	246.9
Eggs & Poultry Meat	8.4	85.5	178.5
Total	**3,815.5**	**10,656.2**	**22,900.8**

Source: The Agricultural Situation in the Community, 1976, 1981 and 1991

It also meant that in real terms, i.e the quantity of other goods a given volume of agricultural goods would buy, agricultural prices varied greatly between member countries.

Fourth, the expansion of EC production damaged the interests of third country exporters. As production increased it replaced goods from the rest of the world with domestic production and then, with the aid of export subsidies, undercut these exporters in third country markets. The Community was not the only offender against the rules of 'free trade'. Almost every developed country had a policy which protected its own farmers but the EC was the largest world importer and, from the early 1980s, its second largest exporter The level of protection it offered farmers was much higher than in most non-European countries. Disputes developed between the EC and in particular the US. Conflicts about trade in chicken, in maize and in restrictions placed on imports of beef from countries which permitted the use of growth promoting hormones caused considerable acrimony. As a whole the EC economy is very trade dependent. Agriculture is a declining proportion of total economic activity, from 4.5 per cent in 1972 to 2.8 per cent of GDP in 1993. The broader interests of the EC were in a smoothly working trade system and the development and improvement of the General Agreement on Tariffs and Trade, GATT. By the late 1980s it was becoming clear that without major concessions in relation to agricultural policy it was improbable that the Uruguay Round of trade negotiations, which began in the mid-eighties, could end successfully.

Fifth, when the Treaty of Rome was signed public opinion was sympathetic to farmers. Not only were they valued as food producers but their activities were thought to be essential to protect the rural way of life, the countryside and the culture associated with it. Increasingly, during the 1960s and 1970s this view was questioned by a variety of 'Green' movements. It was noted that modern farming methods destroyed the habitats essential for the survival of many wild species of plant and animal. The use of farm chemicals could give rise to pollution of both surface and ground water, whilst the misuse of pesticides and herbicides damaged not only wild life but might lead to unwanted and potentially harmful residues in the food supply. Rural communities, also, were changing. Agriculture was now a minority activity even in most country areas. Residents who moved from urban to rural centres were unwilling to put up with the noise, smells and transformation of the landscape which derived from some forms of modern farming. Rural communities were no longer farming communities and understanding and sympathy for farmers' problems were often missing. As a result politicians looked with an increasingly critical attitude at an agriculture whose expansion gave rise not only to budgetary, income, and trade problems but also to political embarrassment as articulate 'green' movements who captured much media attention.

Sixth, the admission of new members to the EC created fresh difficulties and amplified some of the existing problems. In 1973 Denmark, Ireland and the UK joined the Community. Both Denmark and Ireland were substantial exporters of agricultural products and benefited from access to protected markets in the EC. The UK was a substantial net food importer. Whilst the CAP would increase returns to British farming and encourage agricultural expansion, it substantially increased the real cost of food and transferred UK income to the rest of the Community. The policy seriously damaged some traditional suppliers, many of whom were long-standing allies or Commonwealth members. Some adjustments were made, for example in relation to the import of sugar from some developing Commonwealth countries, and the policy was phased in over a period of years. However, the emergence of substantial surpluses and the remorseless growth in the budget cost of the CAP have continued to sour relations between Britain and the rest of the Community.

In the 1980s three more countries joined the EC, Greece, Spain and Portugal. Again the CAP caused problems. The policy had tended to give greatest protection to the products typical of North West European agriculture, cereals, milk and sugar. Its support for fruit and vegetables and for products such as tobacco, products more typical of the Mediterranean region, was much more limited. The countries concerned had many small farms and a relatively high proportion of the workforce still engaged in farming. Without adjustment the CAP would result in a situation in which these countries found themselves net contributors to the support of farmers in relatively rich countries to the North.

In his 1968 Memorandum on the Reform of Agriculture within the European Economic Community, Dr Mansholt, then Commissioner for Agriculture, argued that the CAP could not rely on price policy alone but needed to complement it with an active 'structural policy'. He pointed out that prices could not be raised to meet the social aspirations of farmers because the result would be surplus production on a scale which could outstrip budgetary resources. Equally, without some alternative system of support, prices could not be cut because the damage to millions of farmers who had few other employment opportunities was politically unacceptable. Since then a series of papers from the Commission and outside commentators have addressed the 'reform of the CAP'. The more important of these are listed at the end of this chapter.[10] The process of reform is on-going but its main features are:

(i) Greater emphasis on structural policy:

In 1972 three directives relating to agricultural structural policy were adopted in a much attenuated form.[11] These followed the logic of the Mansholt Plan, seeking to help farmers to modernize, to retire or to move out of farming. In addition to these directives special arrangements were proposed to encourage farmers to move out of dairy farming.

(ii) Improvements in marketing:

Aids to farmers seeking to set up co-operative marketing organizations (1978).[12]

(iii) Assistance to specific regions:

Aids to 'less favoured areas' (75/268)[13] were introduced to compensate especially farmers in the Hills and Mountains of the Community where physical conditions made it difficult for farmers to compete.

Special assistance for farmers in the Mediterranean region. This included special investment programmes for irrigation, forestry, the development of rural infrastructure and a programme for the development of rural information services. These arrangements, introduced in 1977, were intended to help existing farmers within the EC to cope with the further enlargement of the Community to include Greece, Spain and Portugal.

Integrated development programmes for a number of regions where agriculture was a major part of the economy but incomes were low, infra-structure poor and alternative employment scarce. These allowed for assistance in non-farming as well as farming developments which would strengthen the rural economy.

These initiatives, although often justified in their own right, did little to arrest the growing crisis of overproduction within the Community. As a result the more recent development of the EC has been concerned primarily with the introduction of a series of supply control measures for major product areas. Confronted by a choice between allowing prices to fall to a point at which competition would have brought supply into line with demand or seeking to keep prices up but choke off supply by administrative devices, the Council of Ministers have consistently opted for the second approach. The reasons for this are political. A competitive agriculture would require very many fewer people than are currently engaged in the sector, farms would be larger and a substantial shift would occur in the distribution of production within the EC. All these outcomes are in principle benefits to the operation of the EC economy but governments have given preference to sustaining a non-economic agriculture in order to assuage a variety of pressure groups. These include not only farmers but also conservationists, first stage agricultural processors and those who seek to sustain self-sufficiency not merely on a EC wide basis but within member countries themselves.

A decisive move in this direction occurred in 1984 with the introduction of a quota regime for milk. Earlier attempts to check the flow of milk by the introduction of co-responsibility levies had failed. The cost of the milk regime reached ECU 5.8 Billion. The Council of Ministers decided to allocate quotas, based on past production, and to charge a penal levy on any milk marketed beyond that quota. The effect was not only to check current milk deliveries but to create a new capital asset in the hands of existing producers. Newcomers or those who sought to expand would have to purchase quota and so faced additional costs. Details of the administration of the milk regime are complicated. Some EC governments had failed to introduce a quota scheme as late as 1992.[14] Elsewhere quotas had become tradable and their price indicated the very considerable degree to which the protected milk price over-rewarded farmers in relation to market demand.

The CAP Reforms of 1992 and the Implications of the Uruguay Round

A precondition for the Uruguay Round of negotiations within GATT which began in 1986 was that agriculture should be included. For the European Community this posed a sharp conflict of interest. The world market is critically important for many of its industries. The reduction of barriers to trade, whether in the form of tariffs or other restrictions, the extension of GATT principles to issues such as intellectual property and trade related capital investment, promised great benefits for these sectors of the EC economy upon which its growth largely depended. In contrast the CAP operated on a basis which conflicted with GATT principles. Market access was limited, export subsidies were openly provided, discriminatory trade practices applied to some exporters and substantial tariffs were imposed even where variable levies did not prevent price competition. In the past the Community had argued that the CAP was an internal policy and as such not subject to negotiation in international fora. However, it was quite clear that without some significant changes to the policy no trade deal was likely to be attainable.

The CAP was also under internal pressure. At a European Council meeting in 1988 in Luxembourg the heads of state or Government had agreed to limit the growth of agricultural budgetary expenditure to 74 per cent of real GDP growth plus 100 per cent of inflation. Given the tendency for supply to grow more rapidly than domestic demand, without some change in the policy expenses for export restitutions and intervention purchase might be expected to grow at a rate which would outstrip this provision. The orthodox response to such pressure would have been to lower the price. However, the incomes of many farmers remained relatively low and their political influence seemed undiminished. In 1991 the Commissioner for Agriculture, Mr Ray MacSharry, proposed a radical shift in the policy. This took account of both internal and external pressures on the policy. After a protracted debate this package of measures was accepted by the Council of Agricultural Ministers in May 1992. The reforms proposed, and outlined below, were to be phased in during a three year period from 1993 to 1996.

The centre piece of the new policy is a shift in the mechanisms for the support of arable crops, cereals and oilseeds. For these products prices are to be cut and compensation payments made to farmers on an area basis. All but the smaller farmers are required, as a condition for the receipt of compensation, to 'set aside' some proportion of their arable land. Compensation is based on the arable area in the base period, (31 December 1991), the difference of price before and after the change in policy and the average yield of the region in which the farm is situated. The use of the area to be 'set aside' by all farmers whose output at standard yields was in excess of 92 tonnes, was strictly controlled to ensure that it did not add to the volume of supported products reaching the market. Initially this was set at 15 per cent on the basis that the fields set aside would be rotated around the farm. The proportion to be set aside under this arrangement can be varied from year to year, for 1994/5 it has been cut to 12.5 per cent. In a later development farmers were allowed to set aside a rather larger area, (20 per cent in most EC countries but only 18 per cent in the UK) as permanently set aside.

Although the centre of the policy is a cut in cereal and oilseed prices, these changes had 'knock-on' effects for other parts of the Community's agriculture. As a result adjustments had to be made in a number of livestock regimes.

Beef competes in the market place with pig and poultry meat. The lower prices of cereals used in feeding stuffs meant that these products could now be produced more cheaply. As a result their prices were likely to fall and their share of the market to increase. In order to enable the beef sector to compete, support prices for the product were reduced by 15 per cent and a system of compensation paid through the Special Beef Premium and the Suckler Cow Premium. To qualify for this premium, stocking density ceilings, which are reduced from 3.5 LSU (Livestock Units) per ha in.1993 to 2 LSU in 1996, must not be exceeded. Additionally, the volume of beef which will be bought at the full intervention price is being reduced from 750,000 tonnes in 1993 to 350,000 tonnes in 1997.

Sheep are in a somewhat similar position to beef but the regime already allowed for ewe premia payments in order to maintain farmers receipts. In this case the 1992 package limited the claims a producer could make to the number actually made in 1992 and enforced ceilings of 1000 ewes in less favoured areas and 500 ewes elsewhere.

Milk production was already limited by quota but supplies still exceeded Community requirements so in 1992 it was decided to reduce quota by 4 per cent and prices by 2.3 per cent. Compensation for quota loss has been paid at 0.1 ECU/kg for the first 2 per cent and 0.05 ECU/kg for the remainder.

Although CAP reform was an internal issue for the Community its outcome was clearly relevant to the debate within the GATT. There an impasse appeared to have been reached over agriculture. When the parties met, for what had been intended to be the final session of the Uruguay in

1990, no settlement was in sight and the outcome of the entire round remained in doubt. Although GATT involved 117 countries in a multilateral negotiation, the role of the US and the EC was crucial to its outcome. Community and US negotiators met at Blair House in Washington. There they arrived at a set of agreed proposals which formed the basis of the final settlement which was not attained until the end of 1993[15].

Under this arrangement some important changes in relation to international trade in agricultural goods are to be phased in over a six year period. In order to improve market access non-tariff border measures are to be replaced by tariffs that produce substantially the same level of protection. These tariffs are to be reduced by an average of 36 per cent, and with a minimum for each product covered, over the six year period of adjustment. Current access is to be maintained and where this is less than 3 per cent of domestic consumption, tariff quotas at reduced rate are to be provided.

Domestic support is to be measured in terms of the Aggregate Measure of Support (AMS), and to be reduced over the six year period by 20 per cent. However, in assessing the AMS, payments labelled as 'green box' are to be excluded. These include support for research, disease control, infrastructure and food security.

Direct income payments to producers which are decoupled, for example as part of structural adjustment assistance or under an environmental programme can also be excluded. Still more, direct payments under production limiting programmes are not counted in the AMS. In essence this means that the compensation payments introduced in the CAP in 1992 do not have to be counted.

At the heart of the dispute between the EC and many other GATT members were the export subsidies which it provided in order to allow its farm products to be sold at prices much lower than prevailed within the Community. As part of the settlement it was agreed that such subsidies should be reduced by 36 per cent in value and 21 per cent in volume compared with a 1986-90 base period, again over a six year period. In principle the lower prices proposed for the CAP under the 1992 arrangements should make the value criterion readily attainable. More problematical is the 21 per cent cut in volume. Here the outcome depends on the trend in yields and the impact of the set aside programme.

Table 3. A Summary of the 1992 Changes in the CAP

Policy Instrument	Product	Change by 1995/96
Price Policy	cereals	-32.3 per cent
	oilseeds	-61.8 per cent
	milk	-2.3 per cent
	beef	-15 per cent
Co-responsibility levies	cereals	abolished (1992)
	milk	abolished (1993)
Production Quotas	sugar	unchanged
	milk	-4 per cent
Compensation	milk quota reduction	0.1 ECU/kg for first 2 per cent
		0.05 ECU/kg for remaining 2 per cent
	Area payments cereals	207 ECU/ha
	Area payments oilseeds	359 ECU/ha
	beef premia male	180 ECU/head on first 90 animals*
	beef premia suckler cows	120 ECU/head on first 90 animals*
	sheep premia	limited to 1992 reference flock and not to exceed 500 ewes in lowlands or 1000 ewes in LFAs
Set aside	cereals and oilseeds area	15 per cent

*limited by herd size and stocking rate

Taken together the introduction of milk quotas in 1984, the CAP reforms of 1992 and the GATT settlement amount to a fundamental change in the operation of the Common Agricultural Policy. The initial arrangements provided open ended support. Current support is tied to supply control. The original concept kept some high cost producers in business but did not prevent lower cost farmers expanding. The present arrangement means that if lower cost farmers wish to expand they have to acquire the right to do so by buying quota. In effect the producer costs are raised and their ability to compete diminished. The initial arrangements made no specific mention of environmental objectives while after, the new policies involve not only environmental limits in the form of stocking density controls but also a specific agri-environmental package designed to facilitate farming systems which are judged to be favourable to the natural environment. When the CAP was originally negotiated it was as an arrangement internal to the Community. Now it is on the table of international trade negotiations and must expect this to lead to further calls for concessions in the future.

In the final section of this chapter some of the implications of these changes for the future of the policy and of EU agriculture will be considered. Before doing so, however, it is helpful to look a little more carefully at the way in which the policy has affected member states and countries elsewhere in the world.

The Impact of the CAP on Member States

The Common Agricultural Policy has markedly uncommon impacts on member countries. The key to whether they gain or lose is their trade balance in the products the CAP protects. Diagrams 5 and 6 illustrate the situation.

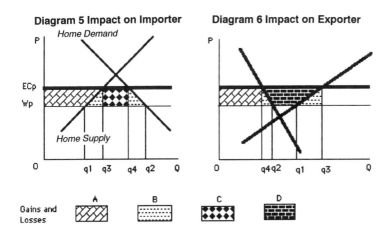

Diagram 5 examines the position of a country which before the CAP consumed 0q2 and produced 0q1 at home. The remainder it acquired at the world price, Wp, from third country suppliers. Having joined the EC it now has to apply the CAP ECp internally. Its producers gain the area shaded A. Its consumers lose all the shaded areas in the form of increased cost of food reduced consumption. The area C constitutes additional payments made to the rest of the Community, either in the form of payments for imports of EC origin or of levies on goods which are bought from third countries. The losses to the economy as a whole include not only C but also areas shaded B which arise because of a sub-optimal allocation of resources and as a reduction in consumers' welfare not captured by anyone else. Clearly the country as a whole loses from this policy, even though its farmers may derive some benefit.

Diagram 6 provides a similar formal analysis of the position of a country which initially produced 0q1, consumed 0q2 and exported the difference. Joining the EC and applying CAP prices means an increase in exports both because production increases, 0q1 to 0q3, and because of a reduction in consumption, 0q2 to 0q4. The whole of the shaded area, A,B,D is extra revenue to producers. Area A constitutes higher prices paid by domestic consumers, but B and D are made up of higher prices paid for exports within the Community or of export refunds paid by the EC on sales to third countries. The losses, due to resource misallocation and reduced consumer welfare are relatively small. Overall the country concerned is a substantial gainer from the CAP.

Such diagrams help to explain the asymmetry of the CAP and the reason why it is an instrument of substantial resource re-distribution within the Community. Transfers occur not according to need but in relation to the net trade situation of the countries concerned. As a result the system encourages member countries to re-inforce the impact of higher CAP prices by taking what action they can to stimulate extra production by their own farmers. In practice this logic provides a rational basis for continued national aids, which seem inconsistent with a truly common policy.

This table can give only a broad indication of the direction of resource flows brought about by the CAP's market policies. A more accurate calculation would need to decompose total figures into those affected by the CAP, to estimate the extent to which internal prices are higher than those which would have been available in a world without the CAP and to weight the impact on each nation according to its mix of trade in these products. Despite this, some important differences in the position of member countries merit attention.

Table 4. Net Trade Position of Member Countries in Agricultural and Food Products, 1992

Member Country	Exports Mio ECU			Imports Mio ECU			Exports minus Imports Mio ECU
	External	Intra	Total	External	Intra	Total	
BLEU*	1,642	9,520	11,162	2,825	9,519	12,344	S -1,182
Denmark	3,218	5,560	8,778	2,182	1,984	4,166	4,612
Germany	6,476	13,412	19,888	12,852	25,335	38,187	-18,299
Greece	817	1,744	2,561	735	2,169	2,904	-343
Spain	2,774	5,707	8,481	5,516	4,984	10,500	-2,019
France	8,172	21,651	29,823	7,031	15,331	22,362	7,461
Ireland	1,150	4,432	5,582	412	1,794	2,206	3,376
Italy	3,673	6,686	10,359	8,025	15,428	23,453	-13,094
Netherlands	5,599	21,953	27,552	7,269	10,337	17,606	10,347
Portugal	402	826	1,228	1,462	1,901	3,363	-2,135
UK	4,827	7,711	12,538	8,696	13,077	21,773	-9,235

* Belgium and Luxembourg
Source: The Agricultural Situation in the Community, 1993

Four countries, Denmark, France, Ireland and Netherlands are substantial net exporters. The largest is Netherlands, but for Denmark and Ireland agricultural exports are a major economic concern. They matter, too, for France, but their economic significance may be less than their political weight. Germany, Italy and the UK, are the main net food importers to the EC. They carry a large share of the total cost of the CAP but for Portugal and Greece, losses as a result of the trade flows implicit are proportionately damaging.

However, for Greece especially, transfers under the CAP's structural policies alleviate the situation. Table 4 shows these receipts for 1989 to 1992. Despite this, there is a prima-facie case for arguing that the Greek economy, if not Greek farmers, would benefit if the CAP were replaced by a less protective policy for agriculture.

Table 5. Receipts by Member States under the Guidance Policy of the CAP

Member state	1989 Mio ECU	1990 Mio ECU	1992 Mio ECU
Belgium	31.6	23.1	28.2
Denmark	17.2	16.9	23.5
Germany	133.0	204.1	253.8
Greece	235.3	270.2	392.2
Spain	203.9	301.8	633.6
France	179.8	383.8	554.3
Ireland	121.9	125.0	194.5
Italy	263.6	282.7	375.9
Luxembourg	3.6	4.6	6.3
Netherlands	20.7	11.4	21.9
Portugal	179.4	241.6	289.8
United Kingdom	78.0	102.8	100.8

Source: The Agricultural Situation in the Community, 1993

The Impact of the CAP on the Rest of the World

It is unrealistic to assume that in the absence of the CAP, member countries of the Community would have adopted agricultural policies which were consistent with global 'free trade'. Judged by the policies of some non-EC European market economies protection might well have been much higher for some EC member countries.[16] It is also unsafe to assume that, in the absence of the CAP, other countries would have adopted policies of agricultural free trade. Certainly, current world market prices do not represent what might reasonably be expected to be the price of agricultural commodities in the absence of government induced distortions. However, by starting from current world price levels there is a clear indication of the changing degree to which the CAP distorts markets and its contribution to global distortions compared with other countries. Other approaches involve arbitrary guesses about how far other countries would change their policies, should the CAP be modified.

Because the CAP provides prices which are both higher and more stable than those available in a free market, EC agricultural output is larger than would otherwise have been the case. This means that there are smaller markets within the Community for third countries and that the total quantity seeking an outlet in the world market will be larger. Thus the first consequence of the CAP is a lower level of world prices than would otherwise have been the case. Those countries in the world which import food benefit as a result, those who export lose.

This account is too simple in a number of ways:-

(i)   The CAP sets, for the EC, not only the level of prices but the hierarchy of prices for different products. Because it made cereals relatively expensive and allowed imports of cereal substitutes, such as cassava and soya beans, to enter relatively freely, the world market has been reshaped. Countries such as Thailand and the USA have become major suppliers of cereal substitutes. In a less distorted world the opportunity costs of supply would determine what fodder was used for animals. Where, as in this case, this is not possible, it represents a wastage of global resource. It also denies countries which could produce cereals at competitive prices opportunities to make best use of their resources.

(ii)   A growing number of Less Developed Countries have become net food importers. The availability of low priced food, whether by trade or in the form of aid, is an important benefit for relatively poor people who might otherwise be hungry. However, against this short-run gain must be set the potential of long-term loss. Because markets are depressed, because access to the richest markets in the world is denied for some agricultural products, investment in food production is discouraged in some developing countries. Such investment would lead to higher incomes in the countries concerned, would enable them to improve the potential of their own agriculture and to play a fuller part in world trade generally. The net balance of the impact of the CAP on the poorer countries of the world is not clear, but there are reasons to be anxious about some of its potentially damaging aspects.[17]

(iii)   The Community has special relationships with a number of less developed countries who were associated with some of its members. Under the Lome Convention these Associates of the EC enjoy somewhat better access to EC markets than other third countries. Of particular importance in relation to the CAP is the protocol which requires the Community to import some 6 million tonnes of sugar from some former dependencies of the UK. This guarantees the countries concerned EC prices for this part of their production. However, since the EC's own sugar production is more than sufficient for its needs, an equivalent extra volume of sugar is exported, with the aid of EC funds. Given the very low short run price elasticity of demand for sugar on the world market, these exports may so reduce revenues on sales of sugar from LDCs as a whole as to make them poorer.

(iv)   The most urgent complaint about the CAP by third countries at the time of the GATT negotiations was the use the Community made of export subsidies. These have been applied in ways which enabled EC exporters to undercut traditional suppliers in their established markets. In essence competition has been between governments and budgets rather than between commercial enterprises. In the process smaller, poorer countries have been unable to defend their market share and their industries have contracted. The EC, from this point of view, has exported its adjustment problems rather than solving them. The reaction of the other major world agricultural power, the USA, was to introduce an 'Export Enhancement Programme'. This has intensified the problems for the rest of the world. The GATT settlement reached in 1993 will limit the further expansion of subsidised exports and in due course lead to their reduction. However, in the long run, it must be expected that other exporters will seek the complete elimination of export subsidies and the removal of all internal supports which are not clearly de-coupled from production.

(v)   Since the Six Founder Members established the CAP in the early 1960s, the Community has grown greatly. It has attracted new members, the most recent addition which added Sweden, Finland and Austria taking place at the beginning of 1995. It has also grown in economic power. Real income levels, even if they have not expanded at the rates of some Pacific Rim countries, have continued to grow. It has become the second largest food exporter as well as the world's largest food importer. As a result the domestic policies of what has become the European Union are of importance for all other participants in the global trading system. To a growing extent this increases the responsibilities of the Union to give effect to article 110 of the Treaty of Rome.[18] Agriculture cannot be excluded from this process.

Issues for the CAP in the 1990s

Unfinished business

Much of the agenda for the 1990s is already on the table. The reform package introduced in 1992 has extended considerably the apparatus of supply control. However, the operation of this system and its ability both to contain budget costs and meet the social priorities of the Community remain to be demonstrated. For some products, sugar, wine and tobacco, further revisions of existing arrangements remain to be completed. Minimally there will have to be adjustments, for example to the detail of 'set aside' arrangements and the application of quotas, as the regulatory process is applied. More worryingly there is a built in inconsistency between policies which preserve existing farm businesses and requirements to adopt a more competitive stance in relation to world trade. It may be that, as managed markets proved unmanageable in the 1980s, so supply control will prove increasingly at variance with the need of the Community to cope with the world of the late 1990s. Should that be the case, the debate about the 'reform of the CAP' which started with Dr Mansholt is likely to continue.

A Community of 15

At the beginning of 1995 Austria, Finland and Sweden became full members of the European Union. In doing so they agreed to apply the CAP as it now stands. Traditionally Finland and Austria, with difficult natural conditions, have aimed to maintain their farming populations and have practised high price supports. Sweden has pursued a more market-oriented agricultural policy and has encouraged structural change.

The new members are relatively small in relation to the EU of 12. Table 6 sets out some of their principle agricultural characteristics and compares these with those of the EU.

In general terms the new members contribute six to seven per cent to the size of the Community's agriculture and enjoy incomes which, although they vary considerably, lie within the range presently experienced among member countries. They do, however, have some common characteristics which influenced the terms upon which they have entered. The new members were expected to apply the CAP price level from the point of entry. However, this was often substantially below their existing prices and by January their farmers were too late to apply for compensation in the normal way. Thus special provision was made for temporary compensation. Each of the member countries had substantial areas of land which were mountainous or lay in extreme northerly latitudes. Part of their needs could be met under Objective 5b of the existing structural policy but a new Objective 6 was added to allow structural funds to be applied in areas of extremely low population density.

Table 6. The Agriculture of the Members who Joined in 1995 before Entry

	Utilized Agricultural Area (000ha)	Gross Value Added by agriculture million ECU	Employment in agriculture (000)	Gross Value added per person ECU
Austria	3519	3758	190	19777
Finland	2647	2241	186	12049
Sweden	3358	1245	153	8136
New members	9524	7244	529	13693
EU 12	130340	109188	7626	14297
New as % 12	7.3	6.6	6.9	95.8

Data relate to 1992 or 1991
Sources:- Commission, the Agricultural Situation in the Community 1993 report; Eurostat, Basic Statistics of the Community, 1993; OECD, Economic Accounts for Agriculture, 1978-91.

Despite such specific modifications the economic impact of the new entrants on the CAP will be relatively modest. Collectively they will become net contributors to the EU budget. However, their influence on policy may be much more important. They share a concern for environmental issues and the role of agricultural policy in this area. Finland and Austria have high price traditions and may be expected to side with those who seek to maintain internal EU prices. Sweden, in contrast, had already embarked upon a much lower price policy and may add its voice to those seeking to reduce prices and refocus the CAP on social and environmental issues.

GATT and the future of the CAP

An account of the agricultural settlement which concluded the Uruguay Round of GATT trade talks was provided earlier in this chapter. The immediate effect is likely to be small. The CAP reforms of 1992 will enable the EU to meet most if not all of the requirements this places upon the Community up to the end of this decade. The more important questions lie beyond the implementation period of this agreement. At that stage further negotiations are likely to take place. The purpose of such negotiations will be to carry further the modest steps towards liberalization which have been agreed so far. The Community is likely to face a choice between accommodating the aspirations of other countries by placing ever stricter limits on its own agriculture, so as to make space in the market for goods produced elsewhere, or of seeking to create a genuinely competitive international framework for agriculture. Within such a system both the EU and other countries would have to abandon those aspects of agricultural policies which distort trade.

This poses difficult questions about the reconciliation of the various goals which have been embodied in the past arrangements for the CAP. There is no physical or economic reason why agriculture in the EU should not be powerfully competitive. It is situated close to its affluent markets, it possesses some excellent soils and a benign climate and it is well endowed with capital both on and off the farm. However, to create a competitive agriculture out of the present industry would imply very considerable structural change. Fewer people would be engaged in the industry, farms would become larger and there would be some visible changes in landscapes and in the appearance of many villages and small country towns. Such changes would be resisted, not only by farmers but by others who wish to preserve traditional patterns of rural life.

Europe after Communism

The end of the cold war and the break-up of the Soviet bloc will have profound implications for the future of the Common Agricultural Policy. The immediate result has been a major dislocation in the patterns of production and trade in Eastern Europe and the former USSR. Agricultural exporting countries, within this group, have faced reduced markets as former customers have been unable to pay for the products they want. Their own production has been deeply affected by the wish to move towards a market system and to privatize farms which had been collectively owned. Real incomes have fallen so that the ability to buy food, and other goods has reduced, whilst rampant inflation has created great difficulties for ordinary citizens.

From the perspective of the European Union these changes, although welcome in the sense that military tensions have been reduced, pose far reaching questions. Minimally there is anxiety that economic disruption may lead to a return of authoritarian governments and a rejection of democratic systems and the growth of genuinely market economies. More positively there is a sense that, as European Countries, many of them should become part of an enlarged Union. In economic terms there is a realistic prospect that as market economies develop, there will be profitable opportunities for trade and investment for businesses within the EU.

Agriculture forms a proportionately larger part of the economy of these countries than it does of the European Union. Table 7 provides basic data for those countries which currently seem most likely to become members of the Union within the foreseeable future.

The immediate response of the Community has been to negotiate Europe Agreements with these countries. These arrangements allow for tariff free entry for a limited quantity of products from the countries concerned. So far their impact has been small. Their balance of agricultural trade with the Community has remained in deficit. However, such modest concessions do not face up to the problems which would arise for the CAP were the countries concerned to attain full membership. In that situation three strategies can be considered:

Table 7. Agriculture in some Central and Eastern European Countries 1993

	Agricul - ture Area (000 ha)	Population million	Share of agricul- ture in GDP per cent	Share of Agricul- ture in employ- ment per cent	No of People employed in Agriculture (000)	Share of household income spent on food
Bulgaria	4576	8.9	9.2	17.4	485	35.9
Czech Republic	4550	10.3	4.5	6.5	724*	31-32
Hungary	6484	10.3	8.5	9.9	517	25.1
Poland	18700	38.5	6.8	25.2	3700	36.0
Romania	14790	22.8	23.7	32.2	2053	58
Slovak Republic	2877	5.3	5.9	8.6		27.2
Total 6	51977	96.1	9.0	19.0	7479	36.1
EU12	130340	346.2	2.8	5.8	8353	21.7

* Czechoslovakia
Source: Buckwell et al.[19]

To apply the CAP in full to the new members. To admit the new members to the Community but exclude them from the CAP. To adjust the CAP so as to avoid the problems resulting from either of the other approaches. These difficulties are not negligible.[20]

To apply the CAP in full to the new members involves financial, administrative and trade policies. The policy currently involves supply control, support buying, export subsidies and direct payments to farmers to compensate for price reductions since 1992. Assuming that under the incentives offered by the CAP production in the new members would be likely to expand, the cost of disposing of this together with the payments to individual farmers would impose substantial new claims on the budget. Administratively there would be a complex task of determining the basis for supply control measures such as set aside and sheep and beef premia. The fact that these countries were not operating in a free market in 1988 and that since then many of the assets have been privatized makes data relating to the communist era of little help. Equally, current levels of activity reflect the depressed state of the economies concerned and their agricultures. This would not seem a fair basis for distributing quotas, in effect future rights to produce. In trade terms further problems would arise. The GATT settlement limits exports from the EU and the potential new members. The CAP would tend to stimulate production but would not create any additional markets. As a result, in order to keep within the commitments made in 1993, there would have to be a further tightening of the supply control measures.

Given these difficulties it might seem tempting to exclude the new members from the CAP. This would be inconsistent with the Rome Treaty and with a single market in the Union. It would also seem to discriminate against the new central and eastern European members in an area of particular importance for their economies and society. Such a rebuff would clash with the strategic goals of the EU and the aspirations of its industry, most of which is not agricultural.

The alternative approach is to seek to converge on policy arrangements different from those which presently prevail in the Union and in the aspiring members but which correspond better to the financial capacity, the administrative abilities and the diplomatic requirements of an enlarged Community. Reports prepared for DG1 have explored this possibility and visualize a shift away from price support towards freer markets and the redirection of support in de-coupled forms to ease the problems of adjustment.[21]

Environmental constraint

The 1980s saw the awakening of public concern to a number of environmental issues. Some important policy initiatives have been made to encourage environmentally favourable farming but policy making has only begun to take account of the wide range of issues involved. Agriculture is likely to have to accommodate an increasing number of restrictions designed to protect the environment. Measures to limit pollution and to penalize those who cause it are likely to affect both crop and animal production. The increased demands made by non-farming interests on the countryside, for housing, for recreation and for sites for 'clean technology' industries will not only mean the loss of land to farming but tougher standards in relation to such nuisances as noise, smells, mud on roads and unsightly farm buildings. Concerns of a longer term nature about 'global warming' and the exhaustion of minerals and fossil fuels may lead to increasing intervention in the form of carbon taxes and the control of emissions from agriculture. Measures of this nature add to the cost of food production. Countries where they are not applied may be able to undercut Community producers as a result. Thus the EC will have to decide to what extent it can reconcile the need to retain a competitive agriculture with the demands of environmental lobby groups.

The development of the Community

Apart from the further enlargement of the EC referred to above, there is also a continued demand for 'deepening' - the development of the existing EC in the direction of a federal state. The arguments surrounding this issue are complex and seem to be unpopular among many EC citizens. However, they are increasingly urgent. Community action already profoundly affects the functioning of the economies of all member states, the employment opportunities open to EC citizens and economic relations with the rest of the world. The need to match economic decision taking with political structures suggests that demands for a strengthening of the central institutions are likely to grow. For agriculture the introduction of a single currency would do away with the cumbersome business of MCAs. It would also force agriculture to participate in the adjustment implicit in the differing rates of growth which exist within the Community.

Summary

This chapter has shown how a policy which was designed for Six has had to adapt to accommodate a Community of Fifteen. It has indicated how adjustment has been forced on the policy by the process of technical change within the agricultural industry itself. It indicates how new concerns about the environment and about diet and health have come to play a larger part in the process of policy making and how the Community has had to respond to the pressures of the outside world.

Such changes are not at an end. The test of the policy must be its ability to serve the interests of the Community as a whole. For all its problems it can fairly claim some important achievements. First, it enabled the Community to come into existence and to grow into a major economic and political power in the world. Second, it has managed agriculture during a period of relatively rapid change and contraction, during which the labour force has more than halved, without major civil disorders resulting. Third, although the internal market it has created is distorted, internal trade has grown and with the coming of the Single Market the opportunities for further integration of the Community's agriculture and food sector should increase. Finally, it has shown that in the end, reluctantly, sluggishly and yet just sufficiently it has been able to change. These are significant achievements and the Community will need to continue to build on them in the future.

Notes

1   See for a straightforward explanation Swann, Dennis, 'The Economics of the Common Market' 6th Ed Ch 4. Penguin, 1988.

2   For a discussion of this subject see for example Martin A, 'Economics and Agriculture', Ch 7 - Routledge and Kegan Paul, 1968.

3   The concept of 'gains from trade' which spring from exploiting comparative advantage was developed in the 19th Century by Ricardo and others. For a modern account see for example Lipsey Richard G, 'An Introduction to Positive Economics' 7th Ed Ch 21. - Weidenfeld and Nicholson, 1989.

4   There has also been a long-standing professional debate - see for example Blagburn, C H, 'Import-replacement by British agriculture', Economic Journal Vol. LX Mar 1950, and the arguments of Robinson, E A G & Marris, R L, 'The use of home resources to save imports' Economic Journal Vol. LX Mar 1950.

5   For discussion of these issues see for example Hoderness B. A., 'British Agriculture since 1945' Manchester University Press 1985. Chapter 5.

6   For further reading see Errington, AJ, 'Investigating rural employment in England', Journal of rural studies Vol 6, No 1, 1990 and also series edited by Lowe, Philip, Marsden, Terry and Whatmore, Sarah 'Critical perspectives on rural change series', Nos 1, 2, 3, 4. London, Fulton.

7   For a discussion see Alexandratos, N, 'European agriculture: policy issues and options to 2000', Belhaven Press for FAO 1990.

8   For an account of the regimes applied to specific products see Harris, Simon, Swinbank, Alan and Wilkinson, Guy, 'The Food and Farm Policies of the European Community', Wiley, 1983. A Wiley, Interscience publication.

9   CEC (1968) Memorandum on the Reform of Agriculture in the European Economic Community COM(68) 1000 Part A Brussels.

10 CEC (1968) *Ibid*; CEC (1973) Improvement of the Common Agricultural Policy, COM(73)1850, Brussels; CEC(1975A) Stocktaking of the Common Agricultural Policy, COM(75)100, Brussels; CEC (1980) Reflections on the Common Agricultural Policy, COM(80)800, Brussels; CEC (1981a) Commission Report on the Mandate of 30 May 1980, COM(81)300, Brussels; CEC (1981b) Guideline's for European Agriculture COM(81) 608, Brussels; CEC (1985) Green Paper on perspectives for the Common Agricultural Policy; COM (85)333, Brussels; CEC (1985) A future for Community agriculture; Commission guidelines following the consultations in connection with

the Green Paper, COM(85)750, Brussels; CEC (1991a) The Development and Future of the CAP, COM(91)100, Brussels; CEC (1991b) The Development and Future of the CAP; Follow-up to the Reflections Paper COM(91)100 of 1 February 1991, COM(91)258/3, Brussels.

[11] 72/159/EEC Directive on the modernization of farms; 72/160/EEC Directive on the cessation of farming and the reallocation of the utilized agricultural area for structural improvement; 72/161/EEC Directive on the provision of socio-economic guidance for the acquisition of occupational skills by persons engaged in agriculture.

[12] 219/78/EEC Community Regulation on application for aid from the Guidance Section of the European Agricultural Guidance and Guarantee Fund for projects to improve the conditions under which agricultural products are processed and marketed.

[13] 75/268/EEC Directive on mountains and hill farming and farming in less favoured areas.

[14] See Agra Europe, No 1494, June 5, 1992, E/3; No 1522, December 18, 1992, N/3.

[15] See GATT Newsletter No 104 Dec 1993 Geneva.

[16] Measurement of the degree of protection is complex and controversial. A widely respected method is that used to estimate Producer Subsidy Equivalents and Consumer Subsidy Equivalents by OECD. Their 1991 calculation showed per cent PSEs of 49 for the EC, 59 for Sweden, 71 for Finland and 52 for Austria, 15 for Australia, 4 for New Zealand and 30 for the US.

[17] For further details see Matthews, A.,'The Common Agricultural Policy and Less Developed Countries', Trocaire, 1985.

[18] Treaty Establishing the European Community - Article 110: By establishing a customs union between themselves the Member States intend to contribute, in conformity with the common interest, to the harmonious development of world trade, the progressive abolition of restrictions on international exchanges and the lowering of customs barriers.The common commercial policy shall take into account the favourable incidence which the abolition of customs duties as between Member States may have on the increase of the competitive strength of the enterprises in those States.

[19] Buckwell A. Davidova S. University of London, Haynes J. CEAS Consultants (Wye) Ltd and Kwiecinski A Warsaw. 'Feasibility of an Agricultural Strategy to prepare the Countries of Central and Eastern Europe for EU Accession'.

[20]   See Tarditi S., Senior-Nello S. University of Siena, and Marsh J. University of Reading. 'Agricultural Strategies for the Enlargement of the European Union to Central and Eastern European Countries'. Tangerman S. University of Gottingen, Josling T. E. Stanford University, 'Pre-accession Agricultural Policies for Central Europe and the European Union'.

[21]   Mahé, L P. 'Ecole Nationale Supérieure Agronomique de Rennes. L'agriculture et l'elargissement de l'Union Européene aux pays d'Europe Centrale et Orientale: transition envoie de l'intégration ou intégration pour la transition?'

16   Regional Policy in the European Union

JOHN LOUGHLIN

Introduction

Since the signing of the Single European Act in 1986, European integration has quickened its pace. This has been confirmed by the ratification of the Treaty on Political Union signed at Maastricht. European Regional policy, implicit in the Treaty of Rome but made explicit only in 1975, has taken on a new significance in this context of accelerated integration. There is even talk of the establishment of a 'Europe of the Regions' as the form future integration will have.

There are two important aspects to these developments. First, it is clear that the refurbished Regional policy of the European Union is closely related to the institution of the Single Market as a compensatory mechanism to those states and regions which are lagging behind the core states and regions of the EU.[1] Second, the 'federalist' dynamic of integration has been given a renewed impulse and the slogan 'Europe of the Regions' is closely related to this conception of a federal Europe.[2] However, the current prevalence of the slogan is also rather confusing in that the movement towards federalism and the strengthening of regional policy are related but not identical.

To help sort out this confusion, a distinction ought to be made between *regionalization* and *regionalism*.[3] *Regionalization* refers to the regional policies developed by central states and by the European Community with a view to bringing about the development of backward regions. Although the models of regional development have changed over time[4] what is constant is that *regionalization* is an approach to the needs of regions perceived from the point of view of, and in relation to, the centre (that is, national governments or Brussels). Sometimes, local regional actors may be brought into the policy process on a consultative basis or as

439

policy implementors. However, final decisions are made by the centre in the context of the (national or European) society as a whole. *Regionalism*, on the other hand, refers to an ideology as well as to political movements emanating from the regions, sometimes with the support of groups at the centre such as those sympathetic to decentralization or even federalism.[5] The ideology, based on the notion of subsidiarity, states that it is regional actors rather than those at the centre who ought to be in control of the affairs of the region. Sometimes, these two aspects of the regional problem coincide: regional policy, whose objectives and priorities are formulated by the centre, may attempt to incorporate some of the demands of regionalists in the regions and even collaborate with them in the formulation and implementation of the policy as happened in France during the Fourth Republic or more recently with the decentralization/regionalization programme which began in 1982; regionalists, on the other hand, may see the existence of a regional policy as an opportunity to obtain some of their demands even if the regional policy falls short of these. However it is often the case that regional policy is developed without a real regionalist basis and this may lead to disappointment and even conflict between the regions and the centre.

This is why the slogan 'Europe of the Regions' may be so confusing: its origin lies in the demands of regionalism and federalism but it is sometimes used to refer to the growing importance of European Regional policy. However, the latter was not originally designed to bring about a 'Europe of the Regions' in the sense of a Europe in which the role of nation-states is diminished and that of regions is enhanced. Rather, as we shall see below, its underlying rationale is to bring about the social and economic cohesion of both states and regions, for example, parts of the UK, France, Italy and Spain and the whole of Ireland, Greece and Portugal, that are lagging behind the most advanced states and regions. This was also the rationale of those states which developed a Regional policy in the 1950s and 1960s.[6] While regionalists do attempt to use Regional policy to bring about a 'Europe of the Regions', and while the recent reforms of EC regional policy have attempted to incorporate a regionalist dimension (see below), it is important to keep the distinction in mind.

The Development of Regional Policy in Western Europe

It is not the intention of this chapter to give a history of regional policy but rather to describe and explain the current developments within Europe and to attempt to discern possible future developments. Nevertheless, a brief glance at the past will help us to grasp the nature of current regional policy at the European level.

The first striking aspect of this development is that regional policy was developed first, not by the European Community, but by individual states within Europe.[7] This occurred in the late 1950s and 1960s in relation to two other developments. The first was the development of *social policy* through the rise of the welfare state.[8] The second was the rise of *national planning* which, towards the end of the 1950s, began to incorporate a regional dimension to the national plans. This was particularly the case in France which was the leader in this field of national planning.[9] These two aspects of European policy development are closely related and this relationship is important for understanding the nature of regional policy. Underlying them is the Keynesian notion that the state can intervene in the economy to effect economic growth and to achieve goals such as full employment but also the social democratic idea that the state ought to do so. One can also discern an attempt to bring about an equalization and harmonization - that is, convergence - of national societies at different levels. Social policy attempts to do this at the level of individuals and social groups which have been disadvantaged in the past - workers, women, children, handicapped people, sick. Planning is an attempt to promote the harmonization of society through economic development. Social policy and economic development have in practice gone hand in hand. Most modern European welfare states were built on the wave of economic prosperity that characterized these states from the mid-1950s until the early 1970s.

Regional policy may be seen as following the same logic as social and economic development but on a territorial level. There were two aspects to this. First, it was thought that backward regions represented a loss to the overall productivity of the society. There were high levels of unemployment with a drain of labour to the more developed regions and a consequent transfer of welfare resources (unemployment benefits and pensions) to the backward regions. It was argued, from an economic perspective, that regional development would bring about growth in employment and a subsequent reduction in these transfers. There would also be an increase in purchasing power and the generation of new industries through a multiplier effect.[10] Second, from the point of view of social policy it was thought that, just as the state had a responsibility to intervene to improve the life-chances of individuals and groups on a national basis, so it should intervene to improve the life-chances of territorially based communities. The means of intervention included giving subsidies of various kinds to attract large-scale investments but also improving infrastructural facilities such as roads, ports, telecommunications systems as well as local training facilities in an effort to 'bring work to the workers'.

Although these policies brought about significant changes in the societies concerned, the literature suggests that, on the whole, the expected economic take-off did not happen.[11] Instead, many multinational companies exploited the possibility of attractive subsidies, tax-free breaks and cheap labour to invest in a region for a short period and then leave the region which was no better in economic terms. Indeed, now it is widely agreed that the gap between the richer regions and states and the poorer has grown despite the efforts of governments to intervene. In the 1980s, regional policy at the national level was rather discredited because of these failures and also because, since the Thatcher - Reagan years beginning in 1979/80, there has been less willingness to accept government intervention whether at the social or economic levels. Thus, in the UK, for example, regional policy has withered and in other countries has been seriously cut back.

Regional Policy at the European Level

The one level where regional policy has not been cut back but, on the contrary, has continued to grow is that of the European Community/Union. To some extent, this has involved taking over from national governments responsibility for formulating regional policy even for regions within particular states although implementation of this remained in the hands of the national governments and those sub-national authorities designated by them. However, it is important to remember that a regional dimension has been present in the European integration project right from the beginning although it has taken many years to be operationalized.

The history of European Regional policy has been well documented by Vanhove and Klaassen (1987) and it is not necessary to repeat this here. It is, however, useful to remember that a reference to the regional problem is found in the preamble to the Treaty of Rome of 1957 which states that it is 'anxious to strengthen the unity of [the member states'] economies and to ensure their harmonious development by reducing both the differences existing between the various regions and the backwardness of the less favoured regions'. The key word here is 'harmonious' and this is developed in Article 2 of the Treaty:

> 'The Community shall have as its task, by establishing a Common Market and progressively approximating the economic policies of Member States, to promote throughout the Community a harmonious development of economic activities, a continuous and balanced expansion, an increase in stability, an accelerated raising of the standard of living and closer relations between the States belonging to it'.

It is difficult to see how this 'harmonious development' and 'continuous and balanced expansion' could occur given the extent of regional disparities even in the Europe of the Six. Thus, the very idea of European economic integration as a 'harmonious development' implies also a regional policy. As Vanhove and Klaassen exhaustively demonstrate, the explicit references referred to above are supplemented by numerous other implicit references in other articles. Furthermore, referring to the above distinction between regionalization and regionalism, while these explicit and implicit references are more in relation to regionalization, the founding fathers of the Community such as Jean Monnet and Robert Schuman were also sympathetic to regionalism of a moderate kind which in turn was related to their federalist sympathies.[12]

However, in the early years of integration, two factors hindered the development of an explicit regional policy. The first was that the prevailing economic philosophy of the time assumed that the development of backward regions would occur as a consequence of general economic development through a kind of trickle-down effect where the workings of the market would ensure that, while stronger regions became stronger, beneficial effects would also percolate down to the weaker regions.[13] It was thought therefore that, at least at the European level, there would be little need for intervention. And, in any case, this could be left to national governments. Secondly, although there existed regional disparities within the Six, only the problem of the Italian South was of sufficient proportions to justify explicit intervention and this was done through the Protocol on Italy appended to the Rome Treaty. Nevertheless, although an explicit Common Regional Policy did not exist, a number of instruments of regional policy at the Community level were created. The most important was the European Investment Bank (EIB), created in 1958, which had as an explicit task the assistance of underdeveloped regions through loans. The Common Agricultural Policy (CAP) which encouraged the development of large-scale industrialized agriculture and the decline of smaller holdings and more traditional farming methods also had consequences for the more peripheral regions of the Community and instruments were developed to counteract the damaging social effects of the CAP.[14] Finally, at a much later date, the development of a European Social Policy was also related to regions in decline and affected by high levels of unemployment.

The development of an explicit Common regional policy may be related to the enlargement of the Community in 1973 with the addition of the United Kingdom, Ireland and Denmark. All three countries, but particularly the first two, possessed serious problem regions, and the question of the activation of a Common Regional Policy was raised during the negotiations for entry in 1971-72. This was supported by Italy for obvious reasons. Another rationale for the development of a Community regional policy was to ensure that economic divergence did not threaten the political and social cohesion of a unified Europe.[15] Finally, it was acknowledged that the *laissez faire* approach to regional development with the expectation that this would come about as a consequence of general economic development had not occurred. The approval for the establishment of a Common Regional policy was finally given at the Paris Summit of the Council of Ministers in October 1972.

The first step in setting up a Common regional policy was to define the Community's problem regions. This task was given to George Thomson, Commissioner responsible for regional policy, who published his Report in May 1973.[16] Although the *Thomson Report* needs to be interpreted with caution because of the unevenness of the reliability of the statistical data it used,[17] it was an important step in the direction of quantifying the regional problem with a view to applying concrete solutions. Regions in need of help were defined as those with a *per capita* Gross Domestic Product (GDP) below the EC average plus one of the following characteristics: more workers in agriculture than the EC average; at least 20 per cent of the work-force in coal-mining or textiles; persistently high unemployment or protracted out-migration. A second important feature of the *Report* is that it insisted on a harmonization of national regional policies although the CRP was originally seen to be complementary rather than a replacement of these.[18] Indeed, the regional policy Committee set up in 1975 'was entirely inspired by the idea of, and the willingness to, facilitate Community co-ordination of Member States' regional policies'.[19]

Whatever the good intentions of the initial formulators of the CRP, this was established at an inauspicious period: the economic crisis and recession of the early 1970s when most western governments were increasingly unwilling to devote more funds or powers either to regions in difficulty or to the European Community let alone a combination of both of these things. The CRP, however, was based on the notion of a transfer of some national powers over regional policy to the European level and also on that of a transfer of national resources between member states on the basis of the ability to pay and of need. Beneficiary Member States such as Ireland, the UK and Italy were strongly in favour of this. The 'paymaster' Member States, especially West Germany, were very reluctant. Thus, the actual funding of the CRP led to a great deal of acrimony among the states. It was only at the Paris Summit of December 1974 that an agreement was reached to set up the European Regional Development Fund (ERDF) which would come into operation for a three-year trial period beginning on 1 January 1975. However, the amount of finance agreed to operate the Fund was very small in comparison with the scale of the problems to be solved. Nevertheless, an explicit CRP was at last in operation.

During this first period, the key actors were national governments and the Commission in Brussels. The former presented plans for the individual development projects to the latter, received grants in return providing certain criteria were met and then distributed the grants to firms, local authorities or development agencies. In the late 1970s, the worsening economic situation led the Commission to devise a more ambitious Regional policy at the European level with an increase in funding and a refinement of the policy instruments being used. The first reform of the

Fund occurred in 1979, when a division was made between a quota section and a non-quota section (5 per cent of the total budget) 'for specific regional development measures' under the control of the Commission.

Guidelines were adopted by the Council with regard to the publication of a Periodic Report, regional impact assessment of other Community policies and the coordination of national regional policies. The introduction of a non-quota section was the most important change. Under the quota section national states were allocated ERDF funds on the basis of a quota decided on the basis of the seriousness of a country's regional problems.

Table 1. National Quotas of ERDF, 1975 - 1985 and ERDF Grants per Member - State, 1975 - 1985

	Quota 1975-77 (100% of budget)	Quota 1987-80 (95% of budget)	Quota 1981-84 (95% of budget*)	ERDF Grants 1975-85 (in m ECU)
	1.5	1.39	1.11	137
Denmark	1.3	1.20	1.06	146
Germany	6.4	6.00	4.65	628
France	15.0	16.86	13.64	2007
Ireland	6.0	6.46	5.94	882
Italy	40.0	39.39	35.49	5233
Luxembourg	0.1	0.09	0.07	12
Netherlands	1.7	1.58	1.24	175
UK	28.0	27.03	23.80	3463
Totals	100.0	100.0	87.0	12683

* *From 1982 onwards there was no longer a legal basis for these quotas.*
Source: Adapted from Vanhove and Klaassen, Official Journal of the European Communities and ERDF 11th Annual Report (1986).

It was still the national governments which had the initiative in deciding what these problems were and in administering the funds granted to attempt to alleviate them. However, the non-quota section gave the Commission an input into the definition of, and attempted solutions to, regional problems. Using this opportunity, it began to develop a number of new approaches to regional policy which would be expanded in subsequent reforms. Important among these was the 'programme' approach which will be discussed more fully below.

The Common Regional policy came in for harsh criticisms in the early 1980s: the statistical indicators on which it was based were called into question; it was criticized for scattering aid to a multitude of small projects; and there was a dispersal of community finance through other institutions as well as the ERDF.[20] It was clear that more drastic reforms were needed. These were prepared in 1984 and came into operation in 1985.

The 1984 Reforms of the ERDF

The first principal feature of the 1984 reforms is the emphasis on *coordination*.[21] There must be coordination between: Community policies with each other insofar as they affect regional development; Community Regional policy and national regional policies; national regional policies; trans-frontier regional development. This should also take into account the regional impact of Community and national economic and sectoral policies. The second principal feature is the *clearer definition of the tasks of the ERDF*: the development and structural adaptation of underdeveloped regions and the conversion of declining industrial regions as well as other regions affected by some Community policies. The emphasis on the *structural* aspects of regional policy led to the use of the terms 'structural action' and 'structural funds' to describe the broader range of policies and instruments which had a regional dimension. There is also a *concentration* in favour of the countries with peripheral and declining regions. Very importantly there is a switch from an *ad hoc project approach*, which was judged to be wasteful, to a *programme approach*. This had been a feature of the implementation of the non-quota section of the post-1979 ERDF operations as mentioned above. Two types of programme are defined: (a) Community programmes and (b) national programmes of Community interest. A Community programme is defined in Article 7 of the new Regulation as :

> 'a series of consistent multiannual measures directly serving Community objectives and the implementation of Community policies. Its purpose shall be to help in solving serious problems affecting the

> socio-economic situation in one or more regions. It must provide a better link between the Community's objectives for the structural development or conversion of regions and the objectives of other Community policies. A Community programme shall as a rule concern the territory of more than one Member State, with the agreement of the latter' [22]

A national programme of Community interest consists of:

> 'set of consistent multiannual measures corresponding to national and serving Community objectives and policies. In particular it shall assist the convergence of Member States' economies through the reduction of disparities. It shall translate into operational commitments the indications contained in regional development programmes. It may concern part of a region ... [or] one or more regions, in one or more Member States'(*ibid*).

The programme approach included an attempt to ensure a genuine 'additionality', that is, funding from ERDF sources should not be substituted for funding from national sources but be in addition to these. The practice of cheating on the additionality had been rife since the foundation of the ERDF with the United Kingdom as the most notorious example. There had been several alleged cases in the past, but it was not until April / May 1995 that the European Court of Auditors started its first serious probe into the misuse of £400m by the UK government.[23] Under special review are two forms of cheating on additionality: i) to pay 'national' contributions out of the funds received, and ii) to commit national funds appropriately, but to divert the ERDF money straight into the pockets of shareholders of the recently privatized utilities suppliers and major transport companies rather than into the budget of the modernization programmes it was intended for. Another important change is the invitation to regional authorities to participate, alongside national governments and the Commission, in the preparation of the programmes. The Integrated Mediterranean Programmes (IMPs) for the period 1985-1990 were the first examples of this new programme approach. Finally, there is again a move away from the 1979 quota/non-quota system, which is abolished, to a more flexible percentage range, with the lower value representing the minimum of each year's ERDF budget guaranteed to that state but where the national governments must negotiate with the Commission to receive amounts above the lower limit up to a predetermined upper limit.[24]

These reforms were accompanied by a significant increase in the financial support available to the Structural Funds. In 1975, the ERDF budget was almost ECU 269 million and by 1984 this was ECU 2,140 million, a spectacular average annual growth of 25.58 per cent. [1]

Table 2. New Regulations ERDF Grants 1985 and 1986

	1985		1986	
	L.L.*	U.L	L.L.	U.L.
Belgium	0.90	1.20	0.61	0.82
Denmark	0.51	0.67	0.34	0.46
Germany	3.76	4.81	2.55	3.40
Greece	12.35	15.74	8.36	10.64
France	11.05	14.74	7.48	9.96
Ireland	5.64	6.83	3.82	4.61
Italy	31.94	42.59	21.63	28.79
Luxembourg	0.06	0.08	0.04	0.06
Netherlands	1.0	1.34	0.68	0.91
UK	21.42	28.56	14.50	19.31
Portugal	-	-	10.66	14.20
Spain	-	-	17.97	23.93

* *L.L. = Lower Limit; U.L. = Upper Limit*

Source: Adapted from Vanhove and Klaassen, and Official Journal of the European Communities

The Single Market and the 1988 reforms

In 1986, the Single European Act was approved by the Council of Ministers. This sought to give an impulse to the process of European integration by creating a single market and laying the basis for economic and monetary union. The architect of this new drive toward a deeper European integration was Jacques Delors, a convinced European and federalist, who had been appointed President of the Commission in 1985. All obstacles to the single market were to be removed by 1 January 1993. However, it was feared that this development would benefit primarily the strongest regions and be socially and economically harmful to the weakest. Although there was a debate about whether such fears were justified,[25] they were felt sufficiently strongly to encourage the European Council, consisting of the Heads of State and Government, to take a decision to reform what were now known as the Structural Funds (ERDF, ESF and the EAGGF Guidance Section) in such a way as to counteract any negative effects the single market might have on the weaker regions of the Community. A reformed Common Regional policy was even more urgent given the accession of Spain and Portugal to the Community in 1986 with the addition of a larger number of regions and populations falling considerably behind the most developed regions of the Community. Finally, the 1988 reforms were in continuity with and sought to further develop those of 1984/5.

According to the *Guide to the Reform of the Community's Structural Funds,* published by the Commission in 1989, the 1988 reforms were necessitated by three imperatives: a *political imperative* based on the notion of solidarity among Member States which demanded that the single market Europe be accompanied by actions designed to promote a harmonious development of Europe as a whole; an *economic imperative* which saw regional disparities as holding back the economic development of the whole; and a *legal imperative* which was based on Article 130d of the EEC Treaty as amended by the Single European Act which demanded that a reform of the Structural Funds take place 'to increase their efficiency with a view to promoting the Community's economic and social cohesion'.[26] This last legal aspect might be seen as an *a posteriori* legitimation of already existing political and economic imperatives.

A key change that had occurred with the 1984 reforms is that Regional policy shifted its emphasis from being based on reactive measures to economic decline to being a proactive pursuit of economic development. Regional measures should have 'a real economic impact' according to the Commission presumably meaning that they should lay the basis for indigenous economic development, a new model of economic development, based on 'bottom-up' approaches involving local actors much more, which replaced the previous 'top-down' approach where solutions were provided by national governments. The 1989 Commission document outlined five principles for the EC's structural action: concentration, partnership, consistency, improved administration of the Funds including attention paid to additionality and simplification.

(i)   Assistance should be *concentrated* on five priority objectives:

-       objective 1 to promote the development of regions lagging behind;
-       objective 2 to convert regions seriously affected by industrial decline;
-       objective 3 to combat long-term unemployment;
-       objective 4 to facilitate the occupational integration of young people (below the age of 25);
-       objective 5 to reform the common agricultural policy; objective 5a to adapt production, processing and marketing structures in agriculture and forestry; objective 5b to promote the development of rural areas.

Regional policy is primarily concerned with objectives 1, 2 and 5b which receive 80 per cent of ERDF resources.

(ii)   *Partnership* is defined by the framework Regulation as 'close consultation between the Commission, the Member States concerned and the competent authorities designated by the latter as national, regional, local or other level, with each party acting as a partner in pursuit of a common goal'. This reflects the principle of subsidiarity which is to be applied according to the culture and traditions of individual Member States.

(iii)   *Consistency*, especially with the Member States' economic policies, is designed to achieve the convergence of economic performances of the Member States.

(iv)   *Improved administration* of the Funds with a substantial increase in financial commitments to them. This would involve: multiannual budgetary planning; increased transparency; additionality; the prevention of duplication; and systematic assessment of the Community's structural action at different levels.

(v)   *Simplification, monitoring and flexibility.* Simplification is designed to reduce the amount of red tape that may hinder the effectiveness of structural action.

Finally, the role of the Commission is enhanced with the development of 'Community initiatives' which enable it to set up its own programmes. These already existed *de facto* as 'programmes' since 1986 with the STAR and VALOREN programmes dealing with telecommunications and renewable energy respectively. However, in 1988, this was expanded to a number of other initiatives.

On 16 June 1993 the Commission published a Green Paper for discussion by the different parties involved on the future of these initiatives. It suggested five topics for future Community initiatives:

- cross-border, transnational and interregional cooperation and networks (Interreg and Regen)
- rural development (Leader)
- assistance to the outermost regions (Regis)
- employment promotion and development of human resources (Now, Horizon, and Euroform)
- management of industrial change (Rechar, Resider, Retex, Konver, but also Prisma, Telematique and Stride in Objective 1 regions).

It may be seen that these reforms are a prolongation of those begun in 1984. They may be summarized as follows:

- more control over EU regional policy by the Commission at the expense of national governments;
- a more integrated and programmatic approach in the context of general economic development;
- greater financial resources for the funds especially the ERDF.

Table 3. Community Initiatives 1989 - 1993

Initiative	Amount in mECU*	Aim of the Initiative
Envireg	500	Protection of the environment and development in the regions
Interreg	800	Cross-border cooperation
Rechar	300	Diversification in coal-mining regions
Regis	200	Integration of the most remote regions
Stride	400	Research, technology, development and innovation in the regions
Regen	300	Energy networks
Telematique	200	Advanced telecommunications services
Prisma	100	Services to businesses in connection with the single market
Euroform	300	New skills and qualifications
Now **	120	Equal opportunities for women on the labour market
Horizon **	180	Access to the labour market for the handicapped and other disadvantaged groups
Leader	400	Rural development
Total	**3,800**	
Retex **		Diversification in regions dependent on the textile industry
Kenver **		Diversification in regions dependent on the military sector.

* in 1989 prices
** An additional sum of ECU 300m was allocated to Retex and Konver, and for the purpose of increasing the funds earmarked for Now and Horizon.

Source: *Community Structural Funds 1994-99*, Commission of the European Communities, p. 28.

The 1993 revisions

Nevertheless, criticisms continued to be levelled at the Regional policy. These are summarized by Harvey Armstrong (1989): the still inadequate size of the ERDF budget despite increases since the 1970s; this is related to the enormous budget of the Common Agricultural Policy which is, in effect, an anti-regional policy (in the sense that it favours wealthy agricultural regions and penalizes the poorer rural areas); the predominance of assistance to infrastructure projects; the slow development of Programme Assistance; the lack of clarity of relations between the EC and Member States with regard to regional policy; the paucity of formal evaluation of ERDF activities. Criticisms such as these led to the revisions of the Regulations in 1993.

The Commission's commentary on these revisions stresses that they are not as far-reaching as the radical reforms of 1988. The 'major principles adopted in 1988: concentration of effort, partnership, programming, additionality, are maintained or strengthened'.[27] Nevertheless, they are still significant and continue the general direction of the previous reforms. The most important feature is the increase of the Structural Funds' budget to ECU 141 billion for the period 1994-99. This brings it to *one third* of the total Union budget. The changes that occurred are primarily concerned with increasing the number of regions eligible for aid under the five priority objectives. These concern principally objectives 3 and 4 which are redefined but only indirectly concern regions. However, Objectives 2 and 5b include new criteria to allow areas suffering from a decline in fishing activity to be included. Some new Objective 1 regions are included: East Berlin and the five new German Länder; the Highlands and Islands Enterprise Area in Scotland; Flevoland in the Netherlands (which was a choice based on political criteria - that is, the Dutch government wished to be seen receiving something from the Structural Funds although Flevoland scarcely merits being classed in the same category as Sicily, Greece, Portugal and Ireland!); the border region of Hainaut in Belgium and Douai-Valenciennes-Avesnes in France; and Cantabria in Northern Spain. Other changes involve the time-tabling of the programmes, measures to strengthen the Community Initiatives, clearer financial guidelines and greater involvement of the European Parliament.

Europe 2000

However, the activities of the Commission with regard to economic and social cohesion and regional policy have not stopped with the revision of the Structural Funds. In 1991, it published a document entitled *Europe*

2000 (Outlook for the Development of the Community's Territory).[28] This was an attempt by the Commission to develop a plan for the entire territory of the Community seen as a whole. As the then Commissioner for Regional policy, Bruce Millan, expressed it in the introduction:

> *'Europe 2000* is a first effort to provide planners with some of the information they need in a reference framework which is Community-wide rather than national or regional'.[29]

This important document identified what the Commission regards as the key issues related to Community-wide planning. First, there are *areas of concentration* of economic activity: (i) the traditional heartlands of the North and (ii) new growth areas of northern Italy, southern France and northern Spain. These areas risked marginalizing the peripheral regions of the Community. However, the document goes on to suggest possibilities for decentralization of economic activities related to changes in economic production which is now less localized, in transport developments and new forms of telecommunication and the costs of congestion in the developed areas. The document departed from the older model of economic development (based on the experience of the United States) which stressed *the geographical mobility of labour* which is no longer effective or desirable and adopted a model based on *the geographical mobility of economic activity.* The document also discerns seven new 'regional groupings' which are of importance to planning on a Europe-wide basis (the countries to which the regions belong are indicated in parenthesis):

-   the Atlantic regions (UK, Ireland, France, Spain, Portugal);
-   the 'Central Capitals' (UK, Germany, the Netherlands, Belgium, Luxembourg, France);
-   the Alpine regions (Germany, France, Italy);
-   the Western Mediterranean (Spain, France, Italy);
-   the Central Mediterranean (Italy, Greece);
-   the North Sea coastal regions (UK, the Netherlands, Germany, and Denmark);
-   the Inland Continental regions (France, Spain);
-   the 5 new Länder (Germany).

(Regions from the new Member States Austria, Finland and Sweden are later to be included in this list as appropriate.)

In 1994, the Commission published a sequel to this document entitled *Europe 2000+ (Cooperation on Spatial Development)* (CEC, 1994).[30] This reiterated the demand contained in *Europe 2000* for Community-wide spatial planning but now took into account the fact that Europe had a new Treaty from 1 November 1993 and a new consultative body in the Committee of the Regions (see below). Three themes are particularly stressed in the new document:

-   economic and social cohesion which should become an element in all Community policies;
-   the development of Trans-European Networks in transport, telecommunications and energy;
-   and the protection of the environment through an approach to economic development based on *sustainable development.*

The document also proposed a more *integrated* approach to spatial planning with spatial issues being included in all policy areas and European inter-regional and transnational co-operation. It called for the setting up of a Committee on Spatial Development by the Council of Ministers which was subsequently carried out by the Council.

The Treaty on European Union (Maastricht) and the Committee of the Regions

The Maastricht Treaty gave a legal basis to an enhanced EC Regional policy and placed it in the context of Economic and Social Cohesion (Title XIV). Article 130a stated that the

> 'Community shall aim at reducing disparities between the levels of development of the various regions and backwardness of the least favoured regions, including rural areas'

while Article 130b provides a legal basis to the revised Structural Funds. Following intense lobbying, particularly by the German Länder, the Treaty (Chapter 4) also allowed for the setting up of a Committee 'consisting of representatives of regional and local bodies, hereinafter referred to as "the Committee of the Regions" ... with advisory status'.

Members of the Committee are proposed by the Member States and appointed by a unanimous decision of the Council. Their numbers are proportional to the size of the states:

Table 4. Distribution of Seats on the Committee of the Regions

Country	Number of Seats
Belgium	12
Denmark	9
France	24
Germany	24
Greece	12
Ireland	9
Italy	24
Luxembourg	6
Netherlands	12
Portugal	12
Spain	21
United Kingdom	24
Austria*	12
Finland*	9
Sweden*	12

* *Since 1995*
Source: Committee of the Regions, Directorate for Press and Communication, February 1995.

The Maastricht Treaty laid down (Article 198c) that the 'Committee of the Regions' shall be consulted by the Council or the Commission where this Treaty so provides and in all other cases in which one of these two institutions considers it appropriate. The issues on which the COR must be consulted were: education and youth (Title VIII, art. 124); culture (Title IX, art. 128); public health (Title X, art. 129); trans-European networks; and economic and social cohesion. In addition, the COR must be informed when the Economic and Social Committee is consulted and may give an opinion where specific regional interests are involved.

In February 1995, the COR issued a Press Release in which it laid out its functions and role. It saw itself as existing to strengthen economic and social cohesion among the Member States. It also saw its setting up as a significant step in continuing the process of creating an ever closer union among the peoples of Europe, in which decisions are taken as close as possible to the citizen in accordance with the principle of subsidiarity. Thus, the COR is to help bring about *cohesion* and to promote *democracy* within the Union. The inaugural session of the Committee took place in March 1994 and saw the election of Jacques Blanc as President. Blanc is also President of the Languedoc-Roussillon Regional Council in France. The Vice-President chosen was Pasquall Maragall i Mira, the Mayor of Barcelona.

The internal administration of the COR is modelled on that of the other EU institutions. There is a Secretariat-General with a Cabinet. Within the S-G there are four Directorates (consultative work; registry, administration and finance; press and communications; and inter-institutional and external relations). The COR shares a number of services with the Economic and Social Committee. The actual work of the COR is carried out in eight Commissions and one Special Commission.

The membership, functions and role of the COR have been a considerable disappointment to many of those political actors who espouse the regionalist and federalist causes and who wish to see a federal Europe with regions having an entrenched role in the politics and policy-making of the Union. These had hoped that the Committee of the Regions might be a kind of European Senate representing sub-national levels of government while the European Parliament would represent European citizens on the basis of numerical majorities. The COR which emerged from the Maastricht Treaty was, in fact, a much tamer and less political entity. First, it is simply a consultative rather than a decision-making body. Second, its membership is open to levels of government other than regions (for example local authorities such as county councils, départements, and municipalities) as well as non-elected appointees. This mixture diminishes the importance of the region as a political force. Third, the COR shares many administrative services with the Economic and Social Committee and is, to some extent, in the shadow of the latter which has been in existence

16 Thomson Report, (Commission of the European Communities), (1973), *Report on Regional Problems of the Enlarged Community*, Brussels: CEC.

17 Thomson Report, (Commission of the European Communities), (1973), *Report on Regional Problems of the Enlarged Community*, Brussels: Commission of the European Communities.

18 Clout, Hugh. D., (1987) *op.cit.*

19 Vanhove, N., Klassen, L.H., (1987) *op.cit.* p. 461.

20 Clout, Hugh. D., (1987) *op.cit.*

21 Vanhove, N., Klassen, L.H., (1987) *op.cit.*

22 Quoted in Vanhove, N., Klassen, L.H., (1987) *op.cit.* p. 453.

23 Palmer, John., (1995), 'EU probes 'misuse' of £400 m', *The Guardian*, 10 July 1995.

24 Clout, Hugh. D., (1987) *op.cit.*

25 Marks, G., 1992. *op.cit.* See the debate between Michael Keating and Robert Leonardi: Keating, Michael, (1995), 'A comment on Robert Leonardi, 'Cohesion in the EC: Illusion or Reality?'', *West European Politics*, Vol. 18, no. 2, April: Leonardi, Robert, (1993), 'The Role of Sub - National Institutions in European Integration', in Leonardi, Robert, (editor), *The Regions and the EC: The regional response to the single market in the underdeveloped areas*, London: Frank Cass: Leonardi, Robert, (1993a), 'Cohesion in the EC: Illusion or Reality?', *West European Politics*, Vol. 16, no. 4, October: Leonardi, Robert, (1995), ' A Response to Michael Keating', *West European Politics*, Vol. 18 no. 2, April.

26 (CEC) Commission of the European Communities, (1989), *Guide to the reform of the Community's structural funds*, Luxembourg: Office for Official Publications of the European Communities. p. 11.

27 CEC., (1993), *Community Structural Funds* 1994 - 1999, Luxembourg: Office for Official Publications for the European Communities. p. 7.

28 Publisher: Luxembourg: Office for Official Publications of the European Communities.

29 CEC (1991), *op.cit.* p. 3.

30 Publisher: Luxembourg: Office for Official Publications of the European Communities.

[31] Van der Knapp, P., (1994), 'The Committee of the Regions', *Regional Politics and Policy,* Vol. 4, no. 3.

[32] Anderson, J., (1991) *op.cit.*; Borras, S. Christiansen, T. and Rodriguez-Pose, A., (1994), 'Towards a 'Europe of the Regions'? Visions and Reality from a Critical Perspective.' *Regional Politics and Policy,* Vol. 4, No.2.

[33] *European Report,* No. 2034, 19 April 1995.

[34] Marks, G., 1992, *op.cit.*

[35] Burgess, M., 1989, *op.cit.*; Loughlin, J., 1994, *op.cit.*

[36] Anderson, J., 1991, *op.cit.*

[37] Loughlin, J., 1994, *op.cit.*

[38] Milward, A., (1992), *The European Rescue of the Nation-State,* London: Routledge.

17 Transport Policy: The Role of Trans-European Networks (TENs)

DEBRA JOHNSON, COLIN TURNER

The potential importance of transport to European integration was recognized at the beginning of the Community's existence when it was accorded its own section within the Treaty of Rome (Articles 74-84[1]), the only individual sector apart from agriculture to receive this treatment. Economically significant in its own right,[2] the transport sector supports all other forms of economic activity and facilitates trade - a key consideration in the creation of a customs union and, latterly, a single market. An effective transport policy also increases competition by extending the geographical range of business and has ramifications for the environment, health and safety, regional development and relations with third countries. This chapter examines the progress which has been made towards a common transport policy and how the programme of trans-European transport networks is increasingly viewed as the means whereby the European Union (EU) can take maximum advantage of the single market.

Progress Towards a Common Transport Policy

Despite such strong reasons for pursuing an active transport policy, the first three decades of the Community's existence saw very little progress towards achievement of the transport goals of the Treaty. The emphasis was on harmonization of regulations relating to working hours, lorry weights and dimensions. These efforts achieved little but proved very time consuming. Deregulation and liberalization only started to dominate policy with the advent of the single market.

Transport was a highly regulated (i.e. protected) sector in virtually all member states. Road haulage, for example, was subject to a host of regulations, including national quotas for cross-border traffic, cabotage[3]

467

restrictions, compulsory tariffs, licensing and widely differing tax systems and rates. In aggregate, these regulations isolated and protected domestic markets and proved highly resistant to change for many years. All other transport modes were subject to similar restrictions, although specific details varied by mode. Different modal preferences, ownership structures and approaches to transport policy in member states also made it difficult to find common ground.

The stagnation in transport policy was such that, in 1982, the European Parliament took the Council of Ministers to the European Court of Justice for failing to fulfil its Treaty obligations regarding the introduction of a common transport policy. In its May 1985 ruling, the Court supported the European Parliament's position and required the Council to bring forward measures to liberalize transport services.

The Court judgement coincided with wider developments in member states and the Community which were to result in important breakthroughs in European transport policy during the following years. The 1985 White Paper *Completing the Internal Market*[4] was essentially about removing non-tariff barriers to trade within the Community. Such barriers, as shown above, were rife in the transport sector. Although it took some time, the single market programme did take hold and capture the imagination of businessmen and policymakers. To a large extent this was because the single market benefited from the spread of economic liberalism and supply-side economics, which emphasizes deregulation and liberalization, from the United States to Europe.

As a result of this seachange in attitude, the legal underpinnings of a single market in transport in the form of service liberalization had, in theory at least, been largely agreed for all modes by the single market deadline of 31 December 1992. In road haulage, the key decision was the December 1989 transitional agreement on cabotage which represented the first breakthrough, albeit limited, on cabotage restrictions in any transport sector. Once the principle of lifting such restrictions was agreed, it was only a matter of time before the task was completed, not only in road haulage but also in all other transport modes. Road haulage also experienced a gradual removal of quotas by 1 January 1993, harmonization of technical and social standards and, as a result of an agreement in June 1993, some limited fiscal harmonization.

AIRLINES

The three airline liberalization packages of 1987, 1990 and 1992 combined to grant freedom to set fares on both scheduled and charter services; to open intra-EU air routes to authorized EU operators; and to end all cabotage restrictions by April 1997 (with an additional ten year transition period for the Azores and the Greek islands). The First Package made several breakthroughs: member states were no longer able to insist that 50 per cent of the traffic on a particular route be reserved for the national airline; limited fifth freedom rights were granted enabling airlines to provide services linking points in two or more other member states; more flexible procedures for fare approval made it more difficult for member states to block proposals for lower fares and single designation provisions were removed. The Second Package extended the liberalization but made important breakthroughs of principle. The Third Package completed the task of creating a deregulated, internal civil aviation market. Licensed EU operators consequently now have access to all international routes within the EU and are more or less free to charge the fares they wish. The domestic markets of member states will also be fully open by 1997 and, following the abolition of the regulatory distinction between scheduled and chartered airlines, member states are requred to grant charter airlines access on the same basis as scheduled services.

Rail

The key development in the rail sector was Directive 91/440. This legislation required separation of management of the rail infrastructure from management of services operating on the infrastructure and the opening of access to the use of rail systems within the EU to groupings operating rail services between member states.

Sea

Although shipping was subject to international competition in deep sea trades,[5] short sea coastal shipping, which carries up to one third of freight traffic within the EU, was hampered by the persistence of cabotage restrictions. These restrictions were, with some exceptions, lifted on this trade from 1993.[6] Cabotage restrictions have also been removed in the inland waterway sector.

Transport service liberalization has not yielded immediate large-scale efficiency improvements or consumer benefits. In part, this is because measures such as the lifting of cabotage restrictions are being phased in over relatively long transition periods. However, it is clear that the removal of internal trade barriers is not, in itself, sufficient to generate the expected single market benefits of increased competition, lower fares and costs, and enhanced choice and services for passengers and freight. The continued existence of large quantities of state aid in the airline sector, for example, inhibited the creation of a genuine civil aviation market. The implementation of and compliance with single market measures is also essential for full attainment of single market benefits and is, in a number of cases, in doubt.[7]

Problems of Transport Infrastructure

Inadequacies in transport infrastructure are widely perceived as serious obstacles to achieving the full benefits of the liberalization of transport services and European integration generally. Such perceptions lie behind the birth of the 'trans-European networks' (TENs) concept which dominates many aspects of European policy debate during the mid-1990s. The TENs initiative is concerned with the creation of comprehensive, cohesive and efficient telecommunication, energy and transport infrastructure networks throughout the whole of the European Union - known as the 'dimension effect'[8]. Transport and other networks have been developed by the nation state to serve national needs and consequently, the argument goes, trans-border aspects of transport requirements have been neglected and the efficacy of the single market is endangered.

Companies and other economic operators have, via the single market, been given legal rights to operate throughout the European Union. However, the existence of physical bottlenecks, missing infrastructure links and generally inadequate links potentially makes these new rights less powerful and reduces the power of the single market to revitalize the European economy by refragmenting the market. This is not a propitious scenario: traffic growth has been strong during the last twenty five years. In addition to these long term trends, which are expected to continue, the single European market and further European integration is expected to contribute to increased intra-European Union journeys and to increased demand for infrastructure to meet that demand - the volume effect.[9]

Traffic congestion is a particular problem in the core areas of the EU and affects road transport and civil aviation in particular. In the latter case, congestion covers a range of problems, including too few landing and take-off slots, shortage of terminal and runway capacity and aircraft stands and inadequate surface access. The existence of over fifty air traffic management centres in the EU also contributes to excessive market fragmentation and rationalization and more efficient use of existing infrastructure would help overcome current problems.[10]

Inadequate infrastructure also penalizes peripheral regions. Indeed the Treaty on European Union cites trans-European networks as necessary *'to link island, landlocked and peripheral regions with the landlocked regions of the Community* '[11] - the cohesion effect.[12] The push to improve social and economic cohesion within the European Union has been an important part of the TENs programme which is based on the assumption that there is a strong direct link between levels of infrastructure and levels of economic development. Reduction of travel times between the core and periphery are intended to offset the impact of physical distances on competitiveness. Furthermore, it has always been acknowledged[13] that the benefits of the single market would not be spread equally across the European Union and part of the trans-European network role is to compensate for these perceived disadvantages.

Not only does infrastructure serve internal objectives of the European Union but it also plays an important role in delivering the external objectives of the Union. Construction of appropriate transport infrastructure facilitates trade, not simply within the European Union but also with neighbouring countries. Issues of transit through Switzerland and members of the new Euro-Mediterranean Partnership are on the third country agenda. However, the external infrastructure emphasis is firmly on links with the countries of Central and Eastern Europe (CEE). The old ties binding them politically and economically to the former Soviet Union have been broken and fundamental market-led economic restructuring is underway. This requires, among other things, improvements in the quantity and quality of CEE infrastructure, which for many years needed to face eastwards only, and to create links westward. Economic reorientation is pushing ahead: the bulk of trade of Central and Eastern European countries is now primarily with the countries of the European Union rather than the former Soviet Union and other former CMEA members.[14] Appropriate infrastructure is needed to meet the requirements of economic reform, new trade patterns and to ensure that the probable accession of a number of these states to the European Union takes place as smoothly as possible.

The EU's Response to Infrastructure Problems: The TENs Initiative

The EU response to the perceived problems of the lack of infrastructure with a European dimension is the TENs programme. However, the origins of a European infrastructure policy go back to the earliest days of the Community. The 1961 Schaus memorandum represented the Community's first attempts to establish objectives for a Common Transport Policy. Whilst concentrating mostly on the need to introduce competition into the transport sector, the Memorandum did assert that

> 'the co-ordination of communication networks ... should be carried out in the light of the future economic integration of Europe '.[15]

European Investment Bank loans were also extended to transport infrastructure projects with a Community dimension from the early 1960s.

In 1966, a formal procedure was agreed for consultation on infrastructure projects of Community importance - a step which recognized the importance of Community-wide infrastructure but which lacked teeth to initiate or take action on a Community basis. A Council Decision[16] of 1978 took European infrastructure policy a stage further: the consultation procedure was expanded and a Committee of Transport Infrastructure was set up with the power to examine 'any question concerning the development of a transport network of interest to the Community.'

The first fears about inadequate infrastructure damaging the single market were expressed most effectively by the European Round Table of Industrialists,[17] a think tank comprising the heads of several major European companies, from the mid-1980s. Similar concerns were expressed by heads of government at the 1989 Strasbourg Council which lead, in turn, to the 1990 Action Programme which contained the first systematic elaboration of the principles which have evolved into the full-blown trans-European network programme.

Through Articles 129b-d, the Maastricht Treaty transformed the Action Programme's statement of general principles into the legal basis for EU action on infrastructure in the areas of transport, telecommunications and energy. In particular, the Treaty states that through '*open* and *competitive* markets, action by the Community shall aim at promoting the *interconnection* and *interoperability* of national networks as well as access to such networks' [italics our own]. In other words, given the emphasis on openness, competitiveness and access, the trans-European network initiative is aimed at providing support to the objectives of the single market and at taking it further.

In order to achieve these objectives, the Treaty authorized the Community to take three types of action. First to establish guidelines for the sectors which set out the objectives, priorities and broad lines of TENs measures to facilitate the identification of projects of common interest. Such guidelines[18] were brought forward in the transport sector in April 1994, and amended in early 1995 to take account of the 1995 enlargement. Secondly, the Community was required to implement any measures necessary to ensure the interoperability of networks, especially regarding technical standardization. Transport Commissioner Kinnock has consequently requested a series of proposals on interoperability in various transport modes. Finally, as discussed at greater length later, the Treaty authorized the Community to support financial efforts by member states to develop projects of common interest, particularly through feasibility studies, loan guarantees or interest subsidies and set up the Cohesion Fund which can be used for transport infrastructure projects. The Treaty also required projects to be economically viable and gave the Community the green light to cooperate with third countries on the development of projects of common interest.

Subsequent to the Maastricht Treaty, TENs has become the latest 'European big idea'. In the mid 1980s, the apparently stagnant process of European integration was revitalized by the single market. As the 1992 deadline for this passed and a majority of the single market programme fell into place, the European Union suffered a crisis of confidence. European economies were in recession, a state which has never favoured integration, and economic and monetary union (EMU), the main 'big idea' candidate, became becalmed in technical disputes and concerns about the role of the nation state in an economically unified Europe. TENs complements EMU by promoting a 'European vision'.

This vision has been incorporated into a number of key policy documents. In the 1993 *Strategic Programme*,[19] TENs was identified as a major element in the campaign to make the most of the single market. The 1993 White Paper on Growth, Competitiveness, Employment also accorded TENs a significant role in solving Europe's employment and competitiveness problems. In fact, following the Maastricht Treaty, most policy documents pay obeisance to the need to develop TENs. Other examples include the 1994 Competition Report and the Fifth Periodic Report on Regional Policy.

The major transport TENs initiative subsequent to the Maastricht Treaty is the work of the Christophersen Group, an intergovernmental group which worked under the aegis of Commisioner Henning Christophersen for the purpose of identifying priority projects in the transport and energy sectors. The Group identified 14 priority transport projects (see table) and ten energy projects, priorities which were confirmed by the December 1994 Essen European Council meeting. Priority appears to have been determined not by the demands of a truly European network but by how far advanced individual projects were and by their attainability within a short period of time. The Christophersen Report also identified 21 other projects which were less well advanced and a number of much less well specified projects which are likely to move quickly up the agenda as EU enlargement to the east becomes closer.

Table 1. Christophersen Group Transport Projects with Costings

Priority projects: work begun or to begin by end of 1996

1. High-speed train/combined transport North-South	ECU Million
Berlin-Halle/Leipzig-Erfurt-Nuremberg	8430
Brenner axis: Munich Verona	12400

2. High-speed train: Paris-Brussels-Koln-Amsterdam-London	
Belgian section	3734
Dutch section	2740
German section	3950
UK section	5239

3. High-speed train South	
Madrid-Barcelona-Perpignan-Montpellier	8430
Madrid-Vitoria-Dax	4500

4. High-speed train East:	
Paris-eastern France-southern Germany	4460

5. Conventional rail/combined transport
   Betuwe line   3291

6. High-speed train/combined transport
   Lyons-Turin-Milan-Venice-Trieste   13550

7. Greek motorways: north-south; east-west   5860

8. Motorway: Lisbon-Valladolid   1070

9. Conventional rail:
   Cork-Dublin-Belfast-Larne-Stranraer   238

10. Malpensa airport, Milan   1047

11. Fixed rail/road link:
    Sweden-Denmark (Oresund)   6431

12. Rail/road: Nordic triangle   4400

13. Road: Ireland-UK-Benelux   2920

14. Rail: UK - West Coast main line   600

TOTAL   **93290**

Source: Trans-European Networks; The Group of Personal Representatives of the Heads of Government Report (The Christophersen Report)

Elements to be Incorporated into TENs Projects

The 14 priority transport projects are dominated by rail and fall into two categories: those which are designed to relieve congestion in the core of the European Union, such as the PBKAL high speed train initiative; and those which are intended to lessen the isolation of peripheral regions. Road projects also figure strongly, especially on the supplementary list of projects. Inland waterways, more important in mainland Europe than in the

UK, also figure prominently on the second list. Ports, which are already subject to intra-port competition, are absent from the TENs initiative. The only airport project to appear on the list of priority projects is Malpensa Airport, Milan - a controversial move which has given rise to a campaign within the European Parliament to get it removed from the list. The proposed new airports for Berlin and for Athens (Spata) appear on the secondary list. The biggest single TENs-related initiative which will affect the civil aviation sector is the proposed reform of the air traffic management system in Europe.

In order to achieve genuine, seamless trans-European networks, the transport sector has to confront and overcome certain challenges. First, interoperability[20] is a major target for TENs policymakers. Currently, different electric voltages, standard container dimensions and rail gauges, for example, create delays and costs at the point at which different national networks interconnect. Some of these differences can be overcome by technical means, albeit at a cost. The Commission is aware of the problem and is preparing White Paper on interoperability for different transport modes due for publication in late 1995 or early 1996. Action to harmonize standards in appropriate cases can be expected.

Secondly, whereas interoperability relates to linkages between different national networks, intermodalism[21] comes into play at the point at which passengers or freight switch from one transport mode to another. For example, freight which is carried by short sea coasters has to reach the port: access roads or the location of the nearest rail terminal or the frequency of services can also have a serious impact on the efficacy of different transport methods. Good practice in this respect can represent major improvements in the operation of networks. At Charles De Gaulle Airport in Paris, it is now possible to catch a TGV to Lille, Lyons and other important destinations. For example, it is now possible to be in Lille in just over one hour after landing in Paris. Previously it would have been necessary to take a bus or taxi into central Paris and, in the case of the former, take another bus, metro or taxi to reach the appropriate railway station to catch a slower train to Lille. Extending innovations of this kind across frontiers is obviously desirable or even necessary, but there is a problem of interoperability since the various High Speed Train technologies have been developed by national manufacturers: although there are signs of increasing alliances and joint ventures among such manufacturers, a big prize potentially still awaits the manufacturer whose technology is eventually adopted as the European norm. The interoperability directive adopts the new approach of 'essential requirements' but it is probable that, at some point, given the expense of producing multi-purpose trains and the fact that this is unnecessary for many export markets, there will be a settling around one of the technologies.

Thirdly, major transport projects need authorization. This can be a lengthy process and, given that trans-European transport networks involve two or more member states, is highly complex. The challenge is to find an appropriate balance between ensuring that all aspects of a particular project are given due consideration and that the authorization process does not impose lengthy delays on projects which are needed and which do receive the go-ahead.

Fourthly, the involvement of more than one member state in trans-European networks can raise important and complex legal issues. The Channel Tunnel, for example, required the negotiation of a treaty between the United Kingdom and France to cover adequately some of the legal issues raised by the project.

Finally, the biggest challenge facing transport TENs is finance. The sums involved are much greater than for the energy and telecommunications projects and relate to large-scale, high risk projects with long payback periods and low profitability - characteristics which make investment in transport TENs problematic for the private sector. Nevertheless, the European Commission is anxious to foster public sector-private partnerships. Without private sector participation many of the trans-European projects will not get off the ground as member states find it increasingly difficult to finance infrastructure investment from their own resources, especially if they are striving to meet the Maastricht convergence criteria on public debt and budget deficits. In view of the importance of these issues, finance is now discussed in more detail.

The Financing of Trans-European Transport Networks

The grand plans of the European Union are only as effective as its ability to raise the finance to pay for them. One of the key themes within the entire TENs initiative is that, given the declining capability and willingness of the state to invest in infrastructure, there is a clear desire to broaden the provision and finance of infrastructure to include the private sector. For economic and regulatory reasons, commercial investment has never flowed into transport infrastructure. In theory the signals sent by the market should lead to private finance coming forward. In this sense, if the Commission's plans are realized, the development of TENs within this sector represents an important watershed which could lead to a fundamental reappraisal of the role and function of transport networks within the EU economy. As a result, it is possible that the broader role of infrastructure, such as public service obligations and job creation which would not appear in a purely financial appraisal of a project, may become secondary to commercial considerations.

The Maastricht Treaty and the Financing Issue

As indicated above, Title XII of the Treaty gives the Community the right to initiate action on the development of TENs, however its capabilities in terms of financing are less clear cut. Funding for the development of infrastructure has been available from the regional funds for some time, although this was, at best, only indirectly linked to the establishment of TENs. The Maastricht Treaty created the possibility of supporting ...*the financial efforts made by the member states for projects of common interest financed by the member states...'.*[22] In particular, it opened up the prospect of support for TENs from the newly established Cohesion Fund.

Two further important points emerge from the Maastricht Treaty's provisions on financing. First, Community action is largely complementary to that of the member states, hence curtailing the Commission's scope for activism. Secondly, the need for proper assessment of economic viability of a project means that a TENs project will not be pursued for itself but because it is needed. It should not be forgotten that the development of TENs is a response to the economic need of the single market. Therefore the market alone should dictate what infrastructure is needed. Of course 'economic viability' as a term is sufficiently opaque to represent a catch-all phrase that can justify the development and support of projects on any number of grounds, apart from profitability. Accordingly, a project may be economically although not commercially viable. It is likely that European Union funding will be prioritized to those projects where market failure is greatest, notably in the peripheral states. Cohesion Fund spending is limited to those member states with GDP per capita less than 90 per cent of the Community's average - namely Spain, Portugal, Greece and Ireland. Non-cohesion countries however can apply for infrastructure funding from other sources such as the Structural Funds.

The Financing of Transport TENs beyond Maastricht

The Maastricht Treaty set the agenda for the development of TENs. The subsequent need was to ensure that the new capabilities given to the Community were utilized to achieve the set objectives. The promotion of such action was given added impetus with the emergence of TENs as one of the Commission's 'big ideas' for economic integration and renewal. The December 1992 Edinburgh and June 1993 Copenhagen European Council meetings gave greater impetus to development of these networks by giving the European Investment Bank greater room for manoeuvre and by creating the European Investment Fund (EIF).[23] Whilst these two summits addressed the problem of finance, publication of the White Paper upon Growth, Competitiveness and Employment,[24] an important milestone, raised the profile of TENs as an economic instrument. Perhaps the most important contribution of the White Paper was to highlight how far from reality these projects actually were by focusing on the immensity of the financing challenge.

The White Paper on Growth Competitiveness and Employment

A key theme in the White Paper is that it is an unrealistic strategy to rely on the market to provide all the funding needed to develop TENs in the desired fashion. Given the level of resources needed (some ECU 220 billion just up to the end of the century), the emphasis is placed upon developing private/public partnerships (PPPs) and financial engineering devices that facilitate some form of private investment. These methods are aimed at reducing the inherent risks involved in the commercial provision of infrastructure by creating a more stable and predictable financing environment.

    Whilst establishing an appropriate regulatory environment is important, the bottom line is about the public sector cushioning the financial risks borne by the private financiers. Any assistance to be provided by the public sector should, according to the White Paper, be based on the following criteria:

- financial equilibrium: put simply, no project should disregard the relative costs and benefits of its development;
- compatibility with public finance: any support from the public sector, be it national or supranational, has to be in line with existing commitments (for example the Maastricht convergence criteria);
- subsidiarity: the Community's involvement in project development is limited to those areas where action by member states or private operators is unlikely to be forthcoming.

Community funding has tended to focus upon preparatory action for the development of projects. This is largely incidental to the overall resources needed. As a result, within the White Paper the Commission sought to facilitate greater public sector support for private sector action by borrowing long term in its own right on the financial markets. Predictably, this proposal was given short shrift from the member states who believed such action was inappropriate. Many felt that the extra funds given to the European Investment Bank were sufficient. In the discussions in the aftermath of the White Paper it became apparent that the public sector's abilities, in terms of financing, were severely limited. As a consequence new ways had to be found to attract private funding into TENs: this was one of the major remits of the Christophersen Group.

The Christophersen Report and Finance

At the heart of the Christophersen report is the desire to create the conditions under which funding for TENs projects would be forthcoming. The report prioritizes, initially, some fourteen projects at a cost of over ECU 90 billion, of which approximately half would be spent up to the end of the century. The intention was to provoke the major public institutions to establish a regulatory framework that would facilitate private sector funding and offer some form of political support for the major initiatives. It is evident from the report that funding remains the key issue for the Group. Indeed by mid-1995, only three of the fourteen priority projects had full funding in place with another two, at best, being partially funded.[25]

The problem, as viewed by the group, is that funding to achieve these projects exists: it is a matter of attracting it into projects linked to the development of TENs. It seems that existing financial devices are limited in their ability to fulfil this function. In relation to the funding proposals for the ten most mature priority projects, conservative estimates assess there to be a financing gap of ECU 4 - 5 billion up to 1999 - some 16 per cent of the total required. If the anticipated private finance is not forthcoming, the financing gap could rise to as much as 40 per cent of the total cost of these projects. Whilst the breakdown of who pays what varies on a case by case basis, it is already evident that all parties are looking at the European Investment Bank to be a prime mover in developing the financial means that will entice private sector funding into these projects. The eventual size of the financing gap depends on how much the European Investment Bank contributes to the development of projects.

European Investment Bank (EIB)

The EIB has always played a fairly prominent role in the provision of finance for the development of the EU's infrastructure. As TENs have moved up the EU's agenda, member states have resisted the potential power grab by other Community institutions by raising the financing capabilities of the EIB. In general, member states see the gradual extension of the capabilities of the EIB as the appropriate supranational response to the financing problem.

Overall, the major function of the EIB is to offer long term finance to projects mainly in the peripheral areas of the EU. Over time the EIB has established a reputation for prudent investment which lends credibility to its enhanced role in the development of TENs. As the need to find a financial solution for the development of TENs became more pressing, so the EIB and the support it offers have proved flexible. For example in some instances the upper limit upon how much finance the EIB can offer as a proportion of total cost has been raised as has its ability to offer finance over longer periods. However the EIB's effectiveness will be limited due to its strategy of spreading its resources across a wide number of projects in order to limit its exposure to risk.

The Christophersen Report remains unconvinced that enhancing the capabilities of the EIB is the right solution. Commercial constraints over the quantities lent and period of lending do not appear to be able to offer the degree of resources needed to entice private sector involvement.

The Future Challenges for Finance

It is apparent that the private sector funding for projects is slow in coming forward. This situation could be due to a number of factors, notably:

- the general economic climate: the call for funding came at the depth of Europe's deepest post war recession and as the economy picks up more funding could be forthcoming;
- the general lack of experience of the private sector in financing projects of this nature: this creates a natural reticence for involvement on behalf of commercial enterprises
- current or proposed PPPs are inadequate leaving the private sector exposed to a prohibitive degree of risk.

There are clear interlinkages between these three. The short term solution would be to offer more funding from the public sector to break the vicious cycle of poor private provision. However offering more money is not the only problem. There has to be a clearer regulatory environment by, for example, harmonizing the differing priorities of the member states in the development of infrastructure. An insistence by member states on placing excessive public service commitments upon private operators would be an obvious impediment to TENs. In turn the Commission should get a firmer grip on what it can realistically achieve via the current TENs financing strategy. Despite the financing problems of the existing priority projects, the Commission has decided, as noted above, to propose another twenty one priority transport schemes raising the total cost to ECU 140 billion. Such a strategy risks rendering the TENs initiative unattainable. The Commission should draw a more distinct difference between what is needed and what is desired.

A number of challenges lie ahead in the longer term. Firstly, Community institutions need to gain experience in joint undertakings. This has to be complemented by a second factor of developing instruments that meet the financing objectives of the TENs programme more fully. There has to be greater flexibility from financing institutions to offer the right level of finance over the period required. Past experience has shown that most institutions, including the EIB and western banks, have been unwilling to offer such a commitment. A step in the right direction would be to offer, either via the member states or via the Community institutions, greater political support to TENs projects. In turn these have to be complemented by financial engineering devices that allow markets for bonds linked to the development of particular projects to emerge. Without a commitment to develop such innovative methods of finance, TENs, as an issue for transport policy, is as good as dead in the water.

The Future of Transport and TENs

Much of the EU's broader agenda (economy, competitiveness, transport, energy, telecommunications, social and economic cohesion, external relations) is being pursued through the TENs programme which cuts across many broader political and economic issues of the day. The future transport policy is therefore closely tied up with TENs and many implications of the TENs programme are only just being appreciated.

Environmental issues in particular fall into this category. TENs projects are subject to environmental impact assessment in the normal way but the whole programme requires new ways of estimating environmental impact. Evaluation of TENs from the environmental point of view requires not only a full assessment of individual projects but an assessment of the networks themselves. The Christophersen priority projects are dominated by high speed train projects. In order to estimate the impact of such projects, it is necessary to assess the impact on modal shifts: will, for example, high speed trains pull passengers and freight from the road networks; will high speed trains become competitive with flights within the European Union? The appropriate framework to answer such questions does not yet exist.

Therefore, a range of TENs related proposals and initiatives can be expected from the European Commission to facilitate achievement of the programme. Transport Commissioner Kinnock has started his five year term of office with a strong commitment to the TENs programme and has promised to bring forward a number policy initiatives within the first year or eighteen months of taking office. These include possible amendments to public procurement rules to facilitate TENs; interoperability; reform of air traffic control in Europe; internalization of external costs of project development and a strategy for the maritime industry.

The TENs initiative will also be kept under constant vigilance with projects moving up or onto the priority list. As the focus of general EU policy shifts, the role of TENs is likely to shift with it. The big challenge for the European Union in the years ahead is the political and economic integration of Central and Eastern European states into the Union. Given the poor quality of infrastructure in that region and its orientation towards the east, the strengthening of networks connecting east and west is likely to become a major priority.

As the programme unfolds, more fundamental questions are likely to be asked of TENs. Much is being asked of the programme: to improve social and economic cohesion; to boost the competitiveness of Europe's economies; to complete the single market process; to act as a factor in economic convergence in preparation for economic and monetary union; to help integrate new member states into the Union and to serve a number of external policy objectives. The realization of these ambitions from the TENs initiative relies upon the financing issue being resolved. Without a resolution of this issue, the entire TENs programme in this sector lacks credibility. The finance issue aside, there are other considerations which will test the evolution of TENs such as practical limits to mobility and access, developing infrastructure that has a practical effect on regional development and introducing a strategy for their realization that is practical. Overall the TENs initiative is in an embryonic phase and, as such, many issues are as yet unresolved. Resolving them has to be a key feature of, and challenge for, the post-Maastricht era.

Notes

[1] The Treaty required the Council to pursue a common transport policy by establishing common rules for transport passing between or through member states, to specify the conditions under which non-resident carriers may operate transport services within a member state and any other provisions deemed appropriate to achieve the objectives of the Treaty. Initially, the CTP applied only to roads, rail and inland waterways (Article 84) but ECJ decisions of 1974 and 1978 and the Nouvelles Frontières case of 1986 have made the inclusion of air and sea in the CTP incontrovertible.

[2] Transport activity accounts for 5 per cent of EU GDP, 5 per cent of EU employment, 28 per cent of EU energy consumption and 40 per cent of EU public investment (Source: European Commission, Transport in Europe, 1992).

[3] Cabotage is the reservation for a country's carriers of domestic traffic.

[4] Commission of the European Communities, *Completing the Internal Market,* Com(85) 310.

[5] Conference trades have benefited from exemptions from competition rules but such exemptions are increasingly under attack.

[6] Exemptions to Council Regulation 3577/92 on maritime cabotage included, for trades in the Mediterranean and along the coasts of Spain, Portugal and France, cruise services - extended transition period until 1 January 1995, strategic goods (oil, oil products and drinking water) - 1 January 1997, services by ships under 650 g.r.t. - 1 January 1998 and regular passenger and ferry services - 1 January 1999; for island cabotage in the Mediterranean and with regard to the Canaries, Azores and Madeira archipelagos, Ceuta and Melilla, French islands on the Atlantic coasts and French overseas departments - 1 January 1999; and for regular passenger and ferry services and services under 650 g.r.t. in Greece - 1 January 2004.

[7] For example, the difficulties experienced by non-French carriers in gaining access to Orly Airport in Paris, the key to the French domestic market, resulted in legal battles in 1994 and stalling tactics by the French authorities. Although forced to give some ground, the French Transport Ministry limited available slots at Orly to existing levels: the Ministry justified this on environmental grounds - critics argue it is a ruse designed to exclude non-French airlines. See *Agence Europe* and *Financial Times* for details.

8   The 1990 Action Programme, *Towards trans-European networks for a Community Action Programme*, Com(90) 585, identifies five main effects and requirements resulting from the development of TENs - the dimension effect; the volume effect; the quality effect; the cohesion effect; and the interoperability and interconnection requirement.

9   Ibid.

10   The existence of such a large number of ATC centres in Europe increases costs and reduces efficiency by requiring high levels of co-ordination of flights between small ATC areas - the greater the number of interfaces between controllers, the more resource intensive and the greater the scope for mistakes. The result is congestion and stacking which costs airlines money, increases pollution and the risk of accidents. Optimal flight paths are also not chosen. Europeanization should represent rationalization and greater efficiency. The land mass of the US is approximately 4 times that of the EU (12) but it makes do with about one third the amount of EU ATC centres - an important factor in the lower costs and higher productivity of US airlines.

11   Article 129b, Treaty on European Union.

12   See note 8.

13   See for instance: The Cecchini Report (1988) *The European Challenge 1992 - The Benefits of the Single Market*, p.105.

14   Poland's exports to former CMEA countries have fallen from 44 per cent of total exports in 1985 to 19 per cent in 1993 whereas exports to the EU have increased from 22 per cent to well over 50 per cent of total during the same period. Imports from CMEA fell from over half total imports in 1985 to about   15 per cent in 1993 - imports from the EU accounted for 70 per cent of total in 1993, up from 19 per cent in 1985. Such shifting trade patterns are repeated in other Central and Eastern European countries.

15   Commission of the European Communities, *Fourth General Report of the Activities of the Community* - 1961, point 137, page 148.

16   Commission of the European Communities, *Council Decision of 20 February 1978 instituting a consultation procedure and setting up a committee in the field of transport infrastructure*, OJL 54 - 25.2.78 (78/174/EC).

17   European Round Table of Industrialists, *Missing Links, Upgrading Europe's Transborder Ground Infrastructure: A Report for the Round Table of European Industrialists* (1984); *Keeping Europe Mobile* (1987); *Need for Renewing Transport Infrastructure in Europe: Proposals for Improving the Decision Making Process* (1988); *Missing*

Networks, A European Challenge, Proposals for the Renewal of Europe's Infrastructure (1991).

[18] Commission of the European Communities, *Proposal for European Parliament and Council Decision on Community Guidelines for the Development of the trans-European Transport Network*, Com (94) 106; amended by Com (95) 48.

[19] Commission of the European Communities, *Making the Most of the Internal Market: Strategic Programme*, Com (93) 632.

[20] The interoperability and interconnection requirement - see note 8.

[21] The interconnection requirement - see note 8.

[22] Paragraph one, Article 129c, *Treaty On European Union*.

[23] One of the major functions of the EIF is the provision of loan guarantees to parties involved in the development of projects linked to TENs.

[24] Commission of the European Communities, *Growth, Competitiveness, Employment, White Paper*, Com (93) 700.

[25] The priority projects that have attained full funding are Malpensa Airport, the Lisbon-Valladolid motorway and the Scotland-Ireland rail link.

18 European Industrial Policy in a Competitive Global Economy

MATTHIAS KIPPING[1]

Introduction

The Treaty on European Union gives the Community for the first time explicit competence in the area of industrial policy. According to Article 130 of the newly inserted Title XIII (Industry), 'the Community and the Member States shall ensure that the conditions necessary for the competitiveness of the Community's industries exist'. The Article's first paragraph then goes on to identify four objectives of industrial policy which consist of facilitating (a) the adjustment to structural changes, (b) business creation and development, especially of small and medium-sized enterprises (SMEs), (c) interfirm cooperation and (d) the commercial application of research results and innovations.

Industrial policy has, however, not become an exclusive domain of Community action. It remains largely in the hands of the individual Member States which are only asked to 'consult each other in liaison with the Commission and, where necessary, [...] co-ordinate their action'. The Commission itself 'may take any useful initiative to promote such co-ordination', and can also make proposals to the Council which then 'may decide on specific measures in support of action taken in the Member States'. The Community has no new fund or tool at its disposal to achieve the above mentioned objectives, but must rely on 'the policies and activities it pursues under other provisions of this Treaty'.

The cautious wording of Article 130 already suggests that it is - like many other provisions of the Maastricht Treaty - a compromise solution. In addition, the Article makes all specific Community action regarding industrial competitiveness subject to a unanimous vote in the Council which indicates that at least some member states see it as a very sensitive area. The extent of the disagreement within the Community about the purpose and the scope of industrial policy becomes even more apparent with the last sentence of Title XIII which introduces a general proviso: 'This Title shall not provide a basis for the introduction by the Community of any measure which could lead to a distortion of competition.'

Efforts to promote the competitiveness of European industry and the discussions about the best way of doing so are as old as the Community itself. And they are likely to continue in the future, especially when it comes to implementing Article 130. After giving an overview on the history of industrial policy in the Community, the following chapter will therefore attempt to:

- identify the potential 'fault lines' among the current member states with regard to the need for and extent of common action,
- give some indications about the success of similar previous efforts in Europe and elsewhere, in order to
- evaluate the opportunities and potential problems facing the European Union in the future.

Beforehand, it is important to clarify which activities fall under the general heading of industrial policy, because definitions for this term are legion.[2] Throughout this chapter three different categories will be distinguished and analyzed: the first one covers all measures involving a direct transfer of funds from the public budget to industry, like subsidies. A second group of measures are those which benefit industry without involving government expenditures. They include mainly trade and competition policy.[3] These two categories constitute industrial policy in the 'traditional' sense, since they are targeted at a limited number of sectors. The third group of measures, usually characterized as 'horizontal', comprises all government action aiming to improve the overall investment conditions, e.g. spending on infrastructure, education, training etc.

Especially with respect to the first category, the Community has obviously fewer policy instruments at its disposal than the individual member states. Not only is its budget much smaller, but it also has to use direct payments to promote, for example, efforts in R&D, whereas the national governments can resort to a wide range of measures, including tax credits, public procurement etc.[4] But even though its own possibilities are limited, the Community has the right to intervene if the actions of national governments are found to distort competition to the detriment of firms from other member states. This has actually been one of the major concerns since the origins of European economic integration.

Historical Overview and Current Status

The Treaties establishing the European Coal and Steel Community (ECSC) and the European Economic Community (EEC) signed respectively in Paris in 1951 and in Rome in 1957 clearly aimed to create equal competitive conditions for industry in all member states. Article 95 of the Treaty of Paris prohibited public subsidies for the coal and steel industries. But most national governments continuously violated these rules, especially since the 1970s when the steel market started experiencing severe downturns. Between 1981 and 1986 state aids accounted for more than 70 per cent of value added in Italian steel production and almost 60 per cent in France and the United Kingdom. Only in the Netherlands and West Germany the percentage remained below 10 per cent.[5] The Commission's attempts to make the approval of further help contingent on efforts to cut the prevailing overcapacity in Europe largely failed. Private producers have also repeatedly protested against the subsidies for the national steel industry in certain countries.[6]

State financial aid and protection also concern other declining industries such as shipbuilding or textiles. In the latter area, a GATT sponsored cartel-like agreement (the Multi-Fibre Arrangement) came into operation in 1974 and still today distorts international trade in favour of the high cost European producers.[7] Many national governments also made extensive use of the right to implement quantitative restrictions against non-EC imports, granted under certain conditions by Article 115 of the Treaty of Rome. Between 1979 and 1987 France was the clear leader with 685 accepted cases, followed by Ireland (409) and Italy (236). In addition, certain (often the same) countries negotiated voluntary export restraints or established other non-tariff barriers against foreign, namely Japanese competitors.[8] Within the framework of the Single Market Programme most of these specific national barriers disappeared, but were sometimes replaced by a joint European approach, like in the case of Japanese car imports.[9] Judging from past experience, the completion of the internal market might also increase the risk of government intervention to protect declining industries in order to prevent large-scale unemployment.

Concerning emerging industries on the other hand, until the 1980s the Community was hardly concerned with promoting common efforts to improve the international competitiveness of European firms. National governments saw this kind of pro-active industrial policy as their clear prerogative. Hopes that Euratom, also established in 1957, would provide a basis and an impetus for joint efforts in civil nuclear energy proved futile, mainly as a result of French reluctance to share its know-how with other member states.[10] In the 'strategic' sectors of the economy, the 1960s and 1970s were actually the heydays of the national champions. Many European governments (most prominently France and the United Kingdom) responded to warnings of a loss in competitiveness of the national producers by actively favouring a regrouping of these firms into a single entity (in the computer industry CII and ICL respectively) and by funding purely national efforts to catch up with rivals in other countries, especially in the United States and Japan.[11]

Early attempts to promote a closer cooperation of European firms in the area of research and development proved, therefore, largely unsuccessful. When the institutions of the ECSC, Euratom and the EEC were merged in 1967, a Directorate General for Industrial Affairs was created. But over the following decade, its proposals for joint European R&D efforts encountered a relatively low enthusiasm from the member states and individual firms, both of whom focused more on national efforts.[12] In 1971, the European Cooperation in the field of Scientific and Technical Research (COST) was established which comprised 19 countries (the current EU members, the EFTA states and Turkey). During the 1970s, it provided a framework for joint European research projects, however without its own financial resources.[13]

Things only changed in the early 1980s, when it became apparent that national efforts in computers and electronic components were insufficient to close the gap with the leading American and the rising Japanese competitors. The initiatives of Etienne Davignon, Commissioner for Industry from 1979 to 1984, finally resulted in the creation of the European Strategic Programme for Research and Development in Information Technology (ESPRIT). In 1982, the relevant ministers agreed on a pilot phase. The positive response from European IT firms and research institutes convinced the member states that these efforts were worth supporting. Phase 1 of the programme was approved in February 1984 and started with a funding of 750 million ECU in 1985. Initially planned to last five years, this budget was already fully allocated by 1987.[14]

Only pre-competitive R&D projects were eligible for support, i.e. the commercialization of marketable products based on the research results had to be several years away. In addition, the participating companies were obliged to match all EC funds. In the following years, the Community launched similar initiatives in other areas considered to be 'strategic' for the future competitiveness of European industry, including RACE (Research and Development in Advanced Communications Technologies for Europe) and BRITE (Basic Research in Industrial Technologies for Europe).[15] In 1987, all the different initiatives were integrated into a multiannual framework programme established by Article 130I of the Single European Act 9SEA). The SEA actually introduced a whole new title 'Research and Technological Development' (Articles 130f to 130q) into the EEC Treaty.

In 1994, the Community adopted its fourth framework programme running until 1998. The approved budge of 12,300 million ECU for the five year period includes 19 specific programmes, subdivided into four activities: (1) research, technological development and demonstration programmes, (2) co-operation with third countries and international organizations, (3) dissemination and optimization of results, and (4) stimulation of the training and mobility of researchers.[16] Compared to its predecessors, the fourth framework programme shows a significant increase in the overall funding. The share of research and development (including energy) in the EC budget actually increased from 2.3 per cent in 1980 to 4.1 per cent in 1993.[17] In addition, as the following table shows, the priorities of the Community's R&D spending underwent important changes over the last twenty years.

Table 1. Amount and Breakdown of Community R&D Funding (in %)[18]

Programme Period	1987-91	1990-94	1994-98
IT and telecommunications	42.2	38.6	27.4
Industrial technologies	15.7	15.4	16.1
Life sciences and technologies	9.3	12.9	12.7
Nuclear energy	19.5	11.4	10.1
Environment	5.8	9.1	8.7
Non-nuclear energy	2.3	2.7	8.1
Transport	0.0	0.0	1.9
Socio-economic research	0.0	0.0	1.4
Training and mobility of researchers	4.3	9.0	6.0
International cooperation	0.0	0.0	4.4
Dissemination of results	1.0	1.0	3.6
Total funds (Mio current ECU)	5,396	5,700[a]	12,300[a,b]

[a] The total includes the budget of the Joint Research Centre (550 Mio ECU for 1990-1994 and 600 for 1994-1998).

[b] There is an additional reserve of 700 Mio ECU to be released before 30 June 1996 under certain conditions.

While IT and telecommunications remained the largest single element and benefited from an increase in absolute terms, their percentage share fell considerably. In addition, unlike the earlier efforts which focused almost exclusively on hardware (computers and components), more emphasis has been put on the integration of information and commmunication technologies, for example in the new areas of telematics and multimedia, receiving respectively 6.9% and 2.6% of total funds. Other important changes in the focus of the common R&D policy concern the shift towards the so-called life sciences (mainly biotechnology and agricultural research) and a significant increase in funding for both environmental research and non-nuclear energies. The share of funds for nuclear energy, on the other hand, has been cut almost in half from the second to the fourth framework programme.

Many of the above changes in the Community's priorities reflect the evolution of technology and innovative activities over the last two decades. But at least partially, they are also a result of the co-decision procedure established by Article 189b of the Maastricht Treaty, which grants the European Parliament the right to shape the broad outline of the EU's science and technology policy. During the drafting of the fourth framework programme the Parliament's Committee on Research, Technological Development and Energy managed, for example, to increase the funding for renewable energies and energy conservation measures. The EP also opposed efforts to subject the Community's Joint Research Centre (JRC) to market pressure.[19] Certain member states however, especially Germany and the United Kingdom, insisted on a greater degree of competition for the institution. The compromise solution was to gradually increase the share of its activities open to competitive bidding, with a target proportion of 22 per cent.[20] The JRC actually submitted several proposals during the first round of tenders for the fourth framework programme.[21]

Other important changes in the focus of the Community's R&D policy concern the role of SMEs and the dissemination of results. ESPRIT had originally been established in close collaboration with the 12 largest European firms in the IT sector.[22] They received about 70 per cent of the funding in the pilot phase. When the programme was officially launched in 1985, already more than half of the 240 industrial participants were smaller companies.[23] SMEs in technology-intensive industries have received even more attention in recent years, partially because of the increasing emphasis put on emerging technologies.[24] The fourth framework programme also incorporates for the first time specific funds for the mobility of researchers, the dissemination of results and international cooperation. Certain observers had actually earlier identified the need to improve the exchange of information.[25] According to the Commission officials interviewed, these questions, viz. the cooperation with Eastern European countries, are very high on the agenda for the preparation of the next, the fifth framework programme.

Regardless of the recent increases however, the Community spending on R&D is still low compared to the efforts undertaken in the individual member states. As the following table shows, the planned annual budget for the 1994-1998 framework programme corresponds to less than a fifth of the money spent in recent years by the French or German governments respectively. And total Community funding still amounts to only 5 per cent of the public spending on R&D in the 12 old EU member states together.

Table 2. Annual R & D spending in the European Union[26]

	Germany	France	UK	EU 12
Domestic R& D (Mio ECU)	37,578	23,790	17,800	104,225
as % of GDP	2.53	2.36	2.12	1.96
% financed by Industry	59.5	42.5	49.7	n.a.
Govt. Expenditure (Mio ECU)	15,265	14,634	6,803	49,914
% of Public Budget	4.31	5.99	3.01	3.26

In a recent communication, the Commission has explicitly realised the predominance of the member states in R&D financing, insisting, however, on the need to co-ordinate the national efforts. Funding for the Community's research programmes has also been consistently lower than government and private spending under the umbrella of the European Research Co-ordinating Agency (Eureka). Following a suggestion from French President François Mitterand, Eureka was launched in 1985 as a response to the American Strategic Defence Initiative ('Star Wars'). Originally, it involved the EC members, the EFTA countries and Turkey.[27] Since 1992 Hungary, Russia and Slovenia joined, bringing the total membership to 23, including the European Commission.[28] Contrary to the framework programme, Eureka projects are not centrally funded. They are approved at meetings of all the members, but the participating firms have to apply to their national governments which follow quite different rules in allocating financial support.[29]

Eureka covers a whole range of technologies, in general closer to the market than the EC sponsored programmes. Among the more important projects are semi-conductors (JESSI), car navigation systems (Prometheus) and high-definition television. The HDTV programme began in 1986, involved in 1993 about 80 companies, research centres and broadcasters, and mobilised over an eight year period 730 million ECU of financial resources. To support these efforts, the European Commission adopted in 1993 an 'Action Plan for the Introduction of Advanced Television Services' with a total budget of 228 million ECU. These European initiatives proved to be largely unsuccessful. The proposed new television standard (called MAC) was contested by broadcasters and firms from the United Kingdom and Germany who would have preferred to improve the current PAL format.[30] More importantly, MAC was based on traditional analogue signals, while the technology moved rapidly towards digital transmission. When the US Federal Communication Commission decided to support the development of a digital standard, the Eureka members abandoned the original plans and, in June 1994, replaced HDTV by a new project called 'Advanced Digital Television Technologies' with a planned R&D spending of 250 million ECU through 1997.[31]

While not always successful, the Eureka projects clearly seem to have a higher profile than the Community's efforts. In addition, many of the European 'showpieces' in the high technology field (such as Airbus or Ariane) stem from inter-firm and inter-governmental cooperation rather than from EU initiatives. Within the Commission more and more criticisms were therefore voiced against the 'dispersed' nature of the Community's R&D spending. The observation that most results never reached the market provided an additional source for discontent. According to one of the officials interviewed some European firms actually see the European Commission as a separate 'buyer' for which they do contract work in addition to their own research and development.

These shortcomings apparently prompted the new Commissioner for Science and Technology, former French prime minister Edith Cresson, to look for a new focus of the Community's R&D policy. Together with her colleague Martin Bangemann, who has been in charge of industry since 1988, she decided in early 1995 to establish 'task forces' in a number of areas. They are composed of officials from the competent EU Directorates and reinforced, at times, by outside experts. Their major purpose is to help launch and prepare R&D projects of industrial interest in close collaboration with those firms or research institutions which will eventually implement and commercialize them.

Through these task forces, the Commission attempts to provide the political impetus for private initiatives in highly visible areas of research and technological development. By April 1995, six of them had been constituted concerning the car, the airplane and the train of the future, the interconnection of transport networks, educational software as well as the development of a vaccine against AIDS. Others might follow in due course. The current task forces are supposed to outline the direction of future European R&D efforts in their field by the end of 1995. At the same time, a decision should be made about the funding of possible projects. Most resources probably have to come from the budget of the fourth framework programme, viz. the 700 million ECU not yet allocated.[32]

Referring to the inclusion of industry in the decision making process, one of the EU officials interviewed characterized the approach of the task forces as 'bottom up, rather than top down'. With respect to the Commission members involved however, these efforts could also be interpreted as an attempt to conduct a more pro-active industrial policy at a European level. During her short term as prime minister in 1991/92, Edith Cresson actually tried to reinforce the traditional involvement of the French government in industrial matters. She advocated for example the merger of the consumer part of the state-owned electronics firm Thomson with the huge public nuclear research laboratory, *Commissariat à l'Energie Atomique.*[33] This plan was, however, criticized by industrialists and experts alike, and ultimately fell through. Industry Commissioner Martin Bangemann, though a member of the German liberal party (FDP) and previously Federal Minister of the Economy, is also known to be a 'microeconomic interventionist'. And the new Transport Commissioner, former Labour leader Neil Kinnock, who is associated with the work of some task forces, can certainly not be accused of having an ultra-liberal attitude.

But while a definite assessment of this new element in the EU's research and development policy seems premature at the current stage, it nevertheless appears quite unlikely that the Commission can pursue a strategy of 'picking winners' with respect to certain sectors or technologies. On the one hand, both in absolute terms and compared to the money spent by the individual member states, the Community's financial resources are clearly insufficient to provide enough support for the necessary R&D efforts (see above). In addition, and more importantly, a significant involvement of the European Commission concerning industrial matters would probably be opposed by a number of national governments.

Conflicting Views and Diverging Interests

The influence of the national governments on the Community's industrial policy remains high. As we saw above, it is one of the few areas left where unanimous voting is still required. And even those observers who see the framework programme and Eureka as proof for the increasing role of the

Commission and industrial pressure groups in the process of policy formulation in Europe, have to admit 'that changing political agendas and divergent national interests still constrain the Commission's independence within the [...] EC R&D policy network'.[34] It is, however, very difficult to gauge from official publications of the European Union where the dividing line between the advocates and the opponents of a more active industrial policy runs. EU press releases, for example, usually mention that 'certain delegations were in favour of ...' or 'objected to ...', but fail to identify their nationality. The following overview of the different beliefs regarding the role of the Community in enhancing the competitiveness of European industry is, therefore, mainly based upon public statements of some national governments and an analysis of the actual policies pursued in the major member states.

The significant differences in opinion among the EU members were highlighted by two officials of the European Commission who declared, in a recent paper, that 'as the goal of a common industrial policy appears within reach, disputes about its shape have heightened among policy-makers'.[35] According to these insiders,

> 'Two camps are violently opposed. The first is in favour of an active industrial policy leading to the creation of pan-European champions able to compete on world markets. This camp recommends a sectorally targeted approach based on a substantial increase in Community R&D support, mandatory common European standards and an accommodating merger policy. [...] The second camp is in favour of a passive industrial policy strictly limited to horizontal measures. It recommends firm adherence to market mechanisms and strong enforcement of policies that prevent the distortion of competition (control of state aids and abuses of dominant positions)'.

These authors identify France and the Southern European countries as members of the first camp, whereas the United Kingdom represents the opposite view. The French government indeed seems the leading advocate of an active Community role in industrial matters. During most of the post-war period, France has intervened significantly and repeatedly in industry, using a broad range of policy instruments. Outright nationalizations in key sectors were carried out immediately after the Second World War as well as in the early 1980s under the new socialist and communist government.[36]

Ailing state-owned enterprises or declining sectors were supported through direct subsidies and protection against foreign competition.[37]

In 1946, France invented the so-called 'indicative planning' whereby private industry agrees on a series of targets (both for production and investment) after extensive consultation with civil servants, outside experts and labour representatives.[38] Especially since the 1960s, the French government tried to promote the development of new technologies or the modernisation of infrastructures. These efforts are often driven by the state bureaucracy and usually crystallized in the so-called *'Grands Projets'*.[39] Some of these projects have been failures, Concorde or the *plan câble* for example, whereas others, such as the high-speed train TGV and the modernisation of the telephone network, obtained rather positive and sometimes quite impressive results.[40]

When the limits of purely national efforts in industrial policy became more and more obvious, French ambitions shifted towards Europe. In 1985, President François Mitterrand initiated Eureka (see above), where firms and research institutions from France continue to play a major role today.[41] The French government was apparently also a driving force behind the efforts to incorporate industrial policy into the Maastricht Treaty and subsequently deplored the fact that these had been only partially successful.[42] And in internal discussions on the European level, the French consistently advocate a more active policy of Community in industrial matters, including increased funding for the joint R&D programmes. These attitudes seem to be independent of internal political considerations, since they did not change when the centre-right parties returned to power in 1993.[43]

For a long time, the French press criticised the Commission, and especially the Directorate General IV (Competition), then under the direction of Leon Brittan, as being dominated by the 'Anglo-Saxon business culture'.[44] Within the Community, France apparently tried to isolate Britain and build a consensus around a limited deregulation, more joint efforts in R&D and increased infrastructure investments, but without much success.[45] Since the early 1980s, the United Kingdom has indeed been a front-runner of market-oriented 'laissez-faire' policies in Europe. The British government under Margaret Thatcher did nothing to defend the national industry, but encouraged the installation of Japanese transplants which created jobs in underdeveloped regions. It also interpreted the 1992 programme for the creation of a single market as an extension of its own privatization and deregulation efforts.[46]

But resistance against an active industrial policy also came from Germany. As one press comment in France noted: 'While the French are somewhat nostalgic because of successes like the TGV, Airbus or Ariane, most other countries share the German allergy against anything which could recall this sectoral interventionism'.[47] In an interview, the head of the Federal Cartel Office, Dieter Wolf, confirmed the significant differences regarding the need for, and the extent of, industrial policy between Germany and its 'romanic neighbours'. Wolf also said he was in favour of the creation of a European Cartel Office, in order to make decisions about mergers more transparent and independent from political influences.[48]

The traditional German approach towards industry since the Second World War has been the so-called '*Ordnungspolitik*' which means that the state only creates a legislative and regulatory framework, leaving the detailed economic decisions about the allocation of resources, investments etc. to the actors in the marketplace. The concept is compatible with public intervention to promote, for example, research and development as long as it does not distort competition among companies. German efforts have therefore concentrated on the creation of favourable conditions for private ·activities. Concrete policy instruments include the fostering of training and exchange of researchers or fiscal incentives for R&D investments, but stop short of promoting national champions.[49] Even too close a cooperation between firms is suspect. As the former president of the Federal Cartel Office, Wolfgang Kartte, put it: 'In a strategic alliance one or both of the partners want to assure that the other cannot have an affair with a stranger. But we cartel officials are more for free love'.[50]

The German government has, however, not always matched its free-market rhetoric with the corresponding policy. In recent years, Germany has been the EU member country which paid the largest subsidies to declining industries. In 1992, the state aids for agriculture, coal mining, the national railways, shipbuilding etc. in the Western Länder alone amounted to more than 28 billion ECU.[51] The problems have been aggravated by the economic and social consequences of German reunification. The EKO steel works in former East Germany provide a good example. In December 1993, the Commission approved a restructuring package for the company which included state subsidies and an increase in production, in spite of the significant overcapacities in Europe.[52] At the meeting of the EU ministers in charge of industry on 8 November 1994, the Commission's suggestion led to 'a broad exchange of opinions about the different aspects of the question'. Certain delegations have required 'additional clarification' from the Commission and the German delegation before making a definite decision.[53]

The disagreement about the Community's industrial policy is not confined to the different member states. The Commission itself also appears divided about the need for, and the extent, of public involvement. These divergences were highlighted in 1991 when an (apparently small) majority of its members decided to block the takeover of the Canadian aircraft producer De Havilland by France's Aérospatiale and Italy's Alenia. It was actually the EU's first and so far only complete interdiction of such an operation.[54] Shortly afterwards, Industry Commissioner Martin Bangemann publicly criticized the 'competition ayatollahs' who seemed to ignore economic realities.[55] Bangemann subsequently advocated an active role of the Community in order to improve the competitiveness of European industry.[56] His views - to no one's surprise - found a positive echo in France, but created frictions with the more liberally minded German Ministry of the Economy.[57]

There are, however, some indications that in recent years the different opinions, both among the member states and within the Commission, about the best ways to promote European industry have tended to converge. According to one of the officials interviewed, during a Council meeting in April 1994, the German representative admitted for the first time ever that a 'sensible' industrial policy and the maintenance of a competitive order did not have to be contradictory. The previous divergences between the Federal Ministry of the Economy and Bangemann have more or less disappeared. The close collaboration between the latter and Edith Cresson has already been mentioned in the context of the recently created task forces (see above). Furthermore, Bangemann has apparently now established a good working relationship with Karel Van Miert, the successor of Leon Brittan as Competition Commissioner.

In France on the other hand, the ruling elite seems to have accepted the market-oriented policies of the Community and its consequences for French industry.[58] For example in 1994 when the EU finally abandoned the European high-definition television standard MAC (see above), the criticisms were relatively limited, even though some had stylized this decision earlier as a question of 'life or death'.[59] The restrained character of this reaction becomes even more apparent when compared to the public outcry against the 'ultra-liberalism' prevailing in Brussels, which followed the Commission's decision in the De Havilland case.[60]

The French government actually complies with the current efforts to deregulate the air transport, telecommunications and energy markets in Europe, even though it shows some reluctance and insists on the need to maintain an adequate level of 'public service' in these areas.[61] But the official and semi-official declarations or publications in this sense aim not only at protecting the few remaining state monopolies, but also, and probably more importantly, at 'soothing' public opinion in France (especially the reluctant trade unions). In its published objectives for the Presidency of the European Union in the first half of 1995, the French government outlined a rather liberal credo: 'The competitiveness and the excellence of the European firms are their best assets in international competition. Their dynamism is the condition for job creation.' Accordingly, the best way to improve the position of European firms is 'to alleviate the [legal and regulatory] constraints to which they are subjected'.[62]

This evolution of the French position might have been fostered by the increasing evidence that an interventionist industrial policy is unlikely to be very successful in the globalizing economy of today.

European Industrial Policy in a Global Context

The question to what extent government involvement might be necessary, or even beneficial, for the competitiveness of industry is subject to considerable debate among researchers. Given the diversity of the empirical evidence (comparing for instance the US and the Japanese example), it seems difficult to determine which kind of public policy is best suited to assure the international success of domestic producers. In addition, the debate contains an important political dimension, since the sectors concerned are usually 'strategic' in nature, i.e. sensitive in terms of employment or national security and are therefore very often at the centre of trade disputes between the countries involved.[63]

According to neo-classical economics, public intervention is only justifiable when the working of market forces alone would not lead to the optimal allocation of resources.[64] A good example for such a 'market failure' is basic research, which would be underprovided by the private sector because of its specific characteristics: high costs relative to a very uncertain outcome in terms of marketable products, the so-called free rider problem, i.e. the fact that outsiders can easily use another company's inventions, and in some cases, like agriculture for instance, the insufficient size and financial strength of the producers. All these considerations reduce the incentives for firms to invest at a level desirable from the point of view of the whole society, thus making it necessary for the government to intervene.[65]

Neo-classical economists, on the other hand, almost unanimously condemn public subsidies, protection against foreign competition (possibly with the exception of so-called infant industries), the creation of national champions and the promotion of investments in specific sectors. Some economists, like Friedrich Hayek and Milton Friedman, oppose government intervention not only for economic reasons, but also because it violates the individuals' right for freedom. According to Hayek, the state should leave the coordination of economic activities to competition,

> 'not only because it is in most circumstances the most efficient method known, but even more because it is the only method by which our activities can be adjusted to each other without coercive or arbitrary intervention of authority'.[66]

In addition, many see the efficiency of public action as being limited by the lack of information, the pursuit of non-economic objectives or the influence of powerful industrial interest groups.[67]

From a neo-classical point of view, it seemed, however, difficult to explain the success of Japan or the Asian NICs over the last decades. Until recently the majority of observers actually attributed their performance in the global market place largely to the involvement of the government, both in promoting the exports of domestic producers and in protecting them against foreign competition.[68] Most of these authors highlighted the leading role of the Ministry of International Trade and Industry (MITI) in new technological developments. During the 1980s Europeans and Americans alike discussed the close cooperation between government and business extensively and also tried to emulate it. MITI's launch of the so-called fifth-generation computer project in 1982 for example, provided an additional impetus for the establishment of ESPRIT and led in the United States to the creation of the Microelectronics and Computer Technology Coorperation (MCC), a joint research laboratory regrouping most of the major computer and semiconductor manufacturers.[69]

This predominant opinion of the government as being crucial for the 'Japanese miracle' has, recently been challenged by a number of authors. In his lastest book on the *Competitive Advantage of Nations*, Michael Porter comes to the rescue of the neo-classical approach. In this comparative study of ten different countries, he identified four interrelated success factors, called the 'diamond', for companies in the global market place. Among them, 'intense domestic rivalry', i.e. competition in the home market, occupies the first place, because it stimulates innovation and productivity improvements.[70] And, according to Porter, 'nowhere is the role of fierce domestic rivalry more important than in Japan, where there are 112 companies competing in machine tools, 34 in semi-conductors, 25 in audio equipment, 15 in cameras [...]'.[71] He therefore categorically rejects any sectorally targeted industrial policy and sees it as the most important role for government to maintain a high level of competition in the country, especially through anti-trust laws and free trade.[72]

Similarly, in an earlier study of the Japanese computer industry and the role played in its development by the MITI, Marie Anchordoguy had concluded that the Ministry's policies 'were, for the most part, sensitive to market incentives'. She highlighted the 'substantial benefits' of inter-firm cooperation, but also stressed the fact that 'domestic competition can be crucial, especially in cases where a decision is made to buffer domestic firms temporarily from foreign competition'.[73] Contrary to Porter with his singular focus on 'domestic rivalry' however, she and most other researchers emphasize the importance of the balance between inter-firm cooperation and competition, both in domestic and export markets.[74] The Japanese success seems indeed largely determined by its unique 'enterprise system', i.e. the complex organizational arrangements between companies, company groups and banks, which enable firms to cooperate without losing their competitive edge.[75]

The completion of the internal market through the so-called 1992 Programme and the ongoing deregulation efforts show that a majority of decision-makers at the national and European level have embraced the idea according to which international competitiveness is furthered by intense competition.[76] Detailed, but still preliminary evaluations show, however, 'a weaker role for the single market than might have been expected from the textbook arguments'. In many cases, the 1992 Programme had apparently little impact on their competitive strategies. For the German machine tool producers for example, 'the most effective competitive threats had come not from within the EC but from outside with the pressure from Japan'.[77] In an interview, the head of strategic planning for a major German chemical firm pointed out that the removal of intra-Community barriers had even made it easier for non-EU competitors to penetrate the European market as a whole.

Today, most of the big firms, whether from Europe, Japan or the United States, actually develop their activities on a global scale.[78] Companies like Alcatel, Siemens, IBM or Sony do not only have assembly plants outside their home countries, but also increasingly high value-added activities, such as research and development. Already in 1982, the world's largest firms undertook about 30 per cent of their production and 12 per cent of their R&D expenditure abroad.[79] Any R&D policy at the Community level has to take these economic realities into account. In semi-conductors for example, European producers often prefer to cooperate with their technologically more advanced US or Japanese competitors. The American firm IBM, on the other hand, is a major player in Japan and in Europe, both in terms of market share and employment. It therefore participates together with Philips, Siemens and SGS Thomson in the Eureka sponsored Joint European Submicron Semiconductor Initiative (JESSI).[80]

In this context, an industrial policy which tries to promote national or European firms will fail, for example, to produce the desired effects on employment. In his study of the French telecommunications policy, Elie Cohen has illustrated the futility of the traditional government efforts in a world of multinational enterprises:

> 'Today, each time one of our diplomats lobbies in an Eastern European country on behalf of Alcatel, he contributes to create jobs in Germany, Italy or Spain, he allows the Belgians and the Germans to develop their technological capabilities and gives the French the hope to obtain dividends one day.'[81]

In his book *The Work of Nations* Robert Reich, now Labour Secretary in the Clinton Administration, had therefore advocated a new approach towards national competitiveness.[82] Since ownership and national origin of firms had become less relevant, the most important objective for public policy, so he argued, was to 'reward *any* global corporation that invests in the American work force'. The US government should invest in commercial R&D, infrastructure, education and training: 'These are the investments that distinguish one nation from another'. According to Reich, they will also help to attract foreign investment, which in turn will improve the skill base and thus lead to more investment - a truly virtuous circle.

His suggestions must also be seen as a response to the industrial policy of the previous Republican administrations which, regardless of a free-market rhetoric, had attempted to favour American big business through a weakening of anti-trust rules and regulations as well as 'voluntary' export restraints imposed on the Japanese car producers. Neither of these measures had, however, been able to slow down the penetration of imports from Japan or the other Asian NICs.[83] While following Reich's proposals to promote foreign investment in the United States, the Clinton Administration also pursues a trade policy different from its predecessors, insisting on 'reciprocity' regarding the opening of foreign markets for the US producers. To no surprise, the countries concerned, whether Japan in the case of cars or the European Union with respect to telecommunications for example, very often contest the American accusations and claims, leading more and more frequently to trade disputes.

The latest relevant communication from the European Commission, entitled 'An Industrial Competitiveness Policy for the European Union', is also a clear expression of this new trend in industrial, competition and trade policy.[84] This document clearly recognizes the fact that governments can no longer 'pick winners': 'The public authorities do not know which products tomorrow's market will demand. However, they must adapt to market trends and ensure that markets are driven by competition.' In order to improve the competitiveness of European industry, the Commission therefore advocates 'horizontal', i.e. cross-sectoral measures. The suggested practical steps are regrouped under four headings: (1) to promote intangible investments, (2) to develop industrial cooperation, (3) to ensure fair competition, and (4) to modernize the role of the public authorities.

With regard to intangible investments, the Commission suggests to give more attention to human resources in general, and vocational training in particular, very similar to the proposal made by Reich in 1990/91.[85] Under the same heading, it is also envisaged 'that research policy takes fuller account of the needs of the market', an idea which, as we have seen, already found a concrete response in the creation of the R&D task forces. Industrial cooperation, for example through the organization of 'round tables', is also on the Commission's agenda. These and similar measures to promote the exchange of information are not limited to firms based in the Community, but also include 'some of the Union's partners', for instance from Eastern and Central Europe or the Mediterranean countries. The Commission also insists on the need to continue its 'extremely active role in removing distortions of competition both inside the Union and at international level'. In doing so, it pursues, on the one hand, previous efforts to reduce state aid and intends, on the other hand, 'to identify the problems encountered by European businesses on markets in third countries'. Judging from the statements of the officials interviewed, the latter efforts could be the prelude to a more active commercial and trade policy following the American example.

In the context of globalizing economic activities, the theoretical discussion and the practical steps undertaken in Europe and the United States seem to indicate a convergence towards an industrial policy favouring investments in infrastructure and training, combined with a commercial policy trying to obtain reciprocal opening of markets. Currently, the criticisms against this combination are relatively limited. Those, mainly in France, nostalgic of a sectorally targeted industrial policy are few and their position seems untenable given the depletion of public budgets (see above). From a neo-classical point of view, Paul Krugman has rather violently criticized what he called the 'obsession' with competitiveness, prevalent within the Clinton Administration and the European Commission.[86] In his opinion, the belief that governments can improve the international position of their country's economy through infrastructure or high technology investments is based on 'careless arithmetic' and therefore at best 'misleading' and in fact quite 'dangerous'.

In his article, Krugman had affirmed that most economists saw strict regulations, high taxes and generous unemployment benefits as being responsible for the low level of job creation in the advanced capitalist economies. However, some of those who he had attacked directly contended his views and accused him in turn of carelessness with numbers.[87] It seems indeed that, at least for the moment, the advocates of a 'horizontal' industrial policy with the objective to maintain or create high-value added activities are in a clear majority, both in the United States and the European Union.

Summary and Outlook

Industrial policy has never been high on the Community's agenda. Initially, the efforts to promote national firms in the international competition were the exclusive domain of the member states. Only in the 1980s, starting with ESPRIT, more common efforts were undertaken in the area of research and development. While the funding for the European R&D framework programme has increased over the last decade, it still remains low compared to the purely national efforts or the co-operation between governments and companies in Eureka or projects such as Ariane and Airbus which, in addition, have received more public attention.

An attempt to re-focus the EU's research programme and to bring it closer to the market is currently under way with the establishment of task forces concerning a limited number of technologies with a high visibility. Given the lack of financial backing, it seems, however, rather unlikely that they would constitute the nucleus of a sectorally targeted industrial policy. Such a development would in any case be firmly opposed by a majority of member states. Especially Germany and Britain are reluctant to follow a possible French lead. The inclusion of industrial policy into the Maastricht Treaty probably has to be considered as the ultimate, but in practical terms, relatively inconsequential achievement of the French government in this area. But even in France, the advocates of an extensive public involvement in industrial matters are becoming more and more rare, discounting for the rhetoric aimed at public opinion.

There and elsewhere, most observers and government officials have actually recognized the futility of any attempts at 'picking winners' and of promoting national or Euro-champions. On the one hand, budget deficits and the rising cost of technological developments do not allow any major public funding for these efforts. On the other hand, the globalisation of economic activities would make it impossible to demonstrate a clear effect of government spending on employment in the national economy. Concerning industrial matters, public action in the European Union, very much like in the United States, is therefore limited to so-called horizontal measures, i.e. those aiming to improve infrastructure and training of the work force in order to attract private investments.

In addition, the European Commission will pursue the removal of internal barriers and distortions of competition. This objective is as old as the Community itself, but received a new impetus with the 1992 Programme for the creation of a single market. According to well-known economic logic, a higher competitive pressure should result in improved productivity and thus increase the competitiveness of European industry world-wide. Following the US example, the European Union will probably also closely monitor the opening of foreign markets to its own firms and, if necessary, ensure 'reciprocity' with a supporting commercial policy.

Given the convergence of opinions about this -rather limited- role for industrial policy, it seems unlikely that in this domain major conflicts of interest will arise among the member states. Some disagreements might be expected with regard to state aids. But since most governments will continue to support a small number of 'sensitive' industries, in the foreseeable future the Commission might be unable to enforce the strict rules laid out in the different treaties. In any case, compared for example to the Common Agricultural Policy, the Community's industrial policy will never be a major source of conflict within the European Union.

Notes

1   The author would like to thank three members of the European Commission who not only granted him an interview, but also made a number of valuable remarks on an earlier draft of this chapter. For reasons of confidentiality, they preferred to remain anonymous. Many thanks also to the referees of this volume as well as Professor Mark Casson for a number of helpful and constructive comments. The usual disclaimer applies.

2   For an overview see Phedon Nicolaides, 'Industrial Policy: the Problem of Reconciling Definitions, Intentions and Effects', in P. Nicolaides (ed.), *Industrial Policy in the European Community: A Necessary Response to Economic Integration?* Dordrecht, Martinus Nijhoff 1993, pp. 1-19.

3   Although they do not necessitate public outlays, their welfare effect on the economy as a whole might be negative, because of the costs they impose on consumers, which usually exceed the benefits accruing to producers (via higher prices) or the budget (through tariff collection).

4   Alain Bucaille and Bérold Costa de Beauregard, *Les Etats, acteurs de la concurrence industrielle. Rapport de la Direction Générale de l'Industrie sur les aides des Etats à leurs industries*, Paris, Economica 1988.

5   Damien J Neven and John Vickers, 'Public Policy Towards Industrial Restructuring: Some Issues Raised by the Internal Market Programme', in K. Cool et al. (eds.), *European Industrial Restructuring in the 1990s*, Basingstoke, Macmillan 1992, p. 178.

6   Lynden Moore, 'Developments in Trade and Trade Policy', in M. Artis and N. Lee (eds.), *The Economics of the European Union*, Oxford, Oxford University Press 1994, pp. 294-327, here pp. 304-305.

7   *Ibid.* Several authors have criticised the Community for this 'inward looking' approach which has not only harmed the outside world, but EC consumers as well, e.g. Alan L Winters, 'The European Community: A Case of Successful Integration?', in J. De Melo and A. Panagariya (eds.), *New Dimensions in Regional Integration*, Cambridge, Cambridge University Press 1993, chapter 7.

8   Neven and Vickers, 'Public Policy', pp. 169 and 172.

9   Matthias Kipping, 'Reaganomics and Wettbewerbsfähigkeit. Deutsche und europäische Lektionen aus einem amerikanischen Experiment', in

C. Jakobeit et al. (eds.), *Die USA am Beginn der neunziger Jahre*, Opladen, Leske & Budrich 1993, pp. 157-175.

[10] Ironically, France had originally required the establishment of Euratom as part of the 'package deal' leading to the Treaties of Rome, Alan S Milward, *The European Rescue of the Nation State*, London, Routledge 1992, pp. 205-211.

[11] Peter A Hall, *Governing the Economy. The Politics of State Intervention in Britain and France*, Oxford, Polity Press 1986; John Zysman *Political Strategies for Industrial Order. State, Market and Industry in France*, Berkeley, University of California Press 1977.

[12] Steven J Warnecke, 'Industrial Policy and the European Community', in S. J. Warnecke and E. N. Suleiman (eds.), *Industrial Policies in Western Europe*, New York, Praeger 1975, pp. 155-191.

[13] *Information and Technology Transfer 6/94.*

[14] Wayne Sandholtz, 'ESPRIT and the Politics of International Collective Action', *Journal of Common Market Studies* 30, No. 1 (March 1992), pp. 1-21.

[15] Margaret Sharp, 'The Single Market and European Technology Policies', in C. Freeman et al. (eds.), *Technology and the Future of Europe*, London, Pinter 1991, pp. 59-76.

[16] Decision No. 1110/94/EC, *Official Journal of the European Communities*, L126, 18 May 1994.

[17] Loukas Tsoukalis, *The New European Economy. The Politics and Economics of Integration*, 2nd rev.ed., Oxford, Oxford University Press 1993, p. 268; EC Financial Report 1993.

[18] Commission des Communautés Européennes, *Les programmes communautaires de recherche*, 3rd rev. ed., Luxembourg, Offices des publications officielles des Communautés Européennes 1992; Decision No 1110/94/EC, Annex I; own calculations.

[19] The JRC which had been established by the Treaties of Rome was initially concerned with research in the field of nuclear energy, but gradually expanded its activities into other areas, viz. the environment and climate. Today it comprises eight institutes at five different locations. One of the Commission officials interviewed   characterised the JRC as a 'remnant from the heroic days of European R&D policy'.

[20] European Parliament, 'The European Parliament and Codecision: The Fourth Framework Program', Directorate General for Research, *Working Papers*, Energy and Research Series W-11 (September 1994).

[21] Presentation of the JRC's Director-General, Jean-Pierre Contzen, to the EP's Research Committee on 24 April 1995.

22   Siemens, Nixdorf and AEG from Germany, Bull, Thomson and CGE from France, GEC, ICL and Plessey from the UK, Olivetti and Stet from Italy as well as Philips from the Netherlands.

23   Sandholtz, 'ESPRIT', pp. 15-17.

24   John Peterson, 'Technology Policy in Europe: Explaining the Framework Programme and Eureka in Theory and Practice', *Journal of Common Market Studies* 29, No. 3 (March 1991), pp. 269-290, here p. 281.

25   Margaret Sharp and Keith Pavitt, 'Technology Policy in the 1990s: Old Trends and New Realities', *Journal of Common Market Studies* 31, No. 2 (June 1993), pp. 129-151.

26   Latest available years; Commission of the European Communities, *Research and Technological Development. Achieving Coordination through Cooperation*, COM(94) 438 final, Brussels, 19 October 1994; own calculations.

27   John Peterson, *High Technology and the Competition State. An Analysis of the Eureka Initiative*, London, Routledge 1993.

28   *Eureka News*, 28, April 1995.

29   Timothy M Collins and Thomas L Doorley, *Teaming Up for the 90s. A Guide to International Joint Ventures and Strategic Alliances*, Homewood, Business One Irwin 1991, pp. 166-169.

30   Elie Cohen, *Le Colbertisme «high tech». Economie des Telecom et du Grand Projet*, Paris, Hachette 1992, pp. 307-351.

31   *Eureka News* 27, January 1995.

32   Presentation of Edith Cresson to the EP's Research Committee on 24 April 1995; Interviews.

33   *L'Usine Nouvelle*, 2 January 1992.

34   Peterson, 'Technology Policy', p. 286.

35   Pierre Buigues and André Sapir, 'Community Industrial Policies', in P. Nicolaides (ed.), '*Industrial Policy*', p. 33.

36   Jack Hayward, *The State and the Market Economy. Industrial Patriotism and Economic Intervention in France*, London, Harvester Wheatsheaf 1986. See also Hall, '*Governing the Economy*'.

37   Elie Cohen, *L'Etat brancardier. Politique du déclin industriel 1974-1984*, Paris, Calmann-Lévy 1989.

38   Stephen S Cohen, *Modern Capitalist Planning: the French Model*, 2nd., updated ed., Berkeley, University of California Press 1977.

39   François Chesnais, 'The French National System of Innovation', in R. R. Nelson (ed.), *National Innovation Systems. Comparative Analysis*, New York, Oxford University Press 1993, pp. 192-229.

40   Cohen, *Le Colbertisme*.

41   The French participated in 45 out of the 144 projects which received the Eureka 'label' in 1994 and thus constituted the single largest national group with respect to absolute numbers and the amount of funding, *Les Echos*, 27 June 1994.

42   *La Tribune*, 4 December 1991; *Les Echos*, 13 May 1992.

43   The opinion of the socialist Minister of Industry, Dominique Strauss-Kahn, and his conservative successor, Gérard Longuet, about the need for the state to promote and defend the national industry are indeed almost identical, see *Le Monde*, 23 October 1992 and *Le Nouvel Economiste*, 30 April 1993 respectively.

44   *La Tribune*, 18 October 1991.

45   *L'Usine Nouvelle*, 11 June 1992; *Le Monde*, 19 June 1992.

46   Tsoukalis, *The New European Economy*, pp. 51-52 and 61-63.

47   *Les Echos*, 2 July 1993.

48   *Handelsblatt*, 16 September 1992. A recent study of the Community's merger control mechanism has indeed highlighted the danger that industrial and national interests could prevent it from functioning effectively, Damien J Neven et al, *Merger in Daylight: The Economics and Politics of European Merger Control*, London, Centre for Economic Policy Research 1993.

49   Peter Katzenstein (ed.), *Industry and Politics in West Germany. Towards the Third Republic*, Ithaca, Cornell University Press 1989; Erhard Kantzenbach and Marisa Pfister, 'National Approaches to Technology Policy in a Globalizing World Economy - the Case of Germany and the European Union', *HWWA-Discussionpaper* 19, Hamburg, February 1995.

50   *Financial Times*, 22 April 1992.

51   Kantzenbach and Pfister, 'National Approaches', p. 9.

52   Moore, 'Developments in Trade', p. 305.

53   Press Release No. 10625/94.

54   Neven et al. *Merger in Daylight*, pp. 102-105.

55   *Financial Times*, 12 February 1992, quoted by Tsoukalis, *The New European Economy*, p. 112.

56   Martin Bangemann, *Les clés de la politique industrielle en Europe*, Paris, Les Editions d'Organisation 1992.

57 *Le Nouvel Economiste*, 29 January 1993; *Les Echos*, 2 July 1993; *Handelsblatt*, 16 September 1992.

58 Cohen, *Le Colbertisme*, pp. 301-384.

59 *Le Monde*, 13 November 1992.

60 *La Tribune*, 18 October 1991.

61 The French government made the establishment of 'public service' requirements at a European level one of its objectives during the EU Presidency in the first half of 1995, *La Lettre de Matignon*, s.d., p. 24. A very detailed development of this argument can be found for example in Christian Stoffaës (ed.), *L'Europe à l'épreuve de l'intérêt général*, Paris, Editions ASPE Europe 1994. For the latest French hesitations see *Financial Times*, 28 November 1994.

62 *La Lettre de Matignon*, s.d., p. 17.

63 Kevin P Phillips, 'U.S. Industrial Policy: Inevitable and Ineffective', *Harvard Business Review*, July-August 1992, pp. 104-112.

64 William J. Baumol, *Welfare Economics and the Theory of the State*, London 1965.

65 Kenneth J. Arrow, 'Economic Welfare and the Allocation of Resources for Invention', in *The Rate and Direction of Inventive Activity: Economic and Social Factors*, Princeton, Princeton University Press 1962, pp. 609-625; Richard R. Nelson, 'The Simple Economics of Basic Scientific Research', *Journal of Political Economy* 67 (1959), pp. 297-306.

66 Quoted by Ha-Joon Chang, *The Political Economy of Industrial Policy*, Basingstoke, Macmillan 1994, p. 14.

67 For a summary of these critical approaches *ibid.*, pp. 18-27.

68 See for example Chalmers Johnson et al. (eds.), *Politics and Productivity.The Real Story of Why Japan Works*, New York, HarperBusiness, 1989; Thomas K. McCraw (ed.), *America versus Japan*, Boston, Harvard Business School Press, 1988.

69 Collins and Doorley, *Teaming Up*, pp. 154-160.

70 Michael E. Porter, *The Competitive Advantage of Nations*, London, Macmillan 1990.

71 Michael E. Porter, 'The Competitive Advantage of Nations', *Harvard Business Review*, March-April 1990, p. 82.

72 Ibid., pp. 86-89.

73   Marie Anchordoguy, 'Mastering the Market. Japanese Government Targeting of the Computer Industry', *International Organization* 42 (Summer 1988), pp. 509-543, here pp. 532 and 539.

74   James E Vestal, *Planning for Change. Industrial Policy and Japanese Economic Development, 1945-1990*, Oxford, Clarendon Press 1993; Hiroyuki Odagiri and Akira Goto, 'The Japanese System of Innovation: Past, Present, and Future', in Nelson (ed.), *National Innovation Systems*, pp. 76-114. The Japanese producers themselves seem to have come to similar conclusions, as the following letter addressed by a Fujitsu vice-president to the company's employees in 1971 shows: 'If we only cooperate and do not compete at all, we will all slide into stagnant waters, which also would be bad. The British and French computer industries are examples of this; quoted by Anchordoguy, 'Mastering the Market', p. 527.

75   For details see W. Mark Fruin, *The Japanese Enterprise System. Competitive Strategies and Cooperative Structures*, Oxford, Clarendon Press 1992. Business historians have highlighted the importance of good inter-firm relations for a number of other countries, see in general Geoffrey Jones (ed.), *Coalitions and Collaboration in International Business*, Aldershot, Elgar 1993; for the German example of 'cooperative managerial capitalism' Alfred D Chandler, *Scale and Scope. The Dynamics of Industrial Capitalism*, Cambridge/Mass., The Belknap Press of Harvard University Press 1990; for a comparison between France and Germany, Matthias Kipping, 'Inter-Firm Relations and Industrial Policy. The French and German Steel Producers and Users in the Twentieth Century', *Business History* 38, No. 1 (January 1996), pp.1-25.

76   Michael Emerson et al., *The Economics of 1992. The EC Commission's Assessment of the Economic Effects of Completing the Internal Market*, Oxford, Oxford University Press 1988.

77   David G Mayes and Peter Hart, *The Single Market Programme as a Stimulus to Change*, Cambridge, Cambridge University Press 1994, p. 207.

78   See for the historical evolution of international business, Geoffrey Jones, *The Evolution of International Business*, London, Routledge 1996.

79   John H Dunning, 'Multinational Enterprises and the Globalization of Innovatory Capacity', *Research Policy* 23 (1994), pp. 67-88, here pp. 72-74. His detailed analysis of US patents obtained by 792 MNEs shows that research in foreign locations increased slightly over the last

decades (from 9.8% in 1969/72 to 10.6% in 1983/86). These data also reveal significant differences between countries and industries. Almost 45% of the patents granted to British companies from 1983 to 1986 for example, originated in locations outside of the UK, whereas this number was below 2% for Japanese firms. Regarding the different sectors, the percentages ranged from a maximum of 24% in food products to a minimum of 2.7% in aircraft.

[80]   Collins and Doorley, *Teaming Up*, p. 88.

[81]   Cohen, *Le Colbertisme*, p. 389.

[82]   Robert B. Reich, *The Work of Nations. Preparing Ourselves for 21st-Century Capitalism*, London, Simon & Schuster 1991; for a summary see Robert B. Reich, 'Who is us?', *Harvard Business Review*, January - February 1990, pp. 53-64.

[83]   Kipping, 'Reaganomics'.

[84]   Commission of the European Communities, *An Industrial Competitiveness Policy for the European Union*, COM(94) 319 final, Brussels, 14 September 1994, here quoted from the publication as Supplement 3/94 of the *Bulletin of the European Union*.

[85]   While the logic is similar between the Commission document and the Reich book, one of the officials interviewed who had played an important role in drafting the document denied any direct influence of the latter.

[86]   Paul Krugman, 'Competitiveness: A Dangerous Obsession', *Foreign Affairs* 73, No. 2, March/April 1994, pp. 28-44.

[87]   *Foreign Affairs*, July/August 1994, pp. 186-197.

19 The Social Security Agenda in the post-Maastricht Union

STEEN MANGEN

'Social policy is at the heart of the process of European integration'.
Social Affairs Commissioner, Padraig Flynn. Action Programme
Launch Speech, 12th April 1995.

In significant ways social security policy offers an important empirical test of
the emerging limits of EU integration. Historically, beyond narrow confines the
Rome Treaty was circumspect about the legitimacy of interventions in this field:
certainly, there was no question of a project to construct a European Welfare
State with strong redistributive goals. Although Article 117 makes explicit
reference to upward harmonization of working conditions, especially in health
and safety affairs, and Article 118 advocates closer cooperation in social
security, it was freedom of movement (Article 51) where coordination
objectives dominated and, latterly, gender equality considerations (Article 119
especially) which were the guiding principles for instigating policy. For much of
the existence of the Common Market social security policy, therefore, has been
formulated within broad and often non-contentious 'technical' objectives rather
than as specific integrating measures.

This chapter reviews policy in this sector, principally from the late
1980s with the articulation of the 'social dimension', which embodied the
Commission's new and expansionary European Social Policy. The Union
Treaty Protocol provided a still stronger focus and, albeit modestly and
constrained by the evolving interpretation of the subsidiarity principle, extended
social policy competences to areas traditionally the reserve of the nation state.
Yet, from 1993, the policy line was again being substantially revised, as
evidenced in the 1993 Social Policy Green Paper (CEC, 1993), the follow-up
1994 White Paper (CEC, 1994), both prepared by the former Commission and,
still more, in the Medium Term Social Action Programme, 1995-97 announced
by the present Commission (CEC, 1995).[1]

Social security - understood here to comprise categorical or unified
social insurance and social assistance - is too expansive for a comprehensive

review of all risks, each of which must confront a specific set of constraints. Nonetheless, what will become apparent is that new and pressing issues are swiftly emerging. To an important degree, these have stimulated a growing consensus among many key actors about the issue, since the rapid series of political and economic events have foreclosed several options for European social security and have encouraged consideration of others. Several factors are at the heart of this policy review. Apart from an electoral movement within the EU to the right, deteriorating economic trends on the eve of the achievement of the Single Market in which so much political investment had been placed with the sharp increase in unemployment rates late in 1992 sapped what little life-blood might have been left out of the 'growth means jobs' argument. In different ways, then, these kinds of events helped to forge a new agenda displacing some of the more ambitious long-term aims of the Social Charter agreed only four years earlier. The firmest indication that a substantial change in policy line was in the air, despite some of the rhetoric of the preamble, was the 1993 White Paper on Competitiveness, Growth and Employment authored by President Delors which was to have a profound impact on the subsequent articulation of the formal social policy proposals reviewed here.

Convergence Through 'Crisis'?

The degree to which there is any real convergence in the operation of social security has long been a contentious issue and is very sensitive to the particular criteria examined. Nonetheless, in broad terms, proponents of the 'logic of industrialism' support a convergence hypothesis whilst political scientists of the 'politics matter' school argue the importance of persisting differences. Although, of course, 'European' social policy is not principally made at Brussels but is the sum of decisions made at the level of the member state and below, enduring differences in welfare traditions among EU countries do not mean that there can be no common European agenda on certain important issues in social security.

As Gretschmann (1986) outlines, there has been a 'convergence of crisis' in terms of the common presenting problems with which EU governments must grapple.[2] The sharp deterioration in the state of public sector finances has been a shared feature, triggering off the inevitable rationalization and cost controls. Adverse demographic projections due to ageing populations in themselves seriously undermine the viability of current expenditure levels and call into question the current generational contract in social security. Whatever the system in operation, funding problems have been further exacerbated by high and sustained levels of long-term unemployment. There has also been deepening concern about the moral hazards presented to recipients tempted into a welfare dependency culture by relatively high decommodification rates which impose heavy burdens on contributors, stimulate tax resistance and, through high non-wage costs, critically endanger international competitiveness. Several member states have experimented by introducing benefits contingent on participation in a range of social 'reinsertion' programmes. Other shared policy constraints arise from increasing female labour market participation rates associated with the changing status of women which produce a critical impulse to renegotiate the gender contract. EU governments have also perceived the need to enhance efficiency in delivery of collective social provisions through more effective targeting and means-testing, privatization and the introduction of 'quasi-markets'.

These shared concerns are not merely episodic: they fundamentally undermine the long-established and, until the 1970s at least, more or less stable reconciliation of overarching welfare principles such as solidarity, equity, universality, equivalence and transparency. Since the 1980s a growing emphasis has been placed on designing more flexible strategies on the part of providers stressing consumer choice and participation, although these have generally meant reductions in statutory rights for recipients through a well rehearsed repertoire of cost containment measures. Nonetheless, European welfare states are still cognate with the reformed structures of the immediate post-war period. Nor have levels of funding significantly changed: only Belgium, Germany and Ireland succeeded in reducing expenditure in terms of GDP ratios in the 1980s and then only by modest amounts.[3]

There are commonalities in social security on other specific, albeit limited counts. Among the northern member states there are some common attributes in terms of coverage and rights, although organizational structures remain distinct. Moreover, social security is the major item of public expenditure: despite sustained efforts at cost control in the 1980s, by international comparison most EU states remain among the highest spenders; as Table 1 shows, the majority allocate between 25 and 30 per cent of GDP to social protection measures.

Table 1. Social Protection Expenditure as Percentage of GDP, 1991

Percentage GDP

Belgium	26.7
Denmark	29.8
France	28.7
Germany	26.6
Greece	19.5
Ireland	21.3
Italy	24.4
Luxembourg	27.5
Netherlands	32.4
Portugal	19.4
Spain	21.4
United Kingdom	24.7
EUR 12	**26.0**

Source: Eurostat (1993a) Table 3.31

However, substantial differences in social security also persist, reflecting not only the stage of economic development but also important social, political and cultural traditions among the member states. At the level of funding a salient north-south divide persists: for example, the share of GDP consumed by social protection in Portugal is only 60 per cent of that of the Netherlands and in real terms per capita expenditure on Dutch benefits is over three times more generous.[4] In terms of institutional arrangements and objectives, several authorities have identified three or even four welfare regimes - Beveridgean, Bismarckian, Nordic and Latin 'rim' - each with distinctive attributes that have been robust over time.[5] In this regard evidence is scant that the institution of the EU has had much of a convergence impact. Montanari (1993), for instance, has demonstrated that on specific criteria the then EFTA countries were closer than her sample of EU states in terms of the quality of pensions, sickness benefit and unemployment compensation.[6]

The consequences of disparities among Member States in the degree to which funding relies on heavy employer contributions has remained a critical issue in the 'social dimension' debate. In 1991 the employer contribution in

France, Italy and Spain comprised over 50 per cent of total receipts and, as such, was almost twice the UK proportion and seven times that of Denmark.[7] Several governments have been attempting to ameliorate the situation by institutionalizing partial fiscalization of social security budgets, although the proportion of tax-funding still varies by almost five-fold.   In this way the traditional distinction between the regimes of Beveridge and Bismarck is being blurred.   The 1993 Competition White Paper recommended that this strategy be accelerated as a means of loosening the connection between insurance and the labour market.   The argument espoused is that such a strategy reinforces a solidarity base for funding universal benefits whilst retaining the insurance link for risks which are employment related. This approach has also been supported by Commissioner Flynn who shared Delors' preference for an accelerated transfer of the burden of non-wage costs from employers to the state, a potential source of funding being some form of eco-tax.

For several governments limiting gross labour costs has assumed explicit priority over maintaining the quality of social protection benefits.[8] From the 1993 European Councils onwards the 'pricing jobs out' argument has been a resonant theme and advanced not only by representatives of the orthodox right. According to this view convergence is an appropriate aim only if it is oriented towards stimulating flexibility and greater deregulation of labour markets. On the other hand, convergence in terms of generosity of benefits or the instigation of minimum income guarantees could provide strong disincentives to work, especially among the marginal labour force and former skilled manual workers being forced to consider low-paid jobs in the service sector. It is further argued that the imposition of a rigidly harmonized 'social' Europe could have perverse effects on convergence and social cohesion by increasing labour costs in the poorer Member States which could produce higher unemployment there and, hence, more acute regional disparities.

From Harmonization to Convergence

The Rome Treaty was clear that social security disparities among Member States were a distortion to the operation of the free market and, as such, an important constraint to be eradicated by a gradual and voluntary evolution in the direction of an upwards, spontaneous harmonization.[9] Clearly such a process has not occurred, nor was it very likely that it would be more than a pious hope. In the intervening years there have been many disputes between the

Council of Ministers and the Commission about the long-term objectives and the appropriate level of intervention, especially in the grey areas between harmonization and coordination, the Council's position being that the prescriptions of the Rome Treaty did not require further harmonization beyond ensuring the interests of migrant labour.[10] The preference for marginality of social policy on the EU agenda has been actively pursued by certain key actors who maintain that a strongly converging social dimension is not necessary to the effective functioning of the Single European Market.

Relations between the Council and Commission on social protection issues have frequently been volatile and it is perhaps the 'most important' policy arena where a certain ingenuity has been required to arrive at accommodations of conflicting views. Reliance on the device of solemn declarations and recommendations, together with a strategy of creating networks have incrementally created precedents to intervene in particular areas regarded as strictly peripheral to EU competence. This 'purposeful opportunism' has stimulated boundary extending 'regulatory' policies at minimum cost to the Commission and, thereby, has created bridgeheads to justify more further intervention later.[11] The strategy has been that, once established, services become objects of pressure group mobilization and, therefore, at risk of incremental extension. Entryism into these policy spaces has been substantially aided by the expansionary rulings of the European Court of Justice, at least until the early 1990s.[12] Such a strategy is not without risk, for it can lull more federally-minded actors into a false sense of confidence. In this regard, the speech of Delors to the TUC in Bournemouth in 1988 is something of a high-water mark in the history of European social policy, since it clearly defined the area as one where the majority of competence in the medium-term would lie at the EU level. Thus, it became one of principal linchpins of Euro-federalism and, as such, a target of criticism from detractors.

The main instrument to advance the social policy remit was to be the 1989 Social Charter which inevitably became enmeshed in controversy. Criticisms of its limitations and lack of innovation,[13] on the one hand, and of its excesses,[14] on the other, have received a wide airing already and cannot be repeated here. Suffice it to say, that in respect of social security it does represent a modest advance on conceptualizing the EU response. By 1993 approximately 60 per cent of the accompanying Action Programme (which expired in 1994) had been adopted, although many of these measures were at the softer end of the intervention continuum.

Significantly, key directives in the Action Programme - in respect of working hours and maternity leave in particular - have been substantially watered down from the original drafts and permit extensive derogations. Crucially, given the trends in European labour markets, two 'atypical' worker directives establishing social security rights for part-time and short-term employees met with hostility from Mr Brittan and the two German commissioners and were long excluded from discussion in council.[15] Although it appeared that they were permanently deadlocked, Mr Flynn, in advance of the Green Paper, urged consideration of means to adapt social security systems to take account of the realities of the dual labour market and advocated that total tax takes from income be made more progressive in order to reduce the cost of employing the less-skilled. The 'atypical' work proposals were carried over into the new Action Programme and in a revised and stricter form, have been referred to the social partners under the Agreement on Social Policy.

Although the specificities of each social policy proposal may be contended, as the dust has settled on the 'social dimension', there appear to be signs of an overall consensus emerging among the major actors, at least, about what the policy line should not be: the aim should not be older, cruder notions of harmonization that some have argued could be an agenda for committing the European Union to an out-of-date 'conservative' model of social security. For example, UNICE[16] (the Union of Industries of the European Community, the employers' organization) developed a set of principles which are articulated in their 1991 submission on social policy and political union. Here it argued for the primacy of subsidiarity which it interpreted as entrusting key decisions to the social partners, especially with regard to insurance contributions, and allocating minimal competence to the Commission. Whilst it is now reconciled to a long-term strategy of some degree of convergence it has argued that harmonization was not a pre-requisite for the achievement of the Single European Market and, indeed, could be detrimental to the interests of the poorer states for the reasons stated earlier.

Accordingly, the approach now espoused by the principal actors is the more modest strategy of celebration of the 'acquis culturel' of each Member State by limiting EU-level legislation, preserving institutional diversity and autonomy and, through it, fostering the interchange of aspects of the best elements of each system and stimulating innovation by providing 'lessons for the homeland'. Thus, although excluded as an explicit convergence criteria for Economic and Monetary Union, an evolving policy of welfare convergence has replaced centralizing harmonization and mere coordination of existing procedures as the favoured strategy. The two principal documents are council recommendations, both concluded in 1992: the first relates to social assistance and declares that the amount of resources available to individuals should be sufficient to cover needs and protect human dignity; the second and more comprehensive on social protection measures in general recommends that the resolution of problems confronting Member States should be achieved by reliance on a set of common objectives, supplemented by review procedures and evaluation. Three overarching objectives were agreed: a guaranteed minimum level of resources; assistance with economic and social integration; and guaranteed minimum benefits for those outside the labour market.

Taken together, these recommendations break new ground. Part of their strength as a long-term strategy lies in forming an 'interface' between legislation and a mere exchange of information because they provide a code of best practice and encourage 'dovetailing' innovations.[17] Significantly, they achieve what the Social Charter could not, that is, support for a de facto income guarantee for all EU residents and not simply workers. Furthermore, the emphasis here was on subsistence rather than the contributory principle which could stimulate further developments down the path of reconciliation of insurance-funded systems, with high non-wage costs, and tax funded systems, thereby addressing the problem of the level playing field: again, Bismarck and Beveridge would be tempted into closer union. Quintin (1992) asserts that these trends, now to be reinforced as an explicit strategy, embody an emerging 'European' model of social protection.[18]

Notwithstanding the positive attributes of the two recommendations, such an assessment appears somewhat precipitate. For one, there is the ambivalent nature of the policy route adopted: recommendations do not have a formal binding status, although the ECJ has ruled that they do have legal effect and the Social Policy Green Paper refers to their 'binding character'. But there can be no doubt that the two recommendations, by accommodating the primacy of subsidiarity represent a considerable retreat from initial conceptualizations implicit in the original 'social dimension' model which would have substantially accelerated converging trends. Detractors can also point to omissions and lack of clarity. For example, the recommendations exclude considerations of organization and funding. Nor is it clear what pace or degree of convergence will be acceptable, although 'value added' is to be the guiding operational principle. Clearly the aim is not one of convergence of processes, yet convergence of outcomes in terms of specific welfare entitlements for the individual guaranteed by the EU remains far from the agenda and, in this way, the key issue of redistribution is inadequately addressed. What appears to be on offer is a convergence of collective relative rights to access to welfare which is largely to be a function of the existing order of things in the Member States, but implying that poorer countries will upgrade their protection systems: a convergence of inputs[19] - and determined, at least in part, by concerns about the possibility of widespread 'social dumping'. In a way the photograph on page 44 of the Social Policy Green Paper which accompanies the caption about convergence best demonstrates its nebulous character: it is a shot of six lanes of a motorway heading into the distance, presumably each being as equidistant in the background as in the foreground.

Considering the long-term character of this still inchoate strategy, it is inevitable that the policy thrust of convergence will wax and wane over time, as various ministers at the Council are delegated by their cabinet colleagues to support or block substantive proposals. Certainly, too much reliance on episodic assessments of policy developments will be misplaced. As stated earlier, there has been a rapid turn of events since convergence displaced the last vestiges of a harmonization strategy as the 1993 Competition White Paper clearly demonstrates. It is apparent that, if Spicker (1993) is correct in his judgement that convergence policy was initially 'directed to something very like a European welfare state' redolent of the principle of institutionalism, the Commission's line has since rapidly evolved into something more circumspect.[20]

The New Phase of European Social Policy

At the turn of the decade Berghman speculated on a range of options for social insurance in the post-1992 era.[21] These range from immobilism, through various forms of harmonization, a form of European 'social' snake to a freestanding 'thirteenth state' solution targeted at what were expected to be an elite corps of migrant workers.

Policy developments since then have become more circumscribed and have certainly moved at least a notch or two towards the more conservative end of Berghman's continuum. The sluggishness of the EU economy in the early Nineties provoked a certain rapprochement between President Delors, as a representative of the social democratic tradition, and the European right. His

Competition White Paper formalized the amended policy line: high non-wage costs had to be curbed, Social Europe had to be reconciled with the current realities of international competition in Market Europe and the threat to jobs and, finally and progressively, with Green Europe. It was a strategy that was reinforced by government heads at the last council of his presidency at Essen in 1994.

It was in this policy climate that the Green Paper on the future of European Social Policy was issued.[22] Although anticipating the sorts of policy constraints later announced in the Competition White Paper, a cautious but still largely sanguine stance was adopted in its speculations about the medium-term future and the tactic of forging policy bridgeheads was still very evident. There was an explicit goal that high standards of social protection must not be sacrificed, since they are an indispensable asset in building a competitive economy. But, inevitably there have to be welfare-fiscal-economic trade-offs negotiated within a 'forward edge' strategy of growth, effective targeting and 'flexibilization' of labour markets and welfare systems. The ultimate goal was a new alignment of relationships between the state, employers and individuals which would determine the appropriate public-private welfare mix.

However, partly as a response to the reactions the Green Paper provoked among certain member states and employer interest groups the 1994 White Paper was altogether a paler affair. The commitment to high quality social protection is reaffirmed as a quintessential element of European citizenship but it is no clearer than the Green Paper on the precise means of sustaining it. Moreover, consideration of a EU-guaranteed framework of welfare rights was put off until after the treaty revisions in 1996. What was clearest was that the next phase of European Social Policy was to rely less on major legislative expansion than on consolidation of what had already been achieved by greater effort in assuring effective implementation: there was to be 'less action, but better action'.

It was evident, then, that the 1995 Medium-Term Social Action Programme, at least in terms of expansionary legislation, would bear no comparison to its predecessor formulated as it was in more optimistic times. Predictably, the new programme provoked vehement criticism from European trades unions and the socialist group of MEPs. But it was given a cautious welcome by employer organizations, such as the CBI, and even by the Conservative Euro-sceptic Minister, Michael Portillo for, in fact, it represents a considerable capitulation to the right-of-centre position and is the product of a growing consensus among the Commission, the Council of Ministers and UNICE that the social policy of the EU for the remainder of this decade will be a more reflective search for variegated welfare solutions complementing the trend towards a complex 'post-fordist' economy: that is, one which decreasingly bears the hallmarks of a heavy industrial, mass production base but, rather, where growth is stimulated by new technology, multi-national companies and, even more so, by small and medium enterprise (SME). Gone, then, are any crude ambitions entertained by the more federally-minded to create a monolithic European welfare state or a tightly EU-supervised social insurance system in sympathy with those national schemes of the post-war genre. Rather, there are to be more post-fordist solutions celebrating flexibility, differentiation, choice and private sector options, and safeguarding the momentum for economic growth located in the SMEs. Subsidiarity will guide routine policy-making; incremental convergence of objectives replaces any notion of organizational harmonization as the long-term strategy.

Both the new President and the Social Affairs Commissioner have repeatedly stressed their strong desire to return to a single legislative basis for social policy. At least in part there is a valid argument that the new action programme is a device to placate the British position. By proposing fewer concrete measures, there is less to argue about; by suggesting few new directives there is less to opt out of. Hence, of the 22 new proposals only five are for new directives and two for amending directives, the argument being that there is no need for a huge corpus of new law. What is stressed is the need for widespread consultation and dialogue to lay the basis for a new model of European Social Policy which will retain the tradition of high quality protection but in which voluntary agreements will increasingly take precedence over measures enforced through legislation.

The document is clearest about proposals for modernization and simplification of regulations governing coordination of social security for migrants, the upgrading of EU data bases and the dissemination of intelligence. As discussed in the next section there are limited welfare advances, principally in gap-filling in intervention areas where the EU remit is already firmly established. There is to be an overarching measure in social security through a communication on its financing and an inventory of advantages that could accrue from increased cooperation among the member states. Dialogue and open debate are firmly established. For example, there is to be a European Forum on Social Policy in 1996 to address the issue of fundamental social rights. More controversially, perhaps, there will be a joint commission and parliamentary hearing to consider the possible extension of the Social Charter to embrace a more comprehensive set of rights. Finally, implementation records are to be monitored, partly through an annual report on national transposition of social directives.

The EU and Target Social Security Groups: Past Performance, Future Priorities

Migrants

The initial target group for EEC action was intra-Community migrants, through provisions to facilitate freedom of movement. Incremental consolidation of transferable coverage and extension of clientele has been the strategy adopted, especially in regulating the grey area of social assistance rights and access to discretionary benefits. It is here that the European Court of Justice has played a crucial role.[23] Meehan demonstrates how, by invoking regulation 1408/71 on the coordination of insurance benefits, plaintiffs have been able to secure key rulings supplementing inadequate insurance-based entitlements by needs-related benefits. This judgement has significantly augmented the range of exportable benefits and has had the progressive effect of blurring the distinction between social insurance and assistance to the extent that, in Meehan's judgement, discrimination against migrants in respect of almost any benefit could now be interpreted as contravening EU law. Taken in conjunction with the Court's extension of the meaning of 'social advantage' under regulation 1612/68 concerning a range of discretionary benefits for migrants and families, these rulings represent a considerable enhancement of social security rights.

Significantly, the Green Paper refers to the unresolved issue of the status of third country migrants who comprise three-quarters of all immigrant labour in the EU and it questions whether it can be justifiable to continue to exclude them from the social security guarantees of freedom of movement. However, this problem is part of the wider, more controversial issue concerning immigration and, given the current political complexion of the council of ministers, the prospects of a substantial relaxation of regulations for this group were scarcely propitious. In the event the 1995 Action Programme restricts itself to extending the provision of immediate medical care to them and, somewhat cryptically, widening coverage of other limited benefits. For the rest, during the lifetime of this programme a white paper on outstanding problems concerning freedom of movement will be published. Associated with it will be an attempt to codify the complexity or regulations in force for EU migants, including a revision of conditions for the receipt of unemployment benefit. There is also to be a draft directive on the protection of individually acquired rights in occupational and supplementary pensions. Action will be sought on the adoption of the Commission's proposal of 1991 to amend regulations on the application of social security schemes to all migrant employees, the self employed, students and civil servants. Finally, there is to be a redrafting of the problematic draft directive with regard to the rights of workers posted abroad.

Women

Both Watson and Meehan concur that within social security issues the gender dimension has been a cornerstone of policy and the one that has made most impact on any movements towards harmonization.[24] Directives were promulgated in 1979 with regard to statutory social security and 1986 for occupational schemes and for the self-employed and maternity provision, albeit with EU sanctioned derogations. One can speculate that gender remains an area where there is a certain momentum for further interventions since related issues in social security have attained more prominence, particularly with regard to, as yet, unresolved problems such as uncompensated child care and the care of the elderly, and the concentration of women in 'atypical' jobs. Thus, as the Green Paper points out there is an urgent need for more flexible and individualized means of accumulating social security rights which take into account part-time and discontinuous employment records.

Although having become more conservative in its judgements in recent years, the European Court of Justice has again fulfilled a critical function in clarifying benefit entitlements, although it has asserted that its rulings apply only to work-related situations. Celebrated judgements setting important precedents have been widely reported in the literature. They include the 1985 ruling against the British government about the exclusion of female spouses from invalid care allowance and the 1990 Barber case which established that derogation from the principle of equal treatment in statutory pensions and redundancy settlements was not permissible for company or private contracted-out schemes. In 1993 a further four test cases came before the European Court of Justice with regard to equalizing treatment in various forms of pension entitlements, in part by seeking clarification on the retrospectivity of the Barber ruling. The 1995 Action Programme announced that these rulings will be incorporated into an amendment of the relevant directive (86/378). In order to specify that equal treatment extends to all forms of occupational pensions and similar benefits. In addition, a five year equal opportunities programme was announced.

By comparison, less progress has been made on family policies relating to social protection. While the Commission has sought to establish a broad strategy on family policy through its 1989 communication which aimed to reconcile family and work commitments, significantly for both parents, if this is to be a serious field of endeavour at EU level, there is a long way to go. Some decisions enacted since the Communication scarcely provide reassuring indications of the kinds of policies likely to secure broad support. Thus, the maternity leave directive as amended on UK insistence must be regarded as something of a setback if one compares the original proposals and those agreed. Controversially carried through on qualified majority voting, the UK minister successfully argued for benefit to be based on prevailing sickness benefits rather than as a percentage of previous income, although a reduction in the qualifying employment period for receipt of the benefit to one year was conceded. The contentious draft directive on parental leave to care for young children was carried over from the old action programme into the new one. British opposition on the grounds of subsidiarity, cost and its potential impact in terms of exacerbation rather than improvement of labour market segmentation by gender has meant that the proposals have become the first collective agreement to be secured by the social partners under the agreement on Social Policy and will now go to the Council of Ministers for satisfaction by the fourteen. On the other hand the possibility raised in the Green Paper of recommending the adoption of the German model of 'baby years' for pension accreditations to acknowledge the investment of women in child care does not find a place in the Action Programme.

The current Action Programme contains proposals for progress on the reconciliation of family and working life and announces a fourth action programme on equal opportunities. Yet convergence of family policy, even as a broad strategy, will be difficult to achieve in any tangible sense because of the substantial variations among Member States with regard to objectives, especially beyond narrow pro-natalist aims. For example, social security systems as well as tax regimes in many Member States have been slow to adapt to the increasing diversity of household structures and there continues to be a preferential treatment for the two parent family, some countries perpetuating discrimination against single parent families.

Pensioners

OECD demographic projections to the year 2040 indicate that, ceteris paribus, statutory pensions expenditure as a proportion of GDP will dramatically rise substantially in the next century, with most Member States requiring to transfer more or less double the volume of their 1980 allocations after 2020.[25] But the demographic element is not the only problem. Growing numbers of men in the EU lack a complete pensions entitlement. This growing dualism adds to the serious disadvantage long accruing to many women. During the 1980s there was also extensive resort to early retirement schemes and disability pensions for the over 55 year olds. Subsequently, governments have acted to restrict access to what have been seen as too costly a provision.

Confronted by these demographic and conjunctural problems pensions policy must be rated as of quintessential importance in any serious moves towards convergence, although as stated earlier, the crucial consideration of funding is specifically excluded from the official convergence programme. Several concerns are either being negotiated or are likely to find their way on the agenda in the next phase of European social policy. Among the most pressing are early retirement, the position of women, the future role of private and occupational pensions and considerations of the means of paying for care in old age.

At the 1993 Brussels summit there was considerable consensus about the need for flexibility at the end stages of working life and for retaining older workers in the labour market, both to improve income in old age and to reduce pressures on pensions expenditure. This approach is reiterated in the Green Paper. Pre-retirement benefits currently remain outside EU regulation and the Green Paper has addressed this issue by arguing for convergence towards more flexible arrangements regarding age of full retirement and means of attractively combining partial pensions with part-time employment. It is likely that these issues will be taken up in the 'framework initiative' announced in the Action Programme which will consider the future of social protection in Europe. Although several member states have moved towards treating women as independent recipients in calculating pension entitlements, as the Green Paper confirms, there is still a substantial policy gap with regard to enabling women to obtain adequate pensions in their own right through improved child care and gender-friendly labour market provisions. Some progress in these areas can be expected in the Fourth Equal Opportunities Programme which commenced in 1996.

Private funded schemes played a relatively marginal role in most Member States, comprising only a small portion of total pensions expenditure. With the achievement of the Single European Market private pension companies can be established throughout the EU and the portable private pension could be an important source of entitlements, particularly for professional migrants. Nonetheless, certain Member States have reservations about the direction such a development should take. A draft directive on liberalization of pension fund investments has been discarded, in part because some countries feared it would encourage investment outside home markets and would circumvent their policy of requiring funds to hold a minimum portfolio in certain domestic assets. Moreover, proposals on promoting portability of personal pensions have been withdrawn because some member states, notably Germany, were concerned about their impact on national pensions systems. The issue has been referred to a working party on outstanding constraints on freedom of movement.

An urgent issue for EU resolution is the correction of the present lack of transferability of occupational pensions, given that this is an area of substantial growth in welfare states. In some Member States there is no statutory preservation of occupational pension rights on change of employment. However, it is a subject on which little progress at the EU level has been made so far. Thus, to date occupational pensions have been excluded from EU coordination. As the Green Paper concedes, this is a difficult issue given the diversity of existing schemes. The Action Programme contains a draft directive on these pensions but this will be restricted to EU cross-national migrants.

Finally, the problem of growing dependency among the 'old old' could be exacerbated for many by the fact that, as non-worker migrants, they do not enjoy automatic de jure access to social assistance.[26] Nor are specific care or attendants allowances transferable. Given the mounting crisis in the funding of care, there may be irresistible pressures on Member States to institute a solution on the lines of the 'heavy risk' care insurance of the Netherlands, Luxembourg and Germany. The current Action Programme mentions the possibility of a recommendation in this area.

The unemployed

In the mid-nineties about 12 per cent of people in the economically active age groups were registered unemployed, not far from half being long-term unemployed. To make matters worse more than four million people - especially among those under 25 years of age and concentrated in the South - have effectively never worked and, thus, do not qualify for unemployment insurance compensation.[27] Neither do many find access to a place on a training scheme or, especially for those under 18, to social assistance.

Unemployment is, thus, an enduring and seemingly insoluable problem. Yet, the Competition White Paper downplayed the clear lesson of the 1980s that 'going for growth' has had a marginal effect on reducing unemployment rates and, still more, a negligible impact on long-term rates. In any case the growth trajectory is currently not a secure option: short-term projections in the EU have not only been depressingly low but volatile. The Competition White Paper, the aim of which was to reduce the rate of unemployment by fifty per cent by the end of the century, takes up the problem that social security and employment policies are operating in ways which discourage too many people from re-entering the labour market and are limiting the potential for job creation. In short, job creation and unemployment indemnification need to be realigned: a reformulation of income support programmes for the unemployed was urged to reinforce incentives for education, retraining and more energetic job searching - all part of what has become known as the 'trampoline' approach to resolving unemployment. Beyond this, as stated earlier, there is a recognition that high non-wage costs are a constraint on employment creation.

The Action Programme is at its most timid in this critical area, although, admittedly policy effort must be interpreted within the wider context of the Competition White Paper and the Essen summit. The document is largely limited to the promise of a report on the impact of the operation of the internal market on employment and, again stressing dialogue, the creation of a European Platform to pool experiences among the member states of local endeavours at job creation. There will also be a report on national efforts at reorientating collective bargaining to programmes generating new employment.

The new poor

One of the fundamental problems in the growing trend of social exclusion since the mid-1970s has been the fact that social security systems have been largely concerned with income maintenance and have largely failed to tackle issues of social integration. Supporting such conclusions, a communication of the Commission has pointed to the quickening pace of extreme social exclusion which is associated with new poverty.[28] Despite enormous expenditures Deleeck and Van den Bosch conclude that social security in Europe has not been substantially successful in alleviating poverty except in the Benelux countries.[29] One of the principal causes is the inefficiency of targeting measures, especially for the lowest income groups. EU poverty statistics suggest that as many as fifty million people in the mid-1980s survived on resources which were below half of the prevailing national average net disposible income. This general situation is particularly acute in the South. More specifically, child poverty has been on the increase in many member states: for example, it is estimated that in Greece, Ireland, Portugal, Spain and the UK more than one in five children were included in this category.[30]

The notion of 'social exclusion', with its stress on processes by which people become marginalized through the 'insider-outsider' effects of contemporary labour markets, has been the integrating conceptualization of poverty since the instigation of the Third Poverty Programme. It is taken up in the convergence recommendation on social assistance where a guarantee of minimum income is espoused. In fact, eleven EU states already have a de jure or de facto national minimum income, with two (Italy and Spain) operating partial local or regional schemes. The exceptions are Portugal and Greece. The most ambitious Europe-wide proposal in this field came from President Delors at the 1993 Copenhagen conference on social exclusion when he suggested a European 'poverty passport' to entitle the EU's poor to a range of benefits in all Member States. The viability of such a passport carries considerable funding implications, since it would necessitate a stronger redistributive fiscal effort on the part of the EU than currently is feasible. It is for these reasons that Leibfried[31] speculates that needs-based benefits will be the most resistant to a stronger form of convergence, since in order to effect it the creation of a EU 'moral economy' would be required which would unambiguously establish European social citizenship. Besides, a passport solution would seriously aggravate existing suspicions entertained by northern states of 'regime shopping'. Several governments are worried about the uptake of social assistance by EU migrant claimants whose access to benefits has been enhanced by European Court of Justice rulings relaxing the definition of current income and the residential qualification for entitlement. The most likely policy scenario, then, has been adumbrated by Vobruba and Chassard both of whom see the way forward as a progressive convergence of the aims of existing schemes towards moderate but guaranteed minimum standards which, significantly, encourage speedy return to more flexible forms of employment.[32] Given the dimensions of these problems and the amount of previous policy effort the measures in the Action Programme are disappointing, all the more so since a proposed Fourth Poverty Programme has been abandoned and replaced by a much smaller initiative on the part of the Commission. However, there is to be a report on the range of the EU's anti-poverty activities to date as a means of specifying future concerted interventions in this field, particularly with regard to the role of the structural funds in alleviating social exclusion.

European Social Security: The Next Phase

The formulation of the 'social dimension' for Springer (1992) broke with crude assumptions of economic spillover and cleared the way for a reinterpretation of social policy which went beyond freedom of movement and, albeit hesitantly, made a step towards a citizenship model of EU welfare policy.[33] But some of the more sanguine speculations about future developments determined by episodic analyses of the sequelae of the Single European Act now need serious revision. The irrestistible redistributive pressures they foresaw in some of their policy trajectories as a result of monetary union will not now materialize in this century or, at least initially, in the next. The subsequent economic events in the post-Maastricht period have made most analysts more sober in their diagnoses of future social security scenarios. We are still a long way off the attainment of even a 'segmented' European welfare state outlined by Leibfried.[34] Indeed, Leibfried[35] more recently has expressed his concern that, given the real or imagined risks of 'social dumping', a levelling down and the gradual destabilization of the universalist welfare tradition is possible. In these circumstances there would be a danger that convergence in social security could threaten standards in the North without measurably improving entitlements in the South. Certainly, the pressures to conform to the convergence criteria for Economic and Monetary Union render this at least a possible scenario. It is not hard to find justifications for this stance. For one, no EU monies to stimulate a positive convergence of income maintenance standards were seriously discussed, still less sanctioned. Welfare regimes with all their differences in priorities and resource allocations have been left intact. The outcome is that we are a long way off any notion of a convergence of welfare rights at the level of the individual based on a common definition of need. Indeed, some southern member states have expressed opposition to such individualization, preferring regional transfers though the structural funds.[36]

What form, then, will convergence assume in the rest of the 1990s? At the EU level gap-filling, updating and upgrading are certainly on the agenda and will have some converging impact. And there may well be occasional 'landmarks', arising particularly from rulings of the European Court of Justice, whose impact will be reinforced, given the greater emphasis now to be placed on ensuring effective implementation of EU legislation. At the level of the member states the increasing reliance on partial fiscalization of national social security schemes will certainly have an important impact on convergence. There is much scope for experimentation and lesson learning profiting, for example, from French and Spanish experiences in implementing a minimum social income linked to reinsertion programmes or Germany's policy of awarding women 'baby years' in assessing pension entitlements. This is the sort of direction that the convergence recommendations encourage.

Future trends in European social security will also manifest less reassuring signs of convergence. Despite the intentions of the recommendations and the repeated commitment of the Commission to maintaining high levels of social protection, it is clear that there will be losers in the spontaneous converging tendencies now in evidence. Future social security is likely to be less firmly established on principles of social solidarity and, unless explicitly checked, a deepening welfare dualism will result. [37] In fact, Overbye has already identified such a convergence trend in respect of pensions where the insurance-assistance axis is being reinforced.[38] The current preferences for a two or three-tier social security system with a basic statutory minimum and voluntary supplementary cover may well incrementally extend beyond pensions and health where several governments are already enthusiastic promoters.

As Molle rightly identifies, appeals to social solidarity have relied on shared cultural identity expressed through nationhood.[39] Even so, such appeals are increasingly being challenged as in many member states 'particularistic' commitments gain precedence over 'universalistic' obligations which may be judged unnecessary or, indeed, undesirable in a contemporary Europe where large sectors of the population can afford to make their own arrangements.[40] Still less likely is a stronger top-down EU redistributive role likely to capture the imagination of sufficently large numbers of its citizens and, more especially, their present political representatives.

Crucially, despite incremental expansion of its remit, the European Union still has 'relatively few powers to improve national social security standards'.[41] Equally important, apart from specific sectors the EU's impact on overall national social protection policies and the systems they address appears minimal. Given the emphasis in the 1995 Action Programme on subsidiarity and the achievement of voluntary agreements, the task for the remainder of the 1990s will be to specify and operationalize a broad and long-term convergence strategy which, to a large degree, will be voluntarily implemented by individual member states; whatever form that strategy assumes the outcome will most definitely not be top-down 'Brussels' imposed commonality for

> 'a common social security system would inevitably imply a transfer of income…to less fortunate countries. Such transfers have proved feasible only when the net contributors…can identify some corresponding quid pro quo elsewhere. No such offset ..(has)..ever..(been)..discovered in…(the EU) context'.[42]

Notes

[1] CEC (1993), *European Social Policy: Options for the Union. Green Paper.* Luxembourg, Commission for the European Communities. CEC (1994), *European Social Policy - the Way Forward for the Union: A White Paper.* Does not contain a reference number. CEC (1995) *Medium Term Social Action Programme,* 1995-1997, Brussels, Commission of the European Communities, COM95/134.

[2] Gretschmann, K., (1986) 'Social Security in Transition' *International Sociology* Vol. 1, pp 223-42.

[3] Eurostat (1993b), *Social Protection Expenditure and Receipts 1980-1991,* Luxembourg: Commission of the European Communities.

[4] Author's reworking of data, Eurostat (1993a) *Basic Statistics of the Community.* Brussels: Commission of the European Communities.

[5] Esping Andersen, G., (1990) *The Three Worlds of Welfare Capitalism,* Cambridge: Polity Press. Leibried, S., (1993) 'Conceptualizing European Social Policy: The EC as Social Actor' in Hantrais, L., & Mangen, S., (eds) *The Policy-Making Process and the Social Actors,* Cross-National Research Papers, Third Series, pp 5-14.

[6] Montanari, I., (1995), 'Harmonization of Social Policies and Social Regulation in the EU' *European Journal of Political Research* Vol. 7. pp. 21-45.

[7] Eurostat (1993a), *op.cit.*

[8] Pfaller, A., Gough, I., and Therborn, G., (1991) 'Welfare Statism and International Competition' in Pfaller, A, Gough, I., and Therborn, G. (eds) *Can the Welfare State Compete?* Basingstoke: Macmillan.

[9] Montanari, I., (1993). *op.cit.*

[10] Molle, W., (1990), *The Economics of European Integration,* Aldershot: Dartmouth.

[11] Cram, L., (1993) 'Calling the Tune without Paying the Piper?: Social Policy Regulation in the Role of the Commission' *Policy and Politics* Vol. 21 pp 135-146.

[12] Bradshaw, J., (1993) 'Developments in Social Security Policy' in Jones, C., (ed.) *New Perspectives on the Welfare State in Europe,* London: Routledge.

13   Kleinman, M., and Piachaud, D., (1993), 'European Social Policy: Conceptions and Choices' *Journal of European Social Policy*, Vol. 3. pp. 1-19.

14   Roberts, B., (1992), 'The Social Charter' in Minford, P. (ed.) *The Cost of Europe*, Manchester: Manchester University Press.

15   EIRR (1992), 'The Social Charter: State of Play'. *European Industrial Relations Review*, Vol. 227, pp. 25-31.

16   UNICE (1991) *Submission to the Inter-governmental Conference on Political Union: Special Considerations as regards Social Policy.* Brussels, 18 March 1991.

17   Chassard, Y., (1992) 'The Convergence of Social Protection Objectives and Policies: A New Approach' in Social Europe: The Convergence of Social Protection Objectives and Policies, Supplement 5/92, Brussels: Commission of the European Communities, pp. 13-20.

18   Quintin, O., (1992) 'The Convergence of Social Protection Objectives and Policies: A Contribution to Solidarity in Europe.' *Social Europe,* Supplement 5/92. pp. 9-12. Brussels: Commission of the European Communities.

19   Le Grand, J., (1992), 'Some Implications of 1992 and Beyond for Social Security in Europe', in *Income Security in Britain: A Research Agenda for the next Ten Years.* Swindon: Economic and Research Council.

20   Spicker, P., (1993), 'Can European Social Policy be Universalist?' *Social Policy Review.* No. 5, pp. 207-26.

21   Berghmann, J., (1990), 'The Implications of 1992 for Social Policy: A Selective Critique of Social Insurance Protection' in Mangen, S., Hantrais, L., and O'Brien, M. (Eds) *The Implications of 1992 for Social Insurance.* Cross-national Research Papers, 2nd Series, pp. 9-17.

22   CEC (1993). *op.cit.*

23   Watson, P., (1993), 'Social Security' in Gold, M. (ed) *The Social Dimension: Employment Policy in the European Community* Basingstoke: Macmillan.

24   Watson, P., (1993) *op.cit.* and Meehan, E. (1993) *Citizenship and the European Community* London:Sage.

25   OECD, (1988), *Reforming Public Pensions* Paris: Organization for Economic Cooperation and Development.

26   Keithley, J., (1991), 'Social Security in a Single European Market' in Room, G., (ed.), *Towards a European Welfare State,* Bristol: SAUS.

27   COMDOC (1992), *Towards a Europe of Solidarity: Intensifying the Fight against Social Exclusion, Fostering Integration,* Communication from the Commission. Brussels: Commission of the European Communities.

28   COMDOC (1992), *op.cit.*

29   Deleeck, H. & van den Bosch, K. (1992), 'Poverty and the Adequacy of Social Security in Europe: A Comparative Analysis' *Journal of European Social Policy* 2, pp. 107-20.

30   CEC (1991), *Financial Report of the Second European Poverty Programme, 1985-1989.* COM(91) 29 final, Brussels: Commission of the European Communities.

31   Leibfried, S., (1989), 'Income Transfers and Poverty Policy in EEC perspective', paper presented to the EEC Poverty Seminar, Florence, September 1989.

32   Voruba, G., (1991) 'The Future of Work and Security' in Room, G., (ed.) *Towards a European Welfare State in Bristol: SAUS.* Chassard, Y., (1992). *op.cit.*

33   Springer, B., (1992), *The Social Dimension of 1992: Europe faces a new EC.* New York: Praeger.

34   Leibfried, S., (1989), *op.cit.*

35   Leibfried, S., (1993), *op.cit.*

36   Majone, G., (1993), 'The EC between Social Policy and Social Regulation' *Journal of Common Market Studies,* Vol. 31. pp. 153-70.

37   Abrahamson, P. (1992), 'Welfare Pluralism: Towards a new Consensus for European Social Policy' in Hantrais, L., O'Brien, M., and Mangen, S., (eds) *The Mixed Economy of Welfare,* Cross-National Research Papers, 2nd Series, pp. 5-22.

38   Overbye, E., (1993), 'Convergence in Policy Outcomes: The Development of Social Security in European and Anglo-Saxon Counties'. Paper presented at the International Sociological Association Conference on Comparative Research on the Welfare State in Transition, University of Oxford, 9 - 12 September 1993.

39   Molle, W., (1990). *op.cit.*

40   Spicker, P., (1993). *op.cit.*

41 Watson, P., (1993) *op.cit.* p. 170.

42 Nevin, E., (1990) *The Economics of Europe*, p. 241. Basingstoke: Macmillan.

20 Energy Policy in the European Community

THOMAS WEYMAN-JONES

Introduction

There has never been a Common Energy Policy in the European Community (EC) in the sense of common policies in agriculture or transport, despite the origins of the European Community in the European Coal and Steel Community and Euratom half a century earlier. Nevertheless energy issues have played a critical role in the evolution of the Community and the shaping of its policies. The European Commission has a specialized Energy Directorate, DG XVII, and this establishes and monitors a set of energy policy objectives, publishes detailed energy statistics and forecasts and suggests guidelines for national policy making. These include a framework for rational pricing of energy and an oil stockpiling programme. The Commission has frequently discussed ad valorem taxes for example to discourage oil imports or more recently to discourage energy consumption or use of fossil fuels for environmental reasons, but policy decisions in this area are still the province of the individual member states. Another important policy issue concerns the regulation and integration of the public energy utilities in the member states and how this fits into the context of the Community's competition policy.

This chapter begins by describing the broad issues underlying current energy policy concerns (section 2) and then examines the supply and demand balance in the EC's energy sources (section 3). Section 4 examines external shocks and individual country responses, before we move on to two important policy issues: environmental aspects of energy consumption (section 5), energy utility regulation and the single market (section 6). This last topic contains two related European policy problems: the breakdown of the barriers to intra European trade in energy and third party access to the EC's energy delivery networks. Finally Section 7 summarizes and concludes the discussion.

Broad Energy Policy Issues

In discussing energy policy in the context of the EC in the 1990s certain themes continually recur. We can group these into external and internal factors. External factors are dominated by the international price of oil. This price has for decades represented the marginal cost of energy to the EC as a whole since the Community is not self-sufficient in its own fuel sources, and oil is the principal fuel in international energy trade. Historically we can think of three broad periods in the evolution of policy that coincide with structural shifts in the trend of oil prices:

1.   pre 1974: cheap oil accompanied by a policy of indigenous fuel (chiefly coal) protectionism

2.   1974-84: the adjustment to high oil prices and the importance of energy conservation and security

3.   post 1985: the collapse of oil prices and the preoccupation with the environmental and competitive aspects of energy markets.

In simplistic terms, we can say that when oil prices are high the EC is concerned with reducing its energy consumption per unit of gross domestic product, and when oil prices are low it can turn to focus on any other pressing energy policy issues. In the early 1990s, the EC was in the middle of a low oil price phase.

A second but less important external factor is the EC's relationship with the countries of Eastern Europe, whose economies are emerging from decades of central planning in which market mechanisms and individualistic incentives have been absent. Even here, the link between the EC and the new democracies of Eastern Europe is conditioned by the price of oil and its substitute in energy trade, natural gas. This is because the old USSR, now the new Russia, was the dominant supplier of oil to these countries and is the largest supplier of natural gas to the EC. Russia's energy pricing policy has changed in the political transition to reflect movements in international fuel prices with consequent changes in its relationship with its previous Comecon partners. The most notable consequence for the Community when the Communist Party began to lose its central control of many of the nations of Eastern Europe was the integration of the former German Democratic Republic with the Federal Republic of Germany. The Community has taken on a large role in the process to liberalize markets in the other countries of Central and Eastern Europe, and this includes work in the area of energy policy as described by the EC Commission in 1993.[1] Technical assistance and budgetary assistance has been provided to improve the efficiency, and the environmental performance of the energy utilities in these countries, as well as to encourage the use of rational energy pricing. The whole package has come under the heading of the European Energy Charter and this is designed to facilitate the large investment programmes needed in those countries if modernization is to succeed. The recipient countries have had only a mixed success in achieving the changeover to market based economies, partly because the distributional consequences of the price restructuring required to reflect demand and supply imbalances has been underestimated. The change is likely to take many years and will provide a continuing area of policy tension for the Community.

However it is internal factors which come to the fore in such low oil price phases, which characterized the early 1990s. The two broad issues that came to dominate the energy policy debate in Europe after the collapse of oil prices at the end of the 1980s concern the environment and the structure of energy markets. Concern for the environment has become a world wide issue and the EC Commission has been at the fore in suggesting polices to cope with environmental externalities, most especially in the shift from the use of centrally determined emission limits to the use of market based mechanisms such as energy and carbon taxes and tradable emission permits. Concern for the competitive structure of energy markets arose both from the EC's commitment to the idea of a single market and from the fact that many member states began to deregulate their previously state dominated energy markets. Amongst the leaders in this was the UK which privatized previously state owned energy network industries under a system of incentive based regulation. Fostering trade between privately (i.e. investor) owned energy networks led the EC Commission to consider the problem of third party access to monopolized markets, which meant a significant link for the first time between the Community's competition policy, which is embodied in the Rome and Maastricht Treaties, and its energy policy which is not mentioned in the Treaties. The Commission was not able to include an energy policy chapter in the Maastricht Treaty, chiefly because member states have pursued independent policies in relation to their own fuel industries. This does not mean Maastricht has had no impact on energy policy issues. Article 129 of the Treaty requires that the Community should contribute to the establishment and development of Trans European Networks (TENs) in the areas of transport, telecommunications and energy. Access to such networks is a primary requirement of the internal market in energy and the access issue has been a critical component of EC discussion about energy policy. I return to this topic below. In a broader perspective, Commission official Jacques Michoux noted that the possibility of including an energy policy chapter in the 1996 revision of the Maastricht Treaty is conditional on the development of much more common ground concerning the objectives and focus of energy policy in member states.[2]

In describing the Commission's view of 'the central pillars' of energy policy Michoux emphasized;

(i)   the recognition of the global nature of energy markets,

(ii)   the application of the market principle, viz. that energy is a commodity and that the internal market ideas especially as related to networks should have a dominant role in energy policy,

(iii)   the relationship between energy and the environment noting that decisions to reduce emissions of greenhouse gases would have to be taken at the international level,

(iv)   the expectation of consumers that the quality of supply service and reliability should continue to be very high - in other words that security of supply could not be ignored.

We see below that these ideas are beginning to characterize energy policy initiatives in the Europe of the 1990s.

The European Energy Balance

Table 1 is an energy balance table for the twelve member states of the EC in 1992 constructed from data published by the Statistical Office of the European Communities.[3] It   includes data for the whole of the unified German economy.

Table 1. Energy Balance Table for the European Community, EUR12 year: 1992, units: million tonnes of oil equivalent (mtoe)

Source/end use	Solid Fuels	Oil	Natural Gas	Electricity	Total
1. primary production	174	120	146	185	625
2. net imports	91	450	88	1	630
3. inland energy consumption (excluding bunkers)	256	535	229	187	1207
4. fuel input in electricity	175	46	35	4	260
5.conversion loss					165
6. final energy consumption of which:	58	382	192	150	782
7. industry	42	43	79	62	226
8. transport	0	242	0	4	246
9. tertiary-domestic	16	97	113	84	310

Source: Eurostat

The structure of the table can be described quite simply. Rows 1 and 2 represent the supply of primary energy to the European Community, split almost equally between the EC's own production and its net imports. As a comparison the share of net imports before the first oil shock of 1973 was about 64 per cent and ten years later in 1983 had fallen to 42 per cent, before rising back to the present figure of about 50 per cent.[4]

The EC's own energy sources are well diversified amongst solid fuels (deep mined black and brown coal), North Sea oil, natural gas production and primary electricity. The entry for primary electricity in row 1 represents the amount of fossil fuel in oil equivalent tonnes that would have to be burnt in order to generate the amount of electricity actually available from nuclear power, geothermal and hydroelectric sources and renewable sources. Nuclear power now accounts for 90 per cent of this primary electricity production.

The amount of primary energy (after subtracting that used in marine bunkers) that is available for consumption in the Community is shown in row 3 of table 1. However, not all of this primary energy is consumed directly, since producers' and consumers' wants necessitate not primary energy but secondary energy, i.e. energy in a form usable in appliances, manufacturing plant and equipment, and this requires that some of the primary energy is transformed into electricity and refined oils. Row 4 shows the amount of primary energy used as input into electricity generation. (The entry under electricity in row 4 simply repeats the amount of renewable energy already included in row 1.) As part of the conversion process from primary to secondary energy, 165 mtoe (row 5) are lost as waste heat reflecting the overall efficiency of energy conversion processes used in the member states. Reading down the total column, the basic arithmetic of the table is as follows:

$$\text{row } 1 + \text{row } 2 - \text{marine bunkers} = \text{row } 3$$
$$\text{row } 3 - \text{row } 4 - \text{row } 5 = \text{row } 6$$
$$\text{row } 6 = \text{row } 7 + \text{row } 8 + \text{row } 9$$

From rows 6 and 8 we can see that oil retains the major share of the EC's energy market at 49 per cent and that 63 per cent of this oil is accounted for by transport usage. In industry and residential markets the portfolio of energy sources is well diversified, although natural gas has become the most used fuel source in both cases with 35 per cent of the industrial energy market and 36 per cent of the tertiary-domestic market.

Surrey sums up the position by noting that the high level of oil import dependence is a major restraint on the Community's freedom of action in energy policy.[5] This is coupled with a wide diversity of fuel use in different member states making agreement on common energy policy objectives difficult to achieve.

EC Responses to the World Price of Oil

For more than forty years the price of oil on world markets has shaped the energy policies of the EC's member states. In the 1950s and 1960s oil from the middle east was diverted to European markets because of import barriers erected in the USA to protect that country's small independent producers. At that time oil was available at $1-$2 per barrel and these prices made much of Europe's indigenous coal production uneconomic. National energy policies in that era were heavily protectionist and featured both heavy subsidies to coal and to national oil companies set up to gain a share of the production and refinery markets.

The years from 1974 to the mid 1980s were the OPEC era when the cartel's prices climbed in nominal terms to $40 per barrel. The Community, as the world's largest oil importing group, experienced very convulsive reactions to the huge shift in world income that this change in the terms of trade with the oil producing countries represented. These reactions comprised four different issues: a) macroeconomic policy responses, b) energy security measures, c) energy conservation, and d) energy supply responses.[6]

The macroeconomic policy responses differed between the two major oil price escalations of 1973-4 and 1979-80. Many member states saw the first oil price shock as a very temporary phenomenon and tried to maintain their permanent consumption streams by allowing monetary policy to expand to accommodate the increase in oil prices. The result was severe inflation. The second oil price shock was regarded as a more permanent drop in income, monetary policy did not accommodate the price rise and inflation was contained at the expense of unemployment.

In terms of energy security the long term response was the establishment of emergency stockpiles and crisis allocation measures. The Community meshed its response strategy with that of the International Energy Agency which had initially been set up as a confrontational counter to the market power of OPEC. These emergency response arrangements have continued to the present day and allow the Community to maintain up to 90 days of oil stocks with provision for pro-rated consumption cuts to contain price rises in the event of an embargo.

Energy conservation became a primary aim of the EC Commission's energy policy statements throughout this period with the central focus on the energy intensity ratio, i.e. the ratio of inland energy consumption (see Table 1) to gross domestic product. Between 1973 and 1983 energy intensity of the then 10 member states fell by 20 per cent.[7] In 1985, as the high oil price era was about to come to an end, the EC Commission's 1985 statement of energy policy objectives for 1995 included the aim of a further reduction of 25 per cent in energy intensity for the Community as a whole.

The most far reaching consequence of the high oil price era was the impetus given to the Community's own energy supplies. Although the Community is likely always to be highly dependent on imports, energy import dependence fell by 35 per cent in the 10 years after 1973 and oil import dependence fell by 27 per cent in the same period. The commercial viability of oil and gas production from the North Sea was so enhanced by the oil price rises that Europe became an important fringe competitor to the OPEC cartel. This factor, together with the long run price elasticity of demand for oil and energy in general, underestimated by OPEC and many other commentators as well, eventually eroded the cartel's market power.

By 1994, the world oil price had fallen to around $15 per barrel, and allowing for US $ inflation this was not far off the 1972-3 price in real terms. The period from 1986 therefore was once again a cheap oil era. The dependence of macroeconomic policy on developments in the world oil market had disappeared, and while energy crisis security measures were still available, much of the urgency in energy conservation had dissipated and oil and gas exploration in the Community's offshore fields was wound down. This showed up most notably in the way the EC Commission's 1985 conservation policy objectives were largely abandoned. The 1985 objective of further reducing energy intensity by 25 per cent turned into an actual reduction by 1994 of 5 per cent. However, oil import dependence increased only marginally above the 1985 actual and objective share to 35 per cent, its place being taken partly by indigenous use of nuclear power for electricity generation.

By 1990, the removal of the constraint of high oil prices had once again allowed the Community to turn its attention to other aspects of energy policy. This see-saw effect, by which energy policy is completely focused on energy conservation when oil prices are high and then is completely directed to other very different issues when oil prices collapse as the producers' temporary market power erodes, is the most characteristic feature of European energy policy. The EC Energy Commissioner made no mention of oil prices or conservation when in 1990 he stated:-

> 'the energy future of the European Community will rely on the development of an energy policy that encompasses a free internal market, encourages technological advance and supports sustainable economic growth with concern for the environment'.[8]

In the years since the oil price collapse of 1986 several developments have characterized the Community's use of energy and the national energy policies of member states. These are set out in detail in EC Commission,[9] and summarized in Table 2. The overall small rise in primary consumption of energy has been accommodated by rising net imports and reduced Community production. Natural gas has shown the largest rise in consumption and about 70 per cent of this has been provided by increased indigenous production. The greatest increase in primary production has been in the form of nuclear electricity, and this has taken over from oil as the fastest growing source of Community energy export, largely from France to the countries of Eastern Europe. Oil consumption has grown marginally since 1986 with higher imports replacing the North Sea production which has declined annually by about 5-6 per cent since 1986. Solid fuel, particularly coal consumption has only just increased compared with the mid 1980s, but hard coal has shown the greatest rate of increase amongst imported fuels. This is both a consequence of cheaper world coal prices compared with those in the Community and because imported coal has a lower sulphur content than most deep mined European coal and hence the Community's environmental targets are more easily met by imported coal for electricity generation.

Amongst the member states, all but one have increased final and primary energy consumption, but the countries which have shown lower growth than the Community average on both measures are Denmark, Germany (former FRG), Netherlands and the UK with Denmark being the leading conservationist country. Only certain member states make use of nuclear power for electricity generation, but of those who do, all but the Netherlands have substantially increased its usage. The most notable feature, however, of the post 1986 period has been the Community's change of emphasis in energy policy towards environmental aspects of energy usage and the competitive structure of its energy markets.

Table 2. Annual Percentage Rates of Change in Energy Indicators, 1986 to 1991

	Final energy consumption	Primary energy consumption	Electricity generation	Nuclear power	Conventional thermal
Belgium	1.7	2.1	4.2	1.7	9.5
Denmark	-0.2	0	3.4		3
France	1.5	2.3	4.6	5.4	7.2
Germany*	1.2	1.3	2.3	4.3	1.7
Greece	4	4.6	4.8		5.6
Ireland	2.3	2.7	3.7		4.5
Italy	3	2.7	2.9		4.9
Luxembourg	4.1	4.1	7.1		4.7
Netherlands	0.6	1.6	2	-4.6	2.4
Portugal	6	6.8	7.9		11.9
Spain	1.4	0.9	1.3	3.6	0.8
UK	1.4	0.9	1.3	3.6	0.8
Community	**1.9**	**2**	**3.1**	**4.5**	**2.9**

* former FRG
Source: Eurostat

Environmental Aspects of Energy Policy

The relationship between increased energy consumption and its environmental consequences has become one of the most critical policy issues in virtually all of the world's developed economies. The environmental damage arising from energy consumption is usually associated with three principal causes: the production of noxious gases (nitrogen oxides and sulphur dioxide and sulphur trioxide), the accumulation of radioactive waste from nuclear power generation, and the production of carbon dioxide emissions mostly from fossil fuel generation of electricity. The oxides of nitrogen (generically NO_x) which form a serious health risk arise from most industrial and transportation fuel combustion processes especially automobile exhausts. Sulphur dioxide, SO_2, is a similar source of respiratory damage and sulphur trioxide can lead to sulphuric acid precipitation in rainwater. These gases are particularly associated with coal burning to raise steam for electricity generation, but they can be removed from generating station chimneys by the fitting of scrubbing equipment, (flue gas desulphurization, FGD). Radioactive waste which has a wide range of half life figures and which often is largely accounted for by benign uses such as hospital treatment, may be disposed of by dumping at sea, burial or temporary water storage. Carbon dioxide is a contributory factor to the 'greenhouse effect' which may in future raise average temperatures around the world causing other climatic changes and raising water levels so that low lying regions are inundated. Consequently most discussions of energy policy must accommodate the various suggestions that economists have made for alleviating these sources of environmental damage associated with energy consumption.

Comparative figures in this area can be very misleading, and summaries are usually very selective. Table 3 shows some selective figures of energy trends and carbon dioxide emissions reported in a recent EC Commission review.[10] The world picture comprises a wide variety of experience. In the table the only under-developed region is Africa, (i.e. Africa excluding North Africa where substantial energy production and consumption occurs).

Energy conservation has been quite widespread over the 1980s. (Both 1980 and 1989 can be regarded as recession years.) Emissions of greenhouse gases are also apparently being controlled, though less successfully in the far east. Nevertheless, there are substantial differences between the developed and the developing world and this may have a policy relevance as suggested below.

Finally economic development as measured by per capita electricity consumption continues, though more slowly in the developing world than in Europe.

Table 3. Some Comparative Figures on Energy Consumption and Carbon Dioxide Emissions

1989					
	World	**USA**	**European Commission**	**East Europe**	**Africa**
Energy/GDP (toe/mecu)	446	329	290	917	689
% change since 1980	-9.60	-23	-12.70	-12.50	19.00
Energy/Capita (toe/inhab)	1.6	7.9	3.4	3.1	0.49
% change since 1980	2.60	-1.20	0.90	0.30	2.00
Elec/Capita (kWh/inhab)	2078	11943	5396	3857	444
% change since 1980	13.40	12.10	22.00	18.00	6.00
CO2/Capita (t/inhab)	0.94	5.64	2.1	2.18	0.41
% change since 1980	4.44 *	-1.20	-6.70	-6.80	-4.70

*compare: Japan = 6.2%, and China = 35.7%
Source: Eurostsat

Environmental economists have developed a substantial analytical framework for dealing with these issues. The first result is that zero pollution is not optimal. Economists measure the effect of pollution on the environment by a so-called damage function, which shows increasing total and marginal cost of environmental damage as pollution increases, but which allows for the environment to have some absorptive properties. Since the marginal benefit of the production which gives rise to pollution is assumed to decrease as pollution rises, there will be a crossover point at which the rising marginal damage curve meets the declining marginal benefit of production curve. This means there is a socially optimal amount of pollution where marginal private benefit of output = marginal social damage of jointly produced pollution. This analysis is at the basis of the World Bank's (1992) *World Development Report*.[11]

Comparing different parts of the world, the amount of pollution shows great variation. Hence it could be argued that there are potential gains to trade in these bads just as there might be gains to trade in goods by relocating some polluting industries; for example, in countries with an environment that is at present much better than the rest of the world's. In return for raising their standard of living these developing countries would import some developed country pollution, until pollution levels were equalized over the world as a whole. This would be a rather extreme economists' position, although it was the subject of some debate between *The Economist* magazine and the World Bank's Chief Economist.[12] Nevertheless, it serves to emphasize that a blanket ban on emissions or an arbitrary upper limit on emissions may fail to take into account the trade-off between costs and benefits of combating pollution. Often, countries begin an environmental policy by using fixed emission limits, and only later do they move on to policy instruments which take account of market incentives and economic trade-offs. Such a policy evolution is characteristic of the EC Commission's approach.

Hahn explains the range of different environmental policy instruments and surveys their use in practice for both European and US markets.[13] The simplest instrument is *command and control* by which the environmental regulation authority imposes an emission limit for a particular pollutant on a company or organizational basis together with a monitoring arrangement and a set of fines or penalties for infringing the limits after a quasi-judicial process. This contrasts with two market-based instruments: *marketable permits* and *emission charges*. As Hahn shows, the implementation of marketable permits, which he calls a 'quantity' instrument, has the following stages: a) a target level of total allowable emissions in a region is determined; b) each firm operating in the region receives a permit to emit a given level of pollution; c) firms can trade or auction these permits amongst themselves and a market clearing price for a permit is established. The contrasting 'pricing' instrument is the emission charge, by which polluters are charged a fixed price for each unit of pollution that is monitored. Each firm has the alternative of paying the charge or installing pollution abatement measures, whichever is cheaper. If the market for permits is competitive, if firms are cost minimizers, and if each firm would pay the same fixed charge, then both of the market-based instruments minimize the costs, of pollution abatement and will show savings in pollution abatement costs, compared with the command and control procedure. Hahn describes these market based instruments as a way of giving firms increased flexibility in taking production decisions while meeting the aims of environmental policy. However, he noted that in both the USA and in Europe their impact to date has been very limited, and that only a small fraction of the theoretical cost savings seem to have been achieved. The cost savings from permits seems to have been greater, with the emphasis in charging being to raise revenue which may then be spent to improve environmental quality in other areas.

In the Community, the primary example of a command and control policy instrument has been the EC Commission's Large Combustion Plant Directive (LCPD) of 1988. As Surrey shows, this concentrated on setting emission reduction targets for different member states.[14] The targets referred to the 1980 levels of SO_2 and NO_x, and required reductions of up to 70 per cent for Germany, France, Belgium and Netherlands, with lower limits for other members including the UK, Italy and Denmark. However, Greece, Portugal and Ireland were allowed to increase emission to take account of their programmes of capital investment in thermal electricity generation. At the same time the EC Council of Ministers has responded to the work of the United Nations Intergovernmental Conference on Climate Change by adopting the objective of reducing CO_2 emissions to 1990 levels by the year 2000, (most member states wanted a closer time limit but the UK argued for the longer period). These emission limits have begun to have an effect on the energy policies of different member states, and one of the strongest effects was on the UK coal industry. This had been in managed decline for several years as its deep mined coal output became increasingly uncompetitive at world coal prices. In an empirical study of coal costs, Newbery shows that at current world prices for coal and oil, UK coal (and this is almost certainly true for the other coal industries in the Community) is very uneconomical compared with oil-fired electricity generation.[15] However, the LCPD rules out the dirty oil option and the UK electricity generation industry (both the large privatized utilities and the new independent power producers) has instead adopted what has become known as a 'dash for gas'. This involves using the combined cycle gas turbine

(CCGT) technology burning natural gas to generate non-baseload electricity. Newbery points out that this might have happened partly as a result of the nature of the UK electricity privatization programme, which gave regional distribution companies a strong incentive to offset the market power of the two major generating utilities. However, he also shows that the LCPD has had a powerful effect on conditioning the response of the electricity generation industry to the choice of fuel source. In fact such has been the switch to gas that the UK can now meet the LCPD without contracting the subsidized coal industry as quickly as it might have had to. Odell has argued that a similar switch from coal to gas is likely to be unavoidable in other member states, particularly Germany, and he anticipates a massive expansion in the Community's gas market.[16]

The EC Commission has however, recently switched the emphasis in the policy discussion to the use of market based instruments, most notably with the proposal for a carbon/energy tax.[17] The principal of the tax was to enable the Community to meet its CO_2 emissions objective, and the EC Commission has recognized that 'fuel switching, especially in power generation is a major policy area for achieving CO_2 stabilization', (op. cit. p.7). The Commission notes that the early 1980s was a rare period in which the level of CO_2 emissions declined and this effect seems to have been almost wholly due to the incentive to conserve energy arising from the increase in the price of oil. Following the decline in oil prices the Commission believes that in the absence of a policy change Community CO_2 emissions could increase by 11 per cent in the period 1990 to 2000. Consequently, the Commission proposed in 1993 that member states should impose a tax weighted at 50 per cent on the energy content and 50 per cent on the carbon content of fuel inputs used in each sector of the economy. The tax would be introduced in seven yearly steps to 2000, (beginning at 0.21 ECU/gigajoule on energy and 2.81 ECU/tonne CO_2, rising to 0.7 ECU and 9.4 ECU respectively). The Commission emphasized that the tax should not be used as an additional revenue raising instrument; it was a tax intended to change behaviour. The revenue should be recycled into the economy so that the overall tax burden remained unchanged. The proposal was met with very strong opposition from the Community's major energy users, on whom the initial burden would fall. In fact energy demand is relatively price inelastic even in the long run, where a range from -0.4 to -1.0 is reported.[18] Consequently, energy consumers are likely to bear most of the final burden. Nevertheless, as with a similar proposal in the USA, the progress towards a Community-wide tax to combat CO_2 emissions is likely to be slow and difficult.

The Single Energy Market and Regulation of Energy Utilities

The European Community instigated the move to a single internal market free from all barriers to trade with the Single act of 1986, but it was not until 1988 that real attention was paid to the idea of a single market in energy. At about this time, some member states, most notably the UK, had been pursuing a programme of deregulation, liberalization and privatization amongst state owned industries, particularly the public utilities involved in the production and distribution of electricity and gas; and the two trends have become interlinked.

It is important to distinguish amongst the three terms we have just used, although they are often wrongly used interchangeably under the catch-all phrase of *privatization*. Deregulation means that an industry, which may contain both state owned companies and investor owned companies, is to be allowed to produce and market its outputs under fewer or less stringent controls on price or quality of supply. It does not imply that there has been any change in ownership of the companies in the industry, or that there have been new entrants to the industry. Liberalization of a market does mean that it is easier for new firms to enter or leave an industry. Privatization, in its more restricted sense, means that majority equity stakes in state owned industries have been sold to private investors. It does not mean that the industry's regulatory regime or the number of its competitors has changed. Nevertheless, these three different policy changes often go together. For example, in the privatization of the British electricity supply industry, when publicly owned utilities were sold to private investors, those utilities' markets were simultaneously opened up to other privately owned companies, and the regulatory controls on their behaviour were changed from the instruction to set price equal to long run marginal cost, which had applied to the former state owned industry, to a system in which the distribution companies could choose their own price structure subject to a cap on the average level of prices. The fixed cap rose at the rate of Retail Price Inflation less an allowance for productivity growth, $(RPI - X)$.

Argyris in defending the EC Commission's approach to the single energy market has nevertheless noted that although it contains no privatization implications, it is likely to have deregulation and liberalization consequences for many member states.[19] The EC Commission's approach to the internal energy market is often said to embody three distinct phases. Phase 1, (1988-92) is relatively innocuous. It concerns transparency of energy prices and the provision of energy price and market information together with a requirement to facilitate the transit of electricity and gas between the national grid transmission systems of different member states. Phase 2 began in 1992 and is much more far reaching. Whish has explained how Phase 2 is grounded in EC law.[20] Articles 30-34 of the Rome Treaty prohibit measures which constitute a barrier to intra-community trade, while Article 37 ensures that the free movement of goods and services under Articles 30-34, also apply to the products of state owned monopolies in member states. It requires that state monopolies do not discriminate against nationals of other member states. The EC Commission has argued that the state electricity and gas monopolies in most of the Community infringe this requirement and in 1992 the Commission began the process of involving the European Court of Justice in determining this position, following the Court's judgement on telecommunications equipment. Article 85 prohibits distortion of competition in the common market, Article 86 prohibits the abuse of a dominant position, and Article 90 prevents any undertaking that has been granted special or exclusive rights by its national Government from infringing the competition requirements of Articles 85 and 86. The exclusive rights that are relevant in energy supply refer to the import and export of fuels, the transmission and distribution of electricity and gas, the supply of electricity and gas consumers in franchise areas, and exclusive rights to generate electricity. In this way the EC Commission has, after many years, finally brought energy policy into the ambit of the competition policy provisions of the Treaties. In addition Articles 92 and 93 are being used to prevent subsidy to a member state's indigenous fuel producers, notably in the coal industry. Finally, the Maastricht Treaty in Article 129 looks forward to the establishment of Trans-European networks in the energy sector.

The details of Phase 2 are set out in EC Commission document *COM(91) 548 final* and there are three principal aims:

(i)   to introduce competition into the generation of electricity,

(ii)   to allow the construction of direct transmission links between energy suppliers, and

(iii)   to allow third party access to electricity and gas networks.

Empirical studies of electricity generation suggest that economies of scale do not persist above the 4-5000 megawatt capacity level, (i.e. about the size of two or three large coal fired generating stations). This means that generation cannot be regarded as a natural monopoly and can be expected to behave more like a competitive industry unless there are artificial barriers to entry. The second provision is likely to be very uneconomic since it provides for a generator and a customer to construct a direct line between them bypassing the established network. It is the third provision that has proved the most contentious and that may bring about far reaching changes in the structure of the Community's energy markets.

There is some debate about what third party access, (TPA) means in the context of Europe's different electricity and gas networks and how it differs from common carriage. The essential idea underlying both terms is that an owner of a gas pipeline or electricity transmission line must offer access to the line in order that another energy supplier (the third party) can deliver energy to one of its own customers. There will be a charge for this facility that may be regulated by the government. The final buyer could have originally been purchasing energy from the transmission system owner so that the latter is now facilitating delivery from a rival to a former customer in return for a carriage charge. Clearly this has enormous implications for increasing the competitiveness of electricity and gas supply. Stern distinguishes between common carriage and TPA in terms of the response that is allowed to the transmission system owner when demand to use the network has expanded to reach the available capacity on the network.[21] He notes that the distinguishing feature of common carriage is that capacity is offered *pro rata* to all parties in proportion to the demand for which each has tendered. Under TPA, on the other hand, the carrier has no obligation to offer access once the capacity of the system has been reached.[22] Stern reports that the EC Commission's estimates of the annual net benefits of introducing TPA to gas supply will amount to about 2 percent of the value in the year 2000 of European gas supply costs.

TPA has provoked a very heated debate about its true costs and benefits and how the consequences will be felt throughout the Community's markets. Argyris argues that the initial proposals may be quite mild since for example in electricity there is a lower limit of 25 megawatts on the maximum demand of those customers who can be served by third parties.[23] This will restrict TPA facilities to about 400-500 very large industrial customers in the Community, in addition to the 100 or so associations of distribution utilities that will be allowed to receive supplies from third parties. The system will operate by each network having a system operator whose transmission business must be at arm's length from its other energy supply business, and who will furnish transparent rules and charges for access to the network. These may be regulated by the operator's national government to ensure that they do not depart too much from long run marginal cost including a reasonable rate of return on capital.

This regulatory problem however is not easy to resolve. Access charges for a network must recover the fixed network costs and relating prices to long run marginal cost will fail to do this. One important recent contribution to the debate on access charges that has also featured in Commission discussion is the idea of efficient component pricing developed by Baumol and Sidak.[24] This extends the concept of marginal cost to include as an opportunity cost the network owner's loss of revenue to the third party supplier. While this resolves many of the entry signalling problems of network industries it still leaves the problem of estimating the revenue losses in a market where the incumbent network owner has more cost information than the regulatory body.

Argyris identifies three arguments used by the opponents of TPA, who unsurprisingly tend to be the major gas and electric utilities in the Community. These are that TPA: a) would reduce security of supply, b) would raise prices especially for small consumers, and c) would require a high degree of regulation in already heavily regulated industries. The security of supply argument arises partly because incumbent utilities may be less willing to take on the risks associated with long lived asset specific investments, especially network reinforcement, in the event that entry barriers are lowered by TPA. Argyris, in defending the Commission, dismisses this argument on the grounds that the network monopolies are simply using their existing market power to pass on business risks to their consumers, and that energy network investment is in fact very profitable in the Community. This may be a correct but optimistic viewpoint. The problem of encouraging asset specific investment is endemic to the regulation of natural monopolies as Williamson has argued, and is one ground for believing that network regulation needs to be strongly interventionist.[25]

The argument that TPA would lead to higher prices for small consumers simply reflects a belief that with TPA large industrial consumers could negotiate price discounts that would have to be recouped from small domestic consumers. The Commission believes that by allowing the regulated local distribution networks who supply domestic consumers to join in the TPA proposals, this risk of cross-subsidy will be minimized. To the argument that with TPA regulation will increase, the Commission can point out that several countries, notably the UK, have demonstrated that TPA can be introduced simultaneously with a privatization and deregulation programme that replaces centralized public ownership with lightly regulated investor-owned utilities.

Phase 2 of the internal energy market began in 1993. Phase 3 in the Commission's proposals is aimed at unbundling the different activities of large scale vertically integrated energy utilities. This is scheduled to begin in 1996, but already the UK has begun the process with its own electricity and, to a lesser extent, gas industries. However, in the process of implementing the internal market, amendments have been made to the original objectives.[26] There is to be a greater reliance on achieving network access by negotiation between the network owner and the third party supplier rather than by regulation. The member State will provide a mechanism for settling disputes using Community law. The management unbundling of vertically integrated utilities is now replaced by the accountancy unbundling of vertically integrated utilities. This would allow, for example, a gas utility to remain as a single entity but with separate accounts for network activities and for gas supply trading activities. This is precisely the decision of the UK Government in respect of British Gas.[27] The UK Government was responding to the suggestion from the UK Monopolies and Mergers Commission that British Gas should be broken up into separate network and supply companies. Supply trading can then be opened up to competition even if the network activity remains as a natural monopoly. These amendments are the direct result of deep opposition by utilities in member states to some of the internal market proposals.

The EC and the Idea of Energy Policy: a Summing Up

Several major themes in EC energy policy and markets have been identified in this chapter, but three seem to stand out: a) the response to oil prices, b) the environmental aspects of energy consumption, and c) the single energy market issue. Surrey however, fears that these issues obscure the Community's fundamental need to have an explicit energy policy, i.e. a set of policies designed to meet the market failures that he believes characterize the energy sector. We need to ask what these market failures are and how they relate to the idea of a Community energy policy. Is it true that energy markets are particularly susceptible to market failure? Many commentators believe there are severe market failures in energy supply, and the most striking arise through uncertainty, natural monopoly or cartelization, depletion of resources if discount rates are distorted, and environmental externalities of energy production. A broad list of possible market failures and their consequences, apart from the question of pollution externalities, includes:

Monopoly - There are natural monopolies in network industries, and artificial or statutory monopolies where there are barriers to entry other than increasing returns to scale. These require regulatory or anti-trust policy rather than energy policy.

Market failures in fuel choices - There may be a coordination failure between individual actions and the social optimum. For example, there may be inadequate entry in competitive parts of the fuel market, but excessive entry in the natural monopoly parts. The emergence of vertically integrated firms that attempt to extend ownership from the natural monopoly parts of an industry to the potentially competitive parts may be another market failure.

A further example is furnished by apparently irrational domestic consumers, who appear not to use the same discount rate for different investments.

Short term horizons - basically this is a discount rate problem. To the extent that energy investments are part of the social infrastructure there is a case for evaluating them by using a social rate of time preference discount rate. However, private opportunity costs of capital are usually higher and therefore desirable energy investments are not carried out by privately owned corporations.

Resource depletion issues - The private capital market may fail to recognize the global resource exhaustion constraint in the optimal depletion of non-renewable resources. This has intergenerational implications because we use as a welfare criterion the present value of welfare changes to generations with no present voice in the market. Put another way, if the future generation's demand for a non-renewable resource is not correctly estimated by today's market, perhaps because its future ownership of the resource is not recognized, then there may be nothing optimal about a particular competitive market depletion path that nevertheless exhibits the correct spot pricing escalation.

Security of supply - there is some debate about whether this is a true market failure. If people differ in their risk preferences, but due to moral hazard or adverse selection problems cannot insure themselves against economic shocks efficiently, then market outcomes will not be satisfactory. Non-existence of spot, future and complete contingent markets shows up in the emergence of long-term contracts. But enforcing competition may actually hinder the emergence of the long-term contracts used to cope with the absence of efficient markets. This is another example of the tension between competition and efficiency when the assumptions of a perfectly competitive world break down.

One of the most frequently heard laments among commentators on European affairs is that the Community lacks an 'energy policy'. The relevant questions from the economist's point of view are:

a)   Does a particular energy market exhibit a market failure? If so, is a 'policy' solution needed or feasible? 'Policy' by definition means some change in today's market clearing price and quantity brought about by Community intervention. The effectiveness of policy is determined by whether it improves economic efficiency, although many policy decisions are driven by the political desire to alter the distribution of income and wealth.

b)   Is there a particular group in society that deserves help or protection for their standard of living? If so, is the distortion of energy prices the only or the best way of providing help?

In this review of European energy policy we have seen how the Community has fluctuated between anxiety about the security of supply market failure when oil prices are high and the income distribution, externality, and monopoly issues when oil prices are low. The early 1990s represent a focus on the second set of issues after the 1980s saw the end of the preoccupation with the first.

Notes

1.   EC Commission (1993b) *Energy in Europe: Community Assistance in the Energy Sector to the Countries of Central and Eastern Europe and the Former Soviet Union,* Luxembourg, Office for Official Publications of the European Communities.

2.   EC Commission (1994) *Energy in Europe: energy policies and trends in the European Union* Luxembourg, Office for Official Publications of the European Communities, July 1994, p. 66.

3.   EC Commission (1993a) *Energy in Europe: Annual Energy Review 1993,* Luxembourg, Office for Official Publications of the European Communities.

4.   See Weyman-Jones, Thomas G. (1986) *Energy in Europe: Issues and Policies,* London, Methuen & Co. p. 13.

5.   Surrey, John (1992) Energy Policy in the European Community, *The Energy Journal,* 13, 3, pp.207-31.

6.   For further detail see Weyman-Jones (1986).

7.   *Ibid* p.88.

8.   EC Commission (1990) *Energy in Europe: Energy for a new century: the European Perspective* Luxembourg, Office for Official Publications of the European Communities.

9.   EC Commission (1993a) *op.cit.*

10.   EC Commission (1991) *Energy in Europe: annual energy review* Luxembourg, Office for Official Publications of the European Communities.

11.   World Bank (1992) *Development and the Environment: World Development Report 1992,* Oxford University Press.

12.   See *The Economist,* 8 February 1992 and 15 February 1992.

13.   Hahn, Robert (1989) Economic Prescriptions for Environmental Problems: How the Patient Followed the Doctor's Orders, *Journal of Economic Perspectives,* 3, 2, pp.95-114.

14.   Surrey , John (1992) *op.cit.*

15.   Newbery, David (1993) The Impact of EC Environmental Policy on British Coal, *Oxford Review of Economic Policy,* 9, 4, pp.66-95.

16.   Odell, Peter, (1992) Prospects for Natural gas in Western Europe, *The Energy Journal,* 13, 3, pp.41-59.

17.   See EC Commission (1993c) *Energy in Europe, (supplement): Consequences of the Proposed Carbon/Energy Tax* Luxembourg, Office for Official Publications of the European Communities.

18.   Weyman-Jones (1986) p.85.

19   Argyris, Nicholas (1993) Regulatory Reform in the Electricity Sector: an Analysis of the Commission's Internal market Proposals *Oxford Review of Economic Policy*, 9, 1, pp.31-44.

20   Whish, Richard (1992) European Commission policies and Technical Change - Competitive Impact and Regulatory Prospects, in   Tony Gilland (ed) *Regulatory Policy and the Energy Sector*, Centre for the Study of Regulated Industries Proceedings 3, London, Chartered Institute of Public Finance and Accountancy.

21   Stern, Johnathan (1993) The Prospects for Third Party Access in European Gas Markets, in Ernst J. Mestmäcker (ed) *Natural Gas in the Internal Market*, London, Graham & Trotman.

22   *Ibid* pp. 184-5.

23   Argyris, 'Regulatory Reform'.

24   Baumol, William J. and G. Sidak, (1994) *Towards Competition in Local Telephony*, MIT Press and the American Enterprise Institute.

25   Williamson, O. E. (1985) *The Economic Institutions of Capitalism*, Glencoe, The Free Press.

26   See Klom, in EC Commission (1994) for details.

27   House of Commons (1994) *Select Committee on Trade and Industry First Report: The Domestic Gas Market*, session 1994-5, HC 23-I, London, HMSO.

21 EC Environment Policy

ALAN MARIN

Historical Background

The Treaty of Rome contained no mention of the Environment - neither as an aim of the EEC nor as an area of common policy. It would have been surprising if there had been any such mention. In the 1950s, there was generally no concern that pollution and the environment were pervasive problems. Particular, harmful, pollution episodes, or particular industries might require remedial action or control, but these were not viewed by most people as aspects of a wider problem requiring an overall framework of policies.

By the late 1960s, the 'environmentalist' movement had begun to take hold in North-Western Europe, possibly slightly later than in the USA and possibly influenced by the latter.[1] The new concerns focused on a series of issues that were seen as inter-related by many of those involved.

The issues included pollution, narrowly defined as harmful effects on human health or amenities and also harmful spillovers from one industry to another. The difference from the 1950s is that pollution came to be seen as a pervasive on-going problem, arising from a wide range of economic activities (both production and consumption), and not limited to an occasional specific episode. On this view, remedial action should no longer be limited to isolated remedies in reaction to isolated episodes, but the aim should be widespread preventative action to control potentially harmful pollutants well before unacceptable damage occurred. In other words, systematic anti-pollution policies were required.

There were also increased concerns about the preservation of biological diversity and the extinction of species. These latter concerns, whether by 'sentimentalists' worried about the disappearance of whales, or by ecologists insistent on the maintenance of diverse habitats in the face of pressure from population growth and industrialization, were not primarily devoted to the effects on human beings. Some even went further and tended to downplay human welfare in any conflict between the two.

571

The present author vividly recalls the first conference that he attended in the early 1970s which was intended to improve the dialogue betweenecologists and economists. He had been working on the control of sulphur dioxide pollution, and one proposal that was being treated seriously, (and was eventually partly incorporated into EC policy) was to burn low sulphur fuels in towns with high levels of pollution. This would protect human health. One result would be the diversion of higher sulphur fuels to rural areas, with the result of raising somewhat the low 'background' levels of the air pollution in those areas, which might damage some forms of lichen - a highly sensitive species. The ecologists were completely opposed to such a proposal - for them it was more important to maintain some habitats for the sensitive lichens, and not take any chances on their complete disappearance.

Both sets of concerns, those about pollution and those about conservation, have continued up to the present, though with varying degrees of intensity over time. In the late 1960s/early 1970s there were another set of concerns which have turned out to be less lasting, but which were also historically important in the initial raising of West European (or at least North-West European) environmental consciousness, and bringing it to political influence. This other set of concerns related to fears about the fairly imminent exhaustion of various natural resources, many of which were essential inputs into the economy - including cultivatable land.

There were a series of influential simulation studies predicting catastrophic results from resource exhaustion, combined, in many cases, with pollution reaching levels that would lead to irreparable damage rather than to the types of temporary damage to the environment that occur with lower pollution, where the environment could regenerate itself once pollution was reduced.[2] In Europe, much of the public discussion and pressure was led by a group of businessmen and other 'VIP's' known as the 'Club of Rome', with a prominent role taken by a leading member of the Fiat Company.

Although fears of resource exhaustion played a role in arousing the consciousness which led to EC environmental policy, for a long time they had no effect on the forms of the policy. One reason was that after the mid-1970s the fears of resource exhaustion became more of a minority concern. They had seemed reasonable, and even urgent, at a time when many raw material prices were rising rapidly - this could be seen as a signal that scarcity constraints were beginning to bite. After the recession of the mid-1970s took hold, the prices of many raw materials collapsed. Even though oil prices continued to rise until the early 1980s, they also fell from 1984. In fact, excess capacity in primary production became the rule.

The other reasons for the waning of interest in resource exhaustion have more relevance for some recent problems. One of these reasons was that effective action would require global cooperation, involving not only the US and Japan but also the poorer countries which were trying to develop. Another reason, perhaps, was that there was something incongruous and unconvincing about groups headed by people who were amongst the most affluent in countries which were the most developed (and therefore had the highest per capita consumption) telling everybody that incomes would have to stop rising, and that poorer countries could not industrialize, because of the insupportable strain it would put on the planet.[3]

More recently, however, similar problems of global coordination, and similar strains between richer and poorer countries, have arisen over the issues of stratospheric ozone depletion and of global warming - the developed countries simultaneously both have higher carbon-dioxide emissions per capita and tell poorer countries to refrain from exploiting their timber resources. Somewhat similar strains on this issue emerged within the EC itself on the Commission's initial proposals for controlling carbon dioxide emissions by means of a tax on fuels according to their carbon content.[4]

As a result of the concerns sketched above, by the early 1970s, the 'Green' movement was becoming politically influential, and this helped to lead to pressure for environmental policies. It was not only the eventual success in managing to have some 'Green Party' M.E.P.s elected, as well as some representatives at national and local levels, but also that some national governments in EC countries have felt obliged to be seen to be responding to public concerns on environmental issues in order to try to prevent the 'Greens' from gaining enough votes to be a threat to government majorities. Such governments, initially primarily in W. Germany and Holland (and possibly Denmark) had, and have, an extra incentive to support EC environmental policies.

The Development of an EC Policy

By 1972, the changes in attitude just sketched led to a report by the Commission, followed at the Paris Summit in October by a call by the Heads of Government for an EC environmental programme. In November 1973, the *1st*

Environmental Action Programme 1973-6 was approved. This was followed by subsequent programmes, up to the *4th Programme 1987-92*. The 5th Action Programme is entitled *Towards Sustainability* and has not been given a formal closing date, but is supposed to cover the period up to 2000 with reviews and 'roll-overs', starting with a 'mid-term'review in 1995.[5]

The programmes have been a somewhat odd mixture of statements about the fundamental principles and aspirations in general terms, together with fairly detailed lists of aspects of environmental protection where action should be taken and to which priority should be given. For example, the 3rd Programme included general statements about the integration of the environmental dimension into other [EC] policies, and a statement on the need to implement a previous Directive on waste from the titanium dioxide industry. The current, 5th, Programme is a similar mix of descriptions of the current position, general principles and detailed proposals.

Although the European Council had agreed to a Programme which committed them to joint policies, which would be binding once specific Directives were agreed, it was not clear whether there was any legal basis for Directives on the environment. In the United Kingdom, in particular, there was some talk of challenging their legality in the European Court, though no case was ever brought challenging the right of the Community to issue Directives.[6] For some Directives, there was clearly a legal competence deriving from the Treaty of Rome. These concerned environmental protection which involved avoiding harm from the use of products, e.g. exhaust emissions from vehicles, noise levels of lawn mowers or packaging and labelling of solvents. The absence of joint standards could lead to differing national standards becoming non-tariff barriers to the free movement of goods between Member States. Joint standards could therefore be justified as product harmonization, and some even predated the *1st Environmental Action Programme*, e.g. the first agreements on exhaust and noise emissions from vehicles go back to 1970, while those on labelling and packing of dangerous substances were in 1967.[7]

Many Directives, however, clearly concerned aspects of pollution and environmental standards that could not hinder inter-State trade. Examples could include the quality of water for swimming, the lead content of drinking water or the requirement for an Environmental Impact Assessment to be undertaken before planning consent is given for large projects.[8] For such Directives, an official justification was required for environmental policy generally, even where trade was not affected, (not even potentially affected).

The claimed justification was from Article 2 of the Treaty of Rome, which stated that

'The Community shall... promote... a harmonious development of economic activities, a continuous and balanced expansion, ... an accelerated raising of the standard of living...'

This was interpreted to include environmental protection on the grounds that such protection would further a balanced expansion and raised standard of living, since people now considered environmental factors and absence of pollution as part of their standard of living and well-being. If the argument were accepted and environmental protection considered as a legitimate objective of the EC, then Article 235 of the Treaty of Rome gave legal backing for binding agreements by the Council.

The legal basis for the Community's environmental actions was finally firmly established, and some of the basic principles spelled out again, in the Single European Act of 1986. Among the Articles inserted into the Treaty by the Act were Articles 130R - 130T, which dealt with the environment.

Allowance for environmental factors was also made elsewhere in the Single European Act. According to Article 100A, actions taken as part of the 'completion of the single market' should take a high level of environmental protection as their base. There is also an explicit allowance for individual Member States to set higher environmental standards, provided that these do not constitute barriers to trade - the precise criteria here are somewhat vague and will require further Court cases to spell out just what constitutes barriers to trade.[9]

There could be conflicts over whether particular Directives were to be treated as relating to product harmonization, which would make them the subject of majority voting by the Council under Article 100A (which deals with completion of the single market) or were to be treated as relating to environmental protection which would require unanimous voting under Article 130S. Such disputes have lead the Commission to refer the Council to the European Court. In one case the Commission and European Parliament had proposed that a new Directive on titanium dioxide pollution should be issued under Article 100A, but the Council treated it according to Article 130S. In this case the Court ruled in favour of the Commission. In subsequent cases involving waste shipments the Court has ruled the other way.[10]

The Maastricht Agreement of 1991, further extended Article 130S to include majority voting on some aspects of environmental policy, though others will still remain subject to unanimous voting. Again, there is scope for interpretation as to which environmental issues will fall within the new Article 130S, Paragraph 2, and therefore still be subject to unanimous voting. The areas which are still subject to unanimous voting are:

-   'Provisions primarily of a fiscal nature;
-   Measures concerning town and country planning, land use with the exception of waste management and measures of a general nature, and management of water resources;
-   Measures significantly affecting a Member State's choice between different energy sources and the general structure of its energy supply'

Another addition of the Maastricht Agreement is to include environmental issues in the revisions of Articles 2 and 3; which are the Articles which set out in general terms the objectives and areas of common policy of the Community.

Article 2 now includes among the aims: 'sustainable... growth respecting the environment'. The phrase 'sustainable development' is currently fashionable, though the precise meaning of the concept is not at all clear, in any but the most trivial sense of the avoidance of intentionally planning to have lower consumption levels in the future because of higher consumption now. Whether the objectives in Article 2 really make any difference to anything that matters or are merely pious non-binding aspirations is a matter of debate. It is therefore unclear whether the new Article 2 will itself make any difference to policies. Article 3 now includes among the list of common policies '(k) a policy in the sphere of the environment'. Again in practice this clause makes no difference to the Community's powers since the Single European Act mentioned above. The present writer's view is that neither the Article 2, nor the Article 3 additions are of any importance in practice.

Insofar as the Single European Act and the Maastricht Treaty increased the power of the European Parliament, this can also lead to stricter environmental policies. The European Parliament is often thought to take a stronger position on environmental issues than the European Council - not only the 'Green' MEPs but also MEPs from other groupings seem to be more concerned about the environment, than their own parties in national governments. Since the Single European Act there has been one case where the European Parliament clearly made a difference leading to much stricter standards.[11] In 1989, the European Parliament amended a proposed Council Directive on exhaust emissions. The Parliament's more stringent limits could only be met by fitting catalytic converters to all new cars, not just to large ones as in the Council's proposal. 1988-89 had been a time of renewed environmentalist public pressure, and even those governments opposed to the more stringent limits were not prepared to end up with no measure at all, as the result of a refusal to accept the amendments.

A final relatively recent innovation to be mentioned at this point is the provision of Community funds for environmental purposes. One fund was set up in May 1992 when the Council established 'a financial instrument for the environment', to be known (with the Community's usual penchant for acronyms) as 'LIFE'.[12] The amounts are trivial compared to other spending programmes financed by the EC Budget: 400 million ECU for 1991-5. Nevertheless, precedents have been set, and with sufficient political pressure an expansion of this, and similar funds, could be possible. The other new EC funding stems from the Maastricht Treaty. Part of the price that the poorer countries extracted for their agreement was the commitment in general terms to further spending on increased 'cohesion'. The actual amount for the new 'Cohesion Fund' was agreed at the Summit at Edinburgh in December 1992, after Spain (in particular) had threatened to block any agreement on other urgent issues without a sufficient increase in regional spending, including the Cohesion Fund. The Cohesion Fund will amount to 2.6 billion ECU per annum by 1999. The fund will be spent on countries with a per capita income which is less than 90 per cent of the EC average; currently these are the four poorest countries viz. Portugal, Greece, Ireland and Spain. One of the two foci of the Cohesion Fund is to help these countries to meet Community environmental standards (the other is for spending on transport infrastructure improvements).

Within the overall framework provided by product harmonization, the Environmental Action Programmes, Articles 130R-T inserted by the Single European Act, as well as by international agreements to which the Members are signatories, and subject to the political pressures indicated above, the EC has passed literally hundreds of Directives and Regulations which affect the environment.

Most of these concern pollution in some form - where the primary purpose is protection of human health or of amenities valued by humans (such as peace and quiet, or forests). Sometimes the Directives have required the collection of information which will be useful in preventing further pollution damage (e.g. the monitoring of forest damage and air pollution or surveys of lead concentrations in people's blood).

There have been relatively few EC measures which attempt to protect species or habitats for their own sakes - though a new Directive on habitat protection was passed in May 1992.[13] This new Directive partly followed from one of the few earlier exceptions, which was a 1979 Directive on the protection of birds.[14] Some Directives are ostensibly for human health or amenity, but may be partly motivated by more ecological motives. For example, some commentators have suggested that the Directives on water quality for rivers and estuaries containing fish or shellfish were not only to protect human health, but also to protect the fish per se - though I personally do not find the suggestion compelling. Other examples would be EC Directives concerning endangered species (e.g. seals and whales) which although motivated by concern about preservation (and repugnance at killing of seal pups) are formally directed at trade in the products of the species, and in some cases result from international Conventions.[15]

One other limited exception to the concentration on pollution is the 1985 Directive which required an Environmental Impact Assessment prior to some large scale developments (mainly industrial or infrastructure). This exception is limited both because it is largely left to Member States to define which projects should be subject to the Assessment and, more importantly, because there is no requirement as to how, or even whether, the results of the Assessment should be used to alter the proposed development.

As stated above, there are hundreds of environmental Directives. There seems little point in trying to list them all here - even a brief but comprehensive coverage would take a whole book on its own.[16] Instead, in the remainder of this Chapter, I shall deal with a number of general issues and problems with EC environmental policies, and use specific Directives and pollution problems as examples.

Issues

Joint Policies

A fundamental question is *why* should there be any EC level environmental policies at all?

This question (at least implicitly) resurfaced during 1992 with the stress on 'subsidiarity'. 'Subsidiarity' may have been a token concession in the Maastricht Agreement itself, to those governments (especially the UK) who were worried about moving too far towards full political union. However, some obeisance towards subsidiarity was already apparent in the Commission draft for the *5th Environmental Action Programme* in March 1992, which proposed aiming at 'sustainable development,' combining 'subsidiarity and a wider concept of shared responsibility'.[17] Just how to combine 'subsidiarity' and 'shared responsibility' is so vague (and possibly self-contradictory) that it seemed no more than lip service.

Although the term 'subsidiarity' was not used, similar lip service has been paid throughout the development of EC environmental policy. The first Commission proposals for the Programme in 1972 stated that

> 'the Community objective must be to preserve as far as possible the freedom of judgment of national, regional and local authorities...' and '...it is necessary to determine the nature and limits of Community responsibilities as compared to those of Member States.'[18]

Similarly, Article 130R inserted by the SEA stated

> 'The Community shall take action relating to the environment to the extent to which the objectives... can be attained better at Community level than at the level of the Member States.'

Nevertheless, despite such statements, the provisos were not taken very seriously.

During the second half of 1992, however, following the problems over the ratification of the Maastricht Treaty, and under the impetus of the British Presidency, there were moves to make 'subsidiarity' into a prime criterion in deciding on Community policies. Even the chastened Commission seemed to take subsidiarity seriously for a while and agreed that EC policies should be examined to see if jointly determined action was really essential. Although, following the Edinburgh Council in December 1992, the stress on subsidiarity has receded somewhat, and it now seems unlikely that existing Directives will be amended to unravel already accepted joint environmental policies, it remains the case that any new proposals are likely to be more closely scrutinized than before. The question of whether there should be joint policies at all remains crucial.

There are a few types of cases, where the need for joint policy seems obvious. One, already mentioned, is where trade in products is directly affected, e.g. exhaust emission standards on cars, but (as also indicated already) most of these could be dealt with under product harmonization programmes, without any requirement for a separate environmental programme. Other cases fall under common external trade requirements, e.g. some of the trade in endangered species.

Another type of case where joint EC policy seems 'obviously' a suitable solution to a problem, is where there are transfrontier pollution flows. With such pollution, there is a need for joint agreements if 'downstream' countries are not to suffer unacceptably high levels of pollution, and the Community would seem to be the natural forum for obtaining agreement when its Member States are involved.[19]

However, most of the EC environmental policy actions do not fall within 'obvious' categories. From public discussions when the policies started in the early 1970s, it seems that there were two main motivations for joint policies, both of which have continued to the present, with varying strengths.

One motivation was the need for the Community to be seen to respond to the public's concerns, and not just be pre-occupied with arcane issues of no interest to the 'man-in-the-street', or even with issues resented by the public. Something more than debates on the technicalities of Monetary Compensation. Amount changes, or the standardizing of varieties of apples, was needed if the public were to be attracted by the 'European Ideal'. In many Member States, at least, EC action on the environment at a time when it had become a newsworthy issue arousing considerable concern, would demonstrate the relevance of the Community and its ability to respond to widely perceived needs.

The second main motivation is itself also partly a concomitant of increased public pressure on environmental issues. As indicated above, by the 1970s it was clear to some EC governments that they would have to take anti-pollution action on a fairly systematic basis in response to domestic political pressures. Many such actions would inevitably result in increased costs for their industries.[20] For example, firms which had previously simply emitted smoke would have to fit filters, others might have to either buy the more expensive low sulphur fuels or fit desulphurization equipment which had a high capital and running cost. Similarly, some industries which had previously poured toxic or noxious waste into sewers and rivers would have to install and run expensive waste treatment facilities.

The worry was, and is, that if some countries imposed tougher anti-pollution controls on a particular industry, and others did not, then firms in the former countries would face 'unfair' or 'distorted' competition from firms located in the other States who would have lower costs because of their laxer anti-pollution requirements. Agreements on common, uniform, emission standards (often referred to as UES) would avoid this threat to competitiveness. This provided a strong motivation for at least some EC states to press for acceptance of the principle that there should be common EC environmental programmes, including detailed Directives on specific pollution standards, and not just vague expressions of aspirations.

This motivation was already clearly indicated in the initial proposals leading to the *1st Environmental Action Programme*.[21] The Commission's proposal referred to the need to avoid distortion of competition in the common market and continued

> 'Marked disparities between the measures taken by the authorities in different Member States (in particular the establishment of maximum permissable levels for pollutants or waste)... are bound to cause distortion of competition.'

Directives on all sorts of pollution, e.g. harmonizing standards of water for drinking, contain what the Advocate General of the European Court (in Case C-300/89) called a 'stereotyped formula' in their preambles. They invoke Article 100 and justify its relevance by claiming

> '... any disparity between provisions [...] in various Member States may create unequal conditions of competition and thus directly affect the functioning of the Common Market'.[22]

Although worries about 'unfair' competition (and subsequent loss of sales and employment) due to different environmental standards in different countries are generally taken as justifiable by politicians, trade unions and businessmen, it is possible to argue from an economic analysis that these worries are misconceived.[23] In the long-run they could reduce social welfare, if the following line of argument is correct.

It is likely that different countries will want different levels of environmental purity and exposure to pollutants.[24] These differences could result from cultural distinctions and 'tastes'. They could also result from different income levels. In general it would be expected that those with a higher level of income will demand (and be prepared to pay more for) higher levels of amenity and health. Whatever the reasons, in some cases different countries left to themselves would choose different environmental qualities.

Living standards fully defined will comprise both goods and services bought by individuals and also those provided publicly, but not paid for by individual consumers. The latter include environmental quality. At any given level of national productivity, if more publicly provided goods are consumed, then less privately purchased ones can be consumed, and vice versa. Conventional measurements of net real wages and real personal incomes only account for privately purchased consumption possibilities. Thus if a country wishes to have a higher standard of environmental quality, the level of real wages will have to be below those possible with lower environmental standards.

If a country raises its environmental standards, one route by which real wages could fall is that at existing levels of real wages but higher costs of meeting the more stringent levels of pollution controls, firms will try to raise prices and thus become uncompetitive, so that they have to lay off workers.[25] As unemployment levels begin to rise, wage reductions will be needed to restore full employment. These wage cuts will enable firms to cut prices and to compete again. The final situation will be full employment and capacity output, with lower incomes defined in terms of privately purchased goods, despite possibly higher living standards when these are viewed as including enjoyment of environmental amenities and reduced pollution.

Since not all industries are equally polluting, the country which wants less pollution will also have to end up with an industrial structure which comprises fewer industries which are heavily polluting per unit value of output, and more of its production in industries which emit less pollution. The changes in relative prices of goods, which occur because the more heavily polluting industries would be uncompetitive at the initial prices (plus more stringent pollution controls), is part of the mechanism by which the reallocation occurs;

as well as the direct closing down of some of the uncompetitive polluting firms. In order for those who were employed in the more heavily polluting industries to be deployed into other industries, their wages may have to fall as a result of temporary unemployment.

In the scenario just sketched out, the interim period of 'unfair competition' is part of the market mechanism leading to the correct result. The problem is that if, as many (but not all) economists believe is the case in the EC, wages are rigid downwards even in the face of protracted high unemployment, the unemployment may last a long time, together with its attendant social and economic troubles. Hence the pressure for common EC emission standards.[26]

On this analysis, the imposition of common standards involves forcing some countries to have more stringent pollution and other environmental standards than they themselves want, in order to reduce the adjustment problems in other countries with different demands for environmental quality. Similarly those countries which would prefer even stricter controls than those agreed in the EC, trade-off lower environmental standards now and in the future for higher employment levels in the short-run. As indicated, the problem arises because the 'short-run' during which wages would be too high, and thus unemployment be too high also, might last a long time. The long-run result of differing national environmental standards would eventually be higher social welfare, but it takes too long to be waited for passively. In Keynes' famous phrase 'In the long-run we are all dead'.

UES or EQS

An issue closely related to that just discussed, is whether common EC standards should be defined in terms of uniform emission standards (UES) or of common levels of ambient environmental qualities, known as environmental quality standards (EQS).

From an economist's viewpoint in particular, but also more generally, it would seem that since the aim of environmental policy is not the limiting of emissions for its own sake, but because the pollution has undesirable effects, it is the effects which should be the criteria, and the controlling of emissions viewed merely as a means. Hence EQS would be generally preferred to UES.[27]

Furthermore, insofar as the relative costs of different ways of controlling the pollution differed between States, then minimizing the costs of achieving any given ambient quality standard should lead to different patterns of emissions in the different States. Only if other criteria were involved, such as product standards (to allow unhindered trade in the absence of sufficient 'mutual recognition'), would there be a case for uniform EC controls.

However, the issue of EQS versus UES arose in the 1970s, in a heated clash between the UK (which favoured EQS) and the rest of the States plus Commission (who favoured UES defined as a maximum 'limit value' so that individual States could have even stricter limits if they wished). The trigger for the clash was a series of industry/pollutant specific Directives on water quality in rivers and estuaries, within a Framework Directive finally agreed in 1976 on 'Dangerous substances discharged into the aquatic environment.'[28]

The reasons why the other States and Commission favoured UES were largely those mentioned in the previous section as the reasons for wanting joint EC policies at all: i.e. the fears of 'unfair competition' plus transfrontier pollution.

'Unfair competition' would result if different countries could meet the EQS for industrial effluents with different emission standards. The UK, with a large coastline and fast flowing rivers and estuaries, would be able to achieve EQS within laxer controls on the industries concerned, and hence less increase in costs. In addition the UK, due to its geographic position, is not generally worried about transfrontier pollution. Other countries, which share river systems (e.g. along the Rhine), would find it difficult to actually agree on the way to achieve an EQS: countries would not feel it necessary to accept more stringent controls on their emissions of effluents to help those downstream.[29]

On the other hand, the UK put arguments in favour of EQS that were similar to those laid out at the beginning of this Section. The UK approach to pollution control had for very many years been summed-up as 'There are no harmful substances, only harmful concentrations'. The UK negotiators rejected the notion of unfair competition in this case. They said it was no more unfair that the UK could benefit from its estuaries than that Italy could benefit from its sunshine as compared to Holland - it would be absurd to insist that the Italians grew tomatoes only in artificially heated greenhouses just to stop them 'competing unfairly' with the Dutch.

In this particular case, a typical EC compromise was reached. Countries were allowed to choose *either* to have 'limit values' *or* EQS. The subsequent specific Directives following this Framework Directive followed the same compromise of allowing countries to choose between UES and EQS, with only the UK choosing the latter.

Although both sides took strongly opposed positions in this debate, neither side consistently followed one approach only. The UK had often applied uniform emission standards to whole industries, and still does in many cases. Conversely EQS were accepted by all Member States with no demur in other areas of EC environmental policy, e.g. the air quality standards for nitrogen dioxide, sulphur dioxide and particulates, or the Directives on nitrates in water for drinking.

Designated areas

One way of mitigating the clash between joint policies and subsidiarity and between EQS and UES, which it is also appealing in its own right, is to limit the areas to which a particular EQS or UES applies. It is appealing in its own right, because the harm done by pollution depends on the use of the medium into which it is emitted, or into which it finds its way. It therefore seems sensible to vary the standard according to the use of the medium. For example, the EC imposes stricter standards on nitrate concentrations in water to be used for drinking than in water not so used, e.g. used for boating.

Where the use of the medium is not obvious, in some cases the EC allows individual States to designate particular areas for the application of particular standards. Examples include the areas where a water quality EQS needs to be applied to protect shellfish, or the EQS concerning bacteria limits for stretches of water where large numbers of people traditionally bathe. Similarly, the Directive (mentioned near the beginning of this chapter) for differing sulphur content of oils according to where the oil is burned, allowed Member States to choose the areas to which the tougher UES would apply (except the limits applied to the sulphur content of oils, effectively it was a UES as the sulphur content of the oil determined the amount of sulphur dioxide emitted).

Despite the apparent reasonableness of the approach, its results might at first not seem so sensible. Governments have at times been able to use their discretion over which areas to designate, as a way of avoiding the implementation of Directives they oppose.[30] In the water standards for shellfish case mentioned above, and in those for water supporting different sorts of freshwater fish, some Member States simply did not designate any waters at all.

Similarly, some beaches, which to many observers were clearly heavily used for swimming, were excluded by means of the discretion States had over how to assess where 'large numbers' traditionally bathed.[31]

In the case of the 1975 Directive on the sulphur contents of gas/diesel oils, the aim was that the higher sulphur content oil should only be burned in areas where sulphur dioxide pollution was not a problem. However, the UK government decided that the whole of the UK should be designated as suitable for higher sulphur content gas/diesel oil, *except for the roadways* - since diesel oil for vehicles was already lower sulphur than other gas/diesel oils.[32] In 1992, a new Directive was agreed which set uniform levels for all gas oils for burning, with lower limits for automotive gas/diesel oil (and an exclusion for aviation kerosene).

Polluter Pays Principle and subsidization

From the very beginnings of the EC environmental policy, in the *First Environmental Action Program* of 1973, the Community accepted a principle agreed by the OECD which is known as the Polluter Pays Principle (PPP). This PPP was also included in Article 130R inserted into the Treaty of Rome by the SEA.

The PPP was initially widely misinterpreted as implying a commitment to control pollution by instituting a system of 'pollution taxes', i.e. charging firms according to the amount of pollution they emit, and thus inducing them to abate their pollution. Although many economists do favour controlling pollution by such pollution taxes rather than by imposing emission standards (whether uniform or not), this was not the meaning of the PPP.[33]

Instead, the meaning of the PPP is an agreement that governments should not subsidize firms in order to compensate them for the extra costs of meeting environmental standards - whatever the means by which the abatement is induced, and whether by regulations or charges. It is thus a no-subsidization policy, and is connected, once again, with 'unfair competition' rather than economic efficiency.

As far as Member States' own environmental policies are concerned, a similar result to the PPP is achieved by the Commission's powers on subsidies under Articles 92-93 of the Treaty of Rome.

Despite the PPP for EC policies, and the control under Articles 92-93 for national policies, some subsidies for pollution abatement have been allowed.

Although subsidies for the higher production (running) costs associated with the use of abatement equipment or procedures which reduce emissions have generally been forbidden, permission has been given for limited assistance with investment costs. Under Article 93.2(b) the Commission has allowed some subsidization for the initial investment costs of installing new abatement equipment when standards have been tightened, or to speed-up the implementation of agreed standards in advance of the last agreed date for compliance.[34]

Conclusions

From initially not even being a question of EC policy at all, Environmental Policy has become a joint policy with major impacts on what happens within individual Member States. Despite the prospect of some limited slow-down in the adoption of new jointly determined standards (whether UES or common EQS) as a result of the new stress on subsidiarity, it is likely that EU policies will continue, with ever more new Directives.

In this chapter, I have indicated reasons why I think that the justification for an EU environmental policy is more tenuous than is often thought, at least from the perspective of a standard approach to economics, for those pollutants involving neither trans-frontier spill-overs nor product standards.[35] However, similiar reasoning would also apply to many other areas where the EC and, for that matter, GATT and other international trade bargaining, stress the importance of a 'level playing field'. This goes against recent trends in trade relations. Such doubts, in some ways striking at what has been seen to be a fundamental principle of the EC, are unlikely to affect policy.

For EU environmental policy, the general belief in the prevention of 'distorted competition', coupled with the control of subsidization by the Commission, will keep up the pressure for EU policies from those States with active environmentalist movements. The result will be tougher environmental standards than would have otherwise been accepted in some countries, while others will often complain of the slowness of reaching agreement but still be unwilling to move too far ahead on their own, even when there is no legal impediment to so doing.

Notes

1   I have not seen any systematic study of the comparative chronology and international spread of the growth in environmental movements.

2   For example, Meadows, D.H., Meadows, D.L., Randers, J. and Behrens, W.W., *The Limits to Growth* (Earth Island) (1972).

3   Many readers will remember being struck as the present writer was, by reading statements frequently made by Ivan Illich, a noted figure at the time, as he travelled by jet plane from conference to conference where he preached the need for everybody to use bicycles and to give up other modern transport.

4   During the subsequent bargaining, before the proposals for an EC harmonized carbon tax were finally blocked by the UK, it was agreed that the poorest States could apply the proposed tax at a lower rate.

5   For details of the five programmes see the Official Journals OJ Nos. C112 of 20/12/73, C139 of 13/6/77, C46 of 17/2/83, C328 of 7/12/87, and C138 of 17/5/93. *Towards Sustainability* was also separately published by Commission of the EC (1993).

6   In several ways, both the strength of protection from pollution and the approach towards methods of pollution control that were favoured by the UK differed from that in most other Member States in the 1970s and 1980s. For an example see Guruswamy, I. D., Papps, I. and Storey D. (1983) who discuss one particular Directive on river pollution. ('The Development and Impact of an EC Directive: The Control of Discharges of Mercury to the Aquatic Environment' *Journal of Common Market Studies,* Vol. XXII.1).

7   For references in the Official Journals for particular Directives see Economic & Social Committee, Economic Consultative Assembly, *European Environmental Policy* (1987), Commission (1984) *Ten Years of Commending Environmental Policy* or Press, A. and Taylor, C., *Europe and the Environment* (Industrial Society) (1990). The annual Reports by the Commission also have brief sections on the Environment, as do the monthly Bulletins. Many of the main Directives are reprinted in the 7 volume series published by the Commission in 1992 under the general heading *European Community Environmental Legislation.* [CEC Vols. 1-7 (1992)].

8   Some of these and similar Directives also referred to Article 100; but this related to notions of distorted competition due to costs of polluting industries differing between Member States - as will be discussed later.

9   There have been some cases in which the Court has taken a reasonably permissive view, e.g. on a Danish law requiring the use of returnable bottles. This case, and similar ones, involve Article 30 as well as 100a. See L. Kramer (*EEC Treaty and Environmental* Protection (Sweet & Maxwell) (1990) Chapter 3 for other examples and a more detailed discussion. A more recent case is the 1992 Court decision on Case C-2/90, involving a ban on imports of waste into Wallonia, where the Court again took a permissive view on those aspects that were not covered by an existing Directive.

10 Cases C-155/91 and C-187/93. It is debatable whether the Court's decisions in these cases and Case C-300/89 (titanium dioxide) are compatible - see, for example, Griffin, D. 'The Legal Basis of the Waste Directive', *European Law Review* Vol. 18 (October 1993).

11 In addition to the dispute over the titanium dioxide, where the issue made no difference to the actual terms of the Directive - merely to the procedure used, which could set a precedent for the future. The disputes over which Article is used may be more important since the ratification of the Maastricht Treaty. Now, the European Parliament can block the adoption of a Directive when the procedure is on the basis of Article 100A.

12 Details are in Official Journal L206 of 22/7/92, page 1. An earlier, even smaller fund, was the 'ACE' fund set up in 1984 (13 million ECU for first three years). Kramer, L, *Focus on European Environmental Fair* (Sweet & Maxwell) (1992), Chapter 4, contains details of environmental spending within EC Structural Funds.

13 Directive 92/443/EC of 21st May 1992, published in OJ L206 of 22/7/92 page 7.

14 The earlier Directive is also interesting as showing divergencies of public opinion on what constitutes acceptable behaviour. It was initially motivated in the early 1970s by Northern European repugnance at the mass shooting of wild birds, especially songbirds and migratory species, in Southern Europe, particularly Italy. In the end, Italian and French insistence ensured that sky-larks could still be hunted in these countries.

15 Unlike the Directives referred to in footnotes 13 and 14, which were explicitly justified by a Community desire for conservation.

16 As well as the references in footnote 7, there are books such as Haigh, N *EEC Environmental Legislation and Britain* (Longman, 2nd revised edition (1989), Johnson, S. and Corcelle, G. *The Environmental Policy of the EC* (Graham & Trotman, 1989) Kramer L., *Focus on European*

Environmental Law, (Sweet & Maxwell) (1992) or EC Committee of the American Chamber of Commerce *The EC Environment Guide*, Kogan Page (1994).

[17] COM(92)23, which seems to have been reprinted unchanged in the final Programme.

[18] Supplement 5/72 to the *Bulletin of the European Communities*.

[19] From an economic analysis, the 'Coase Theorem' [see Coase, R H 'The Problem of Social Cost', *Journal of Law & Economics, Vol. III* (October 1960)] suggests that obtaining correct, i.e. efficient, levels of pollution may involve the downstream country paying the upstream polluter to cut-back, if the polluter has the right to pollute. Trade-offs between pollution control and other EC policies desired by the polluter may allow disguised 'payments' to be made in the form of concessions on other policies, in situations where explicit monetary payments might be politically unacceptable.

[20] See the later section on the 'Polluter Pays Principle' and on EC anti-subsidization rules, as to why governments could not simply compensate the industries affected.

[21] See footnote 18 above.

[22] For example, in the water for drinking Directive, 76/160/EEC, the phase in the middle [...] is 'on the quality required of surface water intended for the abstraction of drinking water already applicable or in preparation'.

[23] These worries apply to all sorts of areas of policy e.g. subsidization of firms' research costs (Articles 92-93 of the Treaty of Rome on State Aids) and to all sorts of countries, e.g. US groups who have objected to the North American Free Trade Area in the absence of stricter environmental standards in Mexico.

[24] Referring to 'different countries' itself begs the question of how the wishes of a country taken as a whole are to be decided on for items which are public goods in the economic definition - i.e. where all individuals have to have similar levels rather than each person being able to decide the level of consumption for themselves, e.g. I cannot arrange to breathe in different levels of air pollution than the person sitting next to me on a park bench. Economic analysis has some insights on how such decisions should be made, just as political analysis has insights on how such decisions are made.

For simplicity I am not going to discuss the further interesting point of whether the historically determined boundaries which define any particular national state constitute the optimal areas for such decisions, or whether decisions should be further decentralized. The argument to be made would best apply to the smallest area in which the level of the pollutant has to be the same, e.g. a single river system or the borders of a single lake.

[25] Firms may also have to accept lower profits. Whether or not this happens depends on how internationally mobile capital is. In the EC now, since the ultimate owners of firms may reside in other countries, it may be that profit rates cannot be forced down. In this context there is also an important proviso to the general argument that I am making, which has assumed competitive product markets. If, however, some firms are producing traded products where the international competition is oligopolistic, issues of 'strategic trade policy' could possibly arise.

[26] If exchange rates are flexible, the change in the aggregate real wage may be hastened by changes in nominal exchange rates, provided that money wages do not respond fully to the changes in the price of imports - the usual 'money illusion' condition for devaluations to have any real effects. However, the relative sectoral re-allocations of resources cannot generally just be achieved by this route (the exception would be if all traded goods were uniformly more polluting than non-traded goods).

[27] For a discussion of the material in this Section in a framework which is more explicitly economic, see my Chapter in El-Agraa, A (ed). *The Economics of the EC* (4th ed., Harvester Wheatsheaf) (1994).

[28] A full and lucid discussion of this particular controversy is in the article referred to in footnote 6.

[29] In terms of footnote 19, the difficulties of actually reaching agreements meant that 'inefficient' but 'simple' solutions seemed preferable - the costs of negotiations involving several parties are often cited as an objection to the practicability of the Coase Theorem.

[30] In some cases one feels that this result was not unforeseen by the Governments concerned - the knowledge that effective implementation could largely be avoided induced Governments to agree to Directives they would have vetoed otherwise. See the next two endnotes.

[31] In the UK, this initial exclusion reflected both worries about the public expenditure on sewage treatment required to meet the EQS, and the view that the Directive was scientifically unsound and that there were no health hazards involved in breaking the standard.

[32] As in the previous footnote, this decision reflected a belief that the Directive was misplaced. UK health scientists did not feel that ambient levels of sulphur dioxide and its derivatives were harmful to health.

[33] The advantages of pollution taxes are discussed in textbooks on environmental economics (a very sketchy discussion can be also found in my article referred to in footnote 27). At the time of writing the EC has not used pollution taxes as part of its own policy - the UK having blocked agreement on the proposed carbon tax. Some Member States have used pollution taxes as part of their own policies, e.g. on leaded petrol, and such taxes have been encouraged in the pre-ambles to some recent Directives (e.g. the 1994 Directive on car emissions, 94/12/EC).

[34] The maximum limit on subsidies is 15% of the investment costs. The Commission's position was briefly restated in Paragraph 284 of the *20th Report on Competition Policy* (CEC 1991). In the *22nd Report on Competition Policy* (CEC 1993), the Commission stated that it was in the process of drawing up new guidelines on environmental aid.

[35] The proviso in footnote 25 above may be relevant here.

Index